Streaming Media Bible

Steve Mack

Hungry Minds™

Best-Selling Books • Digital Downloads • e-Books • Answer Networks • e-Newsletters • Branded Web Sites • e-Learning

New York, NY ✦ Cleveland, OH ✦ Indianapolis, IN

Streaming Media Bible

Published by
Hungry Minds, Inc.
909 Third Avenue
New York, NY 10022
www.hungryminds.com

Library of Congress Control Number: 2002100248

ISBN: 0-7645-3650-8

Printed in the United States of America

10 9 8 7 6 5 4 3 2 1

1B/SU/QU/QS/IN

Distributed in the United States by Hungry Minds, Inc.

Distributed by CDG Books Canada Inc. for Canada; by Transworld Publishers Limited in the United Kingdom; by IDG Norge Books for Norway; by IDG Sweden Books for Sweden; by IDG Books Australia Publishing Corporation Pty. Ltd. for Australia and New Zealand; by TransQuest Publishers Pte Ltd. for Singapore, Malaysia, Thailand, Indonesia, and Hong Kong; by Gotop Information Inc. for Taiwan; by ICG Muse, Inc. for Japan; by Intersoft for South Africa; by Eyrolles for France; by International Thomson Publishing for Germany, Austria, and Switzerland; by Distribuidora Cuspide for Argentina; by LR International for Brazil; by Galileo Libros for Chile; by Ediciones ZETA S.C.R. Ltda. for Peru; by WS Computer Publishing Corporation, Inc., for the Philippines; by Contemporanea de Ediciones for Venezuela; by Express Computer Distributors for the Caribbean and West Indies; by Micronesia Media Distributor, Inc. for Micronesia; by Chips Computadoras S.A. de C.V. for Mexico; by Editorial Norma de Panama S.A. for Panama; by American Bookshops for Finland.

For general information on Hungry Minds' products and services please contact our Customer Care department within the U.S. at 800-762-2974, outside the U.S. at 317-572-3993 or fax 317-572-4002.

For sales inquiries and reseller information, including discounts, premium and bulk quantity sales, and foreign-language translations, please contact our Customer Care department at 800-434-3422, fax 317-572-4002 or write to Hungry Minds, Inc., Attn: Customer Care Department, 10475 Crosspoint Boulevard, Indianapolis, IN 46256.

For information on licensing foreign or domestic rights, please contact our Sub-Rights Customer Care department at 212-884-5000.

For information on using Hungry Minds' products and services in the classroom or for ordering examination copies, please contact our Educational Sales department at 800-434-2086 or fax 317-572-4005.

For press review copies, author interviews, or other publicity information, please contact our Public Relations department at 317-572-3168 or fax 317-572-4168.

For authorization to photocopy items for corporate, personal, or educational use, please contact Copyright Clearance Center, 222 Rosewood Drive, Danvers, MA 01923, or fax 978-750-4470.

Hungry Minds™ is a trademark of Hungry Minds, Inc.

About the Author

Steve Mack — Steve's fascination with audio can be classified to some extent as a family trait. Many Saturday mornings were spent with his father, first watching cartoons and then listening to classical music at extreme volumes. His grandfather, when not teaching history and English, composed in his music room, which also came equipped with a state-of-the-art hi-fi system. Steve's musical obsession soon combined with a curiosity that led him to take apart many more things than he could successfully put back together.

During the last four years of Steve's London sojourn he built, maintained, and operated Bang Bang Studios, a professional 24-track recording studio. Steve personally engineered and produced hundreds of releases. Steve also produced, directed, and edited several music videos for That Petrol Emotion.

Steve returned to Seattle in 1995 and was tipped off by a friend to apply at a small software start-up called Progressive Networks. After an interview that lasted all of five minutes and ended with "Can you start tomorrow?" Steve became employee number 30 at the company that would eventually become RealNetworks.

During his 5 years at RealNetworks, Steve worked closely with the codec and tools developers as well as running the media lab where all the audiovisual content for the RealNetworks family of Web sites was produced. Steve was involved in some of the earliest and most prestigious Internet broadcasts, including the Rolling Stones, Elton John's Oscar Party, the WOMAD festival, the Tibetan Freedom Festivals, The Digital Club Network Festivals, the MTV Europe Awards, President Clinton's Inaugural Address, and the first ever public live Internet broadcast, a Seattle Mariners game in 1995.

Steve decided to move on to other challenges in 2000, when he started his own consulting company, Smacktastic (http://smacktastic.tv). Smacktastic specializes in all things related to streaming media, in particular the intersection between traditional media and streaming media applications.

Steve is a popular and sought-after public speaker, having presented and given workshops at the National Association of Broadcasters, Internet World, the Real Conference, Streaming Media West, and South by Southwest. He chaired the Internet Audio Workshop at the 105th Audio Engineering Society conference in September 1998.

Though this is his first full-length book, Steve has previously published in numerous music magazines and the Wiley Encyclopedia of Electrical and Electronics Engineering.

Steve splits his time between Seattle and Bigfork, Montana. He is still active in the local music community, both as a producer and a performer.

Credits

Acquisitions Editor
Michael Roney

Project Editor
Mica Johnson

Technical Editor
Ben Houston

Copy Editors
Beth Taylor and Suzanne Thomas

Editorial Manager
Rev Mengle

Permissions Editor
Laura Moss

Media Development Specialist
Angela Denney

Senior Vice President and Group Executive Publisher for Technology Publishing
Richard Swadley

Vice President and Publisher
Barry Pruett

Project Coordinator
Jennifer Bingham

Graphics and Production Specialists
Melanie DesJardins, Sean Decker, Brian Drumm, Gabriele McCann, Kelly Hardesty, Joyce Haughey, Barry Offringa, Betty Schulte, Rashelle Smith

Quality Control Technician
Laura Albert, John Greenough, Andy Hollandbeck, Carl Pierce, Charles Spencer

Book Designer
Murder by Design

Special Help
Amanda Munz Peterson

Proofreading and Indexing
TECHBOOKS Production Services

Cover Image
Anthony Bunyan

For Erin, who patiently endured
while I learned how to write.

S.

Foreword

It seems only yesterday that I was walking through our first office in Seattle's Pioneer Square and glimpsed a dreadlocked figure waiting by the elevators. My first reaction was that one of the famed Pioneer Square derelicts had tailgated his way up into our offices.

But after someone told me who Steve was, I became incredibly excited. At first, I admit, this was because I had been a fan of Steve's band That Petrol Emotion. The idea that a bona-fide alternative music rock star had joined our young team felt like validation that we were truly on to something big.

Quickly, my excitement for Steve-as-symbol was replaced by the reality of Steve's incredible talent and commitment. Steve combines a passion for music and video as art with a deep understanding for the science of what makes music and video sound and look great. And, as you will soon read, a rare ability to communicate complex subjects with great clarity and lucidity.

Back when we were bringing audio to the Internet for the first time, we were truly inventing technology on a daily basis, and being able to think quickly and intuitively was absolutely paramount. Without Steve's hard work, and indeed the unbelievable talent and commitment of all the people I've had the honor of working with over the last eight years, RealNetworks, and indeed the whole streaming media industry would not be making the impact and enjoying the success it does today.

When I founded RealNetworks in 1994, it was because I believed that the Internet would be the next great mass medium. We have seen this idea become reality. The past few years in particular have provided galvanizing events that have proven how integral a part of people's daily media experience the Internet has become.

We have seen Internet streaming media usage skyrocket during President Clinton's testimony, during the Election turmoil of 2000, and most recently during the tragic events of September 2001. More and more people use the Internet as their primary source for news and entertainment.

However, our industry is young. Both radio and television took full generation before they became fully mature industries. As technology innovators, we must continue to push the limits of this new medium to provide the highest possible quality and to enable fundamentally new kinds of experiences. As business innovators, we must provide value to our customers in ways that traditional media outlets cannot.

Understanding the full potential of our medium is the first step towards that goal. This long overdue book provides the firm technical grounding that everyone in our industry should have — and that leaders in other media businesses would do well to gain. Kudos to Hungry Minds for having the foresight to commission this book, and many thanks to Steve for taking on such a colossal task and delivering such a useful, thorough, and thoughtful book. It's going to be music to a lot of people's ears.

Rob Glaser
Founder and CEO
RealNetworks

Preface

In April 1995, a small company from Seattle, Washington called Progressive Networks announced at the National Association of Broadcasters' conference the release of RealAudio, a software program for transferring audio across the Internet in real-time, a process that would become known as *streaming*. Although this was not the first example of audio being transmitted across the Internet in real-time, it was the first time anyone using a PC could join in simply by downloading a free piece of software.

In the ensuing years, Progressive Networks became RealNetworks, Microsoft released NetShow and eventually renamed it Windows Media Technologies, and Apple released a streaming server for their renowned QuickTime player. Countless other streaming media technologies have appeared and have either been bought out or have fallen by the wayside. Standards organizations continue to wrestle over how to steer the nascent industry away from the balkanization that it currently suffers.

Throughout this process, the industry continues to mature, and the technology continues to improve. Scratchy audio that was once state-of-the-art has been replaced by CD quality audio. Postage stamp sized video windows are being replaced by full-screen video that continues to approach broadcast quality. Whether you choose to believe the hype or not, streaming media is here to stay and it will continue to improve.

Competition for this emerging market is intense. It is often very hard to separate the facts from the mudslinging in product press releases. This should be taken as an indicator of how important this market is going to be. Harnessing the seemingly infinite powers of the Internet to distribute media is an idea whose time has come.

What This Book Tries to Do

Streaming media is a multidisciplined process. To think that a single book could be the final word in any one of these areas, let alone all of them, would be mere folly. Instead, what this book tries to do is provide a firm theoretical grounding in all aspects of streaming media, while showing you in a step-by-step manner how basic tasks are accomplished.

From this foundation, you should be able to create high-quality source material, encode it to the highest specifications, showcase it in a number of different manners, and serve it using a robust streaming server architecture. After you've become comfortable with the basics, you should be able to dig deeper into the areas that interest you most. Depending on what area this is, you can either buy more reference books or do cutting-edge research online.

Because streaming media is multi-disciplinary, it stretches across different departments in large organizations, or forces the small company owner to wear many hats. The book is divided into sections that roughly approximate different disciplines. If you don't have to worry about every facet of the streaming media production chain, read what you need and pass it along.

One of the more frustrating things about streaming media, particularly for those who are trying to support more than one platform, is finding documentation when you need it. One goal of this book is to assemble the most useful information for each streaming media platform and place it within arm's reach. None of the major streaming media platforms has outstanding documentation, and some seem to go to absurd lengths to make it hard to find. Hopefully this book goes some way toward addressing that need.

Because of the rapid product cycle most software companies are caught up in, this book cannot hope to be absolutely up to date. As the book is being written, one manufacturer is coming out with a new player, with the others soon to follow in one form or another. Some parts of this book will date more quickly than others. The basic rules, however, always apply. Create compelling, high-quality content that people want to see or hear and they will find you. Although this book cannot tell you what content is compelling, it can certainly help you produce your content to a high standard.

Streaming platform wars

This book has tried to remain as neutral as possible. In an effort to keep the book cohesive, coverage has been limited to the three major streaming media platforms — QuickTime, the RealSystem, and Windows Media Technology. There are other fringe players in the streaming market, but the line had to be drawn somewhere and this seemed like the logical choice.

Because each streaming media software manufacturer has a slightly different approach, there are some areas where each platform outshines the others. There are also areas where some platforms fall short. In an effort to stay above the belt, the book concentrates on the strengths of each as opposed to pointing out the weaknesses. To counter charges of favoritism, examples for each platform are listed in alphabetical order.

PC versus Mac

For the most part, this conundrum should not interfere with the concepts explained in this book. Efforts were made to be as non-platform specific as possible, but it must be said that the book was written and tested on a PC. As much as the author would have loved to test every last item in the book on both platforms, it nearly killed him trying to test for one.

How to Get the Most Out of This Book

The sections and chapters of this book are organized so that the neophyte can take it from the beginning, step-by-step. However, each chapter should also stand on its own, so if you really want to learn about one topic in particular, skip straight to that chapter and find what you need.

Additionally, if you are just looking for reference materials, try the Appendixes. Several references have been included there on the CD-ROM specifically for that purpose.

Icons: What Do They Mean?

Throughout the book you'll see icons in the margins that point out certain details in the writing. Although these icons are relatively self-explanatory, here is what each one indicates:

Tips provide extra information about certain topics, or provide special workarounds or alternatives to a listed procedure.

Notes are for background or supplementary information that may not be crucial to the understanding of the concept, but interesting nonetheless.

Caution icons generally mean you should be paying attention. This icon either point out crucial steps or possible pitfalls.

Cross-reference icons point out where you can find additional information about a topic elsewhere in the book.

Indicates that supplementary material for the topic at hand is included on the CD-ROM.

This handy icon points out material graciously contributed by the many experts I've worked with in the field. Take note of the advice and information they provided — it will save you some headaches.

How This Book Is Organized

Streaming media can be overwhelming to the beginner because there are so many things to consider. Taking this into consideration, the book has been organized to break the streaming media process into its component parts, which roughly divides it into the different disciplines necessary. An introductory section is also included to set the stage, define some terms, and give people a broad understanding of the technical challenges streaming media faces. Working within a medium is much easier if the limitations are understood.

Because the majority of streaming media today is audio and video, the early part of this book is dedicated to producing high quality audio and video streams. After you hit Part IV, however, the concepts are applicable to all forms of streaming media. Part VI specifically deals with other data types that are currently available to streaming media authors, and Part VII explains SMIL, the language that is used to synchronize different data types within a single presentation.

Broadcasting on the Internet receives its own section, which is followed by a couple of case studies that illustrate how streaming media is being used in real-life situations.

Part I — Streaming Media: An Introduction

The first section deals with the fundamentals. Chapter 1 is about the streaming media process and the different pieces of software that are involved. It also discusses why streaming media is such a challenge. Chapter 2 talks about the basics of audio and video, including how we see and hear. This leads into a discussion about how we've recorded audio and video over the years, and how it is now done digitally. Chapter 3 looks at codecs, which are the basic building blocks of all audio and video streaming. Codecs are what enable you to overcome the challenges presented in Chapters 1 and 2.

Part II — Creation: Working Within the Internet's Limitations

Part II covers all aspects of media production. Chapters 4 and 5 set the stage, describing the basics of audio and video production. Chapter 6 talks about the tools you use to produce your media. Chapters 7 and 8 focus on audio, first on how to get the best possible recordings, and then how to optimize them for the best possible quality. Chapters 9 and 10 shift the focus to video, again covering how to get the best video recordings and then how you can optimize your quality. Chapter 11 talks about how you can automate some of the more mundane creation tasks.

Part III — Encoding: Reducing Media Files to a Stream-Friendly Size

In Part III, you learn about how to take your pristine audio and video files and turn them into streaming formats while sacrificing as little quality as possible. Chapter 12 starts off the section with an explanation of the limitations involved and what tradeoffs you can make. Chapter 13 shows you how to use the encoding software for each of the three major streaming platforms. Chapter 14 teaches you how to automate your encoding, as well as a few tricks you can do with your encoded files.

Part IV — Authoring: Different Ways to Showcase Your Media

Part IV discusses the various options you have at your disposal to showcase your streaming media. Authoring is the process whereby you make your streaming media files available to the public. Starting with Chapter 15, you learn how to create simple Web links to your streaming media content. In Chapter 16, embedding streaming media players into Web pages is covered. JavaScript is covered in Chapter 17, which allows you advanced control of your embedded streaming media players.

Part V — Serving: Making Your Media Available on the Internet

If you want to learn about serving streams, Part V is the place to go. Chapter 18 discusses setting up streaming media servers. Chapter 19 discusses managing your media assets, which can be a considerable task for a large-scale streaming media producer. To find out who is watching your content and for how long, you can learn what is hiding in your streaming media server log files and how to extract meaningful data from them. Log files are covered in Chapter 20. Advertising, much maligned of late but still essential, is covered in Chapter 21.

Part VI — Other Data Types: It Is Not Just Audio and Video Anymore

After you've got a firm grasp of the streaming media process, you may want to branch out into more exotic data types. This section starts off with streaming animation via RealFlash in Chapter 22. Chapter 23 covers streaming text using RealText, while Chapter 24 covers streaming images with RealPix. The last chapter in this section, Chapter 25, rounds up a handful of other data types and talks briefly about how they can be used.

Part VII — SMIL (Synchronized Multimedia Integration Language)

SMIL was developed to address the special needs of authors when creating multimedia presentations for the Internet. It's an open standard that has degrees of support from all three streaming platforms covered in the book and is an extremely powerful authoring environment. Chapter 26 provides an overview of SMIL, followed by Chapter 27, which talks about SMIL syntax. Chapter 28 talks about layout design in SMIL; Chapter 29 details the timing models used in SMIL. Chapters 30 and 31 teach you how to author effective SMIL files and how to use advanced SMIL programming techniques. Chapter 32 gives an introduction to SMIL 2.0, which has just been released as of the writing of this book.

Part VIII — Broadcasting on the Internet

Broadcasting on the Internet is given its own section, because although the theory is the same, the practice differs slightly from non-live situations. This section is arranged much the way the book is arranged; the process is broken down into the 4 component parts and each dealt with in a chapter. Chapter 33 is an introduction to broadcasting on the Internet. Chapters 34 through 37 talk about creating content for, encoding, authoring for, and serving live broadcasts, respectively.

Part IX — Case studies

The final section of the book includes a few case studies. Chapter 38 studies a radio station that also broadcasts live on the Internet. Chapter 39 looks at a large-scale live broadcast.

Part X — Appendixes

The appendixes are where you should go for quick information. Some only include a few tables, while others are fairly thorough references for languages detailed in the book. Due to space constraints, some of the appendixes are available only in electronic form on the CD-ROM. You should install these on your computer for convenient access. Additional resources are also listed here, as well as a listing of what is included on the CD-ROM.

Getting in Touch with the Author

Before you write, check the book's accompanying Web site for tips, tricks, FAQs, and other useful tidbits at www.streamingmediabible.com

Although I shudder to think what I may be getting myself into, you can reach me at smack@streamingmediabible.com. I can't promise I'll answer every e-mail, but I shall endeavor to do so. If you find any errors in the book, please send them my way and I'll post them on the Web site.

Making a Positive Contribution

We can all make streaming media better by creating better quality presentations and by sharing our knowledge with others. Get involved online with the many e-mail discussion forums and Web sites that specialize in streaming media. If you have tips you'd like to share, send them my way for inclusion on the book's Web site. If they're clever enough, they'll be considered for the second edition of this book.

Another positive thing you can do is to give the software manufacturers feedback on their products. If you think that they're doing a great job, let them know. Suggest features for future releases. Even more important, make them aware of product shortcomings and let them know what you need out of their products to make them more useful. Speaking as someone who worked on the other side of the fence, nothing drives software development more than feature requests from actual paying customers.

Have Fun

Last, but certainly not least, I've tried to make this book as readable as possible. I've attempted to put as friendly a face on this technology as I could. I've worked with audio and film or video as long as I can remember, and I do it because it's fun. I hope I'm successful in transferring at least some of my enthusiasm for the industry to you, the patient reader.

Acknowledgments

Had I known what I was getting myself into, I might not have accepted the commission to write this book. At the least, I would have rolled on the floor laughing when Michael Roney, my acquisitions editor asked "Can you do it in four months?" Here we are at the six-month mark and I still feel like I could have used more time. A lot more. Michael, thanks for the opportunity.

My name is the only one on the cover, but this book certainly could not have been written without help and input from many people. Before I start naming names, I would like to briefly state that over the years I have learned so much from so many amazing people. I hope that I can return the favor by passing on some of this knowledge to other folks.

In the planning stages of this book I received invaluable help from a number of people, but Pat Boyle, Halley Bock, and Dan Rayburn in particular provided a lot of feedback. Halley really helped me hammer the outline into shape — the outline that landed the book deal. Larry Levitsky gave me the inside scoop on the publishing world and encouraged me to take on the project. Larry and Halley, a big thank you to you both.

A number of great folks contributed sidebars and expert tutorials. They're all listed in the experts/contributors section. Thanks one and all.

Of course this book could not have been written without input from the "Big 3" streaming media platform manufacturers. I received invaluable help from Shelley McIntyre, Rob Banga, Eric Hyche, Erik Hodge, Paul Ellis, Steve McMillen, Bridie Saccocio, Eddie Sams, and David Wheeler from RealNetworks. Jerry Black deserves a special mention, because a) he's Dr. Glomph, and b) he has taught me so much.

Amir Mejidimehr from Microsoft was always available for technical minutiae. An absolutely huge thank you must also go to David Caulton, who answered literally hundreds of my questions, and always found the time to point me in the right direction. I didn't need to talk to twenty different people because David always took care of me, even during their product launch.

Were it not for Francesco Schiavon, I would have spent even more time trawling through the Apple discussion forums. Francesco, who teaches multimedia authoring, knew my pain and was an immense help. QuickTime is an amazing product. I just wish that the engineers there could spare a little time for us laypeople.

Both Ken Hostettler from Silicon Mechanics and Zach Jenkins from Groovetech helped me out at a moment's notice when I really needed it — thanks guys.

Mica Johnson, my project editor, deserves special thanks for her patience and understanding with a first-time author. I'm told it gets easier — for Mica's sake I can only hope so.

Most of all, thanks to Erin who put up with a raving lunatic for six months.

Steve Mack

Contents at a Glance

Contents

Part II: Creation: Working Within the Internet's Limitations   89

Chapter 4: Internet Audio Basics 91

Chapter 5: Internet Video Basics 105

Part IV: Authoring: Different Ways to Showcase Your Media — 341

Part V: Serving: Making Your Media Available on the Internet **411**

Chapter 28: Laying Out Your Presentation Using SMIL 609

Chapter 29: Synchronizing Your Streams in SMIL 621

Chapter 30: Authoring Effective SMIL Files 631

Part X: Appendixes   793

Bonus Chapters   On the CD-ROM

Quick Start

This quick start section gives you a brief overview of what is involved in the streaming media process and how it differs on the different streaming media platforms. If you've already played around with streaming media, you may not find anything too revealing in this section. This section is intended for the absolute novice who wants a hint of what lies ahead.

The Streaming Media Process

Behind every link you click to watch or listen to streaming media on the Internet lies a production chain. Every piece of content must go through four main stages:

- ✦ **Creation:** The audio or video must be created or obtained in some raw form
- ✦ **Encoding:** This raw material must be converted to a format that can be streamed
- ✦ **Authoring:** The access to the streaming media must be provided via a Web page link or presentation
- ✦ **Serving:** The files must be placed on streaming servers

Audiovisual production is not covered in this Quick Start. Instead, small video and audio clips are included on the accompanying CD. Though A/V production is a very important part of the streaming process, it isn't something that can be covered quickly — your production chain depends on the type of content you are creating and the editing software you choose to run.

The other three stages of the streaming media process are covered. A lot of detail is left out at this point. The idea is to give an overall impression without worrying about the details just yet.

In the encoding section, you'll see how software from each manufacturer is used to convert raw audio and video files into streaming formats.

The authoring section covers how you can link to your streaming media files from Web pages by using simple links to metafiles. All examples in this section refer to local files.

In the final section of this introductory section, you create Web pages that link to files residing on actual streaming media servers. Doing so enables you to hear streaming media in action.

Before You Start

You should make sure that you have the latest versions of the three streaming media players installed, as well as their respective encoders. If you plan on working in only one or two of the platforms, make sure that you have the players and encoders you need.

 The CD-ROM includes a page that has links to the three major streaming media software manufacturers to download players and encoders.

Install streaming media players

You may already have all three players installed. You should check to make sure that you have the latest version. All three players now have some form of auto-detection built in that cues you if a newer version is available. Although installing a manufacturer's beta releases is not always wise, having their latest "official" release installed is a good idea.

All three streaming media software manufacturers offer a free version of their player, though RealNetworks generally makes it somewhat hard to find. A little perseverance rewards you with a player that has all the basic functionality you need for this book.

Install the player according to the manufacturer's instructions. You generally do this by downloading an installation program that either contains all the bits you need or downloads the software you need piece by piece.

As you install your streaming media players, you may witness first-hand the battle that is being waged for your media files. Each streaming media player offers to be the default application for just about every file type under the sun. If you're an advanced user, you may want to run a custom installation procedure and select the file types you want to be associated with each player. If you're not sure, install by using the default settings. When you're more familiar with what is going on, you can alter your various media player settings accordingly.

Install streaming media encoders

Encoding is a key part of the streaming media process, and each platform has a piece of software to accomplish this task. Encoding functionality for all three platforms is also built into many of the audio and video editing software programs available, including the trial software included on the CD-ROM. This introductory section uses the software that each manufacturer provides to illustrate the examples.

Unfortunately, this introduces a slight problem. QuickTime does not offer a free version of their encoder. Their encoding software is included with QuickTime Pro, which is available for purchase from the Apple Web site. If you plan on doing any work with QuickTime, you should buy QuickTime Pro. It's cheap, and it's money well spent.

RealNetworks offers their RealSystem Producer software for free, and also offers the RealSystem Producer Plus. The RealSystem Producer Plus offers some advanced functionality that comes in handy if you plan on doing a lot of encoding. You may find the RealSystem Producer Plus exclusive features useful as your streaming media prowess increases.

The Windows Media Encoder is a free product. In addition to the Windows Media Encoder, you should also download and install the Windows Media Resource Kit, which has a lot of utilities that you'll find useful later.

Install the encoders according to the manufacturer's instructions. You don't have to worry about the encoders fighting over file types like the players do. Encoders are more of a hands-on piece of software. You can use the default install parameters for all of them.

Pay attention to where each encoder is installed. You should probably say yes when the install software asks if you want an icon on your desktop or start bar. The easier these programs are to find, the less grief you'll have down the road.

Encoding Your First Streaming Media Files

Now that you've installed all the software you need, you can get down to the business of encoding. In general, encoding a file entails selecting the file you want to encode, choosing the parameters for your encoded file, and then clicking OK and waiting for the software to do it's thing. Encoding is really that simple.

 Example files have been included on the CD-ROM in the Quick Start directory.

These examples show how to encode the audio_example.wav file by using a setting appropriate for a 56K modem. You should play around with the other files in the directory to get a feel for how files look and sound when you encode them using different encoder settings.

> **Tip** Get into the habit of giving your encoded files useful names. For example, if you encode the audio file for a 28.8 audience, name the encoded version audio_example_28 or audio_example_20 (because 20 kilobits per second is the targeted bit rate for 28.8 modems).

The authoring section later assumes that you're going to save the streaming media files you create in a folder called encoded on your C: drive. You don't have to, of course, but if you don't you'll have to pay more attention later.

Encoding your first streaming QuickTime file

QuickTime encoding is done by using QuickTime Pro. As mentioned earlier, it's not free, but it's cheap and extremely useful. All you have to do to encode a file into a QuickTime streaming format is to *import* it into QuickTime Pro and then *export* it using appropriate encoding settings.

1. **Open up your QuickTime Pro player.** Depending on which streaming media players you installed and what order you installed them in, the QuickTime player may inform you that it is not the default player for some filetypes (see Figure QS-1).

   If you want the QuickTime player to be your default player, click Yes. Otherwise, click No. Note that this choice does not affect playback of files that the QuickTime player cannot play back, such as RealMedia or Windows Media files. This choice only affects file types, such as .WAV files that can be played back by many different programs.

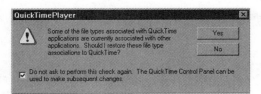

Figure QS-1: The QuickTime player wants to be your media player of choice.

2. **From the File menu, choose Import.** This action opens the Import window (see Figure QS-2). The QuickTime player defaults to opening movie files. Make sure that you choose the appropriate file type you are trying to encode from the Files of type drop-down menu. For example, if you want to encode a raw audio file choose "Audio files" from the drop down menu. Or, just select "All files" from the drop down menu to see all available files.

Play preview button

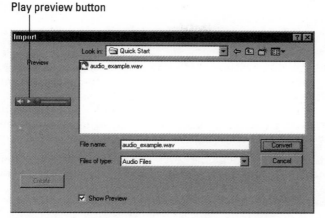

Figure QS-2: Importing a file into the QuickTime player

3. **Highlight the audio_example file and click Convert.**

Note

Make sure that you choose the appropriate file type to encode from the Files of type drop-down menu.

4. **Because this is just an audio file, the QuickTime player hides the video display pane and shrinks in size.** You can play the file by using the QuickTime player controls.

5. **To encode the file into a streaming QuickTime file, choose Export from the File menu.** Doing this brings up the Save exported file as window (see Figure QS-3).

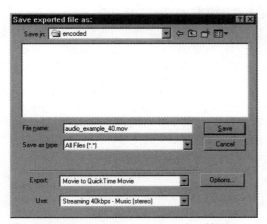

Figure QS-3: Exporting a streaming file from the QuickTime player

6. **Choose an appropriate directory and type in an appropriate file name for your streaming QuickTime file.** Because we're targeting a 56K modem, we'll use a 40 Kbps setting, so appending _40 to the end of the original file name makes sense.

7. **Choose an appropriate audio encoding preset.** For this example, choose the Streaming 40 Kbps - Music (stereo) preset from the Use: drop-down menu. This setting is appropriate to stream to people with 56K modems. Make sure that you don't choose any settings that say High Motion or Low Motion — these video presets use a lower quality audio setting because they reserve bits for the video portion of the signal.

   Make sure that Movie to QuickTime Movie is selected from the Export: drop-down menu. Click the Save button. A small progress window pops up to indicate that your file is being exported (see Figure QS-4).

Figure QS-4: The QuickTime player Export progress bar

8. **After the progress bar disappears, your streaming QuickTime file is ready to play back.** QuickTime remembers the last directory you were working in, so choose Open from the File menu and open up the file you just encoded. Play it back by using the QuickTime player controls.

That's all there is to it. Feel free to play around with other encoding settings by selecting different presets from the Use: drop-down menu on the Export window.

Encoding your first RealMedia file

RealMedia encoding is done using the RealSystem Producer. To encode a file, you must set up an encoding session. For each session, you specify your inputs and outputs and then choose encoding settings. After the session has been set up, you click the Start button and the encoding process begins.

The RealSystem Producer has a Wizard mode that steps you through the process. Eventually, you'll probably want to skip the recording wizard, but the first couple of times you may want to use it.

1. **Open up the RealSystem Producer.** Because this is most likely the first time you've used the software, it should default to offering you a choice of what recording wizard you want to use (see Figure QS-5). The three recording wizards are the following:

- **Record From File:** Choose this option to encode a file.
- **Record From Media Device:** Choose this option to encode directly from your sound card and/or video capture card to a file on your computer.
- **Live Broadcast:** Choose this option when you are doing a live broadcast directly to the Internet.

If the wizards selection window does not appear, choose File ⇨ Recording Wizards ⇨ Record from File.

2. **Choose the Record From File option.** In this example you're going to encode a short audio file.

3. **Click OK to begin using the recording wizard.** This takes you to the first step of the Record From File Wizard where you choose the file you want to encode.

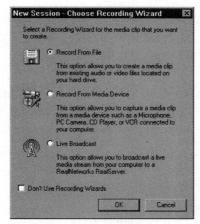

Figure QS-5: The RealSystem Producer New Session - Choose Recording Wizard window

4. **Choose the file you want to encode by clicking the Browse button.** Select the audio_example.wav file on the CD in the Quick Start directory as shown in Figure QS-6.

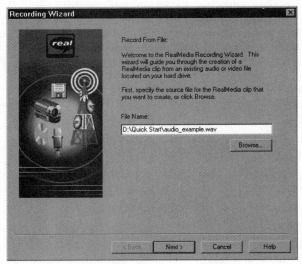

Figure QS-6: Choosing your input file using the RealSystem Producer Recording Wizard

5. **After selecting your file, click Next to move on to the next step.** The next screen allows you to specify information about your clip, such as title, author, copyright, description, and keywords (see Figure QS-7).

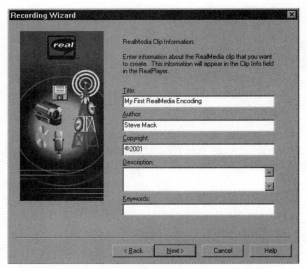

Figure QS-7: Supplying file information using the RealSystem Producer Recording Wizard

6. **Fill in as much information as you want and click Next to proceed.**

7. **Specify one of the following options (see Figure QS-8).**

- **Multi-rate SureStream for RealServer G2.** SureStream files combine a number of streams encoded at different bit rates into a single file. When serving SureStream files, a RealServer can dynamically adjust the bit rate of the file being served depending on the user's Internet connection. In the next step of the Wizard you can determine how many streams are contained within the SureStream file by choosing a number of target audiences.

- **Single-rate for Web servers.** Single rate streams contain a single stream encoded at the bit rate you specify. These streams are appropriate for downloading or streaming from Web servers, because they are smaller in size and Web servers do not have SureStream functionality.

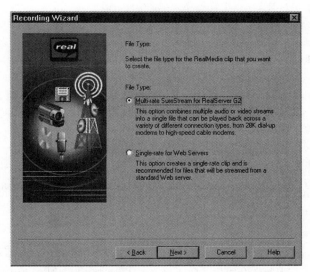

Figure QS-8: Choosing the encode type using the RealSystem Producer Recording Wizard

8. **Choose the SureStream option and click Next to move on.**

9. **Click the 28K Modem and 56K Modem checkboxes and then click Next to move on** (see Figure QS-9). The resulting encoded file will contain streams appropriate for both target audiences.

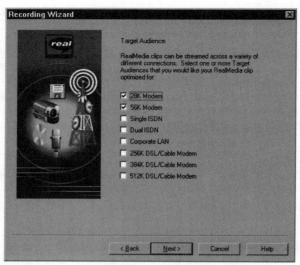

Figure QS-9: Selecting target audiences using the
RealSystem Producer Recording Wizard

10. **Next select the codec you want to use to encode the audio portion of your
    file (see Figure QS-10).** Keep the following notes in mind as you select the
    audio format for your audio file:

    • **Voice Only.** Choose this option for any content that contains voice
      content or music that is only in the background.

    • **Voice with Background Music.** Ignore this option. It uses the same
      codecs as the Voice Only setting.

    • **Music.** Choose this option for all low bit rate content that includes
      music.

    • **Stereo Music.** Choose this option if you want your encoded file to
      preserve the stereo information in the original signal. Files encoded in
      stereo have slightly lower frequency response and fidelity than mono
      recordings.

11. **The audio_example.wav has voice and music, so select the Music setting
    and click Next.**

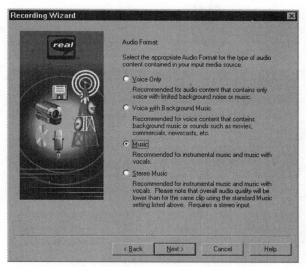

Figure QS-10: Selecting the audio codec using the RealSystem Producer Recording Wizard

12. **The last step is to specify a name and location for the encoded file (see Figure QS-11) by clicking Save As and navigating to the directory you want to save your file and providing a name for the file.** A good rule of thumb is to give your encoded file an informative name, such as audio_example_56_ss.rm. I added _ss to represent SureStream and added _56 to represent 56K Modem as my highest target audience.

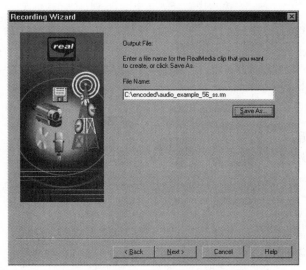

Figure QS-11: Specifying the output file using the RealSystem Producer Recording Wizard

13. After choosing a directory and filename for your RealMedia clip, click Next.
You are presented with a screen that summarizes all the settings you have just selected. Take a quick glance at them to make sure you did not make a mistake (see Figure QS-12).

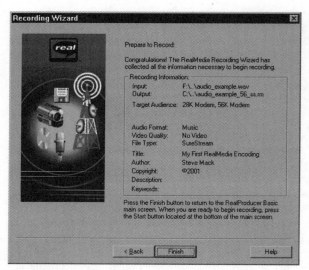

Figure QS-12: The RealSystem Producer settings summary

14. If you are satisfied with the settings, click the Finish button. The Recording Wizard closes and returns you to the main screen of the RealSystem Producer, with all your settings entered (see Figure QS-13).

Any clip information you specified for the file is visible on the left side of the window, and the name of your output file is shown at the top of the RealSystem Producer window.

Note　If you think that you may have made a mistake, you can always back up using the Back buttons, or restart the wizard by choosing File ➪ Recording Wizards ➪ Record from the File menu.

Output file name

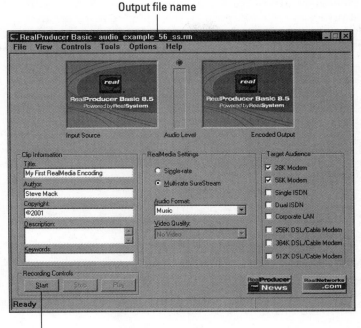

Click Start to begin the encoding process.

Figure QS-13: The RealSystem Producer after using the
Recording Wizard

15. **Click the Start button in the lower-left corner to begin the encoding
    process.** After the file is encoded, the Processing Complete window pops up
    to let you know that the file has finished encoding (see Figure QS-14).

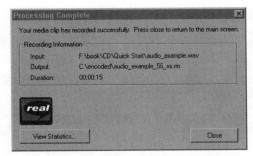

Figure QS-14: The RealSystem Producer
Processing Complete window

16. **Click Close to return to the RealSystem Producer main screen, or click View Statistics to see what streams are included in your SureStream file.** If you choose to view the statistics, the Statistics window pops up as shown in Figure QS-15. If you don't want to look at the Statistics window please skip to step 18.

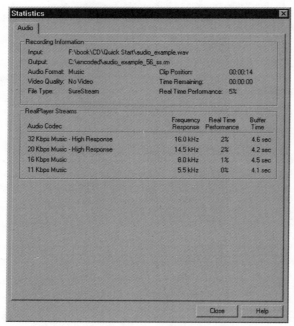

Figure QS-15: The RealSystem Producer Statistics window

The Statistics window indicates that not only are there 32 Kbps and 20 Kbps versions of the stream, but also 16 Kbps and 11 Kbps versions as well. These versions enable the RealServer to fall back to lower-quality streams in lieu of rebuffering.

17. **Click Close to return to the Processing Complete window and click close again to return to the RealSystem Producer main screen.**

18. **If you want to hear what the encoded file sounds like, click the Play button (see Figure QS-16).** This action opens up the RealPlayer and plays the encoded file.

You can re-encode the file using different settings by changing settings directly on the main screen or starting up the Recording Wizard again. If you want to change the name of your output file, you must start a new session. Do this by choosing File ⇨ New Session.

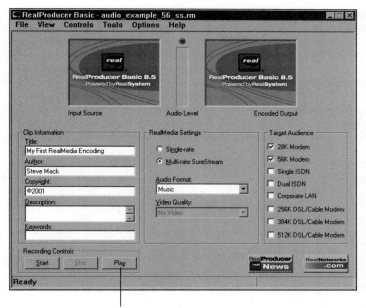

After encoding, the Play button becomes active.

Figure QS-16: Click the Play button to play your encoded file.

Encoding your first Windows Media file

Encoding Windows Media files is done using the Windows Media Encoder. The encoder has a wizard mode much like the RealSystem Producer. After you are more familiar with the encoding process, you will probably avoid using the wizard mode, but it is not a bad idea to stick with it for your first few encodes.

Encoding files with the Windows Media Encoder involves setting up a session, in which you specify the inputs, outputs, and then choosing an encoding *profile*, which determines the bit rate and quality settings of your encoded file. After you have specified all the settings, click the Start button to encode your file.

1. **Open up the Windows Media Encoder and create a new session by choosing Session menu ⇨ New Session Wizard or typing ⌘+W.** This action brings up the New Session Wizard window as shown in Figure QS-17. The following three options are available to you:

   - **Broadcast a live event from attached devices or computer screen.** Choose this option when you are broadcasting a live event.

   - **Capture audio or video from attached devices or computer screen.** Choose this option for a live encode from your sound card and/or video capture card to a file on your computer.

   - **Convert an audio or video file into a Windows Media file.** Choose this option to encode a file.

2. **Choose the Convert an audio of video file into a Windows Media file option and click Next.** The next screen requires you to specify your input and output files.

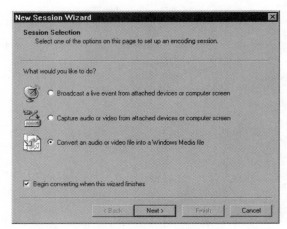

Figure QS-17: The Windows Media Encoder New Session Wizard window

3. **Choose the audio_example.wav file from the Quick Start directory on the sample CD and choose an appropriate output directory on your computer (see Figure QS-18) and click Next.** Make sure to use a sensible naming convention for your file, such as using _56 to represent 56K modem.

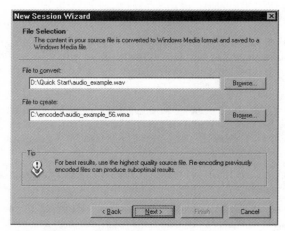

Figure QS-18: Setting your input and output files using the Windows Media Encoder

4. **In the next screen, choose the profile you want to use for this encoding session (see Figure QS-19).** Windows Media offers a whole slew of presets for encoding audio. For this example, choose the Audio for dial-up modems (56 Kbps stereo) option, because we're trying to encode a file for 56K modem users. Feel free to experiment with other profiles.

Choose the profile you want to use from the drop-down menu

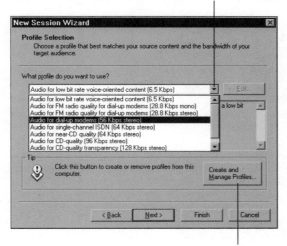

Create your own custom profiles by clicking on this button

Figure QS-19: Choosing and encoding profile using the Windows Media Encoder

5. **Click the Next button to move on to the next screen.** In the next screen, you can enter information about the file.

6. **Enter information about the file in the Display Information screen (see Figure QS-20) and click the Next button.**

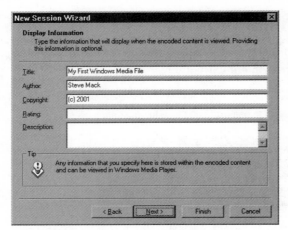

Figure QS-20: Specifying file information using
the Windows Media Encoder

The last screen of the session wizard is a summary of all the settings you have
just specified as reflected in Figure QS-21.

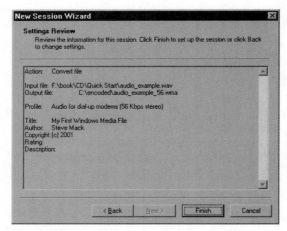

Figure QS-21: The Windows Media Encoder
settings review

7. **After having a quick look over the settings to make sure that they are
   correct, click the Finish button.** Depending on what you specified on the
   first wizard screen, the file either immediately begins encoding or you are
   returned to the Windows Media Encoder main window.

If some of the settings look suspect, reset them by clicking the Back button until you get to the screen you need.

8. **When you return to the Windows Media Encoder main screen, the information you just entered should be reflected in the display (see Figure QS-22).** All of the information you entered via the wizard can be accessed on the Windows Media Encoder main screen via the General and Display Information tabs.

   • **General tab.** Displays the input and output files as well as the encoding profile being used.

   • **Display Information tab.** Contains the clip information you specified for the file.

   If the encoder did not automatically begin encoding your file, click the Start button to begin the encoding process.

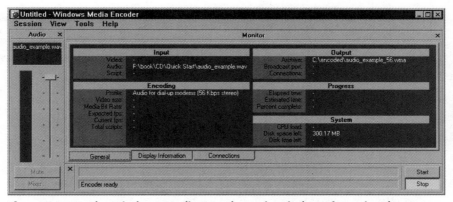

Figure QS-22: The Windows Media Encoder main window after using the New Session Wizard

9. **After your file has finished encoding, the Encoding Results window appears similar to the window shown in Figure QS-23.** From this window, you can play your encoded file by clicking the View Output File button or start a new encoding session by clicking the New Session button.

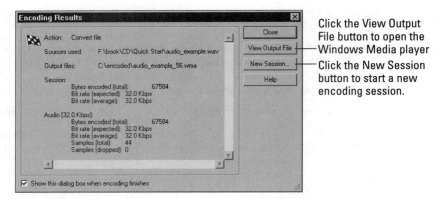

Click the View Output File button to open the Windows Media player

Click the New Session button to start a new encoding session.

Figure QS-23: The Windows Media Encoder results window

You should try encoding a few other files with various settings to become comfortable with the encoding process. After you've got a feeling for the three encoders and how they work, you'll want to showcase your encoded files. The next section describes how to create a Web page on your computer that links to your streaming media files.

Authoring Your First Local Streaming Media Presentation

Now that you've got some streaming media files, you probably want to show them off to the world. Therefore, you have to give the rest of the world some sort of link to them. The easiest way to do this is via a Web page.

There's a slight hitch, though. Due to a number of reasons that won't be explained in detail here (this is the Quick Start section, after all) you can't link directly to streaming media files from Web pages. What you have to do is create a tiny little text file that contains the location of the streaming media file. These little files are called *metafiles*.

Each streaming media software manufacturer has a slightly different approach to metafiles. QuickTime refers to them as *reference movies*, the RealSystem calls them RAM files (RealAudio metafiles), and Windows Media Technologies refers to them as *redirector files*. To make reference movies, you use the QuickTime player. To make RAM files and redirector files, you use a text editor.

After you've made your metafiles, place them on your Web server. Your HTML is then authored to link to the metafiles, and the metafiles in turn open up the appropriate streaming media player. Before you try linking from a Web server, read the following examples to find out how to link to files on your own hard drive.

Creating a QuickTime reference movie

Creating a QuickTime reference movie is very similar to encoding a file, but instead of Importing and Exporting, you simply Open and Save. The distinction is subtle but absolutely crucial.

When you Save a file from the QuickTime player, instead of saving the whole file, it instead saves a reference movie that contains the locations of all the parts of the movie. It's better than saving the individual parts because it takes up so much less room on your hard drive.

1. **Open up QuickTime player.**

2. **Open up the audio_example_40.mov file you encoded earlier by choosing File ⇨ Open and browsing to find the file.** You may have saved it in the C:\encoded directory. If you named your streaming QuickTime file differently, browse to find that file.

3. **Highlight the file and click the Open button.**

4. **Play the file to make sure that it is the right one.**

5. **When you have the right file, stop the playback and move the playback indicator all the way to the left, to the beginning of the file.**

6. **Create your reference movie by choosing Save from the File menu.** The Save window (see Figure QS-24) appears with the default set save to the same file name. Make sure that you give the reference movie a new name or save it in another directory. Otherwise, QuickTime does not allow you to save the file as a reference movie.

   As you change the file name, the options on the bottom half of the screen change. The file size of the Save normally changes drastically, and the Make Movie self-contained option is no longer grayed out.

   Make sure that the Save normally checkbox is checked. Otherwise, you are just saving a complete copy of the movie, which is not what you want. You only want to create a metafile that points to the actual encoded movie.

Tip

Good practice would be to add _ref to the original file name so that there is no confusion about what the file is. As a safety check, the size of your reference movie should be very small, in the 1-4K range.

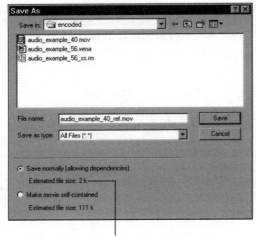

Your reference movie should be in the 1-4 K range

Figure QS-24: Saving a QuickTime reference movie

To save a QuickTime reference movie, you must either save to a different file name or save in a different directory.

7. Click save to save your reference movie.

That's it. You now have a metafile (reference movie in QuickTime-speak) that you use to link to your streaming file. The section "A simple HTML page using metafile links to your encoded files" details how to use it in an HTML page.

Creating a RealSystem RAM file

Creating a RealMedia metafile is very straightforward. All you have to do is type in a single line of code into a text editor and save the file with the .ram file extension. The line of code uses the following syntax:

```
{protocol}://{server}/{filename including directories}
```

Because this first example is going to link to a local file, you do not specify a server. Also, local files use a special syntax for the protocol, so your link should look like this (assuming the file name and directory information are correct):

```
file://C:\encoded\audio_example_56_ss.rm
```

Type the previous bit of code into a text editor and save it as audio_example_56_ss. ram. That's all there is to creating a RealSystem RAM file. You now have a metafile that points to your encoded file. You can move it anywhere on your computer because you specified the full path to the streaming file. Stay tuned for "A simple HTML page using metafile links to your encoded files" later in this chapter to find out how to use this file in an HTML page.

Creating a Windows Media redirector file

Windows Media redirector files are also small text files. The files are XML-compliant, so they are slightly more involved, in that they use special tags enclosed in angle brackets. Here is what you should type into your text editor:

```
<asx version="3.0">
    <entry>
        <ref href="file://C:\encoded\audio_example_56.wma" />
    </entry>
</asx>
```

This simple code breaks down as follows:

+ The redirector file begins and ends with the `<asx>` and `</asx>` tags. These tags are required in every Windows Media redirector file.

+ The redirector file has a single entry, which is enclosed by the `<entry>` and `</entry>` files.

+ The file to be played back is specified in the `href` *attribute* of the <ref> tag

You'll see later in Chapter 15 that Windows Media redirector files can do much more than link to a single file. For the time being, save this file with a `.asx` file extension. This metafile (redirector file in Windows Media-speak) can be moved anywhere on your computer because it contains the full path to the Windows Media file. In the next section, you create a simple Web page by using the metafiles you have created.

A simple HTML page using metafile links to your encoded files

Now that you have metafiles, it's time to create a very simple HTML page that uses them. This page isn't beautiful, but it gets the job done. All you have to do is use your metafiles in anchor tags. Code listing QS-1 shows how this is done.

Code Listing QS-1: A Simple HTML Page Linking to Local Streaming Media Files

```html
<html>

<body>
<h1>A Simple (ugly) Web Page with Streaming Media Links</h1>

<!-- link to the QuickTime file -->
<p>
<a href="file://c:\encoded\audio_example_40_ref.mov">Click here to
    play the QuickTime version</a>

<!-- link to the RealMedia file -->
<p>
<a href="file://c:\encoded\audio_example_56_ss.ram">Click here to
    play the RealMedia version</a>

<!-- link to the Windows Media File -->
<p>
<a href="file://c:\encoded\audio_example_56.asx">Click here to
    play the Windows Media version</a>
</body>


</html>
```

If you take the time to type this code in, substituting any file and directory name differences for your files, you'll see that this is indeed a no-frills HTML page. However, all the links should work just fine.

 Depending on which browser you're running, and in what order you installed your streaming media players, there's a slight chance that the Windows Media Player may attempt to hijack your QuickTime link and fail miserably. Chapter 16 provides the scoop on how to prevent this.

There is a slight difference to how the QuickTime file plays back compared to the other two. The QuickTime plays back centered in a new Web page, whereas the RealMedia and Windows Media files play back in pop-up players. This difference is a result of how the players are integrated into Web browsers.

There are, of course, other ways to showcase your streaming media files. You can embed the players in the Web page, and even control them via JavaScript — but that comes later, in Chapters 16 and 17.

Using a Streaming Media Server

Up to this point, all the examples have dealt with files being played locally. Because this is the *Streaming Media Bible*, you are probably wondering when the streaming part is going to start. To stream files from one machine to another, you use a streaming media server.

A streaming media server is similar to a Web server in that it takes requests from users and sends files in return. However, a streaming server is different in that it enables interactivity, such as being able to fast forward, rewind, and pause the media. In short, streaming servers are built to deliver media files, unlike Web servers.

Because most people still browse the Internet via their Web browsers, streaming servers must interact seamlessly with Web servers. This need for fluid interaction is one reason that metafiles are used — metafiles are the handoff point between the Web server and the streaming server.

After you have created your encoded files, place them on a streaming server and then create your metafiles. Your metafiles must contain the address of the files on the streaming servers. The addresses contained in your metafiles should be fully qualified URLs such as:

```
rtsp://my.quicktimeserver.com/movies/MyMovie.mov
rtsp://my.realserver.com/mediafiles/MyRealVideo.rm
mms://my.wmtserver.com/mediafiles/MyWMTVideo.wmv
```

The actual contents of your metafiles depends on the name of your streaming server, your directory structure, and of course the file name. After you have your metafiles, you author an HTML page that links to the metafiles. You could use code almost exactly like the previous example (see Code Listing QS-2).

Code Listing QS-2: A Simple HTML Page Linking to Streaming Media Files

```
<html>

<body>
<h1>A Simple (ugly) Web Page with Streaming Media Links</h1>

<!-- link to the QuickTime file -->
<p>
<a href="audio_example_40_ref.mov">Click here to
    play the QuickTime version</a>
```

Continued

Code Listing QS-2 *(continued)*

```html
<!-- link to the RealMedia file -->
<p>
<a href="audio_example_56_ss.ram">Click here to
    play the RealMedia version</a>

<!-- link to the Windows Media File -->
<p>
<a href="audio_example_56.asx">Click here to
    play the Windows Media version</a>
</body>
</html>
```

Both the HTML and the metafiles should be placed on the Web server — Code Listing QS-2 assumes that the metafiles are placed in the same directory as the HTML.

When you click on the links on the HTML page, the Web server sends your browser the small metafile, which your browser then hands off to the appropriate media player. The media player then opens up the metafile, and using the address contained within, requests the file from the streaming server.

This Quick Start doesn't include a concrete example of how to do all this — it depends a little too much on your streaming media architecture. If you've done any work with servers or HTML before, you shouldn't have too much trouble figuring out what goes where.

If this all seems a little confusing, don't worry. That's what this book is for — to teach you the streaming media ropes so that you can stream with the pros.

✦   ✦   ✦

Streaming Media: An Introduction

✦ ✦ ✦ ✦

✦ ✦ ✦ ✦

What Is Streaming Media?

These days, finding a Web site that does not include some type of streaming media is hard. Internet radio stations, movie trailers, and distance learning applications are all prime examples. Other examples include sample-before-you-buy music retail sites and online news sites, where stories are often released hours before the evening news.

In the midst of this media-rich information overload, you can easily forget that the Internet was not originally designed to transmit media, nor was it designed to support the number of users it does today. Today's Internet is a massive credit to the original architects whose design has proven to be so remarkably flexible, and to the innovators that continue to stretch the boundaries of the Internet experience.

The Origins of Streaming Media

With the release of Mosaic, the first graphical browser in 1993, Internet use skyrocketed. This explosive growth turned a simple, efficient way of sharing and linking together disparate resources into something altogether new. Suddenly people could place images on their Web pages, and links to virtually any kind of file, including audio files.

However, these new file types that people began to exchange were much larger than the text files that were originally zipping around the globe. This combined with the daily exponential growth in popularity of the Internet translated into huge traffic increases, forcing people to wait long periods of time to download and send files. The World Wide Web was soon dubbed the "World Wide Wait" by the nascent online press.

This wait was particularly painful for people trying to listen to audio files because of an audio file's size. The combination of slow connection speeds (14.4Kbps modems) and large file sizes meant a person trying to listen to a low-quality, one-minute-long file would have to wait at least five minutes for the privilege. For CD quality sound, you'd be waiting closer to two hours — which was completely impractical.

The main problem was that the listener had to wait until the *complete* audio file had been written to the hard drive before they could listen to it. They couldn't listen *as it downloaded* (this isn't strictly true — sometimes you could fool your computer but the results were unpredictable at best). This was due in part to the HTTP protocol, but mostly because browsers were not equipped to play back audio files. This had to be done by a separate application residing on the user's computer. This separate application could not access the file until the browser was finished downloading it.

There was also no simple mechanism to broadcast a live signal over the Internet. A few broadcasts had been done over the MBONE (multicast backbone), a highly specialized subset of the Internet, but to participate in one of these events required a high level of expertise and connectivity. It was at this point in the Internet's history, circa 1995, that streaming media was developed to address these problems.

Basic Streaming Media Concepts

Streaming offers a whole new approach to media on the Internet. Instead of waiting for the whole file to download to a user's computer before playback begins, streaming media playback occurs *as the file is being transferred*. The data travels across the Internet, is played back and then discarded. Streaming media also offers the user control over the stream during playback, something not possible with a Web server.

One of the great things about streaming media is that you can use it for live broadcasts or archived files that can be watched *on-demand*. This way folks who miss the live shows don't have to miss out on the great content — they can watch it when they get the chance.

Regardless of whether you're broadcasting live or streaming archives on-demand, streaming media files are always limited by a user's bandwidth. Because streaming media happens in real-time, you can only send as many bits as the user is capable of receiving.

This section introduces some of the key concepts of streaming media, such as the difference between streaming and downloading and the importance of a user's bandwidth. You need to understand these before moving on to the different components of a streaming media system.

Streaming versus downloading

Streaming media is real-time; you click on a link and a few seconds later you see or hear something. This functionality also enables live broadcasts, an impossibility with downloaded files. And because the bits are discarded after playback, streaming media offers a reasonable degree of copyright protection. Streaming media never touches the user's hard drive.

Downloaded files are by definition not real-time. When you click on a link to a downloaded file, you must wait until the whole file is transferred before you can play it. Downloaded files can easily be copied, because a full copy sits on your hard drive. This renders copyright holders defenseless against piracy unless some form of encryption or a Digital Rights Management (DRM) scheme is used.

Streaming media servers offer the user control over the stream. The user can control playback as if it were a VCR or tape deck. This type of control is not available with downloaded files until, of course, the whole file is downloaded. User interactivity is one of the great advantages of streaming media.

Progressive download

Sometimes a hybrid technology known as progressive download is used. *Progressive download* technology enables a file to be watched as it is downloaded. To accomplish this, progressive download technology utilizes what is known as a *buffer*. A buffer is a temporary area in your computer's memory used to store data. Progressive download files eventually store the whole file in a buffer, but playback is allowed to begin before the entire file is downloaded.

Progressive downloading is most often used when the subject matter is short, and the broadcaster wants to deliver slightly higher quality than a streaming media file would allow due to bandwidth restrictions. Many movie trailers are delivered in this fashion, because people are willing to wait the extra time for a higher quality version.

Progressive download technology is not true streaming in the strict sense, because the user has limited control over the stream. In some situations, a progressively downloaded file may be entirely appropriate, but for many applications, such as live broadcasts or radio stations, streaming media is the only way to go.

On-Demand files

As soon as files have been encoded into a format suitable for streaming and put on a server, they can be listened to at any time, by anyone, anywhere. As long as you create links to the files, people can access them.

In fact, many people can listen to the same file at the same time, and each person has control over their own presentation. Users can pause, fast-forward, rewind, or replay the file as they choose. A good example of on-demand streaming is distance learning. People can take a course from many different locations. Streaming media enables students to access files at different times and to move through the material at their own pace.

On-demand files can extend the usefulness and reach of live events. Though a lot of people may want to watch a particular live event as it is happening, many more may watch it after the fact. A large benefit of on-demand files is that because the file usage is spread out over time, you don't need to have as much connectivity to service a large number of people. Ten thousand people watching a small 28.8 video stream concurrently would take more bandwidth than most people have access to or care to pay for. However, over the course of a month those same ten thousand people could easily watch the same video consuming only modest connectivity.

On-demand files take full advantage of the Internet's flexibility as a medium. However, some events are so time-sensitive that they need to be broadcast live. No one wants to watch the World Series the day after it was played, nor does anyone want to watch the Oscars if they know who won. These types of events warrant a live broadcast.

Live broadcasting

Live broadcasting on the Internet involves encoding an event as it is happening, and sending the stream directly to the server. The server, in turn, broadcasts the stream straight out to the audience.

Live broadcasts require much more bandwidth than on demand files, because everyone tunes in at the same time. In addition to more bandwidth, live broadcasts also require multiple streaming servers so the load can be distributed across many different computers.

By spreading the load across many computers, you reduce the chance of a server crashing and the event grinding to an unexpected halt for anyone receiving their stream from that server. The larger the event, the more servers you need. In fact, you should have *extra* servers available for redundancy purposes. That way, if one server goes down, you can steer the traffic to a back-up server. Some degree of redundancy should be built into every server infrastructure, but it is particularly important in live broadcasts where you don't get a second chance.

Bandwidth issues

One of the problems that streaming media systems have to deal with is the stochastic nature of bandwidth on the Internet. Even though a user's available bandwidth appears constant, in practice it rarely is. It fluctuates wildly between zero and some maximum rate. To deal with this, streaming media players utilize a *buffer*. The first few seconds of the file are stored in the computer's memory before playback begins. This gives the media player a reserve of bits to fall back on when the user's bandwidth becomes constricted.

Think of the food you keep in your house. Each day you need to consume approximately the same amount. You know this, so you stock up your refrigerator with tasty treats, and replenish it from time to time. Sometimes you fill your refrigerator to capacity, other times you throw in leftovers. The food supply chain is not constant, so you use the refrigerator and your pantry as a buffer. If the food supply runs out, you go hungry.

So it is with streaming. The streaming media player plays back streams at a constant rate. If a user's bandwidth becomes constricted and new data stops arriving, the media player dips into the buffer and plays back those bits. If the buffer runs out, the media player must stop playback and wait for the buffer to be replenished.

Streaming media players are generally able to hide the random nature of Internet delivery by constantly keeping the buffer full. At least that's how the theory goes. Anyone who watches streaming media knows that sometimes a buffer isn't enough, particularly when the Internet is having a bad hair day.

Downloaded files suffer the same bandwidth issues as streaming files, but because they are not played back until they are completely transferred, you don't experience the re-buffering that streaming media files sometimes do. Instead, you have to wait longer when the bandwidth becomes constricted.

One thing you're probably well aware of is that few things are more frustrating than waiting for things to happen on the Internet. This is why streaming media is the clear winner in so many applications, because it is designed to provide a more or less instantaneous experience. To understand how this happens, the next section explains the three basic components of a streaming media system.

Streaming Media System Components

Streaming media is made possible by different pieces of software that communicate on a number of different levels. A basic streaming media system has three components:

✦ **Player.** The software that viewers use to watch or listen to streaming media

✦ **Server.** The software that delivers streams to audience members

✦ **Encoder.** The software that converts raw audio and video files into a format that can be streamed

These components communicate with each other using specific *protocols*, and exchange files in particular *formats*. Some files contain data that has been encoded using a particular *codec*, which is an algorithm designed to reduce the size of files.

The following two sections discuss in more detail the software components of a streaming media system, and the different ways in which they communicate.

Encoders, servers, and players

Encoders, servers and players are the three basic building blocks of a streaming media system. The audience uses a streaming media player to watch the streaming media content. This content is requested and received from a server, which is a specialized piece of software designed to deliver media streams. Encoders are used to create the streams that sit on servers. Figure 1-1 shows a diagram of these three components and how they interact in a streaming media system.

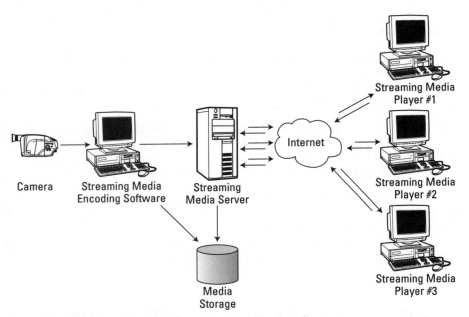

Figure 1-1: The basic components of a streaming media system

Encoders

Before anyone can watch or listen to streaming media, raw audio and video files must be converted to a format that can be streamed across the Internet. This is done using a streaming media encoder, and is known as *encoding*.

Encoding involves reducing the amount of data contained in the raw file while maintaining as much of the original quality as possible. In addition to reducing the file size, the encoder must package the resultant file in an error-resistant format to protect against potential losses in transit. Encoders and encoding are covered in detail in Part III of this book

Servers

As soon as the files have been encoded, they must be placed on a streaming media server. Streaming media servers are similar to Web servers in that they deal with file requests coming from multiple clients, but the similarity ends there.

Web servers are designed to service a large number of short requests. As soon as a Web server delivers a Web page to your browser, the communication between the Web server and your browser ends. Streaming servers, on the other hand, maintain a two-way connection to the user's player throughout the duration of the stream. They have to do this, because the user may decide to pause or fast-forward the program.

In addition to servicing requests from players, streaming media servers must also process incoming live broadcasts from encoders. In fact, streaming media severs may be processing multiple incoming live broadcasts and serving them to audience members simultaneously, along with serving archived streams that reside on the server's hard drives.

Many streaming media servers also offer additional features such as DRM (digital rights management), advertisement insertion, splitting or reflecting of other servers' streams, or multicasting. All the features of streaming servers are covered in more detail in Part V of the book.

Players

A streaming media player is a piece of software that knows how to communicate with a streaming media server, and how to play back, or *render* the streams it receives. A streaming media player can function as a stand-alone application, or as a plug-in inside a Web browser.

Streaming media players generally offer interactive control over streams, such as play, pause, fast-forward, and so on. Some players offer additional features, such as the ability to record streams, the ability to adjust the audio or video, and some sort of filing system to catalog your favorite streams.

Most of you reading this book probably already have at least one if not several streaming media players installed on your computer. The most common streaming media players are RealNetworks' RealPlayer, Microsoft's Windows Media Player, and Apple's QuickTime player. Each has its own set of strengths and weaknesses, as you will discover throughout this book. Other streaming technologies are out there, but in the interest of scope, this book sticks to the manufacturers that are referred to as "the Big 3."

Protocols, file formats, and codecs

The components of a streaming media system must communicate with each other on a number of different levels. Protocols, file formats and codecs provide the framework for this interaction:

✦ **Protocols.** Set the ground rules for how information is exchanged between the components

✦ **File formats.** The standardized way in which this data is exchanged

✦ **Codecs.** Used to encode and decode information contained within the file formats

Current streaming media systems are for the most part closed. Software for one system does not work with any other, except in special situations, because of proprietary protocols, file formats, or codecs. This is slowly beginning to change as standards begin to emerge and gain momentum. Standardized protocols and file formats benefit both the audience and streaming media creators, because they mean a wider selection for viewers and less work for content creators.

Protocols

At the lowest level, you must first have a method for sending streaming media files across the Internet and a way for players and encoders to talk to the server. HTTP, the protocol used to deliver Web pages, is not particularly well suited to streaming media for various reasons. Other protocols are available, but the problem is that a unified standard does not exist.

Little to no interoperability exists between the three main streaming platforms. Both Apple QuickTime and the RealSystem use RTSP (Real Time Streaming Protocol), while Microsoft uses it's own proprietary protocol known as MMS (Microsoft Media Services). It's not the end of the world, because they all work well, but it does present additional challenges.

From a content creation standpoint, supporting multiple formats to cover the widest possible audience can be time consuming and expensive. On the users' side, it can be frustrating having multiple media players on the desktop, each trying to play back all your media files (and sometimes failing). The situation is further complicated by the next layer — file formats.

File formats

When a player or server receives streaming media data, it must be unpacked and rearranged according to a specific set of rules. These rules are known as the file format. Unfortunately, each streaming media platform has its own file format, which is another reason why they don't work with each other.

Note   The MPEG-4 specification, which was approved in January 1999 by the ISO (International Standards Organization), includes an attempt to standardize a streaming media file format that is based on the QuickTime file format. It remains to be seen whether the format will be widely adopted or not. Both Apple and RealNetworks have pledged to support MPEG 4.

Codecs

Last but not least, after the streaming media data is unpacked and reassembled, the streaming media player must decode the data during playback. This is done using a piece of software known as a codec. The word codec is a contraction of *co*der/*dec*oder or *co*mpressor/*dec*ompressor, depending on who you ask.

Codecs are used because raw audio and video files contain too much data to stream over the Internet. Codecs use advanced mathematical models to reduce the size of A/V files to anywhere from one-fourth to one-fiftieth the size of the original. Of course, drastic size reduction cannot occur without some loss in quality. File compression is not a perfect science, but it has improved by leaps and bounds, due in large part to the extreme competition between the major streaming platforms.

Each of the major streaming platforms has a suite of supported codecs, for both audio and video. Each platform claims its codecs are superior, but in reality they are all very close in quality and performance. Quality varies between platforms, but not by much.

Now that you know about the software components that make up a streaming media system, and a little bit about how they all work together, it's time to learn about the streaming media process. When you begin this process, you'll utilize all the streaming media system components, plus additional hardware and software tools.

The Streaming Media Process

Setting up streaming media system components is only the first step towards a complete streaming media system. You also have to create streaming media content, put it up on your servers, and offer some sort of link to your audience so that they can enjoy it. The whole process breaks down into four main stages:

✦ **Creation.** Making the audio/video content that you want to stream

✦ **Encoding.** Converting the raw content it to a format that can be streamed

✦ **Authoring.** Designing how you're going to showcase your media

✦ **Serving.** Placing the files on a server and letting the world have a look-see

These four stages are in rough chronological order if you're creating a single piece of streaming content. If you're creating new content on a regular basis, however, these stages can overlap. For the purposes of organization, this book treats each stage separately. In fact, each stage gets its own Part in the book:

✦ Part II. Creation: Creating High Quality Source Material

✦ Part III. Encoding: Getting the Most Out of Your Encoder

✦ Part IV. Authoring: Going Public with Your Streams

✦ Part V. Serving: Delivering Your Presentation

To give you a hint of what is contained in these parts of the book, the four stages of the creation process are briefly explained here.

Creation

The creation phase is where it all begins. Before you can stream anything, you need content, and that content has to come from somewhere. Creating content for streaming media starts off with the basics — solid audio and video production skills. For the most part, making content for the Internet is the same as making content for any other broadcast medium, such as radio or television. There are a few notable exceptions, which are discussed in depth in Part II of this book.

You may want to use more than just audio and video in your presentations. Streaming media can also include images, text, or even animation. Animation and image creation are not covered in this book, partially due to space constraints, but also because there are already other good reference books available on the subject. What those books do not cover is how to use those data types in streaming media presentations. That *is* covered in this book, in Part VI and Part VII.

Encoding

After you create content, you need to convert the content to a streaming media format. As mentioned earlier, this is known as encoding.

When you encode your files, you have to make some decisions about who your target audience is. Is your audience at home on dial-up modem connections? Or is your audience an internal corporate audience on a high speed LAN? Your target audience dictates the maximum bit rate of your streaming media, which in turn dictates the overall size and quality of your encoded files.

The best part about encoding is that after you make the decisions as to what works best with your content, you can automate the process. This can be done in a number of different ways, such as using special batch processing software or running simple encoding scripts. You may want to single out a particularly difficult file for special treatment, but for the most part, you won't have to worry about the details of encoding on a regular basis. All the wonders of encoding, including automation, are covered in depth in Part III of this book.

Authoring

During the authoring phase, you decide how to present streaming files to the world. The simplest way to showcase your streams is to place a link on a Web page. On the other hand, you may decide that you want the presentation to play inside of a Web page as a plug-in. You may also want your streaming files to interact with other elements on the Web page.

Many options are available for showcasing media. Each option requires a slightly different approach and slightly different code to implement. All of this is covered in detail in Part V of this book.

As your requirements become more complex, or you decide to use multiple data types, you may want to use SMIL (Synchronized Multimedia Integration Language) to author your presentations. SMIL is a standards-based language that is supported by Apple and RealNetworks, and to certain extent Microsoft. SMIL provides control over the layout and timing of presentations in streaming media players. SMIL is a very powerful and flexible language, and is treated to its own section in Part VII of this book.

Serving

Last but certainly not least, serving is the interface between your streaming media files and your audience. After you create, encode, and author a presentation, you need to put the presentation on a server, so users can see it.

The serving stage involves design, implementation, maintenance, and analysis stages that interact with each other in a somewhat cyclical manner. First, you need to design and implement a robust streaming server infrastructure. After the servers are up and running, you want to make sure that they are performing well. And of course you want to analyze the data that the servers provide in their log files to see who the audience is, what they are listening to, and when they are listening. This might lead you back to the design stage to add to your infrastructure.

Designing a streaming media server infrastructure to meet your needs is relatively straightforward, assuming you're starting with modest goals. As your streaming media needs grow, so too must your server infrastructure. Live events in particular place strenuous demands upon streaming servers because the audience comes all at once, instead of spread out over the course of a whole day.

Maintaining your server infrastructure involves not only making sure the servers are up and running, but also managing the assets that are being served. You may run some sort of Digital Asset Management (DAM) software, and if you're charging for your content, you might need to invest in a Digital Rights Management (DRM) system. Of course, each of these systems provides reams of data in the form of log files for you to analyze to make sure your system is performing how it should.

The information extracted from these log files provides invaluable feedback about your content and your server performance. You may find after reviewing the log file data that certain types of content are more popular, indicating where new programming resources should be invested. You can also get a good idea of how your servers are handling the traffic load. You may find that you need to add more servers to handle the load, or that you need to purchase more bandwidth.

All of the above streaming media server considerations are dealt with in much more detail in Part V of this book.

Streaming Media Tools

In the previous section the streaming media process was broken into four distinct stages. In each of these stages, you'll be using a number of different tools, both hardware and software. Some tools are used in more than one stage, while others are more specialized.

You'll find out more about all these tools as you encounter them in various parts of this book. In the meantime, here's a quick overview of the tools you'll be using.

Creation tools

By far, the tools that get the most attention from your co-workers are the creation tools. Many of these tools you are probably already familiar with, such as cameras, tripods, microphones, and headphones. Others tools may be new to you, but will quickly become your favorites, such as a mixing desk or a compressor. Best of all, audio and video tools are without a doubt, well . . . cool!

In addition to the flashy hardware tools, you'll find a lot of great software tools, some of which are on the CD-ROM. For complete information on what is on the CD-ROM, check out the What's On the CD-ROM appendix located at the back of this book.

You'll be using audio editing software, video editing software, and perhaps also some image manipulation tools. After you become proficient at using these software tools, you'll find a lot of other uses for them. Beware — audio and video production is addictive.

Having a camera and tripod sitting in the corner of your office is sure to turn some heads. Throw in a microphone and a decent set of speakers, and you'll be the center of attention. Then, when everyone starts hearing about your new toys and newly acquired streaming media prowess, the requests for favors will start rolling in. My advice — only partly in jest — is to keep these tools hidden and locked up.

Encoding tools

In comparison to the creation tools, most encoding tools are downright dull. Without them, however, streaming media wouldn't exist. Encoders are stand-alone pieces of software put out by each platform. These utilitarian pieces of software are designed to do just one thing — encode. Because of the growing popularity of streaming media, many audio and video editing platforms are building encoding capabilities into their software. This makes your job as a streaming media creator that much easier, because you no longer have to use two separate applications. In this case, your editing software doubles as a creation and an encoding tool.

As briefly mentioned in the last section, you may also decide to take advantage of some form of batch processing. Batch processing automates the encoding process, and can be done using separate dedicated software applications or using the batch processing capabilities of your audio and video editing software.

Encoding tools are covered in more depth in Part III of this book.

Authoring tools

The authoring tools you use can be as simple as a rudimentary text editor or an advanced graphical WYSIWYG (what-you-see-is-what-you-get) editor. Your choice depends on how you want to showcase your media. Simple Web page links are the most straightforward; advanced presentations are going to require a combination of layout tools for the design and text editors to hack the code.

Some platforms offer tools that can author basic presentations, but for my money, you can't beat getting under the hood and cutting the code yourself. Some technologies covered in this book are fairly immature, and consequently the tools available can leave much to be desired.

Authoring is definitely where platforms begin to differentiate themselves. Some platforms have excellent support in a number of tools; others have pitifully little support and demand patience, some require programming skill, or both.

You'll soon discover that making the streaming media process easy involves reusing as much of your previous work as possible. When you find a template that works, stick with it. There's no shame in that — most Web sites use templates liberally. Television and radio stations have formats that they rigidly adhere to. This structure makes it easier to create a large quantity of output.

The authoring process and accompanying tools are covered in more depth in Part IV.

Serving tools

The most obvious tool you use in the serving stage is the server itself. Each streaming media platform has its own server software, which comes bundled with a set of utilities that allow you to manage the day-to-day operational tasks, as well as monitor server performance.

Since serving is all about your network, you may also use tools to monitor the network itself. To improve network performance, you can use special hardware such as Layer 4 switches and hardware caches. If you're really brave, you might actually play around with the hardware routers and switches to fine-tune your network.

Digital Asset Management (DAM) and Digital Rights Management (DRM) solutions are specialized software tools that help keep your streaming media files organized and protected. Some streaming media platforms come with these features built in, while others require third-party solutions.

Perhaps most important is some sort of tool to help you analyze your log files, so you can make intelligent decisions about your content strategy and your server infrastructure. There are off the shelf software tools to help you do this, or you can hire third-party vendors to do it for you.

All of these tools are discussed in more detail in Part V of this book.

Platform considerations

When it comes to deciding which streaming media platform to use, you need to consider many different factors. Some of the things for you to take into consideration are:

✦ The feature sets of the system components

✦ Amount of tool support from third-party vendors

✦ Size of audience install base

✦ Associated license fees

✦ Operating system platform support

Your choice of streaming media platform will depend on which of these factors is most important to you and/or your company. The three major streaming media software manufacturers (Apple, RealNetworks, Microsoft) provide enough free software on their Web sites for you to test out their systems, and I highly recommend you do so. On paper, all three streaming media platforms look wonderful — in practice, they can be downright frustrating. The best way to find out which one is best for you is to take them all for a test drive.

As different as the three streaming media platforms are, streaming media software manufacturers all share the same underlying goal: to provide the users and audience with the best possible streaming media experience. To do that, you need to create the highest-quality programming. That's true no matter which platform you end up choosing.

Summary

Even though the Internet was not designed to deliver streaming media, enough time and effort has been invested into the problem that streaming media has become an integral part of the Internet experience. Now that you've been introduced to the basics of streaming media, the next chapter deals with some of the basics of audio and video.

✦ Streaming is different from downloading.

✦ A user's bandwidth limits the quality of the file that can be streamed to them.

✦ Web servers can only download files and offer no user control.

✦ Streaming servers offer VCR-type control over streams.

✦ A streaming media system has three components: encoders, servers, and players.

✦ Encoders take raw audio and video files and convert them into a format that can be streamed.

✦ Streaming servers broadcast live and on-demand files across the Internet to streaming media players.

✦ Streaming media players request and receive files from streaming servers, and decompress the files as they play them back.

✦ Streaming media components communicate using special *protocols*, exchange files in specific *formats*, and use *codecs* to compress and decompress files.

✦ The streaming process has four stages — creation, encoding, authoring and serving.

✦ Different tools are used at each stage of the streaming media process, though some tools are used at more than one stage.

✦   ✦   ✦

Before You Stream: The Basics

Before you jump headfirst into the world of streaming
media, it's helpful to have a thorough understanding of
audio and video technology. Much of the technology used in
streaming media systems is directly descended from earlier
research in audio and video broadcasting.

Because streaming media derives from the world of broadcast, you should acquaint yourself with the various standards
used in broadcasting. Not only does it help you understand
the challenges in streaming media, but also these standards
were established to make it possible to produce broadcasts to
a unified high standard. You should ascribe to this standard in
your streaming media productions.

Many methods have been developed to store and transmit
audiovisual data over the years. Initially analog, then electronic,
and finally digital technologies have all been harnessed to this
end. Each technological advance has generally corresponded
with an increase in fidelity.

Ironically, streaming media reversed this trend. While consumers and content creators demand the highest possible
quality, the bandwidth limitations of streaming media impose
severe restrictions on bit rates, which in turn affect quality.
The inherent tug-of-war between quality and bandwidth is
what drives streaming media development. As technology
improves and available bandwidth increases, this trend will
be seen as a temporary setback during the early development
phase of streaming media.

In addition to broadcast formats and standards, this chapter
discusses the importance of your recording environment. It is
very difficult to produce high-quality streaming media without

an appropriate environment to work in. This chapter begins with a brief discussion of the history of recorded audio and video to put the broadcast standards of today into historical context.

Analog Recording and Reproduction

Folks have been recording sounds and pictures for over a century. Initially these methods were crude, but the past one hundred years or so have allowed people to refine the processes considerably.

Recorded sound

The earliest attempts at recording sound were strictly mechanical affairs. People spoke or played music in front of a large cone, at the end of which was attached a thin diaphragm. The diaphragm was connected to a needle, which sat on a soft cylinder of wax. Sound striking the diaphragm caused it to vibrate, which in turn made the needle move back and forth. This back and forth motion of the needle could be etched into the wax cylinder as it rotated. After the wax hardened, you could reverse the process and play back the cylinders, where the etchings in the wax cylinder would be converted back into sound.

Along came electricity, and the mechanical system was augmented with electronic components. Instead of a mechanical diaphragm, microphones converted the vibrations of sound waves into electrical signals. The back and forth motion could be represented as a positive and negative voltage, which more precisely controlled the needle. On playback, the needle's movement created electrical impulses that moved a speaker back and forth. These electrical systems and their components were far more accurate than the original mechanical systems, though ultimately the recording was still a mechanical rendition of the signal etched into a wax platter.

With the introduction of magnetic tape systems, the electronic information could be converted into magnetic impulses and stored on a strip of plastic coated with magnetized particles. Initially used solely as a studio-recording medium, it eventually surfaced on the consumer market, first as reel-to-reel and later as cassette tapes. Removing the mechanical component from the recording process greatly improved quality, because less audio quality was lost in the electro-magnetic conversion of tape than in the electro-mechanical transfer of discs.

As a recording medium, magnetic recording offered new flexibility. The tape could be re-used, unlike wax platters. It was also possible to edit by cutting and splicing the tape back together. Soon multitrack recorders arrived which allowed instruments to be recorded onto different tracks and also allowed the luxury of re-recording instruments individually. No longer did everyone have to record a perfect take at the same time.

Until the advent of digital audio technology, the recording process changed very little over the years. Equipment improved and new tricks were devised, but the process remained essentially the same.

Pictures

Film and video have their origins in the still photo. There were many different early versions, but the one that became the standard and the basis of all film stocks and cameras today involved exposing film containing a chemical coating impregnated with silver particles to a light source. The exposure to light caused a chemical reaction in the coating such that a representation of the original scene was recorded by the tiny silver particles. Depending on the type of film used, different development processes could be used to create printed versions of the photo, or versions that could be projected onto a white surface and viewed.

The size of the silver particles in the coating determined the film's sensitivity to light. Larger particles were more apt to catch the incoming light — that is, were more sensitive — and therefore able to be used in lower light conditions. Smaller particles were less sensitive and better suited to brighter scenes. Even though the particles were too small to be seen by the naked eye, the difference between film stocks was clearly visible, as the larger particles displayed a pronounced graininess. This is still the case today; film is now available to shoot in very low light conditions, but the less light it requires, the bigger the grain in the resulting print. You also see this behavior in video cameras.

Moving pictures, or movies, are essentially a series of still photos, taken in rapid succession. After the film is developed, a film projector displays them in sequence. Each photo, or frame, is shown for a split second. Between each frame the projection beam is interrupted while the projector advances the film. When this happens fast enough, it appears to be constant motion because of a phenomenon known as persistence of vision — anything that happens faster than somewhere around 20 times per second is perceived as continuous motion.

To give the illusion of smooth motion, motion pictures are shot and projected at 24 fps (frames per second). A quick look at some old films shows that this was not always the case — films were originally shot at somewhere around 18 frames per second. The frame rate was approximate because before the invention of the electric movie camera, the film was advanced by means of a hand crank on the side of the camera or via a spring mechanism — neither of which produced the smoothest frame rates. The combination of the slower, unsteady frame rates and being projected back at a frame rate faster than that at which they were originally shot is what gives old films that jerky, sped-up feel you see today.

Just as electrical components crept into the audio world, they slowly found their way into cameras and projectors. Video cameras were developed, where the incoming picture was scanned, measured, and converted into a series of electrical values.

These values could then be broadcast, received, and converted back into pictures, much like radio had been doing for some time. But unlike audio, which was a continuous stream of information, video had to be divided into frames and each frame broken down into units that could be measured.

The NTSC (National Television Standards Committee) decided on 30 frames per second as the standard (based on the 60 Hz alternating electrical current), with each frame divided into 525 horizontal lines. A video camera would scan a scene line by line, starting at the top left corner and assign electrical values depending on how bright each portion of the line was. At the end of each line, the scan would zip across the screen and start at the next line. At the bottom of the screen, the scan would return to the top left-hand corner and start again on the next frame. The time that it takes for the scan to return to the top left-hand corner is known as the vertical-blanking interval (VBI). Figure 2-1 shows how this works.

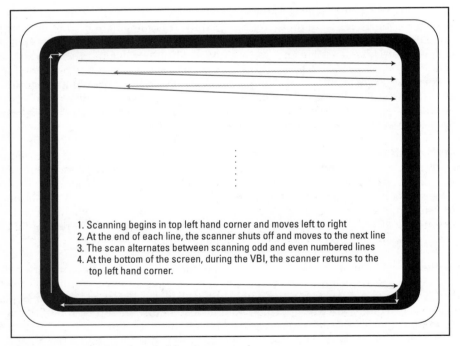

Figure 2-1: How interlaced video is scanned.

In general, the process works as follows:

1. Each frame is divided into two fields. The odd field consists of odd numbered lines and the even field consists of even numbered fields.

2. Scanning begins in the top-left corner and moves left to right.

3. At the end of each line, the scanner shuts off and moves to the next odd or even lines, depending on whether the odd or even field is being scanned.

4. At the bottom of the frame, the scanner returns to the top-left corner and scans the other field.

Even at this rapid frame rate, the television appeared to "flicker." Flicker is a function of screen brightness and frame rate, and is not noticeable at approximately 40 frames per second. To combat this, it was decided to double the scan rate, but scanning only the odd lines on the first pass, followed by the even lines on the second. Each scan was called a *field*. By projecting first the odd field and then the even at 60 fields per second, the flicker problem was eliminated. This form of scanning and display is known as *interlacing*. This will be a problem for us later on, because computer screens are not interlaced displays; when the two fields are combined and projected on a computer screen, interlacing artifacts can appear (see Figure 2-2). Artifacts are distortions introduced into digital audio or video during the digitization or compression process.

Cross-Reference For a deeper discussion about interlacing artifacts (including an example) please turn to the discussion about de-interlacing filters in Chapter 10.

Most European electrical current is 50 cycles per second, which makes their frame rate 25 frames per second. Complicating things even further, there are different standards for assigning values for color and brightness (PAL [Phase Alternation by Line] and SECAM [Sequential Color and Memory]). You'll see later on that converting between film and video or between different video standards can be tricky.

Digital Audio and Video

Along with the electronics revolution of the last 50 years has come the introduction of digital audio and video. Instead of storing audio and video signals as electrical impulses or magnetic waves, the signal is represented as a series of numbers stored in a digital format.

Digital formats have a number of benefits, the key one being that copies don't degrade. When you're copying zeroes and ones it is very simple to make a perfect copy. With analog recordings, each copy, or generation, exhibits some loss in quality.

Digital formats are also very malleable. After you've got the material digitized, it is easy to edit and process. One of the key benefits to editing and processing digital audio and video is that it is non-destructive; if you don't like what you've done, you can simply "undo" the action or re-digitize the original. This was most definitely not the case with magnetic audio tape or film — after an edit was made, you pretty much had to live with it.

Of course, with the advent of satellite and now Internet transmission, digital formats are extremely portable. Plummeting memory prices and increasingly dense storage formats like CD-ROM and DVD now allow digital formats to be stored cheaply and efficiently.

Digital audio

When you digitize audio, you have to find a way of converting the electrical wave into digital information. To do this, you can take measurements of the wave at different points in time and store the resulting values sequentially (see Figure 2-2).

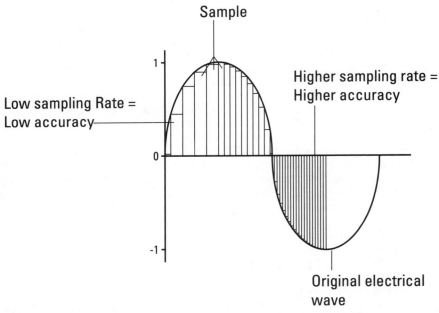

Figure 2-2: A sound wave and how it is digitized using discrete samples.

Each box under the original waveform in Figure 2-2 represents a sample. The higher the sampling rate, the more accurate the digitized waveform.

The original electrical wave is the continuous curving line. Underneath it are boxes representing measurements of the amplitude of the wave at precise intervals. These values, or *samples*, are stored sequentially in memory. To play back the digitized version of the wave, these stored values are retrieved and sent to the playback device. In Figure 2-2, the first quarter of the wave has five boxes underneath it; the second quarter ten, and the third 20. These represent different sampling rates.

Sampling rates

By its nature, digital audio involves discrete samples, each sample being a measurement of the voltage of the wave at that point in time. The sampling rate is the rate at which these measurements are taken. The higher the sampling rate, the more accurate the digital representation of the original electrical wave.

You can see in Figure 2-1 that the digital rendition results in a stair-stepped representation of the original curve. As the sampling rate increases, the stair-stepping effect is less pronounced, and the digital rendition approaches the original curve.

Compact discs are sampled at a rate of 44,100 samples per second. This is considered sufficient to capture the full audible spectrum of 20–20,000 cycles per second. There are audio professionals who feel the original CD standard short-changed the listener and that a higher standard is necessary. There are now proposed formats with higher sampling rates and bit depths, but it remains to be seen whether or not they will be accepted as a consumer standard (see the "Digital audio: How High is Enough?" sidebar).

Bit depth

Every time you sample the incoming signal, you have to assign a number to the electrical value. *Bit depth* refers to the number of bits used to store that numeric value. The more bits used, the higher the accuracy.

As an example, if you measure how wide your desk is, you could say approximately six feet, or 72 inches, or 1,828 millimeters; the smaller the unit of measurement you use, the higher the degree of accuracy. However, smaller units mean larger measurement values. To use millimeters in this case, you would have to be able to store four digits.

Computers use binary numbers to store values. The word *bit* refers to a binary digit that can be stored. If eight bits are used to store the value, you actually have the ability to store up to 256 different values. This is because

```
2^8 = 2 * 2 * 2 * 2 * 2 * 2 * 2 * 2 = 256
```

Sixteen bits yields 65,536 different values. Twenty-four bits yields over 16 million values. The greater the number of bits, the larger the number that can be stored, and the more accurate the measurement is.

Compact discs use 16 bit samples. The same audio engineers that complain about the sampling rate may also be heard pontificating upon the subject of bit depths. Today, it is not uncommon to see 20 bit and 24 bit systems in the professional arena. Whether either takes off as a consumer standard remains to be seen.

Sampling audio at 44,100 times a second using a 16 bits for the left- and right-hand side of a stereo signal gives a data rate of

```
44,100 samples/second * 16 bits/sample * 2 = 1,411,200 bps

1,411,200 bits/second / 1024 bits/Kb = 1,378 Kbps
```

Digital Audio: How High Is Enough?

Ever since the CD audio standard emerged, there has been controversy as to whether it was accurate enough to truly represent the full audio spectrum. In theory, the sample rate of 44,100 Hz is high enough to represent the full frequency range from 20–20,000 Hz. A bit depth of 16 bits gives an enormous amount of detail — or does it?

Look at the sample rate first. Audiophiles feel it isn't high enough. Though virtually no one can hear sounds above 20 kHz, there are harmonic overtones in music that reside above the range of human hearing. Some people feel that artificially imposing a ceiling on the frequency range changes the character of the experience, which in turn changes how the music "feels." There is some evidence to support that even though people can't hear above a certain frequency, higher frequencies do affect the listening experience, though this evidence is highly subjective. As a solution, sampling rates of 48 kHz and 96 kHz have been proposed as new standards.

The argument for a higher bit depth is more scientific. With binary data, each bit added doubles the resolution that the data representation is capable of. The problem is that even though 16 bits are capable of over 65 thousand unique values, only the very loudest peaks use the top bits of resolution. The bulk of the audio signal ends up being represented by only 14 bits.

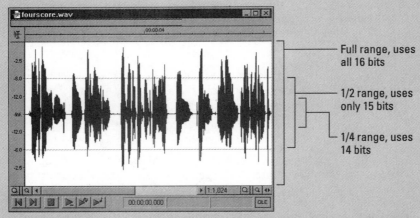

16-bit audio systems are effectively 14 bit systems, because the top two bits are rarely used.

The solution is to use more bits. Twenty-four bits allows over 16 million unique values. Even if the top two bits aren't used, the effective resolution is still 22 bits, which is more than enough to capture the full dynamic range the human ear is capable of handling.

The problem is that using higher sampling rates and bit depth increases the amount of data. Increasing the bit depth to 24 bits leads to a 50 percent increase in the amount of data; using a 48 kHz-sample rate leads to 10 percent more data, while using 96 kHz more than doubles the data. Twenty-four bit/96 kHz more than triples the data rate.

In the pursuit of pure audio, nothing is ever enough, of course. The argument for increased bit depth is rock solid; increased sample rates a bit less so. Because your eventual destination is streaming media files, the last thing you want is more data. But in the interest of posterity, fidelity should be job #1.

The simple answer? The CD standard works — use it. If you're a purist and interested in true audiophile quality, 24/96 sounds better.

This is considerably more than the 34 Kbps that a 56K-modem user can receive — forty times more, more or less. (The actual measured throughput of data on a 56K-modem is closer to 34 Kbps before compression). So to be able to stream audio to a dial-up user, significant data reduction is going to have to occur, which is where the encoding process comes in later.

Digital video

Digitizing video involves dividing each video frame into horizontal lines of resolution, and each line into a discrete number of picture elements (pixels). Each pixel must be sampled, and the resultant values stored. The problem is that digitizing high quality video means using the highest possible resolution. The higher the resolution, the more individual pixels there are, which means more data to be stored.

Earlier in the chapter broadcast video was defined to have 525 lines of resolution. In fact, not all of these lines contain video information. Anyone old enough to remember when his television picture needed the vertical hold adjusted will remember the black stripe moving up or down the screen. This is known as the vertical-blanking interval (VBI). In addition to the VBI, some lines are hidden by the television set's frame, which covers some of the top, bottom, and sides of the screen. After all this is taken into account, you are left with approximately 480 lines of resolution.

What about the horizontal resolution? Unfortunately, horizontal resolution varies depending who you talk to. Broadcast standards are analog; each line on your television screen is a continuous stripe of light. It isn't rigidly divided up into a discrete number pixels.

With digital video, you have to decide how to break that line up. For now, once everything has been taken into account, it is generally accepted that there are about 640 pixels in each line. The question now is, how much information is digitizing all this information going to generate, and where are you going to put it?

Frame sizes and frame rates

To start off, assume you're going to capture the full frame, all 640 × 480 pixels, at 30 frames per second. That means a second's worth of video contains:

```
640 * 480 * 30 = 9,216,000 pixels
```

And that's not all. Each of those nine million pixels needs 24 bits to record uncompressed RGB (8 bits each for red, green, and blue) color information. Which translates to the following:

```
9,216,000 * 24 bits = 221,184,000 bits
221,184,000 bits / 8 bits/byte = 27,648,000bytes
27,648,000bytes / 1024 bytes/KB = 27000KB
27,000 KB / 1024 KB/MB = 26.4 MB
```

This is over 26MB of information per second, which quickly adds up to 1.5GB for a minute of full screen, uncompressed video. Think about that for a brief second. This means your wonderful 20GB drive would be bursting at the seams after only 13 minutes of video capture. Scary, isn't it? Additionally, most, if not all standard hard drives are not capable of sustaining a transfer rate that high. They'll simply choke, gasp, wheeze, and then eventually give up.

There are a number of things you can do to alleviate the situation. First of all, you can change the frame size. If your destination for the media is the Internet, you probably won't be broadcasting at a screen size larger than 320 × 240 pixels. If you reduce your capture size accordingly, you cut the amount of data you're capturing by three-quarters.

Reducing the frame rate also drops the data rate. Obviously 30 frames per second is the ideal, but film looks just fine at 24 frames per second, and for many applications like low-motion video, 15 frames per second is just fine. Cutting the frame rate by one-half cuts the amount of data you need to capture in half.

Colorspace

The last thing to consider is the video colorspace. Uncompressed RGB encoding is actually very inefficient, because it allots the same number of pixels to the red, green, and blue values of each pixel even though your eyes are not as sensitive to each color.

Alternative color schemes, such as YUV use the limitations of our vision to pack the same amount of *perceived* information into 16 bits, or into 12, 9, or 6 bits with some picture degradation. The YUV color scheme divides the visible spectrum up into luminance and chrominance, much the way our eyes perceive color. Table 2-1 provides a quick comparison of data rates for different screen sizes and color encoding schemes.

Table 2-1
Sample Data Rates for Different Screen Sizes and Color Encoding Schemes at 30 Frames per Second

Screen size	RGB (24 bits per pixel)	YUV 4:2:2 (16 bits per pixel)	YUV 12 (12 bits per pixel)	YUV 9 (9 bits per pixel)
720 × 486 (ITU* -R 601 Standard)	30 Mbytes/sec	20 Mbytes/sec	15 Mbytes/sec	11.3 Mbytes/sec
640 × 480 (approx. NTSC resolution)	26.4 Mbytes/sec	17.6 Mbytes/sec	13.2 Mbytes/sec	9.9 Mbytes/sec
320 × 240	6.6 Mbytes/sec	4.4 Mbytes/sec	3.3 Mbytes/sec	2.5 Mbytes/sec

* ITU - The International Telecommunication Union, a standards body

Digitizing tradeoffs — file size versus fidelity

You're going to spend a good deal of time producing your video to a high standard, so the last thing you want to do is compromise it when you digitize. In an ideal world, you want to be able to capture full screen, uncompressed video. However, your capture system may place real world limitations on you. If so, there are a number of sensible steps you can take to reduce your data rate without impacting your quality too much:

✦ If you're capturing for the Internet circa 2002, a screen size of 320 × 240 should be sufficient. This cuts your data rate down considerably, and should allow you to capture at the highest quality your capture card allows. It also avoids any interlacing problems.

✦ You can reduce your frame rate to 15fps for low motion content, such as newscast content or lectures.

✦ Capture uncompressed or using the least amount of compression your capture card supports. In particular, avoid any software codecs.

These simple steps should enable you to capture video and produce streaming media to a consistently high standard.

Cross-Reference

This is all covered in more detail in Chapter 9.

Streaming audio and video

Digital audio and video are very portable. No longer does a physical copy have to change hands. Instead of a company having to send out VCR tapes to every branch office, video files could be distributed via satellite or virtual private networks (VPNs). Alternatively, the media could be streamed. The blessing and curse of streaming media is that it is real-time; this means that the files must be able to stream at a data rate corresponding to the user's available bandwidth.

Bandwidth restrictions

Earlier I mentioned that the data rate of uncompressed audio was over 1,000 kilobits per second (Kbps) and that uncompressed video data rates are on the order of 25–30 megabytes per second. This is over 4 orders of magnitude more data than the average 56K-modem user can receive. If you're going to make streaming media, something has got to give with the data rates. This is where encoders come in — to reduce the bitrates of files low enough to be streamed. But what happens to the quality of the files? How do they compare to the pristine audio and video that you so painstakingly captured?

Table 2-2 shows the kinds of quality you can expect from your streaming media files at different bitrates. Note the liberal use of the word "approximately," especially when pertaining to video files. The judgments in the table are very subjective. Try reading your favorite streaming media company's latest press release and your hyperbole meter will go off the scale. Ignoring the hype for a minute, I want to talk about what you can really expect and why.

Table 2-2		
Streaming Media Quality at Various Bitrates		
(Your Mileage May Vary)		
Access speed	*Audio quality*	*Video quality*
28.8K-modem	Equivalent to mono FM radio, slightly lower quality in stereo	Acceptable for low-motion content, poor for high motion content
		Very small screen (160×120, 176×132, 176×144)
		Approximately 1–10 frames per second
56K-modem	Equivalent to FM radio, possibly in stereo	Acceptable for low-motion content, poor for high motion content
		Very small screen (160×120, 176×132, 176×144)
		5–12 frames per second

Access speed	Audio quality	Video quality
ISDN (64–128 Kbps)	Equivalent to CD quality, that is, "as good as or like a CD"	Good for low-motion content, acceptable for high-motion content
		Screen size will determine performance — very small screens will have higher fidelity; medium sized screens (240 × 180, 320 × 240) will be compromised
		10–30 frames per second, depending on bitrate and screen size
xDSL/ Cable Modem (128–768 Kbps)	CD-transparent audio, that is, "exactly like a CD"	VHS-quality at approximately 300 Kbps; DVD quality at approximately 700 Kbps
		320 × 240 screen size at lower end of range, full screen becomes feasible at approximately 300 Kbps

Cross-Reference For a discussion on access speeds and what they really mean, please refer to Chapter 12.

Quality equivalents

Whenever you talk about an equivalent, you're talking about a subjective judgment. The question is who is making the judgment? To have even the slightest air of authenticity at all, any company's claims should be backed up by an independent study (preferably not funded by the company issuing the press release). In these studies, subjects are shown or played clips and asked to choose which one they preferred or if they noticed a difference. With any luck the questions and clips shown are not skewed to bias the subjects in any manner.

There is little controversy about audio quality these days because it has improved so dramatically in the last five years. It is fairly straightforward to analyze encoded clips for harmonic content to verify frequency range claims. Fidelity, or how faithful the encoded file is to the original, is another matter. The bit rate at which each company claims to achieve "CD quality" changes every day, but suffice it to say that at 64 Kbps, audio should sound pretty darn good. And at lower bit rates, provided there is no interruption in bandwidth to cause re-buffering, the experience should still be entirely enjoyable. There is no excuse for low-quality audio.

Video, as always, is a bit more involved. There are more variables in the equation. An encoded file can look entirely different on two different machines, or the same machine using two different display monitors. Claims of "VHS quality" or "DVD quality" should be taken with an extremely large grain of salt. Most of the video clips used to illustrate "amazing new quality" are hand picked to showcase a company's strengths. And of course these claims assume viewers will have perfect, uninterrupted bandwidth as they try to back haul these 700 Kbps DVD-quality clips across the Internet, which is highly unlikely.

The basic problem is trying to maintain a level of quality at a drastically reduced data rate, which is a bit like trying to fit a swimming pool into a glass — yes, it's water and it's wet and cool and refreshing, but it ain't no swimming pool. While this comparison may be a bit unfair, the fact remains that just because a company claims its video is DVD quality doesn't mean that it is.

The main side effects of encoding are lowered frame rate, reduced fidelity, and blocking artifacts.

✦ Lowered frame rates are noticeable because the video appears jerky as opposed to smooth.

✦ Reduced fidelity means the level of detail is not as great as the original. This happens mostly when there is a large amount of motion in the original video. If the section is short enough, the eye may not perceive a difference, which is what streaming companies really mean when they make their claims.

✦ Blocking artifacts are little blocks of color where things should be smooth. An example would be a wall in the background that appears to be made of square blocks, instead of a smooth surface. They are especially annoying because the brain knows they're not supposed to be there and is therefore drawn to them.

For more discussion about blocking artifacts, including an illustration, please see Chapter 3.

The term "DVD quality" is not necessarily the highest of accolades. While it does represent a significant increase in quality and longevity over VHS tapes, blocking artifacts can be seen on many DVD releases. The amount will vary according to the DVD player and television used to display the picture, but don't be fooled: DVD video is compressed video (MPEG-2 to be exact) and by no means perfect.

Video streaming quality is improving at a steady pace due to the intense competition. Combined with the ever-expanding bandwidths available, the petty bickering about video quality should soon be a thing of the past.

Non-standards

Currently there is no universal standard for streaming audio or video files. Each of the major streaming companies has its own file format, player, server, and set of codecs. Codecs are algorithms used to reduce the data rates of streaming media files. There has been a lot of moaning about this, often by people who have a vested interest in an existing standard.

Codecs are the subject of the next chapter, Chapter 3.

The streaming media industry is still extremely young and the technology imma-ture. Shackling the industry to standards at this early stage of the game is not necessarily the best idea. Having the freedom to try new approaches and, just as important, the fierce competition that currently exists in the industry will catapult the industry to greater heights in the short term. In the long term, certain stan-dards will be helpful to grow the industry as a whole.

Then again, when you talk about standards, you have to be clear about what you're talking about and why you need them. Standards set up a framework within which multiple manufacturers can operate. Having a broadcast standard and a standard for DVDs is helpful; imagine needing a different television for each channel you wanted to watch.

With streaming media, the situation is slightly different. Downloading a player or a software upgrade just isn't that difficult, and is for the most part free. Codecs are improving on a near-daily basis, along with a host of other new innovations. Sure, things are a bit confusing at the moment with three different streaming media play-ers, and the players don't always work as advertised, but these are the growing pains of a new industry.

Standards can be extremely helpful, as HTML was for the World Wide Web, but they're obviously not entirely necessary, as the rapid growth of the streaming industry thus far has shown. In the world of software, standardized protocols and file formats are helpful; standardized codecs are not. There is little doubt that some sort of standards framework will evolve over time.

The last few years have seen the industry slowly moving towards standardization. Both SMIL (Streaming Media Integration Language) and MPEG-4 are open standards. SMIL is a language for authoring streaming media presentations, and MPEG-4 is an open framework for creating any kind of interactive media presentation. All three major streaming media software manufacturers offer some type of support for SMIL; both RealNetworks and Apple have pledged support for MPEG-4.

It remains to be seen whether either of these standards becomes pervasive throughout the industry. SMIL is covered in depth in Part VII of this book. As of the writing of this book there are only a handful of MPEG-4 implementations, and none supported by any of the main three major streaming media manufacturers. I suspect this may change by the time the second edition of this book comes out.

Broadcast Standards, Resolutions, and Recording Formats

Now that you know a little bit about audio and video, both in and out of the com-puter, it's time to take a look at the broadcast standards that have developed over the years. Because a considerable amount of history is behind these standards, they have the mixed blessing of being mature standards. And note that "standards" is plural — there is more than one.

Broadcast standards

NTSC was briefly mentioned earlier as standard for television broadcasts in the United States. It was adopted in 1941, with the color standard being added in 1955. The NTSC standard divides the screen up into 525 lines of resolution, with approximately 480 of those lines visible. The rest of the lines are the vertical blanking interval (VBI), which is used for synchronization purposes.

There are many other television standards in use around the world, but for the most part they are all slight variations on one of the three main standards that are considered Standard Definition Television (SDTV):

✦ **NTSC (National Television Standards Committee):** Used in the United States, Mexico, Canada, Central and most of South America, the Philippines, and Japan.

✦ **PAL (Phase Alternating Line):** Developed in Germany and is used in Britain, most of Western Europe excluding France, and much of Asia.

✦ **SECAM (Sequential Color and Memory).** Developed in France and is used in Russia, Eastern Europe, and in Australia.

Both PAL and SECAM offer 625 lines of resolution at 25 frames per second. They are both interlaced standards, so each frame consists of two fields for a total of 50 fields per second. The additional lines of resolution add a significant amount of detail, but the lower frame rate is slightly more susceptible to "flicker." Both are considered to offer slightly better color than NTSC, having been developed specifically to address NTSC's shortcomings in this area.

Converting between different broadcast standards is not something you will generally have to worry about. Video capture systems are designed to capture the broadcast standard of the countries they are sold in, which is what you'll want 99.9 percent of the time.

The telecine process

When content that originated on film is broadcast on television, it must first be transferred to videotape. Because film is shot at 24 frames per second, and NTSC video is broadcast at 30 frames per second, when you transfer film content to video, you have to find some way of filling up the extra frames in a way that appears natural. This process of transferring film to videotape and creating new frames is known as the telecine process.

The simplest way to do this would be to repeat every fourth frame; this would generate the necessary extra six frames every second. However, it turns out that this method yields unacceptable results. A better way of doing it is to generate new frames by combining fields from different frames. This is done using the scanned video fields.

During the telecine process, each frame has to be scanned twice, once for the odd field and once for the even field that video requires. To create the extra six frames of video, four frames are scanned and then combined as per Figure 2-3 to create five frames of video. Over the course of 24 frames, six extra frames are added, for a total of 30.

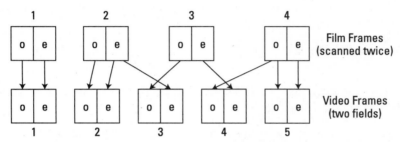

Figure 2-3: How the telecine process converts 24fps film content into 30fps NTSC video.

As you can see in Figure 2-3, three of the frames are exactly as they were in the film version, but two of them are now combinations of two frames. When this is shown on an NTSC display, the result is smoother than if a frame were repeated every four frames.

With PAL and SECAM transfers, the frames are transferred as is. But because the video runs at 25fps instead of 24fps, it results in a slight "speeding up" of the original. The slight change is not noticeable visually; however, since the audio is also sped up, voices sound a bit higher — approximately a half-tone — which can be annoying to the discerning listener.

There are other ways of handling the telecine process, but the general idea remains the same — some field data is repeated and combined to create the additional frames required. The problem arises later when you try to encode video that has been converted in this manner. You will be exerting precious encoding resources and bandwidth to video frames that were artificially created. A better approach would be to remove the redundant information, and to encode the result. This is precisely what inverse telecine filters do, which is covered later.

Cross-Reference For more on inverse telecine filters please refer to Chapter 10.

HDTV

HDTV (High Definition Television) is a new, higher-quality standard that is supposed to eventually replace SDTV (Standard Definition Television). In the United States, the FCC has mandated a complete phase-out of SDTV broadcasts by the year 2006, though many feel that this schedule may be a bit aggressive. HDTV is said to offer six times the resolution and ten times the color information that SDTV currently does. It has a 16:9 aspect ratio, which is compatible with most wide-screen film formats.

The HDTV standard is fairly flexible, and offers a number (some say too many) of different options:

✦ Number of active lines, 1080 or 720

✦ Progressive or interlaced scan

✦ Scan rates — 60 or 50 Hz for interlaced, 30 or 25 for progressive, 24 for film-style progressive

HDTV is a big, ugly can of worms at this point. Televisions that are capable of playing HDTV signals are hideously expensive and the broadcast experiments thus far disastrous. A full discussion of all the issues involved is far beyond the scope of this book. If you're reading this, you probably don't give a hoot about HDTV anyway. Some folks feel the Internet may be able to outrun HDTV, while others maintain the Internet will never be the broadcast medium that television is. Which one are you betting on?

Recording formats

Unless you're planning on using your computer as the master recorder, you're going to have to record your raw audio and video onto some intermediate format before you transfer it to your computer. You may also want something you can carry around with you, which rules out your desktop machine. Luckily a number of excellent formats are at your disposal in both the audio and video worlds.

Audio

The most common portable audio recording format would be the cassette. Ironically enough, the cassette was never really supposed to be high-quality — it was designed as a cheap stenographer's tool. But it caught on like wildfire, and with the development of noise reduction schemes and better quality tape, it became passable as well as convenient. As long you use good quality chrome tape and a professional recorder, the cassette is a reasonable format. It is nowhere near as good as digital audio tape, but if you're on a tight budget and prepared to use it carefully, it will do.

Digital audio tape (DAT), as shown in Figure 2-4, appeared in the mid-1980's not long after the compact disc. It was originally designed as a consumer format but scared the music industry so much that crippling legislative debate pretty much killed it — except as a tool in recording studios. It was embraced by the professional audio community, where it continues to thrive today. Prices have dropped to the point where it is a relatively cost efficient medium offering extremely high quality.

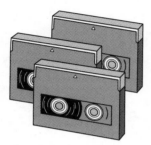

Figure 2-4: A Digital Audio Tape (DAT)

Recent developments have made MiniDisc an interesting solution for the cost conscious. Portable recording units are now aggressively priced, and blank discs are relatively cheap. The only problem is that MiniDisc uses a proprietary compression scheme, which is totally adequate for voice applications, but not high enough quality for recording music.

Many multitrack digital audio formats, such as ADAT, D-88, and hard disk recorders, are more than adequate for the task at hand. It will probably only be a matter of time before portable hard disk recorders appear to complement the current rash of MP3 players. When they do, provided they can record a high-quality uncompressed signal, they will be excellent streaming media tools.

Video

In the past ten years the number of options available to us as video producers have blossomed. Powerful, small electrical components combined with a huge increase in the quality of plastic lenses and an explosion in consumer demand have driven all the major manufacturers into a stampede of research and development on the consumer front. The DV format in particular has seen a lot of innovation in the last few years, which is continuing to drive quality up and prices down. Table 2-3 compares the most common formats.

Table 2-3
Comparison of Different Video Formats

Format	Data format	Quality/Resolution	Price (cameras unless otherwise noted)
Uncompressed Digital (D-1, D-2, and so on)	Digital	Excellent/broadcast	Astronomical ($100,000+)
DigiBeta	Component digital	Excellent/broadcast	Very expensive ($40,000+)
Betacam SP	Analog	Excellent/broadcast	Expensive ($10,000 - $30,000 +)
DV formats: DVCPro, DVCAM, MiniDV	Digital	Very good/near-broadcast Approximately 500 lines of resolution	Reasonable to expensive ($700 - $10,000)
Digital 8	Digital	Good Approximately 500 lines of resolution	Cheapish ($400 - $1200)
3/4" Umatic	Analog	Good Only 330 lines of resolution, but good subjective picture quality	Cheapish ($1500 for a second hand Umatic recorder)
S-VHS/Hi-8mm	Analog	Barely acceptable Approximately 400 lines of resolution	Cheap to expensive ($250 - $6000)
VHS/8mm	Analog	Unacceptable — very noisy, poor resolution (approximately 250–270 lines)	Too cheap — avoid at any cost

A cursory glance at Table 2-3 shows that the most cost-effective entry point into video production is probably some sort of DV system, though I would highly recommend a Betacam system if you can at all afford it. It has been the broadcast standard for the last 20 years or so for a reason. The quality of the cameras, recorders, and playback systems are extremely high, and there isn't a post-production house in the world that won't accept a beta tape.

If a beta system is out of your reach, a good quality DV system should take care of all your video needs. DV cameras come in all shapes, sizes, and price ranges. You generally get what you pay for. Don't look for useless options such as digital zoom or in-camera editing facilities — instead spend your money on the highest quality optics you can get, glass if possible, interchangeable lenses, broadcast standard connectors, and solid build quality. You're going to be putting some mileage on your camera. It's the last place you want to compromise, because it's the first link in your production chain.

Cables and connectors

After you start building an array of production hardware, you're going to have to connect them somehow or other. There are lots of different types of cables to choose from, some better than others. You may have heard it from a salesman at your local hi-fi store and not believed it, but cables do make a difference, sometimes a dramatic difference.

All good quality cables are shielded. This means that in addition to the wires carrying signals inside the insulation, a metal foil or braid surrounds the wires to help isolate the signal from outside interference. Cheap cables, and many of the cables that come with your computer, are not shielded. If you're experiencing any problems with noise or poor quality and you're not sure about your cables, it's a good cost-effective place to start improving your signal chain.

While shielding can do a lot to improve your signal quality, there are some things that even shielding will not stop. Computer monitors and power cables generate extremely strong magnetic fields. It's always a good idea to try and keep your signal cables as far away from power and data lines as possible. Dimmer switches and fluorescent lights are other culprits.

Audio

Audio cables come in two basic flavors: balanced and unbalanced. In a nutshell, balanced cables have two signal wires and a ground wire, while unbalanced have only one signal wire and a ground wire. Two signals are better than one, right? You bet. There's actually a bit more to it than that, but in general, balanced is always better than unbalanced. (For those of you who want the full story, see "Balanced Cables — The Real Deal" sidebar.)

Figure 2-5 illustrates the five main audio connecting plugs. The first three, male and female XLR and ¼" TRS (tip-ring-sleeve) plugs, are all balanced connections. The remaining two, ¼" TS (tip-sleeve) and RCA plugs, are unbalanced. Mini-jack plugs, commonly used to connect to computer soundcards, are not shown because they cannot be considered a professional connector by any stretch of the imagination. Avoid mini-jack plugs if at all possible.

Balanced Cables — The Real Deal

All wires are susceptible to electro-magnetic interference. The longer they are, the more interference they are likely to pick up. Shielded cables are less susceptible, but they still pick up noise. Audio cables are particularly sensitive to this because the signal level is relatively low. Balanced wiring is a simple, elegant solution to this problem.

Balanced cable utilizes cable with three wires, one ground and two signal wires, referred to as the positive and the negative. The original signal is sent on the positive wire, while the signal on the negative wire is sent with the opposite polarity. These signals are referred to as being *out of phase.*

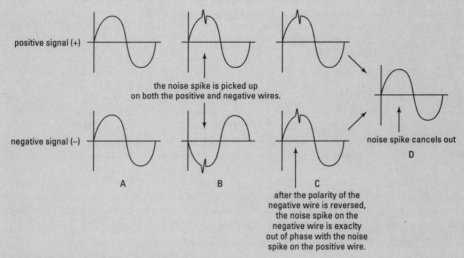

positive signal (+)

the noise spike is picked up
on both the positive and negative wires.

negative signal (−)

noise spike cancels out

D

A   B   C

after the polarity of the
negative wire is reversed,
the noise spike on the
negative wire is exaclty
out of phase with the noise
spike on the positive wire.

How balanced cables eliminate noise.

In the previous figure, each wave is designated as the following:

✦ A: The original positive and negative signals.

✦ B: Both signals pick up a noise spike.

✦ C: At the destination, the polarity of the negative wire is reversed.

✦ D: When the signals are added together, the noise spikes cancel each other out.

If there is any interference along the cable run, both signal wires pick it up equally. At the destination, the negative signal's polarity is reversed (it is put back into phase) and added to the positive signal. Any interference picked up by the two wires is now out of phase, so that when the signals are added, the interference cancels out.

What's not to love about balanced cables? You don't have to fully understand how balanced cables work — just use them.

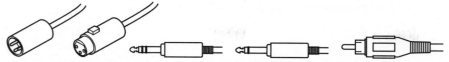

Figure 2-5: Professional audio connectors: male XLR, female XLR, ¼" TRS, ¼" TS, and RCA plugs.

 Note Headphones use ¼" TRS plugs, but do not use balanced wiring. Instead of a positive and negative wire, they send the left and right channels.

Use balanced cable to interconnect your audio equipment. You may end up spending a bit more up front, but you'll more than make up for it with less time spent chasing down hums and buzzes. One of the problems of the streaming media space is that many people use a mixture of professional and consumer equipment, which means a mixture of balanced and unbalanced connections. In theory, balanced equipment is not compatible with unbalanced. In practice, they can be mixed together, but with mixed results.

Unbalanced connections only become a problem when cable runs are long or there is an inordinate amount of interference nearby. If there is, you may want to consider changing the location of your capture system. If your cable runs are fairly short, that is, 3 feet or less, you can get away with unbalanced connections. But don't say I didn't warn you.

Video

With video equipment, it isn't so much the type of wire the equipment is connected with, it's the way in which the signal is transmitted that determines the connector used. There are four main ways of sending video signals:

✦ **Composite:** All signal information is sent down a single wire, terminated with either RCA connectors or higher quality BNC connectors.

✦ **S-Video:** The signal is divided into black and white content (luminance) and color content (chrominance) and sent down two separate wires inside the same cable. S-Video uses a small multiple cable. Some feel S-video is the best video connection to use for streaming video (see "Why S-Video is Best for Encoding" side bar).

✦ **Component:** The signal is broken up into black and white content and two color components and sent on three separate, high-quality cables using BNC connectors.

✦ **Serial Digital:** The video signal is sent over coaxial cables with BNC connectors or optically using special fiber optic cables as digital information, over a single wire.

Figure 2-6 illustrates the most common video connectors.

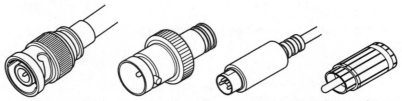

Figure 2-6: Video connectors: male BNC, female BNC, S-Video, and RCA.

Video today is also transferred via FireWire (IEEE 1394), which isn't strictly a video connection, but rather a computer connection that is utilized to send large quantities of data. It uses a specific cable. As more and more manufacturers take advantage of this new standard, you'll see many different kinds of equipment communicating via FireWire.

Note   FireWire was originally designed by people at Apple Computer, and was later adopted by the IEEE (Institute of Electrical and Electronic Engineers) as a standard. Apple trademarked the name FireWire, even though the standard is open and not platform-specific. Other manufacturers have IEEE 1394 implementations, but because of branding concerns, they may be called something else, such as Sony's iLink, which ironically uses a proprietary cable.

Choose professional cables whenever possible. Not only will you sleep better at night, but you'll make fewer trips back to the local A/V store replacing the cheap cables you thought would suffice. And whatever you do, try to avoid using adapters. Not only do they add another point of failure into your signal chain, but the added weight hanging off the back of your equipment could damage it — especially because the extra length added to adapters makes them more likely to be bumped into. Summing up:

✦ Use the best cables you can afford.

✦ Check the cable connectors — bad connector = bad cable.

✦ Keep your cables as far away from interference sources such as power leads and computer monitor cables.

✦ Keep your cable runs as short as possible.

Television displays versus computer monitors

The differences between film and video were discussed earlier in the chapter: Film is projected in sequence, 24 frames per second, while television is displayed at 30 frames per second, which are divided into 60 interlaced fields. This creates problems when converting film to video because of the extra frames required, which is what the telecine process was designed to solve. When we try to display this video on a computer monitor, another problem arises.

Why S-Video is Best for Encoding by Chip Ruhnke

Broadcast formats such as SDI produce beautiful high-resolution television pictures. Paradoxically, these broadcast formats may be counter-productive for making high quality streaming video.

Side-by-side comparisons prove it. S-video is the ideal video signal for creating 320 × 240 Internet video because of the way the discrete cosine transform (DCT) compression algorithm works. S-video is not as high resolution as DV/FireWire, SDI, or Betacam, and that is its blessing.

To reduce the size of digital video files for streaming over the Internet, the picture is divided into 8 × 8 pixel blocks. The picture is more easily dissected into 8 × 8 blocks if the image is a little soft to begin with. With high-resolution video sources, more information is required to describe the pixel block. Encoding horsepower is lost as the software spends a lot of effort determining what details should be discarded, and what details should be added to the description.

When there is action in the video, the DCT algorithm tries to describe motion as simply as possible, for example by saying "The 8 × 8 pixel block moved ten pixels to the left." This is more difficult with high-resolution video, because the extra details can make it harder for the algorithm to find the block's new location. Instead of a simple motion vector, the DCT algorithm may describe the block's location in complex terms: "The pixel block with two dimples moved ten pixels to the left, however the shadows on the dimples are now not in exactly the same relationship so use part of the original pixel block definition but rebuild the dimpled portion."

With high-resolution input video, each 8 × 8 pixel block requires more information to describe it, and even more information to describe motion. Not only does this increase the data rate, but high-resolution video also inhibits the player — leaving the player unable to fully unravel the description in the time allotted to the video frame. As a result, the 8 × 8 blocks are not fully described and tiling artifacts arise. Sometimes the player dwells so long on the description, that it drops frames (although this is not the primary reason for frame drop).

Although you may want your video input to have slightly less detail, you do want your video to be as clean as possible. Chroma noise, NTSC artifacts, low-light camera grain, interlace artifacts, velocity errors from videotape, and RF noise are all random and therefore different on every frame. With DCT, describing moving images takes priority over describing static images. Because random noise is seen as motion, the DCT algorithm spends more effort trying to reproduce the noise than reproducing the underlying picture.

S-video is the ideal input, provided your capture card does a good A-to-D (analog-to-digital) conversion. "S" is free of NTSC artifacts, has ample detail for creating 320 × 240 images, and has analog rise times so the DCT can fudge the edges a bit to make better 8 × 8 pixel blocks. DV cameras, Betacam VCRs and many other professional and pro-sumer devices offer the "S" output. Use this for better streaming.

Chip Ruhnke holds a Masters in media from NYC's New School University, is a Certified Technical Specialist from the International Communications Industries Association, chairs the technical subcommittee of the Streaming Media Alliance, and is co-leader of the streaming media special interest group for the New York New Media Association. He is the CEO and founder of iStreamWebcasting.com.

Computer monitor designers, who had the advantage of an extra 30 years of technology behind them, opted against an interlaced display and chose instead a progressive-scan display. Progressive scan is more film-like in that the display is drawn starting at the top left hand corner, line by line, until the bottom corner is reached. There are no odd or even fields. The scan rates and screen qualities are high enough that flicker is not a problem.

There is a problem, however, when you try to display interlaced video on a non-interlaced display (watching a DVD on your computer monitor). When the odd and even fields are merged into one frame and displayed at the same time, areas of high motion display artifacts where the fields appear to tear apart. This is because the two fields are being displayed at the same time instead of a split second apart.

In clips with low motion and in particular without drastic side-to-side motion, the artifacts are not too noticeable. Also, at screen sizes of 320 × 240 or less, video editing platforms throw away one of the fields. When interlacing artifacts are a problem, de-interlacing filters can attempt to mitigate the situation somewhat, but it is a fundamental problem that interlaced and progressive scan displays are entirely different beasts. If and when HDTV makes any headway, or if the HDTV equipment becomes more affordable, material can be shot in progressive-scan mode natively, which eliminates the problem once and for all. Until then, it's something you're going to have to live with.

Cross-Reference For more on interlacing artifacts, please refer to the section on de-interlace filters in Chapter 10.

Last but not least, the pixels on a computer monitor are square — not so with a television screen. They are rectangular, slightly taller than wide, and technically referred to as "nonsquare." (I am not making this up) So when you capture a full screen of video and display it on a computer monitor, it will appear ever so slightly stretched horizontally. In fact, it isn't stretched horizontally so much as "not stretched" vertically — as it would be when displayed on a television screen.

This isn't a major problem because editing platforms can resize the video to restore the correct aspect ratio. If the eventual destination is broadcast on traditional networks, the aspect ratio should be left the way it is. If, however, the content is to be streamed across the Internet and displayed on computer monitors, then the picture should be resized either during the rendering or encoding phase.

Cross-Reference Aspect ratios and non-square pixels are dealt with in more detail in Chapter 10.

The Recording Environment

With all this discussion about equipment, formats, standards, and whatnot, it is easy to forget one of the most basic elements of the equation: location. Location is everything, as they say, and it's no different when creating content, for traditional broadcast or for streaming.

If you've ever had the opportunity to see the inside of a television studio or a music recording studio, you'll notice a few things:

✦ They're quiet and isolated from noisy areas.

✦ They're roomy — plenty of space for equipment and room to move.

✦ The ceilings are high — this allows the lights to be placed where they won't cast objectionable shadows.

✦ They're laid out sensibly so that everything is within arms' reach.

✦ They're comfortable so that people won't mind spending ridiculous amounts of time in them.

No one expects you to shell out the kind of money that building a professional studio would cost, but there are a number of sensible steps you can take to make sure you get the most out of the limited resources you have. First and foremost is making sure you have a quiet place to work. Remember that noises like air conditioning and computer fans are easily ignored when you listen to them all day, but can be extremely annoying and/or problematic later on.

Go into the rooms you have earmarked for recording and editing, close the doors, and listen. Just how quiet is it? Is there an employee break area nearby? Are there windows that face a busy street? Is there a bathroom nearby? A fire exit with a squeaky door? All these are potential showstoppers. Imagine broadcasting quarterly results to your company's stockholders while a siren is blaring in the background, or having to record take after take because someone is playing a video game in the next room.

After you've found a good spot for your facilities, stand in the center of the room and clap your hands. Is there an echo? Does it sound like you're in a small room when you talk? If it does, it's going to sound that way when you record, which is a big no-no. This can easily be cured with acoustic panels. A few on each wall in a checkerboard pattern will quiet down the room and get rid of any nasty echoes. Heavy curtains on bare walls will also work wonders.

Don't forget the floor or the furniture. Carpeted floors are absolutely necessary. Padded chairs are good. If you have a big table that people sit at while you're recording, make sure you put a tablecloth on it. Not only will it make the room sound better by eliminating another reflective surface, but it also protects against noises such as people putting glasses of water down on the table, or tapping pencils nervously.

When it comes to light, windows can actually be your enemy. The best approach is to avoid them and have a studio equipped with enough lights so that you can control the lighting completely. Small lighting kits can be very cost effective.

If your recording environment is going to be separate from the editing space, as it should be, consider having professional wiring installed between the rooms, so that you don't have to run cables under doors or through ceiling tiles.

All in all, it might not be a bad idea to have someone come in and give you some advice. There are plenty of good acoustic designers around, and as with most things, a little money spent up front can save a lot of woe in the long run.

Summary

Audio and video have been recorded and reproduced for over a century now. Streaming media is descended in large part from this rich history, and therefore should aspire to the same high standards.

It's important as you delve deeper into the streaming media process to have a firm grasp of the basics to understand why things are the way they are today, and where they're going to be tomorrow. Streaming media is still an extremely young field — things will change very rapidly over the next ten years.

✦ Audio and video are digitized by sampling the analog signals at discrete intervals and assigning numeric values to these samples.

✦ By playing the samples back in sequence, a digital approximation of the original signal can be reconstructed.

✦ In the case of audio, these intervals are referred to as the sample rate; with video each frame divided up into pixels.

✦ Digital video generates an enormous amount of data. To reduce this you can adjust the screen size, the frame rate, or the amount of compression.

✦ Capture the highest possible quality video your systems will accommodate.

✦ There are three major broadcast standards around the world today — NTSC, PAL, and SECAM. Converting from film to NTSC in particular is tricky and generates redundant information you'll want to remove later.

✦ Use the highest quality audio and video equipment you can afford.

✦ Don't scrimp on cables — and avoid ⅛" mini-jacks.

✦ Television monitors are interlaced and have non-square pixels; computer monitors use a progressive scan system and have square pixels.

✦   ✦   ✦

Codecs – An Overview

Now that you know a little bit about audio and video and a bit about the streaming media creation process, it's time to introduce you to the piece of software that makes streaming media possible — the codec.

What Is a Codec?

In its simplest form, a codec (coder-decoder or compressor-de-compressor) is a software algorithm that transforms data from one format to another. In the streaming media process, codecs are used to reduce the size of raw media files so they can be streamed across the Internet, and to convert the files back into audio or video on the receiving end.

Streaming media encoders use codecs during the encoding process to create streaming media files, and streaming media players use codecs when playing back streaming media files. The codec that was used to compress the file must also be used to decompress the file.

Codecs break down into two main types: *lossless* codecs, where the original can be recreated exactly from the compressed file and *lossy* codecs, where the decompressed file is an approximation of the original file — how approximate a recreation depends on the amount of compression used.

Many familiar file formats use codecs; JPEG images, GIF images, ZIP files, and StuffIt archives all use a codec to compress the data down to a more manageable size. ZIP files and StuffIt archives are examples of lossless codecs because the original files can be recreated exactly; JPEG and GIF files are examples of lossy codecs since they are only an approximation of the original image.

Lossless codecs

Lossless codecs take advantage of the large amount of redundant information in many files. This redundancy can be represented in a more efficient manner. For example, the sequence AAAAAAAA can be stored as 8A. This technique is known as run-length coding. In this example, instead of storing eight characters, you would only have to store two characters. Your storage requirements are reduced by 75 percent.

Another lossless encoding method is known as entropy or Huffman coding, named after its creator David Huffman. Huffman coding replaces frequently occurring sequences with shorter code words. Acronyms are an example of Huffman coding; instead of writing out hypertext markup language, most people use the acronym HTML.

Alternatively, in a digital version of this book, you could realize some typographical savings if a codec was to replace streaming media with SM, when the file was stored. As long as the words streaming media were reinserted when anyone opened up the file, the encoded version would be an exact copy of the printed version.

Programs like WinZip and StuffIt use lossless compression schemes. The original files can be recreated exactly from the compressed versions. Lossless codecs are great for quality concerns but can only accomplish moderate compression ratios. For the kind of data reduction that streaming media files require, a drastic reduction in the amount of data is needed, which is where lossy codecs come in.

Lossy codecs

Lossy codecs achieve much higher rates of file size reduction by discarding data that is deemed redundant or unnecessary. Because information is discarded, recreating the original file exactly is impossible when the file is decompressed. The idea behind lossy codecs is that some data can be discarded and not missed.

Sometimes lossy codecs have to be ruthless. In cases of extreme compression, lossy codecs do the best they can to retain the quality of the original, but may be forced to discard a large amount of data. The goal in cases like these is to try to keep the most important information in the file, and to discard the rest.

If you've listened to any streaming media, you've heard lossy codecs at work. You may have listened to music or a sporting event happening far away. The quality was probably not pristine, but you listened anyway. In this case, premium quality audio wasn't necessary — the quality was good enough to keep you interested.

You've probably had a similar experience with streaming video. Many news events are available online hours before the evening news, particularly if you live on the West Coast like I do. Though the video quality may leave something to be desired, the fact is that people tolerate lossy codecs in certain situations.

How Streaming Media Codecs Work

Streaming media codecs have a tough job. In Chapter 2, the data rate of raw, uncompressed audio was reported to be 1.4Mbits per second, while raw video clocked in at over 25Mbytes per second for full-screen NTSC. Somewhere on the other end of a phone line sits a viewer with a 56K modem, dying to listen to or watch whatever you have to offer. This staggering divide between the raw bit rates of audio and video and the bit rates available to Internet users is what streaming codecs attempt to bridge.

Bridging this gap involves using very high compression ratios. If a 56K modem user can get a sustained 34K data rate, CD-quality audio has to be compressed using a ratio of approximately 40:1. With video, the numbers become ludicrous. Suffice it to say that dial-up users aren't going to get full-screen, full-motion video — they have to settle for something a little less ambitious.

Streaming codecs bring a whole arsenal of compression tools to the table, both lossless and lossy. Because you need extreme compression ratios, you'll use the more powerful lossy techniques. Some information is going to be discarded. By using models about how humans perceive audio and video, codecs can make reasonably intelligent decisions about what information to keep and what to throw away. This technique is known as perceptual coding.

Perceptual coding

When audio and video is digitized, the goal is to be able to accurately represent the input signal. For audio, this means sampling the input 44,100 times a second, using 16-bit words to represent each sample. This assumes that our ears give equal attention to each and every frequency, which is not the case. Similarly, digitizing video assumes that 24 bits of information are needed for each and every pixel on the screen, all 640×480 of them, 30 times a second, which is not true.

Eyes and ears register an extremely wide range of audio and visual inputs, though both are more sensitive to particular ranges of the audio and visual spectrum. Additionally, what is actually *perceived* is determined by the brain, which filters the raw information. Often, because of the amount of information, some of the content is ignored or overlooked. If you can predict with some degree of accuracy what will be ignored in an audio or video signal, you can use this information to help choose what information to discard.

Perceptual coding enables us to make decisions about how to compress audio and video data based on our knowledge of how humans perceive sights and sounds. With sound, loud sounds take precedence over quieter sounds in the brain. With sight, humans are more apt to notice bright objects and movement. If you think about this concept for a brief second, these traits evolved for very practical reasons — to find food to eat and to avoid being eaten. Even though our eyes and ears are no longer used for primitive survival purposes, humans still retain these perceptual characteristics, which is why perceptual coding works.

Audio codecs

When encoding audio, the goal is to maintain the frequency range and dynamics of the original. If the bit rate is high enough this is easily achieved, but as the bit rate is reduced, compromises must be made in a number of areas, such as frequency response and the number of channels reproduced. Perceptual audio codecs help maintain the fidelity by making decisions about what can safely be discarded and where to allot the bits to be of most use.

Reducing the data rate

Audio codecs do an amazing job of reducing the data rate, but only within sensible limitations. A delicate balance must be struck between fidelity, frequency response, dynamics, and number of channels. Several steps can be taken to reduce the amount of data that the perceptual coder must encode.

Collapsing the audio signal from stereo into mono cuts the amount of data in half immediately. The other two factors that determine our digital audio file's data rate are the sampling rate, which is a function of frequency response, and sample bit depth, which determines the dynamic range of the file. By reducing both of these, you can reduce the amount of data your perceptual coder must process.

The frequency range can be restricted according to the type of content being encoded and the target bit rate. For example, FM radio has a frequency range that only extends up to 12kHz, so a codec can safely drop the frequency response while still maintaining acceptable quality. For voice content, codecs can drop the frequency response even lower, to 8kHz or even 5kHz and still maintain acceptable quality.

Dynamic ranges can also be reduced during encoding. The human ear is capable of perceiving a vast dynamic range, but in practice the listening environment drastically reduce this. Therefore, at the encoding stage it isn't necessary to use the full 16 bits to represent the dynamic range.

As perceptual models improve, the amount of compromise necessary in these two areas decreases. You can already find claims of "CD quality" at 64Kbps, which is one half the bit rate at which MP3 claimed the same quality only a few years ago.

Perceptual audio coding

Perceptual audio coding relies on the concept of *masking* — frequencies at certain volume levels make others inaudible, rendering them somewhat redundant or irrelevant. Masking is best illustrated by an example.

In a crowded restaurant, your ears are being presented with a wide spectrum of frequencies at many different volumes. In the midst of all this noise, you may hear an order of sizzling fajitas being delivered to the next table (your nose may have had a bit of input here as well). If, however, your dinner companion suddenly scrapes his or her chair on the floor upon getting up from the table to go to the restroom, that sound temporarily supercedes or *masks* the quieter sound of the sizzling fajitas. You won't hear the sizzle for that brief period of time — in fact, your attention shifts to your companion, and you completely forget about the next table. The sizzling has not stopped, but your perception of the sound is interrupted.

If you were to make a high-quality recording of this scene, it would include both the sizzling of the fajitas and the scraping of the chair (see Figure 3-1). A perceptual codec determines that the sound of the fajitas will be masked by the chair scrape, and does not allot bits to the frequencies where the sizzling resides when the chair scrape is heard. Those bits are better allocated to the chair scrape. After the chair scrape, the bits can then be used again to encode the sizzling noise.

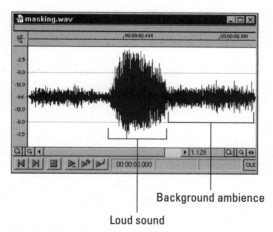

Background ambience

Loud sound

Figure 3-1: Perceptual codecs utilize the fact that loud sounds *mask* quieter sounds.

It's no coincidence that the chair scrape was the loudest sound; after all, that's what caught your attention. As a general rule, perceptual audio codecs allot the most bits to whatever is loudest, so when recording you should ensure that whatever you're interested in is loudest in your files.

Voice codecs versus music codecs

To add an interesting twist and one last level of complexity to audio encoding, the approaches that a codec takes to encoding music and speech are completely different. If you know in advance what sort of content you're dealing with, you can choose the optimal codec for the job.

A codec can make certain assumptions about it a file consists mainly of speech. Speech generally stays at roughly the same pitch and volume. Technically speaking, speech has limited dynamic and frequency ranges, so a speech codec doesn't expect large variations in either range and allots bits accordingly.

Music, on the other hand, has a wide frequency range and can have a wide dynamic range. A music codec has to be prepared for the worst — frequencies ranging from bass guitars to cymbals and sound levels from a whisper to a scream.

You'll find out later in this chapter that encoding software allows you to choose different codecs based on the material. The approaches used to encode music and speech are different enough that using a music codec on speech doesn't sound as good as a pure speech codec, and using a speech codec on music sounds downright horrible.

Video coding

If audio codecs have a hard time, video codecs spend their life in a living hell. Video codecs get a bad rap for doing a poor job, but they're tasked with trying to fit a nearly infinite amount of data down a very narrow pipe. Because the concept is almost laughable to begin with, you have to take some pretty serious steps at reducing the data rate before you hand off to the video codec. You can immediately economize in two areas — the screen size and frame rate.

Reduced screen sizes, frame rates

No doubt about it, when you multiply 640 × 480, you get a big number. Too big — over three hundred thousand pixels that you need to store information about. If you cut both dimensions in half, you end up with a screen size of 320 × 240 pixels and only one-quarter the number of pixels. Although cutting the dimensions in half is a great start, you may need to use even smaller dimensions to strike a balance between screen size and encoded video quality.

You can also economize by reducing the frame rate. Anything above 20 frames per second is adequate to convey smooth motion, but in fact for video content that has little motion, you can safely go below the 20fps threshold, down to 15 or even 10fps. At 10fps, with a 160 × 120 pixel screen size, you're only attempting to encode $\frac{1}{48}$ the amount of information compared to a full-screen, full frame rate file — but you still are nowhere near the amount of compression you need to be able to stream the video in real time.

Much like perceptual audio codecs, perceptual video codecs take advantage of how people perceive visual information to gain economies in other areas. For example, video codecs don't use 24 bits per pixel to represent color because our eyes are less sensitive to certain areas of the color spectrum. And most importantly, codecs use interframe compression to finally achieve the kind of compression needed for streaming video.

Inter-frame compression

Inter-frame compression relies upon the fact that much of the picture content may remain unchanged between frames. Therefore, digitizing every pixel of every frame is unnecessary. Instead, only the section of the picture that has changed needs to be digitized and substituted into the original frame. Figure 3-2 illustrates this concept, using talking head video as an example.

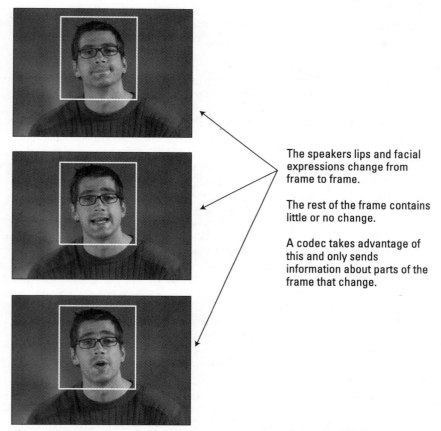

The speakers lips and facial expressions change from frame to frame.

The rest of the frame contains little or no change.

A codec takes advantage of this and only sends information about parts of the frame that change.

Figure 3-2: Inter-frame compression involves encoding only the differences between frames.

Using inter-frame compression, significant savings can be made because often the amount of change between frames is minimal. Bits are not wasted re-encoding static elements, so less bits are used, and the bit used can be focused on what is important — the part of the frame that is changing.

Of course, you can't completely ignore background elements. A video codec must first digitize one complete frame to establish all the elements in the frame. After the background has been established, however, subsequent frames digitize only the changing elements or the differences between frames. The establishing frames are called *keyframes*; the rest are called *difference frames*.

Keyframes versus difference frames

Keyframes are fully digitized, pixel by pixel, to establish the scene. Because keyframes contain encoded information about the entire frame, they are expensive in terms of bit use. Difference frames can be very cheap to digitize, because very little may have changed between frames. Exploiting this characteristic of video can lead to enormous savings in bits and, therefore, to extremely high compression ratios.

A typical encoded video stream starts with a keyframe, followed by a series of difference frames. After a while another keyframe is encoded, followed again by difference frames. In an ideal situation, the keyframes are perfectly crisp, and each difference frame contains an exact record of all the information that changes. When the sequence of frames is played back the result is a perfect recreation of the original video stream.

However, in practice the situation is much different. The limitations of low bit rate streaming force a video codec to compromise the quality of the keyframes and difference frames, as well as limit how often new keyframes are generated.

Take a quick look at some numbers. Assume you're encoding a 160 × 120 picture, and you are using a 12 bits per pixel to describe the color. You can calculate the size of each keyframe using the following equation:

```
160 * 120pixels/frame * 12bits/pixel / 1024 = 225Kb/frame
```

If you tried to watch video encoded at this data rate over a 28.8 modem with an average throughput of 20 Kbps, you'd only be able to receive *one frame every eleven seconds!* Obviously, one frame every eleven seconds is not much of a video presentation. To increase your frame rate, you need to compromise the quality of each individual frame by using intra-frame compression techniques.

Intra-frame compression

Intra-frame compression is compressing the data *within* a frame as opposed to encoding savings between two frames. Intra-frame compression techniques are very similar to the techniques used to compress still images for the Web. By reducing the quality of each individual key and difference frame, the overall bit rate becomes small enough so that you can stream low bit rate video at reasonable frame rates.

A delicate balance has to be struck between the quality and number of keyframes in a low bit rate video stream. A video codec can either send more keyframes, each with degraded quality, or fewer frames at a higher quality. When more frames are sent, the motion appears smoother, but the overall picture quality is less crisp. With fewer keyframes, the motion appears a bit less smooth, but the overall picture quality is higher. Later in the encoding section of this book, you'll learn how to bias your streaming media encoder one way or the other to achieve the desired results.

 Cross-Reference   Chapter 12 talks more about the relationship between keyframe quality and frame rates.

Video codecs try to send as many keyframes as possible, but in reality are limited by the target bit rate. You've probably seen this behavior while watching video streams online — the stream starts off looking fairly crisp, but as time progresses, you see it gradually degrade. Whenever the codec can afford to, it sends a new keyframe, which makes the stream snap into focus and then begin the slow process of degradation again. If the video content is fairly constant, this results in the stream "pulsing" as it snaps into focus with the arrival of each keyframe.

Motion detection

Another trick that video codecs do to economize on the number of bits used is something called motion detection (also known as motion estimation). Motion detection takes advantage of the fact that it is more economical for a video codec to move sections of a video image rather than re-digitize the frame. Figure 3-3 illustrates how motion detection works. As the ferry in the top-most figure moves across the frame, the control house remains relatively unchanged throughout the frame sequence. The codec simply moves the existing information instead of resampling the frame. In fact, the whole ferry can be moved across the frame.

Figure 3-3: How video codecs use motion detection

Video codecs do motion detection by dividing the video image into small square blocks (anywhere from four to sixteen pixels square). The codec then compares each block with adjacent blocks to see if it has moved. If the codec detects a match (or even a close match), it reuses the data from the previous frame instead of sending new data. This process can be very effective at economizing the number of bits necessary to transmit a frame but is computationally complex because each tiny block has to be compared to many other adjacent blocks.

High frequency information removal

Video codecs reduce the amount of high frequency information contained within frames before they encode them. They do this because our eyes are not as sensitive to high frequency information, and because it takes many more bits to encode high frequency than low frequency information.

Codec Side Effects

Encoding is a series of compromises, each one affecting the quality of the stream. With audio, the signal might be collapsed into mono and have its frequency response and dynamic range reduced. With video, the screen size and frame rate are compromised. The compromises don't end here, however. Because video codecs have to achieve such radical file size reduction ratios, it shouldn't be too surprising that the odd side effect creeps into the final result.

Less of everything

The resulting encoded file is not an exact replica of what went in, particularly at lower bit rates. Audio files generally have a smaller frequency range and certainly have less of a dynamic range. The codec may have converted the signal into mono, even if you didn't.

Video screen sizes are smaller. The colors may not be as vivid as the original. And almost certainly, the frame rate is stepped on if the target audience is sitting on the other end of a phone line. All these things are somewhat understandable, even to be expected. What is surprising is when things appear that weren't there in the first place. These are known as artifacts.

Artifacts

Artifacts are distortions in the encoded versions of files that weren't in the original file. Artifacts come in all shapes and sizes and are annoying to varying degrees.

In encoded audio files, the bit depth is reduced, which reduces the dynamic range. Therefore, quiet passages do not have the same resolution as previously and can sound grainy or distorted. Voice codecs can sometimes add a lisping quality to files.

Perceptual codecs do their best to remove audio content that is deemed redundant, but the resulting files can sometimes sound hollow or thin. The distortion, graininess, lisping quality, and hollowness are all artifacts of the encoding process.

Because video compression is more intensive, video artifacts can be very annoying. The two most common artifacts are interlacing artifacts and blocking artifacts. *Interlacing artifacts* arise due to the fact that each video frame is comprised of two fields that are scanned $\frac{1}{60}$ of a second apart. If you're trying to encode full-screen video and want all 480 lines of resolution, you need both fields. With static content the time difference between the interlaced fields is not a problem, but if objects in the video screen move, particularly across the frame, the slight timing difference between the fields shows up as a separation. Interlacing artifacts are particularly hard for codecs to deal with and are why de-interlacing filters exist to mitigate the worst of the artifacts.

Cross-Reference De-interlacing filters, which are used to reduce interlacing artifacts, are discussed in Chapter 10.

Blocking artifacts arise due to the fact that video codecs divide the screen into small squares to do motion estimation. Each block is treated separately, so when the blocks are compressed, the colors may not match across the block boundaries. This makes the blocks noticeable, particularly where areas of the frame should be smooth, but appear to be made of little blocks. These blocks are left over from motion estimation and intra-frame compression. Please refer to Figure 3-4 for an example of blocking artifacts.

These blocks are left over from motion estimation and intra-frame estimation.

Figure 3-4: An example of blocking artifacts

Other artifacts can appear when the file is streamed across the Internet. Because the Internet is far from a perfect transport medium, sometimes packets of data are lost. When loss occurs, the streaming media player has to try to reconstruct the missing information. All good streaming file formats have a certain amount of redundancy built into them to help alleviate these situations, but if a large chunk of data goes missing, it does horrible things to the picture. Streaks, holes, gray spots, you name it.

Combating Artifacts

Although a certain amount of picture degradation is to be expected, your streaming media files should not be filled with artifacts. If they are, chances are that something is fundamentally wrong at some point in your production chain. The purpose of this book is to make sure that you're not compromising your streams in any way. (This is covered in more detail in each respective section.) Each part of the production chain is important to maintaining artifact-free (or at least artifact-reduced) streams.

Each stage of the streaming media creation process has its own section in this book, where you can learn ways to get rid of the worst artifacts and reduce all the others to an acceptable level.

At the creation stage

Streaming codecs can only work with what they are given. If you hand a noisy, hissy low-level audio file to an encoder, you can't expect CD quality from the streaming version. Similarly with video, if you don't have good color, contrast, and composition to start off with, your encoder is not going to magically add it for you.

Using high-quality tools and solid engineering practice from the start prevents the worst problems. Much of what causes artifacts in streaming video and audio files can be virtually eliminated in this way. Sensible use of some signal processing can also add that extra bit of polish, which separates the true broadcast professionals from the hobbyists. It's a somewhat over-used adage in the computer biz but just as relevant: garbage in = garbage out.

Cross-Reference   The creation stage is covered in more detail in Part II of this book.

At the encoding stage

Encoding your streaming media files is done by using the encoding software provided by your streaming media platform, or using the encoding functionality built in to your audio or video editing software. Both methods involve using either an encoding preset or manually setting the encoding parameters. This, of course, is a double-edged sword — not only are you free to optimize the factory settings in the encoder as much as you want, but you are also free to completely mess things up.

If you tell the encoder to try to encode a full-screen, full frame rate file for a 56K-modem user, it will do the best that it can, given the parameters you set. In this case the resulting file is not worth watching. Granted, this is an extreme example, but it makes the point that if you make the wrong choices at the encoding stage, you could be setting yourself up for failure.

 The encoding stage is covered in more detail in Part III of this book.

At the authoring stage

You may want to combine different kinds of media in your streaming presentations or combine streaming media with server push technologies and who knows what else. If you're not careful, you could end up exceeding the audience's bandwidth limitations. If this happens, you could ruin the whole presentation.

You'll see later that every stream has its own bit rate along with some overhead, and that streaming technologies have to fight with other applications for bandwidth. All this has to be taken into account when authoring for your files.

 The authoring stage is covered in more detail in Part IV of this book.

At the serving stage

Though it may seem obvious, you have to make sure that you've got enough bandwidth for your server to stream a number of streams concurrently. Although your servers can serve thousands and thousands of streams over the course of a day, serving 60 concurrent 20Kbps streams will plug up a T1 line. For those of you focused on broadband, 25 concurrent 300Kbps streams will grind your company's internal LAN to a halt.

Packets get dropped on crowded networks and overtaxed routers, and packet loss means poor-quality streaming files. Planning ahead for bandwidth or putting a cap on your streaming server capacity helps ensure maximum stream quality.

 The serving stage is covered in more detail in Part V of this book.

Common Streaming Media Codecs

Talk about streaming media codecs can get a little confusing, because the term is a bit of a misnomer. In fact, any codec can be streamed as long as one of the streaming systems supports it. Some commonly used codecs claim to be more robust than others in streaming situations, because they were designed from the ground up as streaming codecs rather than just data reduction schemes.

The difference is subtle and not necessarily universally agreed upon. For the most part, the difference is academic, because by the time you get to the end of this page, someone will come out with yet another new codec heralded as "the best yet." So for now, take a quick look at the codecs you're most likely to encounter and let the codec developers get on with their work.

H.261, H.263

H.261 and H.263 are two early video conferencing standards that were developed by the ITU (International Telecommunication Union) when it became obvious that telecommunications and the computer industry were moving closer and closer together. These two standards form the basis of many codecs today.

MPEG

The name MPEG derives from the Moving Picture Experts Group that was formed in the late 1980s to come up with a system to encode video to be used in CD-ROM applications. MPEG-1 debuted in 1992 and was initially designed to work at a maximum of 1.5Mbits per second (the maximum transfer rate of single-speed CD-ROMs) and provide VHS quality. MPEG-2, released in 1995, was a progression from the initial specification to deal with larger picture sizes and higher data rates. MP3 audio is actually a contraction of "MPEG-1, Level III" and is, therefore, a subset of the MPEG-1 specification. Though not originally developed as streaming codecs, MPEG-1, MPEG-2 and MP3 files be streamed and played back by numerous platforms.

MPEG-4 is the latest standard to come from the ISO (International Organization for Standardization). MPEG-4 is a framework within which different types of multimedia can be combined for different kinds of presentations, including streaming. MPEG-4 includes new standards for audio and video coding as well as a new approach to video coding that treats different elements in the video as separate objects. Several vendors are now coming out with versions of MPEG-4 video implementations.

Note   As of 2002, both Apple and RealNetworks have committed to supporting the MPEG-4 standard.

RealAudio, RealVideo

RealAudio and RealVideo are the generic names for the family of audio and video codecs used by RealNetworks products. These codecs incorporate a large amount of in-house codec research along with technologies purchased or licensed from third parties.

The RealSystem natively supports a number of codecs:

- ✦ **Video:** RealVideo 8 and RealVideo G2.
- ✦ **Audio:** RealAudio 8.0; RealAudio G2; ACELP.net voice codec; RealAudio 1.0, 2.0 and 3.0 legacy codecs.

In addition, using plug-ins to their player and server allows them to also stream and play back a number of other codecs:

✦ **Video:** MPEG1, MPEG2; H.261 and H.263; ObjectVideo; Vivo video; On2's VP3 and VP4 .

✦ **Audio:** MP3, Liquid Audio, Vivo audio, Audible audio.

Windows Media Technology

Microsoft's Windows Media Technology, much like the RealSystem, has a family of codecs that combines in-house developed codecs with some third-party technology. Native encoding support currently includes:

✦ **Video:** Windows Media Video 8, Windows Media Video 7, Microsoft MPEG-4 V3, and ISO MPEG-4 V1.

✦ **Audio:** Windows Media Audio V7 and the ACELP.net voice codec.

Using what Windows Media Technology refers to as filters, the Windows Media Player also supports other third party codecs:

✦ **Video:** VP3, ClearVideo, VDOnet, Vivo video codecs

✦ **Audio:** Voxware MetaSound and MetaVoice; Lernout & Hauspie; MP3 audio codecs, Vivo audio, and all legacy Microsoft codecs, including all Pre-G2 RealAudio and RealVideo codecs.

Note Windows Media Technologies got its start as NetShow, which licensed RealNetworks technology, hence the legacy support for the early RealNetworks codecs.

QuickTime

Apple has arguably been at the computer multimedia game longer than anyone has, but it was sluggish getting into the streaming game. QuickTime technology has been used to create multimedia for many years, and in fact, the QuickTime file format was used as the basis for the MPEG-4 file format standard.

With the release of QuickTime Version 4, Apple finally offered a true streaming solution that included support for a number of codecs.

✦ **Video:** H.261 and H.263; Radius' Cinepak; Sorenson Video; VP3 files.

✦ **Audio:** Qdesign music codec; QualComm PureVoice codec; MP3; IMA 4:1.

All of the preceding technologies also play back and stream other file types, such as .AVI and .WAV; however, these file types aren't really suitable for streaming purposes. They can be used in local playback situations, but for the purposes of this book, I'll skip over them.

Summary

Codecs are what make streaming audio and video possible. Codecs are necessary to reduce the size of the huge raw data files to something that can be sent out across the Internet at a constant low bit rate. They do this by making intelligent choices about what information to discard, based on models that describe how sights and sounds are perceived. Lowering the amount of data used to represent the audio and video can lead to signal degradation and artifacts, distortions in the file that weren't there before. The worst artifacts can be eliminated or made irrelevant by being careful at each stage of the production process, particularly the creation stage.

✦ Codecs are algorithms used by streaming media encoders and players to compress and decompress encoded media files.

✦ Codecs can be lossless or lossy; however lossless codecs do not provide enough compression for streaming media purposes.

✦ Lossy codecs use perceptual models to help them decide what information can be discarded.

✦ Lossy codecs produce artifacts, which are distortions in the stream that weren't present before.

✦ Using high-quality tools and good engineering practice minimizes artifacts.

✦ Each of the major streaming platforms supports a number of different codecs.

✦   ✦   ✦

Creation: Working Within the Internet's Limitations

Internet Audio Basics

If you took the time to read Part I, you now have an idea of how audio has been recorded and reproduced over the years. Perhaps you skipped over it because you felt like you already had a handle on the basics. Either way, you're probably eager to get going at this point. Before you start pushing buttons, this chapter takes a look at audio on the Internet today and some of the basics of audio production.

Producing High-Quality Audio Is Easy

There's no question about it — audio has come of age on the Internet. This isn't too surprising, because encoded audio sounds great, even at dial-up bit rates. Audio codecs do a good job of preserving audio fidelity, because the amount of data reduction necessary to convert raw audio into a streaming format is nowhere near as great as with video. The preponderance of Internet radio stations and the ubiquity of MP3 audio are testaments to the popularity and acceptance of encoded audio.

Another contributing factor to the popularity of encoded audio is that the explosion in the home recording market and the plummeting prices of electrical components have made high-quality audio equipment much more affordable. Most multimedia computers these days come out of the box with soundcards, speakers, and microphones, but to be honest, they're generally not worth the plastic they're made of. For a few dollars more you can equip yourself with the tools you'll need to produce world-class streaming audio.

What makes all this even better is that working with audio is a simple and straightforward task. There is virtually only one variable that you have to control — the level, or loudness of the signal. If you do a good job of that, you're 90 percent of the way to great sounding streaming files, or downloadable files if that's what you're after. They're not necessarily the same.

Streaming Versus Downloading

Streaming and downloading are two completely different things. When a file is streamed, the player begins playback after it buffers a few seconds of content. Streaming media players also allow the listener to fast-forward or rewind to *any* point in a stream, just as you would with a cassette tape or CD player. The player re-buffers for a few seconds, and playback resumes.

Streams can also be encoded and broadcast in real time, as is the case with Internet radio stations and live concerts. Of course, you can't fast-forward or rewind when you're listening to live streams.

Pure download files, such as MP3 files downloaded off of a Web server, offer no such interactivity. These files do not begin playback nor can there be any interaction until the complete file has been downloaded. This obviously precludes any sort of live applications, and downloading long presentations is simply impractical.

Progressively downloaded files offer a degree of interactivity. The media player usually begins playback automatically after enough data has been downloaded. You can also pause or rewind the presentation once playback begins. You cannot, however, fast-forward the presentation beyond the data that has been downloaded. This limited interaction is fine for short clips, but impractical for longer formats. You also cannot progressively download live broadcasts.

Even though the three processes are different, the files need not be. In some cases the same audio file could be streamed, downloaded, or progressively downloaded. For instance, you could download an MP3 file and play it back when it finished downloading, use an MP3 player that supported progressive download, or you could listen to a streamed version of the same file, provided you had sufficient bandwidth. So when should you stream files and when should you offer files for download?

Well, this is the *Streaming Media Bible*, not *Downloading For Dummies*. But a case can be made for downloading, specifically when you want to offer higher quality files to people with restricted bandwidths. As long as the files are not too long, the resulting encoded file will not be too large and therefore the download not too painful. But with audio files, I'd still have to ask — why download?

Both Microsoft and RealNetworks are claiming CD-quality at 64 Kbps. Whether or not this is true is beside the point. Audio files sound so good at low bit rates these days, it is questionable whether the higher quality that downloading can offer is necessary. The only benefit to downloading a file is that the user has a physical copy of the file on his or her hard drive. After downloading, the file can be placed in a jukebox program, transferred to a portable player, or burned to CD, or — as you may have heard about lately — swapped between users using Napster-like services, such as Aimster or Gnutella.

Therein lies the problem with downloadable files. After there is a copy on the hard drive, you can do pretty much anything you want with it as long as it is in an unsecured file format, such as MP3. Although some folks may relish the thought of millions of copies of their music being swapped on the Internet, record companies are none too keen on the idea, which is fair enough because they invest hundreds of thousands of dollars on artists that they hope to recoup somehow.

Streaming files offer a degree of protection because the digital information is never saved on the hard drive. The bits are discarded as they are played. But no matter how advantageous streaming may be for copyright owners, folks still get pretty attached to having their own copy of something, even if it is a collection of bits on their hard drive.

A lot of work is being done now to protect copyright, particularly when it comes to music on the Internet. To do this, the file format has to include some sort of rules for how, when, where, and for how long rights are granted to the listener. For instance, these rules may specify that a limited number of CD copies may be made and that the song may only be played back on one computer, which helps combat the file-swapping problem. Both Microsoft and RealNetworks have Digital Rights Management (DRM) solutions that work with their systems, and Liquid Audio has had an end-to-end system for years. DRM has been one of the hottest topics of the last few years — you'll see a lot of developments in this area in the very short term.

If you do decide to offer some files for download, the audio pre-production that is discussed in this book will still help you get high quality results. Even if folks have to wait awhile to hear them.

Simple Steps to Ensure Success

Producing audio for streaming media is in reality no different than producing audio for traditional broadcast. Basic audio production values are where it's at, and those start with level.

Level is everything

That's right, level is everything. Say it out loud. Again. Print it out in big letters and tape it to the wall. When it comes to audio, if you look after your levels, you'll always be in great shape. So what's a level?

Dynamic range

Every piece of audio gear has a limited range in which it can operate. This is known as its dynamic range, which stretches from the loudest sound it can reproduce without distortion down to its own internal noise floor. The noise floor is the level of the noise inherent to the piece of equipment. Any signals below this level are indistinguishable.

Anything electronic, by nature of being plugged into the wall and having electricity coursing through it, has an internal noise level. The higher the quality, the quieter the equipment. The quieter the equipment, the lower the noise floor, and therefore the greater its dynamic range. This is generally measured in decibels (dB). Human hearing spans a range of about 130 dB; 16-bit digital recordings, a maximum of 96 dB; FM radio only about 50 dB.

You want to get the best performance out of every piece of equipment you use, so you have to work within their dynamic ranges. You want to avoid signals that are too low, because they will be close to the noise floor — which means the noise may be audible. You also want to avoid signals that are too loud because they may cause the equipment to distort.

Distortion occurs when the equipment cannot faithfully reproduce the required waveform. Distortions of very short duration are often not audible; longer periods of distortion are. In particular, digital distortion sounds absolutely horrible. In the good old days of analog, you could get away with being a little sloppier with your levels, as analog circuits were designed to operate far above their stated dynamic ranges. Analog distortion is not as unpleasant, and in fact can be quite enjoyable, as any rock music fan knows. But that distortion is used as an effect. You'd hardly want your evening news read through a distortion pedal. So in practice, you're going to want to avoid distortion.

Meters

Because equipment can only operate in a given range, you need some way of determining how much signal you're working with. Most pieces of equipment these days come with some sort of meter to give you an idea of what's going on inside. These can either be old-fashioned VU (Volume Units) meters with a needle flicking back and forth, or a more modern style with LED lights as indicators. They are calibrated either in Volume Units, a measure of how loud the signal is, or in decibels (dB) if they are peak meters. Figure 4-1 shows a few different types of meters.

VU meters measure average loudness levels as opposed to peak levels. It gives you an idea of how "loud" the signal is. Using VU meters, 0 VU is considered the standard operating level.

The LED peak meter is typical of what you'll see on a lot of audio hardware. A peak meter, as you'd expect, gives a visual indication of the signal peaks. It is not as good at conveying the overall loudness of a signal, because the way you perceive loudness doesn't have much to do with peak levels, but it is excellent for preventing distortion, which is important when working in a digital format.

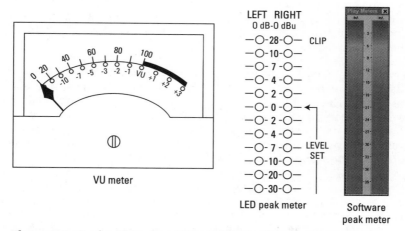

Figure 4-1: Analog VU meter; LED peak meter (Mackie 1202 VLZ Pro mixing desk), software peak meter (Sonic Foundry's Sound Forge)

Last but not least are software peak meters. The biggest difference between a software meter and the other two is that it doesn't go above zero; if the signal goes above zero, a small indicator at the top of the meter lights up to let you know that the signal has *clipped*, that is, gone into distortion. Usually this means resetting your levels and starting again; although, as mentioned previously, if it's short enough, it may not be audible.

The other two meters have *headroom* above zero. Headroom is the amount of room between standard operating level and where distortion begins. Analog equipment is designed to have headroom above zero to accommodate temporary peaks. Digital equipment, on the other hand, does not have this luxury. Anything above the maximum (0 dB) produces distortion.

Setting levels

Now that you have a visual representation of the input signal, make sure that you're using as much of the equipment's available signal range as possible without straying into distortion. For all analog equipment, that means running the signal level at around 0 dB. For the digital equipment, it means running as close to 0 dB as possible *without ever going over*. You can control the levels in each piece of equipment by setting the input and output levels.

Most every piece of audio equipment allows you to adjust the input and output levels using a knob or a *fader*. A fader is merely a knob that slides back and forth as opposed to being rotated. These controls generally allow you to amplify (turn up/boost), attenuate (turn down/cut), or leave the input signal just as it is. To set a level, you simply adjust the level using the knob or fader while watching the display on the meter.

For analog audio equipment, you want to set the level so that the signal is regularly hitting 0 dB, with occasional peaks over that. There is generally an input level and an output level setting. The output level setting is separate from the input because the processing that the equipment is doing affects overall signal level. If it's a compressor, it will be turning parts of the signal down, which means you want to compensate at the output stage by increasing signal level. If the processing has added to the signal level, attenuate the signal a bit to bring the output level back down to 0 dB.

Digital equipment works similarly, but with a hard cut-off at 0 dB. Because you never want to go above 0 dB, set your levels somewhere between –10 dB and –3 dB. Doing so will leave some headroom for unexpected peaks that would otherwise send the signal into distortion. With digital equipment, it is better to be safe than sorry, especially during live events where you have only one chance to get it right.

If for some reason your level is too high, you'll hear it: A crackling noise will be audible. The question is whether it is too loud on input or too loud on output. Because digital equipment is generally at the end of the chain, you generally only have to worry about their input stage. With analog processing equipment, you have to be careful to check both the input and output stages. Some equipment has separate meters for input and output; some share one meter that has to be flipped into input or output mode. Be absolutely sure you check both stages of every piece of equipment.

Note   It is very important to check the levels at each and every point in the signal chain. It does no good whatsoever if you have the input level to your computer set just right if it is set incorrectly at another point in your audio signal chain. Poorly set levels mean lower quality and possibly distortion.

Digital inputs

Digital inputs are a special case. With digital inputs, there are no levels to set. Because digital information is being exchanged, no amplification takes place, so you don't have to make any adjustments. Of course, there has to be at least one input level setting somewhere — there's no such thing as a digital microphone yet. So you're not completely off the hook if you're creating content from scratch.

If someone is handing you finished DAT tapes and you can connect digitally between your DAT machine and your soundcard, you are a lucky soul indeed. In this case, there would be no levels to set — just hit play on the DAT and record in your software. In most cases, though, you'll have to do some knob twisting somewhere in the signal chain.

Setting up a gain structure: A step-by-step example

Your audio signal chain comprises all your audio equipment. As signal flows through the chain, its level, or *gain,* is affected by each piece of equipment. How the gain is affected throughout the signal chain is referred to as the *gain structure*. Setting up a proper gain structure is the first step towards producing high-quality audio.

Because no piece of audio equipment operates well at minimum or maximum gain, the idea behind setting up a gain structure is to keep your level as consistent as possible throughout the signal chain. You do this by adjusting the input and output levels for each and every piece of audio equipment.

Setting levels is different for each piece of equipment, but for the sake of argument, this example assumes you have a microphone plugged into a mixing desk, which is plugged into your soundcard. A mixing desk is a piece of audio gear that takes multiple inputs, each input being referred to as a *channel*. You can set input levels for each channel, as well as adjust the relative levels between each channel. Finally, you can adjust the overall output level of the mixing desk.

To set up a gain structure for this modest setup, you must first set the input level of the microphone into the mixing desk, then set the output level of the mixing desk, and finally set the input level into the recording software. Figure 4-2 illustrates this using a Mackie 1202 mixing desk as a reference.

1. **To set the input level of the microphone, make sure you're metering only the microphone channel.** Most mixing desks have a button labeled Solo on each channel to ensure this. Either press the Solo button or make sure all other channels are turned down.

4 - Set pan to center

2 - Adjust channel trim

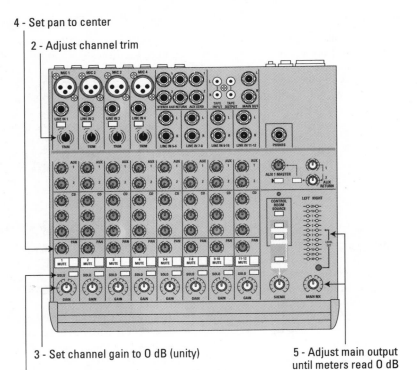

3 - Set channel gain to 0 dB (unity)

5 - Adjust main output until meters read 0 dB

1 - Press solo button to monitor channel level

Figure 4-2: Setting levels using a Mackie 1202 VLZ Pro mixing desk

Image courtesy Mackie Designs, Inc.

2. **There are many places where level can be adjusted on mixing desks (just look at all those knobs!).** What you want to do now is worry only about input levels. To adjust the input level, or *trim,* with your voice talent speaking into the microphone, adjust the Trim knob until the meter indicates an average level of 0 dB.

   Now that you've set the input level for the microphone, it's time to check the output level of the mixing desk. But first make sure nothing is interfering along the way.

3. **If your mixing desk has a Solo button and you were in Solo mode, take the channel out of Solo mode by pressing the Solo button.** Make sure the channel gain is set to zero. If your mixing desk has faders, make sure the fader is set to 0 dB. If your mixing desk has knobs, set the knob to 0 dB. (On a Mackie desk this is labeled as "U" for unity gain.) If your mixing desk has knobs but no markings, set the knob to about three-quarters of the maximum setting — this is usually a save place to start.

4. **Make sure the channel is panned directly center as opposed to left or right.**

5. **To set the output level, adjust the master gain until the meter reads 0 dB (on the Mackie 1202 VLZ Pro, this is labeled as Master Mix).**

   Two down, one to go. The last thing you have to check is the input level to the computer.

6. **Open up your audio editing software and then open up the Recording window.** For this step (and for the illustrations) I'll be using Sound Forge.

   If you're using a high-quality soundcard, you should see levels in your audio recording software that correspond exactly to the levels you see coming out of your mixing desk. Many high-quality soundcards do not offer software adjustment of the input levels. If this is the case with your card and the input levels need to be adjusted, you can adjust the output level of the mixing desk.

   Those of you who are using high-quality sound cards may now be excused. Your level should be set, and you can move on to the next part of this chapter. For the rest of you, it's on to step 7.

7. **If you're using a soundcard that allows software adjustment of the input levels go ahead and open up your Soundcard Mixing window.** For SoundBlaster-compatible cards, you can do this by double-clicking on the speaker icon in the right-hand corner of your task bar (see Figure 4-3).

   If your soundcard's mixing window has high-quality metering, there is no need to open up your audio editing software. If you're stuck using the Microsoft mixer window, use the metering in your audio editing software.

8. **If you're using the Microsoft mixer, you have to make sure you're adjusting the record levels, and not the playback levels.** If you're not using the Microsoft mixer window, please skip to Step 10.

9. **Choose Options ➪ Properties.** When the Properties window opens, select the Recording radio button. Make sure that in the Line-In box is checked, assuming the mixing desk is connected to that soundcard input, and click OK (see Figure 4-3).

Choose Properties from the Options
menu to open the Properties windows

Select Recording properties

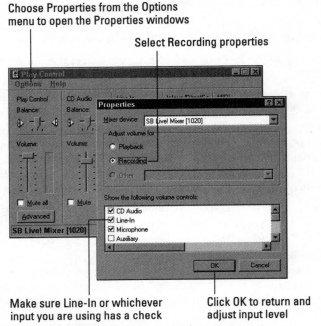

Make sure Line-In or whichever
input you are using has a check

Click OK to return and
adjust input level

Figure 4-3: Getting to the Record window of the
Microsoft Mixer

10. **The Microsoft Mixer window should now say Record Control in the title bar as per Figure 4-4.** Make sure the Line-In input is selected.

11. **If you're using your audio editing program's meters, make sure the meters are enabled.** (In Sound Forge, make sure that the Monitor check box is selected — see Figure 4-4.)

12. **At last you're ready. Have your voice talent speak into the microphone again, and adjust the input level in the Record Control window until it is reading between –10 dB and –6 dB on your meters, with occasional peaks around –3 dB.** Make sure the talent is speaking normally — if they're speaking quietly, you're going to be in for a surprise when your talent speaks up. Figure 4-4 illustrates how to set an input level using the Microsoft Sound Mapper and Sound Forge.

Enable Monitoring and use meters to set level

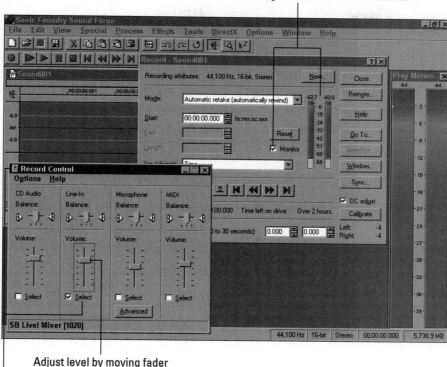

Adjust level by moving fader

Make sure it says Record Window and Line-In
or whichever input you are using is selected

Figure 4-4: Adjusting input levels via the Microsoft Mixer, using the audio editing
software (Sound Forge) meters

That should do it. You've adjusted input and output levels so that you know you're
operating within each piece of audio equipment's dynamic range. In fact, because
you're operating at the top of each dynamic range without going over, you'll get the
best performance out of each piece of equipment, which is what you're after. Noise
will be minimized and sonic clarity maintained. This way, you'll create pristine
audio files to merge with your video or to hand off to your encoders.

You should never have to run any input stage at its maximum or minimum. Two-
thirds to three-quarters of the maximum is where you're going to get the best
performance. If anything is running at an extreme, check the gain stages before
and after it to see if you can get more or less signal. In the preceding step-by-step
example, if the input to the computer was too high ("hot"), instead of turning the
computer input down too far, you should turn down the output of the mixing desk
until you can run the computer input at approximately one-half of the maximum.

Professional versus Consumer Operating Levels — When is 0 dB not 0 dB?

Trick question. Different pieces of equipment define 0 dB differently.

As if you didn't have enough to worry about, the difference comes about because professional and consumer equipment operate at slightly different signal voltages, meaning slightly different operating ranges.

Professional equipment operates at the higher +4 dB standard, while consumer-grade equipment operates at –10 dB. Without getting too technical, this means that when consumer equipment puts out what it references as 0 dB, professional equipment sees it as –14 dB. Conversely, when professional equipment puts out 0 dB, consumer equipment sees it at +14 dB! Yow!

Once upon a time these two standards rarely met; however in today's studios you're quite likely to find a few pieces of consumer gear alongside the professional stuff. Much of the home studio equipment available today runs at the lower –10 dB standard. While mixing and matching like this isn't optimal, it doesn't have to be problematic, provided you are careful about setting your levels.

When you're connecting consumer gear to professional inputs, the professional gear expects +4 dB. Since the consumer gear doesn't put out as much as that, you're going to have to adjust the input trim up to get a good operating level.

Similarly, if you're coming out of professional gear into consumer (as is the case with many soundcards), you're going to have to turn the output level of the professional gear down, as well as turn the input level of the consumer gear down.

In an ideal world, we'd all be running exclusively professional gear, but in practice you have to work with what you can afford.

After you've gone through your equipment and set levels, you won't have to revisit them every day. If you do a daily news report, you'll probably be using the same voiceover talent each day and be recording about the same time each day. You might need to tweak ever so slightly, but for the most part, the levels should be "set and forget."

A little investment goes a long way

If you were going to start a radio station, you wouldn't dream of doing it without investing some money in equipment. Why should it be any different with a streaming media venture? Luckily, bringing your system up to an acceptable level to broadcast quality audio does not need to be expensive.

Today you have a wide range of options when setting up an audio system. The prices have come down not only for digital systems but also for good quality analog gear. There is no reason why you can't set up an excellent quality audio-capture system for under $1,000. An investment of $500 can also work wonders.

You'll need a good set of speakers to be able to hear what you are working on. Even though you may be authoring low bit rate streams that do not utilize the full audio spectrum, you should always aspire to creating the highest quality source files. If you can't hear what you're doing, you won't be able to create the best possible quality.

You'll also want to purchase a good quality soundcard. The soundcard can be the largest source of noise in your signal chain. You'll need to purchase a studio-quality microphone if you plan on doing voiceovers. If your computer came with a microphone, take it and snap it in two right now. Trust me, you won't want to use it.

Other tools you'll probably want to purchase will be a small mixing desk, a compressor, good quality cables, a portable DAT machine, good audio editing software, and maybe some plug-ins. But I don't want to jump ahead; this is all discussed in more detail in Chapter 6. Appendix C also has equipment suggestions for a sample capture suite.

Summary

Audio production is simple as long as you pay attention to your levels. Even though some equipment operates at different levels than others, with a bit of tinkering, you should be able to set up a gain structure that works for most of your situations.

Even though streaming and downloading are different, the files may be the same, and the production process for both is the same. In both cases, you're after the best quality.

✦ Downloading and streaming are different processes, though some file types can be streamed or downloaded.

✦ Every piece of equipment has a dynamic range, which is the difference between the loudest and quietest sounds it can reproduce.

✦ You want to operate at the high end of the dynamic range, without going into distortion.

✦ Levels must be set at every point in the signal chain.

✦ Level is everything in audio production.

✦   ✦   ✦

Internet Video Basics

Audio is fairly straightforward to work with as long as you keep your eye on your levels. Video, on the other hand, is a slightly different beast, because there are more variables to consider. Each one of these variables affects the quality of the encoded file and is, therefore, a point of contact between you and your streaming files.

The variables that determine the quality of your streaming files — lighting, color, focus, contrast, composition — come into play the moment you point the camera at your subject.

Getting It Right from the Start

There a lot of variables to be considered when dealing with video files, and to some extent they are inextricably entwined. Some variables such as color and contrast can be tweaked a bit during the capture and editing phases. Other variables cannot.

For instance, if you shoot without enough light, you can bump up the overall lighting level later, but this will mess up your black level. Not only that, but you probably don't want to add light to the whole scene — just the main subject. Guess what? No can do.

Of course, you can do things to polish your captured video stream. The problem is, when you're working with uncompressed video, you're talking about huge files. So if you decide you're going to change contrast or color balance ever so slightly, it's going to take time to change every pixel of every frame of video. Enough time to grab a cup of coffee, let alone a whole lunch break.

What you really want to do is get it right to begin with. It means not only better raw materials to work with but also less processing time because you'll be doing less tweaking in the processing stage. Given the accelerated time scale the Internet operates on, the last thing you want is for things to take any longer than they have to. So take a look at the three main variables you have to get right from the start: light, color, and composition.

Light

It should come as no surprise that light is everything in video production. It's important for a number of reasons. Let me start with human perception.

Your eyes contain two types of receptor cells — rods and cones. The cones are sensitive to color and detail but require a lot of light; the rods are more sensitive to motion and low light levels but not as sensitive to detail. You can see a demonstration of this every evening at dusk: As the sun goes down and the amount of ambient light slowly decreases, everything starts to turn grayish-blue. You can still see, but colors are no longer as vivid as they were, and things aren't as focused. Consequently, video that is shot without enough light will not appear as colorful, crisp, or focused to us.

Cameras react to lighting levels much the way your eyes do. They can't "see" as well in the dark. Cameras are also not as sensitive as your eyes are and, therefore, require a lot more light. Although equipment nowadays can operate at relatively low light levels, this is not the best approach. Operating at low light levels means operating at the bottom of the equipment's range. Low-level video signals are noisy. Video noise shows up as "grain" or "snow" in the picture. The grain is not only annoying but also inconsistent — it changes from frame to frame. This is an encoder double-whammy. First of all, the codec doesn't know that the grain is noise, and because it is *changing,* it is deemed important. The encoder therefore expends a lot of effort encoding the grain, which is exactly the opposite of what you want. Unsurprisingly, quality of the encode suffers.

Another reason to shoot with plenty of light has to do with how lenses work, and how cameras control the amount of light coming into the lens. Because the frame rate of video is constant, the shutter speed is fixed. Video cameras therefore vary the amount of light coming in by adjusting the size of the aperture. The aperture setting is known as the F-stop. In low lighting situations, the aperture is wide open, which corresponds to a low F-stop. When the aperture is wide open, it allows light to come through the whole lens. In bright light, the aperture is closed down, which corresponds to a high F-stop. When it's closed down, light only travels through the central portion of the lens.

Lenses are never optically perfect, especially the lower-quality plastic lenses you find on most DV cameras today. In particular, lenses are more prone to picture distortion at their edges. Low lighting levels require the aperture to open wide and allow as much light in as possible. However, this means that some of the light travels through the edges of the lens, where the picture quality is lower. This can translate into distortion at the edges of your video frame.

Conversely, if you're shooting in plenty of light, the aperture is closed down. The light entering the camera only travels through the central portion of the lens — where image quality is sharpest. A sharper image results in higher quality encoded files.

Need more reasons? I didn't think so. You need more light. So how do you go about getting enough light on your subject? Well, a full discussion of the myriad possibilities of lighting is beyond the scope of this book, but I go over the basics and give you a sample lighting setup to get you started. If you're serious about your lighting, you should buy a book dedicated to the subject or, better yet, hire someone with some lighting experience. He or she will be able to assess your needs and help come up with a setup that works for you.

Using lights

In nearly every situation you'll be shooting, you'll want more light — the question is where do you get it? The most obvious answer is to use additional lights. They come in all shapes and sizes and are used in a variety of different capacities.

Lights can be hard or soft sources, a concept which refers to the character of the light and the type of shadows they generate. Hard light sources shine directly at the object, with no diffusion or reflection, and cause strong shadows. Soft lighting is either diffused via a translucent substance suspended between the light and the subject, or reflected off a diffusing surface. Breaking up the light this way makes shadows less pronounced.

Soft lights that are diffused or reflected have less intensity than hard, direct lights. So when you're setting up your lights, you have to keep this in mind. Hard lights often have to be dimmed or placed further away from the subject to blend properly with the soft light sources. Many lights have an adjustment to vary the focus of the beam, which changes the character and intensity of the light. The character of each light should be set according to how the light is being used in your lighting setup, which is discussed below.

Though many different approaches to lighting exist, most setups are generally based on a combination of three basic lights: the key light, the fill light, and the back light.

- ✦ **Key light:** The key light is the main light used to light the subject. This is different from the fill light, which lights the whole set. The key light is usually about 45 degrees away from the camera, though this is not a hard-set rule. This light casts shadows on one side of the subject's face, which adds a 3-D quality to the picture.

- ✦ **Fill light:** The fill light is used to brings up the overall light level of the whole set and fill in some of the shadows created by the key light. It shouldn't compete with the key light; rather it should complement it.

- ✦ **Back light:** The back light is designed to separate the subject from the background. If the subject is a person, the back light is positioned behind and above the subject to illuminate the shoulders and top of the head. For inanimate objects the placement is similar, though what you're trying to light varies. Using a back light adds more three-dimensionality to the scene.

By starting with a simple three-point lighting system and augmenting as necessary, you should be able to meet all your lighting requirements.

Using reflectors

Reflectors can be as simple as a white piece of cardboard or a reflective silver sheet specially made for lighting purposes by a lighting supplier. They can be used to reflect light to diffuse the original source, or to get a little more mileage out of an existing light. For existence, you can reflect some of the key light back onto the subject to use as a fill. Or, if your fill light is too strong, you can bounce it off the ceiling to diffuse it and decrease its intensity.

Reflectors can be very helpful when filming outdoors. Outdoors the sun is always your key light. By constructive use of reflectors, it can also be used as the back light and the fill! Figure 5-1 illustrates how you can do this. Without a reflector on a sunny day, your subject will end up with dark shadows under their eyes — which neither of you want.

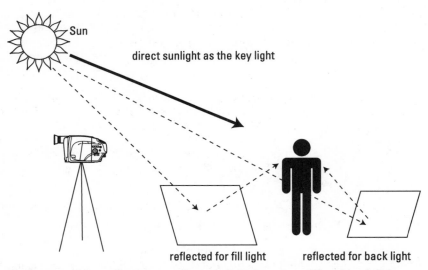

Figure 5-1: Using reflectors to reflect sunlight for use as fill and back light.

Color

Color is an important component in any video production. Your eyes are very sensitive to and react positively to pleasing colors. You also use color to determine what is important. Unfortunately, color is one of the areas where codecs try to economize by using fewer bits to represent the full spectrum of color. It is important to start off with the best possible color information so the encoder can make better decisions about where to economize.

Spending the time to light your scenes correctly is the first step toward good color resolution. The next step involves your camera. Cameras perceive all colors in reference to white. The problem is that white looks different under different lighting conditions. You see a sheet of paper as white whether you're indoors or outdoors, but the amount and color quality of the light it reflects is entirely different in those situations. Your eyes and brain compensate automatically. Cameras must be set properly to make sure they reproduce colors correctly. This is known as "setting the color temperature" or "white balance" of your camera, or simply "white balancing."

By white balancing your camera, that is, setting it up so that it sees white correctly, you'll make sure the scenes you're shooting are reproduced as faithfully as possible. To learn how to white-balance your video camera, please see the section White-Balancing Your Video Camera.

Three-point lighting

Expert This entire section was contributed by Halley Bock, one of this book's expert contributors. Halley's contact information is listed in Bonus Chapter 6 on the book's CD-ROM.

Today's video cameras are capable of shooting under just about any conditions. So what's the big deal? Why should you care about lighting techniques? Well, do you want your streams to stand out or join the ever-expanding pool of "streaming mud?"

No doubt you've seen it — blocks of muddy pixels moving around a postage stamp-sized window, leaving you wondering what, exactly, you're watching. How much more suffering do producers need to ask of their viewers before they step up to the plate? Not only will good lighting help you produce beautiful video, but it will also give your content an edge — and the audience will show its appreciation by coming back for more.

Understanding the problem

"Streaming mud" is most commonly the result of poor lighting. The two most common mistakes are flooding the scene with too much light and not using enough light. Too much light causes a flat, washed out and colorless picture. Insufficient light causes picture-noise (snow or grain) and again leads to a flat, dimensionless image where your subject has no chance of popping out.

With improper lighting, picture contrast will be low and colors will bleed into each other. Without proper contrast, the encoder will have a hard time discerning edges of objects, leading of course to poor quality encodes. What do you get as a result? Mud.

How do you avoid these pitfalls and ensure your time in the studio is well spent? In terms of professional appearance and ensuring your video will not suffer at the hands of the encoder, keep in mind three basic goals:

✦ **Definition:** You want your pictures to be sharply defined.

✦ **Clean Picture:** You want your picture free from picture-noise.

✦ **Color Quality:** You want the camera's interpretation of color quality to match the human eye's translation of the same.

To accomplish all three of the above requires not only proper lighting but also correct color balance in your camera. To find out how to do that, please refer to White-balancing Your Video Camera a little later on in this chapter. This section concentrates on the first half of the equation — lighting.

The fundamentals of three-point lighting

Three-point lighting is highly effective at producing professional results in a multitude of situations. This approach consists of three lights: the key light, fill light, and the back light. While you may not always need all three, you should understand how each lamp contributes to overall picture quality.

The *key light* is the main source of illumination and determines the exposure of the scene. It also establishes the light direction and creates the principal modeling effects (shadow formations). Because the key light determines overall composition, its characteristics tend to be hard and directional to allow maximum control over the light's coverage and focus. Its most effective angle will depend on which aspects of your subject you want to emphasize.

For example, when lighting a person, the temptation is to eliminate all shadows. However, this results in a picture that is flat and without definition. Shadows provide visual cues that suggest depth. In this case, your want to set your key light so that it casts shadows on one side of your subject's face. You'll see in the following section, Setting up three-point lighting, that a good starting point for your key light is 45 degrees away from the camera position.

The *fill light* illuminates the shadow areas produced by the key light. Not too strongly . . . you don't want to negate the modeling effects created by the key light. Remember that the fill light should always play a supplementary role. Therefore, ideally, the fill light should be diffused or soft so as not to compete with the key light. More often than not, bouncing the key light off a reflector board can suffice as your fill.

Going back to the previous example for a moment, a good place to start with your fill light is 45 degrees away from your camera position, on the other side of the camera from your key light. The fill light should be softer than the key, so you should soften the focus, and possibly also use some diffusing material. This is covered in more detail in the following section, "Setting up three-point lighting".

The *back light* illuminates the edge-contours of the subject and helps reveal their depth and form. Back light creates a more three-dimensional illusion, particularly when the subject and background tones are similar. Without it, planes within the picture are liable to merge, so that the overall result is flat and lacking vitality. As with the key, the characteristics of back light are hard and directional. However, as a general rule, the back light should be half the wattage of your key so as not to overwhelm the effects of the key and/or cause lens flare.

Place your back light behind your subject, and either slightly above or below them. This avoids possible lens flares in your camera, while still lighting the edges of your subject. This is covered in more detail in the section below.

Describing light positions

When positioning lights, it is helpful to have a simple way to describe a light's position. Many people find it easiest to describe positions accurately by using a clock face system of reference. In this system, the subject is considered to be at the center of a clock, with the camera at the 6 o'clock position of the horizontal plane and at 3 o'clock in the vertical plane. Figure 5-2 illustrates the clock-face system. Now it is time to move on to the placement of your three lights.

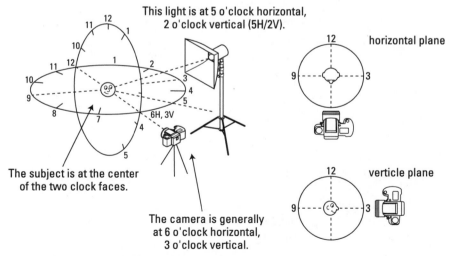

Figure 5-2: Clock Face Reference Diagram

Setting up three-point lighting

1. **Position the key light.** As a starting point, place the key light adjacent to the camera. Now that you see our subject, try moving the key. Move it slightly away from the camera, around your virtual clock face. You will see the shadows move in the opposite direction. Raise the lamp, and the shadows move downward.

Caution Lights are hot. I mean it. Be very careful when handling lighting fixtures. It's also a good idea to turn lights off when you move them more than a few inches — there is less chance of blowing the bulb that way.

The key light determines what the subject looks like by controling how shadows are formed. These shadows define the overall picture dimension. In most cases, the key light should be positioned somewhere between 1–2 hours away from the side of the camera, and between 1–2 hours from the camera's vertical plane (Figure 5-3).

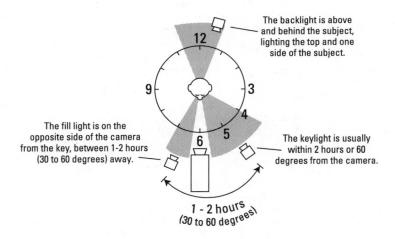

The backlight is above and behind the subject, lighting the top and one side of the subject.

The fill light is on the opposite side of the camera from the key, between 1-2 hours (30 to 60 degrees) away.

The keylight is usually within 2 hours or 60 degrees from the camera.

1 - 2 hours (30 to 60 degrees)

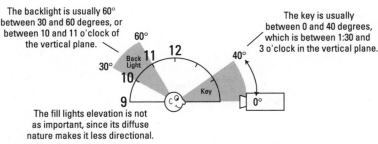

The backlight is usually 60° between 30 and 60 degrees, or between 10 and 11 o'clock of the vertical plane.

The key is usually between 0 and 40 degrees, which is between 1:30 and 3 o'clock in the vertical plane.

Back Light

Key

The fill lights elevation is not as important, since its diffuse nature makes it less directional.

Figure 5-3: Three-Point Lighting Diagram

2. **Adjust for exposure.** After the key light is in position, adjust the light's intensity for the required F-stop. You can do this by adjusting the light output (if you have dimming lights), by adding or subtracting layers of neutral density gel, or by moving the light toward or away from the subject. Light intensity follows the inverse-squared law — twice the distance equals one-quarter the light, half the distance equals four times the light.

   Adjust until your camera's exposure meter reads f/4.5. Generally, an F-stop of f/4.5 achieves sufficient depth of field (most of the scene in focus) without requiring excessively large lighting fixtures. You can shoot at lower F-stops, but you'll have to be extra careful about your focus — the lower the F-stop, the smaller the depth of field.

3. **Position the fill light.** The fill light's position follows from the key light's position. The general rule here is that the fill light should be positioned approximately one to two hours (30–60 degrees) away from the key light, making sure that it is placed on the other side of the camera. For example, for a key light at a 5 o'clock location, the fill light should be between 7 and 8 o'clock. A vertical height of 3–4 feet is also considered standard placement for fill lights, so that it will light both standing and seated subjects.

   Keep in mind that because the fill light falls off in intensity quickly due to it's soft nature, you'll want to place it closer to the subject than the key light to ensure proper illumination.

4. **Position the back light.** The typical back light is a single spotlight placed above and behind the subject, slightly to one side of the subject. If it is too high, it can give your subject a bright nose and black circles under his eyes if you're not careful. If it is too low, it can cause lens flares or even appear in the shot. Placing the back light directly behind a subject (dead back light), tends to light just his upper edges.

   A well-set back light will gently light the top of the subject's head and shoulders, and also rim-light one side of the subject. Take care that it is not offset too much, or it will over-light one side of the face.

5. **Fire away!** You now have now successfully completed your first three-point lighting setup. Understanding this technique gives you a wonderful working basis for any production coming your way. It will also allow you to explore and experiment with the many characteristics and moods that lighting can create.

White-Balancing Your Video Camera

Expert This section was also contributed by Halley Bock. Please refer to Bonus Chapter 6 on the CD-ROM for biographical and contact information.

Alright — if you've been through the three-point lighting explanation, you now have a beautifully lit picture ready to shoot at an appropriate F-stop. This is good news for the encoder and your audience. If you're filming in black and white, you're ready to go. On the other hand, if you're a color-loving videographer like most of us are, you have a few more steps to go before you start yelling "Action!"

It is absolutely critical to ensure that the camera sees the entire color spectrum the same way you do. Your eyes can automatically adjust between outdoor and inside light — cameras cannot. You have to set the camera according to the type of light you're filming under. If you don't set your camera correctly, you're likely to be surprised when you play back your video. What's more, you are in trouble because it is nearly impossible to correct color temperature mistakes later.

Have you ever noticed an orange tint or blue haze to your video? This is a dead giveaway of incorrect color temperature, which results from failing to white balance your camera. Understanding how color temperature works is a necessary skill for any videographer, though a little tricky to explain. Let's begin by taking a look at the color spectrum.

The color spectrum

Remember shining a flashlight through a prism? Remember the spectrum of color that made up white light? What we perceive as white light is actually a combination of all colors. In fact, a deeper analysis of what is considered white light reveals that the actual proportions of the component colors can vary considerably. Even though a lamp is less bright than the sun, you perceive both as being white, whereas a camera set for outdoor shots will see the lamplight as yellow.

The color content of light can be measured and given a value. This value is measured in "degrees Kelvin (°K)." This value is also referred to as the light's *temperature*, but don't confuse color temperature with the temperature outdoors. Once you know the color temperature of the light you're working with, you can set your camera accordingly and ensure that what looks white to us is being recorded as white by the camera.

Where red is cold and blue is hot

You have to think about colors differently when dealing with the Kelvin scale. Where you would normally think of blue as a 'cold' color and red as a 'hot' color, it's just the opposite in terms of color temperature.

Daylight has a *high* color temperature (5600K), which means it contains a high proportion of blue light. Tungsten lamps (household lamps, studio lights) have a *lower* color temperature (3200K) and, therefore, appear more orange or yellow. Table 5-1 lists some common light sources and their approximate color temperatures.

Table 5-1	
Typical Color Temperatures (In Degrees Kelvin)	
Tungsten light sources	*Temperature*
Standard candle	1930°K
Household tungsten lamps (25–250 watts)	2600–2900°K
Studio tungsten lamps (500–1000 watts)	3000°K
Studio tungsten lamps (2000 watts)	3275°K
Studio tungsten lamps (5–10 kilowatts)	3380°K
Fluorescent lamps	3200–7500°K
Natural light	*Temperature*
Sunrise, sunset	2000–3000°K
Sunless early morning, late afternoon	4500–4800°K
Midday sun	5000–5400°K
Overcast sky	6800–7500°K

All video and photographic systems are color-balanced to produce optimum color accuracy when used with white light of a particular chromatic quality. Professional lighting fixtures use different bulbs to handle specific color temperature ranges — either "outdoor" or "tungsten" balanced. Most cameras (from consumer to professional) offer presets specifically designed to deal with most common lighting situations. Our job is to ensure that the camera's color temperature setting matches our lighting situation. We do this by either using equipment presets or by manually adjusting the camera until things look right. The process of setting a camera's color temperature setting is called white balancing.

Using presets to white balance

Different types of light contain different proportions of color. To make sure a camera records the color information accurately, you have to make sure the camera is color balanced for the type of light you're shooting with. This is called white balancing your camera, and is done as follows:

1. **Put your camera into position.** Turn on any your lights and position any reflectors you may be using.

2. **Place a white card where your subject will be filmed, making sure that the card is dense enough so that no light can pass through it.** Any white surface will do.

3. **Zoom in on the white card until it fills the entire video frame.**

4. **Look at the color of the white card through the viewfinder.** Your goal is to get the white in the viewfinder to match the white of the actual card. Toggle through your camera's presets to achieve the best color match.

Even if you know which preset to select, it's a good exercise to step through the other presets and familiarize yourself with the affects an improper setting will have on your white balance. This will hone your abilities to properly correct color temperature problems in a variety of situations. Table 5-2 lists the most common presets, along with when and where they are appropriate.

Table 5-2
White Balance Presets and Their Uses

Preset	Icon	Color temperature	Uses
Indoor	Light bulb	3200–3400°K	Indoor locations using tungsten lights
Daylight	Sun	5400–5600°K	Outdoor locations using higher levels of natural light
Night	Moon	1500–3000°K	Outdoor locations using low levels of natural light

Choose the correct preset according to Table 5-2. The white of the card you see through the viewfinder should be a close match to the actual white of the card. For most applications, this will achieve a satisfactory color balance. However, if the presets didn't quite get you what you were after, your camera should have two other choices to offer when it comes to color correction — automatic white balancing and manual white balancing.

Automatic white balance

Your camera's automatic white balance feature typically resides within the same menu as the presets above. This feature allows the camera to use its circuitry to perform a best guess adjustment to achieve proper color temperature. As you might expect with any feature that is automatic, it may or may not result in the desired effect. If selecting this feature proves unsatisfactory, you still have one last option.

Manual white balance

The manual white balance feature should be available on the same menu set as the preset white balance choices. If not, take a look at your manual — it may be buried in the advanced settings. This function will force the camera to rebalance its circuits based solely on the environment you have created. You're now in a one-to-one relationship with your camera and, for me, there's no better way to have it.

1. **Zoom into your white card, just like you did when attempting to use while balance presets.** It is absolutely imperative that only the white of the card is visible in your viewfinder.

2. **White balance manually according to the instructions in your camera's manual.** Typically you must hold down a designated button until the camera alerts you (in its own unique way, no doubt) that the process has been completed.

Pull back from the card and take a look at the results. The white of the card should match the white you see in the viewfinder. You should have a near-perfect color matching throughout the scene. You are now ready to clap the boards and begin rolling — with no unwanted surprises lurking around the corner.

Note

If you can't achieve a good white balance using any of the techniques described, you either have a problem with the camera itself (and will need to have it serviced), or you are attempting to shoot in an mixed lighting situation where you have too many competing light sources.

If this is the case, a more advanced approach may be necessary (these techniques can be found in almost any video lighting reference book), or you can simply eliminate the offender(s) until a reasonable match is acquired. For example, mixing daylight and tungsten lamps in an indoor situation might confuse your camera. In this case, something as simple as closing the curtains might allow your camera to find a better white balance. That said, most cameras should be able to compensate for most mixed lighting situations.

A closing reminder — recalibrate!

Nothing good lasts forever, right? It's the same with color balance. Every time your lighting situation changes, so does the color temperature. If you change *anything* about the lighting — recalibrate, recalibrate, recalibrate!

Composing Your Shots

Both light, and color have been covered in this chapter. You had a certain amount of control over both of them, but to an extent you were at the mercy of the light source(s) and the quality/temperature of the light. The nice thing about composition is that you have a lot more control over the placement of your subjects and camera. If you don't like the shot, move the camera or zoom in! If you don't like where your subject is sitting or the set decoration, you can change them until you do.

Not only can you choose what elements you want to see though your viewfinder, but you can also choose how they are framed. By zooming in or out, placing the camera low or putting it up high, you can change the feel of your video fairly drastically. There are, however, limitations to what works best on the Internet — and the first rule you must sear into your memory is that unnecessary motion is bad.

Avoiding unnecessary motion

The first rule that codecs follow is that anything in the frame that changes must be re-encoded. Since codecs interpret motion as change, any motion will be encoded. If a lot of motion is in the frame, the quality of the encode will suffer because a limited amount of bits have to be shared across the entire frame. You therefore want to keep unnecessary motion to a minimum. If extraneous motion is minimized, the encoder will spend its time and resources encoding the important parts of the frame.

Using a tripod

Though it may seem obvious, it is absolutely imperative that you use a tripod, at all times if possible. While this may not always be practical, consider your friendly codec for a moment: If the camera moves even one degree in any direction, essentially every pixel in the frame changes. What may have been a simple scene to encode suddenly becomes much more difficult, and the quality of your encode suffers.

Just say no to pans, tilts, and zooms

Similarly, camera moves such as pans, tilts and zooms drive codecs nuts. Codecs interpret camera moves like these as frame after frame of constant change. This is not a recipe for a happy encoder.

Note   Not only are zooms murder on encoders, they're not even a good shot, unless specifically used as a special effect. There's a reason they had "Unnecessary Zooms" in the "Wayne's World" skits on Saturday Night Live — they're stupid. If you want a tighter shot on camera 1, first cut to a different camera. Then have the cameraman on camera 1 zoom in or out to set up his next shot. When you're happy with the new camera angle on camera 1, you can cut back to it.

The problem with avoiding motion is that traditional broadcast media is not faced with the same limitation, and people are becoming more and more accustomed to video content that has extreme amounts of motion in it. Guess how many "cuts," or different shots, are in a 30-second commercial. Five? Ten? Guess again. Modern day commercials can have over a hundred. And each one of those shots might be a "crash zoom" (an extremely fast zoom into a subject), a "whip-pan" (an extremely fast pan), or a wobbly hand-held shot, each of which is a nightmare to encode in its own right. If you combine them in rapid sequence, you virtually guarantee a poor quality encoded file. This is why music videos look so bad when they're encoded for low bit rates. There is simply too much information to try to cram into a low bit rate file.

Ideally, you want a video with long, static shots. A video with completely static shots, however, can look pretty stale. Most cameramen will try to add a small amount of motion, ever so slight, to give their shots some life. While the creative impulse is to be applauded, for Internet shoots, it should also be curbed.

No one is saying that you have to make your productions as stale as yesterday's bread, but if you exercise some restraint, you'll get better results out of your encoder. Use long static shots whenever possible, but don't be afraid to branch out a bit. If you want to put some motion into a shot, make sure the motion is slow and steady. That way, the codec has a better chance of using motion estimation techniques to keep up with the movement. Most importantly, make sure the shot is useful and adds to the presentation, not just thrown in for the heck of it.

Framing for the Internet

If you minimize the amount of the frame that has motion in it, you're maximizing the amount of the frame that has no motion in it — and therefore the area of the frame that the encoder can ignore. If the encoder can concentrate its resources on a smaller area of the frame, the result will be a higher quality encoded file. Figure 5-4 and Figure 5-5 illustrate different framing options. The framing of the shot determines how large the area of motion is, and therefore how available bits will have to be allotted. Smaller areas can be encoded at a higher quality, larger areas will not be as sharp.

Areas of most motion

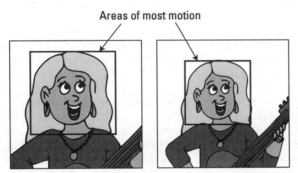

Figure 5-4: A subject framed in two slightly different manners.

In many situations, you should be framing your subject using a mid-shot. You want to strike a balance between the amount of motion that is contained within the screen and the visual interest of the scene. In general, a mid shot will encode better than a close-up because the amount of motion contained in the shot is smaller.

mid shot   close up   extreme close-up

Figure 5-5: Three different framing possibilities. Which would you choose?

In this situation, the extreme close-up is tempting because it gets us as close as possible to the singer. But because of the motion inherent in musical performance, this is a dangerous shot from an encoding standpoint. The mid shot is also not good because it would include the motion of the guitar playing. In this case, the close up is the safest bet.

Then again, there are cases when the mid shot is not the best option. In some cases, the mid shot actually includes more motion than a medium close up would. In that case, you'd want to frame your shot a bit tighter. Remember, you're trying to strike a balance between the amount of motion contained within the frame and the overall visual interest of the shot. Frame your shot the way you want to, and then give a quick thought to your codec.

Quick cuts are taboo

When you cut to a new camera angle, make sure it's a good shot — because you really should stay there awhile. Cutting to a new camera angle changes everything in the frame, so the encoder will require a new keyframe. Keyframes are expensive from a bit rate point of view. Codecs can only economize if there are areas of the frame that are not changing. If you cut from shot to shot too quickly, the encoder will not be able to keep up. The encoder will be forced to drop the overall frame rate drastically, which is not what you want.

Everything about limiting unnecessary motion goes against the grain of modern video production. Again, the problem is that traditional broadcast does not have these limitations, and people already working in the field are used to getting the most extreme shots possible. Also, a pretty good argument can be made that, if everything is filmed in long and medium shots, the viewer's interest will wander and the overall feeling will not be dynamic enough.

There are no hard-set rules. You can film any way you want, but knowing in advance that certain shots will tax the encoder might discourage you from using them. Obviously what you're trying to do is strike a balance between the creative requirements of the subject and the limitations of the Internet. It's not that difficult of a balance to achieve — in fact, if you're having trouble telling your story without fancy camera work, could it be that the story relies a little too heavily on the camera work?

Set decoration, clothing, makeup

You should have no trouble making your subjects stand out using a combination of light and color. You can use back lighting to separate them from the background, and you can make sure that the subject is more colorful than the surroundings. You can also use set decoration to add three-dimensionality to the frame.

Instead of having someone sitting at a desk in front of a blank wall, why not put a bookshelf behind him? How about a plant? By placing something behind your subject, you are putting additional information in the frame that the viewer's brain will use. If the viewer sees something behind the subject, it brings the subject forward by offering perspective. A plain white wall, on the other hand, offers no point of reference and no way for the viewer to figure out perspective.

Clothing

Even if you don't add any fancy decoration to your set, you're at least going to want to make sure your subject is dressed appropriately. Make sure his clothing sets him apart from the background. Avoid clothes with small patterns like pinstripes or checks. These patterns can cause unwanted patterns in the picture called *moires*.

White shirts are usually too bright on camera. If you watch the evening news, you'll see that most newscasters wear light blue shirts and dark blazers. The light blue shirts end up looking nearly white under the lights. Off whites are fine, as are light tans.

Makeup

Makeup is used to compensate for the imperfections that bright studio lights can sometimes highlight. Most people in front of the camera in professional situations wear makeup. The makeup does not have to be overdone — often a light coating of powder or base will suffice. Makeup is not necessary; however, it adds a professional look to your productions.

Perspiration is one thing that always appears when you don't want it to. Studio lights generate a lot of heat, and eventually your subjects are going to feel it and react accordingly. The most visible signs are a reflective gleam on the forehead and upper lip. You should always have some facial powder on hand, along with a small brush or sponge. A light dusting of powder on the subject's forehead before shooting will delay the onset of perspiration; another light dusting when it appears will keep you going for a while longer.

Choosing a Location

The best place to shoot video, provided you have professional lighting available, is indoors. When you shoot in a studio environment you have consistent control over the lighting, which is the most important variable. You'll also have plenty of access to power, and hopefully enough room to move around so that you can compose the shots to your liking.

If you don't have the luxury of a dedicated studio space, make sure you put a little thought into choosing where you're going to shoot. Obviously, you want someplace quiet. You also want as much space as possible, with high ceilings if available. You want high ceilings for a couple of reasons; first high ceilings allow more flexibility when placing lights, and second, the larger the room, the longer it will take to heat up. Studio lights kick out a lot of heat. If you set up in a small room, your subject will be sweating before you can shoot the first frame of video.

Power

Studio lights draw a lot of current. For those of you who took a bit of physics, you may remember that:

```
amps = watts / volts
```

Because wall current is 110 volts in the U.S., you can figure out the current drawn by dividing the wattage of the bulb by 110. A 1K lamp therefore draws about 9 amps of current. If your shoot room is on a 20 amp circuit, and you try to run three 1K lamps, you're going to blow a fuse. If you're trying to run three 650K lamps, you might get away with it — provided that there aren't too many computer monitors in the next room on the same circuit. You would be wise to contact the building electrician to see what your electrical capacity is.

Ventilation

Ventilation is a major concern. You are going to need a lot of it to keep the studio cool, but you also need to consider the noise most air conditioning systems make. Ideally, you want an HVAC system (High Volume Air Conditioning) with noise baffles in the ducts — but unless you're building your studio from scratch, this may not be an option.

Filming outdoors

There are instances when you're going to have to film outdoors — location newscasts, outdoor festivals, and so on. These situations present pretty much the same challenges as an indoor location, with the added complication of having to worry about the elements. Unfortunately, the elements can wreak havoc with every aspect of your shot.

Because your main light source is going to be the sun and the character of sunlight changes throughout the day, your lighting will be constantly changing. You may or may not have the ability to use additional lights or reflectors, depending on the situation. The amount of light you have to work with will constantly be changing. If your camera has automatic exposure control, it will probably deal with this reasonably well, though the constant re-adjustment can be annoying.

You're also going to have to be careful about color balance, particularly in the late afternoon and early morning when the character of sunlight is rapidly changing due to the amount of the earth's atmosphere it has to travel through. You will have to recalibrate your camera frequently — or run the risk of your content slowly changing color.

Composing your shots may also be a challenge. On a windy day, for instance, trees in the background could be a potential nightmare for the encoder if they are waving in the breeze. Strong winds can also vibrate the camera on the tripod, which will defeat your goal of a rock solid shot.

Filming outdoors can be fun, but it can also be a pain in the neck. You'll have to be extra careful, but with a little common sense and some sensible compromise, you should be able to "bring home the shot."

Summary

Because video is a little harder to work with after it has been shot, it's best to get it right from the start. Taking a little extra time to plan the lighting, color, and composition of your shots will save you time in the long run by reducing the amount of work you'll have to do in the capture and editing phases and will produce higher-quality encoded files.

+ Light is the most important thing in video production.
+ Lights and/or reflectors can be used to augment available light.
+ Three-point lighting is a great point to start with lighting.
+ Cameras cannot automatically adjust to color differences the way your eyes can. It is, therefore, necessary to make sure they are properly color-balanced.
+ Color balancing your camera is usually referred to as white balancing
+ Avoid unnecessary motion in your shots.
+ Avoid pans, tilts, and zooms.
+ When choosing a location, remember to think about size, space, power, and ventilation.
+ Filming outdoors is tricky. You have to constantly check your settings in a changing environment.

✦   ✦   ✦

Tools of
the Trade

Streaming media has its own set of tools just like any
other trade. Some of these tools are optional; others are
required. All of the tools discussed in this chapter help you
create higher quality source files, which in turn lead to higher
quality encoded files.

Audio Tools

You can use many tools to produce excellent-sounding audio.
Modern day recording studios may look imposing with their
dazzling arrays of knobs and lights, but essentially all audio
tools fall into a few simple categories:

  ◆ **Microphones:** Microphones convert sounds into electro-
    magnetic signals.

  ◆ **Mixing desk:** A mixing desk routes and balances the
    levels out between different sources.

  ◆ **Signal processing:** Signal processors perform specific
    tasks, such as compression or equalization to make your
    audio sound better.

  ◆ **Recording:** You need something to record your audio.
    This can be an audio editing program, or a dedicated
    piece of audio hardware.

  ◆ **Monitoring:** A good quality pair of speakers ("moni-
    tors") is necessary to verify your audio quality.

You're gong to need all the same elements as a professional
recording studio, starting with a microphone. Microphones
can be plugged directly into computer sound cards, but you'll
get much higher quality if you plug your microphone into mixing desk and then plug the output of the mixing desk into the
sound card.

You may also want to buy some signal processing units, such as a compressor and an equalization (EQ) unit. You'll record using your audio editing software, and monitor the whole process on a good set of speakers. This complete collection, from the microphone through all the other hardware to your computer's sound card is called the audio signal chain.

Each "link" in your audio signal chain contributes to the quality of your source material. The quality is, therefore, limited by the weakest link in the chain; there is no sense in spending $1,000 on a mixing board if you're only using a $20 microphone.

Audio equipment has the advantage of being reasonably priced, due to the explosion in home recording. There is no reason why you shouldn't be able to obtain acceptable results by balancing out your needs with your budget.

Microphones

A good quality microphone (mic) is very important, because it's the first link in the audio signal chain. Any imperfections or limitations of the microphone will be reproduced all the way down the signal chain. A microphone's quality is determined by three main factors:

✦ **Microphone type:** There are two main types of microphones, dynamic and condenser microphones, which have slightly different characteristics.

✦ **Directional response:** Microphones can have varying degrees of sensitivity in different directions.

✦ **Frequency response:** Some microphones are more accurate than others across the full frequency spectrum.

Types of microphones

All microphones share a similar architecture. Incoming sound waves cause an acoustically suspended diaphragm to vibrate. This vibration is converted into an oscillating electrical signal, which is transmitted through a cable to the next piece of equipment in the signal chain.

Dynamic microphones produce the electrical signal by electromagnetic induction. The microphone's diaphragm is attached to a coil of wire, called the *voice coil,* which is suspended between two magnets. When the diaphragm vibrates, the magnets induce a current in the voice coil. This current is an electrical representation of the sound wave.

Condenser microphones operate on an electrostatic principle. The diaphragm inside a condenser microphone consists of two thin plates, one of which can move.

A voltage is placed across the plates to form a capacitor. This voltage is known as *phantom power*. When the diaphragm vibrates, the capacitance between the plates varies, and this variation can be converted into an electrical representation of the sound wave.

Condenser microphones tend to be higher quality than dynamic mics. They are more sensitive and, therefore, do a better job translating sound waves into electrical energy. However, this sensitivity has a downside: Condenser microphones are more sensitive to noise. In controlled studio situations, you should use a condenser mic to take advantage of the higher quality. In noisy situations or outdoors, you should always use a dynamic mic.

Directional response

Microphones can be either directional or omnidirectional. Omnidirectional, or *omni* microphones are equally sensitive to sound coming from all directions, while directional microphones are more sensitive to sound coming from particular directions. This directionality can have a number of different patterns, which are illustrated in Figure 6-1 and noted in the following list:

✦ **Cardioid:** So called because of the heart-shaped directional response. This is the most common response pattern, and good for all applications. For example, the microphones you see news reporters holding are cardioid mics. They are most sensitive to sound coming in directly through the top, which is why reporters point them at the person they're interviewing.

✦ **Supercardioid, hypercardioid:** Variations of the cardioid with a more pronouced directionality. Hypercardioid mics are used in noisy situations or in specialized applications. The microphones mounted on top of video cameras are hypercardioid, because in general you want to record whatever the camera is pointing at. Also, the microphones used on the sidelines of sporting events to capture the live sound of the players are hypercardioid mics. Hypercardioid mics are also known as *shotgun mics*.

✦ **Bi-directional (figure 8):** Looks like a figure eight and is sensitive along a given axis, with little off-axis response. Bi-directional mics are used in special studio applications. For example, you can record two people in a studio with one bi-directional mic as long as the people stand on opposite sides of the microphone.

Most directional microphones have a cardioid response or some variation thereof. This means that they are most sensitive to sounds in front of them, and less so to sounds coming in from other directions. In noisy situations, you should always use a directional microphone to minimize the amount of extraneous noise the microphone transmits. Omni microphones can be excellent choices in quiet studio situations, where noise is not an issue.

Cardioid mike

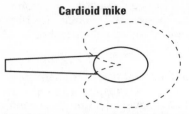

a. Cardioid mikes are mostly sensitive to the front, with some sensitivity on the sides and very little to the rear.

Supercardioid mike

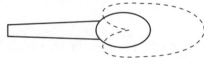

b. Supercardioid mikes are less sensitive to the sides and rear than standard cardioid mikes.

Figure-eight mike

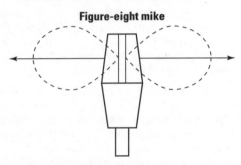

c. Figure-8 microphones are sensitive along a given axis, and much less sensitive off-axis.

Figure 6-1: Directional microphone response patterns

Frequency response

Every microphone has a frequency response curve, which shows how the microphone reacts to frequencies across the entire audible spectrum. Some microphones are capable of responding to the entire spectrum, while others are not. Some frequency response curves are *flatter* than others, meaning the microphone responds to all frequencies equally. Other microphones have frequency responses that are tailored to their particular application.

A microphone used to record speech might have a frequency response curve with a *lift* in the vocal range. This means that the microphone is more sensitive to frequencies in this range of the spectrum. They can also have certain frequencies de-emphasized, or *rolled-off*. Most vocal mics have frequencies below a certain threshold rolled-off to combat noise.

In general you want the best frequency response possible. Condenser mics have better frequency response than dynamic mics, but this increased sensitivity can be troublesome. For example, condenser mics are extremely sensitive to handling noise — they cannot be hand-held. They are also very sensitive to wind noise, so they are unsuitable for most outdoor applications.

How to choose a microphone

When choosing a microphone, a small investment can go a long way. The difference between a professional microphone and the plastic microphone that comes with many multimedia computers is enormous. Professional microphones have far better frequency response characteristics and are much less noisy. You can find a great microphone these days for as little as $100.

Dynamic microphones are an excellent all-around choice. They offer good frequency response and are quite noise-resistant due to their directional responses. They can be hand-held, unlike condenser mics. Dynamic mics can also take a bit of abuse, which is important if you're going to be working in challenging situations.

If you plan on doing any work outdoors, or in noisy rooms, dynamic mics are the way to go. You can carry them around with minimal handling noise, and you can point them at what you want to record. Most dynamic mics also have a degree of built-in protection — if you drop a dynamic mic, you can usually pick it right back up again and continue where you left off.

Condenser mics offer much higher quality but are not suitable for non-studio situations. They cannot be hand-held and, in fact, often require a suspension mount for optimal performance. A suspension mount holds the microphone in place using rubber bands instead of a clamp.

Chances are, you may want to have a few microphones so that you can choose the best one for each situation. In addition to a good, sturdy hand-held dynamic mic, you may want to have a small tie-clip microphone. These are known as lavaliere mics. For studio situations, you should buy a higher quality condenser microphone, a sturdy microphone stand, and a suspension mount if necessary. Figure 6-2 shows different microphone types and a suspension mount.

The Shure SM58®
(Dynamic cardioid
Microphone)

The Audio Technica
AT 4033 SE including
shock mount
(Condenser cardioid
Microphone)

The Audio Technica
AT803b
(Omnidirectional
lavaliere microphone)

Figure 6-2: What dynamic, condenser, and lavaliere microphones look like.
Shure SM58(c) Shure Incorporated, 2001. Used with permission.

Mixing desk

A mixing desk allows you to control a number of different audio sources. Each source is plugged into its own channel, and can be adjusted for level and pan (where the signal sits in the stereo spectrum). Mixing desks also have some signal processing ability. Each channel has equalization controls (see Chapter 8 for more on equalization). These controls allow you to adjust the tonal quality of each channel individually. The channels can then be combined into a master output. Figure 6-3 illustrates the various parts of a mixing desk.

You should buy a mixing desk if you plan on using a number of different audio sources. It not only allows you to combine them but also saves wear and tear on your sound card because you won't be constantly changing what is plugged into the inputs. You merely connect the master output of the mixing desk to the input of the sound card and choose which audio source to use by adjusting levels on the mixing desk.

Mixing desks are also necessary if you plan on using microphones, for a couple of reasons. First, if you plan on purchasing a condenser mic, you're going to need phantom power (a voltage that condenser mics need to operate) — something mixing desks offer but sound cards do not. Second, the microphone inputs on mixing desks are far superior to the microphone inputs on sound cards. In fact, you should never use the microphone input on your sound card unless it is absolutely necessary. Plug the microphone into your mixing desk and the output of your mixing desk into the line level input of your sound card.

Input gain

Channel inputs

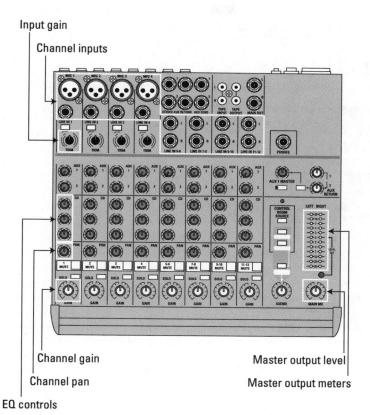

Channel gain   Master output level

Channel pan   Master output meters

EQ controls

Figure 6-3: A typical mixing desk (Mackie 1202 VLZ Pro)
Image design courtesy of Mackie Designs Inc.

Signal processors

In Chapter 8, you learn about the various ways in which audio can be processed for optimal sound quality. Signal processing can take place either in the digital realm via software or in the analog world using dedicated hardware. Software processing can be convenient because it can be automated, but there are instances such as live broadcasts when you may not be able to use software processing. If not, you'll need the hardware to do it. Figure 6-4 is a photo of some common audio signal processors.

Compressor

A compressor helps control signal level by attenuating when a user-defined threshold is exceeded. A compressor can be very helpful in live situations when levels are somewhat unpredictable. In Chapter 8, I go as far as saying that compression is the single most important processing step. If you ever plan on doing any live broadcasts, you'll need a hardware compressor.

The PreSonus DEQ 624, a half-size stereo compressor with presets

The PreSonus ACP-22, a dual channel compressor

The PreSonus Blue Max, a half-size stereo compressor with presets

Figure 6-4: Audio signal processors

Images courtesy of PreSonus Audio Electronics, Inc.

Equalization (EQ) unit

The compact mixing desks that are common in streaming media applications generally offer rudimentary EQ controls, which are fine for moderate adjustments but may not be powerful enough to deal with particular situations. In these instances, you may want the advanced control a dedicated EQ unit can provide.

Effects units

Effects units are not signal processors per se, but often show up in studio settings. They do not modify the original sound; they add additional elements to the sound such as echoes or ambience. Judicious use of special effects such as reverb, echo, and delay can add a professional feel to your productions. Be careful, though — many a decent production has been ruined by the overuse of effects. What may sound good at the time may sound perfectly dreadful the following day. Using too many effects can make your audio sound muddy and confusing. If an effect doesn't make the mix noticeably better, don't use it.

Recorders

If you're working in your studio, you'll most likely use your computer to record your audio. What about if you're in the field? You'll need something relatively portable, perhaps something that is capable of running on battery power alone.

Digital Audio Tape (DAT)

The all-around best option — as far as a portable recorder goes — is a DAT machine (see Figure 6-5). They are available in either desktop or portable versions and offer extremely high performance. Most portable DAT machines have built-in microphone inputs, complete with phantom power. The only bad point is price — a good DAT machine will set you back approximately $1,000. If you're serious about streaming media, you should buy one. If you're a hobbyist or unsure how deep your commitment is, you may want to hold off on this purchase.

Figure 6-5: A portable DAT machine (Tascam DA-P1)
Photograph courtesy of Tascam

MiniDisc

Recently, recordable MiniDisc players have made an appearance on the market. They're reasonably priced and offer fairly good performance. The problem is that they use a proprietary compression scheme, which isn't really suitable for recording broadcast-quality music. For voice applications such as interviews or recording a lecture or presentation, MiniDisc is entirely suitable.

Cassette

Cassette tape has a pretty bad reputation, but considering it was not even developed as a consumer format, it has been incredibly successful. Certainly the price is right. The quality can be acceptable **if and only if** chrome tapes are used, and careful attention is paid to the recording level. Cassettes can never offer the same performance as DAT tape, but if you are budget constrained, they can suffice.

Digital multitracks, hard disc recorders

There have been a number of exciting developments in the digital multitrack arena. A few years ago the first personal digital multi-track, the Alesis' ADAT appeared on the market for the home recording enthusiast, but they were quickly adopted by project studio owners. They offered eight tracks of 16–bit, 48 KHz recording on an S-VHS tape.

More recently, hard disk recorders have come on the market. These machines offer up to 24 tracks of 24–bit, 96 KHz recording quality. It can only be a matter of time before this technology is utilized in a portable recorder. Any one of these machines would be a welcome addition to a streaming media studio, though they probably offer more performance than you'll need.

Monitoring

Speakers, or monitors as they are known as in the business, are crucial because if you can't hear what you're doing, you won't be able to produce top-notch results. Even though some multimedia systems now ship with decent speakers, they don't qualify as studio monitors.

Studio monitors are designed to have as flat a frequency response as possible. They are supposed to give you as accurate a representation of the sound with as little coloration as possible. Most speaker systems, on the other hand, are designed to flatter the sound with exaggerated bass and treble. This might make things sound good on your system, but may hide flaws in your audio.

A good set of monitors costs anywhere from a few hundred dollars to many thousands. The more you spend, the better the frequency response, the more accurate the reproduction. You'll probably want to buy a pair of self-powered monitors to avoid having to purchase an additional amplifier. You should plan on spending at least $250 on your monitors to begin with — you can always upgrade. I have many, many times.

Tip Don't throw away those plastic speakers just yet. Keep them around to check your sounds from time to time. It is very important to have a good set of monitors to be able to hear exaclty what you're doing — but it's just as important that your stuff sounds good to your listeners. Your intended audience will most likely have cheap multimedia speakers. A lot of big-name record producers take copies of their mixes and listen to them in their cars for this exact reason.

If you're on a tight budget, a good set of headphones can be substituted for expensive monitors. If you spend $75–$100, you'll get yourself a good pair. Avoid anything that has "bass boost" or any other fancy features. Headphones are also great because they are portable and private — your office mates may require you to use them.

Additional audio tools

As you assemble your array of audio hardware, you may find you need to add a few odds and ends. Even though I advise against them, you may need to purchase a few adapters to get all your equipment connected properly. If it is at all possible, buy purpose-made cables. There is less chance of failure that way.

You'll want some extra cables in case of cable failure or for special occasions. You may want a cable tester to verify cable integrity. If you're really ambitious, buy a Volt-Ohm meter (VOM) and a soldering iron.

A VOM is used for various electrical measurements, such as voltage, current, and continuity. In particular, you can use a VOM to check you cables. If there's no continuity from end to end, throw it away. Or, if you've bought a soldering iron, you can probably fix it. Soldering irons are used to heat up solder, which in turn is used to connect the wire to the plugs at the end of the cable. Be careful— if you start soldering it's hard to stop.

Microphone stands are always handy. A *pop-shield*, which is designed to protect microphones from the letter "p" is a good, cheap investment. If your mixing desk can't accommodate all of your inputs, you should consider buying a patch bay to interconnect all your audio equipment.

Most of these items are self-explanatory. If you want to know more about any of the others, such as patch bays, you can talk to your local music store representative or check out one of the "Additional Resources" listed in the back of the book.

Video Tools

A wide array of tools is available to videographers. These break down into the following categories:

- ✦ **Camera:** Where the video process begins
- ✦ **Lighting:** Including lights, reflectors, colored gels, and diffusers
- ✦ **Video switching/routing/processing:** Tools to process and/or combine multiple video sources
- ✦ **Recording:** You may want to record your video to something besides your computer
- ✦ **Monitoring:** You need to be able to accurately "see" what you're recording or processing

There are a number of options available to use in each category. Video equipment can get expensive very quickly. If you have budget concerns and tend toward hyperventilation, please keep a paper bag handy during the next few pages.

Camera

Because the camera is the first link in our video signal chain, it is obviously very important. Ideally, broadcast-quality cameras should be used, but due to their crippling price tags, they are generally out of reach to the average streaming media producer. Taking a step down puts you firmly in the realm of DV format cameras.

DV cameras

There are two main things that determine a DV camera's picture quality:

✦ **Lens quality:** The better the lens, the better the image.

✦ **Image capture mechanism:** DV cameras use charge-coupled devices (CCDs) to convert the picture into electronic signals. The number and size of the CCDs affects the quality of the image.

Many DV cameras today have fixed (that is, non-interchangeable) plastic lenses. They usually offer a degree of optical zoom combined with digital zoom. Optical zooming involves physically adjusting the lens mechanism to achieve a different image perspective. Digital zooming is done electronically inside the camera using software. Although digital zoom is a nice feature in theory, you should avoid it in practice. The optical zoom gives you far better quality. Some DV cameras are now beginning to offer an interchangeable lens option.

Lower-end DV cameras use a single CCD to capture the complete image, whereas higher-quality cameras use three separate CCDs to scan the red, blue, and green content of the image giving a better quality scan. CCDs range in size from ¼ inch to ⅔ inch; bigger CCDs give better resolution.

What to look for in a camera

There are a number of excellent DV cameras on the market today. The DVCAM and DVCPro formats generally offer more professional features and higher image quality but at a significant price difference.

Entry-level DV cameras start at around $400 for consumer versions. A decent pro-sumer version (pro-sumer is a neologism that combines professional and consumer) will set you back around $2,000. If you decide to shell out for a DVCAM or DVCPro camera, you're looking at something in the $4-7,000 range.

Pro-sumer DV cameras offer better optics than entry-level DV cameras, and use three CCDs to capture the image instead of one. If you're serious about streaming media, you should consider buying a camera in this range.

As you move up the chain to more expensive DV cameras, including DVCAM and DVCPro, the optics continue to improve, and the size of the CCDs continue to increase. More expensive cameras also offer superior build quality. So if you're planning on creating a lot of content on a daily basis, you should consider investing the extra money and buying a professional camera. If you're just starting out, you're probably better off buying a decent prosumer DV camera and saving some money for a lighting kit.

You should definitely be looking for a 3-CCD camera unless your budget is very tight. It is very important that the camera allows you to manually control as many of the settings as possible. Even though cameras generally do a good job of setting levels automatically, it is important to be able to override this function. You want manual control of exposure, focus, and audio record levels. Interchangeable lenses can be very helpful, but keep in mind that high-quality lenses are very expensive.

You should take a close look at what sort of input and output connections the camera offers. Most cameras have a built-in microphone that is unsuitable for most applications. You'll want to use separate microphones and plug them into the camera. Some cameras accept professional XLR plugs; many do not. A headphone jack is also very handy to be able to monitor the audio input.

Cross-Reference

For a discussion about XLR plugs and why they're superior to those stupid ⅛ in mini-jack connectors, please refer to Chapter 2.

On the video side, the camera may offer a FireWire (IEEE 1394) output, composite video, or S-Video output. If you're going to be using an analog video capture card, S-Video is higher quality than composite. FireWire enables digital transfers and automated capture — something that can save time later.

DV cameras range in price from around $800 to $10,000, with good quality 3-CCD cameras starting at around $2,000. Models are changing and improving all the time. Don't be fooled by useless options such as "200x digital zoom" — buy the best camera you can afford with the best optics and biggest CCDs. There are many sites on the Internet that compare the relative advantages of different camera. The best way to find the latest set is to type in "DV camera reviews" into your search engine, perhaps also with the model number of the model you're considering.

Web site reviews and DV discussion forums are an excellent source of information about model shortcomings. You can also rent a number of DV cameras from professional video rental firms. This is an excellent way to try out models before you purchase. Figure 6-6 is a photo of some common DV cameras and accessories.

The Canon GL-1

The Canon XL-1S

The Panasonic AGDVC 200

The Studio 1 Productions XLR-Pro

Figure 6-6: Canon, Panasonic, and Sony (not pictured) cameras are popular among streaming media professionals, as are accessories such as the Studio 1 Productions XLR Pro.

Images courtesy of Canon, Panasonic, and Studio 1, respectively.

Lighting

Lights come in many different shapes and sizes, each designed for a particular situation. The simplest solution is probably to buy a lighting kit. These are available from a number of manufacturers. The kits generally include three lights and enough accessories for a standard three-point lighting setup, and start around $800. Figure 6-7 is a photo of a lighting kit. This kit includes three lights, a reflective umbrella for fill light purposes, diffusers, gels, and even a hard case, for a list price of $1,065. You won't find them for much less than that, and certainly not with all the accessories.

You also need some lighting accessories. You should buy some diffusion material and colored gels to add control and interest to your lighting setup. Diffusion material is used to soften the character of your lights, which makes shadows less pronounced. Colored gels can be used as special effects or to simply add a little color to an otherwise drab lighting setup.

Cross-Reference For a more thorough discussion of lighting setups, please turn back to Chapter 5.

Figure 6-7: A portable three-point lighting kit (Lowel Basically 3-kit TO-97).
Image courtesy of Lowel-Light.

You'll want an assortment of clamps and stands to cater for non-standard lighting setups. A bag of wooden clothespins is indispensable. Foamcore sheets can be used to bounce light for a more diffused feel. These sheets can also be used to control unwanted light spillage. A fold-up reflector can be extremely handy for outdoor shoots.

Last but not least, you'll need tape. This is perhaps the only situation where duct tape does not work. It cannot stand up to the heat lights put out, and turns into a sticky mess. Spend the extra few bucks and get gaffer's tape.

Video switching/routing/processing

Video switchers are the video equivalent of audio mixing desks. They accept a number of video sources and allow you to switch between them. They usually have built-in software that enables custom transitions between sources, such as fades or wipes. Some also allow you to "blend" video sources together. Video routers simply allow you to select the video source without the fancy transitions. If you have only a single video source, you don't need a switcher or router, but if you have multiple video sources, you should buy some sort of switching or routing system. Figure 6-8 is a photo of a video switcher and a video processing amplifier.

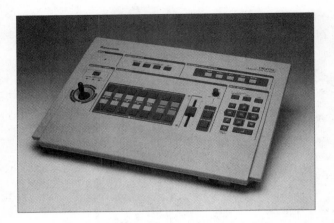

The Panasonic WJMX-20 video switcher

The Studio 1 Productions PA-1 video processing amplifier

Figure 6-8: A video switcher and a video processing amplifiers (*proc amp*).
Images courtesy of Panasonic Corporation and Studio 1 Productions

Video processing amplifiers ("proc amps") allow you to adjust the parameters of your video, such as overall chrominance, luminance, and black levels. Proc amps can be very helpful when trying to match pieces of video shot at different times or in different lighting situations. Video processing can also be done with software though not in real-time. If you are broadcasting live or want quick turn-around times, a proc amp allows you to optimize your video on the fly. Proc amp prices range from about $400 up to many thousands of dollars.

Recording

Most affordable cameras today double as their own recorders. You simply pop in a tape and press the record button. When you are finished recording, rewind the tape and you can play it back for viewing or digitizing.

However, if you plan on using multiple video sources and combine them via a switcher, you're going to need something to record the master output. Another problem with using the camera as the playback/recording device is that it limits your video activities — you can't shoot video while you're using the camera for playback.

There are a number of recording decks available for DV format tapes starting at around $1,000.

Monitoring

A good quality computer monitor is helpful when judging the quality of streaming media files, but to judge the quality of raw, interlaced video, you'll need a good television monitor. It gets confusing because computer folks call computer screens monitors, while video professionals call their screens monitors as well. You need one of each. In this book, they will be referred to as computer monitors and television monitors.

For a discussion about how television monitors differ from computer monitors, please turn to Chapter 2.

Television monitors, unlike regular televisions, are designed to reproduce video signals as faithfully as possible. They don't exaggerate contrast or color saturation like many television sets do. A professional television monitor can be calibrated so that you know you're seeing an accurate representation of what you're working on. Video professionals use them — you should, too.

Computer monitors are completely different from television monitors. They range wildly in quality and are dependent on the quality of the video card. Things that look fine on one monitor may look different on another monitor. Even though you can't control what equipment your viewers are using, you can at least make sure you have a good monitor and video card to make sure your content looks good in streaming format.

Additional video tools

You are going to need an assortment of cables to connect all your equipment. Don't scrimp on cables — good quality cables can really make a difference. Make sure they're as short as possible because longer cables are more susceptible to interference and signal degradation. You may need to buy some adapters for emergency situations, but avoid using them if you can.

If your camera only has a built-in microphone and a tiny ⅛" mini-jack audio input, you should purchase one of the specially made boxes that attach to the bottom of the camera, accept XLR inputs, and have a ⅛" mini-jack output. These boxes are worth their weight in gold.

For a discussion about different kinds of cables and connectors, please turn to Chapter 2.

Computer Hardware

As recently as a few years ago, it was common for software manufacturers to require highly advanced computers to run their programs. This is no longer much of a problem with the ready availability of processor speeds in excess of 1 GHz and 20GB hard drives.

Most streaming media production can be performed on just about any computer these days, with the notable exception of video editing. Audio editing, encoding, authoring, and serving all can be done with fairly standard computers. Video editing requires specialized hardware because of the data rates involved. The rest of this section specifically addresses the requirements of a video editing system.

Tip

Building a video capture system from scratch with off-the-shelf parts can be challenging. Video capture card manufacturers offer turnkey solutions because they are well aware of this fact. A turnkey solution is a system that comes out of a box and just "works." (It comes from auto salesmen — "Just turn the key, and drive it off the lot.") If you choose not to go with a turnkey solution, at least use a systems integrator familiar with video editing systems.

Basic computer considerations

Video processing is extremely processor- and hard drive-intensive because of the data rates. Capturing raw video can generate over 26 MB/sec of data that has to be written to your hard drives. If you decide to do any video processing in software, each pixel on every frame of video must be processed, and that takes time.

You don't *have* to buy the fastest computer or the biggest hard drives, but you probably should because video editing extracts every ounce of performance from your computer. You are going to need as much storage space as possible, and the hard drives need to be extremely fast to accommodate uncompressed video data rates. The two hard drive options available are SCSI and IDE.

SCSI disc drives (Small Computer Systems Interface) are currently the fastest and most robust storage systems available. SCSI systems have a certain amount of intelligence built-in, which allows them to operate somewhat independently from the main computer processor and gives them their speed advantage.

IDE disc drives have sped up considerably in the last few years and offer great performance for the price. ATA100 IDE drives, in particular, claim to equal SCSI performance, but the jury is still out as to whether they are as reliable as SCSI systems. ATA100 IDE drives should be sufficient if you plan on capturing at 320 × 240 or via FireWire. For uncompressed, full-screen capture it is probably wisest to stick with SCSI drives.

You may also want to consider specialized storage solutions such as RAID arrays (Redundant Array of Independent Disks), gigabit Ethernet, or fibre channel networks. These options add redundancy and make possible the sharing of storage between multiple workstations. You should contact your local SAN (storage area network) specialist to find the latest and greatest solutions available.

As a minimum requirement, you should buy at least a Pentium PIII-800 PC or Mac G4 computer, with at least 20GB of storage. You'll need extra slots to accommodate a sound card, a video capture card, and a SCSI controller card if you choose to use SCSI discs. You'll also need a network interface card (NIC), unless your computer has it built in to the motherboard.

Tip   Your network interface is your gateway to the rest of the world. Streaming media production pumps a lot of data through this gateway. You should always make sure there is an extra slot available for a replacement NIC card if you choose to use a built-in interface. Otherwise, when your interface fails, your machine is out of commision — along with all the data on it.

Sound cards

Most computers come equipped with a sound card. These factory-equipped sound cards are fine for playing back streaming media files and listening to MP3 files, but these cards are not of a high enough caliber to serve as the basis of your streaming media production system. You should buy a sound card that has a signal-to-noise ratio (SNR) of at least 96 dB. Cheap sound cards have an SNR of 80 dB or less. While that may not seem like a big difference, it actually means the internal noise is over four times as loud.

Tip   Don't go by published specs alone. Sound cards can sound remarkably different. Buy a sound card recommended for home recording use instead of video gaming — sound cards recommended for home recording are scrutinized more for quality.

Many lower priced sound cards have ⅛" mini-jack connectors mounted on the card. These are not professional connectors and should be avoided. Better sound card-sound cards have RCA connectors, or better yet, a special cable that connects to a separate breakout box with ¼" or XLR connectors. These systems are more robust and infinitely preferable. Figure 6-9 is a photo of two breakout boxes, one for a sound card and one for a video capture card.

Breakout box for the DPS Reality capture card

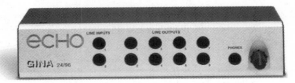

Breakout box for the Echo Gina sound card

Figure 6-9: Breakout boxes for video capture cards and sound cards
Images courtesy of Leitch Technology Corporation and Echo Digital Audio Corporation

Sound cards are also available with digital inputs, either as RCA connectors or the increasingly popular FireWire (IEEE 1394) connector. If your audio equipment has digital outputs, this is an excellent way to record sound. You may also want to see if the sound card can support the emerging 24bit/96 kHz standard. Although it may seem excessive at the moment because streaming media cannot even deal with the current CD standard, the situation may change radically in the next few years.

Be careful about is the sound card's sample rate support. Some professional sound cards have limited sample rate support, particularly sample rates that are multiples of eight. Limited sample rate support is not a problem when recording because you'll be using a sample rate of 44.1 kHz. The problem arises when you try to play back streaming content that has a native sample rate of 8 or 16 kHz. Some media players resample for you, others do not. If the media player does not resample, the result will sound sped up.

Sample rate support can also be problematic in live encoding situations. Some codecs require the sound card to sample incoming sound data at the codec's native sample rate. If the sound card does not support the native sample rate, it cannot be used in live broadcast situations.

Video capture cards

The video capture card sits at the heart of your video editing system, and is one of the largest determinants of the quality of your streaming media files. You can (and should) spend time lighting your subject well and invest money in a high quality camera, but none of it will be worth anything if you don't have a high quality video capture card.

Video capture card quality is determined largely by the amount of data throughput that the card can handle, and also by the quality of the electronics used to convert the video into digital information. Table 6-1 breaks down the main differences between capture cards.

Table 6-1
Video Capture Card Features

Category	Capture quality	Supported capture screensize(s)	Compression used	Price range
Consumer	Acceptable	Scalable to 640 × 480; practically limited to 320 × 240	Uncompressed at 320 × 240, hardware compression at 640 × 480 if supported; up to approx. 12:1 compression	under $200
Mid-price	Very good	Generally ¼, ½, and full screen; some fixed at full screen	MJPEG compression, typically compressed at approximately 2.5:1 to 5:1	$500 – $1000
Premium	Outstanding	Generally fixed at full screen	MJPEG or proprietary compression, true lossless compression (uncompressed)	$1000 and up

Video capture card tradeoffs

A quick glance at Table 6-1 reveals a number of quality tradeoffs. First and most obvious is price. To get the absolute best quality, you need to spend a considerable amount of money. The second tradeoff is supported screen capture sizes. This is not so much an issue for on-demand content, because you'll be capturing at either 320 × 240 or full screen, but is critical in live encoding situations, because some streaming media encoders do not support resizing of the video screen during live encodes.

If your streaming media encoder cannot resize the video image during a live encode. the video capture card must be able to capture at the desired frame size. If you decide on a non-standard screen size, such as 240 × 180 or 176 × 132, you need a video capture card capable of capturing at these sizes. The decision to use a non-standard screen size limits you to a consumer video card, which in turn limits the quality you can expect from live encoding.

Another issue with live encoding is the compression used by video capture cards. Many capture cards utilize MJPEG (Motion-JPEG) compression during capture to reduce the data flow to a more manageable rate. The video must be decompressed upon playback either by the card or via software.

Decompressing MJPEG video in software is CPU-intensive. Because streaming media encoding is also CPU-intensive, most encoders require an uncompressed video input because they cannot simultaneously decompress incoming MJPEG video and encode a streaming media file. Therefore, capture cards that use MJPEG compression schemes are not suitable for live encoding.

FireWire video capture cards are an excellent option, assuming you are working with video equipment with FireWire outputs. FireWire cards allow you to transfer the video digitally, which is a highly desirable option because it is lossless. When you digitize video using an analog capture card, the digital video must be converted to an analog signal, then re-digitized by the capture card. No matter how good a camera or capture card you've got, the signal will be slightly degraded during this process. With a FireWire capture card, the video is transferred digitally, with no loss in quality.

Another benefit is that the FireWire standard provides for some degree of control, which means that the transfer may be able to be automated, provided there is software support in the camera and the video-editing platform.

Caution   The FireWire (IEEE 1394) specification defines a framework but not how it is implemented. Not all FireWire implementations are compatible. Make sure you check with both the video editing platform and the capture card manufacturer to ensure interoperability.

What to look for in a video capture card

You want the best quality video capture card you can get, but you have to think about how you're going to be using your system. Ideally, you should purchase a premium capture card, because they deliver the best quality. Purchasing a premium card entails larger amounts of disc storage because they use less compression, which translates into a higher data rate and larger video files. The higher data rate that premium capture cards generate also means your discs have to be fast enough to be able to write the data to disk. Stepping up to this level means more than just buying the capture card.

Many good mid-priced video capture cards are available that offer an excellent entry point into streaming media. You should make sure that the card has higher quality video inputs, such as S-Video or component video. Many cards come with breakout boxes, which are preferable to inputs mounted directly on the card (see Figure 6-9). You should ensure that the capture card is specifically supported by your chosen video platform. Check the video platform's Web site for compatibility issues.

Tip   When shopping for a video capture card, make sure it supports DirectShow. This enables the card to write files that are larger than 2 GB, which is very important if you plan on working with longer form video projects.

If you plan on doing live encoding, you're going to have to purchase a consumer card. Because they are fairly cheap, you should consider buying a consumer card for live encoding, and a better quality card for on-demand capture. Not only does this increase the quality of your on-demand files, but it also doubles your video capabilities.

Lastly, if you're going to be working in the DV format, you should definitely invest in a FireWire card. You can now purchase them for under $100, and the combination of digital transfer along with being able to control the camcorder from within your video editing platform is priceless. You won't be able to do live broadcasts, but hey, at these prices, you can afford to buy a FireWire card *and* a video capture card.

Note If you've got a G4 Mac, it has FireWire built in — you don't have to buy a capture card at all!

Software

You'll encounter a number of different pieces of software throughout the streaming media process. Some are more exciting than others, but each is necessary in its own way. You're going to need software to capture, edit, and optimize your audio and video. After you're done optimizing, you'll want to encode the results. Encoding is covered in depth in the next part of the book, but I'll touch on it in this part because many audio and video-editing platforms have incorporated streaming media into their core functionality.

Audio and video editing systems

Audio and video editing software is not strictly necessary. If your audio is meticulously pre-processed using audio hardware, your video perfectly lit, and no mistakes happen during the taping, you could in theory encode it directly and be done with it. The chances of this happening are fairly slim, so you'll want the ability to correct the mistakes and polish the rough spots in your audio and video files. For this you need editing software.

There is some crossover between audio and video editing systems. Some audio editing systems open video files, though they won't edit the video. Most video systems have a certain amount of control over the audio, but lack sophisticated processing. To take advantage of all the techniques discussed in this book, you'll need both an audio editor and a video editor.

When looking for an audio editing system, look for a system that is intuitive and easy to use and offers most if not all of the following features:

✦ **Compression (dynamics processing):** Enables you to control the levels of your audio — very important for high quality streaming media.

✦ **Equalization (EQ):** Enables you to control the tonal quality of your audio.

✦ **Noise reduction:** Enables you to reduce unwanted noise levels in your audio.

✦ **CD "ripping" and creation:** Enables you to pull digital information directly off audio CDs, as well as back up any audio work you do to CD.

✦ **Plug-in support for advanced processing:** Enables you to use third-party software in your audio editing system.

✦ **Streaming media support:** Enables you to output streaming media directly from your audio editing system instead of having to use a stand-alone encoder.

✦ **Batch processing:** Enables you to automate repetitive tasks.

Audio editing programs are available as shareware and professional software. Many shareware programs are excellent for recording and editing, but lack some of the advanced features previously listed. While you may not need all the features for your current project, at some point or other, you may find yourself wishing you had them.

When shopping for a video editing system, you should again look for an intuitive interface, and the following features:

✦ **Cropping:** Enables you to trim off unwanted sections of the video.

✦ **Software proc amp:** Enables you to adjust the quality of the video.

✦ **Alpha channel support:** Enables adding graphics and more complex special effects.

✦ **Preview without render:** Enables you to preview effects and transitions without rendering them first.

✦ **Export from timeline:** Enables you to output streaming media directly from you editing timeline without having to pre-render your transitions or special effects.

✦ **Device control:** Enables you to automate the capturing process or print back to tape.

✦ **Batch processing:** Enables you to automate repetitive tasks, especially important with video files, which take time to process.

✦ **Support for files larger than 2GB:** Many systems limit file sizes to 2GB, which goes quickly when capturing full-screen uncompressed.

There are numerous video editing systems out there. Some are tied to a specific capture card, while others support a number of cards.

Encoders

Encoding software is covered in depth later on in Part III, but because many audio and video editing programs include encoding capabilities, I will mention them briefly here.

After your audio and video files are recorded, edited, and optimized, you'll need to encode them into a streaming media format. Each of the major streaming platforms has a stand-alone encoding application. In addition, many audio and video editing programs include export capabilities that include all or part of the stand-alone encoders.

RealNetworks has two stand-alone versions of its encoding software, the RealSystem Producer and the RealSystem Producer Plus. Both encode audio and video into the RealSystem format. The RealSystem Producer Plus has additional encoding functionality and publishing features. The RealSystem Producer is available for free, while the RealProducer Plus costs $199. Both are available from the RealNetworks Web site (www.realnetworks.com).

Windows Media Technology has the Windows Media encoder, which encodes audio and video into the Windows Media format. It is available for free from the Windows Media Web site (www.microsoft.com/windowsmedia).

Upgrading the QuickTime Player to QuickTime Pro enables you to encode audio and video into the QuickTime format. Upgrading to QuickTime Pro costs $29.95 and is available from the Apple Web site (www.apple.com/quicktime). Much of the functionality of these stand-alone programs is included in higher-end video and audio editing software programs. If you are going to buy editing software, don't purchase any encoding software until you give the editing software a spin. Chances are you'll have all the encoding power you'll need.

Summary

Creating high quality source material requires a number of tools, some hardware and some software. There are many reasonably priced tools available today thanks to the explosion of home audio recording and the proliferation of the DV video format. Investing in good quality tools enables you to produce better streaming media files.

✦ A good microphone is important because it's the first link in your audio signal chain.

✦ Dynamic mics are great all-around performers; condenser mics are higher quality but very sensitive to handling noise and therefore only suitable for studio use.

✦ Hardware audio signal processing can be especially helpful in live broadcast situations.

✦ A good set of monitors is necessary to hear the full audio spectrum.

✦ A good camera is very important because it is the first link in your video signal chain.

✦ Buy a good television monitor to check your video.

✦ There is no such thing as too much disc drive storage.

✦ Good quality sound and video capture cards are very important.

✦ If you're working in the DV format, buy a FireWire card if it isn't already built-in to your computer.

✦　　✦　　✦

Recording and Editing Audio

At long last, you are about to begin a streaming media production instead of merely reading about it. In this chapter, you'll start by preparing your audio environment and setting up a studio communication system. Then you'll learn about recording various sources, including how to place and use various types of microphones. Finally you'll learn about the recording process, and how editing can improve your audio files.

This chapter assumes you are only recording audio, in a controlled studio setting. Later on in the book when recording video is covered, you'll learn about some of the limitations video puts on your audio recording technique. For the most part, everything in this chapter is equally applicable in situations that include video.

Preparing to Record

Before you press the record button on your tape machine or audio editing software, there are a few things you should do in preparation. It is always good to have a clean, orderly work environment. Labeling all the inputs and outputs on your equipment makes it easier to diagnose any problems that may arise. Don't forget to label your cables; they have a tendency to get tangled up, leading to unnecessary confusion because they all look exactly the same.

You should set up a communications system, known as a "talkback" system so that you can communicate with your voiceover talent. After your talkback system is in place, you can place your microphones, set your levels, and then begin the recording process.

Setting up a "talkback" system

During the recording process, you should sit in front of the studio monitors and listen carefully to the performance to check the audio quality. The room with the recording equipment is called the control room. Your talent should be in a separate room, referred to as the studio. To be able to communicate with them you need to set up a communication system between the control room and the studio.

To communicate between the two rooms you have to send a mix of all the control room sources into the talent's headphones. You also need to set up a microphone in the control room so the talent can hear you. This microphone is generally not part of the master mix; it is used only for talkback purposes. Many mixing boards have a small microphone incorporated specifically for this purpose.

Tip
Use closed-back headphones in the studio if possible. This prevents *headphone bleed,* where sound leaks out of the headphones and is picked up by the microphone.

Keep the talkback mix completely separate from the master mix being recorded or broadcast. The control room mic should also be kept out of the master mix, to avoid the possibility of the control room microphone mistakenly being recorded.

Most mixing desks have auxiliary sends for this purpose. All you have to do is send some signal from each channel you want in the talkback mix to the auxiliary send. The output of this auxiliary send is then sent to the subject's headphones, sometimes via a small headphone distribution amplifier. Figure 7-1 illustrates how this might be accomplished on a Mackie 1202 VLZ mixing desk — please refer to your mixing desk's manual for specifics about setting up a talkback mix.

One thing to consider when you're constructing a talkback mix is whether the auxiliary send you're using is *pre-fader* or *post-fader.*

- ✦ **Pre-fader:** Means that the auxiliary send is tapped from the signal path before the channel gain is applied. Any adjustments to the level of that channel in the master mix do not affect the level of the auxiliary send. For talkback, it is best to use a pre-fader auxiliary send. This way the engineer can adjust master mix levels independently of the headphone mix.

- ✦ **Post-fader:** Means the auxiliary send follows the channel gain in the signal path. Consequently any change to the channel gain affects the auxiliary send, and therefore your talkback mix as well. Post-fader auxiliary sends are often used for sending audio to effects processors. That way, if you turn down the channel, no signal is sent to the effects processor.

Auxiliary output can be connected to
a headphone distribution amplifier.

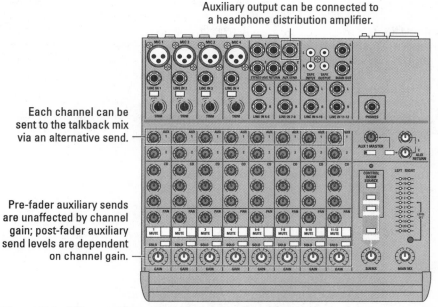

Each channel can be
sent to the talkback mix
via an alternative send.

Pre-fader auxiliary sends
are unaffected by channel
gain; post-fader auxiliary
send levels are dependent
on channel gain.

Figure 7-1: Using auxiliary sends to construct a talkback mix

Using microphones

Microphones come in all shapes and sizes, with different directional and frequency responses. It is important to place them correctly, so that they pick up the sound as best as possible. The most common microphone placements are hand-held microphones, lavaliere (clip-on) microphones, or using some sort of a microphone stand. Each of these options involves a slightly different approach.

Using a hand-held microphone

Most hand-held microphones have a cardioid directional response, which means they are more sensitive to sound coming from one particular direction. This direction is determined by which way the microphone diaphragm or *capsule* is facing. On hand-held microphones, this is the top or front of the mic.

For more information on microphone response patterns (including an illustration) please refer to Chapter 6.

For optimal frequency response sound should enter the mic directly along the capsule's central axis. This means that optimal placement is directly in front of the speaker's mouth. However, you may not want the microphone directly in front of the subject — if you're shooting video, you don't want anything in front of the subject's face. A good compromise is to hold (or have the subject hold) the microphone just in front of the subject, at chest level, pointed toward the subject's mouth (see Figure 7-2).

Figure 7-2: A hand-held microphone should be held directly in front of the mouth at a distance of approximately six inches.

Although it may seem obvious that the subject should speak directly into the mic, it is not always entirely obvious to the subject, particularly when working with people who have no microphone experience. Often people hold the mic in front of them (good) but turn their head back and forth as they speak (bad). This is entirely natural, of course, but poor microphone technique. When they turn their heads, the signal level drops significantly.

Not only is the signal quieter, but it is also different in tone. High frequencies are very directional, so when they turn their head, the microphone picks up some of what they're saying, but it sounds much duller because the high frequencies travel predominantly in the direction the speaker is facing.

This is true of all cardioid microphones. Most podium mics are cardioid and exhibit the same behavior when the speaker turns from side to side. An experienced speaker gestures without turning away from the microphone.

Tip   If your subject is inexperienced, it is better to use an omni-directional lavaliere mic, which is less susceptible to this directional side effect.

Using a lavaliere microphone

Lavaliere mics, also known as tie-clip microphones, attach to the subject's clothing using a small clip. They are available as either directional or omni-directional mics. The main reason they are used is their size; they are usually small enough to be inconspicuous.

Lavaliere mics are extremely common in broadcast situations. Next time you watch a talk show, look closely at the guests, and you'll see a small black dot somewhere on their clothing, probably on a lapel. This is the lavaliere mic. There is a wire connected to it, but the wire is generally inside the guest's clothing and connected to a wireless transceiver clipped to a belt. Most people don't even realize lavalier mics are there.

Placement of lavaliere microphones is fairly simple. You should clip approximately 8 inches away from the mouth, generally as close to the middle of the chest as possible. This assumes that your subject is facing forward. If the subject is going to be turned slightly one way or the other, you should *cheat* the mic in the direction the subject is facing. Omni lavaliere mics are not as directional as cardioid hand-held microphones, but that doesn't make them immune from drops in signal level if the subject turns away from the mic. Figure 7-3 illustrates lavaliere microphone placement.

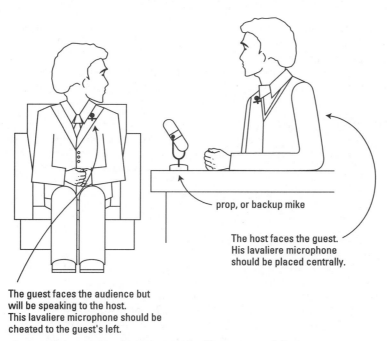

prop, or backup mike

The host faces the guest.
His lavaliere microphone
should be placed centrally.

The guest faces the audience but
will be speaking to the host.
This lavaliere microphone should be
cheated to the guest's left.

Figure 7-3: Correct placement of lavaliere microphones

One thing to beware of with lavaliere mics is noise. Make sure the mic is not near anything that may brush against it, such as clothing or hair. Fabrics that rustle can be a problem. With a bit of patience and planning, you can generally work around any of these problems.

Using condenser microphones

You should only use condenser microphones in controlled situations such as a studio because of their extreme sensitivity to handling noise. Because of this sensitivity, they must always be on a microphone stand, preferably in a suspension mount.

Some condenser mics allow the user to set the directional response. You can generally choose between cardioid, figure eight, or omni-directional. Choose the pattern that suits the situation. For a single speaker, choose cardioid and place the microphone directly in front of the speaker at a distance of six to eight inches. For two people, choose figure eight and place the microphone directly between the two speakers, making sure the speakers are centered on the microphone's directional axis. If more than two people need to share a microphone, choose the omni-directional setting and place everyone at an equal distance from the microphone.

If several people have to share a microphone, adjust each person's distance from the microphone until everyone's voice is at the same volume. Move quiet people slightly toward the microphone; move the louder people slightly away from the mic. It is better if everyone has his own microphone, but if not you should be able to get acceptable levels for each participant. Doing this saves you headaches later on.

Avoiding microphone pops

Certain consonants such as the letters *b* and *p* are formed by expelling a sudden burst of air. This burst can cause the microphone capsule to distort, which is audible as a popping noise. There are three ways to prevent microphone pops:

✦ Move the subject back from the microphone.

✦ Move the subject slightly off-axis.

✦ Use a pop shield.

Most pops occur because the subject is too close to the microphone. In general, the subject should be six to eight inches from the microphone, but people who speak very quietly may be tempted to move too close to the mic, to take advantage of the proximity effect (see "The Proximity Effect Versus Microphone Pops" sidebar). Some people are more prone than others to pop their consonants, even if they are at the proper distance. If the subject's distance from the mic seems right, try moving the subject slightly off-axis.

The best frequency response is obtained by speaking directly into the mic. But this position is also the most prone to microphone pops. It is perfectly acceptable to move the microphone slightly to reduce the chance of popping. Try raising the microphone slightly and angling it down to point to the subject's mouth. Figure 7-4 illustrates this method of reducing pops.

The Proximity Effect Versus Microphone Pops

If a cardioid microphone is very close to a sound source, a curious phenomenon known as the proximity effect occurs whereby the microphone exaggerates bass frequencies. The closer the sound, the more the bass frequencies are boosted.

Singers and announcers hear this pleasing effect in their headphones and naturally move closer to get the "oomph" the proximity effect produces. The problem is that when people move in close to take advantage of the proximity effect they're in the danger zone for microphone pops. Not only that, but the proximity effect adds to the problem by boosting the bass frequencies, which is where microphone pops sit in the frequency spectrum.

Many microphones offer low-frequency roll-off switches to compensate somewhat for the proximity effect, but this isn't enough to stop microphone pops. Another solution, if you're using a microphone that offers different directional responses, is to switch the microphone into omni-mode, because the proximity effect is a side-effect of cardioid microphones. This leaves the microphone open to ambient noise coming in from other directions, but because the subject is so close to the mic, the noise level should be relatively low.

The thing is, most folks like the way the proximity effect makes their voice sound. The next time you hear your favorite full-voiced DJ on FM radio, bear in mind that they're probably sitting on top of the microphone to make themselves sound extra velvety. So if folks like the proximity effect, and are therefore going to keep moving closer to the mics, how can you stop microphone pops?

The simple answer is to use a pop screen. Not only is it effective at stopping most pops, but it forces your subject to back off the mic a bit.

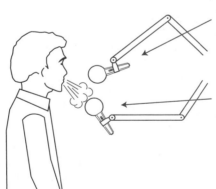

Keeping the microphone directly in front of the subject, move it up slightly and angle it down so it still points at the subject's mouth.

Traditional microphone placement can be vulnerable to popping. Moving the microphone slightly off-axis can reduce the incidence of popping while maintaining acceptable microphone performance.

Figure 7-4: Move the microphone slightly off-axis to reduce pops.

The last method of getting rid of microphone pops involves placing something between the subject and the microphone to break up the airflow before it reaches the capsule. The trick is to use something that is acoustically transparent — that is, something that doesn't change the tonality of the sound, but breaks the air up enough to eliminate popping. These are called *pop shields* or *pop screens* and are available from any decent music store. There are several approaches, three of which are illustrated in Figure 7-5.

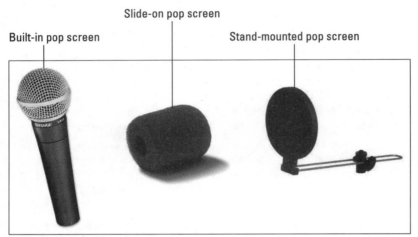

Slide-on pop screen

Built-in pop screen

Stand-mounted pop screen

Figure 7-5: Different pop screens

Recording from line level sources

Most equipment in a recording studio operates at what is known as *line level*. This means the equipment operates at a known, calibrated level. This makes it simple to record from line level equipment. After you set your gain structure (see Chapter 4), you should not have to do much to line-level sources other than minor level adjustments. Contrast this with recording using microphones, where you have to be careful about placement, extraneous noise, microphone pops, and the proximity effect to name a few things.

Of course, you may want to do some signal processing to your line level signals, such as EQ or compression. These optimization techniques are covered in detail in Chapter 8. For example, you could take a raw interview tape recorded in the field and make it sound better. Often material recorded out of the studio needs a little help to make it sound as good as possible.

On most mixing desks, each channel is capable of accepting a line level or microphone input. These two inputs are generally on different types of connectors, with the microphone input being a female XLR connection and the line level a ¼" TRS socket. You may need to toggle a switch to indicate which source you are using. Refer to your mixing desk's manual for specifics about channel source selection.

There is a huge difference in level between microphone and line level sources. Be very careful when switching from one to the other. You should always mute the channel and turn the input gain all the way down before you do. After you've switched sources, unmute the channel and reset your input gain.

Recording Practice

Establish a system to ensure the recording process is as smooth and trouble-free as possible. You're trying to record the best performance using the best technical approach, so it's best to follow a specific regimen to avoid stupid mistakes. Good studio practice, which has evolved in recording studios over the years, breaks the process down into the following steps:

✦ **Soundcheck:** Check the signal level and perform any applicable signal processing.

✦ **Record:** Record one or more versions of the performance.

✦ **Edit/repair:** Choose the best take and polish, or assemble a master take from the various takes.

Soundcheck

There's no sense in recording anything unless it is going to be of an acceptable quality. To ensure a high-quality recording, you need to check your levels and listen critically to judge whether any signal processing is necessary. The recording can also be processed during the optimizing phase, but taking care of potential problems at this stage can save time and effort later.

Make sure you check the signal level at each and every point in your audio chain. You want the signal level registering around 0 dB in all our analog equipment, and peaking in the –10 to –3 dB range in our digital equipment (anything above digital zero causes distortion). Remember that any adjustment to signal levels affects every piece of equipment further down the signal chain.

After you've established a gain structure, listen to the source to see if it needs any processing. Add EQ and compression as necessary, always keeping an eye on the resulting changes in signal level. Don't perform any extreme signal processing in the recording phase — it is difficult to reverse this later on if you change your mind. The goal is to mildly process the signal to obtain a manageable, pleasing sound. Later on in the optimizing phase, you can be more adventurous.

 For a thorough discussion of signal processing, please refer to Chapter 8.

Recording

When you're happy with your signal levels and sounds, it is time to start recording. You'll want to record a number of different versions of the performance. Each version is referred to as a *take*. After you have a few good takes, choose the best one and decide if it is good enough as is. If it is, you're done; if not, you can improve or repair the take by either re-recording a section of it, or moving on to the editing phase and editing sections of different takes into a master take.

You may choose to use your computer as your main recording format, but also purchase a portable recorder for use in the field. If so, the question is which format should you record to in the studio? Though it may take slightly longer to set up, the best approach is to record to both, especially in critical situations. That way, if a problem arises on one format or the other, you'll have a backup version.

Another thing to remember is to save your work often. Audio editing programs do not auto-save like some word processors do. As soon as you are done recording, save your file. A good habit to get into is to name the raw files something descriptive, like myfile_raw.wav or myfile_orig.aif. After you do some work on the file, save it without the "_raw" or "_orig" to differentiate it from the original. That way, if you make a mistake later on, you can go back to the raw audio and start over again.

Sometimes, you might end up with a great take except for a word or line that wasn't quite up to scratch. In this case, it makes more sense to repair the take by re-recording the offending line or word. This is known as *punching-in* or *dropping-in*.

The terminology comes from multitrack tape recording, where the engineer actually has to push the record button during playback to switch the multitrack recorder into record mode on the track that is being fixed *(punching-in)* and then again to take the machine out of record mode *(punching out)*. Multitrack recording is suited to punch-ins because the sound recorded on the other tracks gives the engineer cues when to punch in and out.

If you have a multitrack tape machine, refer to your manual for instructions on how to punch in and out. If you have a DAT machine, punching in isn't very practical because you can't punch in on a single track. With audio software, punching in is a simple process. You simply highlight the audio that you want to re-record and press the record button. The software records over the offending section, and automatically drops out of record mode when the end of the section is reached.

Caution

When using the punch-in functionality, some audio software programs go straight into record mode, which doesn't leave much room for error. Also, some programs will not undo punch-in operations. If you don't have a copy saved to disc, you could be in trouble.

Editing

Editing is where the magic of audio engineering starts to appear. Recording audio is cool, but assembling a perfect take by grabbing sections from different takes, removing all "ums" and "uhs" and tightening up the delivery makes you a god amongst men. Do a few of these for your CEO, and your reputation around the company will soar.

In the "good old days," editing audio meant actually taking a razor blade, slicing the audio tape at precisely the right point, and then rejoining it to another piece of tape with a specially adhesive strip. To find the right splice point meant playing the tape, stopping it at approximately the right point, and then moving the tape back and forth across the playback head to find the beginning of the phrase. This was a little risky, because after the tape was cut, there was no going back. Actually, you can splice the tape back together, but it's a tricky business.

Nowadays with digital editing, it is much simpler. To begin, you get a visual representation of the waveform. The visual representation of the audio makes it pretty easy to pick out where phrases begin and end. Second, and most important, digital editing is non-destructive. If you don't like an edit you can simply undo it and try again. After you get the edit you need, save it to a new file and you're done.

Assembling the perfect take

When you are recording, you'll often get a number of good takes, not one of which stands out as the best. The thing to do is to assemble a new take from scratch, using the best parts from each take. In this respect, audio editors work just like any other program — you simply copy and paste audio from each take into a fresh file.

It is best to take whole sentences or paragraphs when you are assembling takes from multiple sources. It can be very difficult matching a speaker's cadence and inflection between two different takes, particularly if you're grabbing just a word or phrase. Even though you may be choosing the best version of a line or word, there's no guarantee that it will sound right when that piece is placed in the context of the newly assembled take. Be sure to test each edit before moving on to the next.

Cleaning up your files

As you go through and edit your audio, you have a perfect opportunity to clean it up. If for some reason your file ends up with pops or clicks, now is the perfect opportunity to remove them. All you have to do is highlight them in your audio editor and hit the Delete button. While you're at it, you can take this opportunity to clean up the speaker as well.

As much as we'd all love to be well spoken, the fact is that many of you have picked up some terrible speech habits that you may be completely unaware of. Have you ever listened to an interview on the radio or watched one on television where the person being interviewed said "um" so often that you wanted to tear your hair out? This is only one example out of many. The spoken (and written) word has suffered greatly of late — this is your chance to repair some of the damage.

After you begin editing, it is easy to get carried away. You can get rid of "ums," "uhs," "you know," "actually," repeated words, bad English, anything as long as the speaker doesn't mind. When you play back the tidied up version, you'll make a friend for life.

Note All the editing tricks here are extremely easy when working with audio-only files. If you are working with video files, you have much less freedom to edit. Any editing must cut both the audio and video to keep them synchronized. If you remove a few frames of video, the resulting "jump" in the film will be visible and very distracting.

The only way to accomplish this is to cut to a different camera angle that does not show the speaker. You can then edit the speaker's audio track, and then cut back.

Editing an audio-only file

You can use one of your own audio files that needs some work or if you would like a file to practice on, take a look at one of my files on the CD.

On the CD-ROM This example uses a file from the CD, fourscore.wav (fourscore.aif on Mac).

1. **Open up your audio editing program, and open the audio file you want to edit.** If you want to use the file I provided on the CD-ROM, open the four_score.wav file in the Audio folder.

On the CD-ROM If you do not already have audio editing software, there are trial versions of a couple of excellent audio editing programs on the CD-ROM.

2. **Immediately, save the file using a different name.** I renamed my file four_score_edit. In this case, you couldn't possibly overwrite the original, because the original came off the CD, but it's a good habit to get into.

3. **Play the file back.** The speaker means well, but has faltered somewhat in his delivery. See if you can whip this file into shape with a little editing.

4. **Search for any unnecessary and annoying sounds, such as "uh."** In the four_score.wav file, you want to delete the "uh" after "and." If you look at the waveform, it's the fourth "lump" (see Figure 7-6).

5. **Highlight the section of the audio you want to delete and press delete.** See how easy this is?

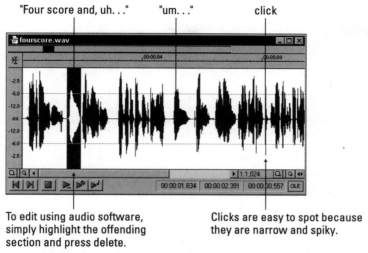

"Four score and, uh. . ."   "um. . ."   click

To edit using audio software,   Clicks are easy to spot because
simply highlight the offending   they are narrow and spiky.
section and press delete.

Figure 7-6: Editing using a software audio editor

6. **Play back the file to test your editing.** You don't have to play back the whole file, just the section where you just did the edit. Listen to a few seconds before and after to make sure the edit sounds good in context. Does it sound okay? Does it sound better? You bet it does.

7. **Go through the rest of your audio file and delete additional mistakes in the audio.** In the four_score.wav file, there's another "um." It's gotta go.

8. **Highlight the parts of the audio you do not want and delete them.**

9. **Test the edit.** Play the section back, being sure to check a few seconds before and after. Does it sound okay? Does it sound better? Depending on how you did this edit, there may now be too long of a gap between "this" and "continent." If so, tighten up the gap by highlighting some of the silence and deleting it. You can estimate how much silence to leave by matching the gap to other gaps in the speech. Be sure to test the edit.

10. **Save your work.** Consider backing it up to DAT tape or burning it to CD for long-term storage.

After this short exercise, you should be left with a reasonable approximation of the first paragraph of Abraham Lincoln's "Gettysburg Address." It may not be a world-class reading, but think about what it sounded like before the editing. Open up the original and see how far you've come. This should give you a small glimpse into the possibilities of audio editing.

Summary

It's best to keep your studio environment clean and tidy, with everything clearly labeled. After you set up your studio system and your daily routine is established, you'll be able to breeze through any audio recording situation.

✦ Using closed headphones in the studio prevents headphone bleed.

✦ Setting up your talkback system on an auxiliary send, preferably one that is pre-fader, avoids potential embarrassment later.

✦ Cardioid microphones should point at the speaker's mouth.

✦ The proximity effect of cardioid microphones is often desirable but can lead to microphone popping.

✦ Microphone pops can be cured using pop screens.

✦ Check your levels at each stage in the audio signal chain.

✦ Signal processing at the recording phase should be minimal and aimed at attaining a controlled, pleasing sound.

✦ Editing can be used constructively to assemble good takes and to clean up the audio.

✦   ✦   ✦

Optimizing Your Audio Files

◆ ◆ ◆ ◆

In This Chapter

Signal processing: what it is and why it is important

Equalization (EQ): What it is, how it can help you, and how to EQ your files

Compression: What it is, how it can help, and how to compress your files

Other audio tools and tricks

◆ ◆ ◆ ◆

This chapter takes a closer look at audio files and discusses a few simple techniques to make them sound much better. If you've been careful up to this point, you should now have a system set up to record and capture good, clean audio signals. But perhaps upon playing them back, you felt that they still lacked something — that little extra oomph that broadcast feeds have. With any luck, you're about to give your files that extra polish that will make them sound as professional as your local radio station.

As an extra-added benefit, the steps you're taking now to produce professional sounding audio are very beneficial when you get to the encoding stage. As powerful as encoders are, they can only work with what they are given. The higher quality the input, the higher quality streaming file you'll end up with.

Signal Processing

One of the wonderful things about working with audio is that it is very malleable. Through the judicious use of equalization (EQ), compression, noise reduction, and a host of other tricks, you can make an audio file recorded in a small closet sound as if it was produced in a professional broadcast studio. These audio tricks are generically referred to as *signal processing* and are employed by audio engineers worldwide.

Earlier, in Chapters 4 and 7, the importance of setting correct input and output levels for each piece of equipment in your audio chain was discussed. This is done to maximize the performance of each piece of equipment and to prevent them from adding any noise to the sound. Now that you've recorded a clean audio file, you're going to be actively molding the sound to achieve the desired result: professional-sounding audio.

If you'd like to review or find out more about setting the input and output levels of your equipment, please refer to Chapter 4. For a discussion about good recording practice, please refer to Chapter 7.

At its most basic, all audio signal processing essentially boils down to one thing: volume, or what audio engineers refer to as level. In dynamics processing (the most common being compression), you'll be adjusting the overall level of the entire audio file. With equalization, you're going to be boosting or attenuating the levels of certain frequencies in your sound files. At each stage of signal processing, you have to be careful with your levels so as not to exceed the maximum level allowed and produce distortion. You also have to make sure that each step is an improvement and that the resulting file is faithful to the original author's intent. Signal processing is extremely powerful, and should be used with caution.

Why Signal Processing Is Important

Signal processing is important because to stand out in a sea of content, your programming has to sound as good or better than your competition. Commercial television and radio stations invest millions of dollars to ensure that their programming meets rigidly defined standards, giving you the quality you expect. On the Internet, this is not the case. No standards exist, and quality varies dramatically.

One of the most powerful features of the Internet is that it makes it possible for just about anyone to become a broadcaster. But this blessing is also a curse: There are already thousands upon thousands of people creating programming for the Internet every day. Ignoring the actual content for a moment, the sonic quality of these programs ranges from excellent to unbearable.

No doubt you've stumbled upon a Web site featuring your favorite music or sports team. You click with baited breath only to find that the audio quality is terrible. Maybe you've been startled out of your chair when a new stream is twice as loud as the last thing you listened to. The problem is that many people who are creating streaming media for the Internet have little or no previous experience with audio or video.

The good news is that because audio is so easy to work with, there is no reason why your audio should not sound as good as your favorite local FM radio station. Although they have no doubt invested a lot of money to ensure that their sound quality is top notch, there is no reason that you can't achieve the same high standard with a minimal investment of time and money. By producing your content to a high standard, you give your programming an edge over your competitors.

All the signal processing techniques described in this chapter are based on solid audio engineering practice. These techniques will make your programming sound better regardless of the eventual streaming format, whether it is an audio-only radio station, a soundtrack to a video presentation, or your latest musical composition available for download.

Equalization (EQ)

Equalization (EQ) changes how your audio sounds by boosting certain frequencies and/or attenuating (or cutting) others. Sometimes you want to boost frequencies to compensate for the shortcomings of streaming media technologies. You may want to add a bit of sparkle to a seemingly lifeless file; audio engineers call this adding *presence* or *punch*. Alternatively you might want to turn up the bass frequencies to make the file sound warmer or fatter.

EQ can also be used as a corrective measure. By turning down certain frequencies you may be able remove certain noises from your audio files, or compensate for an especially noisy environment. Certain consonants known as *plosives* (in particular the letters *p* and *b*) may sound unruly and can be controlled with EQ. Some audio frequencies can make audio sound less intelligible. By finding these frequencies and turning them down, you can make things sound clearer.

Why EQ Is Important

EQ is important because people react to audio quality. People are attracted to things that sound good and are repelled by things that sound bad, even if they aren't consciously aware of it. Even though people listen to ballgames and talk shows on AM radio, given a choice between that and the same program on FM, people always choose FM.

In these days of dirt-cheap DVD players and personal stereos, people are used to hearing high fidelity all the time. Many people have stereo televisions and five-speaker home theater systems. In this day and age you simply cannot get away with poor sounding audio.

Ironically, many Internet broadcasters sound terrible. You may have noticed quality differences between television or radio stations in your neighborhood. In fact, here's a good exercise for you: Turn on your radio and flip through the dial — or for that matter — your television. Try alternating between a large national station and your local public access station. Can you hear the difference? How about between a local FM radio rock station and the local college station?

When you compare your local public stations to their commercial counterparts, do any of the following terms come to mind?

✦ Dull or lifeless

✦ Shrill or harsh

✦ Thin or small

✦ Garbled or unintelligible

All of the above situations can be solved with EQ. By using EQ, you can add high frequencies to add life to your audio or remove frequencies that make your audio sound harsh or unintelligible. You can also add bass frequencies to warm up your sound. In the following sections, you'll learn how to identify the proper frequencies and use the two main kinds of EQ, graphic EQ and parametric EQ.

How to EQ Your Audio File

As mentioned earlier, EQ is simply turning up or down certain frequencies in your audio files. You're probably wondering, "Which frequencies? How do I decide to turn them up or down?" The answer, as it is in all audio engineering situations, is "Use your ears." Even though you can't be expected to become an expert audio engineer overnight, you probably know what you want your audio to sound like.

In fact, you've probably done more than a bit of EQing in your lifetime (see "Gee, Maybe I Am an Audio Engineer" sidebar). What you're trying to do is improve the sound. The questions you need to ask are

✦ Does the sound need anything? Does it sound balanced and full?

✦ Is there anything extraneous in the sound file that could be de-emphasized?

✦ In the case of voice-driven programming, is the narration clear and easy to understand?

Audio engineers working in recording studios often use CDs engineered by other engineers to compare their work to. This is a tried and true technique that you should also employ. Find some programming similar to your own that you think sounds excellent. Play that programming back to back with yours, through the same speakers. Does your audio sound as good as what you're comparing it to? If not, why not?

As you flip back and forth between the two files, break the problem down into frequency ranges. Start with the high frequencies, and work your way down.

✦ Is your audio as *bright*, as the other guy's is? If not, you may want to add a bit of *presence* to your file (both brightness and presence refer to the high frequency content of the audio).

✦ Voices, snare drums, and guitars usually sit in the midrange. Is your midrange clear and intelligible? Or is it cluttered and harsh?

✦ What about the low frequencies? Some folks love a big, warm "bottom end" but beware: Many multimedia speakers have a hard time reproducing this frequency range, and it can also make your midrange less intelligible.

If you've decided that your file could use some equalization, there are two main ways to do it:

✦ **Using a graphic EQ.** This way is simpler to use but not as precise.

✦ **Using a parametric EQ.** This method allows a much greater degree of precision and is therefore better suited for detailed work, where you may be trying to target one particular frequency.

For slight adjustments such as adding a bit of warmth or brightness either one works just as well.

Gee, Maybe I Am an Audio Engineer

Though you may not have noticed it at the time, there are probably numerous times in your life when you've added some EQ unwittingly. Heck, there are probably a number of audio engineering tricks you've done too, but for the time being, I'll stick to EQ.

Here's one situation you probably have experienced: adjusting your car stereo while getting on and off a highway. You're shooting up the on-ramp and merging with traffic, only to find that you can no longer hear your favorite CD or radio station. So you reach over and grab the volume knob and give it a twist.

There's only one problem — you still can't hear the bass on your favorite gangsta rap tunes. This is because the doors, windows, and carpeted floor all do a pretty good job at keeping high frequency noise out of the interior of your car, but can't stop low frequency noise such as the engine and the tires on the pavement. So the low frequencies of the car and highway are interfering with your ability to hear the low frequencies in the music.

If you turn the volume up any further, the mid-frequencies sound too loud (you may also be damaging your hearing). Your ears are much more sensitive to mid-frequencies than to very low frequencies. This partially explains how people can sit in cars with blaring stereo systems that rattle your house windows a block away (or does it?).

So instead, you reach over for the Bass knob and give it a twist. Presto! You've just EQed your system to compensate for the surroundings. You knew what you wanted to hear and kept adjusting until it sounded the way you wanted it to.

And you're about to do it again. As soon as you get off the highway, you'll realize that the stereo is too loud and the bass frequencies are loosening your fillings. Of course, being an expert now, you'll reach over, drop the volume a few notches, and roll off a little bass.

Easy, right?

Finding the right frequencies

Human hearing extends from roughly 20–20,000 cycles per second (Hertz or Hz), though very few people can hear particularly well at either extreme of that range. This range can be roughly divided into the bass frequencies that extend from 20 Hz to 250 Hz; the low midrange between 250 Hz and 2 kHz; the high midrange between 2 kHz and 4 kHz; and the high frequencies above 4 kHz.

It is no mistake that the human ear is most sensitive to midrange frequencies — this is where human speech resides in the audio spectrum. For this reason, it is the most important area to consider when making EQ adjustments.

Using EQ, you can clear up your audio by cutting some of the low midrange. You can make speech more intelligible by boosting the high-mids. You can add presence by boosting frequencies around 5 kHz. Some people have a problem with the letter *s*; their voices are said to be *sibilant*. You can decrease sibilance by cutting 7 kHz. And you can even add that magical audio engineering intangible — *air* — by boosting somewhere in the neighborhood of 16 kHz.

There are a lot of wonderful things that can be done with EQ, but remember — you're trying to gently augment the sound — not change it. Have a good idea what you want your audio to sound like, and compare it to other content repeatedly to make sure it sounds good. Use the information in Table 8-1 as a starting point for your EQ settings, but don't be afraid to strike out on your own.

Table 8-1 Useful EQ ranges	
EQ range	**Contents**
20–60 Hz	Extreme low bass. Most multimedia speakers and, in fact, most home speakers cannot reproduce this. Boosting frequencies in this area can make your audio sound muddy and lead to distortion. It is good practice to roll off these frequencies.
60–250 Hz	This is where the audible low-end lives. Files with the right amount of low end sound *warm* and *fat*. Files without enough bottom end sound *thin*. Files with too much in this range sound *boomy*.
250 Hz–2 kHz	The low-midrange. Files with too much in the low-mids are hard to listen to and sound telephone-like. Sometimes cutting in the 250–350 Hz range can clarify your mix.
2 kHz–4 kHz	The high-midrange. A lot of speech information resides here, consonants in particular, so you don't want to push this range in your background music. In fact, cutting here in the music and boosting around 3 kHz in your narration makes it more intelligible.

EQ range	Contents
4 kHz–6 kHz	The presence range. These frequencies provide the clarity in both voice and musical instruments. In particular, boosting 5 kHz can make your music or voiceover (not both!) seem closer to the listener.
6 kHz–20 kHz	The very high frequencies. Boosting here adds "air" but can also cause sibilance problems.

Using a graphic equalizer for EQ

Note

As with most of the audio processing techniques discussed in this chapter, both graphic and parametric EQ can be done with software or dedicated pieces of audio hardware. The operation is essentially the same. For the purposes of discussion, I will illustrate using software.

With graphic EQ, the audible frequency range is broken down into slices, known as bands, and each band has a corresponding fader (see Figure 8-1) that can be moved up or down to increase or decrease the volume of that particular frequency range.

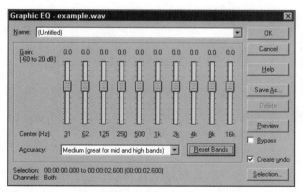

Figure 8-1: A typical graphic EQ (Sound Forge) that divides the frequency spectrum into different "bands." Each band is assigned to a fader that can either boost or attenuate the frequencies contained in the band.

To use graphic EQ, simply grab a fader and move it up or down. If you want to brighten up your audio, slide the faders on the right hand side of your graphic EQ up a bit. To add bass, push up the faders on the left. Remember, if you're pushing faders up, you're adding to the overall volume of the file; be sure you don't push the file into distortion by adding too much at any particular frequency. Plosive consonants like *b* and *p* can get nasty if you add too much bass to your file. Hard vowels like the *a* in *active* or the *o* in *octave* can get ugly if you add too much midrange. Be sure to listen to your file repeatedly and visually inspect the waveform from time to time to make sure that you're not distorting at any part of the file.

If you're not sure exactly which frequency you're after, don't be afraid to experiment. Unless you have been engineering for a good long while, you cannot be expected to know exactly what each frequency sounds like, though you will find with a little practice you'll catch on quickly.

Most audio editing software comes pre-loaded with a few standard graphic EQ settings such as bass boost, presence lift, and loudness. Try a few of these out to see what they sound like, and to see what the fader positions look like. For some suggested EQ settings, please refer to Table 8-2.

Table 8-2	
Suggested Graphic EQ settings	
EQ Desired	*EQ Settings*
Bass boost — music	+ 3 dB at 60 Hz, +6 dB at 120 Hz, + 1.5 dB at 250 Hz
Bass boost — male vocal	+ 3 dB around 100–120 Hz
Bass boost — female vocal	+ 3 dB around 200–250 Hz
Bass roll off	−12 dB at the desired roll off frequency, maximum roll off at all frequencies below that
Vocal lift	+1.5 dB at 1 kHz, +6 dB around 2–2.5 kHz, +3 dB at 4 kHz, +1.5 dB at 8 kHz
Making room in a musical background track for narration (inverse of vocal lift)	−1.5 dB at 1 kHz, −6 dB around 2–2.5 kHz, −3 dB at 4 kHz, −1.5 dB at 8 kHz
Add brightness	+1.5 dB at 4 kHz, +3 dB at 8 kHz and 16 kHz
Add presence	+3 dB at 2K, +6 dB at 4K, +1.5 dB at 8 kHz

Tip When using a graphic EQ, think of adjacent faders as being interdependent. You shouldn't push any fader too far without also pushing its neighbors a bit in the same direction. Similarly, you wouldn't want to add 6 dB of gain to one band and roll off 10 dB in the next. While these are perfectly legal things to do, the result is generally a file that sounds "over-EQed." With graphic EQ, the fader positions should describe a flowing line. If you need to perform highly detailed EQ, do it with a parametric EQ.

Using a parametric equalizer for EQ

In the previous section, you saw how graphic EQ units have the audible frequency range broken into predetermined bands. With parametric EQ, the frequency, the width of the frequency band, and the amount to either boost or cut are all determined by the user. The width of the frequency band in particular is very important and is referred to as the 'Q.'

Note Only fully parametric EQs offer complete user control of the Q — there are various other types of parametric EQs. *Fixed-Q parametric* EQs allow the user to choose the frequency but not the width of the band. *Semi-parametric* EQs offer a mixture of fully parametric and fixed-Q controls. *Paragraphic* EQs have faders instead of knobs. Confused? Don't worry — most audio editing software offers fully parametric EQ. That is what is discussed here and generically referred to as parametric EQ.

Parametric EQ is very powerful in that it gives you the ability to choose the frequency and the Q allows you to adjust some frequencies without affecting others. This allows you to focus on a particular musical instrument or the narration. Controlling the width of the Q is particularly helpful when trying to remove noise from your files.

With a parametric EQ, you are generally given between 2 to 4 bands, represented by a knob or a fader (please refer to Figure 8-2). For each band you must pick both the frequency and the Q. The Q relates to the number of octaves that are affected. A Q of 1 means one octave, so one-half octave on either side of your chosen frequency is boosted or cut. The Q setting can range from very narrow (one-third an octave or less) to very wide (two octaves or more). If you are non-musical and do not understand the concept of octaves, all you have to remember is the smaller the Q, the narrower the band of frequencies you are operating on.

Gain

Four separate bands of EQ

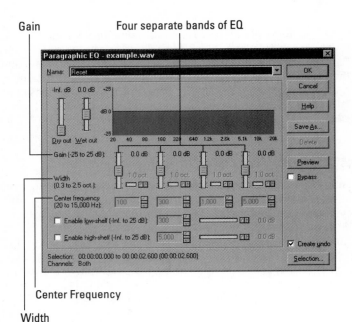

Center Frequency

Width

Figure 8-2: A typical parametric EQ (Sound Forge) gives you a number of different bands. For each band, you must specify the width, center frequency, and amount of boost or cut.

Finding the frequency using parametric EQ

Finding the frequency you want to adjust is the first thing to do when using parametric EQ. To do this, set the Q of your parametric EQ control as small as possible and set the boost to about 10 dB. It doesn't matter whether you are planning on boosting or cutting — when you find the right frequency, if you were planning on boosting, it will sound better, and if you were planning on cutting it will sound a whole lot worse.

Choose an approximate frequency to start with using Table 8-1 as a guide. Adjust the frequency setting until the frequency you're after pops out of the mix. Your software may take a moment to re-calculate after each change to the frequency value. Once you've focused in on the frequency you're looking for, set the boost to zero and set the Q as follows:

✦ If you're boosting the frequency, set the Q to 1.

✦ If you're cutting, set the Q to .5.

✦ If you're trying to get rid of a particularly nasty noise, set the Q as narrow as it will go.

Boosting or cutting to improve your audio

Now that you've found your frequency and have a reasonable Q setting, try boosting or cutting a bit. Compare it to the original. Is it an improvement? Could it stand a bit more or a bit less?

You can also play around with your Q setting to see how it affects the sound. If you're boosting and the frequency you're focused on is too prominent, try increasing the Q. This affects a wider area and makes the center frequency less noticeable. If you're cutting and it sounds a bit hollow, try decreasing your Q setting so that less frequencies are affected.

Tip

"Boost wide, cut narrow" is an audio engineer mnemonic that refers to the Q setting when using parametric EQ. In general, it's better to set your Q wide when you are boosting frequencies, and to set it narrow when cutting. This makes the EQ less noticeable and more pleasing to the ear.

As mentioned before, don't be afraid to experiment and, most of all, use your ears! Most software programs that have parametric EQ have a few presets pre-loaded. Try them out and see how they sound. For some suggested parametric EQ uses and settings, see Table 8-3.

Table 8-3
Suggested Uses and Settings for Parametric EQ

Suggested use	*Setting(s)*
Bass boost — music	+6 dB at 120 Hz, Q=1.5
Bass boost — male vocal	+3 dB at 100 Hz, Q=1
Bass boost — female vocal	+3 dB at 200 Hz, Q=1
Vocal lift	+6 dB at 2.5 kHz, Q=2
Making room in a musical background track for narration (inverse of vocal lift)	−6 dB at 2.5 kHz, Q=2
Add presence	+3 dB at 5 kHz, Q=2
Add "air"	+3 dB at 8 kHz, Q=1.5
Getting rid of ground hum	Maximum cut at 60 Hz (50 in Europe), Q at minimum setting
Clearing up a muddy audio track	−3 dB at 250 Hz, Q=.7
Dealing with sibilance (may be better dealt with by a de-esser.*)	−4 dB at somewhere between 4–8 kHz (depending on voice), Q at minimum setting
Dealing with plosives (deal with each occurrence individually)	−6 dB at 80 Hz, Q at minimum

* A de-esser is a dedicated hardware processor that uses a combination of EQ and compression to address sibilance problems.

EQ — A step-by-step example

With any luck, you've made it through the first few sections of this chapter and are now dying to get your hands on the controls. Alternatively, you've skipped the theory and have cut to the chase. Either way, you're about to do a bit of EQing to illustrate what has been discussed in this chapter.

Hopefully you've read (or at least skimmed) some of the preceding chapters and have taken my advice about getting a good pair of headphones or speakers. Some EQ effects are subtle and may not be as apparent on cheap multimedia speakers. Then again, it is always a good idea to test your audio on speakers that most folks will be using when they listen — so don't throw away those cheap plastic speakers just yet.

 On the CD-ROM This exercise is designed to use sound files from the CD-ROM, which you'll find in the Audio directory.

On the CD-ROM, you'll find two files, well_recorded and needs_eq. Have a listen to them both. Well_recorded sounds full and bright. Needs_eq, on the other hand, sounds small and lifeless. In the following example, you'll learn how EQ can be used to make audio files sound better. The example uses needs_eq, but you should be able to work along with your own audio files.

1. **Open up your audio editing software.** I use Sonic Foundry's Sound Forge to edit audio, and a trial version of that software has been included on the CD-ROM. Of course, if you have another preference for audio editing software feel free to use that.

2. **Open up the audio file you want to equalize, along with a good sounding file for reference.** I opened both well_recorded.wav and needs_eq.wav from the CD-ROM.

3. **Play both files and flip back and forth between them.** Does the file you want to EQ sound as good as the reference file? If not, try to identify what it is about the reference file that makes it sound better.

   If you are listening to the audio files from the CD-ROM, do you notice how well_recorded.wav sounds fuller? A bit wider-spectrum? See if you can make needs_eq sound as good.

4. **Save a copy of the file you're going to EQ.** It's best to give it a new name, such as MyFile_eq, or myFile_o ('o' for optimized).

5. **Compare the bass frequencies.** Listen to the bottom end of the file you're EQing and compare it to your reference file. How do they compare? If your file sounds thin, adding bass will make your file sound warm. If your file sounds boomy or muffled, cutting bass frequencies can help clean up your file.

   If you're working on the files from the CD-ROM, needs_eq could definitely use some more bottom end. Start by boosting everything below 250 Hz.

6. **Open up the EQ window and apply EQ to the bass frequencies.** Using Sound Forge, EQ is available from the Process menu. You can select graphic, parametric, or paragraphic EQ.

   • **Using graphic EQ:** Move the fader at or just above 250 Hz up to the +2 dB mark. If your program doesn't have the decibels marked, then move the fader up about ¹⁄₁₀ of the way to the maximum position. Move all the faders at frequencies below 250 Hz up to the +4 dB mark, or about ⅕ of the way to maximum.

   • **Using parametric or paragraphic EQ and your program has a low-shelf item option:** Set the frequency to 250 Hz and boost 4 dB. If your program doesn't have shelving (or you can't find it), set the frequency of the leftmost knob or fader to 150 Hz, and set the Q to the widest (largest) possible setting. Boost the signal 4 dB — note how the wide Q setting makes the boost wide enough to include a gradual boost at 250 Hz. (Sound Forge users choose Process ⇨ EQ ⇨ Paragraphic. Choose the "Boost Bass Frequencies below 250 Hz by 4 dB" preset. Grab the slider to the right of the shelving option and increase the amount of boost to +6 dB.)

7. **Compare the result to your reference file.** Your file should sound better. Make adjustments as necessary. If you're satisfied with the bass frequencies, save your file and move on to the next step. If you're not happy, either boost or cut more of the bass frequencies until you're happy with the result.

   If you're working with the files from the CD-ROM, you're getting closer, but you could probably add a little more bottom end. Undo the EQ you just applied and try again, this time boosting 6 dB. This should sound much closer to the well_recorded file. Save your file and move on to the next step.

8. **Compare the high frequency content of the files.** Does the file you're EQing sound dull? Or does it sound shrill in comparison to your reference file? Boosting the high frequencies can add life to your files, but if you add too much your files can begin to sound harsh.

   The needs_eq file could definitely use a little presence to make it sound as good as the well_recorded file.

9. **Open up your EQ window again and cut or boost high frequencies:** Depending on what your file needs, adjust the high frequency contents until you're happy with the results. Use Table 8-1 to help you find approximate frequency values for different EQ operations.

   If you're working on needs_eq and consult Table 8-1, you see that presence is centered on 5 kHz. Try boosting that frequency, using one of the following methods:

   • If you're using graphic EQ, move the fader closest to 5 kHz up to 6 dB.

   • If you're using parametric EQ, grab one of the right hand knobs or faders, set the frequency to 5 kHz, set your Q to 2, and boost by 6 dB. (Sound Forge users choose Process ⇨ EQ ⇨ Paragraphic. Grab the fader furthest to the right and move it up by 6 dB. In Sound Forge, this fader defaults to a 5 kHz setting.)

10. **Compare the result to your reference file.** Your high frequencies should sound as good as your reference file. If they don't, keep plugging away, cutting or boosting frequencies until you get the result you're after.

If you're working with the files from the CD-ROM, compare with well_recorded. Perfect! Now you have a good sounding file, with a warm bottom end, and plenty of presence. You're an engineer!

11. **Save your work.**

Advanced EQ — Techniques

The EQ techniques employed in the previous examples are very common. Many files could use a bit of warming up or a little extra presence, especially if they were recorded with an inexpensive microphone. There are also times when EQ can be used as a corrective measure. Sometimes removing offensive frequencies can be just as important as polishing what you've got.

Clearing up a file

Some files can be hard to understand or sound muddy. In this situation, it might be helpful to try and cut around 250 Hz. Use a fairly wide Q in this case, because it isn't a particular frequency you're targeting, but rather, you are just trying to clean things up a bit. Start by cutting 3 dB, and if things improve, try a little more. Don't go hog wild, because you might start to cut into the bottom end. In this situation, a little cut goes a long way toward clearing up the file.

Salvaging a file recorded in a noisy environment

At times, you will not have the luxury of working in a controlled environment, or will not be able to re-record audio that turns out to be very noisy. Perhaps you were trying to record a conference speaker from the back of a room or outside on a windy day. The key here is to try and cut out as many of the extraneous frequencies as possible while retaining as many of the frequencies that contain the speaker's voice.

You can safely roll off everything below 150 Hz; this clears up a lot of rumble and wind noise. You may even be able to start rolling off higher, depending on the speaker and the environment. Rolling off the highs above 4 or 5 kHz might help with air conditioning noise or shuffling paper noise. You can also lift the vocals out of the muck by boosting the 2–3 kHz range. As discussed previously, cutting a bit at 250 Hz can also have a clarifying effect.

As you work with the above suggestions, you may notice the voice starting to sound nasal and thin as you approach the frequency range of the telephone, which is approximately 100 Hz–4 kHz. This is not necessarily a bad thing; people talking on the phone are generally pretty easy to understand. Try to find a good compromise between intelligibility and fidelity. The amount of boost and cut depends on the amount of noise you're trying to combat.

To see how this works, you can try the following steps with a file of your own that has background noise in it, or use the example file included on the CD-ROM.

On the CD-ROM The sound file is in the Audio directory on the CD-ROM.

1. **Open up your audio software and then open up a file that contains background noise.** If you don't have one to use, you can open the noisy_outdoors sound file from the CD-ROM.

   Listen to the file and try to determine if there are some frequencies that could be cut without compromising the main content. In particular, with spoke word content you can usually roll-off the bass frequencies and high frequencies, leaving the midrange, where most of the speech frequencies lie.

   In the noisy_outdoors sound file, notice how you can hear the announcer, but you can also hear some wind and traffic noise. See if you can clean this up a bit.

2. **Save a copy of the file.** Use a sensible file name.

3. **Open up your EQ window and roll off bass frequencies.** With spoken word content, you can usually safely lose quite a bit of bass information while still retaining the bulk of the speech frequencies.

   • If your program has parametric EQ with a low-shelf option, set the frequency to 150 Hz, and roll off the maximum amount. (Sound Forge users, choose the Remove Low Rumble below 80 Hz preset and change the frequency to 150 Hz.)

   • If your program has Parametric EQ but without a low-shelf option, choose the leftmost fader or knob, set the frequency to 80 Hz, set the Q to the widest (largest) possible setting, and roll off the maximum amount. The wide Q setting will actually reach up to 150 Hz.

   • If you're using a graphic EQ, roll off 10 dB at 150 Hz, and the maximum at all frequencies below that.

4. **Click OK and listen to the result.** Hear the difference? You've lost some of the bottom end of the voice, but you've lost a lot of the rumble and whoosh that the outdoor noises were contributing to the file. Now let's see what happens when you slice off the top end.

5. **Open up your EQ window and roll off high frequencies.** Similar to what you just did with the bass frequencies, you can safely lose quite a bit of high frequency information while still retaining the bulk of the speech frequencies. A good place to start is to get rid of everything above 5 kHz.

   • If your program has parametric EQ with a high-shelf option, set the frequency to 5 kHz, and roll off the maximum amount. (Sound Forge users, choose the Reset preset, click the Enable High-shelf check box, and slide the fader all the way to the left.)

- If your program has Parametric EQ but without a low-shelf option, choose the rightmost fader or knob, set the frequency to 10 kHz, the Q as wide as it will go, and roll off the maximum amount. The wide Q setting makes the effect reach down to 5 kHz.

- If you're using a graphic EQ, roll off 10 dB at 5 kHz, and the maximum at all frequencies above that.

6. **Click OK and listen to the result.**

You've lost a lot of the high end of the voice, but along with it, you've reduced the amount of whooshing the traffic noise was generating, and you've cut down the amount of wind noise. The fidelity of the voice has been somewhat compromised, but the overall intelligibility has been improved.

You may notice that the voice is starting to sound like a television news reporter — that's because they're often called upon to report from less than optimal locations. When they do, the engineers on site use this sort of EQ to try and minimize the extraneous noise.

7. **Don't forget to save your work!**

Removing microphone pops

Plosive consonants such as *b* and *p* can sometimes cause the microphone to pop. Ideally, you should use a pop shield and/or reset your gain structure, but you may not always have this luxury. To use EQ to fix this, highlight the offending syllable, and cut about 10 dB at around 80 Hz. Use a fairly narrow Q.

To see how this works, open up a file that you think has unruly plosive consonants.

On the CD-ROM   The sound file is in the Audio directory on the CD-ROM.

1. **Open up your audio software and then open up the offending file.** If you don't have a suitable file, open the pop_goes_the_weasel file.

2. **Save a copy of your file.**

3. **Listen to your file.** In the case of the pop_goes_the_weasel file, do you notice how the *p* in *pop* is too loud? Hear the slight clip where the file goes into distortion? If you look at your levels, you'll also notice that you exceed the maximum allowable level momentarily. This is what distortion sounds like. Generally, you should set your levels so that this doesn't happen, but when it does, you can sometimes alleviate the situation with EQ.

4. **Increase the magnification of the file in your audio program so that you're looking at the word that is causing the distortion.** In the case of the pop_goes_the_weasel file, magnify *pop*. Most programs have a magnifying glass with a plus sign in it that you can click, or a zoom function that you can utilize.

Look at the beginning of the word — notice how the *p* sound is a taller (louder) and longer wavelength (lower frequency). This is the culprit that you're going to fix.

5. **Highlight just the sound.** You can do this by clicking the mouse at the beginning of the waveform and dragging the cursor across the offending section while holding the mouse button down. Make sure you have what you need by previewing the highlighted section. You can do this by clicking on the Play button or in most audio editing programs by hitting the space bar.

6. **To get rid of the pop, open up your EQ window, set your frequency at 80 Hz, your Q at .5, and roll off 10 dB of gain.** Microphone pops are low frequency spikes in you audio file, usually centered around 80 to 100 Hz. If you set your frequency at 80 Hz and use a Q of .5 (one-half octave), you should be able to eliminate virtually any bad pops. 10 dB is quite a bit of attenuation, but because you're only applying it to a split second of the file and at a narrow Q, you won't notice the missing frequencies in the final version.

7. **Click OK.**

8. **Listen to the whole file.** To do this, you're going to have to deselect the highlighted area, which you can do by clicking anywhere in the waveform window.

You should now have a file where the *p* sounds normal and no longer clips. Using EQ, you can repair otherwise unusable files. You can imagine, though, that going through an hour long file and getting rid of all the microphone pops would be an arduous task, which is why setting a proper recording level in the first place can save a lot of heartache later.

9. **Save your work.**

De-essing using EQ

Consonants such as *f, z, s,* and the *th* in *thin* are called sibilants. Pronouncing them involves forcing air through a narrow opening, which makes a hissing noise. Some people have serious problems with sibilants, where the hissing noise is very pronounced, sometimes even evolving into a whistle. The noise may be immediately obvious when the person speaks, or not apparent until you listen later. Because the hissing noise is usually in a very narrow frequency range, it is possible to reduce the sibilants using EQ.

The problem with using EQ to solve this issue is that you don't want to remove the sibilant frequencies altogether, because these high frequencies give your audio clarity. Instead what you want to do is de-emphasize the frequencies *only when the hissing occurs.* What compounds the problem is that there are generally a lot of *s* sounds in any given file. Fixing them all individually can be a time-consuming process.

To solve this problem, audio processors known as *de-essers* have been in use for years. They reduce the high frequency content only when a certain volume threshold is exceeded. You set the threshold so that the de-esser kicks in when the speaker pronounces the letter *s,* so it automatically reduces the high frequency content, thereby making the hissing less noticeable.

You can purchase stand-alone de-esser units, or purchase vocal processors with de-essing built in, along with EQ and compression. These units run anywhere from around $200 to $1000, and of course you can find them used on your favorite auction site. Vocal processors in particular can be a great way to go, because they're designed to be a solution to all your vocal processing needs.

Should you not have a de-esser in your audio arsenal, you can deal with the worst offenders using EQ on an individual basis. Highlight the offending syllable, and try cutting 6 dB at 5 kHz. You may need to adjust the frequency up or down to find where the person's sibilant frequency problem is. Use a fairly narrow Q.

Rolling off bottom end for balance

Full frequency audio stretches from 20 Hz to 20 kHz. Often this frequency range is limited by the transmission medium, be it FM radio or a telephone.

In the interest of providing the best audio experience, research has been done into what people think sounds best when the audible spectrum must be limited. It turns out that when the high frequencies are limited, people prefer a corresponding limitation in the low frequencies. People feel audio that has been limited in both the high and low frequencies sounds more balanced (see "The 400,000 Rule" sidebar).

The 400,000 Rule

Long ago, as legend has it, Bell Labs researched how people hear and why certain sounds were considered pleasing. It was discovered that sound that was lacking in high frequency information sounded unbalanced unless there was also a corresponding lack in the lower frequencies.

An octave (do-re-mi-fa-so-la-ti-do) represents a doubling of the frequency. Looking at the audible frequency range in terms of octaves, human hearing has a range of about ten octaves (20–40 Hz, 40–80 Hz, and so on up to 10–20 kHz).

If a full-range audio signal, such as an orchestra, was played with the top octave missing — that is, no frequencies above 10 kHz — people preferred that the lowest octave (20–40 Hz) was also missing. This gave a frequency range of 40 Hz–10 kHz. Similarly, if the top two octaves were missing — that is, for an AM radio broadcast — people preferred the sound if the bottom two octaves were missing, giving a total frequency range of 80 Hz–5 kHz.

Seeing a pattern? If you multiply the lower frequency by the higher in these balanced frequency ranges, you get the number 400,000. So if you know your broadcast is going to have limited high frequency output, such as radio or low bitrate Internet codecs, you should compensate by rolling off low frequency information to make it sound balanced to human ears.

To figure out where you should roll off your bottom end, simply divide 400,000 by the highest frequency your broadcast medium allows.

Because many common streaming codecs have limited high frequency response, rolling off some of the bottom end may make the file sound more balanced, though this is highly subjective.

You may have already rolled off some bottom end to avoid distortion or for clarity's sake. Then again, you may have inadvertently added too much bottom end when you boosted for warmth. It certainly couldn't hurt to see if it makes your file sound better. Set your parametric EQ to shelf mode, and roll off at the frequency the 400,000 rule indicates. If it sounds better, go with it.

Compression

Compression is the most common form of dynamics processing (don't confuse audio compression with file size compression; that comes later in the encoding section). Think of it as an automatic volume control that operates according to rules you can specify. In most cases, you want to turn the loudest sections of the audio down. You can do this by specifying a "threshold" above which you want the volume attenuated. When you do this you are compressing the dynamic range.

The dynamic range of a program is the difference in volume between the loudest and quietest parts of your audio (see Figure 8-3). Because you are turning down the loudest sections, the measured dynamic range is now smaller. It has been *compressed*.

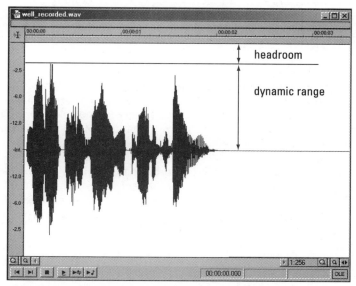

Figure 8-3: The dynamic range and headroom of a file

After the dynamic range has been compressed by turning the loud sections down, you are left with extra *headroom*, the space between the maximum allowable volume before distortion and the loudest sound in your file. When you initially record your file, you try to leave about 3 dB of headroom. After compression, you should turn the overall volume of the file back up to restore the original headroom.

Why Compression Is Important

Compression is important for a number of reasons. First, compression is a good preventative tool because, by turning down the loudest sections of your file, you are taking steps to ensure that the signal level never adds distortion.

Secondly, audio equipment doesn't usually perform optimally at the extremes of its dynamic range. This is particularly true for multimedia systems. Between cheap soundcards and the fidelity of most multimedia speakers, you're operating with a fairly limited dynamic range. It is therefore necessary to compress the natural dynamic range of recordings in order for them to sound better on playback.

The last reason is harder to quantify, but essentially it boils down to this: All broadcast media is compressed to some degree, and most people tend to think of things that sound this way as sounding "professional."

Commercial FM radio is the most obvious culprit. Try this: Turn your radio on, listen to a commercial music station, and then switch to a local community station. The main difference between the huge, full (sometimes crowded) sound of a commercial FM radio station and a small local station is the amount (and type) of compression used.

Compressed audio tends to sound louder and more present than uncompressed audio (see the "Why Television Commercials Are So Loud" sidebar). Since the hunter-gatherer days, people have been conditioned to respond to loud things and are easily fooled into thinking that louder is better. Ask any stereo salesman. The plain fact of the matter is that if someone else's programming sounds louder than yours, the listener usually thinks it sounds better.

All this adds up to one bold statement: Audio compression is probably the single most important step you can take to improve the quality of your streaming content, audio or video. With the quality of audio codecs today, the proliferation of good audio software and reasonably priced audio hardware, there is no reason your audio should not sound as good or better than your favorite local radio station.

Why Television Commercials Are So Loud

Everyone has experienced it. You are sitting in your bed, late at night with the covers drawn up over your shoulders as you drift off watching some silly late night movie you really shouldn't be watching. It's a quiet, tender scene and the main characters are declaring eternal love for each other before the scene gracefully fades to black.

Suddenly: "Yee-haw! I'm Bob Bonehead and I'll do darn near ANYTHING to sell you whatever the heck it is I'm selling..." You're rudely jerked back into semi-consciousness with a singular purpose: finding the mute button. As you search under the blankets, under the bed, finally finding the remote control under your spouse, you wonder to yourself, "Why do television stations play the commercials so much LOUDER than everything else?"

They don't.

Yes, sad to say, you can't pin this one on the local television affiliates. The good news is that there is someone to blame: the advertisers.

Television stations broadcast everything at strictly standardized levels. The broadcast volume remains constant throughout the day. However, the *apparent* loudness of each program may be different.

Movies have very large dynamic ranges. Action scenes are loud, love scenes quiet. It would sound strange if it were otherwise.

Commercials, on the other hand, exist for one purpose — to annoy, oops, get your attention. To this end, they are compressed to within an inch of their lives so that every microsecond of the commercial is as loud as possible. So although they are broadcast at the same level as other programming, the *apparent* loudness is much greater, due to the heavy compression.

Bear this in mind when you're working with compression. Short-form programming is much more compression-tolerant than long form. Programming that is loud all the time is fatiguing to listen to (think drive-time radio).

So the next time you're lying in bed and this happens, don't get mad at the TV, get even: boycott Bonehead Bob.

How to Compress Your Audio Files

Applying compression involves turning down the loudest sections of the file. A compressor does this automatically. All you have to do is specify when and how much you want the compressor to turn things down. The resulting file is therefore quieter. To compensate, you need to apply a bit of gain so that the file is as loud as it previously was. In fact, the apparent loudness will now be greater. Remember, to most people loud = good.

How compressors work

Using a compressor involves setting a threshold, a compression ratio, and an output gain. In addition, you may also need to set an attack and release time, which determines how quickly the compression kicks in and how slowly the compressor returns to the original signal level.

Figure 8-4 illustrates what a few different compression curves look like. All input above the threshold is attenuated (turned down). Higher compression ratios mean more attenuation. Before you actually hear compression in action, take a look at what happens to a typical file when compressed using different settings.

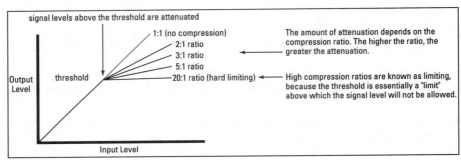

Figure 8-4: Different compression ratios

Setting a threshold

The compression threshold determines *when* you want the compressor to start attenuating. If you've done a good job recording your file, it should look something like Figure 8-5.

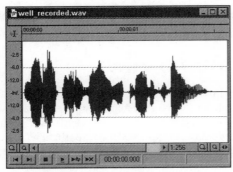

Figure 8-5: A typical well-recorded file

You can see upon casual examination that this file has a few peaks above –3 dB, quite a few around –6 dB, and the bulk of the file peaks around –10 dB. Because you're aiming to attenuate only the loudest peaks, a good threshold in this situation is –10 dB. The few peaks above are attenuated, while the bulk of the file is left relatively unscathed.

In fact, somewhere around –10 dB is generally a good place to start. If you've recorded your audio a bit low, you might need to set your threshold lower, say –12 dB or –15 dB. If the bulk of your audio information is peaking much below –15 dB, you might want to consider re-recording it to get the most out of your soundcard's dynamic range.

You'll get very different results depending on where you set the threshold. As an example, Figure 8-6 shows what the example file looks like after setting the threshold at –6 dB and at –20 dB. If you look at the two results, you see that by setting the threshold lower, at –20 dB, the file gets compressed a great deal more.

In Figure 8-6 on the left, there is about 6 dB of headroom, and it shows about 20 dB. That means the audio pictured on the left can be turned up a lot more than the audio pictured on the right, which means it is going to be a lot louder (see Figure 8-7).

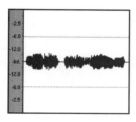
Compressed using
a -20 dB threshold

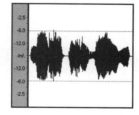
Compressed using
a -6 dB threshold

Figure 8-6: The same file compressed at two different thresholds

In particular, notice how, after adding gain, the beginning and ends of the file in the figure on the left are now as loud as the rest of the file, whereas the figures on the right retains some of the natural dynamics of the original. You will hear this difference later in the step-by-step section.

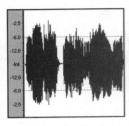
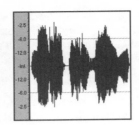

Compressed using
a -20 dB threshold

Compressed using
a -6 dB threshold

Figure 8-7: Two files, compressed using different thresholds, with gain added to restore the original headroom

Setting a ratio

The ratio setting controls *how much* the sound is going to be attenuated. The ratio setting is ratio of input volume to output volume. For example, a compression ratio of 4:1 means that for every 4 dB of input above the threshold, the output level will only be 1 dB. Lower ratios have a lesser effect; higher ratios are much more pronounced. In general, ratios of up to 4:1 are a fairly mild, as long as a reasonable threshold has been set. Ratios between 4:1 and 10:1 are fairly heavy, and any ratio greater than 10:1 is a special type of compression known as limiting.

Limiting can be very helpful preventing distortion. For instance, you could place a limiter at the end of your audio signal chain that limited the final input to your soundcard to –0.5 dB. This way, you would never distort the inputs to your sound card. However, as long as you're careful when you set up your gain structure and use a bit of compression, you don't usually need a limiter.

Cross-Reference   To find out more about setting up your gain structure, please refer to Chapter 4.

When compressing your files, you're generally safe with a starting ratio of 4:1, though different types of content respond to compression differently (see the "Compression: Music Versus Speech" sidebar).

Setting attack and release times

The attack and release times determine how quickly the compressor attenuates signals that surpass the threshold and how slowly the compressor returns to the original signal level after the input signal dips back below the threshold. The words *quickly* and *slowly* are used deliberately:

✦ You want your *attack time* to be fairly swift, say 20 milliseconds; otherwise, you run the risk of the compressor delaying the attenuation too long. Delaying the attenuation too long can lead to sound being attenuated mid-syllable or in the middle of a musical passage.

✦ The *release time* should be gradual or you run the risk of the compression being too noticeable. 100 milliseconds is a good starting point for a release time.

Compression: Music Versus Speech

When you're setting up your compressor, it's worth considering for a moment what sort of content you're trying to compress.

Speech is very compression tolerant, mainly because you're used to hearing compressed speech. The warm, resonant bedroom voices many FM DJs have are not what they were born with; they're a demonstration of what compression and EQ can do.

One of the side effects of compression is a boosting of the low frequency content in the audio. Because high frequencies tend to be spikier, they tend to be the frequencies being compressed. After compression, the relative tonal balance of the audio changes. The high frequencies are attenuated, which makes the low frequencies seem louder.

To most ears, this phenomenon sounds pleasing, particularly on vocals. So compressors change the sound of your files in two ways; first by controlling the levels, and second by warming up the bottom end. Depending on where you set your threshold, you can easily compress speech at 6:1 and above. Most commercial radio stations do so as a matter of routine.

Music is different for a couple of reasons. First, with the exception of classical, most music is already compressed to some degree before it is pressed onto a CD. So what you are doing is adding *additional* compression. Second, when you use compression, you're changing the dynamic range of the piece, as well as the relative tonal balance. This may not be what the artist intended. Hours may have been spent in a recording studio getting the balance just right.

Don't worry too much about adding additional compression — radio stations certainly don't (this is why songs sound different on the radio). You want your programming to sound as good as possible through the given medium. Radio stations process with this in mind, and you should as well. Using a compression ratio of 2 or 3:1 won't be terribly noticeable, makes the music sound more present, and evens out the volume discrepancies between songs.

If your programming is a mixture of speech and music, especially voiceover with background music, beware: compression generally has the effect of blending the two together, which may make the narration harder to understand (EQ can help here).

As usual, the most important advice is "Use your ears."

Using Audio Compression

Enough theory — it's time to hear compression in action. In the following example, you can hear how speech reacts to compression, and how adjusting the ratio and threshold affects the result. You'll be opening a file in your audio editing software and playing around with the settings in the compression window.

On the CD-ROM   This exercise is designed to use sound files from the CD-ROM, which you'll find in the Audio directory.

1. **Start up your audio editing software.** I'll be using Sound Forge.

2. **Open up the file you want to edit.** If you do not have a file to work on, you can open well_recorded from the CD-ROM.

3. **Save a copy of the file using a sensible filename.**

4. **Open up the compression window in your audio editing software, often called Compression or Dynamics Processing.** (Sound Forge users open up the Compression window by selecting Effects ➪ Dynamics ➪ Graphic).

5. **Enter the compression settings.** You should be able to enter numeric values for the threshold and ratio; alternatively, you may be presented with a graphic representation much like Figure 8-5. In this case, you may have to adjust the ratio and threshold settings by grabbing points in the graphical representation and moving them.

   To start off with, compress using a 3:1 ratio with a threshold of –12 dB. (Sound Forge users choose the 3:1 Compression Starting at –12 dB preset from the Presets drop-down menu at the top of the Graphic Dynamics window).

6. **Set your attack and release times.** To start off with, set your attack time to 1 millisecond and your release time to 50 milliseconds. These are fairly standard settings that should work in most situations. Longer attack and release times are used for special effects, such as getting big drum sounds on rock recordings.

7. **Perform the compression and compensate to restore your headroom.** Because compression turns down anything above a certain threshold, you'll want to add some gain after the compression stage to restore the file's original headroom.

   - Some audio editing programs can do this automatically. If your audio editing program adds gain automatically, turn this function on and click OK. (Sound Forge users: Make sure the Auto Gain Compensate check box directly above the attack setting is selected.)

   - If you audio program does not add gain automatically, you need to compensate for the volume change by normalizing the file Find your Normalization function and normalize to –.5 dB (or 95 percent of maximum).

Cross-Reference   For a full discussion of normalization and why to normalize to 95 percent, see the Normalization section in the "Other Processing Tricks" section of this chapter.

8. **Listen to the result.** Hear the difference? It's worth pausing a moment to analyze what has happened. The loudest sections of the file have been turned down, as expected. The Normalization function then brought all the other sections/frequencies up. The result is that the file sounds fatter.

This is because the loud, spiky parts of the file are mid and high frequencies; when you attenuate those sections and bring up the overall level to compensate, the perceived effect is an increase in low frequency content in the file (again, think FM radio DJ).

Next, try changing the ratio and threshold settings in the compression window to see how these changes affect the result:

1. **Undo the previous operations, or re-open the original file** you were working on.

2. **Save a copy.**

3. **Open up the Compression window and set the threshold to –12 dB again, but this time, set your ratio to 10:1.**

4. **Click OK.** Remember to normalize if your audio editing software doesn't automatically compensate the gain.

   Now the file is heavily compressed. It doesn't sound bad; speech is very compression-tolerant. But EVERY SINGLE SYLLABLE IS LOUD. Sounds like a news bulletin, right? Fine if you are putting together a commercial, but overkill for anything of a reasonable duration.

5. **Try messing with the threshold. Undo (or re-open the file), put the ratio back to 3:1, and change the threshold to –30 dB.** Preview it.

Again, it doesn't sound bad, but with the threshold set so low, the space *between* words is being compressed; you can hear the back of the announcer's throat. Compression makes things sound closer, and this is definitely a little too close. So after all this playing around, you should realize that the preset of 3:1 wasn't such a bad place to start.

Okay, time to move on. This time, you'll see how compression affects music.

1. **Open a music file that you want to compress.** If you do not have a file to work with, open music_example from the CD-ROM.

2. **Save a copy.**

3. **Open the Compression window.**

4. **Use the following settings: 3:1 ratio, –12 dB threshold, 1ms attack, 50ms release.** As with the speech example, these are fairly mild settings and should retain most of the original dynamics of the music, while compressing the dynamic range enough so that it will sound better when played back on multimedia systems.

5. **Preview the effect.** As with the speech sample, the music sounds louder and fatter. What you want to listen for is the overall relationship between the instruments in the music. You want to maintain this if at all possible.

   If you're working with the music_example file, the drums took the brunt of the compression because they are the loudest part of the piece. In this case, the overall feel of the piece has been maintained.

6. **As an experiment, change the ratio to 8:1.** An 8:1 compression ratio is very high for music. It is instructive for you to hear what music that has been compressed too heavily sounds like. Preview the effect.

   The sound is much louder, but chances are the relative balance between the instruments has changed. If you're working with the music_example file, the background female vocal, which was very subtle, has now been brought to the foreground. The piece has lost a bit of the punch it had before because the drums have been squashed back into the mix.

   It doesn't sound *bad*; but it does sound *different*. This is too heavy a setting for music if you're trying to maintain the integrity of the original piece. Just for yuks, let's play around with the attack and release settings.

7. **Change the attack time to 250 milliseconds.** Preview the effect. When you set an attack time this high, the beginning of loud sections sneak past the compressor before the attenuation kicks in.

   Wacky, eh? What is happening is the leading edges of the drums are triggering the compressor, but the compressor is waiting 250 milliseconds before it turns the volume down. So the attack of the drums remains unaffected, while what comes 250 milliseconds later is attenuated.

8. **Change the attack time back to 1 millisecond, and the release time to 500 milliseconds.** Preview the effect.

   With these settings, the drums are triggering the compressor, but the slow release is keeping the volume attenuated. And as well, you can hear the volume coming back up; this is known as pumping or breathing and is to be avoided unless you're after a special effect.

Again, you see that the preset wasn't such a bad place to start. Feel free to play around with the settings, and when you find one you like, save it as your own special preset. You're probably going to want to have different presets for speech and music, perhaps even different announcers and different types of music. But once you find what works with your content, you should be able to use your presets consistently.

Stacking your compression

Compression can be very subtle or heavy-handed. In general you want to avoid the latter, but some situations might require a fair amount of compression to achieve the desired result. Instead of heavily compressing the whole file, you can sometimes achieve better results by compressing moderately twice, with slightly different settings to target different problems.

Consider a talk show with two guests: one loud and outspoken, the other mumbling and soft-spoken. It would be tempting to compress the file heavily to try to even out the levels between the two guests. But this would most likely result in the loud guest sounding heavily compressed, with the quieter guest relatively unaffected. Instead a better approach would involve two separate compression stages.

First compress the louder guest's outbursts fairly heavily, say an 8:1 ratio, with a high threshold. Then apply a second pass of compression, this time with a moderate ratio of perhaps 4:1 and a lower threshold. These changes help even out the overall levels between the two speakers. It doesn't matter if the two guests' levels are not perfectly even — they were not even in the first place and it would sound odd if they were now.

Another way compression is commonly stacked is by compressing lightly while recording, and then recompressing the final output.

Multiband compression

Most compressors operate on the audio file as a whole. When the volume level exceeds the threshold, the level is attenuated. Because high and mid frequencies tend to be louder and spikier, they tend to trigger the compression more often than low frequencies. The perceived result is an overall increase in low frequency content, because the high and mid frequencies are attenuated more often.

Multiband compressors divide the audio signal into separate frequency bands and apply compression to them individually. By dividing up the audible spectrum into bands, much higher compression ratios can be achieved while still maintaining a relatively natural tonal balance. Most commercial radio stations use multiband compression in their broadcast chains. These units have traditionally been very pricey, but lately many manufacturers are making consumer versions designed for the home recording market. These units are excellent streaming media processors. They are a bit more expensive than standard compressors, but can be well worth the extra money.

Other Signal Processing Tricks

In addition to EQ and compression, there are a few other tricks that audio engineers have up their sleeves. In fact, these are specialized combinations of EQ and compression, but used so often they are recognized as signal processing techniques in their own right.

Normalization

Normalizing a file occurs when you turn the audio up as loud as it can go without distortion. This is done by finding the loudest peak in the file and calculating the difference between it and 0 dB.

For instance, if your file has its loudest peak at –2.4 dB, you can turn the whole file up exactly 2.4 dB before distortion. If you did, the loudest peak would be at exactly 0 dB (that's okay; you never want to *exceed* 0 dB). This is a very handy function, because it enables you to use all the available headroom in your file without ever going into distortion.

One thing to bear in mind is that you probably want to perform normalization last, because sometimes other signal processing, EQ in particular, adds to the overall signal level of your file. If you normalize and then add EQ, you run the risk of sending your file into distortion.

Tip   Most normalization routines allow you to set a normalization level. Don't set this to 0 dB — this means that at some point in the file you're going to touch 0 dB. While it is perfectly okay to do so, some sound cards/speakers/players have problems handling 0 dB. Instead, set your normalization level to –.5 dB or 95 percent of the maximum. You'll only lose .5 dB of gain, which in theory is inaudible, and you'll have peace of mind knowing you're not running the risk of somebody's system choking on the 0 dB peak.

Gating (noise gates) to remove background noise

Gating is a dynamics processing technique where everything below a threshold is muted. It is used to remove background noise from files. There is no ratio setting, but you do set the threshold and the attack and release times.

The attack time determines how quickly the gate opens to allow the desired audio through; the release determines how quickly it shuts after the audio has dropped below the threshold.

Setting up a noise gate can be tricky when the background noise level is close to the desired audio. In particular, soft consonants such as *h* and *l* can be cut off if your threshold is too high. If your threshold is too low you may hear the gate chatter — this is when the gate is falsely triggered by background noise very close to the threshold level. If your release is too quick, the ends of words can be clipped. If the release is too long, you may hear the background noise creeping in before the gate shuts.

Gates are most useful if the level of the background noise is fairly low. Then again, if the background noise is low enough to be gated easily, it is questionable whether it is necessary to remove it at all. With proper attention paid in the recording stage, you shouldn't need to use a noise gate at all.

Noise reduction

Noise reduction is a process designed to remove extraneous noise without adversely affecting the rest of the file. Noise reduction comes in many shapes and sizes, but they all share a common approach: identifying noise by either frequency or gain characteristics and removing it by a combination of EQ and dynamics processing. Think of noise reduction as signal processing on steroids, or intelligent signal processing.

All the signal processing discussed up to this point involved giving the software a simple set of rules, such as turn everything above −10 dB down using a 3:1 ratio. The software applied those rules to the whole file. Using noise reduction is a bit more complex; it involves giving the software information about what noise sounds like, so that the software can try to remove the noise or at least make it less noticeable.

There are many different approaches to noise reduction. The actual mechanics of how it is done can be both esoteric and proprietary. For the purposes of this discussion, you'll see how to use some of the most common varieties of noise reduction without worrying too much about how they work their magic.

Some software editing programs come with noise reduction, others offer it as an additional plug-in. If you've taken the time to record your content well, you shouldn't have an overwhelming need for noise reduction, but as a salvaging technique, it can be a lifesaver.

Background noise reduction

Background noise reduction works best when the noise is reasonably consistent in both level and frequency. For instance, air conditioning noise would be fairly straightforward to reduce. Lowering the background ambience of a restaurant would not, because it is constantly changing.

To reduce background noise using noise reduction, you identify the noise by highlighting a portion of the audio file that contains only background noise. This is known as generating a noise profile, or print. You then specify how much you want to attenuate. −10 dB to −15 dB of noise reduction is usually more than enough; any more reduction than that and the audio may start to sound hollow. Err on the side of caution.

Click and pop removal

Clicks and pops find their way into audio in a number of ways, such as electrostatic discharges, lip smacks, and so on. If you look at the clicks and pops in a software editing program, they are immediately recognizable in that they are extremely short and very spiky, and appear in a very particular frequency range. This makes it easy for a software program to identify them.

Editing platforms with click and pop removal generally have presets. These routines go through the file, and each time a potential click is found, the user is queried about removing it or skipping to the next offender. Some programs insert silence, others insert an approximation of what the original sound may have been like. Because the duration of these noises is generally very short, this kind of noise reduction can be very effective.

Sample rate conversion

Digitizing audio involves sampling the waveform 44,100 times per second, each sample being 16 bits long. Streaming codecs have internal sample rates and bit lengths. Somewhere along the line, the sample rate has to be converted.

All codecs have some sort of sample rate conversion built into them. But sample rate conversion is a tricky business — and some folks feel that certain software programs do a better job of it than others. In particular, some early low bitrate codecs did a poor job of sample rate conversion, and by doing the sample rate conversion in a professional audio editing software package and feeding the result into the encoding process, some people felt that you would get a better result.

These days, companies have put a substantial amount of effort into their sample rate conversion routines, and performing these conversion routines before you encode is not necessary. Not only that, to do it properly, you have to know the native sampling rate for each codec you wanted to use, and do different sample rate converts for different encoding schemes.

Though some may disagree, I feel it is safe to ignore sample rate conversion as an additional processing step and to leave it to your encoding software.

When to Do Signal Processing

A number of signal processing techniques have been discussed in this chapter. You might at this point be wondering if you should EQ before you compress or vice-versa, or when you should normalize or perform noise reduction. The answer is, of course, that it depends on the source material. But here are a few pointers that should give you an idea of how to proceed:

1. **The first step in optimizing your audio actually comes before the optimization process, and that is to be sure you're recording the best possible quality audio to begin with.** This means setting up a good gain structure, minimizing outside interference, and using good equipment. This may sound redundant, but it bears repeating.

Cross-Reference

If you need a quick refresher course on what setting up a good gain structure is all about, please refer to Chapter 4.

2. **After you've recorded/digitized your audio, it's probably time to think about noise reduction.** Any EQ or compression you apply might make it more difficult to remove extraneous noise later on.

3. **After your file is clean, you can either EQ or compress; the two are rather closely entwined:**

   - If you add EQ to an uncompressed file, the peaks are going to be changed, which affects the compressor later on.

   - When you compress a file, the effect is generally to bring up the bottom end.

   A good approach is to do a light pass of compression to even out the levels, add a bit of sparkle with EQ, and then possibly do a little more compression if necessary.

4. **Last but not least, normalize your file.**

Summary

Audio signal processing is a catchall term to describe the assortment of tools at your disposal to make your audio sound better. Through judicious use of EQ, compression, normalization, and noise reduction, you can turn your ordinary-sounding files into professional-sounding programming.

Signal processing isn't an exact science. Play around with the different tools available and find out what works best for your programming. You are one of the best judges of what your content should sound like, so be sure to "use your ears!"

✦ Signal processing is important because people are used to hearing high-quality audio; in fact people are attracted to good sounding audio and repelled by poor quality.

✦ Equalization (EQ) is changing the tonal balance of your file by adjusting the levels of certain frequencies.

✦ EQ can either be used to accent good frequencies in the file, or to remove bad frequencies.

✦ Compression is changing the sound of the file by adjusting the levels of certain sections.

✦ All professional audio is compressed to a degree; using compression can make your content sound more professional.

✦ Files that require heavy compression may sound better if they are compressed twice moderately instead of once heavily.

✦ Normalization is turning up your file as loud as it can go without distortion; normalize to −.5 dB (95 percent).

✦ Noise reduction shouldn't be necessary if you've been careful in the recording stage but can be helpful when trying to salvage bad recordings.

✦ In general, it's best to do noise reduction first, then EQ and compression, and finish off your audio signal processing with normalization.

✦   ✦   ✦

Capturing, Editing, and Rendering Video

In Chapter 5, I discussed the steps that you must take to create video content that encodes well. Lighting, composition, and minimizing the motion in a frame are all important. Now it's time to digitize this video content so that it can be edited, rendered, and finally encoded. Figure 9-1 provides an illustration of the processes discussed in this chapter.

The process of transferring the video content from a camera or videotape to the computer is called *digitizing,* or *capturing*. This process involves playing back the video content while recording it into the computer by using either a dedicated capture utility or via a video editing platform.

When you've captured all the footage you need, you can begin the editing process. Editing involves trimming the individual shots you have captured and arranging them in some sort of order by using video editing software. You can also add special effects and transitions between scenes at this point; however, special effects in general do not encode well.

When you've finished editing, you must render the final version. *Rendering* means actually writing a new file with the desired special effects or transitions. Many video editing systems can display these effects without rendering; however, they must be rendered before the resulting file can be handed off to a streaming media encoder.

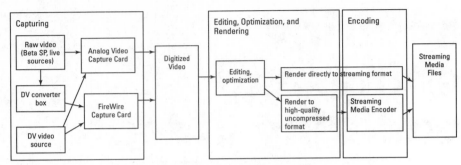

Figure 9-1: The capture, edit, and render process workflow

All three steps discussed in this chapter are fairly time-intensive. Chapter 11 discusses ways that you can automate these steps. But before you start automating your creation process, you need to understand what you're trying to accomplish.

Capturing Video

Before you can begin the process of editing and encoding your video, the video must be transferred to your hard drives in a format you can manipulate. If you're using an analog video source and a capture card, this process is known as capturing and is where a video capture card comes into the equation. Video capture cards take an analog video signal and convert it into digital video data. If you have an IEEE 1394 system, (FireWire/iLink), you simply transfer the information digitally.

One of the most exciting developments in the last few years has been the emergence of the IEEE 1394 standard. Many computers and DV cameras now come with a built-in IEEE 1394 port (FireWire/iLink). Using FireWire, the video can be transferred digitally, directly from the camera to your hard drive.

Because the information transfer is digital and does not rely on a real-time conversion process, the transfer is lossless. You automatically get full frame rate and full screen size, and FireWire is more than fast enough to handle the data rate. If your hard drives are not, the transfer process simply takes a bit longer. No data is lost.

Contrast FireWire transfer to capturing the same video using an analog capture card. An analog capture card requires that your digital video be converted to an analog signal by the camera, and then converted back into digital video by the capture card. Each conversion, from digital to analog and then back again, slightly compromises the video quality where FireWire does not comprise quality at all.

Current FireWire digital video systems use the DV codec, which some engineers do not consider high enough quality for television broadcasts. For streaming media applications, however, it is more than sufficient. The only exception to this is live encoding situations, where streaming media encoders are not capable of taking raw DV input and trans-coding it to a streaming format. For live encoding, you'll need to use an analog capture card.

Analog video capture

If you're using an analog capture card, the quality of your video capture card is one of the largest determinants of the quality of your streaming media files. The video must be digitized as accurately as possible. Different capture cards use different algorithms and different quality components to do this. In general, you get what you pay for with a capture card.

In addition to the challenge of converting the incoming analog signal as accurately as possible, the video capture card must do so within certain limitations, such as hard drive access times and rotation speeds, data bus speeds, and maximum file size restrictions. To work within these limitations, most capture cards must limit the frame size, limit the frame rate, or use a codec to reduce the incoming data rate. Capturing the highest-quality video involves tradeoffs between these three factors.

Finding a good compromise is generally not a problem. Most streaming media at this point is not full screen, and as long as the amount of compression used is minimal, the quality of the resulting streaming media file is not affected much. By selecting an appropriate frame size and using as little compression as possible, you should have no problem creating high-quality streaming media. Figure 9-2 provides a cheat sheet for the next few discussion points.

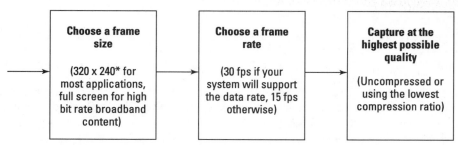

Choose a frame size

(320 x 240* for most applications, full screen for high bit rate broadband content)

Choose a frame rate

(30 fps if your system will support the data rate, 15 fps otherwise)

Capture at the highest possible quality

(Uncompressed or using the lowest compression ratio)

*Note: Some capture cards default to 352 x 240 for quarter-screen capture. Choose this setting if your card offers this as a default.

Figure 9-2: The three main decisions that affect quality when using an analog video capture card

Know the limits of your system

Regardless of whether you're working with a desktop or a laptop, you need to be aware of two main limiting factors to video capture when using an analog video capture card:

✦ The maximum sustainable data rate

✦ The maximum allowable file size on the OS

Maximum sustainable data rate

The maximum sustainable data rate on your system depends on the type of hard drives you're using, your CPU, your PCI bus speed, and a number of other factors, such as whether you're trying to run any other applications in the background, which you should not do. Video capture is an intensive process and requires all available system resources because of the CPU load and the data rate. The data rate is determined by the screen size, the frame rate, and the amount of compression your capture card applies, if any.

If you're capturing at smaller screen sizes and reduced frame rates, you may not bump up against your system's limits. However, if your video-capture utility reports dropped frames, that's a sure-fire indication that you're exceeding the capabilities of your system. Dropping a frame or two here or there can be acceptable, but if you're dropping frames consistently, you must either reduce your frame size or reduce your frame rate until your system can handle the data rate.

Hard drive technology is improving by leaps and bounds, so much so that this problem may disappear in the very near future. In the meantime, sensible hard drive maintenance, coupled with running your capture utility on its own, greatly improves your chances of success.

Maximum allowable file size

If you're running a newer operating system, along with a newer capture card and video editing software, you may not encounter any file size limitations. However, if you're stuck on an older OS or purchased an older generation capture card, read on.

On older operating systems, how large your files can be is limited. Additionally, some files are limited in size by their specification. For a more detailed explanation, please see the "The Two Gigabyte File Size Limitation" sidebar. Suffice it to say, many older video capture systems are limited to two gigabytes per file.

When you're working with video, two gigabytes can be gobbled up very quickly. Table 9-1 lists the approximate length of video that can be captured at different frame sizes, frame rates, and compression rates bearing this limitation in mind. You can see that to capture reasonably long videos, you must capture the video in chunks or reduce your data rate, frame rate, screen size, or some combination of the above.

Table 9-1
2GB Video File Limitations

Quality	Amount of video in a 2GB file (excluding audio)
ITU-R uncompressed RGB (720 × 486, 30fps, 30Mbytes/s)	68 seconds
ITU-R YUV 4:2:2 (720 × 486, 30fps, ~20 Mbytes/s)	2 minutes 30 seconds
ITU-R DV 4:1:1 (720 × 486, 30fps, ~6:1 compression, ~3.5 Mbytes/s)	9 minutes 45 seconds
320 × 240 uncompressed RGB, 30fps (~6.6Mbytes/s)	5 minutes
320 × 240 uncompressed RGB, 15fps (~3.3Mbytes/s)	10 minutes
ITU-R, 30fps, MJPEG 2.5:1 compression	3 minutes
ITU-R, 30fps, MJPEG 5:1 compression	6 minutes
352 × 240, 30fps, MJPEG 2.5:1 compression	12 minutes
352 × 240, 15fps, MJPEG 2.5:1 compression	24 minutes
352 × 240, 30fps, MJPEG 5:1 compression	24 minutes
352 × 240, 15fps, MJPEG 5:1 compression	48 minutes

* ITU - The International Telecommunication Union, a standards body

All of the older, higher priced video editing systems have proprietary workarounds to this limitation, at least on the capture side; many of the older, less expensive and mid-priced capture cards do not. This problem also rears its ugly head later on in the rendering section. Unfortunately, you really have no other choice than to buy newer equipment or to upgrade to a newer operating system. If this is not an option, you must work within the two gigabyte file size limitation when you capture and render.

Choose an appropriate frame size and frame rate

One way to immediately reduce the data rate of your video is to reduce the frame size and the frame rate. If you capture at ¼ screen (320 × 240) and ½ the frame rate (15fps), your data rate is only an eighth of what it was previously. Not only does this reduce the data rate, but it also increases the amount of video you can capture by a factor of eight.

If you are creating high bit rate videos (500 Kbps +) that you intend to display full screen, you should always capture full screen, at the full 30 frames per second. For all other applications, capturing at ¼ screen resolution should suffice.

The Two-Gigabyte File Size Limitation

If you've ever tried to capture a long video or tried to render a bunch of video clips that you've edited together on a timeline, you may have returned to find your computer frozen, having crashed for no particular reason. The reason is that video files are practically limited to two gigabytes. In the world of video editing, that doesn't get you far.

Note that this limitation is only a problem with older operating systems, file systems, video capture cards, and editing software. Newer systems should not have this limitation.

Why are video files limited to two gigabytes, I hear you ask? Well, the answer is a bit complex, involving limitations imposed by the operating system, limitations imposed by the file system you're using, and a programming implementation.

32-bit operating systems can work with files up to four gigabytes. However, Windows 95 and Windows 98 are limited to two gigabytes for compatibility reasons. The same goes for Mac systems running HFS — files sizes are limited to two gigabytes.

If you're running Windows NT or 2000, you can use the NTFS file system, and on the Mac platform, you can use the HFS+ file system. These allow files of up to 1000 gigabytes, but AVI files are still limited to two gigabytes.

That's right — even though newer file systems are capable of working with files of up to 1000 gigabytes, AVI 1.0 files are limited to two gigabytes.

The problem is that the 32-bit number used to describe the size of the AVI file is a *signed* integer, which means that it can represent a value from -2^{32} to 2^{32}. The original specification for AVI files simply ignored the negative values, which limits the maximum file size to two gigabytes. Any capture cards or video editing platforms that are based on the Video for Windows standard are subject to this limitation.

AVI 2.0 is the newest AVI specification and is also known as the OpenDML format. This format allows AVI files to be of unlimited size, along with other file enhancements, such as timecode and support for fields. The OpenDML specification is part of the Microsoft DirectShow package, so if your video capture card and video capture application can use DirectShow, you are not subject to the two gigabyte limit.

Of course, you can use a workaround. A freeware software program called Virtual Dub (www.virtualdub.com) works with Video for Windows capture cards and automatically segments your video captures into two gigabyte chunks that can then be assembled into an OpenDML-compliant AVI file.

You can encounter the same problem when you render your files. If you want to render long video files, your video editing program must be DirectShow enabled. And of course, if you want to encode these huge AVI files, your encoding application must also be DirectShow enabled.

Tip   If you're capturing at less than full screen, choose an even multiple, such as ¼ screen. Even if your eventual goal is another screen size, such as 240 × 180, you get better quality if you capture at ¼ screen and then resize when you render/encode. Resizing is very CPU intensive, which makes it nearly impossible to do in a high-quality manner while capturing.

As far as frame rates are concerned, 15 frames per second should be fine for any content intended for dial-up audiences. It should also be sufficient for low-motion video, such as talking head content. For high-motion content or content that will be encoded at 80 Kbps or above, you may want to consider capturing at 30 frames per second.

Traditionally, the trade off has been between frame rate and file size. With the price of hard drives today, storage is no longer an issue. If you've got sufficient storage, and your capture application can handle the full 30 frames per second at ¼ screen size, you may as well capture at full frame rate.

Low-motion content encoded at 80 Kbps or above should end up close to full frame rate. High-motion content may not encode at higher than 15 frames per second at this point, but this could change rapidly given the advancing nature of codec technology.

Capture at the highest possible quality

The approach to capturing at the highest possible quality varies slightly depending on the type of video capture card you are using. You should avoid using any codecs during capture if at all possible; however, if your capture card uses a built-in hardware codec, use as little compression as possible.

Consumer video capture cards

Consumer-level video capture cards typically offer three different methods of capturing video:

✦ Uncompressed capture at reduced screen sizes

✦ Compressed capture using proprietary hardware codecs

✦ Compressed capture using software codecs

The best approach with these cards is to capture uncompressed at a reduced screen size.

Avoid using the software codecs at all costs. These codecs were designed with data reduction in mind, not video quality. They are perfectly suitable for the home user to conserve file space, but disastrous if you're producing high-quality streaming media.

Tip Many consumer-level capture cards default to using a software codec each time you fire up your capture utility. Be sure to double-check each time that the compression is set to none or uncompressed.

Mid-price and premium capture cards

Practically all mid-price and premium capture cards use built-in hardware codecs. Instead of choosing between a codec or uncompressed, you choose a data rate or compression ratio. You should choose the highest data rate or the lowest amount of compression your setup reliably supports.

Your data rate or compression choice is practically limited by your video capture system. Ideally, you should be using top-quality SCSI drives, in which case you should not encounter any problems. However, you may be limited by budget to IDE drives, so you may need to sacrifice your video quality slightly to achieve rock-solid reliability.

Many video capture cards come with a disk testing utility that measures the maximum throughput that your system can handle. In addition, some manufacturers have motherboard recommendations, or PCI slot configurations. Some motherboards are incompatible with certain capture cards due to the chips used on them. Some capture cards also require a particular PCI slot to function optimally. If your capture card has any such requirements, pay careful attention them. Video capture is extremely data-intensive and time consuming — reliability should be one of your highest priorities.

Tip If your capture card does come with a disk-testing utility, use it and then set your data rate to 75 to 80 percent of the maximum value. Doing so gives your system a little breathing room, which provides you with a higher level of dependability.

IEEE 1394 Capture (FireWire/iLink)

Capturing video via FireWire isn't really capturing at all — it is transferring data. FireWire devices, such as a FireWire compatible camera are seen as devices attached to your computer. The FireWire specification includes device control, so in most situations you can control your camera from your video editing application.

Transferring digital video data from a camera to your hard drives involves using the VCR-like controls of your capture application to find the sections you want to capture and clicking the record button. The video is transferred to your hard drive as full-frame, 30 frames per second video using the DV codec. Even though the video is compressed using the DV codec, it is high enough quality for 99.9 percent of all streaming media applications.

Because the data rate of DV video is only 3.5MB/sec, you should not have a problem with hard drive access rates. And even if you do, most FireWire capture applications are smart enough to recapture any frames that may have been dropped during the transfer. You still may run up against the two gigabyte file size limit, but if you're running a FireWire system, chances are you're using a more recent operating system that is not subject to this limitation.

DV video converter boxes have recently appeared on the market. These hardware boxes have analog inputs and a FireWire output. These converters are designed to take analog audio and video inputs and convert them to a DV video signal, which is output via the FireWire output. The FireWire output can be plugged directly into a FireWire capture card. These boxes provide an extremely cost efficient way of digitizing full-frame video.

The only time FireWire capture is not applicable is during live events. At this stage streaming media encoders are not capable of trans-coding a DV input into a streaming media format in real-time. As processor speeds increase, this restriction is sure to be a thing of the past.

Editing Video

After you've captured your video clips, you can edit them by using your video editing software application. Doing so enables you to trim the beginning and ends of your clips, or to connect multiple clips together into a longer presentation.

The point at which two different clips meet is known as an *edit point*. Choosing the appropriate point for an edit is a skill that takes years to master. Unfortunately, not all of us have that much time.

Editing video is not as simple as editing audio, because of lip sync. To edit out an offending phrase or mistake, you must edit out not only the audio but also the video. If you do not disguise your edit by filling the gap with a cutaway or different camera angle, you end up with what is known as a *jump cut* (see "The Importance of Cutaways" sidebar).

Certain great French film directors have used the jump cut to great effect, but it's generally not something you want in your presentations. To avoid this situation, having some cutaway material is a good idea. Cutaway material is film of your subject or subjects doing something such as nodding or shrugging that you can use as filler material. By using cutaway material, you can hide edits that would otherwise look awkward.

The simplest edit involves a straight cut from one piece of video to the next. Alternately, you can use a transition effect, such as a crossfade or a wipe.

Transition effects are used to soften edit points so that they are less jarring, or they can be used as a special effect. The problem is that transitions do not encode particularly well, especially at low bit rates.

Imagine a transition that fades between two scenes over the course of two seconds. During those two seconds, every pixel in the frame is changing. This situation is particularly difficult for a codec to deal with, and what generally happens is that the quality of the encoded file is degraded, particularly at lower bit rates.

Of course, no one is asking you to do away with transition effects altogether. There are those who believe that 99 percent of all transition effects are completely unnecessary and more of a distraction than anything else. However, we cannot expect to impose our will upon those who feel otherwise.

If you must use transitions, make them quick. This way, the amount of damage they inflict on the encoded version of your files is minimized.

The Importance of Cutaways

Cutaway material can be extremely useful when you're editing your video. Cutaways give you additional flexibility at the editing stage that you wouldn't otherwise have, particularly if you're working with only a single camera angle.

Cutaways are also known as "noddies" in the television news industry. After a reporter does an interview, the cameraman gets 30 seconds or so of the reporter nodding (hence the name), smiling, frowning, and generally reacting to the interviewee, even though the interviewee may have already left. These "noddy" shots can then be used to hide edits to the interviewee's responses.

Here's how it works:

Let's say a guest starts responding to a question, sneezes and utters a swear word, but eventually returns to the topic at hand. If you simply removed the offending section, you end up with a jump cut in the middle of the response, which looks unprofessional if not downright suspect.

You can fix this by using a cutaway as follows (illustrated in the following figure):

1. Start with the guest's response.

2. At somewhere near the edit point, cut to the "noddy" shot of the reporter, while keeping the audio of the guest underneath the shot of the reporter.

3. Because the reporter shot is on-screen, you can then cut back anywhere into the guest's response; lip sync is no longer an issue.

Original, unedited video: One continuous shot of guest speaking, including a sneeze and a swear word...

ONE CONTINUOUS SHOT OF GUEST SPEAKING ───────────────────────────▶

"Thank you very much for inviting me, and I'm glad you asked that question..."	"Achoo!.....$*#&$%*...sorry."	"Our new product is wonderful because..."

You can disguise edits by going to a cutaway where you want to edit:

START WITH SHOT OF GUEST	CUT TO SHOT OF HOST NODDING	CUT BACK TO GUEST
"Thank you very much for inviting me..."	"... and I'm glad you asked that question..."	"Our new product is wonderful because..."

The viewers never see that some of the guest's response was removed.

Without a cutaway, there will be a jump cut if the offending material is cut out, because the speaker will have moved between shots. This is disturbing to viewers.

SHOT OF GUEST SPEAKING, WITH OBVIOUS MISSING SECTION

"Thank you very much for inviting me..."	"... and I'm glad you asked that question..."

Jump Cut

Using a cutaway to disguise an edit

In interview situations, cutaways are almost always shots of the people involved, reacting but not saying anything. However, many other shots can be used as cutaways. Audience shots make great cutaways. Wide shots can be used as cutaways sometimes, because lip sync is hard to decipher.

Whatever you're shooting, cover your bases by grabbing a few minutes' worth of cutaways — you'll be happy you did.

Rendering Video

After you've trimmed and arranged all your shots, you must render the result. Rendering involves writing out a new file with all the edits and transitions you specified in your video editing software. Figure 9-3 is an illustration of the rendering process. Rendering serves a couple of purposes:

✦ Until you render the file, it exists only as a combination of the original files and a bunch of editing/transition commands that only your video editing software can understand.

✦ Some video capture/edit solutions use proprietary codecs or file formats that streaming media encoders do not support. If you can't render streaming versions directly from the timeline, you must render to an intermediate format.

✦ Rendering a new file may be more efficient than keeping all of the original files lying around and can save time later if you need to re-encode.

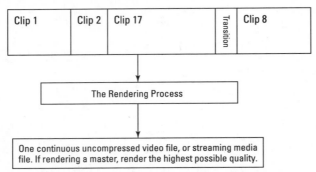

Figure 9-3: Rendering your video involves combining all your video clips and transitions into a single uncompressed video or streaming media file.

Rendering files can be extremely time consuming, taking anywhere from a few minutes to many hours depending on the screen size, the length of the video, the complexity of the transitions, and the speed of your CPU. Having the fastest CPU available can really save you time.

Luckily, many video editing platforms can render streaming versions of your file directly from the timeline so that you do not need to render an intermediate version. Some even use the hardware on board the capture card to speed up the process. This approach is definitely better, and one that you should bear in mind when shopping for a video editing solution.

Rendering a high-quality master

If you can't render a streaming version directly from your video editing software, or if you want to have a master reference, you must render a high-quality version of your edited master. Doing so can save time and space later on if the clip needs to be re-encoded.

You should render your master versions at the highest possible quality. You also want to render to a file type that your streaming media encoder can open up, such as AVI or MOV. If your video capture system uses a proprietary hardware codec, you may need to render an uncompressed version of the file to enable it to be opened by your streaming media encoder.

Depending on which platform you're on, what OS version you're running, and what codec your capture system uses, you may not need to render your files uncompressed. Some codecs are made available to all applications. To see if you need to render an uncompressed version of your file, you should check the specs of the streaming encoder you're running to see if it accepts the native output of your video capture card or editing platform.

Note　If you have DirectX 6.0 or better installed on the Windows platform, most applications can open up AVI files containing compressed video (for example, MJPEG), including all three streaming media encoders.

If you have to render uncompressed files, be careful — uncompressed files take up a lot of room. You may have to beware of the two gigabyte file size limit if you're running an older OS or video editing platform (see "The Two Gigabyte File Size Limit" sidebar). If you are running an older OS or video editing platform, you must render your final video into chunks that are smaller than two gigabytes and encode them separately. The resulting encoded files can be edited together by using the appropriate tool.

Cross-Reference　For more on editing encoded files, please turn to Chapter 14.

Rendering streaming media files

If your video editing software offers it, an excellent timesaving approach is to render streaming media files directly from the timeline. Doing so avoids the intermediate step of rendering an AVI or MOV file. Also, because the data rates of streaming media files are so much lower than raw video data rates, the chances of running into the two gigabyte limit (if applicable) are fairly remote.

Many current video editing platforms offer rendering into multiple streaming formats. Some platforms also offer extensive batch-processing capabilities that enable you to schedule this time-consuming process during times when the computer is not being used, such as overnight.

If you plan on creating a large amount of streaming video, you should seriously analyze the integration of your chosen streaming media platform in the various video editing packages. Some offer far more integration than others, which you'll find incredibly useful.

Capturing, Editing, and Rendering

Although it may seem like a lot of effort and that you have to remember a lot of things, capturing and editing video is simple and enjoyable. Editing video in particular is fun, because good editing can really make presentations come alive.

Rendering isn't very exciting. In fact, it's downright dull, because there's nothing you can do except wait for the results. The faster the CPU, the less you have to wait, but at a minimum, you'll have time to get a cup of coffee.

The following examples demonstrate:

✦ Capturing with a stand-alone capture application that came with the Pinnacle Miro DC50 capture card.

✦ Capturing via the DC 50 from within Adobe Premiere.

✦ Editing by using Sonic Foundry's Vegas Video.

✦ Rendering an uncompressed master using Vegas Video.

✦ Rendering streaming media files directly from Vegas Video.

On the CD-ROM Trial versions of both Adobe Premiere and Sonic Foundry's Vegas Video are included on the CD-ROM.

If you are not using one of the above video editing platforms or capture cards, these examples should still provide you with an example of the workflow involved in the capturing, editing, and rendering processes. Most video editing platforms are remarkably similar, as are video capture cards. You should be able to work through these examples with a little help from your video editing software manual.

Capturing using the DC 50 stand-alone application

When you open up the Miro capture application, you'll see four basic screens, each with a different function:

✦ Overall project settings

✦ Audio and video settings

✦ Recording clips

✦ Verifying and testing clips

I'll start at the beginning:

1. **Open the Miro capture utility and click on the Projects tab.**

2. **Choose a folder to work in, or create a new folder for your project.** As soon as you create a folder and capture video using the settings on this page, you cannot change the settings (see Figure 9-4).

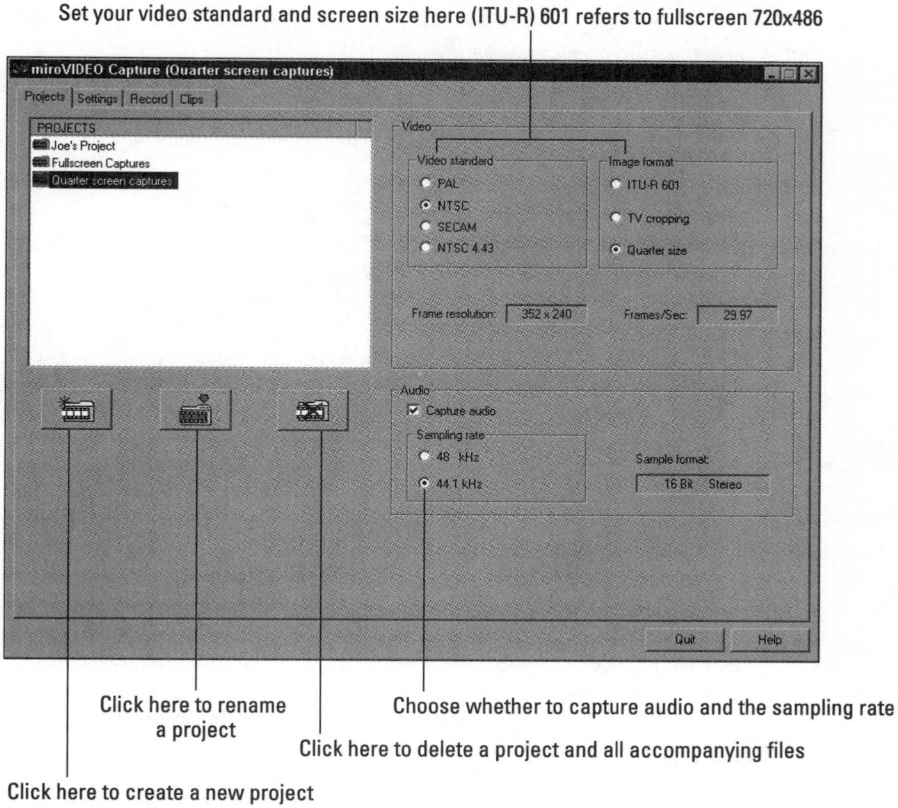

Set your video standard and screen size here (ITU-R) 601 refers to fullscreen 720x486

Click here to rename a project

Choose whether to capture audio and the sampling rate

Click here to delete a project and all accompanying files

Click here to create a new project

Figure 9-4: The Miro capture application's Projects tab

3. **Set your video standard and image format.** Choose ITU-R 601 for full screen captures, Quarter size otherwise. Make sure that the Capture audio checkbox is checked.

4. **Click on the Settings tab.** You can adjust your audio and video quality settings (see Figure 9-5).

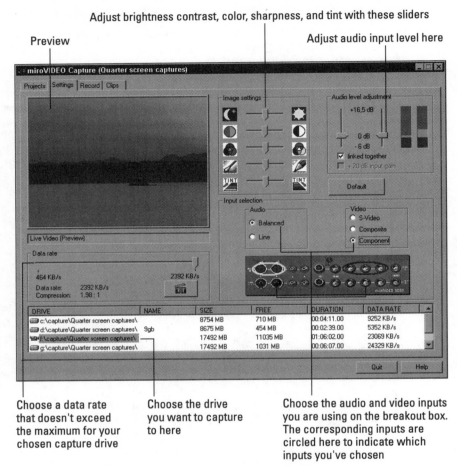

Figure 9-5: The Miro capture application's Settings tab

5. **Choose the audio and video inputs you're using.** After you've selected the correct inputs you should get a preview of your video in the preview window.

6. **You can adjust the audio input level as well as the quality of the video.** These adjustments are anything but precise — you're better off using the meter on your mixing desk and doing any video adjustment in your video editing software where you can have more control.

7. **Set a data rate for your clip.** Make sure this data rate doesn't exceed the maximum data rate for the drive you're capturing to. The maximum tested data rate is displayed on the right side of the drives window. If a data rate isn't listed, simply click on the drive, and the capture application automatically tests the data rate.

8. **Click on the Record tab.** This is where you do all the actual recording of clips (see Figure 9-6).

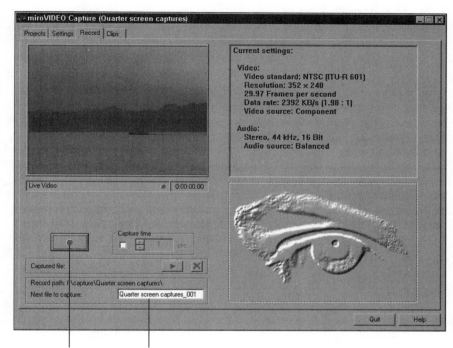

Record files   Unless specified otherwise, captured files are named the
                same as the capture folder, with consecutive number appended.

Figure 9-6: The Miro capture application's Record tab

9. **Type in a name for your captured clip.** You can either type in specific names for each captured clip, or let the application give them default names, which is the name of the project followed by a number that is incremented for each capture.

That's it. You can click on the Clips tab at any time to review the clips that you've captured. When you're satisfied that you've captured everything you need, close the application and open up your video editing software.

Capturing from within Adobe Premiere

If Adobe Premiere supports your capture card, you don't need to capture your clips in a separate application — you can capture from within Premiere. You have to make sure that your project is set up correctly, but after that, capturing your clips should be a snap.

In this case, the Miro DC50 capture card is used again.

1. **Open up Adobe Premiere.** The first thing that happens is the New Project Settings window pops up.

2. **Select General Settings and make sure that the Editing Mode is set appropriately for your capture card (see Figure 9-7).**

3. **Click Next to move on to the Video Settings page.**

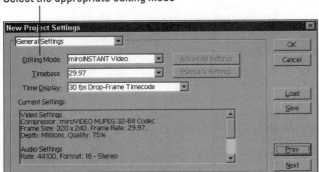

Figure 9-7: Adobe Premiere's New Project Settings window

4. **Set the frame size, frame rate, and compression used.** The video page is where you set the frame size, frame rate, and compression used for your rendered files (see Figure 9-8). The settings here do not affect streaming media files, only rendered masters.

5. **Choose uncompressed for your compressor, unless you're using a card with a hardware codec that your streaming media encoders can understand.**

6. **Choose an appropriate frame size and frame rate.** In most cases, this should be 320 × 240 pixels and 29.97 frames per second unless you're producing full screen content.

7. **Make sure that the quality setting is set at 100% and click Next to move to the Audio Settings page.** On this page, you shouldn't have to make any adjustments.

8. **Make sure that the sampling rate is set to 44.1 kHz, 16-bit Stereo uncompressed.** Click Next to move to the Keyframe and Rendering Options page.

9. **Set the fields rendering option.** On this page, make sure that the drop-down menu is set to No Fields if you're at 320 × 240 pixels or below. If you're creating full screen content, you should choose either Odd first or Even first — this setting is dependent on your content.

Choose the compression you want to use when you render
your files here - this does not affect streaming media files.

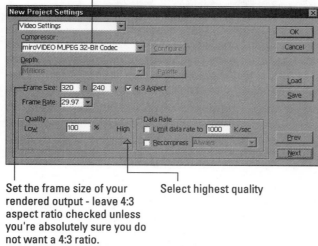

Set the frame size of your
rendered output - leave 4:3
aspect ratio checked unless
you're absolutely sure you do
not want a 4:3 ratio.

Select highest quality

Figure 9-8: Adobe Premiere's Video Settings window

10. **Click Next to move to the Capture Settings page (see Figure 9-9).** On this page, you choose the capture method you're using, and you can adjust the capture card settings by clicking on the Settings button. In the case of the Miro DC50, a window appears with three tabs — Format, Settings, and Input. The Format tab is the same as the Project Settings page of the Miro capture utility, while the Settings and Input tabs are the same as the Settings page of the Miro capture utility.

11. **Click OK to begin working on your project.**

12. **To capture video, choose Capture ⇨ Movie Capture from the File menu.** The movie capture window appears (see Figure 9-10). You should see a preview of your video in the window.

13. **Click the Record button to begin capturing.** To stop the recording, press the Esc button on your keyboard. When you stop the capture process, the captured clip is automatically opened in the Clip window. In this window, you can trim the in and out points for this particular clip before dragging it onto the timeline. If you want to continue capturing more clips, click back into the movie capture window.

Capture Format

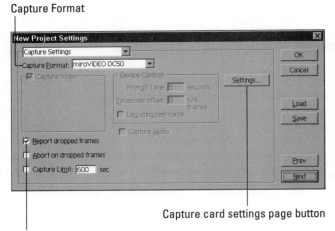

Capture card settings page button

Monitor the preformance of your system

Figure 9-9: Adobe Premiere's Capture Settings window

Click the record button to begin recording;
press the Esc button to stop capturing

Dropped frames are reported
in the bottom of the window

Figure 9-10: Adobe Premiere's Capture window

Editing using Vegas Video

Editing involves arranging all your clips on a timeline, trimming the in and out
points of each clip, perhaps by using transitions between some clips. Remember

that transitions don't encode well if they're too long. If you don't feel the need for transitions, don't use them.

Each video editing platform has its own slightly different approach. In general, you'll find some sort of clip library where you can access all your clips, some sort of timeline for arranging them, and perhaps a small Clip or Trim window where individual clips can be edited. The timeline is usually divided into separate tracks for audio and video. Some systems treat transition effects as a separate track, while others treat transitions as part of the video track.

Rather than try to cover all the possibilities, this section gives an extremely brief overview of editing using Vegas Video. The Vegas Video interface is very simple, with three main work areas (see Figure 9-11):

Note   Vegas Video is a Windows-only application.

✦ The timeline, which can have as many audio and video tracks as you need.

✦ The lower-left side, which is dedicated to inputs and editing individual clips.

✦ The lower-right side, where outputs are monitored.

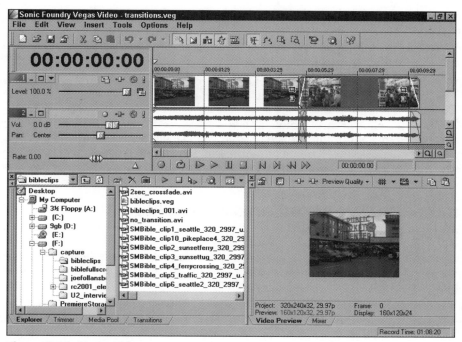

Figure 9-11: Vegas Video

To edit clips, all you have to do is open or drag them onto the timeline. Clips can be dragged back and forth. If you want to change the in or out point of a clip, simply grab the beginning or end of the clip and move it one way or the other. If you want to apply a fade-in or fade-out, simply grab the top corner of any clip and drag it back into the clip.

1. **Open Vegas Video and start a new project by choosing New from the file menu.**

2. **Find clips for your timeline in the explorer window.** Make sure that the Explorer tab in the lower-left corner is selected and browse for clips as you do when you use Windows Explorer.

3. **Grab the first clip you want and drag it onto the timeline.**

4. **Adjust the rough in and out point of the video by grabbing the ends of the clip and dragging back and forth.** You can fine-tune this later when you see what the edit looks like flowing into the next clip. The result is previewed in the preview window. Don't worry — all edits in Vegas Video are non-destructive (unless you specifically perform a permanent edit). The original video is unaffected.

5. **When you're happy with the rough in and out points of the first clip, find the second clip you want in the Explorer window, and drag it onto your timeline.**

6. **Again, find rough in and out points.**

7. **Drag it until it just touches the first clip and test your edit.** You can fine-tune the in and out points of either clip.

8. **If you drag into a position where it overlaps another clip, a crossfade transition is automatically applied.** Try to keep these short if you must use them.

Keep adding clips in this fashion until your video is finished. This example doesn't even begin to scratch the surface of what you can accomplish with Vegas Video or any other decent video editing platform, but you should have enough information to get started. I encourage you to read the manual that came with your software!

Rendering an uncompressed master using Vegas Video

After you've arranged all your clips on your timeline, you have to render the result. Vegas Video doesn't have to render transitions to preview them; however, you must render the result if you want to have a master version.

To render an uncompressed master, choose Render As from the File menu. The Render As window (see Figure 9-12) appears. You should save to either an AVI or a MOV file so that other programs are able to open up the file.

Save masters as either MOV or AVI files for maximum portability

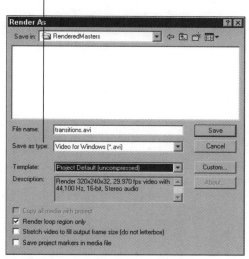

Figure 9-12: Rendering files in Vegas Video

The template defaults to whatever specifications you set up for this particular project, but these can be modified by clicking on the Custom button. For most streaming media applications, you should save a 320 × 240 master at 29.97 frames per second, with 44.1Khz, 16-bit stereo audio.

Rendering streaming media files directly using Vegas Video

By using Vegas Video, you can also render directly from the timeline to all three of the major streaming media formats. All you have to do is select the appropriate file type in the Render As window (see Figure 9-13).

Each streaming media platform has a number of default templates. In addition, you can modify and create your own templates by clicking on the Custom button. By creating standardized templates for all your streaming files, you can avoid confusion as to which template to use.

Choose the template and click OK. That's all you need to do.

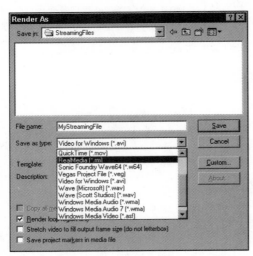

Figure 9-13: Rendering streaming media
files directly from Vegas Video

Summary

Basic capturing, editing, and rendering are easy as long as you follow a few simple principles. In the next chapter, methods of optimizing your video files are discussed so that you can get the most out of your streaming files.

✦ Your video capture card determines the quality of your captures and also the quality of your streaming media files.

✦ The quality of your captures is limited by the maximum data rate your computer and hard drives can sustain reliably.

✦ Capture at ¼ screen unless you're planning on streaming full frame content over very high bit rate connections.

✦ Avoid using any codecs during capture; if your capture card uses a built-in hardware codec, use the lowest compression ratio or highest data rate possible.

✦ If you must use transitions during the editing stage, make them short. Long transitions wreak havoc with streaming codecs.

✦ Be sure to plan ahead by filming some cutaways when filming your content — cutaways give you flexibility in the editing stage.

✦ Render at the highest quality possible or render directly to streaming versions of your files if your video editing software supports it.

✦ Check with your streaming media encoder to see if it accepts compressed (MJPEG) files as input. This determines whether your rendered masters need to be uncompressed files or can be rendered using the capture card's native codec.

✦　　✦　　✦

Optimizing Your Video Files

The basics of capturing, editing, and rendering are simple. If your content is well produced, your streaming files should turn out just fine. In the never-ending quest for quality, you should now be aware of few truths.

Working with video files is tricky. You have many variables to consider, all interrelated, so much so that the corrective measures available are limited. Correcting badly lit video, for example, is incredibly difficult to do. You have no way to correct video that is out of focus, and you cannot remove video "noise" without affecting the quality of the whole video.

The other problem is that video files are very large. Any time you want to adjust something, for example adjusting the contrast, each and every pixel of every frame of your video must be processed. Doing so takes time.

These problems only reinforce the point that I made in the creation section of this book that taking your time when shooting the video is extremely important. There are, however, a few tricks that you can employ to optimize your video files before encoding, and a few issues of which you need to be aware of because they can compromise the quality of your encoded files.

The discussions in this chapter fall into three main categories:

◆ **Video signal processing:** Video signal processing can be used to correct or enhance the video image.

◆ **Sizing issues:** Resizing video can introduce significant distortion to the video if not done carefully

◆ **Cropping issues:** Cropping noise or unwanted areas out of your video can lead to better quality encodes

Video Signal Processing

Video signal processing involves adjusting the way the video looks by manipulating the overall luminance (brightness), contrast, and color balance of the video. Be very careful when doing this, because they are all interrelated, and they depend largely on viewing conditions. The same piece of video looks different when viewed under different conditions.

One challenge of producing streaming video files is that most streaming video is watched in brightly lit offices, which makes it hard to see. Also, many people adjust their computer monitors to compensate for their environment. Because you cannot control either of these factors, you're taking somewhat of a stab in the dark when trying to adjust your video signal.

Another issue is that increasing the contrast and brightness of a video signal can make it more difficult to encode the file. Video noise or insignificant background detail can be made more noticeable, both to the viewer and to the codec, which expends bits trying to encode this excessive detail.

Using caution is the best approach. If you're not absolutely sure that adjusting your video image is helping, don't do it. This method may sound a bit conservative, but to be honest, inexperience can do more harm than good. If you decide that you want to adjust your video, you can do so by using dedicated hardware or by using software.

Hardware proc amps

Video-processing amplifiers, or *proc amps*, are available from a number of manufacturers. Proc amps are desirable because they let you adjust the video picture in real-time, which is a distinct advantage over many software-based proc amps. In live encoding situations, they are indispensable.

Many video capture cards have proc amp controls built-in, but unless you have a premium-quality capture card, they are seldom of as high quality as a dedicated hardware proc amp. Cheap capture card proc amps do not offer the quality or fine level of control available with a hardware proc amp. Also, many capture-card based proc amps do not allow you to adjust the settings after capture begins.

Software proc amps

Software-based proc amps have the advantage of extremely granular control. If you want to apply video processing to one scene of an already edited video, you can simply apply the necessary processing to those frames, leaving the rest of the video unaffected. Doing this with a hardware proc amp involves recapturing the scene with different proc amp settings.

Another advantage to software proc amps is that you can undo an operation if you don't like it. Similarly, with some video editing platforms, you can template video processing operations, so you can repeat video processing operations if necessary.

Using a proc amp

Proc amp controls vary slightly between manufacturers, but essentially they enable the adjustment of the brightness, contrast, and color balance of the incoming video signal. Using a proc amp entails using your eyes and turning knobs or sliding faders in software until the picture looks correct.

One of the reasons proc amps can be useful is that video looks different when displayed on VGA monitors than it does displayed on standard video monitors. A good approach to using a proc amp is to compare how your video looks on a standard video monitor with the same video displayed on a VGA monitor. Video generally looks darker on VGA monitors than it does on standard video monitors. You can compensate for this using a proc amp.

Caution　If your project is going to be rendered back out to tape and played back on a standard monitor in addition to a streaming version, you should *not* adjust the video to look the same on the VGA monitor as it does on the standard monitor during capture. You should only adjust video content that is exclusively for VGA monitor playback. Therefore, you should use a software proc amp to adjust the video for the streaming version only.

If you're using a hardware proc amp, you adjust the video before it is captured. The best way to do this is to split the video signal into two paths, one to a standard video monitor without the proc amp, and the other to the video capture board with the proc amp in-line. Play back the video and adjust the proc amp settings until the video on the computer monitor matches the video on the standard monitor as closely as possible. When you're happy with the quality of the picture on the VGA monitor, rewind the video and capture it as usual.

If you're using a software proc amp, how you use it depends on the particular implementation in your video editing software. Some allow real-time manipulation during capture; others only operate on video that has been captured. As with a hardware proc amp, the idea is to make the video look the same on a VGA monitor as it does on a standard video monitor. Read your video editing software's manual for the recommended approach.

In addition to using a proc amp to make video look the same on VGA monitors as it does on standard monitors, you can also use it to try to salvage poorly lit scenes or to extract detail from washed out scenes.

If a clip seems dark and murky, you can try adding a bit of brightness. Be careful, though, because if you add brightness, the entire clip is brightened — including areas of the screen that are supposed to be black. To add detail, you can try pumping up the contrast. This, too, should also be used with caution. Increased contrast can degrade the encoded versions due to the increased grain.

Using Video Filters

Using filters is another way to optimize your video. These filters are not special effects — they're designed to address specific issues that arise with digitized video. The first two filters, deinterlace and inverse telecine, are used to deal with particular types of video content. The third, noise reduction is used on low quality input.

Deinterlace filter

The deinterlace filter is designed to reduce artifacts that are introduced when interlaced content (TV) is converted to progressive scan (computer monitor). Interlacing artifacts occur when the two fields that make up an interlaced frame are combined and are most noticeable when there is horizontal motion in the frame (see Figure 10-1). The deinterlace filter uses a complex algorithm to make the artifacts less noticeable.

Detail

Both fields of an interlaced video displayed concurrently

Figure 10-1: Why deinterlace filters are necessary

These artifacts are only introduced when the screen size is more than 240 pixels tall. With smaller screens, one of the fields that makes up an interlaced display is discarded and therefore the artifacts do not appear. All content that has a screen height larger than 240 lines should be deinterlaced.

For a discussion about interlaced versus noninterlaced displays, please turn to Chapter 2.

Inverse telecine filter

The inverse telecine filter should be used on content that was originally shot on film and transferred to video. This type of video content has duplicate frames that are inserted during the film-to-video process, because film content is shot at 24 frames per second and video at 30. These extra frames can be detected and removed before the encoding takes place, which prevents bits from being wasted encoding redundant content.

For a discussion about the telecine process, please turn to Chapter 2.

Noise reduction

Low-quality video input is said to be *noisy*. Noise can be visible as grain or snow in the picture, or it can be invisible to the naked eye. Codecs cannot distinguish video noise from other detail and motion in the frame. They expend bits when trying to encode the noise, when in fact they should be ignoring it.

Noise filters can reduce the amount of noise in a video signal and therefore increase the quality of your encoded video. A noise filter is essentially a very slight blur filter. By blurring the content ever so slightly, the video can be made to appear smoother, and the apparent motion of the noise is reduced. This smoothing helps the codec by reducing the amount of detail in the picture. Having less detail in the picture enables the codec to concentrate on more important elements in the video frame.

Noise filters can lead to overall loss of detail in the video frame. Some noise filters are better than others and try to maintain good edge detail; others are less discriminate. Be sure to check that the noise filter isn't doing more harm than good.

Resizing Video

Resizing video is a fairly complicated process. To be as accurate as possible, each pixel of the original video has to be averaged with the ones around it by using complex algorithms. If it is not done correctly, the video image appears distorted. Aliasing, visible as jagged edges on diagonal lines, is a common side effect of poor re-sizing.

Additionally, if you inadvertently stretch the video when resizing, the image distorts. This distortion is passed on to the encoder, which compromises the quality of the encoded file. To minimize this type of distortion, you have to be careful with your aspect ratio.

Aspect ratios

The aspect ratio is the ratio between the width and height of your video image. Video content is shot at a 4:3 aspect ratio, also known as 1.33:1. Therefore, the screen is 1.33 times wider than it is tall. Film is shot at a number of different aspect ratios varying from 1.33:1 to as wide as 2.35:1. The proposed standard for HDTV is 16:9, or 1.78:1.

Regardless of what aspect ratio your content is shot at, maintaining the same aspect ratio when resizing is very important. If you don't, the resulting video is stretched in one dimension or the other. Not only does stretched video look unprofessional, but also the distortion the stretching introduces compromises the quality of the encoded file.

Unless you've invested in an HDTV system, you're going to be shooting and capturing your video at a 4:3 aspect ratio. Therefore, you should always resize to a 4:3 aspect ratio. If you want video that is not a 4:3 aspect ratio, you should crop your frame rather than resizing it.

If you do end up cropping your frame, you have to be careful to crop to a 4:3 aspect ratio, or again, your video ends up being stretched (see the next section, "Cropping Video").

Aspect ratios can be somewhat confusing, especially because some confusion exists as to what the dimensions of a full broadcast frame are, and some streaming media vendors used to recommend encoding at screen sizes that are clearly not 4:3 aspect ratios (176 × 144 pixels).

Note The 176 × 144 pixel screen size was initially recommended by RealNetworks and Microsoft because these dimensions are the standardized size for H.261 encoding algorithms, which derives from ¼ of PAL broadcast size (704 × 576). Neither RealNetworks or Microsoft recommend this size any longer, though for legacy reasons you can still find it in the size choices in the Windows Media Encoder.

For a brief discussion of the differences between 4:3 aspect ratios on TV screens and progressive scan monitors, see the "Square Versus Nonsquare Pixels" side bar. As far as using non 4:3 screen sizes is concerned, any 4:3 video content that is resized and/or encoded at a non-4:3 aspect ratio is distorted — period. Whether this effect is pleasing or not is in the eye of the beholder.

Square Versus Nonsquare Pixels

If you have a medium or high-quality capture card, you may notice that when you capture full screen, it defaults to a screen size of 720 × 480 pixels. On the other hand, you know that a 4:3 aspect ratio dictates that the size *should* be 640 × 480 pixels. What's going on?

Television pixels aren't square; they're slightly taller than they are wide. So even though the pixel dimensions appear to be wrong, when they're projected on a TV screen the resulting picture is actually the proper 4:3 aspect ratio.

However, when you display this video on a VGA monitor, the video appears slightly stretched in the horizontal direction, or more correctly, it *isn't* stretched in the vertical direction like it is on a TV screen. The reason is that the VGA pixels are square, unlike their TV screen counterparts. The following figure illustrates the image distortion that can occur if you aren't careful.

720 x 480 displayed on television screen   720 x 480 displayed on VGA monitor
(non-square pixels)   (square pixels)

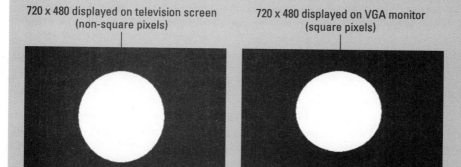

Pixels are slightly taller than they are wide on non-square pixel displays. To maintain the proper aspect ratio on square pixel displays, captured video must be resized to a 4:3 aspect ratio, such as 640 × 480 or 320 × 240.

If you're printing back out to tape, it's academic because you want to maintain the proper pixel dimensions for a TV screen. If, however, you're creating streaming media files, you must resize the video to a proper 4:3 aspect ratio, such as 640 × 480 pixels or 320 × 240 pixels.

Similarly, if you're creating graphics on a computer monitor and want them to display correctly on a television monitor, you have to take the nonsquare pixels into account. The simplest way to do this is to create your graphics at 720 × 540 and then resize to 720 × 480. The graphics will appear slightly squashed on a computer monitor but will look correct when displayed on a television screen.

Cropping Video

Sometimes cropping out part of your video frame is necessary. Cropping is different than resizing in that the cropped material is completely removed from the signal, leaving a smaller video frame. Care must be taken to maintain a 4:3 aspect ratio when cropping.

The two most common examples of when cropping is necessary are when you can see garbage in the overscan area of the video image and when you want to get rid of letter boxing.

Overscan

Overscan is the area around the edges of a video image that is not normally visible when displayed on a television monitor. All television screens have plastic surrounds that cover the extreme edges of the picture tube, in effect *cropping* the image. When you capture video, however, you capture the entire video image and sometimes with low-quality video sources, the overscan can contain video noise. This video noise must be removed.

Letterboxing

In general, when film content is shown on a television screen, the image is cropped to fit into a 4:3 aspect ratio. Alternatively, a wider image can be shown. To maintain the aspect ratio of the original, however, the top and bottom of the screen must be filled with black.

As a streaming media author, the black bars at the top and bottom of the screen are problematic for a couple of reasons:

✦ Even though nothing is happening in the black bars, they must be encoded anyway, which is a waste of encoding bits.

✦ The black bars prevent the codec from doing vertical motion estimation, because objects that bob in and out of the letterboxed frame do not leave the 4:3 aspect ratio frame — they only disappear into the black bars.

You can approach this problem in three different ways:

✦ Crop off the black bars and encode at a different aspect ratio, such as 16:9 (320 × 180)

✦ Crop to a 4:3 aspect ratio that does not include the black bars

✦ Leave the black bars on as a compromise

Visually, the first option is superior because you do not lose any of the video image. One drawback to this approach is that the Real System and Windows Media Technologies require all clips to be of the exact same size and encoding specs if you plan on doing any simulated live broadcasts, so you cannot mix 4:3 content with 16:9.

The second option preserves the compatibility with all the other 4:3 clips, but sacrifices some of the image. These options are demonstrated in the next section.

Video Cropping and Resizing Examples

The following two examples show how cropping and resizing are intimately entwined when trying to keep video quality at its highest. Because each video editing platform (and streaming media encoder) has its own method of cropping, you should refer to the documentation and instructions for cropping video in the video editing software that you use. The following examples illustrate how to use Adobe Premiere and Vegas Video.

Getting rid of overscan

Figure 10-2 shows an extreme example of a low-quality video that is off center and has lots of garbage in the overscan area. The right side has a large black stripe that needs to be removed. In addition the top, bottom, and left side of the screen have a bit of fuzziness that you should crop.

The original was captured at 320×240 pixels; the black stripe down the right side is about 11 pixels or so wide. An additional four pixels or so needs to be cropped from the left side. By adding these numbers, you'll find that a total of 15 pixels must be shaved off the width of this video.

You also must crop the height to maintain the 4:3 aspect ratio, and in this case, you want to crop off a bit anyway to get rid of the fuzziness. The amount you crop is determined by the aspect ratio. For every four pixels you crop off the width, you must crop three pixels off of the height.

If you increase the number of pixels cropped from the width to 16, the number is evenly divisible by 4, indicating that you should crop 12 pixels off the height:

```
16 pixels * (3 pixels width per 4 pixels height) = 12 pixels
```

After the crop, you are left with a frame that is 304×228 pixels, — the proper 4:3 (1.33:1) aspect ratio. This cropped video can be rendered to a 4:3 frame size without spatial distortion.

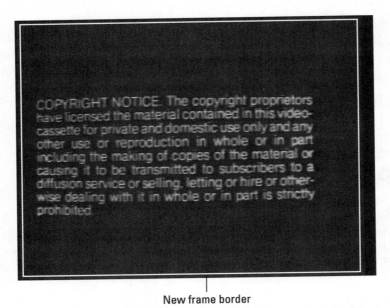

New frame border

Figure 10-2: An example of low-quality video that should have the overscan area cropped out

Note   All resizing involves a certain amount of image distortion, because resizing is never perfect. However, if you stay true to your aspect ratio, the distortion is minimized.

Cropping overscan using Adobe Premiere

Cropping in Adobe Premiere is part of the export process. To crop in Adobe Premiere, follow these steps:

1. **From the Adobe Premiere timeline window, you can export by typing Ctrl+M or choosing Export ⇨ Movie from the File menu.** The Export Movie window appears (see Figure 10-3). The current settings are listed in the lower-left corner, but the crop settings are not listed.

2. **To access the settings dialog box, click the Settings button in the lower-right corner.** The Export Movie Settings window appears (see Figure 10-4).

3. **Click the Modify button to access the Special Processing Settings window (see Figure 10-5).** The actual crop settings are displayed.

4. **You can either specify the settings by typing values manually or by dragging the corners of the crop guides.** Make sure that the total amounts you crop from the height and width correspond to the aspect ratio.

5. **Click OK to return to the Export Movie Settings window.** The settings you entered should be reflected in the display on the left side. If the settings look correct, click OK to return to the Export Movie window.

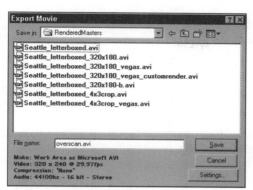

Figure 10-3: The Adobe Premiere Export Movie window

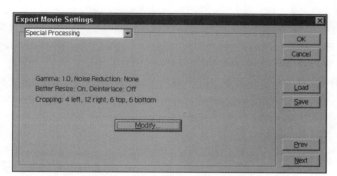

Figure 10-4: The Adobe Premiere Export Movie Settings window

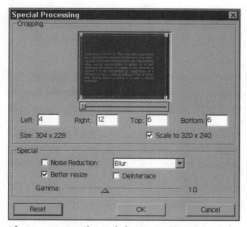

Figure 10-5: The Adobe Premiere Special Processing Settings window

6. **Make sure that the file name is correct or type a new file name.**

7. **Click Save to render the movie that now appears with overscan removed.**

Cropping overscan using Vegas Video

Cropping in Vegas Video is part of each individual video track. To crop in Vegas Video, follow these steps:

1. **To access the crop settings, click the small Event Pan/Crop icon that is located on the right side of your clip (see Figure 10-6).** The Event Pan/Crop window appears (see Figure 10-7) in which you specify the crop settings.

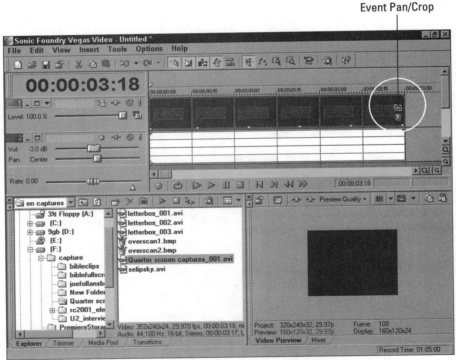

Figure 10-6: Accessing the pan/crop settings in Vegas Video

In this window, you can enter values manually or drag the crop guides to set your crop. As long as the Maintain aspect ratio on the left side is toggled to the on position, you can drag any guide anywhere you like — the aspect ratio is always maintained. In this case, though, you do not want the cropped area centered on the original center, because the overscan is so much worse on one side of the frame.

Aspect ratio button

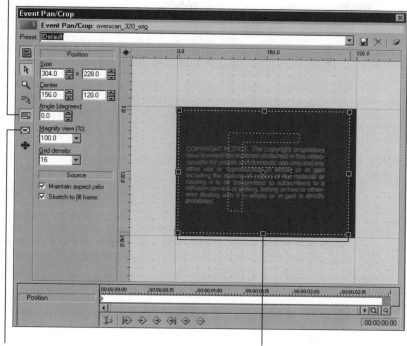

Center crop area button   Crop guides

Figure 10-7: The Vegas Video Event Pan/Crop window

2. **Deselect the centering option (as shown previously in Figure 10-7).**

3. **When you're happy with the crop settings, close the window by clicking on the close window icon (the X) in the top-right corner of the window.** The clip is now cropped in preview mode, so you can check your settings.

Note

You may want to create a template for mild cases of overscan that crops four pixels off the left and right and three pixels off the top and bottom. Then you can simply use the template.

If your video consists of multiple clips, you must specify a crop for each clip individually. Crop settings are unique to each clip; you can't apply a global setting as you can in Premiere. If the clip(s) look good when you preview them, you can either render them as uncompressed master versions or as streaming media versions directly.

Dealing with letterboxed content

Letterboxed content can be dealt with in three different ways, as detailed above. These examples shows how to crop off the black bars to obtain a 16:9 aspect ratio and how to crop into the image maintaining a 4:3 aspect ratio. Letterboxing comes in a number of different aspect ratios. You may need to fine-tune your settings to obtain the best results. The example uses a clip with a standard 16:9 letterbox aspect ratio.

The following examples illustrate dealing with letterboxed content using Adobe Premiere and Vegas Video.

Dealing with letterboxed content using Adobe Premiere

Dealing with letterboxed clips using Adobe Premiere is slightly tricky. You should always leave the project settings at what the video was captured at. If you captured at 4:3 and want to crop to 16:9, leave the project output settings at the default 4:3 aspect ratio.

Leaving the project settings at 4:3 can be confusing because the settings listed in the Export Movie window say 320 × 240 and do not list the crop settings. As long as your crop settings in the Special Processing window are correctly set, the rendered version ends up being the 16:9 version.

Rendering a 16:9 version

To render a 16:9 version, follow these steps:

1. **Open the Export Movie window by typing Ctrl+M or by choosing Export ⇨ Movie from the File menu.** The Export Movie window appears (shown in Figure 10-3 previously).

2. **Click on the Settings button.** The Export Movie Settings window appears (shown previously in Figure 10-4).

3. **Choose Special Processing from the drop-down menu and click on the Modify button to display the Special Processing window (see Figure 10-8).**

4. **Make sure that the Scale to checkbox is _not_ checked; otherwise the video is stretched to fill the entire project screen.**

5. **Adjust the top and bottom crop values until the black bars are no longer in the frame.**

6. **Click OK to return to the Export Movie Settings window and again to return to the Export Movie window.** Note that the settings displayed in this window still indicate that the video is being exported at 320 × 240 pixels — you can ignore this because the crop settings are not taken into account here.

7. **Click Save to render the letterboxed version.**

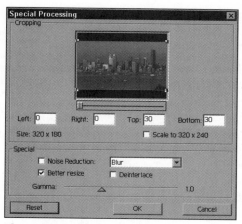

Figure 10-8: Setting up a letterbox crop in the Adobe Premiere Special Processing Settings window

Rendering a 4:3 version

The steps for rendering a 4:3 version are exactly the same as the steps you followed in the preceding section, but with two notable exceptions (see Figure 10-9).

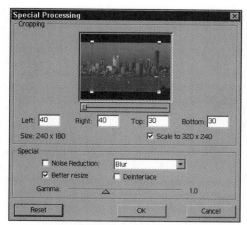

Figure 10-9: Cropping a letterboxed video down to a 4:3 aspect ratio by using Adobe Premiere

This time, you must also crop from the left and right to maintain the 4:3 aspect ratio. And you must check the Scale to... box if you want the resultant video stretched back up to 320 × 240 pixels.

Cropping a letterboxed video and then stretching it back up to full size is not the best idea. If you want to do this, you can obtain better quality by capturing at full screen, cropping, and then rendering a 320 × 240-pixel version.

Dealing with letterboxing using Vegas Video

Because cropping in Vegas Video is a property of each individual clip and occurs before the rendering process, you must set your project settings to reflect the 16:9 aspect ratio. If you don't, clips are rendered with black bars on the top and bottom — which is precisely what you're trying to get rid of!

Rendering a 16:9 version

To render a 16:9 version, follow these steps:

1. **Choose Properties from the File menu or type Alt+Enter to open the project settings window (see Figure 10-10).**

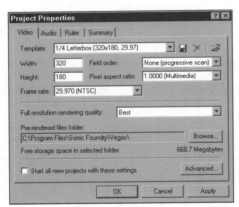

Figure 10-10: The Vegas Video project

2. **Set the appropriate width and height dimensions. Save a template if you're going to do a lot of work with 16:9 video.**

3. **Click Apply and the OK button to return to the main window.**

4. **Open up the Event Pan/Crop window by clicking on the icon on the right side of your clip (as shown in Figure 10-6 previously).** Vegas Video offers a number of letterbox presets.

5. **Choose the 16:9 Widescreen TV Aspect Ratio preset from the drop-down menu at the top of the window (see Figure 10-11).** The preset defaults to the full width of your window and crops enough pixels from the top and bottom of the window to achieve a 16:9 aspect ratio.

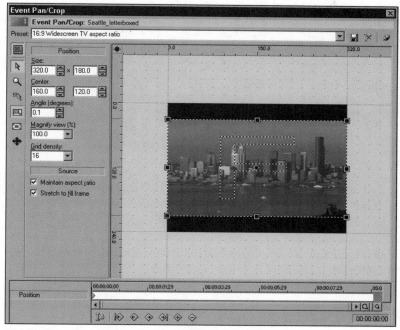

Figure 10-11: Using the Vegas Video 16:9 preset

If the 16:9 preset doesn't quite get rid of the black bars, you can try the 1.85:1 Academy aspect ratio preset. If this looks better, you can either choose to render at the project size using this setting (making sure the Stretch to fit window checkbox is selected), or tweak your project settings to match a 1.85.1 aspect ratio (320 × 172).

6. **Close the window by clicking on the X in the top-right corner.**

7. **Render as usual.**

Rendering a 4:3 version

To render a 4:3 version, you'd follow the same steps as you did when cropping off overscan, however, you'd leave the Centering button checked. All you have to do is grab any crop guide and move it until the crop window fits within the black bars (see Figure 10-12).

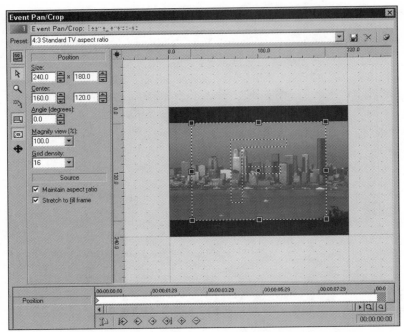

Figure 10-12: Cropping a letterboxed video down to a 4:3 aspect ratio using Vegas Video

Alternative method for rendering 16:9 version

You don't have to have your project properties set up for a 16:9 aspect ratio to render out 16:9 videos. Alternatively, you can set up a custom frame size when you render.

To accomplish this, simply click the Custom button in the Render As window. The Custom Settings window appears as shown in Figure 10-13.

Click on the Video tab to display the video settings window, and set up your window width and height. Save a template if you plan on using the settings often.

It's better to set project settings properly as described previously so that you can preview your video without distortion, but this method certainly produces the proper output.

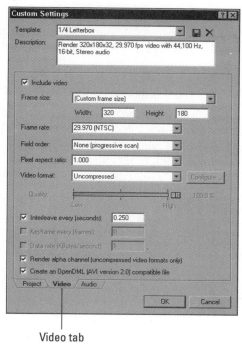

Video tab

Figure 10-13: Setting up custom render settings in Vegas Video

Summary

In this chapter, you learned how to improve the quality of your video. In the next chapter, you explore various methods of automating these video optimization tasks so that you do not become a slave to your video capture station.

✦ Proc amps can be used to adjust video signal quality, but you should use them with caution.

✦ Video displayed on VGA monitors looks different — proc amps can minimize this difference.

✦ Do not adjust video during capture to match video displayed on standard monitors if the video project may be printed back to tape and viewed on standard monitors. In this case, you should use a software proc amp only on the streaming version.

✦ Use a deinterlace filter on all content larger than 320 x 240 pixels.

✦ Use the inverse telecine filter on any content that originated on film to remove the extra frames that are inserted during the telecine process.

✦ Using a noise filter on low quality video can improve encode quality.

✦ When cropping or resizing, always maintain a consistent aspect ratio to avoid image distortion.

✦ Crop out noise in the overscan area.

✦ You can crop the black bars from letterboxed content and render using a different aspect ratio, crop to a 4:3 aspect ratio, or simply leave the video letterboxed.

✦   ✦   ✦

Automation: The Power of Batch Processing

Part II of this book has covered the basics of audio and video capturing, editing, signal processing, and rendering. Each of these steps is important in the creation process, and each can be time consuming. What's more, much of the time consumed is spent waiting for your computer to finish doing something — essentially wasted time.

After you find settings that work for your content, you can standardize your streaming media process by using consistent settings at each stage in the creation process. Doing so not only keeps the quality of your content consistent, but also enables you to automate some parts of the process. Best of all, the automation can often be scheduled to be performed when your computing resources are otherwise idle, such as overnight.

Each stage of the creation process can be automated to some extent. Both audio and video capture can be done unattended. The signal processing that has been discussed can be done via templates in virtually every audio and video editing software program, and many of them offer extensive batch processing built in. Lastly, rendering video, which is extremely time consuming, can be done automatically.

The automation capabilities that are discussed in this chapter are available in many forms, with the implementation varying slightly from program to program. A few examples are discussed in each section. Of course, you should refer to your documentation for details about how batch processing is implemented in your software.

Batch Capturing Media

Capturing your media is time consuming because it generally happens in real-time. If you have a lot of media to digitize, you can end up sitting around for a long time.

On one hand, it's not a bad idea to sit through the capture stage, because it re-acquaints you with your material. If you are planning on editing your content you should be aware of all that you have available. Then again, you may have done an excellent job logging your footage when it was recorded and just want to digitize the sections that you know you're going to use. This is particularly useful when digitizing video.

If you decide you want to try to capture your media unattended, there are a number of options available. Some are as simple as setting a time limit to your captures; others are more involved and involve actual control of external devices.

Batch capturing audio

Most audio editing software programs offer some sort of automated capture, generally timed captures and sometimes also CD "ripping" capabilities (pulling the digital information directly off the CD). Some systems also offer advanced control of external devices via SMPTE code.

Time-limited capture

The simplest way of automating your audio captures is to set a time limit to the recording process. It's easy to set audio levels, press the record button, and walk away from an audio capture, but it's a good idea to specify a length of time for the recording, because if you forget that you are recording:

✦ You end up with a file five times larger than it needs to be

✦ Your hard drive fills up and crashes the computer, forcing you to start over again

Figure 11-1 shows how to set up a time limit for your audio capture using Sound Forge. The implementation may vary slightly, but this capability is available from virtually all audio editing software programs. To specify a timed record in Sound Forge, choose the Punch In mode from the drop-down menu. To specify the length you want to records by, set the Start and End times, or just set the Length value — the recording stops automatically when the time limit is reached.

CD ripping

If you're recording from audio CDs, you can extract or *rip* the digital information directly off the disc instead of recording the audio. Ripping is highly advantageous because modern CD-ROM devices are capable of extracting the information at speeds that are many times faster than real-time. If you're digitizing albums, metadata for each track can also be retrieved from one of the CD music database companies.

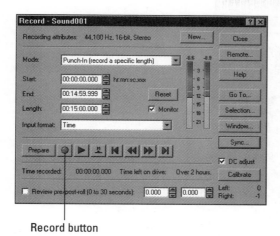

Record button

Figure 11-1: Setting up a time-limited capture using Sound Forge

Figure 11-2 shows how tracks can be extracted using Sound Forge. This is also implemented in Peak and many other audio editing programs. Note that you must have a CD-ROM that supports direct audio extraction — not all CD-ROM drives do. In Sound Forge, you extract the audio directly from the CD by selecting the Extra Audio from CD option from the Tools menu. You need to make sure that the appropriate drive is selected in the drop-down menu and choose Read by tracks to get each track extracted into its own window. You can select individual tracks by highlighting them or select all of the tracks by selecting the first track scrolling to the end of the list and select the last track while holding the shift key down. Remember too that if you choose the Read entire CD button, all of the tracks fall into a single file and this might not be what you intended.

Note   Audio CD extraction is not supported under Mac OS 10.1. Please check the Apple Web site for updates (www.apple.com/macosx).

As soon as your files have been extracted, you can save them as is, or you can process the files and save them in your favorite streaming format.

Synchronizing devices via SMPTE timecode and MIDI machine control

Many audiovisual devices can be synchronized via SMPTE timecode. Synchronizing audiovisual devices involves having a master unit that determines the master time-code to which all the other units *slave to* or *chase*. MIDI machine control is another standard used to send commands from one machine to another. Different hardware units offer different amounts of control, as do different software platforms.

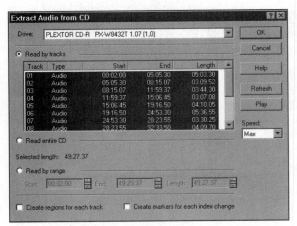

Figure 11-2: Extracting audio directly from CDs using Sound Forge

Setting up a fully automated, SMPTE driven capture system is no simple affair. The problem, as with most tasks involving different manufacturers and a handful of standards, is that not everything always works as advertised.

Of course, I'm not to saying that setting up a fully automated system is impossible. However, automated video editing systems are far more common, and you're probably better off pursuing those options that are tried and true.

Batch capturing video

Much like audio editing programs, most professional video editing software platforms offer some sort of batch-capture functionality that generally involves some sort of device control. Device control enables the software to control the video playback machine so that only the desired sections of videotapes are captured, while the rest is skipped.

Of course, you must have a playback machine that can be controlled — not all can be. In particular, cheaper formats do not offer deck control, unless they have a FireWire port. Device control is built into the FireWire standard, so any device with a FireWire port should be capable of being controlled.

Before you enter into the world of automated batch capturing, however, you probably should play around with the simplest of unattended capture methods — the time-limited capture.

Time-limited capture

If you don't want to have another look at your footage while it is being captured, set a time limit on the footage being captured. This safeguards against the video file being much larger than it needs to be, and also safeguards your file from self-destructing by filling up the hard drive.

Capturing video files can fill up your drives in a hurry. Some software platforms or operating systems handle this gracefully, others do not. Instead of finding out the hard way, set a reasonable time limit on your capture.

Figure 11-3 shows where you can set a maximum capture length using the Vegas Video capture application. You can do the same thing in most other video editing platforms. It's a simple precaution, but one that can save you hours of grief.

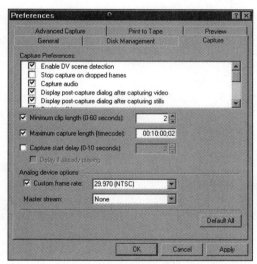

Figure 11-3: Setting a maximum video capture length using Vegas Video

Automating video capture via device control

You can use device control to control many pieces of video machinery remotely. You can choose from a number of device control systems, such as VLAN, MCI, or special third-party plug-ins. These systems have been in place for years at post-production houses and have recently become available on lower-priced, nonlinear editing systems.

With the recent adoption of the FireWire protocol by camera manufacturers and video editing software programs, device control has become much more accessible. Device control is built-in to the protocol, so that any OHCI compliant camera, capture card, and video editing system should be able to communicate via FireWire. This enables batch capture, which can be a large time and file space saver.

With batch capture, you preview the tape, logging the in and out points of the sections you want to capture. The video editing/capture software stores these in and out points. You can fast forward and rewind, choose clips in any order, and even switch tapes as long as you log the name of each reel from which you want to capture.

When you've logged all the footage you want to capture, you simply start the capture process. The system automatically rewinds the tape to the desired points on tape and captures the clips. If you logged clips from more than one reel of tape, the system cues you when you need to switch tapes.

By capturing in this manner, you can avoid having extra scenes lying around taking up valuable disc space. You also do not need to sit in front of the computer while it captures the required scenes. Provided you don't have to switch tapes, capturing can even be done overnight or during your lunch hour.

The following section provides an example of batch capture using a FireWire system.

Using FireWire to batch capture video content

If you're using a DV system to film your video content, a FireWire setup makes a lot of sense — not only because it's cheap, but also because you can generally do a lot of cool things via FireWire including batch capture. The initial setup can be a little tricky, but it's a lot simpler than setting up a VLAN system and a heck of a lot cheaper.

Caution

FireWire support has matured a great deal in the last couple of years, but it is not yet plug and play. Virtually every video editing software system has a Troubleshooting 1394 issues document that you can download from their Web site. Usually, you can solve these problems fairly easily.

The following example uses Adobe Premiere 6.0 and the ADS 1394 DV card to implement batch capture.

1. **Open Adobe Premiere 6.0 and choose appropriate project settings for your project.** Because this example demonstrates capturing standard DV content with 48 kHz audio, the Standard 48 kHz preset was chosen (see Figure 11-4).

2. **Open up the movie capture window by choosing Capture ➪ Movie Capture from the File menu (see Figure 11-5).**

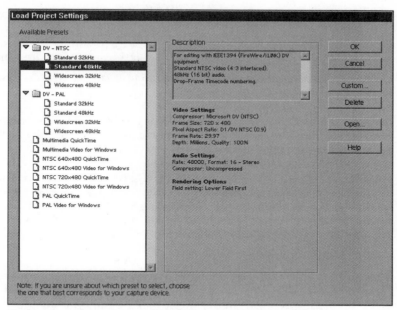

Figure 11-4: Choosing project settings in Adobe Premiere 6.0

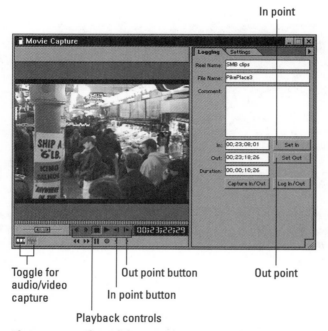

Figure 11-5: The Adobe Premiere 6.0 Movie Capture window

You can use the playback controls in this window to look for the clips you want to capture. If you don't get a preview of what's on your tape, trouble-shoot according to your camera/capture card/video editing software. In most cases you should see video displayed in the movie capture window.

3. **Mark clips you want captured by setting in and out points.** Make sure to leave a little extra on the front and back ends for editing purposes.

 Tip The timecode on DV format cameras is not known for its pinpoint accuracy. For this reason it's a good idea to leave a little breathing room on either side of your desired content.

4. **To use batch capture, you must log each clip by clicking on the Log In/Out button each time you set in and out points for a clip.** Doing so opens a small window that allows you to type in a filename for the captured video, as well as any comments you'd like to include. These comments can be handy later, because they are displayed in the clip bin.

5. **Click OK to finish logging the clip.**

6. **After you log your first clip, the Batch Capture window appears (see Figure 11-6).** As you add clips, you should see them added to the list of files to be captured. When you're done logging all the clips you want to capture, you can edit in and out points, filenames, and just about everything else in this window.

✔	Reel Name	In Point	Out Point	Duration	File Name	Log Comment
✕	SMB clips	00;15;16;13	00;15;27;16	00;00;11;04	Seattle	
✕	SMB clips	00;16;45;02	00;16;57;17	00;00;12;16	SunsetTug	
✕	SMB clips	00;19;33;21	00;20;07;04	00;00;33;14	FerryCrossing	
✔	SMB clips	00;21;24;10	00;21;35;17	00;00;11;08	SpaceNeedle	
✔	SMB clips	00;21;49;11	00;21;59;16	00;00;10;06	PikePlace	
✔	SMB clips	00;23;08;01	00;23;18;26	00;00;10;26	PikePlace2	

Batch Capture: SMBclips.pbl

Total Duration: 00;01;29;16   Uncaptured Duration: 00;00;00;00

Record button

Figure 11-6: The Adobe Premiere 6.0 Batch Capture window

7. **After you've logged all the clips you want to capture off the tape reel, you can either log clips on another tape reel, or you can go ahead and capture all the clips that you logged.** Before you start the batch capture, save your batch capture list by choosing Save As from the File menu and saving the file in .pbl format.

8. **Start the batch capture by clicking on the red record button in the lower-right corner.** It's a good idea to leave the machine alone while the capturing takes place. Any other processes on the machine increase the chance of dropped frames.

 Note In theory, FireWire captures should never have dropped frames, but there is a slight gap between theory and practice. Some FireWire capture utilities are smart enough to go back and recapture the dropped frames, while others are not.

Your clips are digitized and stored in the directory that you specified, and a bin is created in the project containing all the clips, along with any comments that you added. No need to stand around pushing the same buttons over and over — it's taken care of for you.

Batch Processing Media Files

After you've captured a number of media files, you may want to use the same settings to process them all. For example, you should normalize and lightly compress all your audio files, and for consistency's sake you should use the same settings for all your files. Or you may want to take all the video clips in a certain directory and crop off the letterbox bars. Either way, if you want to perform the same thing on a number of files, you should be using batch processing.

Batch processing audio files

In Chapter 8, I discussed various methods of optimizing your audio files. To make sure that the sound quality is consistent, you should:

✦ Normalize your files

✦ Lightly compress them

Most audio editors allow you to save your favorite settings as templates. You can use these templates to signal process all your audio files automatically by using batch processing

Using batch audio signal processing

The following example utilizes the Sonic Foundry Batch Converter, which is a stand-alone application that enables access to all the processing capabilities of Sound Forge.

1. **Open the Batch Converter program (see Figure 11-7).**

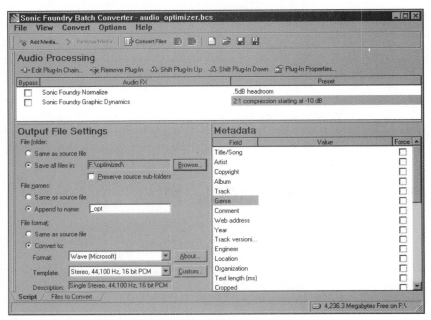

Figure 11-7: The Sonic Foundry Batch Converter

2. **To begin, set your output file settings by selecting a folder to save the processed files in and the format you want the files saved in.** Output file settings are set on the left side of the main screen of the Batch Converter, below the audio processing section. You can save uncompressed masters or save to any streaming format you want. You can also specify a suffix to append to the filename of each processed file to indicate that it has been processed.

   Depending on what output format you choose, you can also enter metadata. Some formats offer more metadata fields than others.

3. **To add plug-ins, click the Edit Plug-In Chain icon.** The Plug-In Chooser window appears (see Figure 11-8).

4. **Scroll through the plug-ins, highlight the Sonic Foundry Normalize plug-in and click the Add button.**

5. **Scroll back and find the Sonic Foundry Graphic Dynamics plug-in, highlight it, and click the Add button.** Now you've got a plug-in chain that includes normalization and compression.

6. **Click the OK button to return to the main window of the batch converter.** You should see that the two plug-ins have been added to the list of audio processing effects, both with Default all parameters in the preset column. Now you need to select the settings for each effect.

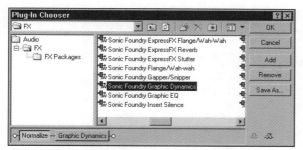

Figure 11-8: The Batch Converter Plug-In Chooser window

7. **Open the Normalize properties window.** Do this by highlighting the Normalize effect and clicking the Plug-In Properties icon or by double-clicking on the current settings for the Normalize effect that are listed in the Preset column. This opens the Properties window (see Figure 11-9).

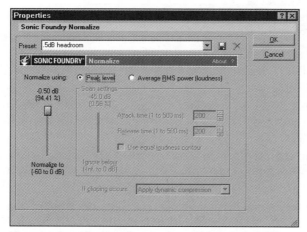

Figure 11-9: The Batch Converter Plug-In Normalize Properties window

If you've played around with Sound Forge at all, you should realize that this is the same window that you see when you use the Normalize effect. Set the mode to Peak level and set the fader to -0.5 dB. Name and save your preset for later use.

8. **Click OK to return to the main window.**

9. **Open the Graphic Dynamics Properties window (highlight and click the icon or double-click the preset).** The Graphic Dynamics Properties window appears as shown in Figure 11-10. Again, you see this window when using this effect in Sound Forge.

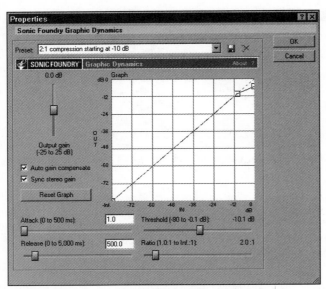

Figure 11-10: The Batch Converter Plug-In Graphic Dynamics Properties window

10. **Choose the 2:1 Compression starting at –10 dB preset. This setting is a mild compression setting.**

11. **Click OK to return to the main window.** You've got a good audio processing plug-in chain set up. Save yourself some work next time by saving these settings as a script.

12. **Choose Save Script from the File menu or type Ctrl+S.** Save this script as audio_optimizer.bcs. Your screen should now look exactly like Figure 11-7 that you saw previously.

13. **Now it's time to add some files to be processed by the Batch Converter using these settings.** You can do this by clicking on the Add Media icon just under the File menu or by typing Ctrl+M. Doing so opens the Add Media window and flips the batch converter into file view mode (see Figure 11-11).

14. **Browse for all the files you want to process and then add them to your list.** As you add files, you should see them appear in the main batch converter window.

15. **After you've added all the files you want, click on the Convert Files icon to start the batch process.** The amount of time it takes to complete the conversion process depends on the number and size of the files and the amount of processing being done to each file. The amount of time spent processing is also dependent on the speed of your CPU.

When the process is complete, your files are saved to the directory you specified, in the format you specified. What a timesaver!

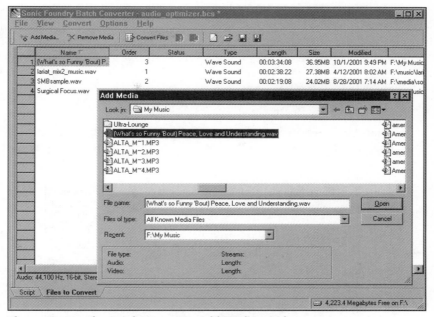

Figure 11-11: The Batch Converter Add Media window

Batch video processing

When processing video files, you also may want to run the same process on a group of clips. For example, you may have captured a number of clips that contain some overscan or that need to have the letterboxing removed. Both of these processes could be done automatically using batch processing.

Some implementations also allow you to run batch processing on whole projects. Batch processing of whole projects enables you to include rendering effects, such as fade ins and outs, transition effects, and anything else you may add during the editing stage.

By using this approach, you can set up projects to be rendered and then save the project file. Before you leave at night, you open up the batch processor and schedule all the projects that need to be rendered instead of rendering them during the day. By doing this process at night, you keep your resources working more hours of the day.

The following example demonstrates the batch processing capabilities of Adobe Premiere 6.0.

Using batch video processing

Adobe Premiere offers comprehensive batch processing functionality, enabling you to time-shift the drudgery of rendering to the wee hours of night. You can create custom templates for each project or file rendered. You cannot, however, render to streaming media formats.

1. **Launch Adobe Premiere.**

2. **Open the batch processor by choosing Utilities ⇨ Batch Processing from the Project menu.** The Batch Processing window is shown in Figure 11-12.

Figure 11-12: The Adobe Premiere Batch Processing window

3. **Add files, projects, or whole directories to the batch process by clicking on the Add button to open the Add Files window (see Figure 11-13).**

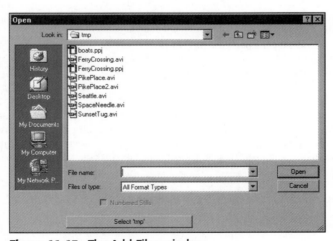

Figure 11-13: The Add Files window

4. **Add as many files, projects, or directories as you want.**

5. **For each item you add, you can specify a different batch processing setting.** To access the settings for an individual item, highlight the item and then click the Settings button. The Export Movie Settings window appears (see Figure 11-14).

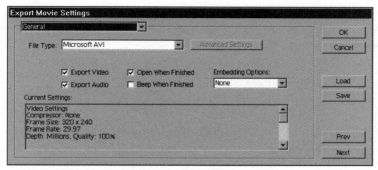

Figure 11-14: The Export Movie Settings window

6. **Choose settings for each item you added to the batch processor.** You can also specify filenames and directories for the output by clicking on the Target button.

7. **After you've chosen output settings for all your items, save the batch process by clicking on the Save button.** This saves a lot of effort later if you encounter any problems.

8. **Before you start up the batch process, click on the Check button to make sure that all the video clips referenced by all the projects are available.** If some clips are not, an appropriate error message is generated. This saves your batch process getting stuck in the middle of the night.

9. **Start up the batch processor by clicking the Make button.** The Batch Choices window appears, which enables you to choose between batch processing all the files or just selected files (see Figure 11-15).

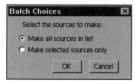

Figure 11-15: The Batch Choices window

10. **Choose the appropriate selection and click OK.**

Summary

Creating media can be a lot of fun, but even the most diligent among us could do with a bit less drudgery. By automating as much of your streaming media processes as possible, you reduce the amount of drudgery as well as lessen the probability of human error that comes with mindless, repetitive tasks. In this chapter, you learned:

✦ The simplest way to capture material without having to stick around is to set a time limit on the capture.

✦ Batch capturing allows you to specify clips on various reels to be captured without you having to perform the actual capturing.

✦ When batch capturing, you preview the reels and log the clips to be captured. The capture application can then be instructed to capture the clips automatically.

✦ If you want to perform the same processing on a number of files, you should use batch processing.

✦ A full-featured batch processor is a must-have for any serious streaming media producer.

✦   ✦   ✦

Encoding: Reducing Media Files to a Stream-Friendly Size

Choosing the Right Encoding Settings

No matter which streaming platform you decide to use, whether it's one of the Big Three (QuickTime, RealNetworks, or Windows Media Technology) or another technology, you have to encode your files before you can stream them across the Internet. To do this, you must employ some sort of encoding software, which is determined by the streaming platform you've decided on.

Of course, because some platforms are capable of streaming standard files, such as MPEG-1 and MPEG-2 files, you may not always need to use a streaming media encoder. However, for the most part your files must be encoded by using the appropriate encoding software.

Encoding software varies little from platform to platform. In general all you have to do is select a bit rate, a screen size, choose an audio codec, and select from the available optimization settings.

After you've specified the settings, the software takes over and processes the file(s). This can take anywhere from a few seconds to a number of hours, depending on the length of the file, the codec being used, and the CPU of the encoding machine.

The encoded files can then be watched locally or placed on a streaming server and made available to the audience. It's important that you test the encoded files across a network, using the type of connectivity that your audience is using to make sure that your settings are not too aggressive. You don't want to use a higher bit rate if the audience is unable to watch the encoded result.

Streaming Media: It's All About Bandwidth

The largest obstacle you face in the encoding process is bandwidth. You have to ensure that the bit rates of your encoded files do not exceed your audience's connection speed. In addition, you have to take two other things into consideration:

✦ How much bandwidth do they *actually* have (as opposed to what their ISP says they have)?

✦ How much of that bandwidth is available to you as a content provider?

The answers to these two questions aren't as straightforward as you may imagine. Before you fire up your encoding software, you need to think about your audience, their connectivity, and how much of it they want to give to you.

Actual versus advertised throughput

The truth of the matter is that very few people have as much bandwidth as they think that they do. This isn't their fault — they're just victims of the marketing hype that accompanies their equipment and home connectivity package. The vendors always conveniently neglect to mention that:

✦ Hardware performance specs are measured under ideal, not real-world conditions

✦ The Internet is a *shared* resource, both at the local (ISP) and the global level

Every piece of networking hardware is tested before it leaves the factory to make sure that it performs as advertised. The equipment must be able to handle the advertised throughput rate. Sure enough, when connected across a LAN or dial-up connection directly to a server, the equipment performs as advertised without a hitch.

Unfortunately, this is never the situation in the real world. It's not entirely fair to blame the hardware manufacturers — their equipment performs as advertised when it can. It's just that the opportunity does not arise that often.

In the real world, you're never directly connected to the server that you're requesting files from. There are routers, switches, LANs, and who knows what else your request must traverse before the server can respond — and the return journey is no better.

In addition, all of these resources are shared by other people, who may be downloading the latest browser software or watching broadband feeds of their favorite sporting event. No matter what route your data packets take, traffic is likely along the way.

When you factor this in, you're faced with a bandwidth picture that isn't as rosy as it was before. This shouldn't discourage you from creating streaming media content, but it should make you think carefully when you choose the settings for your encoding profiles.

Broadband connections

When ISPs sell broadband connectivity, they assume that bandwidth usage is *bursty* — meaning that not everyone uses their computers at the same time, and when they do use it they don't always need their maximum bandwidth. They make intelligent guesses at usage during peak periods and design their infrastructure accordingly. Obviously, ISPs want to minimize their expenditure while maximizing their revenue, like any good company. The problem is that this leads to degraded performance if they oversell their capacity by too large a factor.

As an example, assume an ISP is selling 256 Kbps DSL connectivity. If these connections share a 10 Mbps LAN circuit, they should only sell 28 DSL connections on this circuit (the theoretical maximum of TCP/IP throughput is about 70 percent of the total bandwidth). However, taking a guess at overall usage patterns the ISP may oversell the capacity by as much as 10 to 1.

Normally, this may not be a problem, but if everyone decides to watch a broadband stream at the exact same time, a huge traffic jam ensues. The actual throughput in this scenario is laughable, on the order of a 28.8K modem. This is an extreme example, but not so far removed from reality.

Granted, some ISPs promise to never oversell their capacity, but this should be put in the "believe it when you see it" category. The current economics of Internet delivery practically demand it. If the oversell ratios are low, performance is relatively unaffected. Problems only occur when oversell ratios are too high.

The situation is improving. Customers complain when they don't get the connectivity they pay for, and ISPs need to keep their customers happy. The continuing drop in connectivity costs will slowly trickle down to consumers, and consumers will be more willing to pay for broadband when the content merits it. It's a bit of a chicken-and-the-egg scenario, but one that still shows promise.

Modems

Modems, unlike broadband connectivity, have been around for a very long time. You may remember placing phone handsets into rubber couplings and receiving a staggering 1200 bits per second. Modems have come a long way since then, but the technology remains fundamentally the same.

Because modems use analog phone lines, they must operate in the audible frequency range, which makes them susceptible to noise. When modems encounter noise, they renegotiate, meaning that they slow down. The longer you remain connected via modem, the more likely renegotiation is. The blistering 28.8K connection you started off with is more likely to be 24, 22, or 20K.

When modems renegotiate, they won't reestablish the original connection speed unless a sufficient amount of time passes without noise errors. Usually, they stay slow. This lack of speed can be especially troublesome during live broadcasts because people stay tuned in to the same stream for a long time.

With the gradual proliferation of broadband connectivity (with its own problems — see above) modems are sure to become a thing of the past, but this is not yet the case. As of the writing of this book, broadband connectivity only comprises about ten percent of all household connectivity, which leaves an enormous number of people still using the humble modem. For the foreseeable future, you should continue to cater to dial-up users if you want to reach the largest audience.

The good news is that it isn't too difficult to cater to a wide audience with varying amounts of connectivity. Two of the three biggest streaming media technologies offer methods of including streams catering to different bandwidths in a single file, and you can always simply encode different bit rate streaming media files. This is covered in more depth later in the chapter in the "Catering to the Widest Audience" section.

As the connectivity picture changes over the next few years, your encoding parameters will also change. The best way to keep track of your audience's connectivity is via your server log files. Careful analysis of this data will provide you with a wealth of information not only about what your audience is watching, but also about their connectivity,

Cross-Reference For a full discussion of server log files and how to analyze the data they provide, please turn to Chapter 20.

How much bandwidth should you take?

In addition to the hardware and connectivity limitations, you should also ask yourself, "How much of a customer's available bandwidth should I use?"

Think for a moment of the poor dial-up user, connecting at a paltry 20 to 28 Kbps and attempting to enjoy the Internet to its fullest extent. To just about everyone, surfing the Internet involves checking e-mail, a bit of Web surfing, perhaps accompanied by a musical soundtrack from an online radio station. People like to multi-task and flit from one Web page to the next while doing a number of other tasks.

Measuring Actual Throughput

Although you can't ever know exactly what sort of throughput your audience is getting, there is an experiment you can perform that might open your eyes to their plight: Find out what kind of throughput *you're* actually getting, by doing a little math. After you see the difference between reality and the hype, you may want to take this into consideration when choosing your encoding parameters.

Bandwidth is measured in bits per second, so the best way to measure it is to download a file, see how long it takes, and divide the file size by the number of seconds. For a true test, you should download a large, compressed file (.exe or .zip on PC, .hqx or .sit on Mac). Use a large file because 56K modems get their rating in part by doing some on-the-fly compression that cannot be done on files that are already compressed. Streaming media files are heavily compressed and, therefore, cannot take advantage of this compression. A good file to perform this test with is the latest version of a browser or media player.

One thing to watch out for is that file size is usually measured in kilobytes (KB) as opposed to kilobits (Kb). Therefore to find the throughput, we will first need to multiply the file size by eight (1 byte = 8 bits), and then divide by the number of seconds it took to download the file. This gives us throughput in kilobits per second, or Kbps:

```
throughput (Kbits/second) = F * 8 / S
```

If you don't want to stick around waiting for a full download, most browsers and FTP programs include a display that shows the approximate speed at which the file is being downloaded. You can estimate your throughput in Kbps by multiplying this number by eight.

Simply watching this display while a file downloads can be an educational experience. You'll see the connectivity fluctuate wildly and see that the highest transfer rate is rarely sustained for any length of time. For this reason, measuring the throughput over a sustained period of time with a long, compressed file is better. This way you get an average throughput over time, which is what you should consider representative of your true connection speed.

Another option that you may want to try is repeating the exercise at different times of the day. You may want to try repeating it from different Web sites as well. Internet traffic varies at different times of the day. You may see your connection speed reduced by 50 percent or more during peak usage times.

Regardless of whether you do the full test or not, you'll probably be surprised at what you see. Rarely, if ever, does the bandwidth equal what you're supposed to be paying for. It's one of those quirks about owning a computer — maybe you'll get the full, advertised bandwidth in Version 2.0.

You should, therefore, always leave some overhead for your audience's other Internet activity. If you don't, the other tasks (which the audience is going to do regardless) may force your presentation to rebuffer, because the viewer's computer must divide the available resources among all competing tasks.

You should plan on leaving 20 to 30 percent of users' available bandwidth for overhead, error-correction, and other Internet activity. Appendix B contains a table of recommended target bit rates for various connection rates.

Audio Codec Considerations

Audio codecs come in a number of varieties. Encoding an audio file involves a continual tradeoff between the dynamic range, the frequency range, and the fidelity of the content to the original. If the codec knows in advance what to expect from the content, certain assumptions can be made to get the best result. When you choose an audio codec, you're giving the encoder important information about what to expect from the audio file.

Music versus speech

Music is very dynamic and encompasses a wide frequency range, and it is generally recorded in stereo. All these factors make encoding high-quality audio tricky, particularly at low bit rates. Music codecs have improved dramatically in the last few years, so much so that supposed "CD quality" is available at 64 Kbps.

Speech is much simpler to encode than music. When someone begins speaking, they generally continue speaking at roughly the same volume and in a relatively small frequency range. Speech codecs can take advantage of this, and put more effort into rendering the limited frequency and dynamic ranges as faithfully as possible. Because speech is relatively easy to encode, excellent quality can be obtained at 32 Kbps or less.

The shortcuts that speech codecs take make them particularly unsuitable for music. Music codecs do an acceptable job with speech, but never do as good a job as a dedicated speech codec.

Choosing the proper audio codec for the job is important — otherwise you're condemning your content to inferior audio quality. If your content contains any musical content whatsoever, you should choose a music codec. Speech sounds reasonable when a music codecs is used, however, the same cannot be said about music encoded with a speech codec.

The only time you may be able to get away with using a speech codec with music is if the music is used only in the background, at a very low level.

Tip In general, sticking with music codecs is best, unless you're absolutely sure that the content is a speech-only presentation, or the music is at a very low background level.

Stereo versus mono

When you're encoding musical content, you can do so by retaining the original stereo separation, or you can collapse the mix into mono. Mono codecs provide more fidelity, a wider dynamic range, and a higher frequency range because they only have to encode one channel.

Nowadays the stereo codecs have improved to the point where they're nearly equivalent to mono codecs. Mono codecs still do a better job at reproducing the original, but at the expense of all the stereo information.

Stereo has long been a buzzword, and that reputation accompanies it to this day. In reality, very little stereo information can be found in most modern music, with the exception of dance music that uses exaggerated stereo imaging as an effect. Even so, many people would not be able to tell you whether a recording was in stereo or not. Then again, they probably wouldn't notice the increased fidelity that a mono encoding provides.

These days, you can safely choose a stereo or mono codec. However, as much as the audio purist in me prefers the increased fidelity of mono files, particularly at low bit rates, using stereo codecs is best. If you don't, your competitors will use stereo and claim that their streams are better because of it.

Tip After you decide on a format, stick with it. Some applications, such as creating a playlist, demand that all the files be encoded the exact same way.

Video Encoding Tradeoffs

Video codecs have a tough task. They have to take an immense amount of data and condense it to a size that can be streamed. Everything they do is a compromise, and it is based on the target bit rate that you set for the file.

You have no hard-set rules to follow. If you try to encode a full-screen presentation for a 28.8K modem user, the encoder does the best it can. In this case, you'd get one frame every ten minutes or so. So what you have to do is set some parameters for your encoded file that make sense for the intended audience.

Frame size versus fidelity

Video codecs must employ a strategy when allotting bits to frames. Keyframes have to be encoded, followed by an indeterminate number of difference frames, followed by the next keyframe. Thus video codecs create a "bit budget" that they must adhere to when encoding individual frames.

The larger each individual frame of video is, the more bits it takes to encode faithfully. It's that simple. Video codecs allot a certain amount of bits to each frame, which limits the quality that can be achieved for each frame.

Given the same number of bits, a large frame does not encode as well as a small frame. The question is then how large should the video frame size be for different bit rates? The answer depends on the types of content you're trying to encode. Talking-head content, such as news broadcasts, can generally be encoded at a larger frame size than high-action footage, such as sports.

Table 12-1 lists suggested frame sizes for video at varying bit rates. Try experimenting with different frame sizes, frame rates, and codec combinations until you find a setting that works best for you.

Table 12-1 Suggested Video Frame Sizes		
Type of content	*Bit rate*	*Suggested screen size(s)*
Low action (News, interviews, nature programs, and so on.)	28.8 Kbps	176×132
	56 Kbps	240×180, 176×132
	Dual ISDN (80 Kbps)	320×240, 240×180
	256K DSL	320×240
	384K DSL	640×480, 320×240
	512K DSL	640×480, 320×240
High Action (Sports, music videos, advertisements, movie trailers)	28.8 Kbps	160×120
	56 Kbps	176×132
	Dual ISDN (80 Kbps)	240×180, 176×132
	256K DSL	240×180
	384K DSL	320×240, 240×180
	512K DSL	640×480, 320×240

Frame rate versus fidelity

The strategy that video codecs employ to allot bits to frames also includes the number of frames per second that the codec attempts to encode. For example, at low bit rates, attempting to encode 30 frames per second doesn't make sense. The quality of each frame would be so low as to be laughable.

Therefore, depending on the target bit rate and frame size, the codec decides how many frames per second to encode. This number can vary dynamically depending on the video content. As the codec goes along, it may encode more frames when the action is low, or encode fewer frames and save bits for high action sequences later.

You can influence how the encoder chooses its frame rate by setting a maximum frame rate. You can't force the encoder to encode more frames; that is limited by the bit budget. However, by limiting the number of frames per second the encoder attempts to encode, you can force it to encode higher quality versions of each frame.

This setting interacts with the frame size to determine the final look of your encoded video. Table 12-2 lists some starting points for your encoded content. Find the settings that work best for your content.

Table 12-2
Suggested Maximum Frame Rates

Type of content	Target bit rate	Suggested maximum frame rate
Low action (News, interviews, nature programs, and so on.)	20 Kbps (28.8 modem)	10
	34 Kbps (56K modem)	12
	80 Kbps (Dual ISDN)	15
	200 Kbps and above (DSL/Cable modem)	30
High Action (Sports, music videos, advertisements, movie trailers)	20 Kbps (28.8 modem)	7.5
	34 Kbps (56K modem)	10
	80 Kbps (Dual ISDN)	15
	200 Kbps and above (DSL/Cable modem)	30

Catering to the Widest Audience

If you want to reach a number of people with different connection speeds while providing the highest possible quality to each, you must encode different versions for each target bit rate. That way, you can optimize each file for a particular connection speed by specifying appropriate frame sizes, frame rates, audio codec, and so on.

This may or may not involve additional files, depending on which platform you're using. QuickTime does not support multiple streams inside a single file. However, you can encode multiple versions of a file inside a reference movie and have the player choose the appropriate version based on the available bandwidth.

Both the RealSystem and Windows Media Technologies have technology that embeds multiple streams at various bit rates in a single file. These streams are created automatically in the encoding software, and offer certain fallback capabilities in the serving stage, which are described below.

QuickTime

QuickTime supports choosing between different files based on bandwidth by embedding the choices available in a single reference movie. Two tools are currently available to create these special reference movies:

✦ MakeRefMovie

✦ XMLtoRefMovie

For more information on QuickTime reference movies, please turn to Chapter 15. For information on encoding QuickTime files, turn to Chapter 13.

Using either one of these tools, you specify which stream the streaming media player should choose based on connection speed or CPU speed. You can specify as many alternatives as you want. When a streaming media player opens up a reference movie, it decides which streaming media file to request based on the connection speed that the user sets when installing the player.

After the player decides which file to request, it requests the file from the QuickTime streaming server. The player cannot fall back to a different version if insufficient connectivity is available.

RealSystem

The RealSystem calls its multiple bit rate technology SureStream. SureStream files contain multiple streams, each for a specific *target audience*. You can select your target audiences when you encode the file by using the RealSystem Producer. The free version of RealSystem Producer enables you to select up to two target audiences; the RealSystem Producer Plus up to eight target audiences.

For more information on encoding files with the RealSystem Producer, please turn to Chapter 13.

The screen size for SureStream video files must remain consistent, but all other encoding parameters for each target audience may be set individually, including the audio codec. You can also specify whether the audio or the video content should be *emphasized*, which refers to how the stream is scaled back whenever the server encounters adverse bandwidth conditions.

SureStream technology allows the server to automatically switch to a lower bit rate stream if a viewer's connectivity should drop. The server can degrade the video or audio stream or both, depending on the emphasis setting and how bad conditions are.

The server can switch back up to the original bit rate when the connectivity returns. In fact, if a viewer requests a low bit rate file but has enough bandwidth to receive a higher bit rate version, the server automatically switches to the higher quality stream.

To take advantage of SureStream technology the files must be streamed from a RealServer. Web servers can stream SureStream files, but without any of the stream switching capabilities. For more about SureStream technology, please refer to the documentation available from the RealNetworks Web site (www.realnetworks.com).

Windows Media Technology

Windows Media Technology includes Intelligent Streaming and also uses the concept of *target audiences.* By using Windows Media Encoder, you can select the desired target audiences and specify the frame size and audio codec. Unlike RealNetworks SureStream technology, you cannot specify different audio codecs for different target audiences.

You can select as many target audiences as you want, but if one of your target audiences is under 80 Kbps, the encoder does not allow you to choose a target audience above 300 Kbps. This limitation is not necessarily unreasonable because you should encode streams at different screen sizes for low and high bit rates to provide the optimal experience.

 Cross-Reference For more information about encoding using the Windows Media Encoder, please turn to Chapter 13.

Intelligent Streaming allows the server to adjust to changing connectivity conditions. If the viewer's connectivity drops, the server sends fewer video frames, while maintaining audio quality. If the connectivity drops further, the server stops sending video frames altogether. When the connectivity returns, the server resumes sending video frames.

Only Windows Media Servers can perform Intelligent Streaming. For more on Intelligent Streaming, please refer to the Windows Media Technology section of the Microsoft Web site (www.microsoft.com).

Summary

Before you encode your files, you've got to think about your target audience and make some decisions about your encoding parameters. After you've decided on the settings you're going to use, the next chapter shows you how to encode on all three platforms.

✦ Bandwidth is your single largest concern when encoding.

✦ Actual throughput is rarely as high as the advertised bandwidth.

✦ Leave space for viewers to do other Internet tasks.

✦ 25 to 30 percent bandwidth overhead is a good safety margin.

✦ Make sure that you choose the right audio codec for your content.

✦ If you're not sure about your audio content, use a music codec.

✦ Choose an appropriate frame size and maximum frame rate for your content.

✦ Encode multiple files to cater to different connection speeds.

✦ All three platforms have strategies that incorporate multiple files, some more full-featured than others.

✦   ✦   ✦

Basic Encoding Techniques

As soon as you decide who your target audience is and what you want to send them, you can roll up your sleeves and start encoding the files that you've painstakingly created.

All three of the main streaming platforms offer simple to use encoding software. Each takes a slightly different approach, naturally, but essentially they all accomplish the same result.

This chapter introduces encoding with QuickTime Pro, the RealSystem Producer, and the Windows Media Encoder. In addition to these software packages, many third-party tool manufacturers include the ability to encode raw media files into one or more of the streaming formats.

When encoding files, you should always start with the highest quality input, generally an uncompressed `.avi` or `.mov` file. If your capture card uses a hardware codec, make sure that you use the least amount of compression possible. If you're working with DV video, you may be able to encode directly from the DV format, depending on the encoding application you use.

Even if you plan to encode your files by using a third-party tool, familiarize yourself with the encoding software each platform provides. You still must supply the necessary encoding parameters, and the user interface most third-party tools use for encoding usually closely resembles the streaming platform's own encoding software.

Using QuickTime Pro

Unlike the RealSystem or Windows Media, QuickTime does not use a separate application for encoding files. Encoding is done in the QuickTime Player; however, you must have QuickTime Pro to be able to encode. QuickTime Pro is available as an upgrade to the QuickTime Player from the Apple Web site (www.apple.com/quicktime).

Encoding using QuickTime Pro is simple. All you have to do is open or import the original media file into the QuickTime player. Then you export it as a QuickTime movie and choose the appropriate settings. Last, you must *hint* the movie. Hinting gives the server extra information that it needs to stream the movie.

Note   All QuickTime streaming files are generically referred to as movies, even if they are audio-only.

You can hint QuickTime movies as you encode them. The streaming presets included with QuickTime Pro all hint the movie automatically. If you do not use one of the presets, you can hint a movie while you encode it by clicking the appropriate checkbox in the Movie Settings dialog box. This process is demonstrated in the next section.

Encoding using QuickTime Pro

Sometimes, the easiest way to learn something is by doing it. Encoding files can involve a lot of settings to specify and buttons to push, but it all makes a strange sort of sense when you're doing it.

For the purposes of this example, assume that you want to create a streaming video file that people on a 56 Kbps modem can watch and a higher-quality version that people in your office can watch. A quick glance at the recommended maximum target bit rates in Appendix B indicates that you should use approximately 34 Kbps and 150 Kbps as your target bit rates.

Assuming your video has music in it, you also should use the QDesign Music 2 codec, at 10 or 12 Kbps mono for the lower bit rate, and 32 Kbps stereo for the higher bit rate. QuickTime does not support multiple bit rates inside a single file, so you're going to have to create two separate files to cater to the two audiences.

1. **Open your movie in QuickTime Pro by choosing Open or Import from the File menu.** Browse to find your file and click the Open or Convert button. (If the file is already a QuickTime file, the Open button is displayed; otherwise the Convert button displays and the file is converted to a QuickTime file.)

2. **To create a streaming version of the movie, simply select Export from the File menu or type Ctrl-E.** This brings up the export dialog box (see Figure 13-1).

Figure 13-1: Exporting streaming files from QuickTime Pro

3. **Browse to the directory you want to save your file in and type in a name for your streaming version.** Make sure that the Export box is set to Movie to QuickTime Movie.

4. **Click the Options button to set the encoding parameters.** The Movie Settings dialog box appears. (See Figure 13-2.)

   Working your way from top to bottom, set the video parameters, the audio parameters, and finally make sure that you're going to automatically hint the movie for streaming purposes.

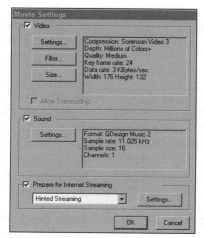

Figure 13-2: The Movie Settings dialog box

Note If you're absolutely positive that you want to use the same encoding parameters as your last encode, you can simply click the Save button.

5. **Click the Settings button to open the Compression Settings dialog box (see Figure 13-3).** Select Sorenson Video 3 for your compressor. You can set a number of other settings in this dialog box, but for the most part, the default settings work just fine. The one setting that you must set is the maximum bit rate.

   You can force a frame rate if you desire; however, leaving the frame rate blank allows the Sorenson codec to choose the optimal frame rate. Click OK to return to the Movie Settings dialog box.

Figure 13-3: The Compression Settings dialog box (left) and the Export Size Settings dialog box (right)

Note Sorenson Video 3 is only available in QuickTime 5. If you're working with an earlier version of QuickTime, you should upgrade to take advantage of the superior quality of Sorenson Video 3. If this is not an option, choose whatever Sorenson video codec is available.

Caution QuickTime uses bytes to describe bit rates instead of bits. Make sure that you divide your target bit rate by eight before entering it here. If you make a mistake and enter a number from Appendix B for your target bit rate, your file will look fantastic when you test it locally, but forget about it streaming smoothly to your target audience — because the bit rate is eight times what it should be.

Setting your video bit rate involves a bit of math — assuming that you want a total bit rate of 34 Kbps, and 10 Kbps is used for your audio, that leaves 24 Kbps for the video. Dividing this by eight gives you a rate of 3 Kbytes per second.

6. **If you want to resize your original video, click the Size button in the Movie Settings dialog box.** Doing so opens the Export Size Settings dialog box (see Figure 13-3).

For the low bit rate file, you should scale your video down to a reasonable size. Table 12-1 in Chapter 12 suggests 160 × 120 pixels or 176 × 132 pixels, depending on the type of content. Set your height and width parameters and click OK.

7. **To adjust your audio encoding parameters, click the Settings button in the sound section of the Movie Settings dialog box.** Doing so opens the Sound Settings dialog box. (see Figure 13-4).

Figure 13-4: The Sound Settings dialog box (top) and the QDesign Music Encoder dialog box (bottom)

8. **Select the Qdesign Music 2 or Qualcomm PureVoice codec depending on your audio content. Set a sampling rate by clicking the down-arrow to the right of the Rate box.** Click the Options button to set the bit rate. Doing so opens the Qdesign Music Encoder dialog box (see Figure 13-4) or the PureVoice Option dialog box (see Figure 13-5).

If you're encoding music content, simply choose a bit rate for your audio from the drop-down menu of the QDesign Music Encoder dialog box.

If you're encoding speech, make sure that the Optimize compression for streaming checkbox is checked and then select PureVoice SmartRate or Qualcomm Half Rate, depending on the bit rate you require.

Double-click OK to return to the Movie Settings dialog box.

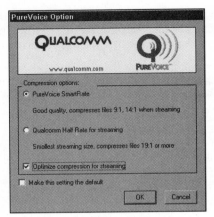

Figure 13-5: The Qualcomm
PureVoice Options dialog box

For more information about the Qualcomm PureVoice codec please turn to
Appendix B.

9. **Last but not least, check to make sure that you are going to export a hinted movie.** Make sure that the Prepare for Internet Streaming checkbox is checked. Click the Settings box to bring up the Hint Exporter Settings dialog box (see Figure 13-6).

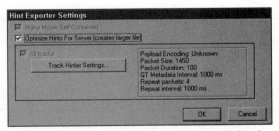

Figure 13-6: The Hint Exporter Settings dialog box

10. **Make sure that the Optimize Hints for Server checkbox is checked.** Click OK to close the Hint Exporter Settings dialog box, and then click OK again to return to the original Save Exported File as dialog box.

11. **Click the Save button.**

The encoding process for the first file is now complete. For the second file, you'll repeat the whole process, this time choosing encoding settings appropriate for a 150 Kbps file.

The encoding process takes anything from a few moments to a few hours, depending on the length of your file and the encoding settings. After you encode your file, create your reference movie. Then place the streaming file on your streaming server and place the reference movie on your Web server.

 Creating reference files is covered in Chapter 15; streaming servers are covered in Chapters 18 and 19.

Streaming noncompressed data types

Certain data types, such as text and MIDI tracks, can be streamed but should not be encoded. If your QuickTime presentation uses either of these data types, remove the tracks before encoding, add them back in after the audio and video have been encoded, and then hint the movie.

If you added tracks to your movie after encoding, you need to rehint the movie. This is simple enough:

1. **Open your movie in QuickTime Player Pro and choose Export from the File menu (or press Ctrl-E).**

2. **Make sure that only the Prepare for Internet Streaming checkbox is checked.** Click the Settings box to open the Hint Exporter Settings dialog box (see Figure 13-6).

3. **Make sure that the Optimize Hints for Server checkbox is checked.** Click OK to close the Hint Exporter Settings window and then click OK again to return to the original Save Exported File as dialog box.

4. **Click the Save button.**

Using RealSystem Producer

The RealSystem Producer is the encoding software used to produce RealMedia files. This software is a completely separate application from the RealPlayer and is available from the RealNetworks Web site (www.realnetworks.com/).

Two versions are available, RealSystem Producer and RealSystem Producer Plus. RealSystem Producer is free to download, while RealSystem Producer Plus is available for purchase from the RealNetworks Web site (www.realnetworks.com/). RealSystem Producer Plus has a number of additional features:

✦ Up to eight target audience settings allowed per file instead of just two

✦ Target audience and codec settings that you can edit

✦ Video cropping and scaling

✦ Batch scripting

✦ RealMedia Editor, a GUI utility to edit RealMedia files

✦ Bandwidth Simulator

✦ Backwards compatibility with RealPlayer 5.0

✦ Publishing support

Everything that you need to encode audio and video is included in the RealSystem Producer, but a few of the features included with the RealSystem Producer Plus can be very useful.

In particular, being able to edit the target audience settings can be crucial, particularly if your audio or video files are part of a SMIL presentation that uses other streaming data types. Video cropping and scaling can save a lot of time because you don't need to render separate versions of your video at different sizes — the RealSystem Producer Plus resizes them.

The batch scripting capability is described in the next chapter. This feature can be a great time saver. The Bandwidth Simulator lets you view your encoded files at different bit rates and even allows you to simulate packet loss on the Internet. The RealMedia Editor can also be handy when doing simple edits on previously encoded files.

This section covers the basic RealSystem Producer functionality, along with some of the most useful features of RealSystem Producer Plus. As your production needs increase, you may want to consider purchasing the Plus version to take advantage of the added functionality.

RealSystem Producer overview

The RealSystem Producer uses the concepts of *sessions* and *target audiences*. A session describes the inputs and outputs that you are using. The three types of sessions are:

✦ Encoding an existing file

✦ Encoding directly from the audio and video inputs to a file (a local live encode)

✦ Encoding directly from the audio and video inputs to a server (live broadcast)

Note   You cannot encode from a file directly to a server. If you want to broadcast static files in a live fashion, use the G2SLTA application on the server. (See Chapter 37 for more information.)

If you want to change anything about your inputs or outputs, such as the name of the output file, you have to create a new session.

Target audiences are used to specify how files are encoded. The RealSystem Producer Basic has predefined templates for each target audience. These templates include the total bit rate, the audio bit rate, and the maximum frames per second the encoder tries to encode. If you have RealSystem Producer Plus, these templates can be modified.

The RealSystem enables you to choose multiple target audiences if you decide to create a SureStream file. SureStream enables you to embed multiple streams at different bit rates into a single file. SureStream simplifies the authoring process, because only a single link is needed for all audience members, and also enables the RealServer to do some fancy footwork if a user's connection suddenly becomes constricted.

Cross-Reference The RealServer is the software application used to stream RealMedia files across the Internet. Chapter 1 introduces the concept of a streaming media server, and Chapter 18 introduces the three main streaming media servers.

Regardless of whether you use SureStream, you still must specify the type of audio content in your file and the video encoding quality (see Figure 13-7). You can also enter metadata for the file, such as title, author, copyright, and a file description.

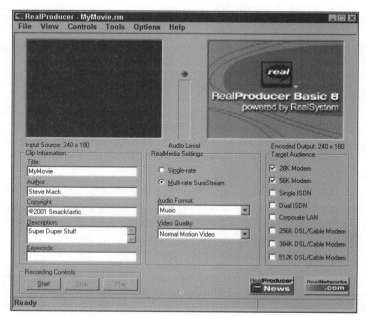

Figure 13-7: The RealSystem Producer main window

After you choose all your settings, simply click the Start button. You can test the file when it is done encoding by clicking the Play button. If you want to encode it again using different settings, simply change the settings and click Start again. If you want to encode another version while keeping the original, you have to start a new session to change the name of your output file.

When you finally have a version that you're happy with, all you have to do is move it to a server, and it's ready to stream. Of course, you should test your streaming file before sending out the link to anyone — nothing is worse than sending out a dead link.

Choosing an audio format

The RealSystem Producer lets you choose among four audio formats:

✦ **Voice Only:** Use this setting with audio content that contains only speech.

✦ **Voice with Background Music:** This setting uses the same codecs as the Voice Only setting. Only use this setting if the background music is much lower than the voice content. Otherwise use a music setting.

✦ **Music:** Use this setting for music content that you want encoded in mono.

✦ **Stereo Music:** Use this setting with music content you want encoded in stereo. Be sure to choose an appropriate codec for your content. You can also use the No Audio setting if you do not want the audio portion of your signal encoded.

Cross-Reference   For additional information about how to choose an appropriate audio codec, please refer to the Audio Codec considerations section in Chapter 12.

Setting the video quality

You can choose from four different video qualities when encoding video files. If you remember the discussion about keyframes and difference frames in Chapter 3, these choices affect how many keyframes are generated and the sharpness of each keyframe.

✦ **Normal Motion Video:** This is the default setting and is good for most content.

✦ **Smoothest Motion Video:** This setting is better for high action content and generates more keyframes but at a slightly reduced quality.

✦ **Sharpest Image Video:** Use this setting for low-motion content. It generates fewer keyframes but each one is higher quality

✦ **SlideShow:** This setting avoids trying to encode full motion video and instead generates high-quality frames. The frame rate is dependent on the frame size and bit rate.

For most applications, use the Normal Motion Video setting. If you're dissatisfied with the quality, play around with this setting to see if the result is more to your liking. For instance, I generally prefer the Sharpest Image Video setting. I'd rather receive fewer frames but have them be high quality, as opposed to more blurry frames. But that's just me.

SureStream versus single rate files

As mentioned above, SureStream files include multiple streams inside a single file. This can be advantageous for a couple of reasons:

✦ A single file can be used for multiple connection speeds, so only a single link is necessary on a Web page.

✦ The RealServer can switch between the streams inside the file, according to a user's available bandwidth.

In addition to the streams for each target audience, the RealSystem Producer inserts intermediate streams between the target bit rate streams. These streams give the RealServer the ability to tailor the stream being served to the available bandwidth.

The RealServer can detect when a player's available bandwidth is constricted and shift down to a lower-quality stream without any interruption in playback. When the bandwidth opens back up, the RealServer can shift up to the original stream. In fact, if the player has additional bandwidth, the server can send an even higher-quality stream. The entire process is invisible to the viewer, other than the change in quality that occurs when the RealServer shifts from stream to stream.

Only a RealServer can take advantage of SureStream functionality. SureStream files may be placed on a Web server, but only the lowest-quality stream in the file is served.

SureStream file sizes

One drawback to SureStream files is that they are much larger than a single rate file. As an example, a one-minute single rate file encoded for a 28.8K modem is about 150 KB. The same file encoded in SureStream mode is over 350 KB.

Inside the 28.8 SureStream file, are a 20 Kbps stream, a 15 Kbps stream, and a 12 Kbps stream. Including these three streams in the same file allows the RealServer to shift down twice, first to a lower-quality video stream and then to a slideshow stream. This functionality comes at a price — the file size doubles. SureStream file sizes depend on the number of target audiences you want to cater to. For each target audience, you have a maximum bit rate stream and a "fallback" stream. This fallback stream is the stream the server switches to when bandwidth becomes constricted.

Sometimes one target audience's stream is another's fallback stream. The 56K modem target audience generates a 32 Kbps stream and a 20 Kbps stream. The 20 Kbps stream is also the main stream for 28.8K modem audiences. In this case, adding a 56K target audience to the 28.8K target audience only adds one additional stream, but generally you should count on each target audience adding a considerable amount to the overall file size.

SureStream limitations

When encoding SureStream files, the video frame size must remain consistent. Although having to keep the video frame size consistent does not place any hard limits on your files, it may limit the number of target audiences you choose to include in your file. In general, you want to send your viewers the largest possible frame size. Because SureStream files must use a consistent frame size, this can cheat some of your audience. If the target audiences in your file are too far apart, the higher bit rate target audiences get a smaller screen than they could receive or the lower bit rate target audiences get compromised quality because the frame size is too large for their bit rate.

As a rule of thumb, you should include target audiences in the same SureStream file that have similar maximum bit rate limitations to take advantage of the stream shifting. For example, if you want to cater to users on 28.8K modems and 56K modems, definitely use a single SureStream file to cater to both of them. This file will contains streams to serve both audiences, making file management easier, and the target bit rates for both audiences dictate a small video screen size.

If you are trying to cater to dial-up users *and* users on the corporate LAN, you should encode one SureStream file for the dial-up users, and one SureStream file for the audience on the corporate LAN, for a couple of reasons:

✦ Using SureStream for both files gives the server the ability to fall back to a lower bit rate stream if necessary.

✦ By creating two separate files, you can encode the higher bit rate file at a larger screen size, giving the corporate LAN users a better experience.

Setting global Preferences

In addition to the session details and encoding parameters, you can set a number of global parameters for the RealSystem Producer. To access these, choose Preferences from the Options menu. Doing so brings up the Preferences dialog box (see Figure 13-8).

The Preferences window has six separate tabs, and each contains a different set of options. Most of these settings are simple checkboxes or drop-down menus. For the most part the settings in this window are set once and then used for all your content. A brief discussion of each tab follows.

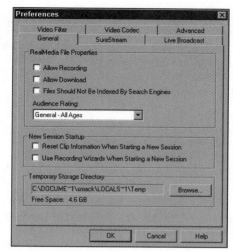

Figure 13-8: The RealSystem Producer Preferences window.

General settings

This page allows you to set whether or not your files should be recordable, downloaded, or indexed by search engines. Most people do not want their content recorded or downloaded but do want it to be indexed by search engines.

Note Audience members who want to record your content must have RealPlayer Plus. The standard RealPlayer does not have record functionality enabled.

This page also enables you to specify a rating for your streaming media file and allows you to choose a temporary directory to use during the encoding process. The last two settings on this page determine whether clip metadata is reset each time you start a new session and whether the recording wizard should be used when you create new sessions.

SureStream settings

This page enables you to set whether SureStream files should include a RealPlayer 5.0 stream for compatibility purposes and whether audio or video is favored during the SureStream shifting process.

Including a 5.0 stream may extend your audience, though by now the number of audience members with old RealPlayer versions should be quite low. Setting the SureStream emphasis determines which stream degraded first when adverse bandwidth conditions are encountered — the audio stream or the video stream.

LiveBroadcast settings

On this page, you can set whether the Producer uses UDP or TCP to connect to the server during live broadcasts. For most purposes, you want to use UDP. However, certain circumstances require that you use TCP, such as during live broadcasts when a firewall exists between your encoding machine and the RealServer you're trying to encode to.

Video Filter settings

This page allows you to do some advanced filtering of your streams during the encoding process. You can apply video noise reduction, determine the quality of the resize filter applied, and choose to use De-interlace and Inverse Telecine filters.

Noise filter

Using a noise filter can be very useful during live broadcasts. In low light conditions, cameras can generate fairly noisy video signals. This noise shows up as a grainy picture. By applying a bit of noise reduction, you can smooth out the picture and get a better quality encode.

You don't want to use the noise filter if you're working with high-quality video input. The slight blur that is applied does more harm than good in this case.

Resize filter

You can also choose the fast resize filter or the high-quality resize filter. For most applications, you should use the high-quality resize filter. You should use the fast resize filter only if you're doing a live encode on a low-powered machine.

Caution   Video resizing is available only in the RealSystem Producer Plus.

Inverse telecine filter

Use the inverse telecine filter on content that was originally shot on film and then transferred to video. This type of video content has duplicate frames that are inserted during the film-to-video process. These frames are removed before the encoding takes place, therefore, preventing bits from being wasted encoding redundant content.

Cross-Reference   For more information on the De-interlacing filter, please turn to the Using Video Filters section of Chapter 10.

The inverse telecine can safely be used on all content. Content that does not have extra frames is not affected.

De-interlace filter

The de-interlace filter reduces artifacts that are introduced when interlaced content (TV) is converted to progressive scan (computer monitor). Interlacing artifacts occur when the two fields that make up an interlaced frame are combined and are most noticeable when there is motion across the frame. The de-interlace filter uses complex heuristics to make the artifacts less noticeable.

These artifacts are only introduced when the screen size is more than 240 pixels tall. With smaller screens, one of the fields is discarded and the artifacts do not appear. All content that uses a screen size larger than 320 × 240 pixels should be de-interlaced.

Video codec settings

This page allows you to set the RealVideo codec that is used. The latest version provides the highest quality, but generally requires the latest player. Audience members without the latest player version receive an upgrade notice that may involve a sizeable download and install process.

You can also choose whether to use 2-pass encoding, Variable Bit Rate encoding, and Loss Protection. Each of these settings offers improved performance, but a couple of these settings do have drawbacks.

   ✦ **2-pass encoding:** 2-pass encoding offers improved encoding quality, but it takes longer than a standard encode because during the first pass the encoder decides where bits should be allotted, before actually encoding the file. The encoding time is roughly doubled, but the quality is much improved.

   ✦ **Variable Bit Rate (VBR):** VBR encoding also offers improved encoding quality, but these files can have much higher prebuffer times. The additional prebuffer time is necessary to compensate for the large bit rate variations that can occur with VBR files.

   ✦ **Loss Protection:** This option should always be used for streaming content. It provides additional protection against packets being lost in transmission with virtually no increase in encoding time or reduction in quality.

Advanced settings

This page allows you to adjust advanced encoding parameters for variable bit rate (VBR) encoding. If you knew how to set these, you wouldn't be reading this book. I don't even know how to set them. Leave them alone.

RealSystem Producer Plus Features

The RealSystem Producer Plus has a number of extra features. Two of these features are particularly useful.

Customizing Target Audience settings

The presets that come with the RealSystem Producer Basic are fine for most applications, but occasionally you may want to customize the settings. RealSystem Producer Plus allows you to change the target bit rate for each audience, the audio codec, and the maximum frame rate for each target audience.

To access this feature, choose Target Audience Settings from the Options menu, then select either RealAudio clips or RealVideo clips. Doing so brings up a window where you can choose settings for each individual target audience (see Figure 13-9). The settings for RealAudio clips and RealVideo clips are separate so that you can specify different settings for clips that include video and clips that are audio-only.

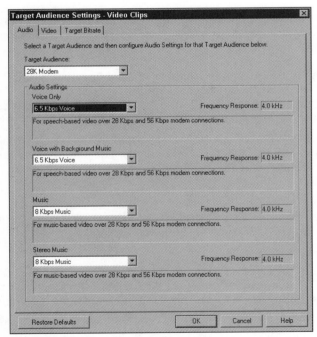

Figure 13-9: Customizing Target Audience settings

If you modify your target audience settings, those settings remain until you modify them again. In general, this should not present a problem unless you change the target audience settings for a unique situation. For unique situations you might be better off using the command line encoder along with an encoding profile instead of modifying the target audience settings.

The command line encoder and encoding profiles are covered in the next chapter.

When you find settings that work for your content, you should standardize them. This enables you to encode your content to consistently high standards and also allows you to take advantage of certain RealServer features, such as the G2SLTA, which allows you to broadcast a list of archived files as if they were a live stream. If you plan on doing any broadcasting with the G2SLTA, all your files must be encoded with exactly the same parameters.

For a brief discussion about broadcasting using the G2SLTA, please turn to Chapter 37.

If you find yourself encoding files with a special template, reset the target audience settings afterwards. Doing so helps to avoid confusion later on when you may have forgotten that you changed your target audience settings.

Video cropping and resizing

The most time consuming aspect of streaming media creation is rendering the raw video files. Depending on the screen size and your hardware configuration, rendering the raw video files can take anywhere from a few minutes to overnight.

If you're catering to audiences with different connection speeds and want to offer two different screen sizes, you need to render two separate video files if you're using RealSystem Producer Basic. RealSystem Producer Plus lets you resize and crop while you encode, making multiple video renders unnecessary. Instead, you only render the largest video screen size you require and resize for the smaller versions while you encode using RealSystem Producer Plus. You still must encode two separate versions, but the encoding process is much faster than rendering. To access the cropping and resizing features, choose Video Settings from the Options menu (see Figure 13-10). Doing so opens the Video Settings window.

In the video settings window, you can resize your video content by checking the Enable Resizing checkbox and entering the desired size in the boxes below. You can also crop your video in this window by checking the Enable Cropping checkbox and entering the desired crop settings.

Choosing your crop settings can be a little tricky because the codec requires that both dimensions be divisible by four. The best way to set your crop parameters is by reducing the width and height parameters a notch or two using the down arrows next to the Width and Height parameters (each notch is four pixels) and then centering the resulting area by using the Left and Top parameters.

The video window at the bottom of the Video Settings window gives you a live preview of how your settings affect the input.

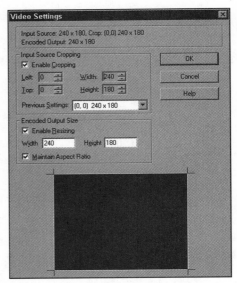

Figure 13-10: Cropping and resizing your video using RealSystem Producer Plus.

Using Windows Media Encoder

The Windows Media Encoder is the software used to encode all audio and video files for use with Windows Media technologies. This software is free and is available from the Windows Media Web site (www.microsoft.com/windowsmedia).

In addition to encoding raw audio and video, the Windows Media Encoder also offers the ability to encode what happens on-screen using the Windows Media Screen Capture codec. The Screen Capture codec can be very useful in educational and business settings.

Windows Media also lets you embed URLs into the encoded stream, via the Windows Media Encoder interface, as opposed to the RealSystem, where URLs are embedded into streams via SMIL or using events files.

The Windows Media Encoder is a powerful piece of software that can appear daunting at first, but using this software is simple. All you really have to do is create a session, choose a profile, and start encoding — but first you need to become familiar with the user interface and the terminology of the Windows Media Encoder.

Windows Media Encoder overview

The Windows Media Encoder is divided into five *panels*, each containing information about a different part of the encoding process (see Figure 13-11):

✦ **The Sources Panel:** This panel contains all the source groups you define for an encoding session.

✦ **The Audio Panel:** Use this panel to control the master audio input levels.

✦ **The Monitor Panel:** This panel shows information about the encoding process.

✦ **The Script Panel:** In this panel, you can enter URLs to be encoded into the stream.

✦ **The Control Panel:** In this panel you control the encoder and status information is displayed here.

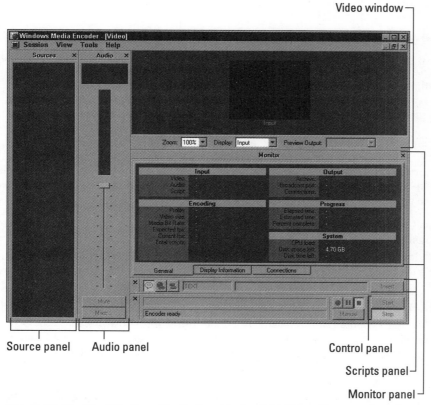

Figure 13-11: The Windows Media Encoder is divided into five panels and a video window.

The video window displays your video as it is being encoded. When you create a new encoding session, the Windows Media Encoder automatically hides panels that are not being used. Alternatively, you can always show or hide a panel by toggling the panel display name in the View menu.

Sessions

The Windows Media Encoder uses the concept of *sessions* to describe all the information required to encode a file. The three types of sessions are:

✦ Encoding an existing file (a single *source group*)

✦ Encoding directly from *source groups* to a file (a local live encode)

✦ Encoding directly from *source groups* to a server (live broadcast)

Session information can be saved as .wme files. These XML-compliant files contain all the source group and *profile* information, so that the session can later be duplicated if necessary.

Source groups

Source groups define the inputs to the Windows Media Encoder. If you're encoding a single file, you define a single source group that contains the file. In broadcast situations, you can define multiple source groups.

Each group includes an audio and a video source. These sources can come from audio and video input cards, files, or the output of your screen. You can even select the video track from one video file and the audio track from another.

Only one source group at a time can be active. Each source group you define has a corresponding button in the Source Panel. As you encode, you can switch between source groups.

During broadcasts, source groups that consist of a file are looped until another source group is chosen. If you specify more than a single source group, the Windows Media Encoder assumes that you're doing a live encode by broadcasting to a server or to a local file. To encode a single file, you must specify only a single source group.

Profiles and target audiences

The Windows Media Encoder uses *profiles* to determine how files or source groups are encoded. Each profile may contain a number of target audiences, along with the video and audio codec information. You can edit and save profiles for later use.

Windows Media deals with target audiences slightly differently than the RealSystem. Multiple versions of the video stream are encoded, but only a single version of the audio. Because the audio codec is shared, the lowest target audience in the profile limits the audio codec bit rate. All target audiences in a profile also share a video screen size.

Profiles may include multiple target audiences. Multiple Bit Rate (MBR) files are files that are encoded with a profile that contains multiple target audiences.

Creating a new session

You can create new sessions in the Windows Media Encoder by using the wizard interface or by using the New Session window. Using the wizard approach is simple and self-explanatory. To use the wizard to create a new session, choose New Session Wizard from the Session menu or press Ctrl-W.

This section covers how to create new sessions by using the New Session window. To use this method, choose New from the Session menu or press Ctrl-N. Doing so opens the New Session window, with the Sources tab displayed (see Figure 13-12).

Setting up source groups

First, you need to specify what types of sources you're going to be using during this encoding session. The type of sources you specify affects the profiles that are made available to you later when you choose an encoding profile.

Select the sources by checking or unchecking the Video, Audio and Scripts boxes at the bottom of the Sources tab of the New Session window (see Figure 13-12). All source groups must have the same number and types of sources.

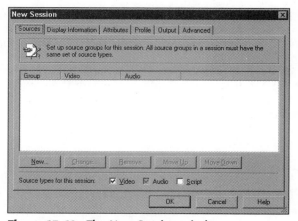

Figure 13-12: The New Session window.

Every source group must include an audio source. If you don't want to include audio in the stream you can set the audio bit rate to zero later on when you create your profile. Choose an audio source regardless of whether you want audio in you encoded file or not.

After you select the type of sources that you're going to use, you can add source groups by clicking the New button. Doing so opens the New Source Group window (see Figure 13-13). You can select sources for audio and video from the drop-down menu.

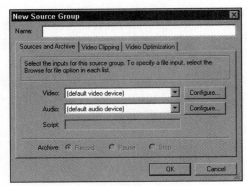

Figure 13-13: Adding new source groups.

If you want to use a file for your source, choose Browse for file from the drop-down menus. You can specify different files for the audio and video sources. If one file is longer than the other, the resulting stream is as long as the longest source; the extra space is filled with silence or black screen.

Hardware sources cannot be shared among source groups. If you're doing a live broadcast and want to use multiple video sources that share the same audio signal, each source needs an additional audio card.

After you specify the sources for a group, you can enter a name for the group if you want. Click OK to return to the New Sessions window, where you can add additional source groups or set other parameters for the encoding session.

Entering metadata

You can add two types of metadata to your presentation — *displayed information* and *attributes*. The displayed information is visible to the audience, such as the title and copyright. Attributes, on the other hand, are encoded into the stream and available to anyone but must be accessed via search tools and other custom applications.

Entering displayed Information

To add metadata that is displayed to your audience, click the Displayed Information tab in the New Session window. Doing so opens the Displayed Information tab, where you can enter title, author, copyright, rating, and description information.

Attributes

To add attributes to your file or broadcast, click the Attributes tab in the New Session Window. Here you enter name and value pairs to be encoded into the stream. These attributes can be accessed by anyone using tools created with the Windows Media SDK.

For example, you might want to include an attribute called "publisher" for a music track. This attribute value could be queried using a custom Windows Media application so that the publisher could be credited and perhaps even paid when the music track was played.

Choosing a profile

Profiles contain the codec information for your encoding session. To choose a profile, click the Profile tab in the New Session Window. The Profile tab opens (see Figure 13-14).

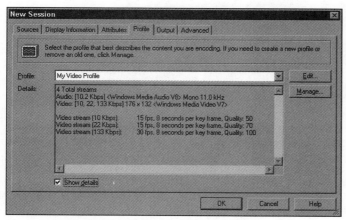

Figure 13-14: Choosing an encoding profile.

Only profiles that are suitable to the type of sources you specified in the Sources tab are displayed. For example, you cannot choose a profile that includes a video codec if you did not specify a video source.

Choose a profile from the drop-down menu for the session. If you check the Show details check box in the lower-left corner, all the encoding parameters are displayed instead of just the profile description. It's a good idea to leave this box checked so that you can always see exactly what encoding parameters are used.

If you want to edit a single profile, click the Edit button. You can also manage all your profiles by clicking the Manage button. Managing profiles enables not only editing of all your profiles but also the creation of new profiles. You can choose target audiences, select the audio and video codec, as well as specify maximum frame rates and keyframe quality for each target audience.

Specifying an output

The Output tab is where you specify whether you are doing a live broadcast or encoding to a file. Click the Output tab to open it (see Figure 13-15).

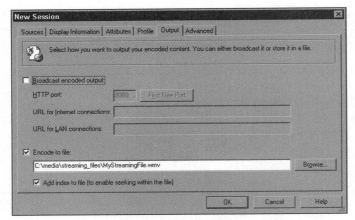

Figure 13-15: Specifying the session output

This tab has two checkboxes, one for a live broadcast and one for a local version of the encoded output. The local version checkbox toggles between Archive to file and Encode to file, depending on whether you're broadcasting or not.

If you are broadcasting, you can use the default port (8080) or specify a different port. If you choose a different port, you must be sure to specify the right port in the Windows Media Administrator when you set up your publishing point (see Chapter 37). URLs for both LAN and Internet connections are displayed immediately below the port specification. Use this URL when setting up your publishing point.

If you're archiving a broadcast or merely encoding to a local file, click the Browse button to specify a location for the encoded file. Be sure that the Add index to file checkbox is checked so that you can fast-forward and rewind through the file later.

Managing profiles

Windows Media Encoder profiles offer a powerful and flexible way to manage all your encoding needs. The encoder comes with a number of useful presets, but you may find that you want to modify some of these settings to get the best quality.

You can do this by editing the presets and saving them under a different name, or you can create a whole new profile from scratch. Come up with standardized profiles for your content and name them sensibly so that if you bring in interns to encode five hundred video clips, the correct profile to use is clear.

In fact, profiles can be exchanged between machines. When you create a new profile, a file with a .prx extension is created in the Windows Media Encoder Profiles folder. This file can be copied and distributed to other encoding machines, so that your encoding specifications remain consistent across multiple machines.

Creating a new profile

Creating or editing a profile is done in the Manage Profiles window (see Figure 13-16), where you can edit an existing profile or create a new one. Either way, you have to specify the source types you're using, select target audiences, choose audio and video codecs, and set individual video stream settings, such as frame rate and keyframe quality.

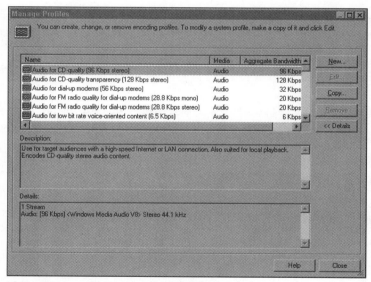

Figure 13-16: The Manage Profiles window.

1. **Open the Windows Media Encoder and then open the Manage Profiles window by choosing Manage Profiles from the Tools menu or by pressing Ctrl-M.** Click New to create a new profile. The New Profile window appears (see Figure 13-17).

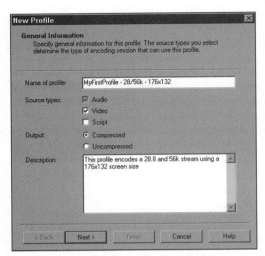

Figure 13-17: The New Profile window

2. **Give your new profile a name, specify your source types, make sure that the Compressed radio button is selected, and enter a description for your profile.** Click the Next button to move on to the Audience Selection window.

It's a good idea to enter a description for your profile. It can save confusion later, especially when someone else uses your profiles.

3. **Select your desired target audiences by checking the appropriate boxes (see Figure 13-18).** Click the Next button to move on to the Common Stream settings screen, where you can choose the audio and video codecs.

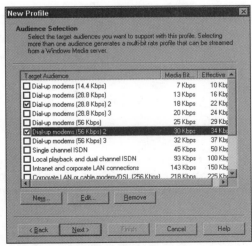

Figure 13-18: The Audience Selection screen

4. **On the Common Stream settings screen (see Figure 13-19), you can choose an audio codec, a video codec, and a screen size.** Select the codecs from the choices offered in the drop-down menus.

You can also choose one of the predefined screen sizes or set a custom screen size by choosing Custom from the drop-down menu. A screen pops up in which you can enter a custom width and height.

After you enter the settings on this screen, you can click Finish if you are done, or you can click Next if you want to adjust the individual screen settings.

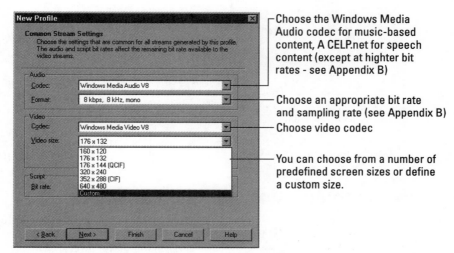

Choose the Windows Media Audio codec for music-based content, A CELP.net for speech content (except at highter bit rates - see Appendix B)

Choose an appropriate bit rate and sampling rate (see Appendix B)

Choose video codec

You can choose from a number of predefined screen sizes or define a custom size.

Figure 13-19: The Common Stream settings screen

5. If you want to adjust individual stream settings, you can do so on the Individual Video Stream Settings screen (see Figure 13-20). On this screen, you can adjust the frame rate, the keyframe interval, and the image quality.

The settings on this screen can have a serious effect on the video quality — better or worse. Don't mess around with these settings unless you know what you're doing.

Cross-Reference

For more information on how to vary the settings on this screen and how to get the most out of your Windows Media video files, please refer to the "Advanced Video Encoding with Windows Media" sidebar at the end of this chapter.

6. **Click Finish.** You now can use this profile in any encoding session or share it with other machines by copying the .prx file.

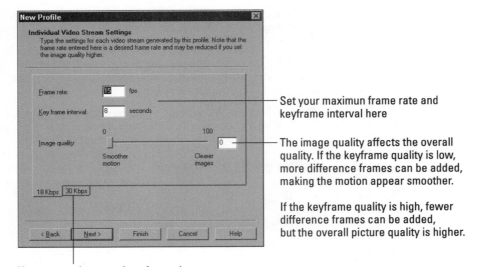

Set your maximun frame rate and keyframe interval here

The image quality affects the overall quality. If the keyframe quality is low, more difference frames can be added, making the motion appear smoother.

If the keyframe quality is high, fewer difference frames can be added, but the overall picture quality is higher.

You can set these settings for each target audience you specify.

Figure 13-20: The Individual Stream Settings screen

Video preprocessing

The windows media encoder offers additional processing of your video files. You can adjust the quality of the video input by using the video proc amp, crop your video, and perform advanced optimization by using video filters.

Video proc amp

The video proc amp enables you to change the quality of the incoming video by adjusting the brightness, contrast, hue, and saturation. To open the video proc amp, you can do one of three things:

✦ Click the Configure button next to the video source on the New Source Group Screen (see Figure 13-13)

✦ Choose Configure Devices from the Tools menu on the main screen of the Windows Media Encoder

✦ Press Ctrl-D

Video cropping

You can crop your video when you set up a new source group. When you add new source groups, you can click the Video Clipping tab, which brings that screen forward. It's a simple interface where you can specify pixel values to be cropped off the left, right, top and bottom of the video screen. The cropping values must always be multiples of two, and the overall dimensions of the video screen must always be multiples of eight.

Video optimization filters

The Windows Media encoder also offers de-interlacing and inverse telecine filters. Like cropping, you can set up these filters when you configure new sources. Click the Video Optimization tab on the New Source Group screen, and you can specify a pixel format and whether you want to use one of the filters.

The Windows Media Encoder does not allow you to use the de-interlace filter at the same time as the inverse telecine filter.

For more information on de-interlacing and the inverse telecine process, please turn to Chapter 10.

De-interlace filter

The de-interlace filter reduces artifacts that are introduced when interlaced content (TV) is converted to progressive scan (computer monitor). This filter should only be used on content that uses a screen size larger than 320×240 pixels.

Inverse telecine

The inverse telecine filter should be used on content that was originally shot on film and transferred to video. This filter removes the extra frames that are added during the telecine process.

Using Windows Media Encoder

The previous sections detail how to set up source groups and profiles for the Windows Media Encoder. After you've done that, the actual encoding process is extremely simple:

1. **Choose a source group.**

2. **Choose a profile.**

3. **Start the encoder.**

Even if you haven't set up source groups or created custom profiles, encoding with the Windows Media Encoder is straightforward. The following example uses the same raw file that you encoded using QuickTime Pro and the RealSystem Producer. Assume you want to create Windows Media versions that cater to 28.8K and 56K modem users as well as a version for people on the office LAN.

The target bit rates for these audiences are probably a bit far apart to use the same screen size, but you do not need to render two separate versions from your video editing program. You *will* have to encode two separate versions, but you can resize while you encode.

1. **Open the Windows Media Encoder and start a new session by pressing Ctrl-N or choosing New from the Session menu (refer to Figure 13-12).**

2. **Define a single source group that contains the file that you want to encode.**

   On the New Session screen, click New to bring up the New Source Group screen (see Figure 13-13). Choose Browse for file from the Video drop-down menu and find your file. The name of your source group defaults to the name of your file, which is fine.

   If you want to crop the file or use any video filters, now is the time. Click the Video Clipping and/or Video Optimization tabs and choose your settings accordingly.

   Click OK to return to the New Session screen.

3. **If you want to enter any metadata, do so by clicking the Display Information and Attributes tabs.** Enter appropriate metadata on these screens.

4. **Choose an encoding profile.**

   Click the Profile tab to open the Profile screen (refer to Figure 13-14) and choose a profile from the drop-down menu. Use a profile that you created earlier or one appropriate to your needs. Two presets are appropriate:

   • Video for dial-up modems or single channel ISDN

   • Video for dial-up modems or LAN

Both these presets use a video screen size of 176 × 144 pixels, which is not a true 4:3 aspect ratio when displayed on a square-pixel monitor. You may want to edit these presets to use a 176 × 132 pixel screen size to avoid image distortion.

   If you're going to use a larger screen size for the LAN audience, choose a preset that includes only the 28.8K and 56K dialup audiences.

5. **Click the Output tab to specify your output.**

   Make sure that the Broadcast box is unchecked and the Encode to file box is checked. Specify a name for your encoded file by entering the full path information or by clicking the Browse button (refer to Figure 13-15).

6. **Essentially that's it for the first file.** Click OK to return to the main encoder window and click the Start button in the lower-right corner.

7. **When the file is done encoding, you must start a new session to encode a different version.** Go back to step one and repeat the steps, but this time choose a profile (and screen size) to suit a LAN audience. When you finish, click Start again to encode the second version of the file.

Now that you have two streaming versions of the file, you need to put them on a server and test them to make sure that they work correctly.

Testing Lower Bit Rate Streams in Multiple Bit Rate Windows Media Files

It's important to test all the streams in your multiple bit rate files to ensure the quality lives up to your expectation. However, when you connect locally or across a LAN, your player connects at a high speed and all you see is the highest quality stream. If you really want to know what your audience sees you should connect via the same methods your audience uses, but if the prospect of dialing in on 28.8 modem sounds unappealing, you can sample the quality of the lower bit rate streams in a couple of ways.

Forcing connection speeds in the Windows Media Player

When you install the Windows Media Player, you are asked to supply a connection speed. The player passes this parameter to the server when requesting files. You can temporarily reset this parameter to force the server to send a lower quality stream to you. Even though the server senses a higher speed connection, it will not override this setting.

To change your connection speed, choose Options from the Tools menu and click on the Performance tab. This action brings up the performance window. Simply change your connection speed to the speed of the stream(s) you want to test and re-request the file from the server.

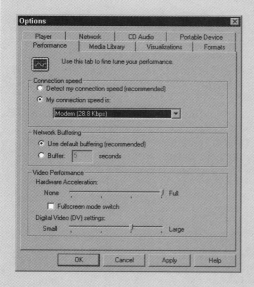

Changing your connection speed preference in the Windows Media Player

Continued

Continued

Using the WMBitrate modifier

Alternately, you can specify a bit rate to be sent via the `WMBitrate` modifier, either in an `.asx` file or entered directly into the player. To use the modifier, simply follow your stream URL with a question mark and the modifier, as follows:

```
mms://my.server.com/MyMBRFile.asf?WMBitrate=32000
```

This forces the server to send a stream at or below the specified bit rate, which is specified in bits per second.

Advanced Video Encoding with Windows Media codec

Expert   The following material was contributed by Amir Majidimehr of the Windows Media Group at Microsoft.

The Microsoft Windows Media Video codec is a state-of-the-art video compression technology. It is designed to provide far higher compression efficiency and lower visual artifacts than traditional video codecs such as those based on the H.263 and MPEG-4 codecs. As a result, you can achieve either better quality video at the same data rate or equivalent quality at much lower rates compared to earlier technologies.

In addition to the more efficient compression engine, the Microsoft Windows Media Software Development Kit (SDK), Windows Media Encoder, and Windows Media Encoding Script provide an additional set of tools for extracting higher levels of quality from encoded material. This side bar covers the overall operational details of Windows Media Video together with best use of the encoding technologies to create great looking video.

Windows Media Video Codec Overview

The Windows Media Video codec is a video compression engine that takes advantage of redundancy within a frame (intraframe coding) and between frames (interframe coding). The combination of these two modes enables very high compression ratios that can be in excess of 1,000:1.

The codec starts with compressing the initial frame and then produces incremental *delta* frames that follow. However, if there are sufficient image changes, the codec may produce a full frame (known as a key frame), instead of incremental frames.

Constant Bit Rate Encoding

Although Windows Media Video has very efficient intraframe compression, the compressed key frames generate more bits than the delta frames. As a result, the output of the Windows Media Video core compression engine is a variable-bit-rate (VBR) stream.

Typically, when streaming over fixed bandwidth channels such as modems, it is desirable to have a fixed bandwidth codec. Windows Media Video has a built-in "rate control" module that uses an intermediate buffer to smooth out the peaks and valleys to produce a constant bit rate. The codec monitors the available buffer space and dynamically varies the amount of compression to *guarantee* the target bit rate is met. This mode of encoding is referred to as constant-bit-rate (CBR) encoding.

The amount of buffering used to create a constant bit rate is customizable in Windows Media Encoder and Windows Media Encoding Script. However, setting this value on the encoding side means that you must adjust the start-up buffer in the player by at least the same amount. Otherwise, the user will experience variations in the bit rate that can result in potential starvation or buffer underflow that will stop playback and require rebuffering. For this reason, Windows Media Encoder or Windows Media Encoding Script stores the amount of buffering in the header of the stream so that the player can use it to allocate and fill the buffer accordingly.

Because a player cannot start playing until it fills its buffer, the start of a video clip is delayed. For this reason, the encoder buffer time is also known as the *delay* buffer. The delay buffer usually causes a corresponding delay in the player. So, if you set the encoder to buffer for 10 seconds, the player needs 10 seconds of buffering before starting.

It makes sense that the larger the buffer, the better the quality of the encoded video because, in complex video scenes, the buffer will be able to absorb larger bit rate peaks, which will avoid higher compression levels (and more artifacts) in those scenes. The default delay of 5 seconds is used as a balance between the need for good quality and shorter buffering time.

Variable Bit Rate Encoding

CBR encoding must be used when the transfer rate of the network or device is constant and not much higher than the expected data rate of the encoded video. However, there are cases when the network or device has far higher capacity than the clip data rate. For example, even the slowest hard disk today can handle in excess of 50 Mbps, which is far faster than the encoding rate of most video clips. The same is true in high-speed networks, such as 100 Mbps Ethernet or even 11 Mbps 802.11b wireless networks.

For these situations, using another encoding method, VBR encoding, is best. In this mode, the codec lets its output data rate fluctuate based on the source content. As such, the quality can be better controlled because there are no fixed buffer size constraints.

Note that VBR is most advantageous when encoding a combination of easy and difficult scenes. VBR mode naturally allocates fewer bits to the easy scenes, leaving enough to produce good quality for the difficult ones. Therefore, a clip that is easy to encode, such as a "talking head" news story or a very difficult clip, such as a 30-second commercial, would not benefit from VBR.

The best application for VBR is long-format content such as movies. The long format means that there will be many fluctuations in scene complexity providing plenty of places where bits can be conserved.

Constant Quality Encoding with VBR

One of the choices you have with VBR encoding is *quality-based* encoding, which enables you to set a constant compression quality level, and the codec picks the appropriate data rate. Windows Media Video has a calibrated quality scale of 1 to 100, with 1 representing the lowest quality and 100 representing the absolute best quality the codec can achieve. When the codec uses any of these quality levels, it attempts to achieve the same level of quality throughout the clip. So, there will be fewer artifacts during high motion sequences, which is typical of the CBR encoding mode (where the larger data rate required for complex video frames causes the compression ratio to increase substantially, leading to more artifacts).

So, if your goal is to arrive at a certain quality and your network and device can handle the peak data generated by the codec, then quality-based VBR is the main mode to use.

The quality-based VBR mode has been calibrated based on a set of objective and subjective tests to arrive at roughly the required quality level. So, when you set the quality level to 50, it will be close to half the quality of 100. Of course, this can never be exact because the objective measurements made by the codec may not agree with your (subjective) opinion of the output quality. But the rate should be close enough to allow for simple fine-tuning from there on.

Note that VBR files should not be streamed because the network load will be totally unpredictable. Imagine the scenario of 100 people watching different clips and they all hit a scene change roughly at the same time. The network load jumps by a large factor when you consider the peak requirements of each clip. However, you can use file sharing capabilities from the operating system to play VBR clips across a network.

Two-pass CBR Encoding

When encoding video in CBR mode, knowing what will occur in future frames is very useful. That way, the codec can make a more optimal selection as to how many bits it should allocate to each frame. For example, imagine a news story with a "talking head" that switches to a commercial. The talking head is easy to encode due to lack of motion. The commercials, on the other hand, tend to have a very high number of scene changes to catch the viewers' attention. If the codec does not know that a commercial will follow the talking head, it may allocate too many bits to the talking head in an attempt to make the content look as best as it can, only to run out of bits when the commercial arrives, leading to potentially visible artifacts.

Increasing the buffer amount helps the bit allocation problem, but this solution becomes impractical when the clip duration becomes lengthy. For example, setting the buffer period to 1.5 hours when encoding a movie with the same length is unrealistic. Doing so means that the player will allocate a buffer large enough to capture the entire movie before playing. For a 300 Kbps, 1.5 hour clip, the buffer will be in excess of 200MB. Even if the amount of start up delay does not disappoint the user, the amount of memory required by the player definitely will.

Two-pass encoding solves the allocation problem by letting the code "see the future" by scanning the entire clip before encoding any of it. The encoder feeds the entire clip to the codec, which makes an analysis of the theoretical bit rate needed to encode the various frames. This information is then used in the second pass to decide how many bits should be allocated to each frame.

Because the codec has full visibility into the "future" in two-pass encoding, it is able to better deal with sudden scene changes, meaning that the overall quality will vary a lot less than it would in single pass encoding.

The main drawback to two-pass encoding is that you need access to the source file, which rules out using this type of encoding for live content. By using this mode, you can also increase the encoding time by roughly a factor of two. But if these restrictions are not a factor, then two-pass CBR is an ideal tool to use to increase the video quality while still staying in CBR mode.

Bit Rate-Based VBR Encoding

The VBR mode allows you to specify an average bit rate rather than a quality level. This mode requires a two-pass mechanism. In the first pass, the codec analyzes the video frame complexities (using a similar process as two-pass CBR encoding). In the second pass, the codec automatically determines the quality level that will achieve the average bit rate.

Note that the results are not the same as with CBR encoding. The file could still have massive peaks that last for a considerable amount of time. So, the network needs to be fast enough to handle such peaks.

The main reason to use bit-rate-based (two-pass) VBR encoding is to arrive at the desired file length because quality-based VBR encoding can result in unpredictable (that is, content dependent) output file size.

Note that bit-rate-based VBR shares the same restrictions as quality-based VBR in that it is not suitable for streaming and will require long and varied content to show its advantages.

Picking the Encoding Mode

By now it should be clear that picking the right encoding mode is critical in arriving at the best quality encoding. No amount of optimization can make up for a poor choice here.

The decision making process should start with VBR, then two-pass CBR, and then finally one-pass CBR. VBR, when used on proper content (again, content that is long and varied in complexity), will produce a much better encoded clip given the same file size when compared to CBR. The difference can be as high as 2:1, meaning that you may be able to get a VBR file that has the same quality as CBR in just half the file size.

Likewise, if the source is a file and not a live source, then it is highly recommended that you use two-pass CBR. You will get higher quality than one-pass without losing the advantages of CBR mode.

Finally, when encoding live to a streaming audience, one-pass CBR is the only available option.

Optimizing Parameters for CBR Encoding

Your main tool for optimizing content for CBR encoding is using the delay buffer mentioned previously. Increasing the buffer period from the default 5 seconds — much longer can significantly increase quality. You can almost call this "pseudo" VBR as it will simulate the same effect as VBR encoding, but over a shorter time period.

An example of when larger buffering sizes may be useful is with feature length movies that you are *streaming*. It is probably reasonable to have a higher start-up delay, for example, 30 seconds, because relative to the length of the movie, it will not seem too large.

You can also be aggressive with the buffer length when the content is distributed by a server running Microsoft Windows Media Services in Windows .NET Standard Server or Windows Media Services in Windows .NET Enterprise Server. This technology includes a new streaming mode called Fast Start. Fast Start will enable a player to fill its buffer faster than real-time, bandwidth permitting. Therefore, the initial buffer may be much shorter in reality. For example, when a user clicks 56 Kbps encoded content on a DSL or cable modem, the start-up delay may just be a second or two, even if the buffer delay is set to tens of seconds.

When the bit rate is too low for a given (complex) video scene, the codec may need to skip frames to maintain the peak bit rate fluctuations within the CBR buffering constraints. You can control the tradeoff between frame skipping and image quality by using the quality parameter (for example, the `-v_quality` command in the Windows Media Encoding Script), which accepts values between 0 and 100. A smaller quality value will improve the temporal video smoothness at the expense of reducing video quality. The best value for this quality setting is somewhat subjective because you may prefer to maintain a full frame rate and tolerate some drops in video quality in difficult scenes; hence, setting a low quality value. Or you may tolerate some frame skipping and prefer a higher image quality; hence, setting a high quality value. One good way of tuning this parameter is to encode a clip multiple times while increasing the quality value from 0 to 100 in small increments, and then picking the largest quality value that results in little or no frame skipping in the encoded video.

When tuning buffer delay and quality, remember that a longer buffer delay can accommodate higher values of quality for the same level of frame skipping. You may want to select the buffer size first, and then the quality parameter.

Another parameter that is worth tuning is the key frame distance. A longer distance usually results in better video quality because the codec only inserts key frames whenever it makes sense from a compression standpoint, such as in scene changes. However, key frames are synchronization points for streaming (if the user temporarily loses the connection), and earlier players seek only to key frames within a file, so you should not place key frames too far apart. This encoding technique applies to all CBR and VBR encoding modes.

Beyond the delay buffer, quality, and key frame parameters, there are really no other direct codec parameters to optimize. However, you can achieve much more by modifying other encoding parameters. One key parameter is the overall image size. For example, instead of encoding content at 320 × 240 resolution, you could clip five lines from the top and bottom of a clip for a displayed resolution of 320 × 230. This may not sound like much, but you have to remember that each line has 320 pixels, so the overall data reduction is much more substantial than it seems at first.

Note that reducing the vertical resolution is required sometimes for proper encoding (for example, with standard TV signals, which have embedded the time code in the video signal itself). This Vertical Interval Time Code (VITC) is not normally visible because TVs overscan and in general, do not display this part of the image area. However, computer capture cards faithfully capture these lines and the player shows them as dashed white lines that seem to follow some pattern. Needless to say, this area should be clipped and not encoded as it simply wastes bits and makes it look like there is extra material on top of the image.

You should use the cropping and resizing controls in the encoding tools to reduce the output image size rather than changing the input image size. If you simply change the image size, the output image will become distorted and no clipping will occur. If you are using Windows Media Encoding Script, the `-v_clip` command can be used to do this. Alternatively, you can use the crop and resize controls on the Video Size tab in Windows Media Encoder.

Optimizing the Bit Rate for CBR Encoding

When setting the bit rate in CBR mode, the codec does not actually try to use all of the available bit rate if it is not needed. For example, if you set the bit rate to 1 Mbps and the frame size to 320 × 240 and then feed the encoder a single stationary frame for one minute, the Windows Media Video codec will not generate anything close to 1 Mbps. Instead, the codec generates the best quality it can for the frame size, and then pads the rest of the output. The resulting file will appear to be at 1 Mbps, but in reality, the actual data encoded in it will be far lower.

You can tell when the bit rate is set too high if the output frame rate is far lower than you have specified (for example, 1 fps versus 30 fps) and ample CPU cycles are in the system. Alternatively, you can determine the same thing if you compress the file with a program such as WinZip or PKZip, and the resulting file is much smaller than the original. This is because the output of the codec itself cannot be further compressed by such programs because all such redundancy has already been removed from it by the video codec. What can be compressed is the additional padding in the file.

By now, you may be wondering if extra bandwidth is wasted when you stream such files. The answer is no; bandwidth is not wasted. A Windows Media server will discard the padding when streaming these files so there is no efficiency loss there. The only loss is in the actual encoded file.

Encoder CPU Requirements

Encoding audio and video is one of the most CPU-intensive tasks that you can run on a computer. A codec, such as Windows Media Video, is asymmetrical in that it uses far more CPU while encoding than when decoding the image. This is the proper trade off as it is much more reasonable to assume that someone encoding a clip will be better prepared to get a faster computer, than expecting millions of users to do the same.

Fortunately, Windows Media codecs are highly optimized for a wide range of CPUs and architectures. Specifically, Windows Media Video is optimized to take advantage of special MMX and SSE instructions in *x*86 processors such as Pentium, Pentium II/II and 4, and Advanced Micro Devices (AMD).

In addition to specific processor optimizations, the Windows Media Video codec is multi-threaded, meaning that it can take advantage of more than one CPU to accelerate encoding. Specifically, Windows Media Video can use up to four processors simultaneously, although most people opt for dual-CPU systems due to the much better price to performance ratio of these systems compared to quad-process computers.

As an aside, the Windows Media Audio codec is optimized to take advantage of two CPUs when encoding in stereo.

Even if a single CPU is fast enough to handle the video encoding, it is recommended that you use a dual-CPU system instead when encoding live content. This is because the extra CPU decreases the chance that video frames are dropped on the way into the system when the other CPU is busy with encoding. With a single CPU, it is much more probable that captured frames get lost during high-motion video sequences (which require the most CPU cycles).

Note that Task Manager in the Microsoft Windows operating system is not a reliable measure of CPU requirements for the Windows Media Video codec as it will average the CPU usage and will not represent the instantaneous, peak usage. So, if Task Manager reports 80 percent usage, it does not necessarily mean that you have 20 percent CPU left. It is entirely possible that during high motion video sequences, the system could be falling behind, causing frames to be dropped.

Encoding Audio for Video

When encoding a video clip, it is important to pay particular attention to the audio settings. This is important for two reasons: first, a better sounding clip will always "look" better than another with identical video quality; secondly, optimizing the audio data rate can help increase the data rate for video, making it look better in the process.

The strategy for audio encoding falls into two categories: low-data rate (for example, modems) and high data rates.

When encoding at low data rates, (for example, 37 Kbps for a 56 Kbps modem), it is critical to pick the lowest audio data rate that gives adequate quality. For example, if you reduce the audio data rate from 8 Kbps to 5 Kbps, you will be actually adding 10 percent more bandwidth to the video in a 37 Kbps clip, which can produce a noticeable quality difference. Lower audio data rates also enable the system to maintain the audio stream at even lower data rates should it become necessary during congestion or data loss. You may also consider encoding in mono at lower bit rate settings rather than encoding in stereo.

At high data rates, the opposite is true. When encoding at broadband data rates, you should maximize the audio data rate as much as you can because small incremental increases can substantially improve audio quality, with negligible impact on video quality. For example, by moving from 32 Kbps to 48 Kbps with the Windows Media Audio codec, you lose only 16 Kbps, which is just 6 percent less of a data rate for video when encoding at 300 Kbps. But the increased audio quality, especially when encoding in stereo, will be substantial because the Windows Media Audio codec at 48 Kbps provides near CD-quality compared to FM quality at 32 Kbps.

In general, at higher data rates (greater than 300 Kbps), it is recommended that up to 15 to 20 percent of the overall data rate be allocated to audio, perhaps stopping once the audio rate gets to beyond 64 Kbps.

Finally, be sure to use the latest version of the Windows Media Audio codec because recent releases have far better quality than earlier versions of the codec. As such, you get higher quality without spending as many bits on audio.

Getting great looking video starts with a deep understanding of the various encoding options available, such as VBR and two-pass CBR. Using the proper mode will result in far better quality than any hand tuning. Further optimization of encoding parameters, such as buffer delay, video resolution, and audio data rate, can generate even better results.

Summary

With any luck you should now be able to navigate your way around the encoding software for all three streaming platforms. In the next chapter, you'll learn ways to automate the encoding process, as well as a few more tricks you can do with encoded files.

✦ QuickTime Pro can convert QuickTime movies into streaming versions.

✦ All QuickTime movies must be hinted to be streamed.

✦ You can hint while you encode or hint movies separately.

✦ If your QuickTime presentation includes noncompressed data types, such as text or MIDI, remove the tracks before encoding and then add them back in before you hint your files.

✦ RealMedia files are encoded by using the RealSystem Producer software. This software is available in a free version and a Plus version that includes additional functionality.

✦ The RealSystem uses target audiences to determine which codecs to use when encoding. These settings are fully configurable in the Plus version of the RealSystem Producer.

✦ The RealSystem SureStream functionality embeds multiple streams at different bit rates into a single file. The RealServer can switch between streams depending on network conditions.

✦ The RealSystem Producer enables you to set whether the encoded file should be recordable or downloaded.

✦ Both the RealSystem Producer and the Windows Media Encoder offer de-interlace and inverse telecine filters to improve video quality.

✦ Resizing and cropping functionality is available in both the RealSystem Producer Plus and Windows Media Encoder.

✦ The Windows Media Encoder uses sessions to describe what is encoded and how it is encoded. Sessions can be saved for reuse.

✦ Windows Media Encoder sessions contain profiles that describe the parameters used to encode the source.

✦ A Windows Media Encoder profile may contain multiple target audiences. These target audiences must share the same screen size and audio codec. Profiles also can be saved to disk and shared among machines.

✦   ✦   ✦

Working with Encoded Files

By now, you should have a grasp of how to use the
encoding software for all three platforms. At a minimum, you should at least know how to use the encoder for
the platform you're most interested in. In this chapter, you
learn a little more about how you can speed up the encoding
process and what you can do with your encoded files.

You may have already realized that encoding can involve a lot
of repetition. If you have a large number of files you want to
encode using the same encoding parameters, encoding the
files as a batch instead of one at a time would be easier.

Batch encoding software does exactly this. It enables you to
encode whole directories of files instead of having to encode
each file individually.

Many commercial software applications are available that offer
batch encoding capabilities, and some software also offers
video and audio preprocessing and automation. Windows
Media Technologies and the RealSystem offer native batch
encoding by using a command line version of their encoders.
Windows Media also offers a simple batch encoder in the
Windows Media Resource Kit.

Even though editing your encoded files is not the best idea,
you may need to do some simple editing, such as pasting two
encoded files together or removing an objectionable section.
This type of editing really should be done during the
creation phase, but sometimes you don't have that option.
Conveniently, all three platforms offer simple editing tools.

If want to embed URLs into your streams, you can do so in a
number of ways. The Windows Media Encoder lets you insert
URLs as you encode, while both QuickTime and the
RealSystem let you add them to an encoded file.

Using Batch Encoding

You could spend hours tweaking the encoding settings to obtain the highest quality for each of your audio and video clips. But, if you're like most people, you do not have that kind of time, nor does the content require it. When you find encoding settings that work for your content, establish those settings as the standard and stick with them.

When you've established a standard, you can take advantage of batch encoding. Batch encoding rids you of much of the drudgery of large scale encoding projects. Although nothing's wrong with encoding a few files every day, if you have hundreds to do, you need a way to minimize the amount of interaction you have with the encoder.

Occasionally, you may want to tweak a particular file that merits the extra attention, but for the most part, your standardized settings should work just fine. Best of all, you can set your batch encoding processes to run overnight when computers usually lie idle, instead of during the day when encoding can tie up valuable resources.

Third-party batch encoding platforms are available, such as Media Cleaner and Sonic Foundry's Batch Converter as well as batch processing capabilities built-in to powerful video and/or audio editing platforms such as Adobe Premiere. These capabilities are extremely useful, and I'd highly recommend that you make batch processing one of your requirements when shopping around for an audio or video editing system. However, this book deals only with the native batch encoding available with each streaming platform.

Two of our platforms offer batch encoding by using a command line interface. Therefore, you have to open up a command window and type a long command that tells the encoder exactly how to encode the files. Every setting you see in the graphic user interface (GUI) versions of the encoders can be set in the command line.

Because typing these long command lines can be tedious and frustrating, the best way to do command line encoding is to type the command in a simple text editor, such as UltraEdit or BBEdit (included on the CD-ROM). You can edit and correct any typing errors, save the file, and then tell the operating system to execute the commands contained in the file.

The following sections detail the steps necessary to batch encode files into each of the three main streaming media platforms. If you're not familiar with command line interfaces, you may find batch encoding a bit daunting at first, but the amount of work batch encoding saves you will more than make up for the time you spend learning how to use the command line.

Batch encoding QuickTime files

QuickTime does not offer a command line encoding utility but does enable you to control QuickTime encoding by using AppleScript. AppleScript is an English-like scripting language that enables you to automate many tasks on an Apple computer. Unfortunately, AppleScript is not available for PCs; it's available for Mac operating systems.

AppleScript falls a bit outside the scope of this book, particularly because AppleScript is not cross-platform. If you are interested in learning more, please refer the Apple Web site (www.apple.com/applescript/).

You can, of course, also use third-party software, such as Adobe Premiere or Cleaner 5, to automate your encoding tasks. These platforms have the additional benefit of offering video and audio pre-processing. You may want to use a third-party platform specifically to take advantage of these pre-processing abilities.

Batch encoding RealMedia files

To batch encode RealMedia files you need a program called rmbatch. This utility has the functionality of the RealSystem producer without the graphic user interface (GUI). To use it, you must open up a command window and type a long command that supplies the encoder with all the parameters needed to encode the file.

Note

The rmbatch **utility is only included with the RealSystem Producer Plus** (www. realnetworks.com).

Every parameter you can set with the RealSystem Producer GUI can be set by using a switch on the command line. For example, to specify the file you want to encode, you use the /I switch, followed by a space, followed by the name of the file. A typical batch encode command looks something like this:

```
rmbatch /I C:\MyMovie.avi /O C:\encoded\MyMovie.rm  /T 0,1 /A 2 /V 2 /F 1
```

The switches used in this command line are as follows:

- ✦ /I: Sets the input file to C:\MyMovie.avi
- ✦ /O: Sets the output file to C:\MyMovie.rm
- ✦ /T: Sets the target audiences to 0 and 1, which corresponds to 28.8 and 56K modems
- ✦ /A: Sets the audio format to 2, which is music
- ✦ /V: Sets the video quality to 2, specifying sharpest image
- ✦ /F: Sets the file type to 1, specifying SureStream

To see the full list of switches, please consult the RealSystem Producer Plus User Guide, or simply type `rmbatch /?` at the command prompt. Doing so creates and opens up a file called RealProducerPlus.txt in a Notepad window. This file contains all the switch definitions and provides a permanent reference for you.

Caution The above example assumes that you are in the RealProducerPlus directory. If you are not, you must specify the full path to the `rmbatch` utility. If any spaces are in the path, you must put quotes around the file specification, as follows:

```
"C:\Program Files\Real\RealProducerPlus\rmbatch.exe"
   /I C:\MyMovie.avi /O C:\MyMovie.rm  /T 0,1
   /A 2 /V 2 /F 1
```

Encoding profiles

You can simplify the encoding command line (and avoid mistakes) by creating encoding profiles. Creating an encoding profile involves specifying the total bit rate, audio codec, video codec, and maximum frame rate for each target audience.

Each target audience must have its parameters specified on a single line, separated by commas, using the same syntax as on the command line. As an example, if you wanted to set up a profile that encoded for 28.8, 56K, and dual ISDN target audiences, your encoding file might look like the following (ignore the line breaks):

```
TARGET=0,TOTAL_BIT_RATE=20,AUDIO_CODEC=cook0,
   VIDEO_CODEC=RV300,MAX_FRAME_RATE=7.5
TARGET=1,TOTAL_BIT_RATE=34,AUDIO_CODEC=cook1,
   VIDEO_CODEC=RV300,MAX_FRAME_RATE=7.5
TARGET=3,TOTAL_BIT_RATE=350,AUDIO_CODEC=cook3,
   VIDEO_CODEC=RV300,MAX_FRAME_RATE=15
```

Caution Parameters and codec names in RealSystem Producer profiles are case-sensitive.

You can save this file as a simple text file, and then used in your command line via the /M switch, as follows:

```
rmbatch /I C:\MyMovie.avi /O C:\encoded\MyMovie.rm
   /M MyProfile.txt /V 0 /F 1
```

Note The above example assumes the profile resides in the same directory as the `rmbatch` utility. If it does not, you need to specify the full path to the profile.

Streamlining your encoding

The real power of the batch encode comes with the /D switch. This switch allows you to specify an input directory instead of a single file. Instead of having to specify a command line for each file that needs to be encoded, you can simply encode a whole directory with the same specifications. When using the /D switch, the encoder expects a directory specified in the /O switch.

If you do a lot of encoding, the best way to set this up is to establish a directory where your un-encoded files are kept and a directory where encoded files are placed. Create profiles for the various kinds of encoding you do and command line files that you can run every night so that encoding doesn't tie up valuable computer resources.

As long as you specify full paths in the command line, you can save the command line anywhere on your computer as a .bat file (for example on the desktop) and simply double-click on the .bat file to run your encodes. You can even put multiple encoding commands in your encoding batch file. For example, your batch file might look something like this:

```
"C:\Program Files\Real\RealProducerPlus\rmbatch.exe"
 /I C:\raw_video /O C:\dialup_encodes
 /M C:\MyProfiles\dialUp_profile.txt /V 0 /F 1
"C:\Program Files\Real\RealProducerPlus\rmbatch.exe"
 /I C:\raw_video /O C:\hibit_encodes
 /M C:\MyProfiles\hiBit_profile.txt /V 0 /F 1
```

This batch file encodes all the videos in the raw_video directory twice, once according to the dialUp_profile.txt file and once according to the hiBit_profile.txt file.

Batch encoding Windows Media Files

Batch encoding Windows Media Files is accomplished by using the Windows Media Batch Encoder or by using a command line utility called wm8eutil. Both ways are capable of the same result — it depends on what you're after. The Batch Encoder provides a convenient GUI interface that is simple to use, but unlike the GUI version the command line utility can be automated for example, by using a .bat file.

The Windows Media Batch Encoder

Figure 14-1 shows the Windows Media Batch Encoder. You can add as many files as you want by dragging and dropping files onto the batch encoder or by clicking the Add File button. You may add files of any type that the Windows Media Encoder supports. An encoding profile must be selected for each file you add. After each file is added, a line with all the encoding information and metadata displays.

Note The Windows Media System refers to metadata as attributes.

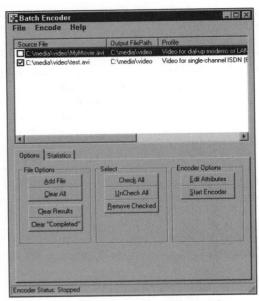

Figure 14-1: The Windows Media Batch Encoder

One nice feature of the Windows Media Batch Encoder is the ability to edit the metadata for a group of files. For example, if you have a group of files that should all have the same copyright, simply check the small box to the left of each file you want to edit (or click the Check All button) and then click the Edit Attributes button. Enter the copyright information and click OK. The copyright information is applied to all checked files.

When you've specified all the files to be encoded, chosen appropriate profiles, and entered all the metadata, simply click the Start Encoder button and go grab a coffee somewhere.

Batch encoding using the command line

wm8eutil is available in the Tools section of the Windows Media Components directory. The command line syntax can be very simple, because all you need to enter is the input file name, the output file name, and the profile that you want to use, as follows:

```
wm8eutil -input c:\MyVideo.avi -output c:\MyVideo.wmv
    -profile av100
```

Caution This example assumes that you are in the same directory as the encoding utility. If you are not in the same directory, you must specify the full path to the utility. If any spaces are in the path, you must put quotes around the path.

The profile, in this case av100, contains all the information necessary to encode the file, including video bit rate, audio codec, filter information, and so on. Each of these parameters can also be specified individually. To get a full list of all the available parameters, open up a command window, change directory to the Tools directory, and type

```
wm8eutil -all?
```

Doing so spits out all the variables that can be specified on the command line. You may want to copy this information to a text file so that you can refer to it later. Every setting that can be accessed through the Windows Media Encoder GUI can be accessed by using a switch on the command line. Because so many switches can be specified, using profiles and configuration files is the easiest way to use the batch encoding utility. When you use profiles and configuration files, the command line syntax is much simpler, as you'll see in the next section.

Working with profiles and configuration files

The Windows Media batch encoding utility comes with a number of preinstalled profiles. These profiles are similar to but not exactly the same as the profiles that are included with the GUI encoder. You cannot use profiles created by the Windows Media Encoder with the command line encoding utility; however, you can create custom configuration files that produce nearly the same encoded result.

Note You cannot generate multiple bit rate (MBR) files with the current windows media encoding utility (wm8eutil.exe). However, you can use the new VBScript, wmcmd.vb to create MBR profiles that can be called from the command line. Please refer to the Microsoft Web site (www.microsoft.com) for documentation for this script.

For a full list of all the pre-installed profiles, please refer to the Windows Media encoding utility help file or by typing the following at the command line:

```
wm8eutil -profile?
```

You can modify preinstalled profiles by adding parameters to the command line. Parameters specified individually override settings in the profile. When you find settings that are appropriate for your content, you can save them to a configuration file by using the -s_config switch. This switch saves all the parameters on the command line to a simple text file with the .weu extension.

Alternatively, you can create a configuration file in a simple text editor. All you have to do is type each parameter on a separate line. For example, if you wanted to encode video files at 100 Kbps with the Windows Media Video 8 codec, a 240 × 176 pixel screen size, and an audio bit rate of 32 Kbps, your configuration file should look like this:

```
-a_setting 32_22_2
-v_bitrate 100000
-v_width 240
-v_height 176
-v_codec WMV8
```

Save this file as `MyConfigFile.weu`, and your command line to encode files becomes very simple:

```
wm8eutil -input <inputfile> -output <outputfile>
    -profile MyConfigFile.weu
```

Note   The above example leaves out all path information for readability and assumes both the batch encoding utility and profile are in the current directory. It's good practice to specify full path for the utility and the profile, as well as the input and output files. Doing so makes your command line portable.

Streamlining your encoding

Just as you saw with the RealProducer, the true power of batch encoding comes into play by specifying whole directories as input. Input and output directories can be specified in the configuration file, in which case your command line encoding becomes the simplest yet:

```
wm8eutil -config MyConfigFile.weu
```

You may want to come up with different configuration files for different target audiences. Then all you have to do is create a batch file with the encoding utility called a number of times, each time using a different configuration file. What could be simpler?

Editing Encoded Files

In general, editing encoded files is not something you should do, particularly encoded video files. The playback of these files relies heavily on information that came previously (namely keyframes), so editing can only happen at certain points in the file to ensure accurate playback. Pinpoint accuracy is simply not possible.

If you can at all avoid it, don't edit encoded files. Do your editing on the raw files and re-encode. Of course, sometimes this is not possible. You may not have the original files, or you may be under severe time constraints. In these cases each platform provides simple tools that enable you to do rudimentary edits on encoded files. These tools are discussed in the following sections. The results may not be optimal, but these editing tools can be sufficient for some applications.

Editing QuickTime files

Editing QuickTime files is done in the QuickTime Player. However, you must have the Pro version; the free version is Playback only. If you've got QuickTime Pro, editing couldn't be easier. All you have to do is set the in and/or out points of the movie, and then copy it to a new file. Figure 14-2 shows where the indicators are located in the QuickTime Pro player.

Figure 14-2: Choosing in and out points using the QuickTime Pro player

Setting in and/or out points is easy. You can drag the in and out point indicators (small triangles under the timeline) or lock an indicator to the playback indicator by clicking near an indicator in the timeline. If you hold the Shift key down you can then scrub through the movie until you find the edit point. Release the shift key and repeat for the other indicator. The selected portion of the file is indicated by the gray shading in the timeline.

To create a new file that includes only the region, between your in and out points, all you have to do is copy the region and then paste it into another instance of the QuickTime player. You can do this in three keystrokes:

1. **Copy the selected region by pressing Ctrl-C.**

2. **Open a new QuickTime player by pressing Ctrl-N.**

3. **Paste the selected region into the new player by pressing Ctrl-V.**

Or you can use the drag-and-drop method:

1. **Open a QuickTime player and select the desired region.**

2. **Open another QuickTime player (Ctrl-N).**

3. **Click on the display screen in the first player, hold the mouse button down, and drag the cursor over to the second player. Release the mouse button to perform the edit.**

4. **Save your edited file, preferably using a different name so you can re-do the edit if you're not happy with it.**

That's all there is to editing files. If you want to paste files together or insert parts of one movie into another, choose the section from one file and then copy and paste it into a second player that has the other file you want to add to. Bear in mind that all regions are pasted *before* the playback indicator, unless the playback indicator is at the end of the movie, in which case the new content is appended to the file.

So, if you wanted to glue two movies together, here's what you do:

1. **Open the first movie and drag the time indicator to the end of the file.**

2. **Open the movie that you want to append to the first movie in a second QuickTime player.** Select all, copy, and paste it back into the first QuickTime player (Ctrl-A, Ctrl-C, Ctrl-V).

3. **Save the new movie using a new filename or continue appending files.**

You can also edit the metadata included with a QuickTime file. Just select Get Movie Properties from the Movie menu or type Ctrl-J. Doing so opens a small window where you can edit any metadata included in the file or add additional metadata (see Figure 14-3).

Metadata display area

Figure 14-3: Adding and editing metadata to QuickTime movies

Editing RealMedia files

RealMedia files can be edited in two ways. You can edit via the command line using `rmeditor` or by using the GUI version that is bundled with the RealProducer Plus. Both ways are easy to use.

Using rmeditor.exe

You can use `rmeditor` to cut and paste RealMedia files as well as changing any metadata included in the file, such as title, author, copyright, and so on. The syntax is straightforward. Some sample editing commands are as follows:

```
rmeditor -i one.rm -i two.rm -o onetwo.rm
rmeditor -i unedited.rm -o edited.rm -s 30 -e 5:45
rmeditor -i oldtitle.rm -t "New Title" -o newtitle.rm
```

The first example pastes two RealMedia files together. You can specify as many input files as you like; the input files are pasted together in the order that they are listed. The second example creates an edited version of the input file that starts at 30 seconds and ends at 5:45. If no start time is supplied, the beginning of the file is assumed; similarly, if no end time is specified, the end of the file is assumed. The last example copies the input file to the output file with a new title.

Caution Only RealMedia files that were encoded using the exact same parameters may be pasted together.

For a full listing of all the switches available please refer to the documentation that installs with the RealProducer. Here are a few things for you to consider:

✦ All start and end times are adjusted to the closest keyframe.

✦ If you are pasting files together, you cannot specify start and end times. First, you must do all your editing and then paste the files together.

✦ The above examples assume you are in the same directory as the `rmeditor` utility, and that all files being edited are also in the same directory. Be sure to supply full path information if this is not the case, being careful to put quotes around any paths that include spaces, as follows:

```
"c:\Program Files\Real\Realproducer\rmeditor"
    -i c:\raw_files\one.rm -i c:\raw_files\two.rm
    -o "d:\edited files\onetwo.rm"
```

Using the RealMedia Editor

The RealProducer Plus includes a GUI-based RealMedia Editor that performs all the functions of the command line utility. The RealMedia Editor also offers the ability to display files as you edit them, and preview the edited video before it is rendered out.

Note   The RealMedia Editor is only available if you purchase the RealSystem Producer Plus.

To open up the RealMedia Editor, choose Edit RealMedia File from the File menu. This opens up the main editing window (see Figure 14-4). Using the RealMedia Editor is fairly self-explanatory. Scroll through the file using the current position indicator and choose input and output points by grabbing the end points of the timeline or by clicking on the In and Out buttons.

Current keyframe

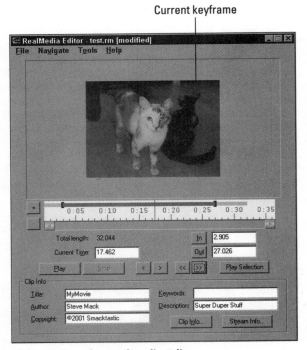

Figure 14-4: The RealMedia Editor

Note   The RealMedia Editor automatically edits video files on the closest available keyframe. To make sure that your edit falls on the correct keyframe, use the << and >> buttons to find the keyframe you want to edit on and then click the In or Out button.

You can preview the edited selection by clicking on the Play Selection button. When you're happy with your selection, you can perform the edit by choosing Save RealMedia File or Save RealMedia File As from the File menu.

Tip   Save your edits to new files so that you can try again if you want to. If you save over your original, that's it — you won't get a second chance.

If you want to paste RealMedia files together, simply open the first file in the RealMedia editor and then select Append RealMedia File from the File menu. Provided the files were encoded using the same specifications, they are pasted together, and the display changed to reflect the new length of the file. You may continue appending as many files as you like.

For full documentation of the RealMedia Editor, please refer to the documentation that is included with the RealSystem Producer Plus.

Editing Windows Media files

You can edit Windows Media files by using a few different methods. Most editing tasks are accomplished by using the ASF Advanced Script Indexer. In addition to working with scripts, the ASF Advanced Script Indexer also performs simple editing tasks, such as editing the start and end points of a video and changing the contents of the metadata fields.

You can also use a couple of command line options, ASFChop and WMVAppend. ASFchop is the command line version of the ASF indexer, and WMVAppend is used to paste Windows Media files together. Both options are available in the Windows Media Resource Kit that is available from the Windows Media site (www.microsoft.com/windowsmedia).

When editing Windows Media files, you may not be able to edit exactly where you want to. Regardless of whether you use the ASX Advanced Script Indexer or ASFchop, the in point (the first frame of your edited video) is adjusted to fall on the nearest keyframe to ensure correct playback.

Advanced Script Indexer

The Advanced Script Indexer is Windows Media's premiere editing tool. With this tool, you can do more than just edit — you can also add script commands and markers and edit metadata.(Scripts are discussed later in the chapter). Figure 14-5 shows the Advanced Script Indexer and where to find the necessary adjustments to edit files.

You can edit individual files using the Advanced Script Indexer, but you cannot paste files together. If you want to paste Windows Media files together, you can use WMVAppend. To edit:

1. **Open up the file in the indexer.**

2. **Choose the in and out points.**

3. **Resave the file.** Save to a different filename so that you can re-edit the original if necessary. After you save the file, you cannot undo.

You can also edit the file metadata by typing in the appropriate fields (refer to Figure 14-5).

Playback position indicators

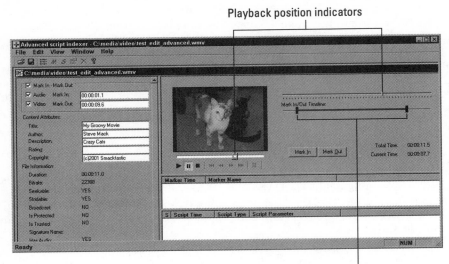

In and out point markers

Set in and out points by scrubbing through the video with either
position indicator and clicking the "Mark in" and "Mark out" buttons,
or simply sliding the in and out point markers.

Figure 14-5: The Windows Media Advanced Script Indexer

The ASF Advanced Indexer allows you to cut out sections of the audio or video
without affecting the other stream. You could cut out a section of objectionable
audio from a video, for example. The video track would be unaffected. If you want
to do any edits like this, simply select the track you want to edit by checking the
appropriate box in the top-left corner (refer to Figure 14-5). For most cases, you'll
want to leave both boxes checked.

ASFchop

ASFchop is a command line version of the Advanced Script Indexer. You can edit
files by specifying an input file name, an output file name, and start and end times
as follows:

```
asfchop -in MyFile.asf -out MyEditedFile.asf -start 30
  -end 3:45
```

To see the full list of available parameters for ASFchop, open up a command window, navigate to the Windows Media Components/Tools directory, and type the
command with no parameters:

```
asfchop
```

Be sure to use full paths if the files you're editing are not in the ASFchop directory and remember to put quotes around paths that contain spaces.

WMVAppend

WMVAppend is a command line program that creates a new Windows Media file by gluing two existing files together. The syntax is very simple:

```
WMVAppend -o <output file name> -i1 <first input file name>
   -i2 <second input file name> [-a <attribute index>]
```

You can specify the parameters in any order, but you may only glue two files together at a time. The attribute index is optional and is used to specify which file to use the metadata from for the new file. The default is 1; if you want to use the metadata from the second file, specify an attribute index of 2.

Windows Media Attribute Editor

The Windows Media Attribute Editor is another simple tool included in the Windows Media Resource Kit. This program lets you open up your Windows Media files and enter or edit any metadata fields (see Figure 14-6).

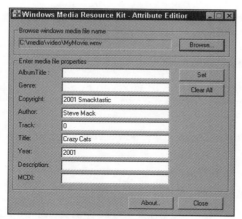

Figure 14-6: The Windows Media Resource Kit — Attribute Editor

Inserting URLs into Your Streams

Embedding URLs into your encoded streams can be useful. By using this functionality, you can have your streaming media player *drive* your browser by sending the URLs embedded in the streaming media file to your browser at appropriate times.

You can use streaming media to narrate tours of your Web site, or you can use Web pages to add to your streaming media presentation.

All three platforms offer this functionality, but of course refer to the ability to embed URLs in streams using different terminology. QuickTime has *HREF tracks* in which URLs are stored on a separate track in the QuickTime presentation. The RealSystem calls URL triggers *events,* which can be merged into your file. You can also use the power of SMIL and various other RN data types to drive presentations. Windows Media calls this functionality *adding scripts,* which can be done live in the Windows Media Encoder, or later on by using the Advanced Script Indexer or `ASFchop`.

Inserting URLs into QuickTime presentations

You can insert URLs into your QuickTime presentations by using HREF tracks or by using SMIL. Both methods are straightforward as the following two sections show.

QuickTime HREF tracks

QuickTime uses HREF tracks to insert URLs into encoded streams. You can use HREF tracks to specify movies to replace the current movie, target movies or Web pages to a specific frame in a browser, or even trigger JavaScript functions. For full HREF track documentation, please refer to the Apple Web site (`www.apple.com/quicktime`) or Stephen Gulie's excellent book, *QuickTime for the Web.*

To use HREF tracks, you must do the following:

1. **Create your streaming file without the HREF track.** (You don't want to compress the HREF track — QuickTime by default merges any text tracks into the video when compressing.)

2. **Create a text file that contains the URLs or commands you want to incorporate into the stream.**

3. **Import the text file into a QuickTime Player as a text track.**

4. **Copy the file and add it to the streaming file.**

5. **Modify the text track properties so that the track is recognized as an HREF track and not displayed like a normal text track.**

6. **Export the combined movie as a self-contained, hinted movie so that it streams from a server.**

The process sounds a bit complicated, but actually it isn't. When you understand the approach, the steps are really quite simple.

Note   Only Steps 2, 3, and 5 are expanded on below. Step 1 is the subject of Chapters 4–11 of this book; Step 4 is covered in the "Editing QuickTime files" section of this chapter, and Step 6 is covered in Chapter 13.

Creating the text file

First, create the text file that specifies the URLs you want embedded in the stream. The first line takes care of some global parameters and looks like this:

```
{QTtext}{timeScale:30}{timeStamps:absolute}
```

The above line of code specifies three separate things:

✦ {QTtext}: Specifies that the track is a QuickTime text track

✦ {timescale:30}: Specifies the time scale you wish to use (in this case 30 frames per second)

✦ {timestamps:absolute}: Specifies what the time line is referenced to, in this case the master time line of the whole QuickTime presentation.

After this line, you can put as many URL references as you like. The syntax for each URL is as follows:

```
[hh:mm:ss:ff]<URL, relative or absolute>
[hh:mm:ss:ff]
```

The first time reference specifies when the URL becomes active, and the second time reference, which should be on the next line, specifies when the URL ceases being active. Two additional optional parameters can be included with these URLs:

✦ A: Specifies that the URL should be loaded automatically

✦ T <target>: Specifies where to load the URL into. Use _blank for a new browser window. Other options are frame objects, window objects, <myself> and <quicktimeplayer>.

A URL entry including these optional parameters looks like this:

```
[00:00:30.00]A<http://www.apple.com> T<_blank>
[00:05:00.00]
```

Note   If the URL is relative, it is relative to the *streaming file* not to the Web page in which it may be embedded. It's always safest to use fully qualified URLs.

Save your text file as plain text, and you're ready for the next step.

Importing and modifying the HREF track

When you finish creating the text track, you need to import it into a QuickTime player and then add it to the intended movie. Along the way you need to change the name of the track to HREFTrack so the QuickTime player knows that the track contains URLs, and disable it so the URLs are not displayed in the video window like normal text tracks.

1. **Open the movie you want to add the URLs to in a QuickTime player.**

2. **Open another QuickTime player and import your text file by choosing File ⇨ Import.**

3. **Select the text movie and copy it.**

4. **Switch to the Quicktime player with the movie you are adding the URLs to.** Choose Add from the Edit menu. You've just added a text track to your original movie.

5. **To give this text track HREF functionality, you must change the name of the text track.** Open the Movie Properties window (Ctrl+J) and change the name by selecting the text track's general properties (see Figure 14-7). Change the track name to HREFTrack.

Note

There is no space in "HREFTrack." If you mistakenly add a space, the QuickTime player will not treat the text as URLs.

Figure 14-7: Changing the name of a text track to obtain HREF functionality

6. **Now you want to disable the track, which simply means turning off the display of the text in the video window.** Disabling the track does not affect the HREF functionality. Choose Enable Tracks from the Edit menu and disable the HREFTrack (see Figure 14-8).

Figure 14-8: Disabling the HREFTrack so that it is not displayed

7. **Save your movie as a self-contained movie, and you're ready to go.** Be sure to hint your movie if you're placing it on a streaming server.

 Note The QuickTime player does not let you save a self-contained movie unless you change the name of the file or save it to a different directory from the original.

Now all you need to do is embed the movie in a Web page, and the URLs are automatically sent to the target frame or to a new browser, depending on what you specified.

There's a slight catch, though. For HREF tracks to work, they must be played within a browser with the QuickTime Plug In or streamed using RTSP.

So to test a file that includes HREF tracks locally, you have to embed them in a Web page. Alternatively, you can put the file on a QuickTime or Darwin Streaming Server and test it in a stand-alone player.

 Note QuickTime Player Pro 5.0.2 has a bug whereby it does not hint HREFTracks properly, which means they cannot be streamed. The workaround is to deploy a hybrid QuickTime movie, streaming the video via RTSP, and the text via HTTP. To do this, create a reference move for the streaming portion of the QuickTime presentation, then add the HREF track to the reference movie. Place the reference movie on a Web server, and the HREF track will stream via HTTP.

Using SMIL to insert URLs in QuickTime presentations

URLs can be embedded into SMIL presentations in a number of ways. For a full discussion of using URLs in SMIL please turn to Chapter 31.

Working with URLs in the RealSystem

The RealSystem offers a couple of different ways of embedding URLs in your presentations. You can embed URLs directly into the audio or video file, or include URLs as part of a SMIL presentation. When merged into the actual media files URLs are referred to as events.

URLs embedded in SMIL presentations generally require the user to click a link or region (not true of SMIL 2.0 — see Chapter 32), whereas events embedded into RealMedia files are automatically executed upon playback.

Events files

To embed events into your RealMedia files, you create a text file containing a listing of the events and then use the rmevents command line utility to merge them with a RealMedia file. The syntax for the events file is as follows:

```
{letter code} {start time} {end time} {data}
```

✦ **Letter code:** One of four letters, u for a URL event, t for a title change, a for an author change, and c for a copyright change.

✦ **Start time:** The time the event becomes active, in dd:hh:mm:ss.xx format. Time specifications without colons or decimal points are assumed to be seconds.

✦ **End time:** Same syntax as start time.

✦ **Data:** The necessary data, for example, the URL or text for any other event.

A typical events file entry looks like this:

```
u 30 5:00 http://smacktastic.tv
```

This entry, when merged with a RealMedia file, makes the RealPlayer throw the URL to the user's default browser. In addition to URLs, you can also insert changes to the title, author, and copyright information that are displayed in the RealPlayer information bar.

To merge your events file with your RealMedia file, open a command window and navigate to the RealSystem Producer directory. Then use the following syntax:

```
rmevents -i {RealMedia file} -e {events file}
  -o {output file}
```

Don't forget to use full path information for files that are not in the same directory as rmevents, and be sure to use quotes around paths that include spaces. You can also use rmevents to merge an image map into your video files. For full documentation of the rmevents utility, please see the documentation that installs with the RealSystem Producer.

Using SMIL to trigger events

URLs can be embedded into SMIL presentations and other RealSystem data types in a number of ways. See Chapter 31for SMIL considerations and Chapters 23 and 24 for RealText and RealPix considerations, respectively.

Windows Media scripts

Windows Media refers to embedded URLs as scripts. Scripts can be embedded directly into Windows Media files using the ASF Advanced Indexer or the ASFchop command line utility. During live broadcasts, scripts can be inserted directly into streams using the Windows Media Encoder.

ASF Advanced Indexer

Earlier in this chapter you saw how the ASF Advanced Indexer could be used to edit Windows Media files. The ASF Advanced Indexer can also be used to add scripts to files. Figure 14-9 illustrates how the ASF Advanced Indexer can be used to add or edit scripts.

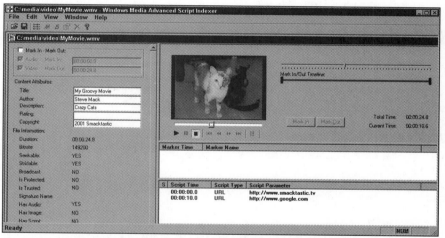

Figure 14-9: Adding and editing scripts using the ASF Advanced Indexer

To add a script, simply click the green S or press Ctrl+P. Doing so pops up the New Script Properties window where you can enter the URL information (see Figure 14-10). Be sure to select URL from the drop-down Type menu.

Figure 14-10: Entering new script properties

When you're done adding or editing scripts, save your file and you're done. One nice feature that the Advanced Indexer provides is the ability to export the script information as a text file. This text file can then be imported and used for other files. This feature is particularly useful if you have a number of files that you want to have the same scripts or if you want to use ASFchop.

ASFchop

You can also use ASFchop to embed scripts in your Windows Media Files, although you must have a preexisting script file. You cannot specify the URL and start time as separate parameters. Provided you do have a valid script file, the syntax to use is as follows:

```
asfchop -in MyMovie.asf -out MyMovieWithScripts.asf
     -script MyScriptFile.txt
```

Note   The above example assumes you're in the same directory as the asfchop utility and that all the necessary files are also in that directory. Be sure to specify full path information if this is not the case.

If you don't have a preexisting script file, you can create one using the ASF Advanced Indexer as detailed in the preceding section.

Windows Media Encoder

The Windows Media Encoder enables you to enter script commands directly into live streams. To obtain this functionality, you have to choose a profile that includes a script component in it. Specifying a profile that includes a script component ensures that the script panel is visible when you begin your broadcast.

To insert URLs into your live stream, choose the URL event type by clicking on the middle icon (a blue globe, presumably for the World Wide Web) at the left of the script panel, type the appropriate URL into the text field. Click the Insert button when you want the URL script inserted into your live broadcast.

If you create an archive of this file you can edit these scripts later using the Advanced Indexer.

Summary

After you've established standardized settings for your encoded files, use batch encoding to automate your encoding process. Editing encoded files isn't the greatest idea, but it can be done using utilities included with all three of the main streaming media platforms. URLs can also be embedded in all three streaming media platforms, using slightly different methods.

✦ Batch encoding can be done with third-party software or using the utilities supplied with each platform.

✦ If you're in the market for a third party editing platform, make batch processing one of your requirements.

✦ All three platforms allow you to edit files, although editing encoded files is not an exact science.

✦ The three mains streaming platforms use different terminology for inserting URLs into presentations: QuickTime uses HREF tracks, the RealSystem calls them events, and Windows Media refers to them as scripts.

✦ You can also insert URLs into presentations using SMIL, which is supported by QuickTime and the RealSystem.

✦ Windows Media enables you to insert scripts into live streams by using the Windows Media Encoder.

✦   ✦   ✦

Authoring: Different Ways to Showcase Your Media

Authoring Basics

◆   ◆   ◆   ◆

In This Chapter

How Web browsers
and Web servers
work

Linking to streaming
media files

Linking examples

◆   ◆   ◆   ◆

Now that you've learned how to create and encode good
looking and good sounding streaming media files,
you're probably anxious to foist them upon an unsuspecting
public. The question is . . . how?

You've probably clicked on many streaming media links and
not even given a second thought to the process that leads to
the eventual playback of the streaming media. This is how it
should be — as an audience member you don't need to know
how or why the process works. Streaming media should be as
seamless as possible. Television audiences are not expected
to know how antennas or cable reception works. The same
should apply to streaming media.

Unfortunately, you no longer have that luxury. Because you've
decided to become a streaming media author, you need to
understand how the streaming media linking and serving
process works. Before you take the leap into streaming media
links, it's instructional to take a step back and look at how
your browser works.

How Web Browsers and Servers Work

Have you ever thought for a moment about what happens
when you fire up your browser in the morning, coffee in
one hand, and mouse in the other? Probably not. When you
double-click on your browser icon, the program starts up, and
after a bit of activity your home page magically appears. What
you may not realize is that the page you're looking at is not a
single file. In fact, one page is probably anywhere from 20 to
50 different files, all assembled and displayed for you without
you even knowing it.

More importantly, these files can come from many different servers in disparate locations. Figure 15-1 is a simplified diagram of how a Web page is requested and assembled for you by your browser. Not only that, but your browser can request and assemble a page for you while you're doing a bunch of other things that are querying the network. The typical process as illustrated in Figure 15-1 is the following:

1. Your browser requests your homepage from your favorite site.

2. The server returns the HTML code, which may contain references to images, text, animation, and other elements that may or may not come off disparate servers.

3. Your browser parses the file and issues requests for the files referenced within the HTML code.

4. Servers receive the requests and send the appropriate files, along with the appropriate MIME types.

5. Using the MIME type information, your browser renders the files or hands them off to plug-ins, and your home page is displayed.

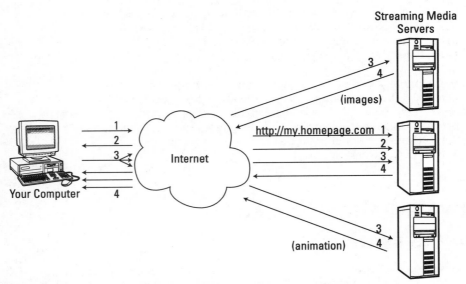

Figure 15-1: How browsers request and assemble a typical Web page

I think this is laboring the point a bit. It's supposed to be getting the point across that different elements **can** come off different servers. Yes, text is usually included in the original HTML doc. But what if it's a frames-based page? Of course, that would involve more requests, more arrows, etc. but do we really need to be that granular in this representation? If it absolutely has to be changed, then change it to "more text" or "advertising." I would leave it as is. SMAs you skim your home page, you may decide to fire up your e-mail program and check for new messages. You may also be running an instant messaging program or listening to a streaming radio station. All these programs request data from the network. Your computer uses *ports, protocols, and MIME* types to ensure that when data arrives, it is forwarded to the correct application.

Ports and protocols

Every data packet that traverses a network carries with it a number of important pieces of information. Among these pieces of information are the IP address of the requesting computer, the destination IP address of the server that is being asked for data, and a port number. You can think of a port number as a virtual mail slot — as data packets arrive, the computer uses the port number to determine which application should receive the packet.

Many port numbers are reserved for particular kinds of traffic. For example, port 80 on a Web server is reserved for HTTP traffic requests. When your browser requests data from a Web server, it addresses the packets to port 80 on the server. The server knows that because the requests are addressed to port 80 they should be routed to the Web server application. In fact, any application can run on port 80, and a Web server can run on any port; port 80 is merely the accepted standard. Other port numbers are reserved for processes such as FTP, Telnet, sending and receiving e-mail, and a host of other networking functions.

Firewalls can use port numbers to determine whether or not data packets are allowed to traverse the intranet. For example, if port 23 is the standard Telnet port, a system administrator may use a firewall to block incoming requests on port 23 to prevent people from logging in remotely to his servers.

In addition to port numbers, different applications may use different *protocols* to communicate with each other. A protocol is a set of rules that determines how data is sent back and forth between two applications. HTTP, for example, is the protocol that Web browsers and Web servers use to send data back and forth.

A number of applications can use the network simultaneously by using different ports and protocols. For example, many streaming media servers can stream via HTTP to avoid firewall issues as well as another protocol such as RTSP. Streaming media servers using HTTP must use a different port, such as 8080, if a Web server on the same machine is using port 80. In this case you have one application running two protocols, and two applications on the same computer using the HTTP protocol, but using different port numbers to keep things straight.

Streaming servers use special protocols to communicate with players. HTTP is not particularly well suited to streaming media because of the high amount of overhead built into it and the lack of a control channel. The absence of a control channel is why you can't fast forward or rewind clips that are being served by a Web server.

Instead, streaming servers use RTSP (Real Time Streaming Protocol), or in Microsoft's case, MMS (Microsoft Media Server protocol). These protocols were designed specifically to deal with the rigors of streaming media delivery, and they offer the two-way communication necessary for interactive streaming media presentations.

MIME types

MIME types are used to specify the contents of a document. A MIME type is a simple string of text that is included in a file header. Your browser compares this text string to a list of known (*registered*) MIME types to determine what type of data is contained within a file.

Your home page may contain text, pictures, and maybe even animation. Your browser is capable of displaying all these different data types, if it knows in advance what type of data each file contains. By knowing the type of contents, the browser can determine whether it can rendered the data natively or if a helper application or plug-in must be used. For example, a Web page may contain Flash animation. This animation is sent with a MIME type that identifies the contents as being Flash animation. When your browser looks at the MIME type, it realizes that it must load the Shockwave Flash player to render the animation content. Without the MIME type, the browser would attempt to render as text, which is the default. In fact, you may have encountered this behavior — incorrectly set MIME types often result in your browser filling up with garbage text.

MIME type registration

For the MIME type process to work properly, all the applications involved must be configured properly. In particular, the user's browser(s) and media player(s) must work together. Media players must register with all installed browsers for the MIME types they are capable of rendering. This can be a problem because a battle is constantly being waged for ownership of MIME types.

For example, when a browser encounters a file with a QuickTime MIME type, it determines that the QuickTime player must be used to play back the contents. Similarly, RealMedia files are handed off to the RealPlayer or the RealPlayer plug-in.

However, some data types can be played back by a number of different applications. Many programs attempt to register for as many different MIME types as possible. If you have two programs on your computer that are both capable of rendering a particular type of file, they may fight for the right to be the default application for that MIME type. You may have seen a message that more or less says, "This program is no longer the default <whatever> application." This message is displayed when an application senses that a second program has registered for MIME types that the first application was previously registered for.

Another problem is that streaming media players can only register for MIME types with browsers that are already installed. If you install or reinstall a browser after you've installed your streaming media players, you have to reinstall all the plug-ins so that they can re-register for the MIME types. For example, if you install the RealPlayer and then install Netscape, the Netscape browser will not be aware of the installed RealPlayer. Nor will it be aware of any other plug-ins that you may have previously installed, such as Adobe Acrobat or Macromedia Shockwave.

Finally, Web servers must also have all the appropriate MIME types registered so that when a file is requested, the correct MIME type is sent with it. Most Web servers come preconfigured to deal with most standard MIME types but often must be specially configured to work with streaming media files.

Streaming Media MIME Types

For browsers to be able to interact with streaming media players and servers, two main things need to happen:

✦ The Web server must be configured to send the correct MIME type for redirector files (or streaming media files if you're streaming from your Web server).

✦ The player(s) must be properly registered to play back these MIME types.

Unfortunately, you have no control over the audience's machines, so all you can do is hope that they installed their media players correctly. You do (or should) have control over the MIME types that are registered on your Web server.

You don't have to know how to register MIME types, and moreover, the process is different depending on what Web server you're running. A quick chat with your system administrator to make sure that the appropriate MIME types are configured should fix the problem.

You can easily tell when MIME types are not properly configured, because the files receive a default MIME type, which tricks the browser into trying to render the file. Use of the default MIME type usually results in a screen full of gibberish. Whenever that happens, you've got a MIME type problem.

Table 15-1 lists the most common required MIME types for the major streaming platforms. Please note that many other file types are supported by one or more platform.

Table 15-1
Web Server MIME Types

Platform	File Extension	MIME type
QuickTime	.qt, .mov	video/quicktime
	.qti, .qtif	image/x-quicktime
RealSystem	.ra, .ram	audio/x-pn-realaudio
	.rm	application/x-pn-realmedia
	.rpm	audio/x-pn-realaudio-plugin
	.rp	image/vnd.rn-realpix
	.rt	text/vnd.rn-realtext
Windows Media Technologies	.asf, .asx	video/x-ms-asf
	.wma	audio/x-ms-wma
	.wax	audio/x-ms-wax
	.wmv	audio/x-ms-wmv
	.wvx	video/x-ms-wvx
	.wm	video/x-ms-wm
	.wmx	video/x-ms-wmx
	.wmz	application/x-ms-wmz
	.wmd	application/x-ms-wmd
Non-Platform Specific MIME types	.smil, .smi	application/smil
	.swf	application/x-shockwave-flash
	.mp3	audio/mpeg3
	.mpeg, .mpg, .mpe	video/mpeg

Unfortunately, the answers to the MIME type problems that pop up from time to time are not simple. MIME types are standardized, but how they are implemented on different machines and browser platforms is not. Perhaps some day a standard will emerge that enables some sort of centralized control of MIME types. Don't hold your breath.

Linking to Streaming Media Files

Now that you understand how a browser requests and receives files, you can explore what needs to happen to link streaming media files from Web pages. A number of different scenarios can arise:

✦ The file is streamed via HTTP, and the browser has a renderer or plug-in that can decode the stream.

✦ The file is streamed via HTTP, and the browser hands off the file to a separate streaming media player.

✦ The file is streamed via a different protocol and handed off by the browser to a separate streaming media player.

✦ The file is streamed via a different protocol and played back in the browser via a plug-in.

The original request must be made via HTTP, because browsers use the HTTP protocol. If the file is then streamed or progressively downloaded via HTTP, the Web browser can play it back by using a plug-in or hand it off to a separate streaming media player.

Browsers use the HTTP protocol, so the initial request for a streaming media file always uses HTTP. What is needed is some way to transfer control from the browser to the streaming media player. This control transfer is done using *metafiles*. When the streaming media player takes over, it can use a different protocol to receive the file.

Using metafiles

Metafiles are small files that are earmarked for streaming media player playback using MIME types. These files are referred to alternately as metafiles (RealSystem), redirector files (Windows Media Files), or reference movies (QuickTime). Metafiles are small text files that contain the address to the actual streaming file. Metafiles can also contain other information, such as metadata, a playlist, or conditional statements that offer the player choices about what file to play back.

When the Web browser receives a metafile, it hands off the metafile to the streaming media application appropriate for the MIME type of the file. The streaming media player opens the metafile, finds the address of the streaming file, and begins a separate communication with a streaming server on another port, using a different protocol. This handoff from the browser to the streaming media player, combined with different port numbers and protocols is why you can listen to streaming radio stations while continuing to browse the Internet. This process is illustrated in Figure 15-2.

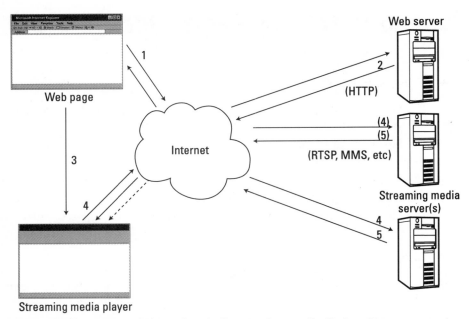

Figure 15-2: Using metafiles to hand off streaming media file locations to streaming media players

Problems with metafiles

Metafiles are a clever solution to a problem, but they can also generate their own share of problems. If you have a handful of streaming media files, a handful of accompanying metafiles is not a big deal. However, if you're a large content provider and have thousands of streaming media files, having the additional responsibility of an equal number of metafiles only adds to the infrastructure and file management headache.

Additionally, metafiles can easily be copied or e-mailed because they are small, plain text files. Having copies of metafiles floating around that are not under your control can present file management problems. For example, if your system administrator decides to do a little house cleaning and move a few files around or to add new servers to your server farm, the distributed copies of the metafile are out of your control and may steer people to an incorrect file location. In essence, you can end up painting yourself into a corner or end up with a lot of dissatisfied customers when their favorite files are moved.

The solution to the static metafile nightmare is to dynamically generate your metafiles. You can do this by querying a database, by using server-side scripts, or by using simple text scripting languages.

You can accomplish this several ways; however, the best approach is to repurpose existing code that you use on your site. Once again, you need to sit down with your system administrator and work out a mutually beneficial solution.

You probably just want to know what to put where to make it all work. In this section, you find out the syntax for linking to your streaming files from your Web pages. Each platform has a slightly different approach and slightly different behavior, so they are discussed separately.

QuickTime

You can link QuickTime movies from Web pages in a number of different ways:

✦ Using the `<a href>` tag

✦ Using the `<embed>` tag

✦ Using reference movies

✦ Linking via SMIL

Linking a QuickTime movie using the HTML `<a href>` tag causes the movie to be loaded into a new browser page, centered, with nothing in the background. This way of linking to QuickTime movies is very crude and not recommended at all. Anyone who uses this style of linking in this day and age gets an "F" for effort and presentation.

You can improve your presentation by using frames and by using the `<a href>` tag to target specific frames. Targeting your QuickTime player to a frame is certainly an improvement on simple links but still offers only minimal control over the results. A much better approach is to use the `<embed>` tag.

The `<embed>` and `<a href>` tags can link to self-contained QuickTime movies or reference movies as their source. When used with self-contained QuickTime movies, the movies stream via HTTP. For RTSP streaming, you must use reference movies with embedded players or specify RTSP URLs and target external QuickTime players using `href` or `qtnext` parameters, as explained in the following sections.

Embedded playback using the `<embed>` tag

The `<embed>` tag is a much more powerful way to link to your QuickTime presentations, because it gives you a large degree of control over the presentation of your streaming media file. Similar to the `<img>` tag, you can specify the height and width of the QuickTime player. A typical link to a QuickTime movie using the `<embed>` tag looks like this:

```
<embed src="MyMovie.mov" width="160" height="136">
```

Caution   When calculating the height parameter for your embedded QuickTime movie remember to add 16 pixels to the height parameter to include room for the controller.

In addition to width and height, you can specify a number of other parameters, such as

✦ **autoplay:** When set to true, causes your movie to play automatically.

✦ **starttime/endtime:** Enables you to play back only part of a movie by specifying begin and end times.

✦ **loop:** Enables you to set the movie into loop mode.

✦ **controller:** When set to false, this parameter hides the controller bar.

✦ **hidden:** Similar to controller, this can be set to false to hide the QuickTime player. This can be useful when using the QuickTime player to play background music.

✦ **qtnext:** A useful feature that allows you to specify a playlist inside an ⟨embed⟩ tag. You can even loop playback lists by using a goto statement, as follows:

```
<embed src="MeFirst.mov" width="160" height="136"
       qtnext1="<IPlaySecond.mov> T<myself>"
       qtnext2="<IplayThird.mov> T<myself>"
       qtnext3="goto0" >
```

Note how you specify targets in the qtnext value.

✦ **target:** Enables you to specify where to load the URL specified in the src parameter.

Many more parameters are available. I've merely scratched the surface. For a full listing please consult the QuickTime Web site (www.apple.com/quicktime/authoring/embed.html). Embedding the QuickTime player is also covered in the next chapter.

Bear in mind that Web browsers use HTTP, so whatever file is used in the src parameter is delivered using HTTP. If you want to stream your files using RTSP, use a reference movie as your src parameter and reference a streaming movie using RTSP in the reference movie.

Launching movies into the QuickTime player

You can launch QuickTime presentations directly into the QuickTime player in a couple of ways, using slightly different combinations of the ⟨embed⟩ tag parameters. Both approaches assume you use a placeholder image with a .mov extension to load the QuickTime plug-in. The first example uses the qtnext parameter with the target set to quicktimeplayer:

```
<embed src="placeholder.mov" height="320" width="240"
controller="false" autoplay="true"
qtnext1="<rtsp://my.server.com/MyStreaming.mov>
T<quicktimeplayer>" >
```

This next example uses a combination of the `href`, `autohref`, and `target` parameters to accomplish the same thing:

```
<embed src="placeholder.mov" height="320" width="240"
controller="false" autoplay="true"
href="rtsp://my.server.com/MyStreaming.mov"
target="quicktimeplayer" autohref="True" >
```

Usually users must click on a movie to trigger the `href` URL, but in this case the `autohref` parameter causes the URL to load immediately.

Using reference movies

Reference movies are QuickTime's version of metafiles. Reference movies can be as simple as a single reference to a streaming movie, or very complex, offering different movie choices to be played back depending on specific criteria to be met.

The simplest way to make a reference movie is by using QuickTime Pro (refer to Figure 15-3). Follow these steps:

1. **Place your streaming QuickTime movie on a streaming server.**

2. **Open the stream in a QuickTime Pro player by using the Open URL option from the File menu.** The URL should look something like this:

   ```
   rtsp://your.quicktimeserver.com/MyStream.mov
   ```

3. **If the movie buffers and plays back properly, stop the movie playback and move the playback head to the beginning of the movie.**

4. **Choose Save As from the File menu and give it an appropriate name, such as** MyMovie_ref.mov.

That's all you need to do. This reference movie file can now be put on a Web server, e-mailed, or distributed across a LAN to provide access to your streaming file.

Creating reference files using the QuickTime player is simple but unsophisticated. If you use this method, you have no way of offering viewers choices if their QuickTime players do not have the appropriate components installed or if they are on slow connections. For that, you have to use either `MakeRefMovie` or `XMLtoRefMovie`. To find out how to use these programs, please see the "Creating Advanced Reference Movies" Expert Tutorial.

Figure 15-3: Using QuickTime Pro to create simple reference movies

Expert Tutorial: Creating Advanced Reference Movies

Francesco Schiavon was kind to share his expertise and provides the inside scoop on what you need to know to get up and running with MakeRevMovie. Francesco Schiavon is an instructor at the Vancouver Film School, New Media where he specializes in interactive media. He has extensive experience with all things QuickTime and offers expert training and consulting. Francesco can be found contributing on many of the QuickTime and streaming media lists on the Web.

Creating Reference Movies with MakeRefMovie

MakeRefMovie is a free application provided by Apple that is used to make reference movies. Use MakeRefMovie when you want to embed logic within the reference movie. With MakeRefMovie, you can create reference movies that enable the QuickTime player to choose between different files depending on connection speed or language preference. You can download the latest version of MakeRefMovie (Mac OS9–X, Windows) from Apple's Web site at: http://developer.apple.com/quicktime/ quicktimeintro/tools/.

To create a reference movie with MakeRefMovie, follow these simple steps:

1. **Open MakeRefMovie (see Figure 15-4) and type a name for the reference movie at the prompt.** Saving this reference movie in the same directory as the other movies that it refers to is a good idea.

2. **From the Movie menu, choose Add Movie File... and select one of the movies that the reference movie will point to.** The movie you select here can be a movie that contains media or another reference movie, for example, a reference movie that points to streaming content.

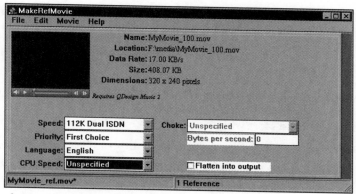

Figure 15-4: Using MakeRefMovie

3. **Select the criteria that must be met for this selected movie to play back.** In addition to the criteria, you should specify a Priority parameter, which is used if more than one movie in the reference file meets the criteria.

4. **Repeat Steps 2 and 3 for the other movie choices in this reference file.**

   You can also add movies to a reference file by simply dragging them onto the MakeRefMovie program. Alternatively, you can enter a URL that points to any QuickTime supported media type by choosing Add Movie URL... from the Movie menu. The URL can be an absolute or a relative URL and can use any QuickTime supported protocol (http://, rtsp://, ftp://, and so on). Keep in mind that relative URLs are relative to the location of the reference movie.

   If the reference movie is going to reside on a different server from the streaming files, be sure to use fully qualified URLs.

5. **When you are done adding movies and criteria, save your file and choose Quit from the File menu.**

When the reference movie has been saved, you can distribute it by any method you choose.

Creating Reference Movies with XMLtoRefMovie

XMLtoRefMovie is a free utility written by Peter Hoddie. This utility is available for the Macintosh OS X and Windows. You can download it from Peter's Web site (www.hoddie.net/xmltorefmovie/). Using XMLtoRefMovie is the most flexible and powerful way to create reference movies because it handles criteria that MakeRefMovie cannot. An example of this is a reference movie that chooses between different movies depending on the QuickTime components installed on the user's machine.

XMLtoRefMovie, unlike the methods described above, does not have a graphical user interface. You author a QTRM file and then XMLtoRefMovie converts this text file into a reference movie. A QTRM file is an XML document that describes the criteria that must be met for each movie being referenced. You create this QTRM file with any text editor, such as UltraEdit or BBEdit.

Because the QTRM file is based on XML, you need to follow a few syntax rules:

✦ The document must start with `<qtrefmovie>` and finish with `</qtrefmovie>`.

✦ At least one `<refmovie>` tag must be inside the `<qtrefmovie>` tags.

✦ Each `<refmovie>` tag must have a src attribute, whose value is the URL of the media being referenced, and one or more criteria to be met to trigger that specific `<refmovie>`.

This example uses XMLtoRefMovie to make a reference movie that chooses between an MP3 file (my_mp3_file.mp3) and a movie with a skin (skinned.mov). If the user's QuickTime player is capable of playing back both movies (both criteria are met), then the skinned movie has higher priority than the MP3 file.

1. **Open a text editor and create a blank document.**

2. **Start the document by typing** `<qtrefmovie>`.

3. **On the next line specify the first choice by typing**

   ```
   <refmovie src="my_mp3_file.mp3" priority="low">
   ```

4. **Now add a condition for this movie. On the next line, type**

   ```
   <component type="movie-importer" subtype="mp3" />
   ```

   Conditions are unary tags, so they must end with a forward slash.

5. **After the conditions, close this movie reference by typing a** `</refmovie>` **tag.**

   All this translates to "This reference points to a document called my_mp3_file.mp3, which requires an MP3 component to play back. If more than one file in this reference movie meets the criteria, this file has low priority."

6. **Create another choice, starting with the file and priority.**

   ```
   <refmovie src="skinned.mov" priority="high">
   ```

7. **Followed by the criteria**

   ```
   <component type="movie-importer" subtype="SKIN" />
   ```

8. **Close this movie definition by typing a** `</refmovie>` **tag.**

   This movie reference requires the skin component, and if more than one movie reference meets the criteria, this file has high priority.

9. **Close the QTRM file by typing** `</qtrefmovie>` **on the last line.** Your code should now look like this:

```
<qtrefmovie>
       <refmovie src="my_mp3_file.mp3" priority="low">
             <component type="movie-importer" subtype="mp3"
/>
       </refmovie>
       <refmovie src="skinned.mov" priority="high">
             <component type="movie-importer" subtype="SKIN"
/>
       </refmovie>
</qtrefmovie>
```

At this point, you are done creating the QTRM file.

10. **Save the file with the** `.qtrm` **extension.** XMLtoRefMovie takes files with the `.qtrm` extension and outputs reference movies of the same name with a `.mov` extension.

11. **To use XMLtoRefMovie, drag and drop the QTRM file on top of the XMLtoRefMovie application.**

On Windows machines, double-click on the XMLtoRefMovie.exe file. This brings up an Open File dialog box. Find your QTRM file and click the Open button. The confusing part is that the Open File dialogue box stays open. Believe it or not, your reference movie has been created and XMLtoRefMovie is asking if you want to convert another QTRM file. It only takes a fraction of a second to create a reference movie from a QTRM file. If you have no other movies to convert, exit the utility.

Please note that this example uses relative URLs for the files being referenced. This assumes the reference movie is on the same server and in the same directory as the QuickTime movies. You can just as easily use fully qualified URLs so that your reference movie is portable.

For a complete explanation of all the different elements and attributes that a QTRM file can have, please refer to the documentation provided when you download the XMLtoRefMovie application. The documentation is also available on Peter Hoddie's Web site.

Creating Streaming Movie Reference Files From Text Files

Being able to create a reference movie from a plain text file is a little known but very powerful feature. You can create reference movies that point to RTSP media (delivered only via a streaming server) with any text editor, back-end application or middleware that can generate a text document. The only catch with this method is that you can only reference RTSP content and not to content delivered via a Web server. To make references to content on a Web server via a text file you need to use SMIL.

1. **Open a text editor or a script that can output a text file.**

2. **Start the text document with the following eight characters:** `rtsptext`.

3. **On the next line, type the absolute URL to your RTSP content. For example:**

   ```
   rtsp://your.quicktimeserver.com/MyStream.mov
   ```

4. **(Optional) On the next line, type** `autoplay` **so that the movie starts streaming as soon as it's opened.**

5. **Close the file and save it with a .mov extension.**

   Your text file should look like this:

   ```
   rtsptext
   rtsp://your.quicktimeserver.com/MyStream.mov
   autoplay
   ```

No matter how you choose to distribute this document, it will always point to the media on your streaming server.

Linking via SMIL

QuickTime supports both relative and absolute URLs in SMIL files. For more information about SMIL, please refer to Chapters 26 through 31 of this book. For more information about SMIL support in the QuickTime player, please refer to Chapter 31 and the QuickTime Web site.

Note   As of December 2001, the QuickTime player cannot resolve relative URLs in SMIL files unless the files reside in the same directory as the SMIL file. Don't use subfolders or the dot-dot (" . . / ") construct.

RealSystem

RealSystem content can be linked in a number of ways:

✦ Using .ram metafiles to play back files in a standalone RealPlayer

✦ Using .rpm metafiles to play back files in an embedded RealPlayer

✦ Using the RealServer `ramgen` feature to automatically generate metafiles

✦ Using the linking capabilities of SMIL

Using .ram/.rpm files

The RealSystem originally used static metafiles, known as RAM and RPM files (RealAudio Metafile, Real Plug-in Metafile) to link to content. Metafiles are simple text files that contain the location of the file(s) to be streamed. Metafiles can contain references to a number of files, as well as a number of simple modifiers. RAM files are used to open a separate RealPlayer application; RPM files are used to embed the RealPlayer in a Web page.

Note The contents of a RAM and RPM file are exactly the same. They have slightly different MIME types that cause the stand-alone or embedded RealPlayer to be opened, respectively.

For the most part the use of RAM and RPM files is now deprecated in favor of the ramgen function included with the RealServer (discussed in the next section). There is, however, one situation when you still have to use metafiles — when you're "streaming" from a Web server.

Streaming from a Web server is not recommended for a number of reasons, such as users being unable to fast-forward the stream and lack of any advanced streaming media server features such as QuickTime Skip Protection or Windows Media Intelligent Streaming, but if you have no alternative it does work. Make sure you use the HTTP protocol when you specify the URL to the file.

Creating .ram/.rpm files

Creating a RealSystem metafiles involves little more than typing the URL of a file into a text editor and saving it with either a .ram or .rpm extension, depending on whether you want it to play back in a stand-alone player or an embedded player. The syntax is as follows:

```
{protocol}://{server}/{filename}[?{option}][&{option}]...
```

✦ **protocol** — rtsp, http, pnm, or file for local playback

✦ **server** — An IP address or a server name, such as my.server.com

✦ **filename** — The name of the file, including any directory information

✦ **option** — A number of optional parameters can be specified. The first one is separated from the URL by a question mark; any further options are separated by ampersands.

Table 15-2 lists the available optional parameters that can be used in RealSystem metafiles.

Table 15-2
Optional RealSystem Metafile Parameters

Parameter	Values	Use
start	Any time written in dd:hh:mm: ss.xyz format where dd = days hh = hours mm = minutes ss = seconds xyz = milliseconds	Specifies a start time for the file.
end	Any time written in dd:hh:mm: ss.xyz format where dd = days hh = hours mm = minutes ss = seconds xyz = milliseconds	Specifies an end time for the file.
screensize	original	Causes the RealPlayer to play back the file at its originally authored size.
	double	Causes the RealPlayer to play back the file at twice its originally authored size.
	full	Causes the RealPlayer to play back the file in full-screen mode.
mode	compact	Causes the RealPlayer to play back the file in compact mode. *
title	Any text string	Specifies an alternative title for the presentation. **
Author	Any text string	Specifies an alternative title for the presentation. **
Copyright	Any text string	Specifies an alternative title for the presentation. **

* Only affects RealPlayer 8 and later — earlier versions ignore this parameter.

** Alternative title, author, and copyright information takes precedence over the information contained within the file.

A RealSystem metafile may contain more than one URL. When RealSystem metafiles contain more than one URL, the files are played back in sequence, with the player rebuffering between each file. Some sample ramfile URLs are as follows:

```
rtsp://my.server.com/media/concert.ra?start="30"
rtsp://your.server.com/MyBigPres.smil?screensize="full"
rtsp://big.server.com/keynote.rm?start="1:00"&end="11:20"
    &title="Product Launch (edit)"
http://a.webserver.com/noControl.rm
```

RealSystem metafiles can also specify older RealSystem files for backwards compatibility with pre-G2 players. The syntax is as follows:

```
rtsp://my.server.com/SuperDuper.smil
--stop--
pnm://my.server.com/UpgradeNowDangIt.ra
```

Newer versions of the RealPlayer play back the first file and then stop when they hit the "--stop--" line. Older players ignore the first two lines, which they do not understand, and simply play the last file in the sequence. The last file must also be encoded with old audio and/or video codecs to ensure backwards compatibility.

Using ramgen on the RealServer

To alleviate the problems that having thousands of metafiles lying around can create, RealNetworks added ramgen functionality to their server. This functionality allows the server to accept an HTTP request from a browser or a RealPlayer and return a metafile that the server generates on the fly, complete with the proper MIME type. This HTTP call can be used as a link in any Web page as part of an <a href> or <embed> tag. The syntax is as follows:

```
http://{RealServer}:{RealServer HTTP port}/ramgen/{file path/name}
    [? option][& option]...
```

There are two crucial ingredients, and a couple of extra optional parameters in ramgen URLs:

✦ **Specifying the RealServer HTTP port (required):** Sends the request to the port the RealServer uses for HTTP requests. The default is 8080, but check with your system administrator to be sure.

✦ **Specifying ramgen/ before the file path/name (required):** Instructs the RealServer to use ramgen functionality.

✦ **embed (optional):** If specified as an optional parameter, it causes the RealServer to return the metafile with a RPM MIME type, causing playback in the embedded player.

✦ **altplay="filename":** If specified, ramgen generates a backwards compatible metafile as described in the last section.

`ramgen` URLs can also include any of the optional RealSystem metafile parameters from Table 15-2. As an example, consider the following `ramgen` URL used in an `<a href>` tag:

```
<a href="http://my.realserver.com:8080/ramgen/keynote.rm?start=30
     &screensize=double&altplay=UpgradeDangIt.ra>Click me</a>
```

If the viewer clicked on this link, a metafile would be returned to the browser that used the RAM MIME type and contained the following:

```
rtsp://my.realserver.com/keynote.rm?start=30&screensize=double
--stop--
pnm://my.realserver.com/UpgradeDangIt.ra
```

Pretty clever, eh? You no longer need to worry about RAM or RPM files because all the information that you need is contained in the URL.

Linking to RealMedia files using SMIL

The RealSystem has extensive SMIL support built in. SMIL files, being simple text files, can either be served off of a RealServer or Web server. Inside the SMIL file, URLs can be relative or absolute, and use the RTSP or HTTP protocol. For more information about linking via SMIL, please refer to Chapters 26 through 31 of this book.

Windows Media Technologies

Windows Media Technologies uses a number of different metafiles, including all files with the `.wax`, `.wvx`, `.wmx`, and `.asx` extension. In general, `.wax` metafiles should be used to refer to audio files or metafiles; `.wvx` files should be used to refer to video files or metafiles, and `.asx` files can be used to refer to just about anything. The `.wmx` extension has been reserved for future use. The different file extensions mildly confuse the fact that essentially their contents are indistinguishable.

Windows Media metafiles are XML-based text files. The contents of the Windows Media metafiles can be as simple as a single URL, or they can be much more complex. They can contain references to a number of files arranged in a playlist as well as metadata, references to graphic elements, hyperlinks, instructions for ad insertion, and more. You can use any text editor to author Windows Media metafiles or by using the Windows Media Metafile Creator utility that is included in the Windows Media Resource Kit.

A simple ASX file

Because Windows Media Technologies metafiles are XML-based, the files consist of a number of tags enclosed in angled brackets. Some tags are binary, meaning they require a matching closing tag, such as `<asx></asx>`. Other tags are unary and instead take a closing slash, like `<ref/>`. The following is an example of a simple ASX file:

```
<asx version="3.0">
<!--A simple asx file with a single entry.-->
    <title>Super Simple</title>
    <entry>
        <ref href="mms://my.server.com/AnyFile.wma" />
    </entry>
</asx>
```

The whole file is enclosed by the `<asx></asx>` tags. The opening `<asx>` tag includes a version number. The second line is a comment, using the familiar HTML comment syntax. Next, a title is specified, which is enclosed by the `<title></title>` tags. Then a file is referenced inside a `<ref>` tag, which is enclosed by the `<entry></entry>` tags. Notice how the `<ref>` tag is unary and, therefore, takes the closing slash.

This file can be saved with any metafile extension and then placed on a Web server. Because it references an audio file, you should use the `.wax` or `.asx` extension. You can link to this audio file from a Web page by using this metafile as the source of an `<a href>` or an `<embed>` tag. When the link is clicked, the Web server sends this small metafile to the browser, which hands it off to the Windows Media Player because of the MIME type. The Windows Media Player then parses the file and begins a separate networking session with the Windows Media Server, requesting `AnyFile.wma`.

Windows Media metafile tags

Windows Media supports a number of different tags in their metafiles. These tags can be mixed and matched to design complex metafiles. Table 15-3 contains a list of all the tags that are available in Windows Media metafiles and a brief description of each. For full Windows Media metafile documentation, please refer to the Microsoft Web site (`http://msdn.microsoft.com/library/default.asp?url=/library/en-us/wmplay/mmp_sdk/asx_elementsintro.asp`).

Note   Binary metafile tags that require a closing tag are listed in pairs, such as `<asx></asx>`. Unary tags that require a trailing slash are listed with the trailing slash, such as `<ref/>`.

Table 15-3
Windows Media Metafile Tags

Parameter	Parameters	Use
`<abstract>` `</abstract>`	None.	Used to specify text that appears when you mouse over an element. For instance, if you specify an `<abstract>` inside an `<entry>` tag, the text contained within the `<abstract>` tags appears when your mouse hovers over the clip title.
`<asx></asx>`	`Version` (required) — can be either 3 or 3.0. `Previewmode` (optional) — either yes or no, determines whether the presentation is played in preview mode or not. In preview mode, each clip is played back only for a short duration specified by the `previewduration` tag. `bannerbar` (optional) — either `auto` or `fixed`, determines whether the Windows Media Player reserves space for a banner bar graphic element or not. The default is `auto`, where space is reserved only if banner graphics are present.	Used to enclose the entire metafile.
`<author>` `</author>`	None.	Used to specify author information. Can be specified for the whole metafile or for individual entries or events.
`<banner/>` *	`href` — Specifies the URL of the graphic element, which should be 32 pixels by 194 pixels.	The Windows Media Player can reserve space to display an ad. This tag is used to specify the location of the graphic to be displayed. Can be specified for the whole playlist or for individual entries or events.
`<base/>`	`href` — Specifies the URL string.	Used to specify a URL string that is pre-pended to all URLs referenced in the metafile.
`<copyright>` `</copyright>`	None.	Used to specify copyright information. Can be specified for the whole metafile or for individual entries or events.

Parameter	Parameters	Use
`<duration/>`	`value` — Any time reference specified in dd:hh:mm:ss.xx format.	Can be used to set a duration for the playback of a file.
`<endmarker/>`	`number` — The number of an existing marker in the file. `name` — The name of an existing marker in the file.	Specifies a point in the file where the file should stop playback. It must have either the number or name attribute.
`<entry>` `</entry>`	`clientskip` (optional) — viewer is allowed to skip this entry. `skipifref` (optional) — Either "yes" or "no," determines whether this entry is skipped if the metafile is being referenced by another metafile.	Used to specify a clip to be played.
`<entryref>` `</entryref>`	`href` — Specifies the URL of the metafile.	Used to specify the URL of a metafile instead of a file. Metafiles may reference other metafiles. However, any `<entryref>` tags in the referenced metafile are ignored (you can only have one level of recursion).
`<event>` `</event>`	`name` (required) — Specifies the name of the script command required to trigger this event. `whendone` (required) — Specifies the behavior when the clip enclosed by the event tag is through playing. It can be set to "resume," which causes the player to resume playing the stream it was playing before the script event; "next" which causes the player to move on to the next entry in the file; or "break" which is used to break the player out of a loop set up by a `<repeat>` tag.	Used to define how the player should respond when it receives a script command labeled as an event.
`<logurl/>`	`href` (required) — Specifies the URL of the logging . computer	Used to specify the URL of a computer to which log information must be posted.

continued

Table 15-3 *(continued)*

Parameter	Parameters	Use
`<moreinfo/>`	`href` (required) — Specifies the URL for more information `target` (optional) — Used to target the frame or window in which to open the URL. It can be any valid window or frame name, or one of the following: _blank, _self, _parent, or _top.	Used to specify a URL associated with content.
`<param/>`	`name` (required) — A text string defining the name of the custom parameter. `value` (required) — A text string defining the value of the custom parameter.	Enables you to specify custom parameters that can be accessed using advanced programming methods. Each `<param/>` tag requires name and value attributes.
`<preview duration/>`	`value` (required) — Any time reference specified in dd:hh:mm:ss.xx format.	Enables you to specify the length of previews. This tag can apply to every clip in the presentation if specified outside an entry tag, or it can be applied to clips individually.
`<ref/>`	`href` (required) — Specifies the URL of the clip.	Used to specify URLs for actual clips.
`<repeat>` `</repeat>`	`count` (optional) — Any integer value.	Used to specify the number of times a clip or group of clips repeats. An optional parameter count can be specified. If no count is specified, the clip(s) repeat indefinitely.
`<skin/>`	`href` (required) — Specifies the URL of the skin.	Used to specify the URL of a Windows Media Player skin. Only works for Windows Media Player 7 and higher.
`<startmarker/>`	`number` — The number of an existing marker in the file. `name` — The name of an existing marker in the file.	Specifies that playback of a clip should begin at a particular marker contained within the file. This tag must have either the number or the name parameter.

Parameter	Parameters	Use
`<starttime/>`	value **(required)** — Any time reference specified in dd:hh: mm:ss.xx format.	Specifies the point in a given file at which playback should begin.
`<title>` `</title>`	None.	Enables you to specify title information for an entire metafile or individually for clips.

Metafile tag scope

The *scope* of a tag or attribute is the time during which it is active. The scope is determined by its location in the metafile. For example, in the first ASX example listed above, the `<title>` tag remains active for the whole file, because it is defined outside of the individual entries. Scope can be overridden in certain situations. Consider the following code:

```
<asx version="3.0">
    <title>My Playlist</title>
    <entry>
      <!-- intro clip for station branding -->
      <ref href="mms://my.server.com/intro.wma" />
    </entry>
    <entry>
      <title>Title #1</title>
      <ref href="mms://my.server.com/song1.wma" />
    </entry>
    <entry>
      <title>Title #2</title>
      <ref href="mms://my.server.com/song2.wma" />
    </entry>
    <entry>
      <!-- no title for this song -->
      <ref href="mms://my.server.com/song3.wma" />
    </entry>
</asx>
```

In this example, the presentation starts out with the title My Playlist, which remains active throughout the entire presentation. My Playlist is displayed during the intro clip. After the intro, when the first song begins playback, the title tag in the second entry overrides the scope of the original title tag. Therefore, the title changes to Title #1 and stays that way until the second song, when it changes to Title #2. Because the third song has no title specified, the title defaults back to My Playlist, because the scope of the original title tag would no longer be overridden.

Attributes specified at the ⟨ref/⟩ level take highest precedence. Attributes that are specified at the ⟨entry⟩ or ⟨event⟩ level come next in the order. Finally, attributes specified at the ⟨asx⟩ (global) level are last. It's usually pretty simple to figure out the order of precedence of tags (and consequently their scope) if your code is properly indented.

Windows Media URLs

Windows Media Technologies uses slightly different terminology for different kinds of streams. On-demand content is referred to as files or clips and can be referred to directly. Broadcast content falls into two separate categories:

✦ **Unicast content.** This type of content is accessed via Publishing Points on a Windows Media Server.

✦ **Multicast content.** This kind of content is called Stations and is accessed via a NSC file that is created by the Windows Media Server and placed on a Web server.

Unsurprisingly, you use a slightly different syntax for linking to each type of stream. Table 15-4 lists the different sources and the syntax to use in your metafiles to link to each.

Table 15-4
URL Sytax for Different Windows Media Stream Types

Type of Stream	Syntax
On-demand file on a Windows Media Server	mms://{server IP or name}/{path}/{filename}
On-demand file on a Web server	http://{server IP or name}/{path}/{filename}
Unicast content	mms://{server IP or name}/{publishing point alias}
Mutlicast content (assumes that the NSC file has been uploaded to a Web server)	http://{web server}/{path}/{filename.nsc}

Media file roll-over using multiple ⟨ref⟩ tags

Sometimes a streaming media player can have trouble connecting to a server to play back a particular clip. To safeguard against this, you can specify additional files for the player to attempt to connect to when troubles arise. When the player encounters difficulties and tries the alternative files, it is said to be *rolling-over*.

You can specify roll-over files in Windows Media metafiles by specifying more than one clip inside an `<entry>` or `<event>` tag by using multiple `<ref/>` tags. When the Windows Media Player encounters difficulty connecting to a server, it tries to connect to the next file, and so on until it is either successful or all possibilities are exhausted.

As soon as a successful connection is made, the Windows Media Player plays that stream until the end and then moves on to the next entry in the metafile. The rest of the streams referenced in that particular entry are ignored. If you want all the streams to be played, you must put them in separate entries. This method should only be used for redundancy purposes.

Note also that this method is not attempted until the player has exhausted all possible methods of connection, such as multicast, unicast via RTSP, unicast via UDP, and finally TCP/IP.

Using `<event>` tags

When the Windows Media Player receives a script command labeled as an event, it looks for an entry in the metafile whose name matches the name of the event it received. If it finds a match, it plays the media enclosed by the `<event>` tags and then behaves according to how the `whendone` attribute is set.

For example, a live broadcast could send out an event called "Ad1." The metafile might have an entry as follows:

```
<event name="Ad1" whendone="resume">
        <ref href="mms://ads.server.com/OurSponsor.wmv"/>
</event>
```

The player would play the video ad, and when it was done, return to the live broadcast. In addition to "resume," the `whendone` attribute can also be set to "next" and "break." If it is set to "next," the player plays the next entry in the file after the event has finished playback. "Break" is used to break the player out of a loop set with the `<repeat>` tag.

Creating Windows Media metafiles

Windows Media metafiles can be created by using any text editor or by using the Windows Media Metafile Creator, which is included with the Windows Media Resource Kit. To create a metafile by hand, follow these simple steps:

1. **Open up a text editor and start by entering the necessary opening and closing `<asx>` tags.**

```
<asx version="3.0">
</asx>
```

2. **If you want to specify any global metadata, such as title, author, copyright, or a Web site to go for more information, add that just after the opening `<asx>` tag.**

```
<author>smack</author>
<moreinfo href="http://smacktastic.tv" />
```

3. **Create your metafile entries.** Each entry requires a clip reference. You can also specify other tags within an entry group, such as title, author, repeat, duration, and so on.

```
<entry>
        <title>Crazy Cats</title>
        <ref href="mms://my.server.com/media/crazycats.wmv" />
</entry>
<entry>
        <title>Tune in Next Week for...</title>
        <duration value="30" />
        <ref href="mms://my.server.com/media/episode2.wmv" />
</entry>
```

4. **If you wish, you can get fancy by referencing other metafiles.** Doing so causes the Windows Media Player to insert the contents of the referenced metafile into the current metafile. Any secondary metafile references are ignored (you're only allowed one level of recursion). Entries from the referenced metafile that have the `skipifref` attribute set to yes are also ignored.

5. **You can also get super fancy by inserting events entries (see the previous section, "Using <event> tags").**

6. **Save your file with an appropriate metafile extension.** You're always safe with `.asx`.

Put your metafile up on a Web server, and you're ready to go. Reference your metafile via a `<a href>` or `<embed>` tag. If more than one entry is included in the metafile, the Windows Media Player does not need to rebuffer between files; the buffering is transparent to the end-user.

When creating metafiles, you *can* use relative URLs but be careful. The paths are relative to the metafile, not the files being streamed. Plus, if you're serving the metafile from a Web server, you have to use full path URLS to use the MMS protocol.

Summary

This chapter gave you a good overview of metafiles and how they are created for the three platforms. In the next chapter, you're going to find out how to embed players into Web pages, so you can have more control over the presentation of your media files.

✦ Web pages often consist of many different files that can be of different types and even come off different servers.

✦ Browsers ascertain the content a file contains via the file's MIME type.

✦ Different programs can use the network simultaneously by using different ports.

✦ Metafiles are used so that the browser can hand off the address of the streaming presentation to the appropriate media player.

✦ Dynamically generating metafiles avoids the file management problems of thousands of metafiles.

✦ QuickTime movies can be embedded straight into Web pages by using the <a href> or <embed> tags. However, doing so only gets your HTTP streaming. You have to use reference movies to get RTSP streaming.

✦ QuickTime metafiles are called reference movies.

✦ Reference movies can be created in the QuickTime Pro player or by using the MakeRefMovie or XMLtoRef utilities.

✦ The RealSystem uses RAM or RPM metafiles, or the ramgen function on the RealServer, to dynamically generate metafiles.

✦ RAM files open stand-alone RealPlayers, RPM files are used for embedded players.

✦ Windows Media Technologies metafiles are XML-based text files that can be created by hand or by using the Windows Media Metafile Creator utility.

✦ Windows Media metafiles can include a number of different tags that provide a wealth of different behaviors.

✦   ✦   ✦

Embedding Your Presentation in a Web Page

By now, you should have an understanding of metafiles and why they are necessary to connect the audience to your streams. Hopefully, you've authored a few metafiles and figured out how to launch your streams into a stand-alone streaming media player.

Playing streams in a separate media player has advantages and disadvantages. On the plus side, playing streams in a separate media player is easy to do and virtually guaranteed to work. On the minus side, you're pretty much stuck with the look and feel of whatever media player you're streaming to. Ignoring the branding, the extra features, and other doodads such as equalizers, visualizations, and advertising that streaming media players abound with these days can be hard.

Some streaming media players support *skins*, whereby the author can create a custom look and feel for the player. Unfortunately, time and space constraints preclude a full discussion of this ability in this book.

 Cross-Reference For a discussion of media player skins, please refer to the companion Web site for this book (www.streaming mediabible.com).

The alternative is to embed your media player into a Web page. Doing so gives you control over what surrounds your presentation — the surrounding Web page real estate is yours to design.

Embedding streaming media players enables you to choose which elements of the media player are visible and where you want to lay them out. You can create a custom look for any streaming media player using images arranged in an HTML table or by using frames.

Authoring in HTML brings up an added benefit — it allows you to use a multitude of WYSIWYG (What You See Is What You Get) authoring tools that *may* make your life a lot easier.

However, embedded players do have a down side. When you embed a streaming media player, you run the risk that compatibility issues may prevent some of your audience from seeing your content. For example, if you author your a Web page using the ActiveX control for a streaming media player, the Web page may not be compatible with the Netscape navigator browser. If you're careful, though, you can reach the majority of your audience. This chapter takes a look at how browsers communicate with embedded players before delving into the code necessary to embed each of the three major streaming media players.

How Embedded Players Work

When you click on a Web page link that opens a stand-alone player, the browser actually hands off the metafile to the player. After that, the browser has nothing to do with the process. Embedded players work slightly differently. They have all the functionality of stand-alone players but are controlled, to some extent, by the browser.

Browsers communicate with embedded players in one of two ways — either by using the Netscape plug-in architecture or by using the Microsoft ActiveX control. Unsurprisingly, Netscape Navigator provides no support for ActiveX, and Internet Explorer no longer supports the Netscape plug-in.

The RealSystem and QuickTime provide support for both embedding technologies, while Windows Media only supports the Active X control. The question is, how can you author your embedded presentations so that they can be seen by the largest audience? The best way to reach the widest audience is to write code that supports both the Netscape plug-in *and* the ActiveX control.

Luckily, doing so isn't too tough. Most browsers ignore code that they can't understand and use the code they can understand. By authoring your pages with code for both the Netscape plug-in *and* the ActiveX control, all your bases are covered. Authoring your code in this manner takes a bit more time and effort, but after you've authored a page that works, you can use it as a template and reuse it over and over again.

On the CD-ROM   Many of the code examples in this chapter are available on the CD in the Authoring directory for your viewing pleasure.

The Microsoft ActiveX control model

Using the Microsoft ActiveX control involves using the `<object>` tag, along with a number of additional parameters. The parameters are specified individually by using `<param>` tags that contain name-value pairs. The following code embeds the Windows Media Player in a Web page using the ActiveX control:

```
<object id="WMTPlayer" width="160" height="120"
  classid="CLSID:6BF52A52-394A-11d3-B153-00C04F79FAA6">
  <param name="url" value="MyMovie_160x120.asx">
  <param name="autoStart" value="true" >
  <param name="uiMode" value="none" >
</object>
```

The code breaks down as follows:

✦ **object** — The `<object>` tag specifies that an ActiveX control is being used.

✦ **id** — The `id` attribute gives a name to the object that can be referenced by ActiveX or JavaScript controls.

✦ **width** — The `width` attribute specifies the width of the embedded media player display window.

✦ **height** — The `height` attribute specifies the height of the embedded media player display window.

✦ **classid** — The `classid` attribute identifies which ActiveX control to use, in this case the Windows Media Player 7.0.

✦ **param** — The `<param>` tag is used to specify additional parameters in name-value pairs. In this case, three `<param>` tags are used, one to specify the location of the file, one to specify that that the file should begin playback automatically, and one to specify that the Windows Media Player controls should not be visible.

When a browser comes across this code, it loads the ActiveX control for the Windows Media Player 7.0, reserving a display area 160 pixels wide by 120 pixels tall. The extra parameters specified in the `<param>` tags are handed off to the Windows Media ActiveX control.

Embedding the QuickTime player or RealPlayer by using the ActiveX control works similarly, the main (and crucial) difference being a different string specified in the `classid` parameter. The three players also have different sets of parameters that can be specified. These different parameters are discussed later in this chapter in the player-specific sections.

The Netscape plug-in model

The Netscape plug-in model works very similarly to the ActiveX model, but instead uses the `<embed>` tag. The `<embed>` tag works slightly differently in that it does not use `<param>` tags, and the closing `</embed>` tag is optional. The following code embeds the RealPlayer in a Web page by using the Netscape plug-in (line breaks inserted for clarity but not required):

```
<embed width="240" height="180"
    src="MyMovie_240x180.rpm"
    autostart="true"
    controls="ImageWindow">
</embed>
```

This code snippet breaks down as follows:

✦ **embed** — The `<embed>` tag specifies that a Netscape plug-in is being used.

✦ **width** — Specifies the width of the embedded media player display window.

✦ **height** — Specifies the height of the embedded media player display window.

✦ **src** — Specifies the source file for the plug-in. Note the `.rpm` file extension — the MIME type of the source file triggers the appropriate plug-in, in this case the RealPlayer.

✦ **autostart** — All additional parameters are specified directly in the embed tag. In this case, the file is set to begin playback automatically by setting this parameter to "true."

✦ **controls** — The RealPlayer can be broken into separate pieces when embedded into a Web page. Each piece required is defined with a "controls" parameter. In this case, the display window is specified.

When a browser encounters the `<embed>` tag listed above (provided it supports the Netscape plug-in model), it uses the MIME type of the file specified in the `src` parameter to determine which plug-in to use. The browser then loads the plug-in and hands off the specified parameters.

You can also embed the QuickTime player and older versions of the Windows Media Player by using the Netscape plug-in; however, Windows Media Player 7.0 and Internet Explorer 5.5 and later no longer support the Netscape plug-in architecture.

Building cross-platform Web pages with embedded media players

As mentioned previously, both the ActiveX control and the Netscape plug-in can be supported at the same time. To do this, you place the `<embed>` tag within an `<object>` tag. Browsers that use the ActiveX control use the object tag content and ignore the embed tag; browsers that use the Netscape plug-in ignore the object and parameter tags and use the information contained in the embed tag.

The following code is an example embedding the QuickTime player:

```
<object classid="clsid:02BF25D5-8C17-4B23-BC80-D3488ABDDC6B"
    width="160" height="136" >
    <param name="src" value="media/MyMovie_ref.mov">
    <param name="autoplay" value="true">

    <embed src="media/MyMovie_ref.mov"
        width="160" height="136" autoplay="true" >
    </embed>
</object>
```

The code includes not only the object tag but also an embed tag *inside* the object tag. Because the two methods of embedding use different ways of specifying parameters, all parameters must be specified twice — once for the object tag using name-value pairs inside `<param>` tags and once for the embed tag, specifying the parameters directly in the embed tag.

Be careful with the parameters you specify when embedding players. Each of the players has a rich set of parameters that you can use to customize the functionality of the embedded player. The problem is that some parameters only work in specific versions of a player.

If you stick to the basics (such as `width`, `height`, `autoplay` or `autostart`, `src` or `url`), you stand a better chance of your Web pages not breaking when support for an obscure parameter is dropped a few months down the line. This example is not an exaggeration — one of the major streaming platforms recently dropped support for a number of its embedded player parameters. The simpler you keep your code, the wider your audience can be, and the longer your pages last.

Embedding the QuickTime Player

The QuickTime player provides support for both the Netscape plug-in and the ActiveX control methods of embedding. QuickTime also provides a rich set of parameters to customize the functionality of the embedded player.

You can use all embedded QuickTime parameters with the ActiveX control or Netscape plug-in, with the exception of a handful that are specific to one method or the other. Table 16-1 lists all the parameters available for the embedded QuickTime player along with a brief description of each. For the most part, the parameters should be self-explanatory. For full embedding documentation, please refer to the Apple Web site (`www.apple.com/quicktime/authoring/embed.html`).

Table 16-1
Embedded QuickTime Player Parameters

Parameter	Values	Use
autohref *	True or false	Specifies whether the URL specified in the href parameter should be loaded automatically or not (see href).
autoplay	True or false	Specifies whether the QuickTime movie should play back automatically or not.
bgcolor *	Any hex value (or predefined color in QuickTime 4.0 or later)	Specifies a color to fill in the background of the display window. This color is only visible if a movie does not take up the whole display window.
cache *	True or false	Specifies whether a movie should be cached or not (not supported by Internet Explorer).
classid (required) (ActiveX control only)	clsid:02BF25D5-8C17-4B23-BC80-D3488ABDDC6B" **	Unique string used by the ActiveX control to identify the embedded QuickTime player; not recognized by the Netscape plug-in.
codebase (ActiveX control only)	www.apple.com/qtactivex/qtplugin.cab	If the user does not have the QuickTime ActiveX controller, this parameter enables the browser to direct them to a page to automatically install it.
controller	True or false	Specifies whether the controller bar is visible or not.
dontflattenwhensaving *	No value — you merely specify it as a parameter, i.e. <embed src="MyMovie.mov" width="320" height="240" dontflattenwhensaving>	When specified, the plug in does not flatten the movie before saving.

Parameter	Values	Use
enablejavascript *	True **or** false	Determines whether the presentation can be controlled using JavaScript or not. By default, it is false, so if you wish to use JavaScript to control the QuickTime player you must specify enablejavascript="true"
endtime	Any valid time reference in "dd:hh:mm:ss.xy" format.	Specifies the point in the movie that playback should end.
goto *	Used with any valid integer value, i.e. goto3, goto24, and so on.	Used in conjunction with the qtnext parameter — see qtnext.
height **(required)**	Any integer value.	Specifies the height of the player in pixels. Be sure to add 16 to the height parameter if you're including the controller bar.
hidden	True **or** false, **or use without a value to specify hidden, i.e.** <embed src="MyMovie.mov" width="2" height="2" hidden autoplay="true">	Specifies whether the QuickTime player should be isible or not. Set both height vand width parameters to 2 and autoplay="true" when using this parameter.
href	Any valid relative or fully qualified URL.	Provides the URL that should be opened if the movie is clicked on.
kioskmode *	True **or** false	When in kiosk mode, the player does not allow the movie to be saved and does not enable the pop-up menu in the movie controller.
loop	True, false, **or** palindrome	Specifies whether the movie should be looped or not. In palindrome mode the movie is first played forwards, then backwards, and so on.

Continued

	Table 16-1 *(continued)*	
Parameter	**Values**	**Use**
`movieid` *	Any valid integer	Used when you want to control movies via Wired Sprites. You can then control this movie by its `movieid` value.
`moviename` *	Any valid string	Used when you want to control movies via Wired Sprites. You can then control this movie by its name.
`playeveryframe`	`True` or `false`	By default the QuickTime player drops frames if necessary to keep up with real-time playback. Setting this value to true forces the player to play every frame of a movie, even if that forces the playback to slow down. Note that the audio is muted when this parameter is set to true.
`pluginspage` (Netscape plug-in only)	`www.apple.com/ quicktime/download`	The URL where users without the QuickTime plug in are directed.
`qtnext` *	Any valid relative or fully qualified URL, specified as follows: `<embed src= "MyMovie_ref.mov" width="160" height= "120" qtnext1= "<Movie2_ref.mov> T<myself>" qtnext2= "goto0" >`	Enables you to specify a number of different movies to be played back consecutively. Each `qtnext` parameter should have a consecutive integer assigned to it, such as `qtnext1`, `qtnext2`, and so on. Each movie can be targeted using the T parameter. The `goto` statement can be used to create looping.
`qtsrc` *	Any valid relative or fully qualified URL	Enables you to force the browser to use the embedded QuickTime player regardless of MIME type.

Parameter	Values	Use
qtsrcchokespeed *	Any valid integer	Enables the author to specify specifying bits per second a maximum download speed for a file.
qtsrcdontusebrowser *	True **or** false	By default this parameter is false, which means the browser fetches the file before handing off to the QuickTime player. If set to true, the QuickTime player retrieves the file, which speeds up access to local files. Also, by not using the browser the file is not cached, which can make it more difficult to make illegal copies.
scale	tofit, aspect, **or any valid number**	Specifies how a movie should be scaled to fit into the QuickTime player's display. tofit specifies the movie be stretched to fit the embedded window size. aspect specifies the movie should be stretched or shrunk to fit the display window while retaining the movie's original aspect ratio. if the aspect ratio of the display window and the movie are different, the extra space in the display window is filled with black if no bgcolor attribute was specified. If a number is specified, the movie is scaled by that number. For example, to play back a movie at double it's original size, you would set scale="2."
src (required)	Any valid relative or fully qualified URL	Specifies the location of the file or reference movie to be played.

Continued

Table 16-1 (continued)

Parameter	Values	Use
starttime *	Any valid time reference in "dd:hh:mm:ss.xy" format	Specifies the point in the movie that playback should begin.
target *	frame name, myself, quicktimeplayer	When set to myself, the movie specified in the href parameter is played when the screen is clicked on. When set to quicktimeplayer, the movie specified in the href parameter is loaded into a stand-alone QuickTime player. When a frame name is specified, a QuickTime player is opened in that frame.
targetcache *	True or false	By default false, specifies whether a user is allowed to cache a movie referred to by a poster movie.
type	Any valid QuickTime MIME type, such as "image/x-quicktime"	Used to specify a MIME type. Can be helpful to "force" the loading of the QuickTime player. Not supported by Internet Explorer.
urlsubstitute *	urlsubstitute="<string1> <substitute URL> where string1 is a string appearing in HREF tracks and substitute URL is a valid relative or fully qualified URL.	Used to repurpose QuickTime movies with embedded URLs.
volume	Any percentage between 0 and 100	Sets the initial play back volume. Defaults to 100 percent.
width (required)	Any integer value	Specifies the width of the player in pixels.

*Requires QuickTime 4.0 or later.

**When coding your HTML pages, please make sure the classid value does not have any spaces or carriage returns in it.

Note Never set height or width to less than 2, even if the movie is hidden. Some browsers crash if you do. Don't blame Apple.

QuickTime embedding tips

A few of the tags in Table 16-1 are particularly useful, especially if you want to reach the widest audience possible. Although many people have QuickTime installed on their systems, a few folks out there do not. To give these people an option to install the latest version of QuickTime, you should always use the classid, codebase, and pluginspace parameters.

The classid parameter is absolutely necessary and must have the proper value. This is the only way that the browser knows what ActiveX control to use. If the browser does not have the proper ActiveX control, the codebase parameter specifies where the browser can go to download the necessary ActiveX control.

Similarly, the pluginspace parameter performs the same function for the Netscape plug-in. If the browser does not recognize the MIME type of the embedded file, it can steer the viewer to the appropriate download page to find the latest version of QuickTime. So every time you embed a QuickTime player, your code should look like this (substituting appropriate values for src, width, and height):

```
<object classid="clsid:02BF25D5-8C17-4B23-BC80-D3488ABDDC6B"
    width="160" height="136"
    codebase="http://www.apple.com/qtactivex/qtplugin.cab">
    <param name="src" value="YourRefMovie.mov">

    <embed src="YourRefMovie.mov"
        width="160" height="136"
    pluginspage="http://www.apple.com/quicktime/download/">
    </embed>
</object>
```

 Note When calculating the height parameter for embedded QuickTime movies remember to add 16 pixels to the height parameter if you plan on including the controller.

Preventing QuickTime movies from being hijacked

QuickTime files that are embedded using only the Netscape plug-in (the <embed> tag) run the risk of being hijacked by other media players. The Netscape plug-in utilizes the MIME type of the file specified in the src parameter to determine which plug-in to load. Sometimes media players other than the QuickTime player register themselves as the preferred media player for QuickTime movies.

The problem is that these renegade media players may not be able to play *all* QuickTime movies, and they certainly do not understand QuickTime-specific parameters in the `<embed>` tag. You can employ a number of strategies to prevent this. For the best strategy, please refer to the Apple developer site, in particular on the following Web page (ignoring the line break):

```
http://developer.apple.com/techpubs/quicktime/qtdevdocs/
        QT4WebPage/corrections.htm
```

If you're using the ActiveX control, hijacking is not a problem because the `classid` parameter is unique to the QuickTime player. However, Netscape Navigator ignores the ActiveX control, so if you want to write bulletproof code for the widest possible audience, you should consider employing the strategies discussed on the Apple Web site.

Embedding the RealPlayer

You can also embed the RealPlayer by using the Netscape plug-in or the ActiveX control. By placing the Netscape plug-in tags within the ActiveX tags, you can create Web pages that work across a wide range of browsers.

For the ActiveX control, you must supply the correct `classid` parameter. Unfortunately, the RealPlayer does not make use of the `codebase` parameter, so the ActiveX control cannot be installed automatically. However, you should always provide a link to the RealPlayer download page in case folks need to download the player (`www.real.com/player/index.html`).

Cross-Reference
Table 16-2 lists the available parameters for the embedded player, along with a brief description of each. For full documentation, please refer to the RealSystem Production guide, available from the RealNetworks site (`www.realnetworks.com`). For full documentation, please refer to the RealSystem Production guide.

| | Table 16-2 | |
| | **Embedded RealPlayer Parameters** | |
Parameter	*Values*	*Use*
`autostart`	`True` or `false`	Specifies whether playback of the source file should begin automatically or not.
`backgroundcolor` *	Any hex value preceeded by a "#" sign or any valid predefined color	Specifies the background color for the image window.

Parameter	Values	Use
center *	True or false	Specifies that the clip should be played back at its original encoding size and centered in the image window — this parameter cannot be used with maintainaspect.
classid (required)	"clsid:CFCDAA03-8BE4-11cf-B84B-0020AFBBCCFA" **	The unique string used by the ActiveX control to identify the embedded RealPlayer. Not recognized by the Netscape plug-in.
console	Any string	Enables the author to group various RealPlayer controls on a Web page so that they interoperate, or keep them separate, so they do not affect each other.
controls	ImageWindow, All, ControlPanel, PlayButton, PlayOnlyButton, PauseButton, StopButton, FFCtrl, RWCtrl, MuteCtrl, MuteVolume, VolumeSlider, PositionSlider, TACCtrl, HomeCtrl, InfoVolumePanel, InfoPanel, StatusBar, StatusField, PositionField	Enables the author to specify which controls to make visible. Many different combinations of controls are available. See the "Using selected RealPlayer controls" section or the RealSystem production guide.
height (required)	Any integer value	Specifies the height of the RealPlayer element in pixels.
id	Any string	Specifies a name for the RealPlayer element in <object> tags (use name in <embed> tags).
imagestatus	True or false	Specifies whether status information should be displayed in the image window; default is true.
loop *	True or false	Enables the author to specify that a clip should be looped indefinitely.

Continued

Table 16-2 *(continued)*

Parameter	Values	Use
maintainaspect *	True or false	By default, the RealPlayer stretches all clips to fill the entire image window. If this parameter is set to true, the aspect ratio of the original is maintained, and the video is stretched until one of the dimensions of the image window is met.
name	Any string	Specifies a name for the RealPlayer element in \<embed\> tags (use id in \<object\> tags).
nojava *	True or false	Prevents the Java Virtual Machine from starting up.
nolabels	True or false	Enables the author to suppress the title/author/copyright information from being displayed (only works on RealPlayer 5.0 and earlier).
nologo *	True or false	Prevents the Real logo from being displayed in the Image window at startup.
numloop *	Any integer value	Enables you to specify the number of times a clip should be looped and does not require the loop parameter.
prefetch	True or false	Specifies whether the RealPlayer should get the stream description information before playback; default is false.
region *	Any string	For use with SMIL presentations. Allows the author to specify layout in HTML instead of SMIL.
scriptcallbacks	Comma separated list	Specifies the browser callbacks to monitor.
shuffle *	True or false	For use with multi-clip .ram files or SMIL files. Causes the RealPlayer to randomize the playback of the listed files.
src (required)	Any valid relative or fully qualified URL	Specifies the location of the metafile or file to be played back.

Parameter	Values	Use
type	string	Specifies a MIME type for the embedded plug-in.
width (required)	Any integer	Specifies the width of the RealPlayer element.

*Requires RealPlayer G2 or later.

**When coding your HTML pages, please make sure the classid value does not have any spaces or carriage returns in it.

Embedded RealPlayer examples

Embedding a RealPlayer is slightly different than embedding the QuickTime Player or the Windows Media Player because the RealPlayer can be broken up into separate elements. Every part of the player can be described by a controls parameter, and each of these parameters can be specified in a separate <embed> or <object> tag.

In the previous Netscape plug-in example, only the image window was specified with a controls parameter, and autoplay was set to true. In the following example, a control panel is added so that the viewer can control playback as well as an information panel with a volume control:

```
<embed width="240" height="180" src="MyMovie_240x180.rpm"
    controls="ImageWindow"
    console="_master" >
</embed>
<br>
<embed width="240" height="55" src="MyMovie_240x180.rpm"
    controls="InfoVolumePanel"
    console="_master" >
</embed>
<br>
<embed width="240" height="36" src="MyMovie_240x180.rpm"
    controls="ControlPanel"
    console="_master" >
</embed>
```

When using the Netscape plug-in, you must use a separate <embed> tag for each element of the RealPlayer that is being displayed, and each one of these requires a src parameter. The ActiveX control also requires a separate tag for each element, but the src parameter only needs to be specified in one of them:

```
<object classid="clsid:CFCDAA03-8BE4-11cf-B84B-0020AFBBCCFA"
    width="240" height="148">
    <param NAME="controls" VALUE="ImageWindow">
    <param NAME="console" VALUE="_master">
</object>
```

```
<br>
<object classid="clsid:CFCDAA03-8BE4-11cf-B84B-0020AFBBCCFA"
    width="240" height="55">
    <param NAME="controls" VALUE="InfoVolumePanel">
    <param NAME="console" VALUE="_master">
</object>
<br>
<object classid="clsid:CFCDAA03-8BE4-11cf-B84B-0020AFBBCCFA"
    width="240" height="36">
    <param NAME="SRC" VALUE="media/MyMovie_240x180.rpm">
    <param NAME="controls" VALUE="ControlPanel">
    <param NAME="console" VALUE="_master">
</object>
```

To author a presentation for the widest possible audience, you can combine the previous two code examples so that you have embedded code that works properly with either the Netscape plug-in or the ActiveX control. To do so, you need to nest each embedded element inside its corresponding `<object>` tag as follows:

The following code is available for your viewing (and copying/modifying) pleasure on the CD in the embedded players folder of the Authoring directory. The file is called Real_dual_with_controls.html.

```
<object classid="clsid:CFCDAA03-8BE4-11cf-B84B-0020AFBBCCFA"
    width="240" height="148">
    <param NAME="controls" VALUE="ImageWindow">
    <param NAME="console" VALUE="_master">
    <embed width="240" height="180"
        src="media/MyMovie_240x180.rpm"
        controls="ImageWindow" console="_master" >
    </embed>
</object>
<br>
<object  classid="clsid:CFCDAA03-8BE4-11cf-B84B-0020AFBBCCFA"
    width="240" height="55">
    <param NAME="controls" VALUE="InfoVolumePanel">
    <param NAME="console" VALUE="_master">
    <embed width="240" height="55"
        src="media/MyMovie_240x180.rpm"
        controls="InfoVolumePanel" console="_master" >
    </embed>
</object>
<br>
<object  classid="clsid:CFCDAA03-8BE4-11cf-B84B-0020AFBBCCFA"
    width="240" height="36">
    <param NAME="SRC" VALUE="media/MyMovie_240x180.rpm">
    <param NAME="controls" VALUE="ControlPanel">
    <param NAME="console" VALUE="_master">
    <embed width="240" height="36"
        src="media/MyMovie_240x180.rpm"
        controls="ControlPanel" console="_master" >
    </embed>
</object>
```

Each object has a matching embedded element hidden inside it. Each combined object/emebed tag can be laid out in HTML by using a table or frames or any other HTML layout scheme. The code is a bit verbose and involves a bit of repetition, because the parameters have to be specified for both embedding methods. However, authoring your code this way ensures that the widest possible audience is capable of viewing your content, which is what you want.

Using selected RealPlayer controls

The embedded RealPlayer can be broken up into many pieces. Just about every button, display, or control available on the stand-alone RealPlayer can be embedded separately on a Web page. All you have to do is use a separate object and/or embed statement for the piece of the RealPlayer you want to embed.

To tie the various pieces together, you use the `console` parameter. You can group various RealPlayer elements together by using the same console name or separate them by using different names. You can also use the special name "`_master`" to control all the RealPlayer elements on a page.

Table 16-3 lists all the predefined elements of the RealPlayer that can be embedded separately as well as suggested pixel sizes for each. If smaller or larger regions are specified, the icons displayed scale automatically.

Table 16-3 Embedded RealPlayer Components		
Component	**Description**	**Suggested pixel dimensions**
`ImageWindow`	The video display area.	The RealPlayer automatically scales the video to fit the display. If the stream is significantly different in size or shape scaling can lead to picture degradation and CPU load.
`All`	Embeds all the buttons, sliders, and information panels on the RealPlayer.	375×100
`ControlPanel`	Displays all the control buttons, along with a position slider and a speaker icon that pops-up into a volume slider.	350×36

Continued

Table 16-3 *(continued)*
Embedded RealPlayer Components

Component	Description	Suggested pixel dimensions
PlayButton	Displays the play button and a pause button.	44×26
PlayOnlyButton	Displays only the play button.	26×26
PauseButton	Displays only the pause button.	26×26
StopButton	Displays only the stop button.	26×26
FFCtrl	Displays only the fast forward button.	26×26
RWCtrl	Displays only the rewind button.	26×26
MuteCtrl	Displays only the speaker icon used as a mute button	26×26
MuteVolume	Displays a small speaker icon used for muting and a volume slider above it.	26×88
VolumeSlider	Displays only a vertical v olume slider.	26×65
PositionSlider	Displays the horizontal position slider.	120×26
TACCtrl	Displays the horizontal gray box where the title, author, and copyright information is rotated.	370×32
HomeCtrl	Displays a small Real logo.	45×26
InfoVolumePanel	Displays a black box where title, author, and copyright information is displayed in green; on right-hand side speaker icon and volume slider are included.	325×55
InfoPanel	Same as above, but without the mute button and volume slider.	300×55
StatusBar	Displays a horizontal black box where clip status is displayed, such as clip time, network conditions, and so on.	300×30

Component	Description	Suggested pixel dimensions
StatusField	Similar to the Status bar, but displays only the message area, where network messages such as "Re-buffering..." are displayed. *	200×30
PositionField	A small black box that shows total clip length and current position in the clip.	90×30

*If no status bar is embedded, the status messages are displayed in the browser's status bar, and buffering messages are overlaid on the Image window.

Using these values for the `console` parameter, you can embed as many or as few RealPlayer components as you want. For each component that you wish to embed, you must include a separate object and/or embed tag with the appropriate value for the `console` parameter. To see what the individual components look like, refer to the RealSystem Production Guide or have a look at the RealPlayer_parts.html file included on the CD in the embedded players folder of the Authoring directory.

Embedding the Windows Media Player

Until recently, Windows Media Technologies supported both the Netscape plug-in and the ActiveX control. Sadly, this is no longer the case. The best you can do now is to embed the Windows Media Player 7.0 or later by using the `<object>` tag and the older Player 6.4 by using the Netscape plug-in (see the "Netscape plug-in support" section).

Before delving into how to embed both the 7.x and 6.4 Players at the same time, Table 16-4 lists the Windows Media Player 7.0 parameters available to the ActiveX control, along with parameter values and a brief description of each. For more information, please refer to the documentation that is included with the Windows Media SDK, available from the Windows Media Web site (www.microsoft.com/windowsmedia).

Table 16-4
Embedded Windows Media Player 7.0 Parameters

Parameter	Values	Use
autoStart	True or false	Specifies whether the clip should begin playback automatically; default is true.

Continued

	Table 16-4 *(continued)*	
Parameter	**Values**	**Use**
balance	Any integer between -100 and 100	Specifies the balance between the left and right speaker, with −100 indicating all sound in the left speaker; default is zero.
baseURL	Any valid fully quaified or relative URL	Specifies a string that is prepended to any URLs received via script commands.
currentPosition	Any valid time reference in seconds	Specifies the current position in playback.
currentMarker	Any valid marker number	Specifies the current marker number.
defaultFrame	Any valid frame name	Specifies a default frame name to send URLs received via scripts.
enableContextMenu	True or false	Specifies whether the context menu should be available, which is accessed via a right mouse-click.
enableErrorDialogs	True or false	Specifies whether error dialogs are shown or not.
enabled	True or false	Specifies whether or not the player is enabled.
fullScreen	True or false	Specifies whether content is to be played back full screen or not.
invokeURLs	True or false	Specifies whether URLs should launch a browser or not.
mute	True or false	Specifies whether the audio should be muted or not.
playcount	Any positive integer	Specifies how many times a clip should be played.
rate	Any number, in theory, but practically limited to -10 to 10	Specifies how fast the clip should be played back, with negative numbers indicating reverse play; ASF and WMV files mute the audio when the rate is anything other than 1.

Parameter	Values	Use
SAMIFilename	Any valid relative or fully qualified URL	Specifies the name of the file that contains the closed-captioning information.
uiMode	None, mini, or full	Specifies how much of the Windows Media Player controls to expose; mini exposes only play/pause buttons, mute and volume controls, and Status bar.
url	Any valid relative or fully qualified URL	Specifies the location of the file or metafile to be retrieved.
volume	Any number from 0 to 100	Specifies the volume level, with 100 being full volume; default is to play back the stream at the Windows Media Player's current volume level.

Caution The embedded Windows Media Player 7.0 does not support the "../" structure in the url parameter.

Embedded Windows Media Player examples

I gave a brief example of embedding a minimal Windows Media Player in a Web page earlier in this chapter. Here's another example, this time with some controls thrown in. In fact, this example uses even simpler code, because the default behavior is to show the controls:

```
<object id="WMTPlayer" width="240" height="244"
    classid="CLSID:6BF52A52-394A-11d3-B153-00C04F79FAA6">
    <param name="url" value="media/MyMovie_240x180.asx">
</object>
```

Similar to embedding the QuickTime player, you have to remember to include room in your height parameter for the controls. The player controls are 40 pixels high; the status bar is another 24 pixels high. Therefore, to avoid any image distortion you need to add 64 pixels to your window height.

Note The 6.4 Player has different sized controls. The default is to show the controls, which are 46 pixels high. You can also choose which other player elements to include in your presentation using various parameters. Please refer to the Windows Media SDK for details. The SDK is available from the Microsoft Web site (www.microsoft.com/windowsmedia).

Also, think about which `uiMode` to specify. The default is full, but at widths less than 240 pixels the fast forward and rewind buttons can be partially obscured, so using `mini` mode is better when the width of the presentation is less than 240 pixels.

Netscape plug-in support

The only problem with the code snippet in the previous section is that it only displays on browsers that support the ActiveX control. What you really want is to be able to support both embedding methods. The problem is that Microsoft has dropped support for the Netscape plug-in with Windows Media Player 7.0.

Luckily, you can still use the Netscape plug-in for the Windows Media 6.4 Player as follows:

The following code for embedding a Windows Media Player using both the ActiveX control and the Netscape plug-in is available for you to review on the CD, in the embedded players folder of the Authoring directory. It is called WMT_dual_with_ controls.html .

```
<object id="WMTPlayer" width="240" height="244"
    classid="CLSID:6BF52A52-394A-11d3-B153-00C04F79FAA6">
    <param name="url" value="media/MyMovie_240x180.asx">
    <embed type="application/x-mplayer2"
        src="media/MyMovie_240x180.asx"
        width="240" height="226">
    </embed>
</object>
```

The `classid` in the object tag specifies the Windows Media Player 7.0. The MIME type referred to in the `<embed>` tag is associated with the older Windows Media Player 6.4. This plug-in is not deleted by the new player install.

This example is simplified. You can get a lot fancier, but you're going to have to be very careful. You're mixing two separate methods, and the parameters for each are markedly different. For example, if you want to hide the controls in the above code, you need to set the `uiMode` parameter in the ActiveX portion, while setting the older `ShowControls` parameter in the Netscape plug-in section.

Another thing to be careful of is that some of the newer audio and video codecs cannot be played back in the old 6.4 Player. In some cases you may have to encode different versions of the file for older version players.

You can set many parameters when you use Windows Media Player 6.4. For details, please refer to the documentation that is included with the Windows Media SDK — the 6.4 player documentation comes at the end. The Windows Media SDK is available from the Microsoft Web site (`www.microsoft.com/windowsmedia`).

Sometimes, if Netscape is installed after the Windows Media Player, the plug-ins do not get properly installed. Furthermore, Netscape claims to be able to find a plug-in for you but then fails. To work around this, consider placing a link on your page to the Windows Media Download center and instructions on how to download the plug-in. The download page is: www.microsoft.com/windows/windowsmedia/download/default.asp.

Summary

Embedding players isn't that tricky, but it can be the first step down a long, slippery slope. In the next chapter, you'll explore how to use JavaScript to control embedded players.

✦ Embedded players work closely with the browser, unlike stand-alone players, which are completely separate applications.

✦ You can use two methods to embed players — by using the ActiveX control or by using the Netscape plug-in.

✦ You can write code that utilizes both embedding methods by nesting the <embed> tags used by the Netscape plug-in inside <object> tags, which the ActiveX control uses.

✦ All three streaming media players support the ActiveX control. Microsoft has recently dropped support for the Netscape plug-in; however, you can still utilize the Windows Media Player 6.4 plug-in.

✦ Use the codebase and pluginspage parameters when embedding the QuickTime player so that users without the appropriate ActiveX control are automatically enabled.

✦ The embedded RealPlayer enables you to embed as much or as little of the player as you want. Each player element takes its own object/embed tag and can be laid out by using HTML.

✦　　✦　　✦

Using JavaScript to Control Embedded Players

CHAPTER

17

Embedding players in Web pages is only the first step in creating a customized user interface. This method works well, but it falls short in a couple of ways.

First, you're still stuck with the controls that come with whatever streaming media player you've embedded. Generally speaking, they're not the most attractive interfaces ever designed.

Second, you may want interaction between the player and various other elements of the Web page. Basic embedded player can perform simple interactions, such as targeting HTML pages to frames, by using the built-in capabilities of the players, but more complex interactions require a sophisticated approach.

To accomplish such multifaceted interactions, you need to use JavaScript. JavaScript offers a (reasonably) cross-platform way of controlling and interacting with all the elements of a Web page, including embedded players.

JavaScript is an incredibly rich technology that can do much more than simply enable you to control your embedded streaming media players. This chapter aims to give you an overview of what is possible with JavaScript, and it provides you with some simple code examples that you can repurpose into your Web pages.

If you want to delve deeper into the realms of JavaScript, you can grab a number of good reference books available (my copy of the *JavaScript Bible* by Danny Goodman has seen extensive use). You should also refer to the Apple (www.apple.com), RealNetworks (www.realnetworks.com), and Microsoft (www.microsoft.com) Web sites for their latest and greatest JavaScript implementation information.

How JavaScript Works

JavaScript arose from the desire to make Web pages more dynamic without having to send requests all the way back to the server. For example, if a Web page has a form that needs to be filled out, checking the validity of the individual fields *before* sending the information back to the server for processing makes sense. Not only does doing so lighten the load on the server side, but it also takes advantage of the processing power of the viewer's computer.

Taking advantage of the client computer's processing power also has other benefits. JavaScript can really make a Web page come alive, for example by changing an image when you mouse over it. This type of browser interaction would be totally impractical implemented over a network. Imagine waiting five seconds or more every time you mouse-over an image. You would be more annoyed than interested.

What JavaScript does is add some intelligence to your browser. Instead of being a passive device that merely displays text and images, your browser becomes more of an interface, capable of dynamic interaction with the user.

JavaScript is not part of HTML. It is a separate piece of software that is built-in to your browser that enables the manipulation of HTML and other pieces of software that are contained within the browser window. JavaScript, for the most part, is cross-platform compatible. If you write JavaScript code it should (in theory) work on any JavaScript enabled browser on any platform.

You may have noticed the phrase "in theory" in the preceding paragraph. That's because, although JavaScript is standardized and supposedly cross-platform, different degrees of implementation of the standard exist in different browsers and browser versions.

Don't let this paint too bleak of a picture. Authoring cross-platform/cross-browser JavaScript code is nowhere near as difficult as it was a couple of years ago. The key is to keep your code as simple and as minimal as possible.

Before jumping into the code necessary to control your embedded player, you should know a little bit about how JavaScript works. When you understand the underlying principle, looking at JavaScript code becomes much less intimidating.

Objects, properties, methods, and events

JavaScript treats everything in the browser as an *object*, including the actual browser. Each object has a set of *properties* that can be queried or set. You use different *methods* to access and manipulate an object's *properties* or perform tasks. Last but not least, JavaScript enables you to keep track of browser *events,* for example, if the mouse is clicked or if the cursor moves over a certain object.

Staring at code listings can make even the most stoic streaming media author glaze over. JavaScript attempts to keep things as simple as possible by using hierarchical "dot" syntax when referring to objects, properties, and when calling methods. The results can be surprisingly readable. Some examples are as follows:

```
window.topFrame.adBanner.src
document.images[logo]
window.open("http://www.mysite.com");
onClick="window.close();"
```

The first line references the source URL of an object named `adBanner` that is contained in a frame called `topFrame` in the current window. The second line references an image named `logo` in the current document. The third line calls the `open` method of the `window` object to create a new browser window that loads the site `www.mysite.com`. The final line closes a window when the `onClick` event occurs.

Operators and control statements

JavaScript includes various operators and control statements similar to other programming languages. These operators and control statements are used to query and set the values of object properties, perform tasks based on object property values, or perform tasks when certain events occur.

As a simple example, every browser has an object called `navigator` that in turn has several properties. The `appName` property is particularly useful — it is the name of your browser application, which in general will have the value Microsoft Internet Explorer or Netscape.

Knowing this, you can author Web pages with a script that queries the values of this property and then performs certain functions. The following code gives a simple example:

```
<script language="JavaScript">
    if (navigator.appName == "Microsoft Internet Explorer") {
        document.write("Hi, I'm Internet Explorer.");
    }
    else {
        if (navigator.appName == "Netscape"){
```

```
            document.write("Hi I'm Netscape.");
          }
        else {
          document.write("Who am I?");
        }
      }
    </script>
```

In this script, the value of `navigator.appName` is compared to known values. Depending on the outcome of the comparisons, different code is executed. In this case, a simple message is written to the screen by using the `document.write` method. Notice how this code has "branches" for Internet Explorer, Netscape, and a default branch if no conditions are met (hint, hint).

Hiding JavaScript from older browsers

Older browsers such as Internet Explorer 2.0 do not understand JavaScript. These days, only a very small portion of your intended audience probably uses these browsers. The problem is that some old browsers attempted to execute the code and ended up displaying garbage on the screen. For this reason, most JavaScript code you see uses the following syntax:

```
<script language="JavaScript>
<!-- hide from old browsers
    ...javascript code goes here
// End of HTML comment for old browsers -->
</script>
```

The two script tags are read by old browsers and ignored; the rest of the JavaScript code falls within a large HTML comment. Newer browsers are clever enough to ignore the HTML comment code and to look for valid JavaScript code between the two script tags.

The percentage of browsers out there that do not understand JavaScript is very small at this point, but it doesn't hurt to author your scripts this way for the few that remain.

Working With Embedded Players

JavaScript treats embedded players as objects. Each streaming media player has its own set of methods that you can use to perform certain functions. You can issue commands, such as play or stop. You can also query properties, such as metadata or whether certain parts of the player are visible.

Referring to an embedded object can be done in a couple of ways. When an HTML document is loaded, the browser keeps track of all the elements by using a hierarchical model. Elements of the same type are kept in arrays. So if you knew, for example, that you had a single image in a document, you could refer to it by using the following syntax:

```
document.images[0]
```

JavaScript starts counting at zero, so the first element of any array is element zero. Of course, your Web pages probably have many images, so referring to them via the array element number isn't the best approach. The simplest way by far is to give the elements you want to access via JavaScript unique names. Then all you have to do is refer to them by name:

```
document.qtPlayer
document.realPlayer
document.wmtPlayer
```

As soon as you give your embedded player a name, you can use the specific player's methods to control the player. Each embedded player uses *slightly* different syntax:

```
document.qtplayer.Play();
document.realPlayer.DoPlay();
document.wmtPlayer.controls.Play();
```

Now that you know how to issue the Play command, you can use it in any number of ways. In this example, the Play command is linked to a user clicking on an appropriate link.

```
<a href="javascript:document.realControls.DoPlay();">Play</a>
```

You can use this syntax to link text, buttons created by HTML forms, images, or whatever else you can think of.

Authoring Web pages with embedded streaming media players can be exceedingly tedious, particularly if you're trying to author single pages that cater to multiple streaming platforms and attempt to be reasonably browser-independent. You can easily spend hours trying to debug your code only to find a missing semicolon was the culprit. To avoid wasting your time in this manner, you need to follow a few ground rules that should keep you out of the worst trouble:

✦ Every JavaScript command should end with a semicolon. Doing this isn't strictly necessary, but using them all the time prevents you from forgetting them when they are required.

✦ When naming an embedded object using the Netscape plug-in, be sure to use the name parameter, not the id parameter. When using the ActiveX control, either parameter is acceptable, but the id tag is generally used.

✦ Make absolutely sure that you're using the right parameter names and methods. All three embedded players use extremely similar but sometimes slightly different parameters. If you try to use the `url` parameter with the RealPlayer, or the `src` parameter with the Windows 7.0 embedded player, it won't work. The problem is the code *looks* correct, when in fact it isn't.

✦ Make absolutely sure that the paths to your source files are correct. You can spend hours staring at perfectly good JavaScript code only to find that your metafile isn't where it is supposed to be.

Caution

The embedded Windows Media Player 7.0 does not support the " . . /" structure in the `url` parameter.

✦ If you're working with QuickTime, you must enable JavaScript control by setting `enablejavascript="true"`.

✦ If you're working with the RealPlayer, give each separate embedded element on the page a unique name. You don't have to do this, but it's good coding practice and will help prevent silly mistakes.

✦ If you're working with the Windows Media Player, make sure that you're using the appropriate methods — the 7.0 Player does not understand 6.4 player methods and vice-versa.

You now should have enough to get started. Most of the code explained in this chapter is included on the CD. A good policy is to copy code that you know works, thereby avoiding missing punctuation, incorrect syntax, and so on. Modify the working code to your needs, checking often along the way. After you arrive at code that works for you — template it and reuse it!

QuickTime JavaScript Control

QuickTime offers JavaScript control via the Netscape plug-in. However, JavaScript control via the Netscape plug-in only works in Netscape browsers earlier than the 6.0 version. JavaScript functionality via the Netscape plug-in also does not work in Internet Explorer.

Apple eventually released an ActiveX control for the QuickTime player because Internet Explorer 5.5 and above no longer support the Netscape plug-in. Unfortunately, the ActiveX control does not yet include JavaScript control functionality. Hopefully this will not be the case for long.

Of course, this calls into question whether you'd want to author pages with JavaScript control of the QuickTime player at all but to be thorough, I cover it in this chapter. As a workaround, you can get fancy and dynamically generate pages based on the user's browser (see "An ActiveX workaround," later in this chapter).

Netscape

Caution

JavaScript control of the QuickTime plug-in is not working in Netscape 6.x. With any luck, this situation may be corrected soon. Please check the Apple Web site (www.apple.com/quicktime) and the Netscape developers' Web site (developer.netscape.com) for the latest details.

Because JavaScript control only works in Netscape, you don't have to nest the `<embed>` tag in an `<object>` tag. You can keep your code simple by using only the `<embed>` tag. Remember, however, that doing so makes your code incompatible with Internet Explorer 5.5 and above.

When using JavaScript controls, you need to remember two crucial points:

✦ You must enable JavaScript by setting `enablejavascript="true"`.

✦ Use the `name` parameter, not the `id` parameter to assign a name to the player.

Because you're going to be providing JavaScript controls, you have the option of leaving the QuickTime controls out. If you decide to leave them out, the embed statement should look like this:

```
<embed name="qtPlayer"
   src="../media/MyMovie_160_20k.mov"
   width="160" height="136" autoplay="false"
   enablejavascript="true"
   controller="false"
   pluginspage="http://www.apple.com/quicktime/download/">
</embed>
```

To control the player, you can use the play, stop, and rewind methods that are available (for a full list of all the JavaScript methods, please refer to Bonus Chapter 4 available for easy searching on the CD-ROM). There are two simple ways to use these commands, using the name that you assigned to the embedded player. For example, the previous code example assigns the name `qtPlayer` to the embedded player. You can issue commands to the embedded player in an anchor command as follows:

```
<a href="javascript:document.qtPlayer.Play();">Play</a>
```

Notice how you preface the command with the word `javascript` to let the browser know that this link is not to another document. Alternatively, you can use the `onClick` event to issue the command, as follows:

```
<a href="#" onClick="document.qtPlayer.Play();">Play</a>
```

In this case, `href` parameter is set to #, which means top of the page. If sending the viewer to the top of the browser page is unacceptable, you can also use `"javascript: void();"` which tells the browser to do absolutely nothing — except of course for what you specified in the `onClick` event.

You can use these links to link images or text, or they can be used in a form. An example is included on the CD that uses a number of methods to link to the controls.

On the CD-ROM To see how the code looks and behaves, please see `qt_javascript_controls_` `netscape.html` on the CD in the javascript folder of the authoring directory.

In addition to these simple control commands, you can extract data from the QuickTime player or the QuickTime movie by using JavaScript. For example, you can retrieve the name of the presentation by using the `GetUserData();` method. You can also set the volume, set the movie to loop, or any number of other things.

Cross-Reference For a full list of all the QuickTime JavaScript methods, please refer to Bonus Chapter 4, on the CD-ROM, "Embedded Player JavaScript Reference."

An ActiveX workaround

If you're goal is to author pages that are compatible across the widest range of browsers, you're in a bit of a tricky position with QuickTime. Because you cannot use JavaScript controls in Internet Explorer, you must include the QuickTime controls on your page. This is not tricky; just make sure to include the controller in the `<object>` tag and disable the controller bar in the `<embed>` tag.

The question is what to do with the JavaScript controls? If they don't work in Internet Explorer (IE), then you probably shouldn't even display them. By using the `navigator.appName` property that was discussed at the very start of the chapter, you can write a JavaScript function to decide whether to display the JavaScript controls or not.

The problem isn't that Internet Explorer doesn't understand JavaScript; IE understands most JavaScript just fine. The problem is that the QuickTime player and IE cannot communicate via JavaScript. Bearing this in mind, you can sketch out a JavaScript function that looks something like this:

```
<script language="javascript">
<!-- hide from ancient browsers
    if (navigator.appName != "Microsoft Internet Explorer"){
        ...code to display the JavaSCript controls
    }
// -->
</script>
```

This script essentially says, "If the browser is *not* IE, then go ahead and display the controls. Otherwise, the browser must be IE, so the controls are not written out." Obviously, this solution is not optimal, but with any luck, the QuickTime ActiveX control will soon support JavaScript methods.

A sample Web page that displays JavaScript controls in Netscape and a controller bar in IE is included on the CD in the javascript section of the Authoring directory (qt_javascript_controls_sometimes.html).

RealPlayer JavaScript Control

The RealPlayer can be controlled via JavaScript on both IE and Netscape. Whether you're embedding by using the Netscape plug-in or by using the ActiveX control, the JavaScript methods you use are exactly the same.

JavaScript control of the RealPlayer is not working on Netscape 6.*x.* Hopefully this problem will be corrected soon. Please refer to the Netscape developers' Web site (developer.netscape.com) and the RealNetworks Web site (www.realnet works.com) for the latest details.

You may recall that embedding the RealPlayer is slightly different than the others because you embed all the pieces of the player individually, by using separate <embed> or <object> tags (or one nested inside the other) for each piece. As long as they all have the same console parameter value, you can target any of the embedded pieces with JavaScript commands — all the other parts respond as well.

When embedding the RealPlayer, you should give each embedded element a unique name. It isn't required, but it's good programming practice and there is a case (using <embed> on IE) where it is required to make things work.

The cross-platform approach

Because JavaScript control works on both IE and Netscape, you should embed the player by using the <embed> tag nested in the <object> tag, as follows:

```
<object id="realWindow"
   classid="clsid:CFCDAA03-8BE4-11cf-B84B-0020AFBBCCFA"
   width="240" height="180">
   <param name="src" value="media/MyMovie_240x180.rpm">
   <param name="controls" VALUE="ImageWindow">
   <param name="console" VALUE="_master">
   <embed width="240" height="180" name="realWindow"
         src="media/MyMovie_240x180.rpm"
         controls="ImageWindow" console="_master" >
   </embed>
</object>
```

Note that the embedded player is given the name `realWindow` by using the `id` parameter in the ActiveX control and the `name` parameter in the Netscape plug-in. These names must be the same for the code to work cross-browser. You can embed other pieces of the RealPlayer (other than the image window), but be sure to give each piece a unique name. You should also make sure that all the pieces have the same console name. Doing so ensures that they all respond to JavaScript (or the embedded control panel).

Now you can make JavaScript calls directly to the player by name. To start off with, you can operate the RealPlayer with the following methods:

```
document.realWindow.DoPlay();
document.realWindow.DoPause();
document.realWindow.DoStop();
```

These can be used in anchor tags to link text or custom images, in a form to link the buttons, or in other JavaScript functions. To use them with simple text links, the code would look like this:

```
<a href="javascript:document.realWindow.DoPlay();">Play</a>
<a href="javascript:document.realWindow.DoPause();">Pause</a>
<a href="javascript:document.realWindow.DoStop();">Stop</a>
```

On the CD-ROM Refer to the real_javascript_controls_all.html on the CD in the javascript section of the Authoring directory to see a simple Web page with an embedded RealPlayer.

In addition to controlling the RealPlayer, you can also use JavaScript to access a wide range of information about the RealPlayer. You can query the values of the plug-in parameters and performance statistics, and you can also query and set individual clip properties. For the full set of RealPlayer methods, please refer to Bonus Chapter 4, available on the CD-ROM.

Callbacks

In addition to communicating with the RealPlayer via the browser by using JavaScript, you can also send messages the other way, from the RealPlayer to the browser. These are referred to as callbacks.

All the methods that I've discussed so far have involved a browser event, such as a mouse click, to trigger an embedded player event. The reverse is also possible, whereby an event in the RealPlayer can be used to trigger something in the browser.

For example, if you are playing a list of songs in an embedded player and displaying the current song title in HTML, you could change the title each time a new song begins playing by utilizing a RealPlayer callback that sends out a message every time a new song begins. This could be combined with a JavaScript method that queried the player for the new song title, and the result could be displayed in HTML.

Working with browser callbacks gets a little tricky, not only because IE and Netscape handle callbacks differently, but also because Netscape 6.*x* handles browser callbacks differently than Netscape 4.*x*:

✦ If you're authoring for IE, you use VBScript or Jscript (Microsoft's proprietary implementation of JavaScript) to trap callbacks.

✦ If you're using Netscape 6.*x*, you have to add a special parameter to your embed statement.

✦ If you're authoring for Netscape 4.*x*, you have to trap callbacks by using an appropriate Java applet.

Because working with browser callbacks is pretty advanced coding, I won't discuss it in this book. Instead, a list of RealPlayer callbacks available for your scripting enjoyment is presented:

```
OnAuthorChange, OnBuffering, OnClipClosed, OnClipOpened,
OnContacting, OnCopyrightChange, OnErrorMessage, OnGotoURL,
OnKeyDown, OnKeyPress, OnKeyUp, OnLButtonDown, OnLButtonUp,
OnMouseMove, OnMuteChange, OnPlayStateChange, OnPosLength,
OnPositionChange, OnPostSeek, OnPreFetchComplete, OnPreSeek,
OnPresentationClosed, OnPresentationOpened, OnRButtonDown,
OnRButtonUp, OnShowStatus, OnStateChange, OnTitleChange, and
OnVolumeChange.
```

For more information about callbacks and the various methods used to employ them, refer to the RealPlayer Embedded Player Extended Functionality Guide, available from the RealNetworks site (`http://service.real.com/help/library/index.html`).

Windows Media JavaScript Control

The Windows Media Player presents an interesting conundrum when it comes to JavaScript control. Both Windows Media Player 6.4 and Windows Media Player 7.0 can be controlled via JavaScript by using either the Netscape plug-in or the ActiveX control. But the Windows Media Player 7.0 uses completely different JavaScript methods than the Windows Media Player 6.4.

The fact that the two different player versions use different JavaScript methods isn't a problem if you're sticking with one player or the other. However, if you want to use the latest available player for IE users and want Netscape compatibility to reach the widest audience, you have to embed two separate versions of the player.

Because there is no Netscape plug-in for the Windows Media Player 7.0, you must embed a Windows Media Player 6.4 for Netscape users. IE users may decide to embed the latest and greatest Windows Media 7.*x* version.

Embedding two versions of the Windows Media Player adds a certain amount of complexity to your embedding code, but you'll see in the next section that it isn't that difficult. Plus, after you have a template that works for your content, you can reuse it over and over again.

Windows Media Player 7.0 versus Windows Media Player 6.4

If you're trying to author Web pages that are as cross-platform as possible, you must include an <embed> statement for browsers that use the Netscape plug-in. There's a slight problem — the control methods for the Windows Media Player 7.0 and 6.4 are slightly different. The JavaScript method to issue a play command to Windows Media Player 6.4 is as follows:

```
document.wmtPlayer.Play();
```

Whereas the JavaScript method used to issue a play command to the Windows Media Player 7.0 is

```
document.wmtPlayer.controls.Play();
```

When Microsoft revamped the player object model with the Windows Media Player 7.0 release, some of the JavaScript methods were organized into three subcategories — controls, settings, and network. You can see in the above example that the method is essentially the same — it's just hiding in a different place.

Additionally, in Player 7.0, a number of methods have been added while support for others was dropped. Bonus Chapter 4 (on the CD-ROM) has searchable tables that list the most common methods used for both Player 7.0 and Player 6.4. For full documentation, refer to the Windows Player SDK, which is available from the Microsoft Web site (www.microsoft.com/windows/windowsmedia/download/default.asp).

The cross-platform approach

Because you can control both the Netscape plug-in and the ActiveX control by using JavaScript, start off with the code required for both browsers:

```
<object name="wmtPlayer" width="240" height="180"
    classid="CLSID:6BF52A52-394A-11d3-B153-00C04F79FAA6">
    <param name="url" value="media/MyMovie_240x180.asx">
    <param name="autostart" value="0">
    <param name="uiMode" value="none">
    <embed type="application/x-mplayer2"
        name="wmtPlayer"
        src="media/MyMovie_240x180.asx"
```

```
            autostart="0"
            showcontrols="0"
            width="240" height="180">
        </embed>
    </object>
```

In this code, a 7.0 Player is embedded using the `<object>` tag, and nested inside the `<object>` tag is a 6.4 Player embedded using the `<embed>` tag. Notice that they both have the same name so that no matter which browser you're using you can refer to the player by a single name, in this case `wmtPlayer`.

What you want to do now is issue basic commands to the player, using the appropriate method. All versions of Internet Explorer default to using the ActiveX control, while others use the Netscape plug-in. So by checking the browser type you can determine which player method to use.

Earlier in the chapter, I used the `navigator.appName` property in hypothetical context. In the following code, you can use the `navigator.appName` property to determine which JavaScript method to use:

```
<script language="javascript">
<!-- hide script from older browsers
function PlayMedia () {
    if (navigator.appName == "Microsoft Internet Explorer"){
    // use 7.0 player method since IE uses ActiveX control
        document.wmtPlayer.controls.Play();
    }
    else {
    // use 6.4 player method for Netscape plug-in
        document.wmtPlayer.Play();
    }
}
//-->
</script>
```

The `if` statement determines whether or not the browser is Internet Explorer. If so, the 7.0 method is used. If not, the 6.4 method is used to communicate with the older player.

Using this approach, functions can also be written for the pause and stop functions, as well as many other methods that the Windows Media Player offers.

On the CD-ROM To see a working version of this code, along with functions to pause and stop the Windows Media Player, refer to the wmt_javascript_controls_all.html file in the javascript section of the Authoring directory.

Callbacks

The Windows Media Player also can send events back to the browser, which can be trapped by JavaScript or VBScripts. Handling events is tricky, because the approach to handling callbacks is different in the two browsers.

If you want to find out more about handling Windows Media Player events, the best approach is to start delving through the documentation on the Microsoft Developer's Network (`http://msdn.microsoft.com`). Bonus Chapter 4 on the CD-ROM provides a table with the Media Player 7.0 events and the player 6.4 equivalents. The available Media Player 7.0 events are as follows:

```
buffering. currentItemChange. currentPlaylistChange. error.
markerHit, mediaChange,; mediaCollectionChange, modeChange,
openStateChange, playlistChange, playStateChange,
positionChange, scriptCommand, statusChange.
```

Summary

Using JavaScript can be a great way to customize the user interface of your embedded media players. However, you should use caution when authoring your pages and be sure to test across a full spectrum of browsers and operating systems. JavaScript is standardized, but the implementation on various browsers is not.

✦ JavaScript adds functionality to your browser.

✦ JavaScript treats everything in the browser as an object; objects have properties and methods.

✦ Referring to objects in JavaScript is done by using a hierarchical dot syntax, such as document.realPlayer.Play().

✦ JavaScript control of the QuickTime player is only available via the Netscape plug-in — the current ActiveX control does not include JavaScript fuctionality.

✦ JavaScript control of the RealPlayer works on both IE and Netscape, using the ActiveX and Netscape plug-ins — though there are outstanding issues with Netscape 6.x as of February 2002.

✦ JavaScript control of the Windows Media Player is available for the 7.0 player only via the ActiveX control. JavaScript control via the Netscape plug-in is only available for Player 6.4.

✦ When authoring Web pages for cross platform purposes using the Windows Media Player, you must write functions to call the appropriate methods because the 7.0 and 6.4 player methods are slightly different.

✦   ✦   ✦

Serving: Making Your Media Available on the Internet

Installing and Running a Streaming Server

 Expert This chapter was contributed by Charlie Morris. Charlie has written countless articles and even published a couple of books about Internet technologies. He also writes extensively about digital audio technology. For contact info please refer to Bonus Chapter 6 on the CD-ROM.

If you want to offer streams with true interactive control, or if you intend to stream live broadcasts, you need to use a software package called a *streaming server*. Streaming servers are specifically designed to provide a robust and efficient way to deliver streaming media. Instead of (or in some cases, in addition to) HTTP, streaming servers use protocols such as *Real-Time Streaming Protocol (RTSP)* and *Microsoft Media Server (MMS)*, which are better suited to streaming audio and video.

Like any type of server, a streaming server is an advanced and complex piece of software, and installing and running a streaming server is not a task for the casual computer user. As you will learn in this chapter, serving streaming media at a consistently high level of quality and reliability requires a well-planned network of hardware servers with one or more high-bandwidth Internet connections. Therefore, many streaming media content providers find it more cost-effective to delegate the task of operating their streaming servers to an Internet hosting service than to maintain streaming servers in-house.

Even if you choose to outsource your streaming server operations to a hosting service, you need to know the basics of how streaming servers work, so that you can project your bandwidth requirements and decide which of the available software products is the best choice for your needs. It's also vital that you understand the various ways that a streaming network can be organized to optimize the available bandwidth and to ensure consistent high-quality operation.

Streaming Server Platforms

The QuickTime, RealSystem, and Windows Media streaming servers have roughly similar capabilities. The main differences among them lie in the platforms on which they run and the streaming formats that they deliver. All three products are mature, up-to-date, and full-featured, and all three products are in widespread use.

Both QuickTime and the RealSystem use the RTSP protocol to stream files, while Microsoft uses its own proprietary protocol, MMS. All three servers stream their own proprietary file formats, which can be played on the corresponding media player. Streaming servers can deliver a variety of other multimedia formats such as MP3, .wav, .avi and so on, although these file types are not necessarily best suited for streaming.

Note   The RealServer can also stream QuickTime files to QuickTime players, partly because QuickTime and the RealSystem both stream using the RTSP format. The QuickTime server, however, cannot stream RealMedia files.

Apple QuickTime and Darwin streaming servers

The QuickTime Streaming Server is included with Mac OS X Server and runs only on Mac hardware. The QuickTime server streams files in the QuickTime format. The upcoming Version 4 will also be able to stream MP3 files.

You don't have to use a Mac server to stream in the QuickTime format, however, because Apple also offers the Darwin Streaming Server, which has the same features as the QuickTime Streaming Server and is available for various Unix platforms and Windows NT/2000. Apple also provides the source code for the Darwin Streaming Server so that it can be ported to other platforms if desired. Both the QuickTime and Darwin Streaming Servers are free.

Various other servers can stream QuickTime files, including RealNetworks' RealServer 8.0, and Sun's StorEdge Media Central Streaming Server.

More details about Apple's streaming servers are at www.apple.com/quicktime/products/qtss/.

RealNetworks RealServer 8.0

RealServer 8.0 is available for both Unix and Windows NT/2000. In addition to RealNetworks' streaming format, RealServer 8.0 can stream MP3 and QuickTime files.

RealServer comes in four versions: Basic, Plus, Professional, and Intranet. RealServer is the only one of the three major streaming servers that isn't free. The Basic version is free but is limited to 25 simultaneous streams, and lacks some advanced features. The Plus version currently sells for $1,995, and the Professional version costs $5,995 and up, depending on the number of streams supported. You can find more details at `www.realnetworks.com/products/media_delivery.html`.

Windows Media Services 4.1

Windows Media Services (WMS) runs only on Windows-based servers. Microsoft specifies a minimum requirement of Windows 95 with DCOM95 but recommends NT 4.0 with Service Pack 4 or later. WMS is included at no additional cost in Windows 2000 Server and Advanced Server.

WMS streams Advanced Streaming Format (ASF) files using their proprietary MMS protocol. ASF files may also have a number of other file extensions, such as `.wma`, and `.wmv`. Although the Windows Media Player plays a wide range of audio and video formats, the ASF format is the only one that can be streamed by the WMS. You can find more detail at the Microsoft Web site, `www.microsoft.com/windows/windowsmedia/technologies/services.asp`.

Which streaming server(s) should you choose?

The so-called "big three" are capable of both live and on-demand delivery, and all offer a variety of advanced features, such as caching, multicasting, automatic selection of connection bandwidth, and many other goodies. Their intense competition provides them all with a strong incentive to improve their products on a continual basis. You have little reason to choose one streaming server over another on the basis of features.

For many media providers, the operating system is the deciding factor. If you're running Unix, then your choice is between RealServer and Darwin, as WMS doesn't run on Unix. If you're running Windows 2000 Server, then the fact that WMS is tightly integrated with this operating system and included at no extra cost is likely to be a powerful incentive to make WMS your choice. If you're one of the few who are running Internet servers on the Mac OS, then the QuickTime Streaming Server is your only option.

You need to keep in mind that the server you decide to run dictates the type of files you're going to be able to stream. In addition to the features offered by the serving software, you should take into consideration the audio and video quality offered, support for other data types if you want more than just audio and video, support for the format in third-party tools, and how large the platform's market share is.

Many streaming media professionals have all three media players installed on their computers, but this is not necessarily true of your audience. Therefore, to reach all potential users, you may want to make material available in all three popular formats, which requires running at least two streaming servers (RealServer can serve QuickTime, so a separate QuickTime/Darwin server may not be necessary).

All three players are free, and all three come in both Windows and Mac versions, so a user can easily equip him or herself with all three major media players and eliminate the compatibility issue. However, for various reasons, many users don't do so. Just as some Web users prefer either the Netscape or the Microsoft browser, some streaming media users prefer a particular media player and do not use any of the competing products. Also, some organizations, in the interest of reducing their technical support burden, require their employees to use a particular player. The bottom line is, if you offer media in only one format, you limit your potential audience.

Many streaming media providers offer material in more than one format, but many others don't. Whether reaching the small percentage of users who insist on using only one media player is worth the additional investment of resources required to run more than one streaming platform is a question you must answer in terms of the objectives and unique audience of a particular site.

If you choose to run more than one type of streaming server, each server should have a dedicated machine, or better yet, a cluster of machines. Both Microsoft and RealNetworks strongly recommend that, except for very small installations, a streaming server should run on its own dedicated machine. Later in this chapter, you learn the benefits of server clustering. If you use clustering, each streaming server should have a separate cluster with a load-balancing device.

Other streaming servers

Although the big three together have the lion's share of the market, many other streaming servers are available. Some offer special features that may make them attractive to certain media providers, especially because many work with one or more of the big three players.

SHOUTcast, from Nullsoft (`http://shoutcast.com/`) can stream MP3 files, either live or on-demand. The SHOUTcast server runs not only on Windows but also on several types of Unix (although live broadcasting is possible only on Windows platforms). One attractive feature of SHOUTcast is that it's a free product. SHOUTcast supports the following media players:

✦ Winamp (Windows, available at `http://www.winamp.com/winamp/download`)

✦ Audion (Mac, available at `http://www.panic.com/ppack/audion/index.html`)

✦ XMMS (Linux, available at `http://www.xmms.org/`)

Liquid Audio (`http://liquidaudio.com/`) can stream in both the Windows Media format and their own proprietary format. Liquid Audio can also be streamed by the RealServer and played back in the RealPlayer using the Liquid Audio plug-in. It offers a range of packaged solutions for content providers, including integrated Digital Rights Management (DRM).

Cross-Reference   Refer to Chapter 19 for detailed discussion on DRM.

Sun StorEdge Media Central Streaming Server is a streaming server that runs on Sun's Unix-based Solaris operating system and uses the QuickTime streaming format.

The basic issues involved in setting up and maintaining servers are the same regardless of which streaming server you work with. However, as with most things related to streaming media, bandwidth is the first and most important issue you should consider.

Bandwidth Considerations

Bandwidth is a central issue in any discussion of serving streaming media for two reasons. The most obvious reason is that digital audio and video files are much larger than most types of computer files and delivering them requires large amounts of bandwidth, at least by Internet standards.

Maintaining streams of consistent quality depends on ensuring that every part of the network path has more than enough bandwidth to accommodate the stream(s) that it must carry. The network path can be broken down into three parts:

✦ User Internet connection

✦ Server Internet connection

✦ Data center internal network

Unfortunately, you have no control over the user's connection to the Internet. This is known as the "last mile" problem — it doesn't matter how good your distribution network is if the user has a terrible connection to the Internet. You can, however, provide streams at different bit rates to cater to the widest possible audience.

Many sites offer media at two or more bit rates to accommodate users with different types of Internet connections. Current streaming servers make offering multiple bit rates simple by detecting a user's bandwidth and automatically delivering the appropriate stream.

Additionally, both the RealSystem and Windows Media Technologies are able to combine multiple streams encoded at different bit rates into a single file. This makes encoding and managing data much easier, because you can cater to users on different connection speeds with a single file. QuickTime does not offer multiple streams in a single file, but offers the ability to choose between files via reference movies.

The other two sections of the network path, the server Internet connection and the data center's internal network, can be controlled. Building a robust streaming media architecture involves doing the math to project how much bandwidth you need to provide a high-quality streaming media experience.

Projecting bandwidth requirements

When you set up any type of client/server system, projecting bandwidth requirements is a necessary step. It's particularly important when setting up a streaming media delivery system because of the high bandwidth required and the dire consequences of running out of bandwidth. The amount of bandwidth you'll need at any given time is a function of two factors: the number of simultaneous streams and the bandwidth required for each stream.

Cross-Reference

Projecting bandwidth requirements is something you should do on an ongoing basis, not just when setting up a server for the first time. In Chapter 20, you learn to monitor network usage and use that data to project future requirements.

A simple formula for determining bandwidth requirements for a streaming media delivery system is

```
Number of Simultaneous Users * Average Bandwidth per Stream =
Total Streaming Bandwidth Required.
```

In the real world, of course, things are more complex. You need to include four other important factors in your calculations. These four factors are discussed in depth in the following four sections.

Different users connect at different rates

As explained earlier in this chapter, you can offer streams at different bit rates to accommodate users with different types of Internet connection. Whether your users choose their stream or whether the server does so automatically, the issue of differing data rates is one that you must consider when projecting bandwidth needs, as different sites have different audiences.

For example, a site that caters to entry-level Internet users probably has a high proportion of low-bandwidth users, while a site whose audience consists mainly of power users has a high proportion of people with high-bandwidth connections.

If you modify your bandwidth-projection equation to take this issue into account, you have

```
  Number of Users @ Bandwidth A * Bandwidth A
+ Number of Users @ Bandwidth B * Bandwidth B
+ Number of Users @ Bandwidth N * Bandwidth N
= Total Streaming Bandwidth Required.
```

Bandwidth projections must be based on peak usage, not on average usage

As every Webmaster knows, Internet sites are subject to sudden spikes in traffic for various reasons. A mention in a magazine or on a television show, a news event that causes a lot of interest in a site's subject matter, and securing a listing on a popular search engine are all events that can cause a site's user traffic to multiply instantly.

If a site's infrastructure can't handle the higher traffic levels, this increased level of traffic can be a catastrophe because the site becomes unavailable just when it is most in demand. Many users who are turned away won't come back, and an opportunity to expand the site's audience is lost.

Streaming media sites are subject to all of these possible traffic-boosters. In the case of a live broadcast, you need to take into account another factor: Some programs draw more users than others. Traditional broadcasters have long recognized *prime times*, during which the number of viewers is much higher than average. For radio stations, these tend to be morning and afternoon drive times, when people are in their cars on the way to and from work. For television, prime time tends to be the evening, as people watch television between supper and bedtime.

For the Internet broadcaster, prime-time capacity is a critical issue. A further complication is the lack of geographic limitations for an Internet broadcast. Prime time in one time zone may be the graveyard shift in another. Some Internet broadcasters are more or less geared to a particular geographic market, and some are not, so each broadcaster must weigh this factor according to its own particular situation.

When making forecasts of required bandwidth, you must use figures for peak usage, which unfortunately means that a certain amount of computing resources will be sitting idle much of the time. In trying to smooth out the load, adhere to the following three policies:

✦ Maintain close coordination between programmers and network administrators, making sure that administrators know well in advance about any particular broadcasts that may draw heavy traffic levels.

✦ Follow usage patterns closely and try to establish an accurate model of how usage levels vary at different times of the day or different days of the week.

✦ Have intelligent load-balancing and fault-tolerance systems in place, as described later in this chapter.

Allow for network overhead

No network has 100 percent of its theoretical capacity available for data transfer. You're practically limited to about 70–80 percent of the theoretical maximum because of the way TCP/IP traffic is handled on a network. For example, if you're streaming on your company's internal 10 Mbps LAN, you're practically limited to

```
10,000,000 bps (Ethernet) - 20% Network Overhead
= 8,000,000 bps Available Bandwidth.
```

In addition to this practical limitation, you may want to allot additional bandwidth for other tasks, such as file transfers, backup procedures, and so on. You can generally perform most housekeeping tasks when your streaming usage is low, so another ten percent should suffice. In general, a good equation for calculating the practical capacity of a network is

```
Theoretical Maximum * 70% = Practical Network Capacity
```

This number applies whether you're running your own server on your own network, or paying someone else to run your server infrastructure.

Allow extra capacity for future growth

Internet usage grows quickly, so measuring and analyzing your traffic at frequent intervals is critical. Even so, traffic may grow a significant amount between the beginning and end of a reporting period, especially if a provider is actively marketing its services. To avoid the self-defeating trap in which higher usage triggers service degradation, always err on the high side when forecasting user traffic.

Projecting the capacity of available bandwidth

In the preceding discussion, I've assumed that you'll start with a forecasted number of users and use that figure to calculate your required bandwidth. In the real world, however, applying this equation in reverse may be more useful, because you probably have a fixed budget to work with, and therefore a fixed amount of maximum bandwidth for your network. To calculate the number of streams that a given amount of bandwidth can support, use the following equation:

```
Practical Network Capacity / bit rate per stream
= Maximum Simultaneous Streams.
```

For example, if you have an Ethernet network (10 Mbps) and you want to know how many 20 Kbps (the recommended bandwidth for a user with a 28.8 Kbps modem) streams you can support, the equation is

```
10,000,000 * 70% / 20,000 = 350 Simultaneous Streams.
```

When calculating the maximum number of streams your network can support, you must consider three components:

✦ The capacity of server

✦ The practical capacity of the internal network

✦ The practical capacity of the connection to the Internet (unless you are streaming solely over a LAN)

When planning a network, you must keep these three items in balance. For example, having a server that can handle 9,000 simultaneous streams when your Internet connection can only handle 100 makes little sense.

Calculating the second two items is fairly easy, as described above. Predicting how many streams a particular server can support is difficult, because that number depends on many factors, including the operating system, the processor speed, and the amount of RAM. The only way to get a totally reliable figure is to run a test with a real server.

Fortunately, Microsoft's documentation for WMS provides two examples of server capacity that you can interpolate to get a rough idea of how many WMS streams your server can handle. At the low end of the scale, a 233 Mhz Pentium with 128MB RAM (the minimum recommended configuration for WMS) can serve up to 1,000 28.8 Kbps simultaneous streams. For those with higher budgets, an independent test by ZD Labs showed that a Compaq server with eight 550 MHz processors and 1GB of RAM was capable of serving over 9,000 simultaneous 22 Kbps streams (see `http://etestinglabs.com/main/reports/msstream.pdf`).

If you compare these figures with the bandwidth capacity of various types of network connections, you can see that for most systems, the server is unlikely to be the bottleneck. Earlier in this chapter, you calculated that an Ethernet connection, assuming a 30 percent network overhead, could support about 350 simultaneous streams. And a single T-1 connection can only handle about 55 streams (1,544,000 × 70 percent / 20,000). For this reason, most streaming media data centers use Fast Ethernet and multiple high-bandwidth Internet connections.

If you want to ensure that every user consistently has a high-quality streaming experience, you should limit the number of simultaneous streams the server permits. Both RealServer and WMS let you specify a maximum number of streams or a maximum amount of bandwidth. Users who try to connect after the limit has been reached receive a message that informs them the server has reached its capacity. After you've calculated the maximum number of streams your system can comfortably support, you can set an appropriate limit.

The scarcity of bandwidth is a central constraint in the streaming media field. You can always conserve bandwidth by limiting the quality of your media or limiting access, but these are never optimal solutions. Fortunately, there are several ways in which you can squeeze more streams into your available bandwidth without sacrificing quality. Two of the most important are *multicasting* and *caching*.

Multicasting

Streaming media may be delivered to a user in three ways:

✦ **Unicast:** A server delivers a stream to each individual user. On-demand delivery always uses the unicast model.

✦ **Broadcast:** A single stream is delivered to many users simultaneously, with each user having his/her own connection to the server. Most live broadcasts use the broadcast model.

✦ **Multicast:** A single stream is broadcast on a network using a special multicast IP address. When viewers join the broadcast, their players are instructed to grab copies of the broadcast packets on the network. Multicasting can only be used for live (or simulated live) delivery.

Figure 18-1 shows the relationships among servers and clients under each of the three delivery methods.

Multicasting is much more efficient than broadcasting, because only a single copy of the stream is sent out across a multicast-enabled network, and players on that network merely grab copies of the data. Multicast-enabled routers can send copies of the stream to other multicast-enabled routers, which in turn multicast the stream on the local network.

To take advantage of multicasting, both server and client must be multicast-enabled. All three of the major streaming platforms support multicasting. In addition, if you want the broadcast to extend beyond your local area network, all the routers must also be multicast-enabled. The problem with multicasting across the Internet is that every single router involved must be multicast-enabled, which is not yet the case.

Multicasts make an enormous amount of sense on LANs where a single network administrator has control of all the routers. In situations like these, broadband streams can be multicast across a LAN with minimal impact on traffic congestion. Multicasting across the Internet, however, is still a few years off. Configurations that combine multicast and unicast can be used to minimize bandwidth and maximize coverage. For example, you can multicast inside your LAN, unicast to the public Internet, and send a single stream via unicast to a second server that multicasts to another LAN.

To find out more about implementing multicasting on your network, please refer to each streaming software vendor's site.

Tip   If you'd like to find out more about how multicasting works, there's a wealth of information available on the IP Multicast Initiative's Web site at www.ipmulticast.com.

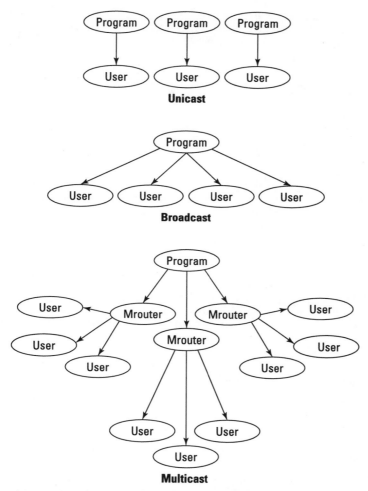

Figure 18-1: Three ways to deliver multimedia over the Internet: unicast, broadcast, and multicast

Caching

Caching should be a familiar concept to most computer users because it is used in many aspects of computing. For any content delivery system, certain content tends to be requested much more often than the rest. If you can store this often-used content in a special place where users can obtain it more quickly, then you can greatly reduce average access time.

A Web browser provides a familiar example of caching: each time a user requests a Web page, a copy is stored on the user's local machine, so that if the user requests the same page again, it can be retrieved much more quickly than if it had to be downloaded over the Internet.

You can often greatly increase bandwidth efficiency by simply replicating content in multiple locations. Later in this chapter you learn the benefits of geographically-dispersed server farms and edge servers. Because disk space tends to be cheaper than network bandwidth, redirecting user requests to a copy of a particular program on a nearby server is often more efficient than sending all requests to a single centrally located server.

True caching, however, is even more efficient. Instead of replicating all your content, you replicate only the most often-requested content. With a caching scheme, the first time a user requests a file, it is delivered from the central server, and a copy is stored on the local network. Whenever a user on the same local network requests the same file, the copy is delivered from the local cache.

You can take advantage of caching in several ways. You can use a hardware caching appliance, or you can set up software-based caching on a server. RealNetworks offers a sophisticated software product called RealSystem Proxy that aggregates and manages client requests for streaming media. RealSystem Proxy can split live broadcasts as well as store on-demand streams in local disk storage. Although the stream is served locally, the system contacts the central server for each request to authenticate the user and to check for updated content.

Note   More information on the RealProxy can be found on the RealNetworks Web site at `www.realnetworks.com/products/proxy/index.html`.

Firewalls

Firewalls are pieces of hardware or software that protect a network by monitoring connections between the network and the Internet. Only data using approved transfer protocols and approved ports is allowed to pass through the firewall.

Streaming servers depend on User Datagram Protocol (UDP), Real Time Transfer Protocol (RTP) and/or Real Time Streaming Protocol (RTSP) to function efficiently, and firewalls typically block these types of requests. Therefore, a firewall on either the client or the server end may interfere with the transmission of streaming media, causing it to be of poor quality or preventing it from being viewed altogether.

Unfortunately, the subject of firewalls can be quite complex. Firewalls work in various ways, and the different streaming server packages deal with them in different ways. Two scenarios in which a firewall may present an issue are:

✦ **Client behind firewall.** You can solve this problem two ways. If possible, configure the firewall so that it permits RTP and RTSP throughput. If you cannot do so, use HTTP streaming or enable Transport Control Protocol (TCP) streaming on port 80.

✦ **Streaming server behind firewall.** The solution to this problem depends on which streaming server you're using, as explained in the following sections.

Firewalls and QuickTime

QuickTime offers two possible ways to get around firewall problems:

✦ The client can set up QuickTime to use a proxy server, by specifying a type of proxy server (SOCKS, RTSP or HTTP) and port number in the QuickTime Settings control panel.

✦ The streaming server administrator can configure the server to stream using HTTP on port 80.

HTTP is the least efficient of the possible streaming protocols, so regardless of which server you're using, you should try the other possible fixes before resorting to HTTP streaming.

Firewalls and RealServer

RealServer cannot stream content from behind a firewall. You can stream content over an intranet to other users behind a firewall, but if you intend to stream over the Internet, then you can't locate your RealServer behind a firewall. For many organizations, doing this would seem to present a problem because the internal network must be protected by a firewall, and the RealServer must be connected to the internal network.

The solution is to implement something called a *screened-subnet firewall*. This type of firewall creates a perimeter network, colorfully called a *Demilitarized Zone (DMZ)*. The DMZ is outside the internal network but is still secured by the firewall. Both the internal network and the Internet can access machines in the DMZ, but traffic can't be directly transferred across the DMZ. The RealServer is located in the DMZ, and it is configured with a less restrictive set of security features than the machines on the internal network.

Note For more information on the RealSystem and firewalls, please refer to the RealNetworks Web site at http://service.real.com/help/library/ guides/ g270/htmfiles/firewall.htm.

Firewalls and WMS

Windows Media normally streams via UDP/IP on several ports; however, doing so causes problems with many firewalls. WMS can get around the problem by using TCP/IP on port 1755 or HTTP on port 80. A WMS streaming server can be operated behind a firewall but only if the ports are configured a certain way. For full details, see www.microsoft.com/windows/windowsmedia/serve/firewall.asp.

Deployment Options

Two factors that determine the value of any computer network are the following:

✦ **Capacity:** How many simultaneous users can be supported

✦ **Reliability:** How much of the time the system is working as desired

Obviously, how much capacity and reliability you can have depends on your budget. A low-budget broadcaster might run a streaming server on a single 266 MHz PC running Windows 95 (according to Microsoft's stated minimum requirements for WMS), connecting to the Internet through an ISDN line. Such a system, however, won't be able to deliver very many simultaneous streams and is likely to be inaccessible frequently.

To provide streaming on a medium-to-large scale and to ensure that a high-quality stream is delivered every time a user requests one, much more than one server is required. A proper Streaming Media Provider (SMP) deploys a carefully designed network, consisting of many powerful servers with high-bandwidth connections to the Internet. Each server is assigned a specific task, and the network is designed to prevent each of many problems that can cause service interruptions. Table 18-1 lists some of these problems and ways you can avoid them through carefully planning your network.

Table 18-1 Forestalling Problems through Network Planning	
Problem	*Solution*
Electrical Failure	Uninterruptible Power Supply (UPS)
Virus on Server	Virus Scanning Software
Server Hardware/Software Failure	Redundant Servers
Internet Connection Failure	Redundant Internet Connections
Encoding Failure (for live broadcasts)	Redundant Encoding
Regional Network Failure	Geographically Diverse Server Farms
Internet Congestion	Edge Servers
Content Delivery Network (CDN) Failure	Multiple CDNs

Having a large network of multiple servers not only enables you to consistently deliver high-quality streams, but it also brings benefits in the form of increased capabilities. For example, it may be desirable to offer streams in several different formats, which requires running two or more streaming server software products, each on its own cluster of servers. Also, analyzing your log files is an important but processor-intensive task that is best accomplished on a dedicated machine.

See Chapter 20 to find out how to analyze your log file data.

Redundancy

Networking experts agree that the key to reliability is redundancy. The concept of redundancy is simple — having duplicate components ensures a high level of reliability. If one component fails, the other can take its place, and the chances of both units failing at the same time are small. In practice, redundancy means not only having two (or more) copies of each component in your network, but also having a means to automatically transfer tasks to a backup unit whenever a component fails.

To build a truly fault-tolerant network, you must incorporate redundancy into every link in the chain. Not only servers, but networking hardware (routers, switches, interface cards), Internet connections, AC power, and even entire data centers should be duplicated. For live broadcasts, you need to have redundant encoders. RealServer and WMS are both capable of automatically switching to a backup if an encoder fails during a live broadcast. In a live situation, you should also have spares for front-end components such as microphones, video cameras, and cabling.

For more information on serving live broadcasts, please refer to Chapter 37.

For many reasons, which are detailed in the next section, having two or more medium-capacity servers is better than having one super-server. Additionally, having several medium-bandwidth Internet connections is better than having one high-bandwidth connection.

Redundancy is often more cost-effective than it may appear at first glance, because having multiple components often delivers other benefits in addition to fault tolerance. For example, having two complete data centers in two different locations gives you two benefits: your audience gets higher quality streams because the data travels a shorter distance, and you have a high level of fault tolerance because even if one entire data center goes out of service, the other can take over.

Even if you outsource your media delivery to a content delivery network (CDN), or your entire Internet operation to an ISP, keep redundancy in mind. In the fast-changing

Internet business world, it's all too common for a service provider to suddenly fail to deliver an adequate level of service, or even to go out of business. If you have contracts with two CDNs and/or two ISPs, you'll be protected.

Tip   The best network planners tend to be a little paranoid, constantly envisioning possible scenarios in which a critical component might fail. These individuals also tend to think in stereo — everything comes in pairs. In fact, you should have two copies of this book and store them in separate bookcases.

Server clusters

To gain the benefits of redundant servers, you must have a way to allocate processing tasks from one server to another dynamically, automatically, and in a way that is transparent to the user. You can use *server clustering* to implement a system for dynamically allocating processing tasks. Clustering means connecting several servers together in such a way that they can be controlled like a single computer. Server clustering has many benefits, but the most important ones for a streaming media network are *load balancing* and *fault tolerance*.

Load balancing is the process of automatically distributing a server load more or less equally among several machines. For example, a site is running on a cluster of four servers and is experiencing a user load of 40 simultaneous streams. Load balancing dynamically allocates the server capacity so that each of the four servers is serving only ten streams, instead of streaming all 40 from one machine. Doing so keeps the machines working well below their maximum capacity, reducing the likelihood of network congestion and software crashes.

Fault tolerance refers to the capability of a network to continue working even if a hardware or software failure occurs. Clustering is a great help in building a fault-tolerant system, because if one server in a cluster fails, the system can automatically shift the load to the other servers. For example, if one of the four servers in the previous example should crash, the operating system could quickly reallocate the streams among the other three servers. This capability is called *failover*.

Note   To be precise, load balancing and failover are two different things. However, the same hardware or software component often provides both features, and the term load balancing is often used in a general sense to include failover as well. For example, a so-called load-balancing server may provide both load balancing and failover capabilities.

You can incorporate load balancing and failover into a network in several ways. One old standby is called *DNS round robin*. Every network connected to the Internet has a *Domain Name Server (DNS)*, which has the job of resolving alphanumeric domain names (for example, hungryminds.com) into numeric Internet Protocol (IP) addresses (for example 168.215.86.100). Using DNS round robin, you can map a single domain name to several IP addresses, each of which corresponds to a single server. The DNS server distributes traffic more or less evenly among the servers. DNS round robin is simple and requires no special hardware or software. But its capabilities are limited, and current networking technology provides more sophisticated tools.

Another way to implement load balancing and failover is through hardware load balancers. Alteon, Cisco CSS, and F5's BIG-IP are some popular lines of network switching devices that offer load-balancing capabilities. Hardware-based load balancing is platform-independent, and may be cheaper than an OS-based solution, because no load-balancing server is required.

Current network operating systems offer integrated load balancing and fault tolerance features. Implementing these capabilities through the operating system requires no specialized hardware, but it does require a separate computer to act as a load-balancing server.

In a Windows 2000 Server environment, Network Load Balancing (NLB) lets you distribute client TCP/IP connections over up to 32 servers, and Microsoft Clustering Service (MSCS) offers failover capabilities. In the Unix world, each vendor (Sun, IBM, HP, DEC/Compaq, and so on) offers its own products for server clustering and load balancing, for example Sun's Sun Cluster 3.0 (www.sun.com/software/cluster/). For Linux, the Backhand Project (www.backhand.org) offers a set of free server clustering tools.

 Cross-Reference For a tutorial about how to load balance the RealServer using the Linux Virtual Server (LVS), please turn to Chapter 38.

Figure 18-2 shows how load balancing works, and Figure 18-3 demonstrates failover.

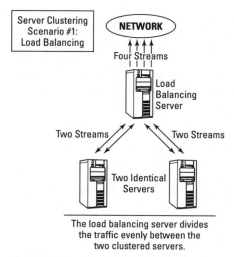

Figure 18-2: Server clustering: load balancing. The load-balancing server divides traffic evenly between the two clustered servers.

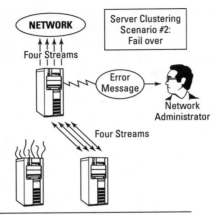

The server on the left has failed, so all traffic
has been automatically shifted to the
remaining server. An error message
is sent to the network administrator.

Figure 18-3: Server clustering: failover.
The server on the left has failed, so the
load-balancing server has automatically
transferred all traffic to the remaining
server, and sent an error message to
the network administrator.

The Data Center

In the preceding sections, I described various ways to improve the capacity and
reliability of a network by addressing each of several problems that may occur. In
practical terms, solving such problems often involves adding more servers to the
network. In a large-scale network, each server performs a single specialized task,
and every major software program runs on its own server or cluster of servers. By
now, you are probably aware that a full-scale streaming media delivery system
requires quite a few servers. These servers are grouped together in what is called a
data center or, more informally, a *server farm*.

The concept of a data center is not the same as that of a server cluster. Servers in a
cluster are logically linked together so that they function as a single computer.
Servers in a server farm are physically located together so that looking after their
physical maintenance requirements is easier. A single server farm may contain more
than one server cluster, and a server cluster can conceivably be spread over more
than one server farm.

Servers require a number of physical support services to function reliably, and providing these services is one of the essential functions of a data center. Setting up a complex and expensive network of servers without arranging to take care of their ongoing support needs is foolish. Some services that a data center must provide are

✦ **Reliable electrical power.** The data center must have line conditioners to ensure a constant voltage free of electrical interference, Uninterruptible Power Supplies (UPSs), which provide battery backup in case of brief power outages, and a backup generator in case of longer power outages.

✦ **Powerful air-conditioning.** Computers work better and last longer when operated at low temperatures.

✦ **Physical security.** Good locks and strict access control are necessary to protect against both theft of valuable equipment and unauthorized access to data.

✦ **Network security.** Network administrators must enforce and periodically update security policies.

✦ **24/7 monitoring.** Although you can do most network administration tasks remotely, having staff on-site is prudent.

✦ **High-bandwidth Internet connections.** As explained earlier in this chapter, a streaming media data center needs to have redundant Internet connections with very high capacity.

✦ **Virus protection.** A virus can spread rapidly throughout a network, shutting down your entire system regardless of how many redundant servers you have, so you need to keep virus protection software up to date and run periodic virus scans.

✦ **Periodic data backups.** You need to back up your valuable data on a permanent storage medium such as tape or CD-ROM, and store the backups in a safe place. As explained in Chapter 19, different types of data require different backup schedules.

✦ **Disaster resistance.** Fires, floods, and earthquakes do occur, which is why most data centers are located in substantial masonry buildings well away from flood zones. Some are located in bombproof underground bunkers.

Having multiple geographically dispersed data centers gives you several benefits, both in terms of bandwidth efficiency and fault tolerance. The high-bandwidth requirements of streaming media mean that the geographic proximity of client and server is a significant factor. And having redundant server farms protects you from disaster at the data center (fire, major network failure) and regional events (Internet backbone failure, widespread power outage, earthquake).

Figure 18-4 shows the relationship among the servers in a fairly basic data center.

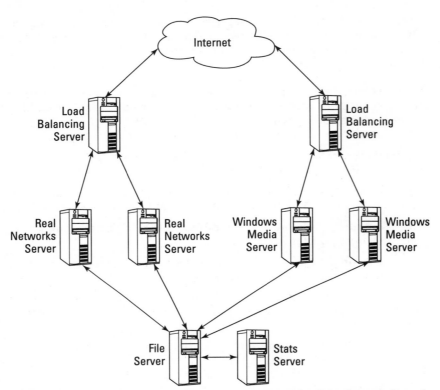

Figure 18-4: This streaming media data center serves both RealNetworks and Windows Media streams, each from its own cluster of two servers. Both clusters share a file server, which contains multiple versions of each media file. A log analysis program runs on its own dedicated server.

Edge servers

The farther a stream must travel, the more likely it is to suffer packet loss or become bogged down by a slow network somewhere along the way. If you can deliver streaming media from a point reasonably close to the end user, you can realize major performance gains.

An *edge server* is so called because it's visualized as being close to the "edge" of the Internet, that is, as close as possible to the end user. In this scenario, when a user requests a stream, it is not delivered from a single centralized data center but rather from whichever one of many edge servers is nearest to the user.

You can enable this streamlined method of data delivery in one of two ways: you can store duplicate content on many edge servers, or you can store data at a central data center, but transmit it to the edge servers through a special super-high-bandwidth network that is separate from the public Internet. Some content delivery networks even use high-bandwidth satellite connections to deliver streams to edge servers around the world.

Earlier in this chapter, I discussed ways of getting the most out of scarce bandwidth (caching, multicasting) as well as ways of increasing network reliability (load balancing, failover). Using edge servers delivers both types of benefits, because a shorter network path from the streaming server to the client means less likelihood of either bandwidth bottlenecks or network malfunctions. Another point in favor of edge servers is that they conserve overall Internet bandwidth: Sending a stream halfway across the country is wasteful when it can be delivered from much closer to the end user. Of course, this bandwidth savings may come at the expense of having to duplicate data on the edge servers, but at the current state of technology, disk storage space is far cheaper than Internet bandwidth.

Note   Edge servers can be used for both live and on-demand applications. Also, edge servers can be used for any type of data, not only streaming media. The data may be delivered to the edge servers from a central point, or it may be stored on the edge servers themselves. Edge servers are often used in conjunction with both multicasting and caching.

Figures 18-5 and 18-6 show the difference between delivering streaming content from a centrally-located data center and delivering content from edge servers.

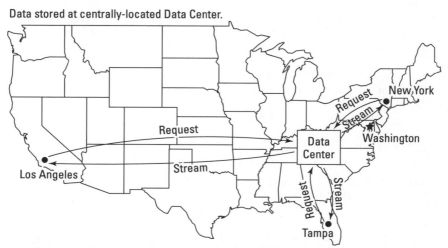

Figure 18-5: Media files stored at a centrally-located data center. Streams must sometimes travel a long way to reach the end user.

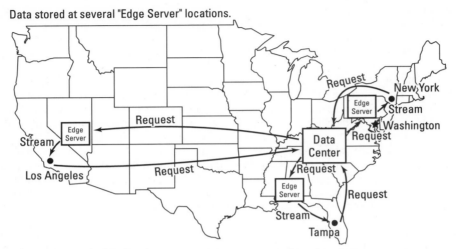

Data stored at several "Edge Server" locations.

Figure 18-6: Media files stored at geographically dispersed edge servers. User requests go to the centralized data center, which redirects them to the edge server nearest the end user. High-bandwidth streams travel only a short distance from the edge server to the end user.

Content Delivery Networks (CDNs)

A *Content Delivery Network (CDN)* is a high-performance network that features edge servers and sells capacity to content providers on an ongoing basis. By hosting content from several clients on a single edge server, a CDN can allocate server resources efficiently while delivering major performance benefits.

Note   For simplicity's sake, an edge server is referred to as if it were a single machine, although in reality it would probably consist of one or more server clusters.

CDNs make sense for a couple of reasons:

✦ **Expertise:** A significant amount of time and expertise is required to build and maintain a large distributed network of edge servers.

✦ **Efficiency:** Although edge servers are very efficient in terms of bandwidth, they may be inefficient in terms of server capacity for a single content provider.

The more edge servers you use, and the more spread out they are geographically, the greater the benefits. However, if edge servers are included in a system, more time and more expertise are required to build and maintain the system. Most streaming media providers don't find it practical to build and maintain a large network of edge servers.

Additionally, a single powerful server can deliver well over 1,000 simultaneous streams. Even a large media provider is unlikely to need this sort of capacity within a small geographical area. For example, if you place 100 servers at ISPs in 100 metropolitan areas, and you only need to deliver 5,000 simultaneous streams, then each of these 100 servers will be operating far below capacity. CDNs can take advantage of their specialization and excess capacity to provide a valuable service to streaming media content providers.

A CDN is not the same as a network service provider (although the same company may offer both services). Using a CDN is an attractive option, even for an organization that hosts streaming content in-house. For a content provider, a CDN offers an alternative to simply connecting to the Internet. CDNs often bypass much of the public Internet in favor of a network that is specially optimized for the needs of streaming media.

Perhaps the best-known CDN is Akamai (www.akamai.com). It offers a turnkey content delivery solution called EdgeSuite, which incorporates multiple data centers, edge servers, and caching. Another CDN is Digital Island, a unit of Cable & Wireless (www.digitalisland.net/services/cont_delivery.shtml). Both these CDNs have servers co-located at hundreds of ISPs all over the world.

CDNs are a fairly recent development, but they have a bright future. CDNs are a part of the all-pervasive trend toward specialization that is summed up by the saying "stick to the business you're in." Few, if any, media providers can or should build a delivery network as powerful as those offered by major CDNs. And even if they did, for the reasons explained earlier in this section, a CDN can probably provide the service more cheaply. Even organizations that run their own large-scale hosting operations may choose to use a CDN as a supplement or a backup to their own networks.

If you think a CDN is the way to go for you, there are a number of things you should look for when shopping for a CDN. For a full discussion of what a good CDN should provide, please see the two sidebars at the end of this chapter, "How to Choose a CDN" and "The Importance of Peering."

Of course, CDNs aren't for everyone. Many smaller-scale streaming media providers simply don't need such a powerful media delivery system. As streaming technology improves, and overall Internet bandwidth increases, media providers are finding that low-bandwidth streaming works quite adequately even with an ordinary Internet connection.

How to Choose a CDN by Christopher Levy

It is estimated that almost 85 percent of the world's web traffic is delivered via what is commonly referred to as a content delivery network, or CDN. If you have watched video news reports on the web or attended a large-scale live event via your computer, there is a high probability that you were serviced by a CDN.

This tutorial provides you with the basics to shop your RFP, Contract, Live Event or upcoming company meeting across the CDN space with the most educated and concise approach possible.

What a CDN Does

A CDN is a service organization that provides reliable storage and delivery of Internet content. CDNs typically deliver a variety of content, including all the major streaming media formats, as well as static content like Flash, banner images, and even whole Web sites.

This is done using a variety of proprietary methodologies for storing the content in multiple locations, managing sessions and content requests, load balancing these requests across multiple interfaces and physical networks/locations. In addition, the CDN must track the data it delivers and manage its resources to accomplish this as effectively as possible, 24 hours a day, 7 days a week, 365 days a year.

CDNs have three basic structures:

✦ **Centralized:** Many machines, in a few origin locations

✦ **De-centralized:** Many machines, dispersed across multiple origin locations

✦ **Hybrid Topology:** Many machines, dispersed across multiple origin locations of mixed bandwidth, including Internet and extranet interfaces

A content publisher should consider his or her audience and required scope of reach, and make a decision based on needs and financial considerations. Three sample scenarios are described below:

✦ **Live Corporate Webcast:** Jane's CEO is getting ready to tell the whole company about their newly completed acquisition of their biggest competitor. Jane decides to go with a centralized CDN due to their good peering with her two regional sales offices and their attractive pricing.

✦ **Ongoing Monthly Sales Training:** Joe has a global sales force of 10,000 employees and channel partners in mixed locations and IT environments and over 1,000 different files. With a hefty budget and revenue goals to meet, Joe decides to use two different global CDNs to provide himself with multiple redundancy and the largest possible reach.

✦ **Large Product Launch:** Pat has worked for over a year at XCorp designing the "Killer App" and with the impending launch there is no room for failure. Pat needs as much redundancy as possible for the nearly 100 million people that will see the XCorp Commercial during the Super Bowl. Pat decides to contract with multiple CDNs to deliver the various different bandwidth and bit rate product info files.

What To Ask For

When shopping for a CDN, you should look for a provider that offers all of the following:

✦ **Web-Based User Interface:** A CDN should provide Web-based file database info, stats and consumption reports, network status, NOC information, technical support, user management, account history, and so on. All of this info should be easily downloadable and in some cases exportable in several formats including HTML, e-mail, CSV, XML, and so on.

✦ **FTP access:** A CDN must provide you with a simple way to upload your media files.

✦ **24/7/365 Support:** A CDN must provide knowledgeable, reliable technical support, available 24 hours a day.

✦ **Redundancy, QoS and PushButton Use:** Look for machine, location and personnel redundancy as well as multiple network providers.

✦ **Additional Services:** Most CDNs have additional services including encoding, live event webcasting, satellite transport, interactive learning interfaces, digital rights management, and eCommerce. If you have no experience in producing live events or moving video and audio around terrestrial and non-terrestrial transports, ask who your potential CDN is using for these services and get a quote for these services.

Pricing

There are a number of metrics that come into play when pricing CDN services:

✦ **Storage:** Storage charges typically hover anywhere from $25 per Gigabyte for localized storage in a few locations to $55 per Gigabyte for global storage across a single CDN. If a provider is utilizing multiple CDNs with a hybrid topology, costs can range as high as $150 per Gigabyte for storage across 100+ locations. If you need a Terabyte or more of storage for your content, most CDNs offer custom pricing and will meet whatever your budget is.

✦ **Delivery:** The actual delivery cost can be priced in a number of different ways. For simplicity's sake, most CDNs have moved to a model that is primarily based on the client paying for the bandwidth they use. This is typically quoted as a dollar per Megabyte rate. Rates can also be quoted in dollars per Gigabyte or Terabyte.

✦ **Reports:** CDNs have come to understand the supreme importance of timely, accurate and accessible reports, because they represent the state of the client/vendor relationship. Depending on the sophistication of the reports, the manner in which they are delivered, the frequency in which the data is updated and the amount of time they are archived, reports can vary from free to upwards of $200 per month.

Continued

Continued

✦ **Setup/Minimums:** More often than not there are some unavoidable minor costs associated with streaming. Setup fees vary — look for at least a $500 to $1,000 minimum monthly fee. A general rule of thumb is that if you are doing more than $5,000 in delivery a month, the minimum should be no more than $500 per month. In some cases you may be charged for your reports and the full minimum fees per month if you do not do much transfer.

The StreamingMedia.com Web site has great up-to-date information available about delivery costs in a report titled "The Cost of Streaming Services" (`www.streamingmedia.com/research`).

Christopher Levy is the Co-founder of DRM Networks and has been a driving force in the Streaming Media industry. After founding ClickHear Productions in 1997, Christopher served as the Sr. Director of Technology for the Streaming Division of NaviSite, and was responsible for the development of streamOS, the industry's first Overlay Content Management and Delivery Platform for publishing content across multiple Content Delivery Networks.

The Importance of Peering by Dan Rayburn

The Role Of Peering In A CDN

Content delivery networks (CDNs) have become very popular for content providers and corporations looking to improve Website and streaming media performance and reliability. Having multiple CDNs linked up and connected to one another allows companies to achieve better performance by giving the content being delivered a wider, speedier reach.

What Is Peering?

Peering is the arrangement of traffic exchange between Internet service providers (ISPs). Larger ISPs allow traffic from other large ISPs to traverse their network in exchange for the same privilege in return. They also exchange traffic with smaller ISPs so that they can reach regional end points. Essentially this is how a number of individual network owners put the original Internet together. To do this, network owners and access providers work out agreements that describe the terms and conditions to which both are subject.

Properly speaking, peering is simply the agreement to interconnect and exchange routing information. Initially, peering arrangements did not include an exchange of money. More recently, however, some larger ISPs have charged smaller ISPs for peering. Each major ISP generally develops a peering policy that states the terms and conditions under which it will peer with other networks for various types of traffic.

There are a number of different kinds of peering arrangements:

✦ **Private peering** is peering between parties that are bypassing part of the public backbone network through which most Internet traffic passes. In a regional area, some ISPs exchange local peering arrangements instead of or in addition to peering with a backbone ISP. In some cases, peering charges include transit charges, or the actual line access charge to the larger network.

✦ **Bilateral peering** is an agreement between two parties.

✦ **Multilateral peering** is an agreement between more than two parties.

How Does Peering Work?

Peering requires the exchange and updating of router information between the peered ISPs, typically using the Border Gateway Protocol (BGP). Peering parties interconnect at network focal points such as the network access points (NAP) in the United States and at regional switching points. Series of network access points (NAPs) were set up by private and public sector interests as neutral meeting grounds for ISPs to interconnect to each other after negotiating arrangements for exchanging traffic.

In the United States, a combination of public sector initiative and private enterprise led to the establishment of independent NAPs like the Palo Alto Internet Exchange and MAE-West. These NAPs were fundamental to the growth of the Internet past its academic roots and into the competitive world of private telecommunications networks.

Why Is Peering Important?

Without peering, the limit of one's delivered content is defined by the scale and reach of the single network that it is hosted on. In the past, companies would typically subscribe to more than one CDN provider so that they would have a wider reach or footprint for their content. Today, most of this can be accomplished by selecting a CDN provider than has extensive peering relationships.

CDN providers that are not doing extensive peering cannot, as a general rule, provide the same quality service as ones that are peering with many other networks. Without proper peering, the packets of data being delivered to the end user must take longer routes on the Internet. The distance the packets have to travel and number of networks they have to traverse are the biggest factors determining the quality of the audio and video to the end user.

What To Ask A CDN About Their Peering

When you're shopping around, you should ask potential vendors a few questions, which should help determine the extent of their peering:

1. **How many "active" peering connections do they have?** Some ISP's have a large number of peering agreements but an agreement does not mean that the ISP has actually has a turned up "active" connection.

2. **How many NAPs are they peered at?** The Network Access Points allow ISP's to be able to exchange traffic at major peering connections where most major networks meet.

3. **What is the extent of their international peering?** Being able to successfully deliver content closer to the end user requires the CDN to be peering on a global basis.

Dan Rayburn, has been on the cutting edge of streaming media technology since its inception in 1995 and was involved in producing some of the first cybercasts on the Internet. Dan is one of the founding board members of the IWA, International Webcasting Association and writes for many publications on streaming media trends and technology.

Summary

This chapter discussed streaming servers and how to incorporate them into a network. You learned that

✦ The QuickTime/Darwin, RealServer, and Windows Media Services products have similar features but differ in the platforms that they run on and the streaming formats that they support.

✦ Bandwidth is a central concern when setting up streaming servers. It's important to calculate the maximum number of simultaneous streams that a particular network connection is able to support.

✦ Multicasting and caching are two important ways to maximize the number of streams you can deliver over a network, without reducing the media quality.

✦ Firewalls at either the client or the server end can interfere with streaming by blocking requests over the protocols that streaming servers use. You can get around firewall-related problems by changing the configuration of the firewall or the streaming server or by relocating the server.

✦ Consistently delivering high-quality streams requires a powerful and well-planned network that includes redundant components. You can arrange redundant servers in a cluster, which enables important features, such as load balancing and failover.

✦ Edge servers can play an important role in optimizing bandwidth and maintaining high-quality streams. Because a network based on edge servers is large and complex, many streaming media providers choose to use the services of a content delivery network (CDN).

✦   ✦   ✦

Managing Your Media Assets

◆　◆　◆　◆

In This Chapter

Digital Asset
Management (DAM)

Digital Rights
Management (DRM)

◆　◆　◆　◆

 Expert　This chapter was contributed by Charlie Morris. Charlie has written countless articles and even published a couple of books about Internet technologies. He also writes extensively about digital audio technology. For contact info please turn to Bonus Chapter 6 located on the CD-ROM.

Managing your media content involves a number of ongoing tasks. Because of the large and complex nature of media files, simply keeping track of them is a major project. Furthermore, because many media files consist of creative work that is subject to copyright laws, you need to keep track of the rights that are associated with all media on your system.

Digital Asset Management

In Chapter 1, you learned that the streaming media process includes creation, encoding, authoring, and serving. Each of these steps generates a lot of files, and you need to be sure that these files are safely stored, backed up, and in some cases updated from time to time. Above all, you need to be able to find them when you need them. Your library of media can quickly become a vast, disorganized, space-wasting monster unless you organize and control your files carefully. This important process is called *digital asset management* (DAM).

Classes of media files

Different files have different functions in your system. To avoid confusion, I'll use the term file *type* to refer to the format of a file, and the term file *class* to refer to the purpose a file serves in your media delivery system. Each class of file has different requirements in terms of who needs to have access to it, how often you need to update it, and what other files are affected if you change it. The key to efficient file management is tracking, storing, and managing each file appropriately based on the class of file to which it belongs.

Raw media files

The process of creating digital media usually involves assembling various types of raw media files into a finished program. Such files may include multitrack audio files, unedited video footage, still photos used in a multimedia program, and so forth. After you've created the final version of a program, some of these files can be discarded, but you may prefer to keep some around in case you decide to go back and re-edit the program someday. These files tend to be huge (especially unedited video footage), and you don't need to have immediate access to them, so the best place to store old raw media files is on CDs, tape backup, or some other cheap offline storage.

If you have old audio or video recordings on tape, keep in mind that tape isn't a permanent storage format. Unless you store the tape in a temperature- and humidity-controlled environment, it will deteriorate in a few years. Also, be careful not to leave media stranded in an obsolete format. For example, for many years two-track, ½ inch audio tape was the industry standard for audio mixes. Now, however, almost all recording studios mix down to a digital format. Sooner or later, manufacturers will stop making two-track ½ inch machines altogether, so if you need to go back and remaster your old two-track mixes, you'll have to find a used machine and face hassles getting service and parts.

Technology marches along a road that's littered with dead and dying formats (Betamax video, 5¼ inch floppy disks, the Atari 1040 computer, and so on), so if even a remote chance exists that you'll need to use a particular bit of media again, digitize it in a generic format and store it on a CD (and plan to transfer it again in a few years when CDs become obsolete).

Master source files

Your master source files are your finished products, and the fruits of your labor. It's important to keep a copy of the finished master of a program in a high-quality general-purpose format, such as `.wav` or `.avi`.

The master source files are the most valuable files you have, so you'll want to keep them carefully backed up in several locations. If you need to re-encode a program for any reason, you'll need to have access to these files, so you may choose to keep them on a network drive accessible to your production staff. By no means should you make them available to the public, however, so they should be on the private network, accessible only to authorized users.

Encoded files

Both the RealSystem and Windows Media Technologies let you encode a file at multiple quality levels and store the results as a single file. Doing so greatly simplifies file management. However, you still may have multiple versions of a stream, for example encoded using different screen sizes. In this case each version of a program must be a separate file. If you're offering two or more streaming ormats, that's double the number of files to keep track of.

In Chapter 18, a sophisticated streaming media delivery network was described, which featured several geographically dispersed servers as well as such bandwidth-saving techniques as caching and multicasting. Taking advantage of these capabilities requires having several copies of each encoded file, all stored permanently or temporarily in various places.

Whenever you make changes to an encoded file, you must change all copies of that file that exist on the system. Alternatively, the system can check to see if an updated version exists at the time when a user requests a file. Checking for updated versions is handled by the network operating system, or by whatever utility you're using to manage file mirroring and replication (for example, RealProxy).

HTML files and metafiles

In Part 4, you learned how to create links to streaming media files from HTML pages using metafiles. Doing this creates a sort of mutually dependent relationship between all three files. If one is modified, the others may need to be updated as well. If you change the filename of a media file, you must change the metafile link to that file too, or you'll have a bad link. If a particular file becomes obsolete, you must be sure to remove not only the link to the file, but also the actual file to free up disk space.

Each media file in your system may have one or more related files, of which a linked HTML file is only one example. Such relationships are one more type of data that you need to keep track of. The task is a bit more complex when more than one person is involved. For example, one staff member may be responsible for updating a media file, and another for maintaining HTML files. Whenever the first staff member changes a media file, the other person must be notified. If you use a dynamic page-generation system to create HTML files automatically, then you'll want to let this system communicate with your media database if possible.

Log files

Servers keep an ongoing record of requests made to the server by creating log files. Server log files can quickly become enormous. To prevent your log files from growing out of control and crashing your server, you need to set up log file cycling.

 For more information about cycling your log files please turn to Chapter 20.

Table 19-1 summarizes the requirements for managing each of the different classes of files described in the previous section.

Table 19-1
Media File Classes

File class	Storage locations	Access requirements	Update schedule	Related files
Raw media	Cheap offline storage (CD, tape)	Media creation staff	None	Master source files
Master files	Private network, secure backup copies	Media creation staff, encoding staff	As desired	Raw media, encoded files
Encoded files	Streaming servers, including mirrored locations, edge servers, and so on	Encoding staff, server administrators	Whenever master source files or encoding parameters change	Master files, linked HTML files
Metafiles	Web servers, including mirrored locations	Encoding staff, authoring staff, server administrators	Whenever encoded files change	Encoded files, HTML files
HTML files	Web servers, including mirrored locations	Authoring staff	Whenever encoded files change	Encoded files
Log files	Generated by the streaming servers, can be moved to reporting machines	Reporting staff, server administrators	Should be automatically cycled	N/A

Organizing a digital media database

If your media library is small, you may be able to keep track of your files simply by organizing them in folders in a logical way and adopting a standard file-naming scheme that incorporates information about the file. For example, the following three filenames represent three versions of an file called cats, which are encoded at 28 Kbps, 56 Kbps, and 300 Kbps, respectively.

```
cats_28.asf
cats_56.asf
cats_300.asf
```

The file extension tells you what kind of file it is, and viewing the file properties tells you the file size and the date it was last modified.

For a media library of any size, however, you need a much more sophisticated way of grouping and searching for files. You need to be able to keep track of the relationships among different files, and you need a complete list of files that may be stored in many different locations. Also, if you're using a dynamic content management tool to make files available through a Web interface, you may not be able to name your files whatever you choose.

For all these reasons and more, you need a proper database to keep track of your media assets. Such a database contains an individual record for every media asset in your library, and each record contains information about the asset (this is called *metadata*). A *media asset* may consist of a single file or a group of files. The database may contain copies of the media files, or the database may merely contain pointers to media stored in various locations. Depending on your needs, you may want to associate various types of metadata with each asset.

File properties

Every computer file has the following properties:

✦ File format

✦ Size

✦ Modification date

✦ Permissions (who is allowed to read and/or modify the file)

You may often need to search for files based on their properties. For example, you may periodically search for files created before a certain date in order to purge outdated files from your system.

Media parameters

You convert media such as images, audio and video to computer files using various parameters, and it's important to be able to identify these parameters for each file when needed. Media parameters include:

✦ For audio source files: sampling rate, resolution, number of channels.

✦ For video source files: frame rate, resolution.

✦ For graphic source files: resolution, image size, color depth.

✦ For encoded files: codec, bit rate.

This information is often contained in the file header. Many DAM database packages can automatically extract and record this information.

Resource description

You can use text fields to store any sort of information you want to associate with a particular media asset. Attaching text fields to files makes it possible to search for files that meet certain criteria. Although you can devise any system you like for creating this information, using one of the standard ways of describing metadata is best. Doing so enables you to use open-standard tools, such as XML to make your database interact with other applications such as Web content management, e-commerce, and search engines.

The Dublin Core Metadata Element Set (DCMES) is a widely used metadata standard that you can use to describe anything from Web pages to books in a library to . . . you guessed it — Media files in your collection. The DCMES is incorporated in some of the advanced DAM solutions, and it comes in handy for communicating with Web-based applications, by using the XML-based resource description protocol (RDP). The Dublin Core provides an extensive set of elements, of which you can use as few or as many as you need. Together with the file properties and media attributes, the DCMES covers most of the information you're likely to need about an individual media asset.

The Dublin Core Metadata Element Set includes the following:

✦ Title

✦ Creator

✦ Subject

✦ Description

✦ Publisher

✦ Contributor

✦ Date

✦ Identifier

✦ Source

✦ Language

✦ Relation (enables you to specify related files)

✦ Coverage

✦ Rights (enables you to provide information for digital rights management (DRM))

 Tip Details of the Dublin Core Metadata Initiative can be found on the Web at http://dublincore.org/documents/dces/.

Copyright information

As you learn later in this chapter, the rights, permissions, licensing, and royalties associated with a single media asset can be complex, especially if it's a multimedia program made up of several individual files. The Dublin Core provides a Rights element.

Text content

You can easily search a text file for keywords to find files related to a certain subject. However, to make an audio or video file text-searchable, you must have a transcription available. If a program includes closed-captioning, some of the DAM database packages can extract this and include it in the asset record.

Related files

The Dublin Core includes an element in which you can list related files. Some DAM packages enable you to view related files together.

Access control

As explained earlier in this chapter, media files fall into different classes, and different personnel need different types of access to each class. For example, the encoding staff needs to have read access to master media files to encode them, but only the creation staff needs to have write access to the masters. Network operating systems let you make file permissions as complex as you want, by setting up groups of users and so on.

Update/archiving schedule

You may choose to update certain assets on a periodic schedule, and/or remove them from the system after a certain date and store them in an archive. You can use DAM software to set up a schedule to notify staff when it's time to carry out these tasks.

Asset classes

Instead of setting up separate fields in your database for access control and update schedule, you can set up a single field for the asset class and associate each class with a particular set of file permissions and a particular file maintenance schedule.

DAM software

You can build your own media asset database by using Oracle, MS Access, or some other database package. Or you may choose to use one of several packaged DAM products.

Idex

Idex (www.idexworld.com/) is a free software product (Figure 19-1) that lets you store, organize, and view media assets in a custom database format. Idex supports many data formats and can extract media parameters to include them in a database record automatically. It also includes powerful search capabilities.

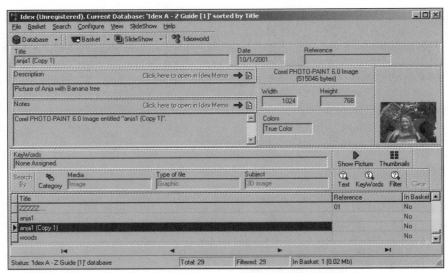

Figure 19-1: Idex is a free digital media database product. This figure shows a record in the database that represents an image file. The screen displays a thumbnail of the image, as well as the image size and other media parameters. You also have the option to display the whole image, to insert a text description and notes, and to specify keywords for search capabilities.

Destiny ContentEZ

Destiny ContentEZ from Centillion Digital Systems (www.centilliondigital.com) is a full-featured DAM software package that supports over 40 file types.

Other Useful DAM Software

More upscale choices include Content BOSS from Bulldog Group Inc. (www.bulldog. com/), and TEAMS 4.3, from Artesia Technologies (www.artesia.com/). These enterprise-level platforms are built on Oracle's database and are designed to handle thousands of users and millions of assets. These platforms can handle any type of digital asset, not only for Internet delivery, but in a broadcast context as well. They automatically extract a wide variety of information from media files and also perform batch format conversions. Both are built around cutting-edge standards, such as XML and Java and are designed to integrate smoothly with other applications.

Like many software products these days, you can buy a DAM software package to run in-house, or you can subscribe to it as a service through an application service provider (ASP). Doing so enables you to outsource your media storage and backup needs at the same time that you implement a DAM system.

Digital Rights Management

If digital distribution of media over the Internet is to reach its potential, we need a way to protect copyrighted media that is truly secure, flexible, easy to use, and can be integrated with existing e-commerce systems. The lack of any widely-accepted technology is one of the reasons that on-demand distribution hasn't caught on, even as other streaming media applications, such as Webcasting, have mushroomed.

Various types of copy protection and access control exist, many developed by software makers to protect their products. For example, a user may need to provide a registration code to install a software package, or enter a password to gain access to a Web site. Such systems are not adequate for digital media applications for several reasons:

✦ **Not secure enough.** A registration code can be copied right along with a supposedly protected file, and passwords can be shared through Internet discussion groups.

✦ **Not flexible enough.** Content providers want to be able to offer different subscription models (monthly, pay-per-view, free trials, and so on), or even make up new ones.

✦ **Inconvenient for users.** A good protection scheme must not only block unauthorized users, but must make it easy for authorized users. Consumers won't be enthusiastic about a system that requires them to remember passwords or write down registration keys.

✦ **Difficult to integrate with other hardware and software.** Content providers need a rights management system that can smoothly communicate with e-commerce and user tracking applications. Consumers want to be able to transfer licensed media to various platforms, such as portable media players.

Clearly what is needed is a *digital* license that is separate from the media file, which conforms to a standard format and can be activated in a variety of flexible ways. For these reasons, the concept of *digital rights management* (DRM) has been developed. A media file protected by DRM is encrypted, and can be played only when a valid digital license is present. To play a protected file, the user requires two things: the file itself and the electronic license.

Note   Some companies and writers use the term DRM in a much broader way, to include any and all forms of copy protection, including digital watermarks. Our narrower definition matches that used by Microsoft, RealNetworks, and other makers of DRM products.

Separating the license from the media has many advantages. You don't have to create different versions of a file to accommodate different licensing scenarios, nor do you need to prevent copying of a protected media file. And because the licenses are stored at the server end, the provider has complete control over them.

Security features of DRM

A DRM system can protect files in various ways. Major DRM systems include some or all of the following features:

✦ **Secure downloads.** Content is encrypted during download to prevent unauthorized interception.

✦ **Secure PC audio path.** Content is encrypted between the user's media player and sound card to prevent users from capturing and recording streams.

✦ **Persistence.** Each digital license is specific to a particular computer, which means that a media file is transferable, but the license is not. A user can distribute a protected file to other users, but each of those users needs a valid license to play the file.

✦ **Individualization.** Each media player is linked to a particular computer. This feature prevents a user from transferring licenses simply by transferring the player software.

✦ **Revocability.** Because the licenses are stored on a license server, a license can be revoked at any time if a user breaches the licensing terms.

✦ **Portable device support.** Some DRM systems allow files to be transferred to hardware players that incorporate the Secure Digital Music Initiative (SDMI) copy-protection scheme.

Business scenarios using DRM

Media is a product that lends itself to a wide variety of pricing models. Different users find different arrangements attractive: some prefer a pay-as-you-go system, and others may prefer to pay a monthly fee for unlimited use. Online media distribution is a new industry, and providers are keen to experiment with different ways of generating revenue. One of the most exciting features of DRM is that, because user licenses are stored at the server end, a provider has almost unlimited flexibility in setting up different kinds of pricing models.

Some of the possibilities include:

✦ **Free access.** Companies often offer media access at no cost to promote a product or service, to attract viewers to an advertising-supported site, or as a prize or premium. Even if you're not collecting fees, DRM can still be useful, because it enables you to require user registration and track usage patterns.

✦ **Pay-per-view access.** The user buys a certain number of accesses to a media file or group of files. For example, a user might pay a fee for the right to download up to 100 media clips from a catalog.

✦ **Timed access.** The user buys access to a file or group of files for a set time period. For example, a user might pay a monthly fee for unlimited access to a catalog.

✦ **Tiered access.** The user receives different levels of service depending on how much he or she pays. For example, a provider may offer low-bandwidth streams with ads for free, ad-free low-bandwidth streams for a low monthly price, high-bandwidth streams for a higher price, and so forth.

✦ **Trial offer.** The user can access media free for a certain time or a certain number of viewings, after which the user must choose a paid access option.

✦ **Reward program.** The user earns free access by performing some desired action, such as buying another product, responding to a questionnaire, or viewing advertisements. Users could even earn points that could be redeemed for access, in the manner of an airline's frequent flyer program.

These options are only a few pricing possibilities, all inspired by arrangements that exist in traditional media. Considering the flexibility that DRM provides, and the competitive nature of the media market, providers will devise various innovative business models that no one has thought of to date.

Implementing DRM

DRM can work with any and all types of files and any type of distribution method: streaming, download, or physical media such as CDs. Each of the major DRM systems (as outlined in Figure 19-2), however, is specific to a particular streaming server/player combination, so if you're delivering more than one streaming format, you may need to implement more than one flavor of DRM.

Delivering media that is protected by DRM involves these steps:

1. The media provider packages a media file, which creates a protected media file and a corresponding digital license.

2. The provider places the protected media file on a streaming server, and the license on a license server.

3. When a user attempts to play the file, his or her media player requests a license from the license server.

4. The user's computer either downloads a license without requiring any action by the user (this is sometimes called *silent licensing*), or directs the user to a Web page, which directs the user to register and/or make payment.

5. After the license is on the user's machine, the user can play the file in accordance with the terms of the license.

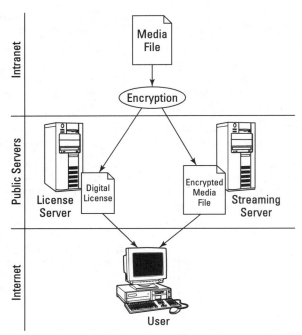

Figure 19-2: This figure shows the architecture of a DRM system. Media files are encrypted and placed on the streaming server. The user must obtain a license from the license server to play the encrypted file.

DRM solutions

Two of the major streaming server makers, Microsoft and RealNetworks, have developed very sophisticated DRM solutions that offer most or all of the features described earlier in this section, and are incorporated into more recent versions of their products. QuickTime does not yet support DRM. The less well-known Liquid Server has included DRM features for several years. Because each DRM solution works only with a particular streaming format, your choice of server platform(s) will probably dictate which DRM system you use.

Although Microsoft's and RealNetworks' DRM products are packed with features and claim to be highly robust and scalable, don't forget that both are comparatively new products. You should expect a certain number of compatibility problems, especially if you're using older servers, or if a large number of your users are using outdated players.

Windows Media Rights Manager 7.1

Windows Media Rights Manager 7.1 (WMRM) is an end-to-end DRM system for the Windows streaming platform. It supports a huge number of security and business-model options, including all those described above and much more.

WMRM delivers protected media files in Windows Media Audio (.wma) or Windows Media Video (.wmv) format. Supported players include Windows Media Player versions 6.4 and up, as well as players from MusicMatch, RioPort, Sonic Foundry and WinAMP.

WMRM includes server and client software development kits (SDKs) that enable developers to write applications to encrypt media files and issue licenses. This gives you a way to integrate WMRM with your existing business applications.

A related technology is Windows Media Device Manager, which enables users to transfer protected files to portable devices such as hardware media players. You can transfer protected Windows Media files to most SDMI-compatible hardware devices.

One caveat about WMRM is that it won't necessarily work with non-Windows operating systems, or even old versions of Windows. There are currently two versions of WMRM available. The older version 1 works with most Windows and Mac versions of Windows Media Player, but the new Version 7.1 works only with clients running Windows 98, ME, 2000 or XP. At the server end, WMRM requires Windows 2000 Server.

For more details, visit the Web site at www.microsoft.com/windows/windowsmedia/drm.asp.

On Demand Distribution (www.ondemanddistribution.com/) is a European music distributor using WMRM. Their site contains some interesting information about the business aspects of implementing WMRM. Other media providers using WMRM include LAUNCH Media (http://launch.com), amplified.com (http://amplified.com) and House of Blues (www.hob.com/).

RealSystem Media Commerce Suite

RealNetworks' DRM offering is called Media Commerce Suite (MCS), and consists of four components: The Packager, which encrypts the media, the License Server, which issues content licenses, the Media Commerce Upgrade for RealPlayer, and a plug-in for RealSystem Server 8.0.

Like WMRM, MCS offers a host of features, enabling you to use many different business models and modes of distribution, and to implement various levels of security. MCS can be integrated with a wide variety of existing applications such as payment systems, e-commerce applications, databases and customer relationship management (CRM) software.

For more details, visit the Web site at www.realnetworks.com/products/commerce/index.html.

The MusicNet content delivery network, of which RealNetworks is a partner, uses MCS, and is now available as part of the RealOne service. Visit the Web site at www.realnetworks.com/solutions/ecosystem/realone.html.

Liquid Audio

Liquid Audio is a format-neutral streaming system that's compatible with both RealNetworks and Microsoft streaming formats. Their Liquid Server, which comes in both Unix and NT versions, incorporates a DRM system that offers a range of security features and supports many business and distribution models.

Although Liquid Audio is not as well-known as the Big Three, the company claims that over 1,500 record labels and 1,000 music retail sites use their services. They also offer a platform called SP3 for secure playback on portable hardware devices.

For more details about Liquid Server's DRM features, visit the Web site at `http://liquidaudio.com/services/distribution/drm/index.asp`.

Summary

This chapter discussed the management of media assets, in terms of managing the files themselves and in terms of managing the intellectual property rights associated with the assets. You learned:

✦ A media provider creates and maintains many different kinds of files, which may serve various different purposes. Managing them efficiently requires understanding the different requirements for storing and maintaining different classes of files.

✦ Managing digital assets requires a sophisticated database. You can create your own, or choose among several specialized media databases that are available.

✦ Unauthorized copying has been a concern of content providers since the advent of mass media. Although the problem can't be totally stamped out, various legal and technological tools are available to keep it to a minimum.

✦ As a user of intellectual property, you must obtain the proper licenses and sometimes pay royalties for the use of copyrighted content. The process of obtaining a license differs depending on the type of media involved.

✦ As a provider of intellectual property, you need to protect your assets from illegal copying. Current streaming platforms provide powerful ways to do this, using digital rights management (DRM) technology.

✦ DRM systems offer a wide range of security features, and enable you to deliver media under a wide range of business models.

✦   ✦   ✦

Using Server Log Files

CHAPTER

20

In This Chapter

How server log files work

Log file analysis software

Analyzing and cycling log files

Learning from your log files

Expert This chapter was contributed by Charlie Morris. Charlie has written countless articles and even published a couple of books about Internet technologies. He also writes extensively about digital audio technology. For contact info please turn to Bonus Chapter 6 on the CD-ROM.

For any type of content provider, knowing as much as you can about your audience, including what they like the best and what they like the least is critical. The Internet makes it far easier than any other medium to get this information, because Internet servers can automatically keep a record of every user request.

The server keeps these records in a file called a *server log file*. Creating server log files is easy. Analyzing and using the information contained in them is more difficult; although it can be a complex task, you'll probably find that doing so is a very rewarding undertaking.

How Server Log Files Work

A streaming media provider can generate log files in two ways. Major streaming servers (including RealServer, WMS and QuickTime) can generate them automatically. Alternatively, you can use the logs generated by an associated Web server. Because most streaming media is delivered through some sort of Web-based interface, your Web server logs can tell you some of what you need to know about requests for streaming files.

Note Although Web server logs give you information about what files were requested and when, they cannot provide any information about your network or streaming sever performance.

The streaming server logs may contain some interesting information, such as bandwidth usage, that the Web server logs do not. However, using the Web server logs can also provide information that the server logs do not. They can give you information about how users find your HTML pages and may reveal HTML errors that aren't apparent from the streaming server logs. Also, if you're using more than one streaming server, the Web server logs provide you with combined usage information for both streaming servers.

In either case, you must enable logging in your server program, and you must make arrangements to store, maintain, and analyze your log files, as described later in this chapter.

Most servers create three different log files:

✦ **Access Log.** Records a variety of information about every request the server receives.

✦ **Error Log.** Records any error messages triggered by unfulfilled requests.

✦ **Referrer Log (Web servers).** Records the page that a user was looking at just before requesting one of your files. You can use this information to determine where your users are coming from.

Some servers give you the option of combining the access and referrer logs. If you can, you should do so, because being able to analyze the access and referrer data together is useful.

Log files are simply ASCII text files, but two different standard formats are in use. The NCSA (National Center for Supercomputing Applications) Common Log File Format has a fixed number of data fields, whereas the W3C Extended Log File Format is customizable, allowing you to configure the server to log only certain data fields. The latter option is preferable, as it enables you to save server resources by not logging data you don't need, and to add special data fields of your own, for example fields that record the content of cookies. In addition to the standard log formats, some servers, such as Microsoft's Internet Information Server (IIS), can create a format readable by an ODBC-compliant database.

Every request to the server is recorded as a separate entry in the log file. For example, an entry in your Web server log file generally looks something like this (ignore the line breaks):

```
200.99.99.99 - - [19/Jul/2001:00:00:04 -0600] "GET
    /directory/file.html HTTP/1.1" 200 20607
    "http://www.yourdomain.com/filename.html"
    "Mozilla/4.0 (compatible; MSIE 5.0; Windows 98)"
```

To see what information is contained in the log, let's examine each of the items in Table 20-1. The example combines access and referrer information.

Table 20-1
Web Server Log File Information

Log file entry	Explanation
`200.99.99.99`	This is the IP address of the user making the request.
`[19/Jul/2001:00:00:04 -0600]`	Date and time of the request. The -0600 at the end indicates that the server is located in a time zone six hours behind Greenwich Mean Time.
`GET`	Request method.
`/directory/file.html`	The local path of the requested file.
`HTTP/1.1`	The protocol that is used for the request. For a streaming file, this might also be RTP or RTSP.
`200`	The response status code. 200 indicates a successful file transfer.
`20607`	The size, in bytes, of the file that was transferred.
`www.`*`yourdomain`*`.com/`*`filename`*`.html`	The URL of the referring file. This is the file from which the user reached this one.
`Mozilla/4.0 (compatible;` `MSIE 5.0; Windows 98)`	The User agent. It reveals the browser or media player version and operating system of the user.

The error log contains entries like these:

```
[19/Jul/2001:00:00:04 -0600]  httpd: send aborted for
    yourdomain.com

[19/Jul/2001:00:01:32 -0600]  httpd: access to
    /directory/file.ram failed for yourdomain.com,
    reason: file does not exist
```

The first entry says "send aborted," which tells you that the user aborted the transfer, either because they got tired of waiting or because their connection went down. The second entry says "file does not exist," which tells you that the link was invalid.

Logging with QuickTime Streaming Server

The QuickTime Streaming server creates two log files, the access history log and the errors log. These log files are generated in the W3C standard format, and are compliant with popular log analysis tools from Lariat, Active Concepts, and WebTrends.

You can change the log file settings via the QuickTime Streaming Administrator. You can also view the current log files using the QuickTime Streaming Administrator. Log files are automatically cycled on a weekly basis.

For a complete description of the access log format, please refer the Apple Web site (www.apple.com/quicktime/authoring/qtss/pgs/qt18.htm).

Logging with RealServer

RealServer creates three types of logs:

✦ **Access log.** Records information about every request the server receives.

✦ **Error log.** Records information about every failed request.

✦ **Cached requests log.** Records all streams that RealServer sends to RealProxy.

Chapter 18 explains how to use RealProxy to optimize bandwidth usage by caching often-requested streams.

If you use .ram files (metafiles) to link to your streaming files, keep in mind that the metafiles are served by a Web server. RealServer records requests for the individual files referenced by the .ram file, but requests for the actual .ram file are logged by the Web server.

Chapter 15 explains how to use metafiles.

RealServer can create reports for specific time periods that let you see usage trends. You can also feed RealServer logs into a traffic analysis program, as explained later in this chapter. RealServer enables you to limit the size of log files by time period or by file size, a process it calls log file rolling. When the log file grows to your preset limit, RealServer begins a new log file. As described later in this chapter, you need to move old log files off the server as new ones are created.

RealServer also includes two applications that enable you to monitor activity real time: Java Monitor and NT Performance Monitor (for NT users). Java Monitor is part of RealSystem Administrator, and can display real-time information about the number of clients connected, resources used, and which files are being streamed, in graphical form. Data you can monitor includes:

✦ CPU usage

✦ Memory usage

✦ Bandwidth

✦ Number of players connected

✦ User IP addresses

✦ Versions of browsers or RealPlayers

✦ Length of connection time

✦ Files being served

Monitoring your server performance in real-time can be very illuminating, particularly during live broadcasts.

Logging with Windows Media Services

WMS creates log files through the Windows Media Administrator, and records the following information:

✦ Unique client ID (assigned automatically by the program)

✦ Client's IP address

✦ Port number

✦ File name

WMS saves log files in W3C standard format and has built-in log cycling capabilities.

Logging with Web servers

Internet Information Server (IIS) lets you choose among four different log file formats. In addition to the standard NCSA Common and W3C Extended formats, you can use the special Microsoft IIS Log Format, which uses a two-digit year format and thus may be handy for backward compatibility with earlier IIS versions, or ODBC logging, which supports using an ODBC-compliant database, such as Microsoft Access or Microsoft SQL Server. IIS also has built-in log cycling capabilities.

Unix Web servers, such as NCSA and Apache, let you choose various logging options by modifying the configuration files. You can specify which of the standard log file formats you want to use, and even define your own custom data fields. To enable log file cycling, you need to set up a *cron job*, a script that the server runs automatically at a time that you specify.

Analyzing and Cycling Log Files

Reading log files directly is of limited use. To get the most out of your log data, you need to be able to see totals for a whole site (or group of sites) and compare the figures over time. A log analysis (also called traffic analysis) software package can condense the information from your log files into an organized, readable report.

Log files get huge very quickly, so you need to *rotate* or *cycle* your log files, which means having the server start a new log file at specified intervals (RealNetworks calls it *rolling*). After a new file is started, you can run the previous one through your analysis software and eventually archive it. It's absolutely critical to manage and organize your log files carefully. Gaps in your data can prevent you from getting an accurate picture of your traffic over time, so make sure that you have a good log file management plan and stick to it.

The life cycle of log files includes the following steps:

1. **The server closes a log file and starts a new one.** You can configure your server to start a new log file when the file reaches a certain size or at the end of a specified time period. Starting a new file periodically is better because you can organize your log file data according to date, which is generally how you'll want to analyze the data.

   How often you start a new file depends on the traffic level of your site. Sites with heavy traffic may need to start a new file daily to prevent the files from reaching an inconvenient size. The time and date of each request is recorded in the log, so it makes no difference to a log analysis program how often the files are cycled, but keeping them to a consistent time period makes it easier to keep track of them.

2. **Remove the old log file from the Web server.** Log files can be extremely large. If you run out of space on your server, it stops logging, and you lose valuable data. When log data is lost, it's gone forever. You need to remove log files from the Web server periodically to make sure your hard drive doesn't fill up. One way to do this is to have the server automatically FTP a copy of the log file to the log file analysis computer or a permanent storage location, and deletes the old log files from the Web server.

   It's best to have the server compress the log files by using a utility such as gzip, before transferring the log files to another machine. It's also not a bad idea to have someone verify that a copy of each log file has been saved before the old file is deleted. If you lose a log file, the data for that particular date range is lost forever.

3. **Perform log analysis on the log file.** Most log analysis programs can be set up to generate reports automatically at specified times. You may want to prepare daily, weekly, and monthly reports. Creating a traffic report from log files takes a lot of time and computer power, so set up your log analysis program to create them at appropriate times, perhaps scheduling daily reports to run in the middle of the night so that your staff members can have them first thing

in the morning. Some simple log analysis tools can run on your Web server, but the more sophisticated ones are very processor-intensive. If you're running one of these beasts, having a dedicated computer for log analysis is a good idea.

4. **Move the old log file to a permanent storage location.** After you've created the desired traffic reports from a set of log files, you can remove the log files to free up disk space, but you should save them permanently on CDs or tape backup for two reasons. First, if you use an audit bureau to verify your traffic information (explained in the next section), it'll want to examine your raw log files periodically. Second, you may devise new and better traffic reports in the future and want to run these reports on historical logs.

Figure 20-1 shows the life cycle of a log file, from creation to archiving.

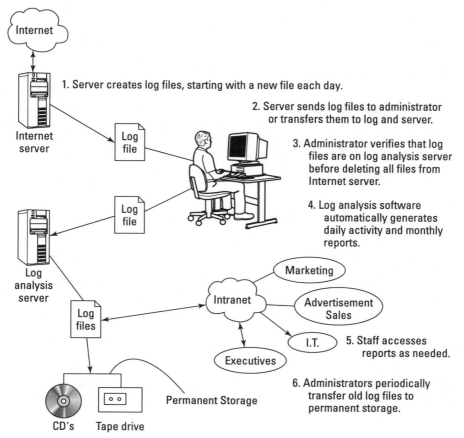

Figure 20-1: Managing log files properly may be complex, but it's absolutely critical. Most of the steps in the process can be automated, but a person should check regularly to make sure that valuable data doesn't get lost.

Log File Analysis Software

A log analysis (or traffic analysis) program takes data from raw log files and arranges it into concise, readable reports that show trends over time. The simplest ones prepare text reports that show basic statistics, such as the numbers of requests for various types of files and the number of site visitors. More sophisticated (and expensive) packages allow you to design custom reports containing attractive charts and graphs, and offer a much wider range of statistics, including information on your most and least popular content and information on search engines and other sites that send you traffic.

Several traffic analysis packages are available, including:

✦ **Analog 5.1:** This free product offers versions for just about every OS platform under the sun. It is available at `www.analog.cx/`.

✦ **The Webalizer:** This free product runs on Linux, just about every flavor of Unix, Mac OS, and even such lesser-known operating systems as OS/2 and BeOS. It is available at `www.mrunix.net/webalizer/`.

✦ **Lariat MediaReports:** This upscale commercial product comes in both installable and hosted versions. For information, see `www.lariat.com/`.

✦ **WebTrends:** This company offers a range of traffic analysis products, from the entry-level Log Analyzer to the advanced WebTrends Reporting Center to the hosted solution WebTrends Live. For information, see `http://webtrends.com/`.

✦ **Accrue Software:** Accrue also offers a range of products, including the venerable midrange product Hit List, formerly sold by Marketwave. For information, see `www.accrue.com/`.

✦ **NetGenesis:** This company offers the upscale NetGenesis 5.5. For information, see `www.netgen.com/`.

Log analysis services

As is the case with many software applications nowadays, many companies now offer log analysis as a service, which gives you an alternative to the complex task of running log analysis software in-house. Lariat Software (`www.lariat.com/`) offers a comprehensive traffic reporting service called MediaReports that's designed for streaming media providers. MediaReports installs a module called a data reader on each of your media servers to collect log file data and forward it to a database. MediaReports then generates your reports from the database at whatever times you specify. A service such as this can greatly simplify the complex task of reporting across multiple servers, multiple streaming platforms, and multiple content accounts.

Audit bureaus

If you intend to use your traffic analysis information as a marketing tool, such as showing it to potential advertisers, for example, you need to have the data audited by an independent audit bureau. Because digital data is easy to falsify or misrepresent, reputable ad agencies require that all traffic statistics be independently audited. An audit bureau performs two functions: they verify your log files to make sure that you aren't making the data up, and they examine your log analysis procedure to make sure that your figures give an accurate picture of your traffic. The two leading organizations in this field are the Audit Bureau of Circulations (www.accessabc.com) and BPA International (www.bpai.com).

Audit bureaus require you to follow certain standard practices to make sure that every request you count is really a valid user request. You can't count anything that automatically refreshes, such as an audio file that loops automatically, you can't count any requests from inside your organization, and you can't count hits from automated programs, such as spiders and robots.

In addition to independent auditors for your log files, you can also have a third-party monitor your streams for quality. It is just as important to monitor the quality of the streams your audience is receiving as it is to know who is watching and when. For a discussion about monitoring stream quality, please see the "Streaming Media Quality Metrics" sidebar.

Streaming Media Quality Metrics by Shai Berger

Assessing the quality and reliability of your streams is an important task for any company deploying a streaming media system. It is also important for any content owner serious about using streaming as a distribution channel. Despite all of the technical advances of recent years, the streaming industry is still plagued by reliability issues and inconsistent quality. In order to address quality issues, you need objective data collected through your own internal processes or by using a Streaming Metrics Provider (SMP).

The role of the SMP is to monitor and measure stream quality using a set of standard metrics. Ideally, these metrics should reflect the experience of the intended end-user of the streaming content. Data generated by an SMP can be used to make objective judgments about streaming delivery. The people interested in this kind of data include the content owner, the streaming service provider, advertisers, and syndication partners. The emergence of the SMP signals an important step in the maturation of the streaming industry.

Why do my streams need to be measured by a third party?
✦ Accurate end-to-end measurement of streaming quality is needed in order to make educated decisions on a stream hosting solution initially and throughout the term of the contract.

✦ Measurement allows a content owner to know if a service provider is meeting expectations throughout the contract. This is especially important if a Service Level Agreement (SLA) is part of the contract.

Continued

Continued

> ✦ Real-time notification should be part of any professional streaming operation. Complaints from customers should not be your company's early warning system.
>
> ✦ Finally, content partners, advertisers and other stakeholders are expecting quality guarantees as part of their streaming arrangements.

How are streaming quality metrics collected?

To measure the quality of a stream, special software is used to mimic the behavior of an end-user by connecting to the stream and viewing or listening to the content for a specific period. This software is often called a "scanner" and runs on computers in different locations and with different Internet connections. In order to provide a true end-user view, some SMPs are employing "edge" scanners, which are connected to the Internet via DSL or cable modems.

Shouldn't my stream host take care of stream quality?

Most stream hosts and Content Delivery Networks (CDNs) have sincere intentions of providing the best possible quality and reliability to their customers. However, an independent source of quality metrics brings unbiased information to the table.

Many stream hosts simply do not have the technology in-house to provide robust and detailed quality data. Quite simply, it isn't their core competency. A third party metrics provider can help both content owner and stream host to understand and address quality issues.

Furthermore, conflicts of interest can arise within the organization when quality measurements yield data that is less than perfect (especially when an SLA is involved). It is in best interest of the stream host to provide the highest quality streams to its customers. This is one reason that stream hosts are partnering with SMPs to provide stream monitoring to their customers.

Metrics to Watch

One of the difficulties in analyzing stream quality is that there are many different ways of measuring it, some of which vary with time throughout the course of the stream. It is important to pick the relevant metrics and consolidate the information into a manageable and actionable form. Below is a list of commonly used metrics that are relevant for a broad number of streaming applications.

Connection Success Rate (CSR)

This percentage represents the number of times a connection was established with a streaming server as a percentage of total attempted checks. Failures to connect can arise due to:

> ✦ **Connectivity problems:** Server couldn't be found
>
> ✦ **Server problems:** Server was down or not accepting further connections
>
> ✦ **Logic problems:** File wasn't found, access was denied, etc.

Average Bit Rate (ABR)

The average bit rate of data transfer is a number that should be compared to the encoded bit rate of the content. If the measured ABR is lower than expected it may indicate that the delivery network doesn't have the necessary bandwidth.

Frustration time

Frustration time is the total time the end-user spends waiting for audio or video content to play. It is made up of three non-playing activities: connecting, buffering and re-buffering. The following figure shows a chart indicating the frustration times associated with a clip on a particular day.

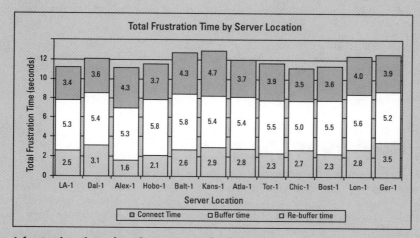

A frustration time chart from Streamcheck

Using frame rate as a quality metric

Frame rate is a well-known, readily understandable measurement of quality in traditional media and broadcasting. Unfortunately, it is not a good metric for streaming video. The frame rate that is reported by the streaming players is based on data analysis of encoder output. It is not based on actual frames displayed on the screen. The "player frame rate" depends on the codec used and the encoding approach. Some streaming media players interpolate frames to provide better video. While technology like this is ultimately beneficial to the end user, it presents problems when trying to collect consistent metrics.

Miscellaneous Metrics

Other metrics that might be useful in certain situations are listed below.

✦ **Packets stats:** Received, dropped, early, late, out of order

✦ **Traceroute:** A list of the hops between each scanner and the origin server

✦ **Protocol:** UDP or TCP or MMS or HHTP

Continued

Continued

Check Duration/Frequency

A common approach to measuring stream quality is to use a 60-second check duration. Tests have shown that multiple 60-second checks closely approximate an end user's experience. In a live event situation, where it is critical to have 100 percent uptime and connectivity, check frequency can be as high as every 15 seconds.

Costs

Although the SMP space is new, some pricing standards are emerging. Typically, stream measurement costs $300 to $1,200 per month per stream, depending on bit rate. Many variables can effect the cost such as checking frequency, check duration and extra analysis.

Shai Berger is the president of Streamcheck, a premier SMP and the creator of the first distributed system for real-time monitoring of streaming media delivery. Streamcheck's service has been in operation since mid-2000, conducting millions of checks on streams of all types using scanners throughout the US, Canada and Europe. For more information, see www.streamcheck.com.

Learning from your Log Files

Preparing reports from your log files is only the second step in the feedback process. The next and most important step is using the information from these reports to find ways to improve your content offerings. The information provided by your log files is factual, objective data. Deciding how to use that information to improve your content and your delivery methods, however, can be very subjective, and two people examining the same traffic information may reach different, even opposite, conclusions about what it means and what should be done about it.

A traffic report can tell you a lot about what's happening with your content, but it usually can't tell you *why* it happens. For example, let's say you notice that a particular piece of content is extremely popular, consistently receiving a high number of user requests. The reason could be because people love this content, or it could be because this content is prominently featured on your site and easy to find. Conversely, if another item ranks among your least popular programs, it could be because your users aren't interested, or because it's buried and they can't find it.

One of the most productive things you can do is to experiment with different content and different ways of organizing and presenting content, using your traffic reports over a period of time to ascertain what works and what doesn't. Obviously, doing so is very time consuming and requires careful planning and record keeping.

For example, you could take the unpopular piece of content from the previous example and give it a prominent link on the front page of your site, keeping a record of when you make the change. A month later, you can compare the traffic it receives to the traffic from the period before the change. If you see a large increase in requests for this item, you may conclude that it's good stuff and was only neglected before because it was hard to find.

Sometimes, even when a trend and its causes are obvious, you may be able to draw two different conclusions as to what action you should take, if any. The business of choosing stock market investments provides a fitting analogy: If a particular stock has gone up in price, one analyst may see this as an indicator of strength, and say that it's time to buy; another analyst may reason that, because what goes up must come down, the stock is ripe for a fall. Either analyst could be right.

Likewise, you may see the relative strength of a particular content area or a particular segment of users, as a reason to develop the area even more (play to your strengths) or as a reason to try to improve other areas to see if they can yield similar success (if it ain't broke, don't fix it). Keep this in mind as you examine each of the different types of statistics in your traffic reports.

A traffic report is usually broken down into several parts, each of which provides a different type of information about your site traffic. Each of the remaining sections of this chapter corresponds to a part of a typical traffic report. In each section, we'll discuss some of the ways in which each type of traffic information might influence your actions as you work on improving your Internet site.

Number of requests and visitors

Obviously, this section of your traffic report can tell you whether your site traffic is growing and can give you an approximate rate of growth, which can help you to project future bandwidth needs. A closer look at the figures in this section can show you several other interesting things.

Comparing daily traffic figures can show you how your traffic varies by the day of the week (most sites experience significantly higher traffic on weekdays). Comparing the number of files requested with the number of visitors can tell you how many media files the average visitor is requesting. A low number of file requests per visitor indicates that people aren't listening or watching many different clips, which could be due to a variety of reasons. Perhaps you don't have enough compelling content to make people stick around. Or maybe you do, but it's poorly organized, and people give up and leave before they can find what they're looking for. Or perhaps people come looking for a particular clip because it was mentioned on another popular site. Figure 20-2 shows a sample report comparing successful requests and unique visitors.

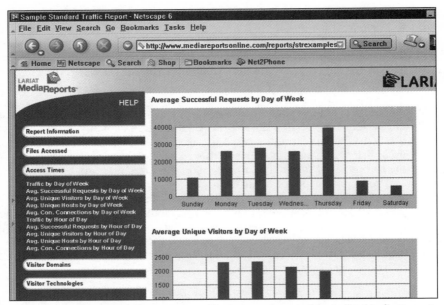

Figure 20-2: A section of a sample traffic report generated by Lariat Media Reports showing the number of successful requests and unique visitors by day of week

Traffic analysis programs can give you a figure for the number of visitors, but it's only an approximation, for a couple of reasons. First, many ISPs assign users floating IP addresses, which means that every time a user logs on, they receive a different IP value. Thus, the same user may appear to be several users. The second problem has to do with firewalls. When a user connects through a firewall, the Web server records the IP address of the firewall system. Thus, many users may appear to be a single user if they're all behind the same firewall. High-end analysis programs are designed to take these issues into account, so their figures for number of visitors should be fairly reliable, though they aren't 100% accurate.

Type of requests

This part of your traffic report can provide very useful information if you offer streaming media in different formats. A breakdown of the types of files that are being requested can tell you how many users are requesting WMS, Real and/or QuickTime streams. Running multiple streaming servers involves a lot of additional work and expense. Knowing if it's worth it is important. Most sites see roughly equal numbers of requests for RealMedia and Windows Media files, with a much smaller number of requests for QuickTime files. Figure 20-3 shows a sample report comparing server usage.

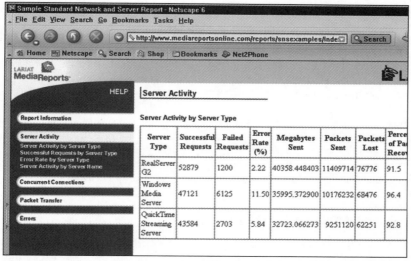

Figure 20-3: A section of a sample traffic report generated by Lariat Media Reports comparing streaming server activity by server type

Most and least requested files

This section of your traffic report can give you a wealth of information. Knowing which *type* of programming is most popular can indicate where you should focus your content creation resources. Conversely, it can indicate what section of your content library needs more promotion. This traffic information can also suggest revisions to your overall Web site design to improve access to your streams.

When analyzing this section of the traffic report, you have to bear in mind a number of things. You should consider the location and prominence of the links to the content on your Web site. Media that is featured on your home page is almost always going to get more traffic than your archived programming. Also, any links to content that are *above the fold* (in the portion of the page that the user can see without having to scroll) will also be more popular. Another major factor in the popularity of a particular item is newness. Any time you post a new media clip to your site, it gets a flurry of traffic that gradually tapers off.

If you keep careful track of when you add new material and when you make changes to the layout of your Web pages, and correlate this information with the number of requests for particular files, you can devise an optimum schedule for rotating material. Over time, you'll learn the perfect spots to place links to material that you want to push. You'll also learn how long you can expect new content to draw a healthy number of hits, and take it out of the prime location once this amount of time has elapsed.

Error types

This part of your traffic report is very important, because errors mean lost traffic and possibly lost revenue. Your log analysis program can give you a breakdown of the different type of errors. A small percentage of errors is inevitable, but a large percentage of errors (more than two or three percent of total requests) may indicate serious problems that need your attention.

When the server can't find a file that a user requests, it generates a 404 error. Track down every 404 that you find in your error report and fix any bad links. If bad links keep cropping up, you may have problems in your site maintenance procedures. For example, staff members may be removing files or changing file names without notifying other staff members to change the corresponding HTML pages.

Browsers and media players

This part of a traffic report gives you a breakdown of what browsers and media players your visitors are using. This information can be useful for two reasons. If you notice that a large majority of your users are using a particular brand of browser, you may choose to optimize your HTML pages to look good in that browser. The breakdown of brands of media players should closely match the breakdown of streaming media file types delivered. As mentioned earlier in this section, if only a small percentage of visitors are using a certain media format, you may question whether it's worth the trouble of supporting that format.

You should also keep track of what version of browsers and media players your audience uses. It's important to keep track of these numbers, because this will tell you how important it is for you to support older client software. If you find that a lot of your viewers are still using older browsers or players, you'll want to continue to support them with compatible codecs and take it easy on implementing cutting-edge features that older systems don't support.

Operating systems

Knowing what operating systems your visitors are using can be useful for a couple of reasons. First, it gives you an idea of how important it is for you to cater for different platforms. For example, if you notice that only a tiny percentage of your visitors are Mac users, then you may decide not to bother offering QuickTime streams. On the other hand, you may decide to add QuickTime to your offerings to try to attract more Mac-heads.

Users, domains, and countries

Your traffic reports can show you the percentage of visitors coming from each type of domain (.com, .net, .org, and so on). You can also find out what countries your visitors are coming from, which can be helpful in planning content.

For U.S. sites, you'll find that most of your traffic comes from the United States, with smaller but significant amounts from the U.K., Canada, and Australia. The next countries on the list are almost always Germany and Sweden, followed by the other countries of Western Europe. Studying the international breakdown of your traffic can be valuable in a couple of situations.

If the percentage of your visitors coming from outside the United States is tiny, then specifically targeting international traffic (for example, by submitting your site to international search engines and directories) may be a good way to boost your overall traffic. In another scenario, you may find that some particular country or region places unusually high on the list. For example, if Spanish-speaking countries are placing in the top ten, you may try to take advantage of this by adding some Spanish-language content.

Some sophisticated programs (including WebTrends Reporting Center) attempt to tell you what cities or zip codes your visitors come from. They do this by comparing user IP addresses against a database containing the locations of various ISPs. This data can be interesting, but it isn't always very accurate because, as explained earlier in this chapter, the IP address that shows up in your log may represent some intermediate point rather than the location from which the user is actually connected. For example, most sites notice a large percentage of visitors from Virginia, which may be puzzling until you realize that America Online (AOL) has a main hub located in Virginia. Always take geographical breakdowns with a grain of salt.

Top referring sites (Web server logs)

One interesting thing that you can get out of your Web server reports that you cannot get out of your streaming server log files is the referring site. This tells you which search engines, directories, and links on other sites are sending you visitors. This information is critical to finding ways to increase traffic to your site.

Search engines and directories

Yahoo is the biggest search site, but obtaining a listing in their directory is tough. Sites fortunate enough to have a listing find that Yahoo sends them more traffic than any other site. Next on the list are the top search engines (Google, Excite, Altavista, Lycos, Infoseek). Each of these has a certain share of overall search engine traffic; you can find the latest figures for their relative importance at Search Engine Watch (http://searchenginewatch.com). The relative amount of traffic you receive from each search engine should roughly correspond to the relative amount of overall traffic each one currently has. If not, you may have a problem with your listing at one or more of these sites.

The most sophisticated log analysis tools can tell you not only which search engines are sending you traffic, but also what keywords people are searching on to find your site. If you analyze this information and use a little imagination, you can come up with all kinds of ideas for boosting your traffic.

Links from other Web sites

Next in the list of top referring sites, after the search engines, you'll find listings for various other sites that have links to yours. This section can be useful for verifying that people who said they'd give you a link actually did, and finding out whether those links are doing you much good. You may also find some sites listed in this section that you never knew had links to your site, so you can track down online reviews and other favorable or unfavorable mentions of your site. Following these links can lead to endless ideas for increasing your traffic and/or improving your content, although of course you'll never have time to pursue all of them.

Summary

This chapter introduced server log files and explained why they constitute an important tool that you can use to improve your content and increase traffic to your Internet site. You learned:

✦ You can generate log files with your streaming server(s) or with an associated Web server. By using a customizable ASCII log format, you can choose to record just the data that you need. You also learned some of the details of logging with different types of server software.

✦ Managing log files is a critical process that includes configuring your server to start new log files at set time periods, removing log files from the server, analyzing them by using a log analysis software package, and archiving historical log files.

✦ Many different log analysis (or traffic analysis) packages are available, from free software that runs on your Web server to highly sophisticated commercial products that consume large amounts of computing resources and should be run on a dedicated computer.

✦ The most important part of the log analysis process is examining the traffic reports that your analysis software generates, and combining that information with your knowledge of your content and your market to come up with ideas to improve your offerings and boost your user traffic.

✦　　✦　　✦

Advertising

Advertising has been a feature of the Internet almost
since the beginning and continues to be the most common way for Internet publishers to generate revenue. Web site
banner ads and text-based e-mail ads are familiar to Internet
users, ad agencies, and ad buyers. Advertising in conjunction
with streaming media is less mature, but because streaming
media incorporates both sequential (audio, video) and static
(text, images) forms of content, the possibilities for innovative
forms of advertising are even more exciting.

As a streaming media provider, you may have prime advertising real estate to offer. If your programming is popular, you
can make a case to an advertiser that it is worth them paying
to place an ad before, during, or after your programming. The
more popular your programming is, the higher premium you
can command for the advertising space.

Many commentators have published doom-and-gloom articles
about Internet advertising, bemoaning its slow growth or even
making the ludicrous assertion that it will never catch on. In
fact, it will be strange indeed if the Internet ever becomes the
only form of media known to man that isn't replete with
advertising. The growth of Internet ad revenues has been
comparable to what the advertising industry experienced
during the early days of other media, such as radio and television, although the recent economic slowdown has slashed
revenues throughout the entire advertising industry. However,
the Internet, and especially streaming media, still has a very
long way to go to achieve market saturation, so the potential
for future growth is gigantic.

On the other hand, it's easy to overestimate the amount of
revenue that you'll be able to realize from selling online ads.
The market is glutted with would-be advertising-supported
Internet properties. By no means are all content providers
who want to sell ads able to do so, and only a tiny fraction are
able to turn a profit. Taking full advantage of the latest ad
delivery technology is one way you can make your Internet
property stand out from the hordes who are trying to sell ads.

Ad Industry Practices and Terminology

In the few years since Internet advertising came into being, the advertising industry has very quickly adapted standards, procedures, and terminology from traditional media to the online world. Some Internet content providers deal with ad buyers directly, but most use the services of an ad agency or ad network. In either case, you need to be familiar with the established norms that govern the selling, creation, delivery, and evaluation of online advertising campaigns.

Terminology

The stereotype of the smooth-talking "ad agency type" in a polyester suit may or may not be accurate, but it's true that people in the ad industry have their own colorful jargon. To be taken seriously as a seller of ads, you need to speak their language, which includes the following terms:

✦ **Impression.** One delivery of one ad to one user.

✦ **Clickthrough.** The act of a user clicking an ad banner or an advertiser's hyperlink.

✦ **Clickthrough rate or click rate.** The number of clickthroughs divided by the number of impressions delivered within a given period. For example, if the clickthrough rate is one percent, that means that for every 100 users who viewed an ad, one user clicked on the advertiser's hyperlink, and presumably visited the advertiser's Web site.

✦ **CPM.** Cost per thousand impressions. This method is used to price advertising campaigns. For example, if an ad seller and buyer agree on a CPM of $10, then $10 buys 1,000 impressions, and $1,000 buys 100,000 impressions.

✦ **Cost per click (CPC).** An alternative pricing scheme by which the ad buyer pays according to the number of clickthroughs that an ad receives. This pricing method is far less attractive to an ad seller than the standard CPM method, so it's generally used only by ad networks that cater for low-value or low-volume Internet properties.

✦ **Creative.** Ad agency professionals use this word as a noun to refer to the actual media (for our purposes, a computer file) that comprises an ad. For example, for an audio ad, the creative consists of an audio clip.

✦ **Rich media.** A banner that consists of anything other than an image file, including banners that employ streaming media, scripting, Java, Flash, or HTML. Most low-end ad management software can deliver only image files.

✦ **Targeting.** The process of delivering a particular ad only to a particular group of users. Well-targeted ad campaigns deliver better value for an ad buyer, because they are delivered only to those users deemed the most likely prospects.

✦ **Branding.** The act of creating a (hopefully favorable) impression of a company in a consumer's mind. A branding element is anything that makes a consumer think of a certain company, such as a logo, symbol, or color scheme. Examples include IBM's blue color scheme, Apple's apple, and Gateway's cows.

✦ **Insertion order (IO).** A contract to purchase advertising. An IO generally specifies a number of impressions to be delivered over a certain time period at an agreed CPM.

✦ **Conversion rate.** The rate at which visitors to a site are converted into paying customers.

Ad agencies and networks

There is nothing stopping you from calling people up and trying to sell them advertising spots in your programming. However, even if you memorize all the terminology in the previous section, you'll probably have better luck if you work with an ad agency. Ad agencies work with both advertisers who want to place ads and the media outlets that have advertising space to sell.

A *full-service ad agency* is one that can deliver any and all advertising-related services that an ad buyer may need. Such an agency plans campaigns, matches ad sellers with buyers, designs and produces ads, and reports on the effectiveness of campaigns across all types of media. A full-service agency may coordinate Internet ads with ads in other media, including print, television, and much more.

Some agencies handle Internet advertising only, although many of these agencies are subsidiaries of a full-service agency. An ad agency may handle the technical business of serving online ads, or they may handle only the sales end, and leave it to you to deliver ads on your Internet site.

Many ad agencies only work with Internet sites that can guarantee a certain minimum amount of traffic, perhaps 100,000 page views per month. The largest, best-known ad agencies generally require minimum traffic of 1,000,000 page views per month. Sites with lower traffic who wish to sell advertising space may consider working with one of the smaller online *ad networks*. Agencies tend to match up ad buyers and sellers on an individual basis, but ad networks aggregate the traffic of many small Internet sites and offer a package deal to both buyers and sellers.

Note　For clarity's sake, we define ad agencies and ad networks here as two different things, but some writers use the terms interchangeably, and some companies offer both business models.

Unless your site has a substantial amount of traffic, your prospects of making money by selling ads are minimal. It's currently a buyer's market for online ads, and ad agencies and networks go in and out of business constantly. The large, reputable agencies won't work with low-traffic sites, and many of the small ad networks are financially shaky or have few clients. Carefully investigate an ad network or agency before you sign a contract and be skeptical of optimistic promises.

A couple of Internet ad agencies with well-established reputations and impressive client lists are:

✦ **RealMedia (**`http://realmedia.com/`**).** Recently merged with fellow giant 24/7 Media. Features their very advanced ad management software Open Ad Stream.

> Although the names are similar, there's no relation between RealMedia and RealNetworks.

✦ **DoubleClick (**`http://doubleclick.com/`**).** Features DART ad management software.

Adbility (`http://adbility.com/`) is a fairly comprehensive resource for everything to do with online advertising. It features a list of ad agencies and ad networks at all levels, including candid assessments of their programs and business prospects.

Gauging the effectiveness of online campaigns

Clickthrough rate is easy to measure, and it can provide a rough indication of the effectiveness of an ad or a campaign. For the first few years of online advertising's existence, agencies and buyers tended to rely on clickthrough figures when deciding how ad dollars should be spent. As the industry has matured, however, people have realized that clickthrough alone isn't a reliable yardstick, for several reasons:

✦ Clickthrough is affected by many factors, including ad content, ad newness, and ad placement (targeting).

✦ Good clickthrough does not guarantee good sales. The conversion rate of an ad buyer's Web site is also an important factor.

✦ When ad banners were a novelty, average clickthrough rates were very high. As Internet users became accustomed to seeing banners, clickthrough rates steadily declined, and currently average well below for the industry as a whole. Ad buyers are looking "beyond the banner" for more compelling advertising vehicles such as streaming media that can deliver better response rates.

✦ Just because an ad isn't directly generating traffic to an advertiser's site doesn't mean that it is worthless. Billboards and magazine ads are not clickable, and yet they yield results. Ad buyers now realize that online ads have branding value, as viewing the ads may reinforce a brand image in a consumer's mind.

Pricing online ads

CPM is the basic unit of pricing for many types of media, including online ads. CPM rates vary widely, from pennies to hundreds of dollars. Factors that influence the price that a particular Internet property can command include:

✦ **Targeting.** The narrower the slice of viewers, the more the ad is worth. Untargeted ads, such as those evenly distributed across a large ad network, command only low prices, but ads that can be shown to reach a small clearly-defined market segment can command very high CPMs.

✦ **Desirability of market segment.** Certain audiences are more highly prized by advertisers. For example, a site whose audience consists of affluent middle-aged viewers commands higher CPMs than a site that caters for cash-strapped college students.

✦ **Type of ad.** Mailing list ads have been shown to deliver better response rates than banner ads, so they command higher CPMs. Streaming audio or video ads enable advertisers to deliver compelling content, so they should command high CPMs.

✦ **Historical response rates.** Ad rates are negotiable, so if you can prove that you've delivered good clickthrough rates or better yet, good sales, you can boost your prices.

Deploying Streaming Media Ads

Streaming media and advertising may interact in three different ways:

✦ Streaming media may be a feature of an ad-supported Web site. Many Web sites contain streaming media content and also feature advertising, but they don't include ads in the actual streaming media content. Most music sites fit into this category.

✦ Streaming video can be used in an ad banner. Web ad banners are getting fancier all the time, and some now feature streaming video instead of the more common animated image format. Only the more advanced ad management systems are capable of serving video banners.

✦ Streaming media can include advertising, which can be static (ad banners) or sequential (in-stream ads).

In this chapter, I'm only concerned with the third scenario.

Types of streaming media ads

Your imagination is the only limit when it comes to creating ads, but all ads that you can insert in streaming media fall into two categories: *in-stream* ads, which consist of audio or video ads that appear either before or during a program and *graphic* or *text* ads that appear within a media player. For an insider's view of the effectiveness of audio ads, see the "Audio Ads Are Better Than Banners" sidebar.

In-stream ads

One unique feature of streaming media is the possibility of including an audio or video ad within a streaming media program. In-stream ads give advertisers more time and space to deliver their messages than banners do, and they also offer the possibility of repurposing existing radio or television ads. In-stream ads can incorporate all types of media, including clickable hyperlinks.

Different streaming servers provide different ways of inserting in-stream ads, as explained later in this chapter. Advanced ad management software packages can serve in-stream ads in addition to banners.

Media player ads

Most media players include one or more windowpanes that can display visual content of various kinds. The Windows Media Player (WMP) calls this the Now Playing pane, and the RealOne Player calls it the Presentation Area. When audio content is playing, the entire display window is available to show content, such as album covers, an artist's Web page — or ads. Even when video content is playing, you can insert banner ads outside or on top of the video display. Don't worry, there's always plenty of room for ads.

Many media players let users and/or Web publishers replace the standard user interface with a custom *skin*, which gives you even more opportunities to present branding elements, including graphical and text ads. However, the user is usually asked whether they want to install the new skin — there's no guarantee they will install your custom skin, particularly if they're attached to the skin they're already using.

Audio Ads Are Better Than Banners by Todd Herman

Banners and audio ads exist for the same reason — to connect people with products. However, only one — audio advertisements — is a proven entity with years of success and billions of dollars behind it. The other — banner advertisements — is a shot in the dark that has yet to really prove its worth. Audio ads put banners to shame, and here is why: correctly executed, Internet audio ads are radio ads on steroids.

Radio ads work, and the biggest brands know it. The easiest way to understand why audio ads are so much better is to examine the differences between the two mediums. For the sake of brevity, I will list the three most important.

✦ Audio ads are harder to ignore than banners.

✦ Audio ads can tell a story and sell, not just tease or trick like a banner.

✦ Because of the self-regulating ecosystem of broadcast entertainment, audio ads will not become junk impressions, as many banners have.

Audio ads: too sexy to ignore?

Want to get a date? Go into a bar sometime and sit in a corner, hold up a sign that says "Ask me why I'm so cool." If that doesn't work, try talking to people to whom you are attracted. Tell them about yourself and then track which method is more effective — and more fun. I'm betting on the latter. Ignoring someone who is talking to you is more difficult than ignoring someone who is holding up a sign. It is particularly hard to ignore a spoken message that is professionally created and well targeted towards you.

Well-done Internet audio ads, as part of an Internet radio broadcast for example, rely on the listener's familiarity with the programming in a way that banners cannot. At my former company, theDial, we achieved this familiarity by insisting that our hosts read the ads. This approach, coupled with a unique method for allowing listeners to respond to an ad ("Click the Go Button") built a huge track record of success with major Fortune 500 clients. Where banners were lucky to pull a 1 percent response rate, our average response rate was 5 percent, and we built campaigns that drew a 25 percent click through rate — an unheard of achievement, and the result of what we called "radio ads on steroids."

Audio ads can tell a story

Attorneys know that the best story wins the case. The same is true with advertising; the best story wins the sale. Now think of the banners you have seen. I'll bet you can't remember a single one of them. There is a reason for this: Banners don't tell stories, they are cheap come-ons. The creators of these banner ads do not have much of a choice — it is virtually impossible to tell a story in five to seven words. Audio ads don't share that limitation; they can tell a story about a product, why you need it and why your wife will track you down and kill you unless you buy it — today!

The only thing to which most banners aspire is tricking you into clicking. Again, try to remember a banner you have seen. In preparation for writing this I began to notice banners. Here are some examples of what I saw: "You have mail!" and "Your computer is running too slowly, click for help!" Which of those messages is selling anything beyond the click? No wonder so many agencies are buying banners on a cost-per-click basis; unless a click occurs, the banner has done nothing to promote a brand.

Audio ads, on the other hand, actually explain a product. They paint a picture and promote brands — even when someone doesn't click! That fact, combined with the well presented audio ad campaigns I have already described allowed my company to refuse cost-per-click advertising buys and instead take much more lucrative cost-per-thousand ad buys. We got paid to run a message and promote brands, not to tease someone into clicking.

Continued

Continued

The failure of banners to tell a story creates one more new phenomenon in advertising: I call it the bum-click. Consider the come-on banner; think of banner ads that use sex, in particular. A beautiful, silken-clad woman stares steamily at you from the top-right side of your computer. Copy reads, "Can you please her?" You look around the office, make sure no one is spying and click, then bammo, copy reads, "She wants color prints, not cheap black and white." How quickly do you surf away? The banner, though, has done its job and someone has collected a paycheck and you don't even remember the name of the printer. That is a bum-click, and agencies shouldn't waste client money on such bunk.

Broadcasting self-regulates against advertising clutter

Now, I don't want to start ranting but I just loaded my favorite home page and counted eight banner ads. I won't mention the advertisers, but the number is important. How many ads did I notice? One, maybe two. How many advertising *impressions* does the page claim to have made? How many do they bill for? Eight.

Officially, an impression occurs when an ad is seen, heard, or somehow absorbed, but almost all media guesses at whether or not an impression has actually been made. The banners on my home page are a bad example of impressions being made because the owner of that page could claim that eight impressions were created — even if I didn't notice a single ad. I call this a Junk Impression, and Junk Impressions have contributed to the ruin of the banner ad.

A *Junk Impression* is one that consumers are unlikely to have seen or, in the case of Web browsers, to even have appeared on the screen. For example, a banner hiding below all the content on a page is, IMHO, unlikely to be seen.

Junk Impressions were born like this: When online companies began to sell banner ads, a funny thing happened . . . they liked getting money. It bought hip stuff like quirky, tech-guy glasses. When the ad inventory "sold out" the banner sellers made a crucial mistake and broke the law of supply and demand. The marketing department said five fateful words: "Make room for more banners." Suddenly ads were appearing everywhere and creating, you guessed it, Junk Impressions.

The proliferation of Junk Impressions contributed to advertisers experiencing lower response rates and, in reaction, advertising rates soon dropped. Think about it: the more Junk Impressions (ads that are never, or rarely, seen), the more ads (money) it takes an advertiser to get a response. The people selling the ad inventory — more than a few of them never having worked in advertising and many now under pressure from Wall Street — said, "Rates are dropping? Well, no problem, we'll put more ads on the page." Do you see the circular logic being applied here? This circular logic was akin to a captain of a ship saying, "Icebergs? Well, speed the ship up and let's get out of here as quick as we can!"

There is no such thing as a bottom of the page audio ad, and because of that audio ads will never suffer the same fate as banners. It's not that radio people wouldn't love to fit more ads in, they would. Yet, unlike a Web page, too many commercials in an audio program spoil the show and radio programmers know this. Radio, by its very nature, limits the clutter and Junk Impressions. There are rare exceptions: I once heard 17 commercials in a row on Howard Stern but, as his sales people would say, Howard is compelling enough that people stay tuned. Web pages may well be just as compelling, but unlike Stern's show, the user can skip all the banner ads they want and never miss a word of content.

One thing about all those ads Stern played that is very important to note is this: He played them one at a time. It simply would not work if — as Web pages do — Stern played all his ads at once. How many audio ads can you absorb and understand at one time? The answer is one. Radio only plays one ad at a time; like the king and queen of the prom in the final, groping dance. The spotlight is on the advertiser. On the Internet, banners are like dancers in a packed disco; you may, or may not, focus on one particular dancer.

Audio ads aren't pixels on a page; they are loud town criers who won't be ignored. These town criers don't trick you with a three-word come on; they tell you a story and draw you in with a message. Audio ads, as town criers, don't stand on soapboxes all yelling at once; they talk to you clearly and one at a time. If you are listening, the impression is made.

Banner versus audio ads? Don't make me laugh.

Todd Herman has been in radio since 1991 and was most recently the CEO of theDial, a groundbreaking Internet Radio company that pioneered a new level of entertainment, interactivity and was among the first to welcome top brands like Proctor & Gamble, Sears, Muzak, and Hewlett Packard into the World of Internet Radio. TheDial, acquired by Loudeye Technologies, continues to provide private labeled Internet Radio to the Web's largest sites, amongst them: Prodigy, Excite, and Salon.com. In the early 90s, before changing Internet Radio, Herman helped modify the world of talk radio as a leading edge purveyor of the Hot Talk format. As a host, he is proud to have been banned from the Utah State House for life. He may be reached at Todd@mediagasm.com.

Integrating your ad servers and streaming servers

Ad management systems are designed to give URLs to Web servers requesting banner ads. With a little intelligence on the part of a streaming server, most ad management systems can also be used to insert advertising into streaming media presentations.

Here's how a typical ad management system works. A special tag on an HTML page instructs the server or browser to request an ad from the ad server. The ad server chooses the most appropriate ad based on various parameters that the site publisher has set in advance. The ad server then generates a snippet of HTML code containing the URL of the ad file (typically an image file) and the clickthrough URL (the address of the site that loads when a user clicks on the ad) and sends it to the Web server or browser to be displayed along with the rest of the HTML page.

Both the RealServer and WMS can pull ads from ad management software systems and dynamically combine them with streaming content. The main difference in the way the two major streaming servers handle ad insertion is that RealServer uses an extended version of the open standard Synchronized Multimedia Integration Language (SMIL), whereas WMS uses Microsoft's ASX language (both languages are based on XML).

Cross-Reference   Part VII discusses SMIL in detail.

WMS inserts advertising into streams by requesting URLs for advertising from an ad server and integrating this information into a .asx file that is sent to the Windows Media Player. This process is illustrated in Figure 21-1.

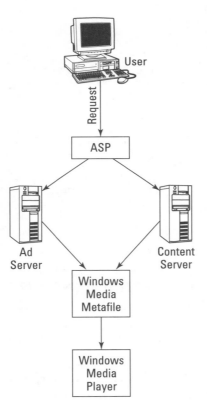

Figure 21-1: When a user requests a program, ASP or some other dynamic content generation tool pulls an ad from the ad server and combines it with a link to the requested content to create a Windows Media metafile.

Similarly, the RealServer can also request advertising URLs from an ad server and dynamically insert this information into a SMIL file that is sent to the RealPlayer. This process is illustrated in Figure 21-2.

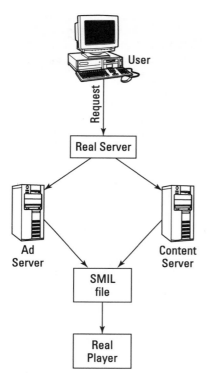

Figure 21-2: When a user requests a program that contains advertising, the RealServer pulls an ad from the ad server and automatically inserts the necessary code into the SMIL file.

These processes are discussed in a bit more depth later in this chapter.

Generating presentations dynamically

One of the simplest ways to insert advertising into streams is via metafiles. Both the RealSystem and Windows Media Technologies allow multiple entries in their metafiles. Windows Media metafiles also allow you to specify an ad banner to display while a particular clip is playing back. Inserting advertising into metafiles can be done by combining the URL of the clip the viewer wants to watch with a URL returned by an ad server.

You can also insert advertising into QuickTime and RealMedia presentations using the layout and timing abilities of SMIL. You can specify regions for banner ads or play ads before the programming. All you have to do is insert the URLs of the ads into the SMIL code.

For this process to be effective, it must be done dynamically because you don't want to serve the same ads in the same presentations over and over again. You need to be able to rotate many different ads, target specific ads to specific groups of users, and keep detailed records of the ads that are served.

There are many ways to do this. The RealServer has automatic file generation capabilities built-in, and Microsoft's Site Server, Commerce Edition, includes a feature called Ad Server, which you can use to schedule ads. You can also use one of the many dynamic content generation tools, which uses scripting to assemble content from pre-existing templates.

If you use Windows as your server platform, it is likely that you also use Active Server Pages (ASP) to serve dynamically generated content. ASP or another dynamic content-generation system can pull ads from any of the commercially available ad management systems (discussed later in this chapter) and combine them with streaming content to create metafiles.

If you use Unix as your server platform, you have a wealth of scripting technologies at your disposal.

Inserting ads with QuickTime

The QuickTime Server has no out of the box support for ad insertion systems. However, given the open source and plug-in architecture of QuickTime's code, a skilled programmer might consider modifying the code to allow the server to pull HTML code from an ad server and insert the necessary URLs into a SMIL file in a way similar to that which RealServer uses. Alternatively, you can write a simple utility that assembles SMIL files dynamically and sends them to the QuickTime player.

QuickTime 4.1 and later can play SMIL presentations, so you can use SMIL to create programs that include both banner and in-stream ads, and you can use dynamic content generation tools to create SMIL files dynamically.

 See Chapter 31 for tips on using SMIL with QuickTime.

Inserting ads with RealServer

There are a number of ways that advertising can be inserted into RealMedia files. The simplest way is to use metafiles to insert advertising streams before the requested streams. This method is somewhat limited, however, because the viewer can skip the advertising by dragging the playback indicator forward. In addition, you cannot implement banners to play in parallel with audio or video streams.

A better approach is to use SMIL to design your presentation, allowing time and/or space in your presentation for advertising. The RealServer has special functionality that enables it to query ad servers for URLs and insert them into the SMIL code using the `<RealAdInsert/>` tag. Both of these methods are discussed below.

Inserting in-stream ads using RealSystem metafiles

RealSystem metafiles can have more than one entry in them. The files included in the metafile are included in order. Therefore, to insert an advertisement before a music video, all you have to do is insert the URL for the advertisement before the URL for the music video:

```
rtsp://my.server.com/ads/zoom-zoom.ra
rtsp://my.server.com/videos/aimee_mann.rv
```

The RealPlayer plays these clips in order, however, the player buffers between each clip. In addition, the viewer can skip the ad by dragging the playback indicator forward, or by hitting the Page Down button. A much better way of implementing advertising is by using SMIL and the <RealAdInsert/> tag.

Inserting in-stream ads using SMIL and the <RealAdInsert/> tag

SMIL is a much more powerful way of inserting ads into RealMedia presentations because using SMIL you have control over the layout and the timing of your presentation. In addition, you can make it so that people cannot skip over the advertising.

SMIL is covered in detail in chapters 27–31 of this book.

The RealServer has an additional feature that works in conjunction with SMIL files to integrate your ad server system with your streaming media files. The way it works is that you author the SMIL code, inserting <RealAdInsert/> tags wherever you want an ad banner. You then place these special files in a special directory of the RealServer named adtag. The RealServer knows that files residing in this directory contain <RealAdInsert/> tags that must be replaced with URLs for ad banners.

When requests are made for files in the adtag directory, the RealServer automatically replaces each <RealAdInsert/> tag in the SMIL code with URLs requested from your ad server.

For a more detailed discussion of the <RealAdInsert/> tag, please turn to Chapter 31.

The <RealAdInsert/> tag is limited to working with images — you cannot insert audio, video, or Flash animation advertisements. To do this, you would have to dynamically generate the SMIL file using an automated content generation system.

Different ad management systems generate HTML code in slightly different ways, so RealServer gives you several options for configuring the ad extension feature. The RealServer Administrator includes a variable called Ad Server Type, which you can set to integrate RealServer with various ad management software products. Available settings include DoubleClick DART, DoubleClick Ad Server (formerly known as NetGravity), Engage, and AdForce, as well as three different generic settings.

RealServer includes a SMIL generation feature that can automatically create SMIL files that include ads. This enables you to insert ads into an entire library of existing streaming media without having to write SMIL files by hand.

Inserting ads using WMS

Linking to Windows Media files is done with metafiles that can control the playback of one or several individual Windows Media (.asf, .wma, .wmv, *et al.*) files. In Windows Media terminology these are known as *redirector* files. In addition to creating a *playlist* of media files that play in a specified order, you can set various parameters in the metafile that affect the behavior of the Windows Media Player during playback. Windows Media metafiles have many uses, one of which is inserting various types of ads into your streaming media programs.

Please turn to Chapter 15 for more information about metafiles.

Inserting in-stream ads using WMS metafiles

To insert audio or video ads into a streaming media program, use a metafile to create a playlist that includes links to the ad clips at the desired points, as in Listing 21-1.

Listing 21-1

```
<asx version="3.0">

<title>Video Clip Including an In-stream Ad</title>

    <entry clientskip="no">
        <ref href="mms://yourdomain.com/video_clips/ad_1.asf"/>
    </entry>

    <entry>
        <ref href="mms://yourdomain.com/video_clips/program.asf"/>
    </entry>

</asx>
```

This playlist contains two entries: the first entry plays our ad, a file called ad_1.asf. Note the clientskip="no" descriptor of the first entry element. This sneaky little feature prevents the user from skipping the ad by disabling three of the Media Player controls: Next Clip, Preview Mode, and the slider bar.

After the first entry has finished playing, the second one begins. This is our program, a file called `program.asf`. As this entry doesn't specify `clientskip="no"`, the user now has access to all the usual transport controls. The Media Player starts buffering the next entry while the first one is playing, which means that entries in a playlist follow one another with no pause in between.

Inserting banner ads using WMS

A Windows Media metafile also enables you to insert a banner ad that appears in the Media Player Now Playing pane, below the normal visual content. You do this by including a `banner` element as a child of the `entry` element, as in Listing 21-2.

Listing 21-2

```
<asx version="3.0">

<title>Video Clip Including a Banner Ad</title>

    <entry>
        <ref href="mms://yourdomain.com/video_clips/program.asf"/>

        <banner href="http://yourdomain.com/ad_banners/banner.gif">

            <moreinfo href="http://www.yourdomain.com"/>

            <abstract>Click here to go to our Web site.</abstract>

        </banner>
    </entry>

</asx>
```

The `banner` element specifies the location of the banner image file. The `banner` element has two child elements: `moreinfo`, which specifies the clickthrough URL for the banner, and `abstract`, which lets you specify a text message that will be shown as a tool tip when the user holds the mouse over the banner. Figure 21-3 shows an example of an ad banner in the Windows Media Player.

Figure 21-3: The Windows Media Player playing a song from a metafile. The Now Playing pane displays the artist and song title at the top, and an ad banner at the bottom. Note the tool tip (Click here to go to our Web site.), which pops up when the user moves the mouse over the banner.

Using skins and borders for advertising

Using the `banner` element in a metafile is an easy way to insert an ad banner into the Media Player Now Playing pane, but it's very limited. The banner appears in a fixed position, and can be no larger than 194 pixels wide by 32 pixels high. Windows Media provides a much more powerful way to add visual content to the Media Player. Using skins and borders is an involved process, but it gives you the power to display advertising or branding elements in just about any way you could want.

A *skin* is a custom user interface for a media player. You can create your own skins for the WMP, enabling you to make it look any way you like. A skin controls the appearance of the WMP application window, playlist, and user controls — everything *except* the Now Playing pane. A *border* is a special type of skin that controls the appearance of the Now Playing pane. The term border may be a bit misleading, because a so-called border enables you to place images not only around the edges of the visual content, but anywhere in the Now Playing pane, including directly on top of streaming video content. Only WMP Versions 7 and later support skins and borders. You can find more information about skins and borders at http://www.microsoft.com/Windows/windowsmedia/software/v7/P7Skins.asp.

Ad Management Software

The Internet makes delivering and tracking ads in extremely sophisticated ways possible, far more so than any other medium. Nowadays advertisers expect media providers to take full advantage of these capabilities, which requires that you use some sort of dynamic system to serve and track advertising.

You can set up an ad management system of your own by using a dynamic content delivery tool, such as CGI scripting or ASP, but most media providers prefer the additional power and convenience that a commercial ad management software package offers. An ad management system runs on your Web server or (preferably) on its own dedicated server, and automatically serves ads according to parameters that you specify.

As explained earlier in this chapter, most ad management systems are designed to serve ads to Web pages, but working together with an advanced streaming server, they are perfectly capable of inserting ads into streaming media programs. One caveat is that some lower-end packages are not capable of serving anything other than image files. Such a package would be able to insert banners into a streaming program, but not to insert streaming ads.

Ad management software features

Systems vary widely in the features that they offer, but basically their capabilities fall into four categories:

✦ Banner rotation

✦ Targeting

✦ Reporting

✦ Inventory management

Banner rotation

Banner rotation is the most basic feature that ad management software offers, but it is an important one. A very simple script can provide the ability to rotate several banners at random, but advanced ad management software can do much more. An advanced package enables you to specify how many impressions are delivered for each advertiser, and also for each individual banner within a campaign. It also delivers impressions evenly over a given time period. For example, if an advertiser buys 100,000 impressions within a month, they don't want to see all 100,000 delivered in the first week. As site traffic fluctuates from day to day, an ad management system must constantly estimate how many daily impressions it must deliver for each ad to deliver the required number within the specified time period.

Targeting

The ability to serve a particular ad to a narrowly defined group of users is the most exciting aspect of online advertising, and advanced targeting features are one of the things that separate the high-end ad management products from the (much) cheaper offerings. As explained earlier in this chapter, the more precise targeting you can do for a campaign, the higher the CPM you can command. Ads can be targeted in several different ways.

Day/time targeting

Targeting ads to specific times and/or specific days of the week is easy and effective. Most ad serving products enable you to specify certain days of the week or times of day when a particular ad is delivered. If you're serving campaigns that target particular geographic regions, try to deliver them during prime Internet usage times within the relevant time zones (9 a.m. to 5 p.m. weekdays for business users, evenings and weekend afternoons for home users).

Content-based targeting

Matching ads to related content is one of the most effective targeting strategies of all. For example, serve an ad for skateboards with the latest boy band video, and serve an ad for Cadillacs with Sinatra (or whatever kind of music Cadillac buyers like). Advertisers often specify the demographic they want to reach. Alternatively, ad agency staff may make the judgments about which content matches which market segment, and tell you exactly what areas of your site they want you to place a particular campaign on.

There are several ways to identify files or groups of files to your ad management program. Simpler systems require you to use different tags for different items of content, but top-end systems maintain a database of all content on your site, automatically extract the URL of each file requested, and choose an appropriate ad.

IP targeting

In Chapter 20, you learned that every time a user requests a file from an Internet server, the server can glean various bits of information about the user, including the domain the user is connecting from, and the user's operating system, browser and/or media player. Advanced ad management systems can use this information for targeting in several ways. For example, you can show localized ads to users based on the country they are connecting from, or operating system-specific ads based on the user's OS.

As discussed in Chapter 20, a user's domain, OS, and software version can give you a rough idea of the demographic group to which the user belongs. For example, you might assume that Unix users are likely to be IT professionals and show them ads for computer products. Stretching your imagination a little further, you may reason that someone connecting through AOL and using an outdated OS version is likely to be an older person; you can show this user ads targeted to an older age group.

User behavior profiling

Some programs can follow a user's path through an Internet site and use this information to build a profile that lists the pages the user visited, the ads they viewed, and so forth. The information can be stored in a cookie and used to select content when the user visits a site again in the future.

Chapter 20 discusses cookies.

One simple use of this information is to serve a visitor a new ad each time he or she requests a stream. A more sophisticated application is to serve targeted ads based on the type of content a user has requested in the past (the Sinatra fan sees the Cadillac ad). Some ad agencies even maintain a database of user profiles collected from many different sites.

Registration-based targeting

Many sites give their users the option to register and provide some information about themselves. This information can be used for targeting. For example, you mayt ask users their gender, age group, and what part of the country they live in. Keep in mind that many Internet users are concerned about privacy and may deliberately provide incorrect information if required to register to use a site. Make any information that you plan to use for targeting optional and tell your users that you plan to use the information to tailor content to their interests. This reduces the incentive to lie and encourages users to provide accurate information.

Well-run Internet sites have a consistent privacy policy that governs how they use information that they collect from users. If you ask users to provide personal information, be sure to provide a prominent link to your site's privacy policy. People are more inclined to provide accurate information if they believe you'll use it responsibly. A user is much more likely to give you a correct e-mail address if you promise not to pass it on to spammers, and also allow them to opt out of any e-mail-based marketing that you do.

As is the case with log file data, which you learned to analyze in Chapter 20, targeting features are only useful to the extent that you make sound judgments about what kind of ads you should target to certain groups of users. Do Sinatra fans really like Cadillacs, or is that just your imagination? Educate yourself with as much market research data as you can and incorporate the information you've gleaned from your traffic reports into your decision-making.

Reporting

The simplest ad management programs generate reports of impressions and clickthroughs. Figure 21-4 shows a basic daily ad report generated by Central Ad 4.0. The fancy products create Web-based reports complete with attractive tables and graphs. A full-featured ad management package can show figures for any desired time period and can break things down by individual banners or groups of banners as well as by any of the targeting criteria discussed in the previous section. The sophisticated products can also generate graphs to show trends, for example, how clickthrough rates fluctuate over time.

Central Ad 4.0 Statistical Report Center - Microsoft Internet Explorer

Daily Report

DATE	REGION	CAMPAIGN	ACCOUNT	BANNER	Views	Clicks	Rate
05/09/1999	n/a	n/a	BURST_Media	f_code	9	0	0.00%
	Default	Default	Default	Default	0	10	0.00%
	Front_page	BURST	BURST_Media	a_code	807	0	0.00%
				b_code	776	0	0.00%
				c_code	1095	0	0.00%
		Flycast	Flycast	tag1	1102	0	0.00%
		MadGames	MadGames	MadGames	29	8	27.59%
	Index_pages	BURST	BURST_Media	a_code	741	0	0.00%
				b_code	726	0	0.00%
				c_code	1036	0	0.00%
		Flycast	Flycast	tag1	622	0	0.00%
		MadGames	MadGames	MadGames	38	1	2.63%
				Total	6981	19	0.27%

DATE	REGION	CAMPAIGN	ACCOUNT	BANNER	Views	Clicks	Rate
05/10/1999	n/a	n/a	BURST_Media	a_code	1	0	0.00%
				f_code	2	2	100.00%
			MadGames	MadGames	4	0	0.00%
		BURST	BURST_Media	b_code	1	0	0.00%
	Default	Default	Default	Default	114	17	14.91%
	Front_page	BURST	BURST_Media	a_code	1170	0	0.00%
				b_code	1167	0	0.00%

Figure 21-4: A daily report generated by Central Ad 4.0, showing impressions, clickthroughs and clickthrough rates for individual banners belonging to several separate campaigns.

Your ad management system needs to generate several different kinds of reports. Each advertiser needs to see figures only for their own ads, whereas you and your staff need to be able to see figures for individual campaigns and for your site as a whole. Ad agency staffers need to see reports that compare results from different sites.

Advanced ad management systems generate reports on an ongoing basis, so you can access up-to-the-minute figures on the Web. They also allow you to customize reports to suit your needs, so you don't have to slog through a bunch of data you don't need. Ad reports are a valuable tool, and if you monitor them continuously, you can often improve the effectiveness of your campaigns, for example, by replacing poorly performing ads with others or by fiddling with the targeting.

Inventory management

Your *ad inventory* is the number of potential ad impressions that you expect to deliver within a certain time period. This is a round figure somewhat lower than your total site traffic. For example, if you have been serving an average of 220,000 streams per month and you insert one ad per stream, then you might calculate your available inventory as 200,000. Ads are usually sold in round figures, and advertisers like to see a little bit of over-delivery (and consider under-delivery a catastrophe).

This may sound simple enough, but if you have several campaigns running, each with different start and end dates and each targeting different sections of a site, it can quickly become impossible to calculate how much inventory you have available off the top of your head. Promising more impressions than you can deliver is a disaster, and so is passing up an ad sale opportunity unnecessarily. When an ad agency calls to find out how much inventory you have available, they generally expect an instant answer. The best ad management systems can tell you how much inventory you have available for any subset of your site's content.

Ad management software products

Available products range from free CGI scripts to extremely sophisticated, expensive solutions. If your needs are very simple, try Random Image Displayer (`www.worldwidemart.com/scripts/image.shtml`), a free product that's been around a long time. Central Ad 4.0 (`http://centralad.com/`) is a very capable product considering its bargain price, and it's been garnering good reviews for a while. If you have a higher budget, you may want to consider Ad Juggler (`http://adjuggler.com/`), a full-featured system in the medium price range that's also stood the test of time. Adbility (`http://adbility.com/`), mentioned earlier in this chapter, features a list of ad management software products in all price ranges.

The really high-end ad management systems are very powerful and complicated software packages. Like high-end log analysis programs, a lot of computing power is needed, and running them on a dedicated machine is best. Some run on Unix, some on Windows, but they can insert ads in content hosted on any OS. The big-time ad programs are notoriously difficult to install, configure, and maintain. Getting them to work with your system is likely to require a good bit of technical support and possibly even some custom programming.

Like most types of software these days, you can buy ad management as a service instead of purchasing and running the software in-house. Considering the complexity of the high-end systems and their enormous price tags, most content providers find this an attractive option. An added incentive to outsource your ad management is the fact that most of the top-end ad management software products are now owned by ad agencies, for example DoubleClick's DART (`http://doubleclick.com`) and Real Media's Open Ad Stream (`http://realmedia.com/`). Although these agencies do offer the software for sale, a more common scenario nowadays is for the agency to host ads and handle all ad management duties as part of the package they offer to their clients. Doing so enables an ad agency to manage ads and report ad traffic across many Internet sites, and in some cases, to share targeting data among different sites.

Summary

This chapter discussed online advertising, especially as it relates to streaming media providers. You learned that:

✦ Online advertising is an established industry with its own generally accepted practices and terminology. Ad agencies and networks handle the business of matching ad sellers with buyers.

✦ Clickthrough rate is easy to measure and is often used to judge the effectiveness of online ad campaigns. Clickthrough rate, however, is not the sole indicator of whether a campaign is achieving its goals.

✦ Ad prices are based on cost per thousand impressions (CPM). The CPM rate that a particular Internet property can command depends on several factors, including the desirability of the audience, the targeting options available, the type of ads offered (text, banner, and streaming), and the property's historical performance.

✦ You can insert two kinds of ads into streaming media: in-stream ads, consisting of audio or video (in some cases Flash animation) ads that appear before or during a streaming program and banner or text ads that appear in the media player window.

✦ WMS, RealServer, and QuickTime all enable you to insert ads into streaming programs and can pull ads from most ad management software products.

✦ To deliver ads in a professional manner, you need some type of ad management software package that offers features such as banner rotation, targeting, reporting, and inventory management.

✦ Ad management products range from free scripts to sophisticated and expensive solutions. Ad management is also available as a service, and this model is the norm for the top-end packages.

✦   ✦   ✦

Other Datatypes: It Is Not Just Audio and Video Anymore

◆ ◆ ◆ ◆

◆ ◆ ◆ ◆

Streaming Animation with Flash

Flash animation is everywhere these days, not only as a streaming media data type but also as the basis of many Web sites. The reason that flash animation is so popular is because it delivers very rich presentations with a minimum amount of data, which makes it an attractive data type for the Internet.

This chapter begins by briefly explaining how Flash works before showing how it is used with two of our streaming systems. You must be careful when authoring for streaming media presentations, because Flash can be CPU intensive, and the bit rate can be uneven. However, with a little planning and extra attention to detail you'll be streaming animation in no time.

Note   This chapter assumes you have a working familiarity with Flash authoring. As much fun as teaching you Flash would be, that is best left to another book, such as the *Flash MX Bible* by Robert Reinhardt and Snow Dowd, coming soon to a store near you.

How Flash Works

Flash is, among other things, a vector-based animation program. Instead of sending pictures across the Internet, the instructions about how to draw the pictures are sent instead.

The simplest way to understand vector animation is to imagine an image with a circle in the middle. Compare the amount of data required to send this via video versus vector-based animation:

✦ A frame of video has to send each and every pixel of information. Even if the frame is heavily compressed, it is still a fairly large file. If the video file has to be heavily compressed for low bit rate streaming, the image quality will suffer.

✦ A vector-based frame only has to send five things: a message saying that a circle is being sent, the location of the center of the circle, the radius, the background color, and the color inside the circle. This information is sent in just a few bytes.

Of course, the streaming media player that receives the information has to know how to draw a circle, and the program has to use CPU cycles to actually draw the circle. This is one of the things that you have to beware of when you author Flash files — a lot less information is sent, but the tradeoff is that the client-side machine has to do work to draw the presentation. This is generally not a problem unless the animation is complex or uses a lot of special effects.

Using vector-based animation allows Flash to scale gracefully. Going back to our circle example, if you double the size of the video, the imperfections in the compression become more obvious. However, with vector-based animation, the circle is described in terms of a radius and a color. If the frame size doubles, all the streaming media player must do is double the radius before it draws the circle. This scalability enables the streaming media player to draw the circle perfectly every time, no matter what the frame size.

Flash does more than just vector-based animation. You can also animate bitmaps (JPEG images, for example) and create all sorts of interactivity by using Flash action scripts.

Most of this power, such as interactivity, is still available when you combine Flash with streaming media. Some things, such as embedded sounds for button rollovers, are not. One of the frustrating things about getting Flash and streaming media to work together is that they are on different development cycles, and the latest version of one may not include the latest improvements of the other.

Streaming Flash with RealFlash

Flash first started streaming in 1997 with the introduction of RealFlash, which combined the streaming technology of RealNetworks with the animation prowess of Macromedia. Since 1997, both companies have come out with many new versions.

Flash support in the RealSystem was limited to Flash 2.0 for a while, but this is no longer the case. You can now render and stream Flash 4 files by using the RealPlayer and RealServer. Flash 5, however, has not yet been implemented.

Note   Streaming Flash 3 or 4 requires RealServer and RealPlayer 8 or later. Earlier versions of the server only stream Flash 2 files; RealPlayer G2 prompts the user to upgrade to the latest RealPlayer when it encounters a Flash 3 or 4 clip.

The following sections provide an overview of how to create and stream RealFlash. You may also control the RealPlayer via Flash, and even perform secure transactions. To find out more about this, please refer to the RealSystem Production guide, available from the RealNetworks Web site (www.realnetworks.com).

Understanding how Flash works with the RealSystem

Streaming Flash in the RealSystem involves streaming the animation as an SWF (Shockwave Flash) file, along with the audio track as a RealAudio file. The two are married together using either a RAM file or SMIL. When a RealPlayer requests the audio and animation files, the server serves them in parallel. The RealPlayer synchronizes the two incoming streams, ensuring synchronized playback.

This is different than Flash animations coming off a Web server. With streaming Flash the viewer may stop, fast forward, rewind, or pause the stream as with any other streaming data type.

Although Flash supports embedded sounds for button clicks, rollovers, and so on, the RealSystem does not support sound embedded in the Flash clip. The audio must all be contained in the accompanying RealAudio file.

RealFlash creation considerations

RealSystem 8 supports Flash 4 files. Therefore, when creating Flash for playback in the RealPlayer, you should not use any Flash 5 features. If you do, this functionality is discarded when you render the animation as a RealFlash file, and your animation may not turn out the way you intended.

Caution RealPlayer does not support Flash 5 features.

Also bear in mind that the RealPlayer only controls the Flash movie's main timeline. If you develop animation on individual Movie Clip timelines, the RealPlayer cannot control them. You have to include separate controls to play back these animations. Therefore, you should probably stick to developing animations for the RealPlayer on the Main Timeline.

Audio

When authoring Flash animations that you plan on streaming, you should stick to using high-quality uncompressed source sounds. Many Flash animators use low quality MP3 files with their animations This is a good approach for non-streaming Flash presentations, because the reduced file sizes of the MP3 files keep the size of the downloadable Flash file relatively small.

Exporting to RealFlash, however, involves encoding the audio into RealAudio format. If you use MP3 files, they must be transcoded to the RealAudio format. Because it is encoded twice (once into MP3, once into RealAudio), transcoded audio doesn't sound as clear.

If you must use a particular MP3 file as your musical backing track, you should reference it directly in the SMIL file, provided you have a high enough bit rate available.

Video

If a Flash animation consists only of vector graphics, the resultant streaming file has a very low bit rate. However, you have to be careful if you use bitmapped images. Each of the bitmapped images must be downloaded to the player before they can be used.

The data rate of Flash tends to be spiky — this is because each new scene generally involves a number of new images, followed by instructions on how to animate the images. The images are relatively high bit rate, and the instructions very low bit rate. If you looked at a graph of the file's bit rate, each scene change would be represented by a spike. This can cause problems if you're not careful, particularly if you have other streams playing in parallel with the animation.

Of course, there are a number of steps you can take to avoid this spiky behavior and get the best performance out of your streaming flash files. To learn more about this, please see the "Optimizing Flash Content for Streaming" Expert Tutorial.

Expert Tutorial: Optimizing Flash Content for Streaming by Janet Galore

Flash is uniquely well suited for delivering great animation at slower than broadband connection speeds. But to get that performance, you need to optimize your content to take advantage of how Flash works and your audience's viewing environment.

Streaming Flash needs to abide by many of the same constraints that streaming video does and has some additional constraints of its own. The big three constraints for streaming Flash are:

✦ Average bit rate must be low

✦ Don't max out the CPU

✦ Bit rate needs to be consistent

Streaming Flash involves splitting the animation and audio components into two separate files, or tracks. The audio track is encoded to stream at a constant rate, but the animation track needs to be optimized by hand so it streams nicely with the audio track. As a Flash author you need to coax your animation files into being as lean and smooth as possible before publishing them with streaming audio.

Don't hog the bandwidth

Because streaming Flash has a separate audio track, the animation track *plus* the audio track must add up to be no more than your overall bit rate constraint. If you are authoring for a 56 Kbps stream, then the overall bit rate should be 34 Kbps maximum (accounting for Internet overhead). If you use 16 Kbps for the audio, that leaves only 18 Kbps (or 2.25 KB/s) for the animation stream! If you are a seasoned Flash animator, you are used to balancing audio versus visual compression. However, you don't get to cheat by preloading data in streaming Flash. You need to keep a close eye on the bandwidth your Flash visuals are consuming.

Note: Check out Appendix B for suggested maximum bit rates for different audiences.

A quick way to calculate the average bit rate of your animation file is to use the Bandwidth Profiler in the Test Movie window in Flash.

1. **First, make sure that you have disabled the sound in the Publish Settings — you are only concerned with the animation track.**

2. **To test your movie in Flash, choose Control ⇨ Test Movie to bring up the Movie Test window.** If the movie starts playing automatically, press Escape or Enter to pause it.

3. **Next, choose View ⇨ Bandwidth Profiler.** Doing so shows you the size (KB) and duration (secs) of your movie.

4. **Divide the size in KB by the duration in seconds and then multiply by 8 to get your bit rate in Kbps.**

```
(size in KB) ( (duration in secs) ( 8 = Average bitrate in Kbps))
```

Because sound often takes up most of the bandwidth in Flash, you'll probably find your animation track is well within your bit rate limit. But if not, it's likely due to one of the following issues:

✦ You've used too many bitmap images, or the images files are too large. Compress JPG images as much as possible, or try using GIF images instead, which often compress to smaller files, though sometimes with an accompanying reduction in quality.

✦ There are a lot of complex vector graphics, often created by tracing bitmaps or importing complex vector files. Complex vector graphics can take a lot of bits to send, thereby increasing your bit rate. You can use the Optimize Curves feature to reduce the number of curves making up vector shapes. Select your shape in edit mode and then use the Modify ⇨ Optimize menu. In general, avoid tracing complex bitmaps in Flash.

✦ Your animation is too complex or uses too many keyframes. Limit your use of keframe animation and use *tweening* in moderation. Tweening is when Flash interpolates between two keyframes to create an effect, which is computationally complex. Be sure that you're using symbols as much as possible. When symbols are downloaded, they do not contribute further to the bandwidth and can be used again for free.

Continued

Continued

Optimizing your Flash file for bandwidth is only the first piece of the streaming puzzle — you also have to make sure that it plays back smoothly on your viewers' computers.

Don't hog the CPU

One reason Flash movies are so small is that data is not repeated over and over throughout the movie — it's object-oriented. A side effect, however, is that Flash needs the user's processor to do a lot of extra work. Whenever you use tweening, a color effect, or a fade up, Flash creates the effect in real time, causing a draw on the user's processor. If you do too much tweening or if the user has a slow processor, your movie will not play back well. This poor-playback problem is particularly noticeable with streaming Flash, because the CPU is already busy decompressing the audio track.

Flash is by definition fairly processor intensive, but some Flash effects are worse than others when it comes to CPU usage:

✦ **Tweens, pans, and zooms.** Tweens create effects, such as fades, zooms, pans, and motion along a curve. The more you tween, the faster the user's processor needs to be to keep up. Keep motion, zooms, and fade up effects to a minimum and test your movie in a streaming environment to see how it performs on a slower machine.

✦ **Big gradient fills.** Gradients and alpha effects also require processing power. Instead of a sky that fades out into darkness, try getting that effect by using a bitmap or use a solid color. Try to avoid using transparent or translucent objects in your movie and be aware of how they might affect playback on a slow computer.

✦ **Frame rate.** The frame rate can tax the user's processor if it is too high. Using a slower frame rate gives the computer a few less calculations to do per second. RealNetworks recommends using between 7–9 frames per second (fps), which works well for simple animation.

Smooth it out

The object-oriented nature of Flash does not naturally generate a file that has a consistent data rate — each time new graphics or event sounds appear in the file, there is a spike in the bit rate. To help combat the uneven nature of Flash's data rate, RealNetworks provides a Flash tuner that helps to smooth out the data rate of your SWF file, and Flash 5 has a Publish to RealPlayer option that tunes your file automatically.

Nevertheless, you'll get much better performance if you do some hand tuning as you author the animation. Before you publish your file, first look for spikes in the Flash Bandwidth Profiler. As outlined earlier, to view your file in the Bandwidth Profiler:

1. **Check that your Export Movie or Publish Settings are what you want them to be (sound should be disabled).**

2. **Click on Control ⇨ Test Movie.** Doing so opens a new window with your Flash movie exported according to your settings.

3. **The movie automatically begins playing, so press Escape or Enter to pause it.**

4. Click on View ⇨ Bandwidth Profiler. Doing so brings up bandwidth profiling information at the top of the window.

5. Click on any of the frames in the profiler to see how much data is being loaded in that frame.

You'll see a graph at the top of the window showing a red line (that's your maximum bit rate, as set in the Debug menu), and how much data each of your frames takes up (see the following figure). Every time a frame goes above the red line, that's a data spike, which you want to minimize as much as possible. Those spikes are going to force the Flash-audio stream to pause for the data to load there and rebuffer.

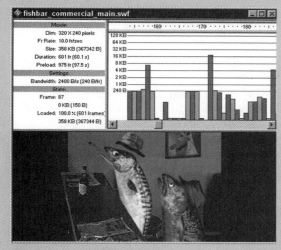

The Flash Bandwidth Profiler
"FishBar" image ©2001 Honkworm International.

Look at which frames are causing spikes. By using the optimization techniques mentioned above, you can reduce the file size of the objects being loaded in those frames.

Another way to smooth out your bit rate is to shift where your objects are loaded. Loading multiple images in the same frame causes huge bandwidth spikes. By loading some of the images in earlier frames, *before* they are needed, you distribute the data so the images aren't loaded all at once.

To do this, find the frame causing the spike and copy one of the symbols you are loading there. Go back 10 or 15 frames (or more if the symbol has a large file size). Paste the symbol into a new layer beneath your background or paste it into a layer and move the symbol to the back, so the symbol is beneath any other symbols on that layer and is completely hidden. Flash will now load the symbol on the earlier frame, before it is needed in the later frame. When you check the movie again in the Bandwidth Profiler, you'll see two much smaller spikes, which are better than one large one.

Continued

Continued

Just remember, to get your Flash file ready to stream, you want to keep the file size small, the bit rate low, and the data rate as smooth as possible. By combining all the techniques outlined in this tutorial, you should be able to get your Flash files streaming without a hitch.

Janet Galore is a digital media maven with a background in virtual reality, computer games, and streaming media. She began animating in Flash in 1997 and has always enjoyed pushing Flash to its limits. She directed and animated nearly 40 animated episodes for Honkworm International, an online entertainment company in Seattle and created the "photosurrealistic" art direction of Honkworm's "FishBar" series. Janet's animation has won numerous awards and has appeared in the Sundance Online Film Festival, ResFEST, and FMX2K in Germany. Janet is currently creating new Flash animations as well as writing, directing, and producing. She can be reached at jgalore@t-minus.com.

Exporting RealFlash files

Prior to Flash 5, creating RealFlash presentations was a time-consuming process that involved separating the audio from the animation, exporting the animation without the audio, exporting the audio as a WAV file, and then tuning the whole presentation to make sure that it streamed well. With Flash 5, you can export tuned SWF files and encoded RealAudio files automatically.

 Caution Please note that although the Flash 5 authoring tool exports tuned SWF files and RealAudio files, the RealPlayer does not support Flash 5 features. If you author your Flash animation using Flash 5 features, they are ignored when you export your tuned SWF file.

To export directly from Flash 5, all you have to do is set your publishing settings correctly. First, you must choose the right publishing formats, then set the parameters for the flash export, and finally choose the encoding parameters for the RealAudio export.

1. **Open the Publish Settings window by choosing Publish Settings from the File menu (see Figure 22-1).**

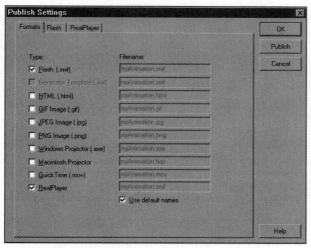

Figure 22-1: The Publish Settings window

2. **Make sure that both the Flash and RealPlayer boxes are checked.** You should see the RealPlayer tab appear after you check the RealPlayer box.

3. **Click on the Flash tab to bring up the Flash export settings (see Figure 22-2).** This page enables you to set the bitmap image qualities and audio export formats. You need to make sure to keep the following points in mind:

   - Choose an appropriate JPEG quality for your images. You can lower the value later if your file does not stream well.

   - Export raw stereo audio for encoding into the RealAudio format.

   - Disable any event audio and override any sound settings you may have specified in your Library.

   - Choose Flash 4 if you have RealServer 8 or higher. If you are using an older version of RealServer, select Flash 2.

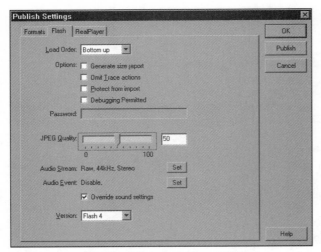

Figure 22-2: The Flash Export Settings window

4. **If you're using bitmapped images, you can specify an export quality on this page.** Set the audio stream export quality to Raw, 44 kHz, stereo and disable the Audio Event stream. To set these, click on the Set button to the right of each setting. Doing this brings up the Sound Settings window (see Figure 22-3).

Figure 22-3: The Sound Settings window

You should also check the Override sound settings box and select an appropriate Flash version to export to.

5. **After you've set the Flash Export settings, click on the RealPlayer tab to bring up the RealFlash Settings window (see Figure 22-4).** With this tab, remember to do the following:

   • Make sure that the Export Tuned Flash is checked and set an approximate bit rate for the flash.

   • Make sure the Adjust bit rate... box is checked. This feature enables you to adjust the bit rate depending on the pre-roll figure quoted.

   • Make sure to check the Export Audio box and choose the encode parameters as you would with the RealSystem Producer.

   • Make a decision as to whether you want to export a simple SMIL file or not.

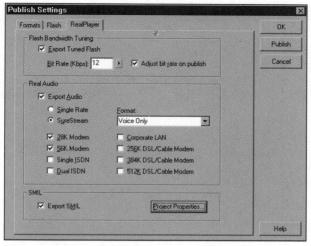

Figure 22-4: The Publish Settings window

Choose settings for the audio just as you would by using the RealSystem Producer. When you're done, click the Publish button.

6. **The program does some calculations and then brings up the Publish for RealPlayer window (see Figure 22-5).** This page enables you to adjust the buffer time by adjusting the bit rate. You should aim for a buffer time of seven seconds or less.

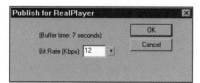

Figure 22-5: The Publish for RealPlayer window

You don't have to have a buffer time of seven seconds — you can buffer for as long as you like, or more importantly as long as you think your audience will wait. Seven seconds is a good target because that is the amount of time the RealPlayer buffers audio and video.

If you can't strike a good balance between the bit rate and the buffer time, you might have to try some optimization techniques, such as reducing the frame rate or reducing the quality of your bitmapped images (see the "Optimizing Flash Content for Streaming" tutorial earlier in the chapter).

7. **Click the OK button, and the program renders out the files.** All you have to do is place the files on a RealServer, and they're ready to stream.

Authoring Real presentations with Flash content

After you have your tuned Flash file and your audio file, you must instruct the RealPlayer to play them back at the same time. To do this, you use a SMIL file.

 Note Flash 5 will automatically generate a SMIL file for you if you check the Export SMIL checkbox at the bottom of the RealPlayer tab of the Publish Settings window (see Figure 22-4).

SMIL (Synchronized Multimedia Integration Language) is an open, standardized language for combining multiple data types into a single multimedia file. SMIL offers both layout and timing control. A simple SMIL file to play back the SWF animation and the RealAudio in parallel looks like this:

Cross-Reference SMIL is covered in detail in Chapter 27 through Chapter 31 of this book.

```
<smil>
<body>
<par>
    <audio src="rtsp://my.realserver.com/myAnimation.rm" />
    <ref src="rtsp://my.realserver.com/myAnimation.swf" />
</par>
</body>
</smil>
```

This code instructs the RealPlayer to play back the audio and animation clips in parallel. The layout section of this file has been left out for simplicity's sake, and in fact, because only one of the clips has a visual element, you can safely leave this section out. The player defaults to opening up to the size of the flash presentation.

This code can be typed into a simple text editor and saved with the `.smil` file extension. The SMIL file can then be placed on a RealServer or a Web server. When the RealPlayer parses this file, it finds two file references inside and requests them from the RealServer.

SMIL enables you to combine more than one visual track and define complex timing for your presentation. You can add text, pictures, and many other data types to your presentation using SMIL.

Using Flash with QuickTime

Beginning with QuickTime 4, you can play Flash files with the QuickTime player. The catch is, however, Flash files cannot be streamed using RTSP; they can only be played locally or downloaded using HTTP. However, there is no law against mixing and matching your protocols. You can easily create a presentation where the audio is streamed off of a QuickTime server while the animation is downloaded from a Web server.

Note Although the QuickTime player plays QuickTime movies streamed off a RealServer, it cannot play Flash movies streamed by a RealServer.

Usually, when watching content streamed off of a Web server you do not have any control over the delivery, such as fast forwarding or rewind. In this case, the QuickTime player synchronizes the two streams — if either stream rebuffers, the other pauses until the other is ready to stream again.

If you seek forward into the stream coming off the media server, the presentation pauses while the player buffers packets from the media server, and also from the Web server if the animation has not yet been completely downloaded. Synchronization is maintained throughout the presentation.

There is a slight catch, in that you can only combine Flash and on-demand streaming QuickTime presentations in QuickTime Player Pro. To add Flash to live streams requires a special tool, such as LiveStage Pro or Adobe GoLive.

The following two sections combine a streaming audio track with a Flash animation. You can also combine Flash tracks with video, for example to create a Flash background for your movie displays. You can also control the playback of the QuickTime movie via embedded Flash commands.

You can combine these two technologies many ways, but this book doesn't have enough space to enumerate them. If, after playing around with the following two examples your curiosity is aroused, you'll find a number of good reference books available that have more space to devote to this particular combination.

Cross-Reference Please turn to Bonus Chapter 5 on the CD-ROM for a list of additional resources.

Combining Flash and streaming QuickTime via reference movies

To combine Flash and QuickTime via reference movies, all you have to do is combine the reference movies by copying and pasting, similar to what we saw in Chapter 14 when adding HREF tracks.

1. **Create both your audio backing track and your Flash animation and put them on the appropriate servers — the animation on a Web server, and the audio on a QuickTime server.**

2. **Open up QuickTime Pro and open up the audio file by using the Open Url... command from the File menu or typing Ctrl+U.** Type in the location of your streaming audio URL. It should look something like this:

   ```
   rtsp://my.qtserver.com/myBackingTrack.mov
   ```

3. **Click OK and wait for the audio to buffer and begin playing.** Stop the playback and move the playback indicator to the beginning of the stream.

4. **Open another QuickTime player and this time open the Flash animation via the Open URL... command.** This time, the URL should look something like this:

```
http://my.webserver.com/myFlash.swf
```

5. **Again, wait for it to begin playback.** Stop the playback. Now the fun begins.

6. **Copy the whole Flash presentation by choosing Select All and then Copy from the Edit menu or simply type Ctrl+A then Ctrl+C.**

   It's worth noting that you're not copying the actual Flash presentation — you're merely copying a *reference* that refers to the whole movie.

7. **Flip over to the player that contains the audio, make sure that the playback indicator is at the beginning of the stream (assuming, of course, you want the Flash to start with the audio), and choose Paste from the Edit menu (or press Ctrl+V).**

8. **You should see the Flash presentation pop into the movie window.** Click Play, and voilà! You now have a movie with a backing track.

   This example assumes your flash is the same length as your backing track. If not, you have two options to consider:

   • **Stretch or shrink the animation to match the length of the audio.** To do this, choose Add Scaled from the Edit menu when pasting. This scales the length of the added presentation to match exactly the length of the original presentation.

   • **Edit the audio to match the length of the animation.** You can always shorten the audio to match the length of the animation, or repeat it if the animation is longer.

9. **Save a reference movie by choosing Save As from the Edit menu.** Again, you're not saving the actual clips, you're only saving a reference to them, one coming off a streaming server and the other a Web server.

10. **You're done.** This reference movie can be placed on a Web server or e-mailed like any other QuickTime reference movie.

Combining Flash and streaming QuickTime via SMIL

The previous section combined two references to QuickTime clips to create a file that referenced two clips coming from two different servers using two different protocols. You had to type the URLs for both streams into the QuickTime player to create the references — you can just as easily type these two references into a SMIL file and play them in parallel.

```
<smil>
<body>
<par>
    <video src="rtsp://my.qtserver.com/myBackingTrack.mov" />
    <ref src="http://my.webserver.com/myFlash.swf" />
```

```
</par>
</body>
</smil>
```

The QuickTime player also supports SMIL. The previous code looks a lot like the SMIL code that you saw earlier for the RealPlayer, with a couple of notable exceptions. First, the video referenced is a QuickTime movie, not a RealAudio file. Second, the animation reference uses the HTTP protocol this time, not RTSP.

 Cross-Reference To learn more about the QuickTime implementation of SMIL, please turn to Chapter 31.

Summary

Flash is a great data type for the Internet because it can have a very low bit rate. You can incorporate it into your Real and QuickTime streaming presentations in a number of ways, and even take advantage of some of the advanced control functionality Flash provides. In the next chapter, streaming text via RealText is explored.

✦ Flash can be a great data type for the Internet because it can have a very low bit rate.

✦ The data rate of Flash is spiky; downloading images is high bit rate, sending instructions to animate them is not.

✦ RealFlash combines Flash animation with RealAudio.

✦ Use SMIL files to play back Flash animation and RealAudio in parallel.

✦ Flash 5 publishes RealFlash files directly.

✦ For optimal streaming Flash files, keep the bit rate low, the CPU use low, and the bit rate consistent.

✦ The QuickTime Player 4 plays Flash files directly.

✦ Flash files cannot be streamed via RTSP to the QuickTime player — you must use HTTP.

✦ You can combine Flash and QuickTime movies via reference files or SMIL.

✦   ✦   ✦

Streaming Text with RealText

Beginning in 1998 with the release of RealSystem G2, RealNetworks opened up their streaming system to include new data types, such as text and pictures, as well as third-party data types. During this process RealNetworks created a proprietary data type for handling streaming text and unsurprisingly called it RealText.

> **Note** RealText is only supported by the RealSystem and requires the RealPlayer G2 (6.0) or above. RealText is a proprietary implementation that is not currently supported by any other streaming platform.

Text is a particularly useful streaming media data type for a number of reasons:

+ **Lightweight:** The data rate of streaming text is extremely low, so it is perfect for bandwidth-constricted applications.

+ **Client-side render:** Computers are already capable of displaying text, and RealText harnesses this built-in ability — no special download is required (other that a recent RealPlayer).

+ **Encoding text in video is difficult:** Because video clarity at low bit rates can be problematic, encoding video that contains text can be especially difficult. By separating the two, quality can be improved.

You can add a significant amount of interest and interactivity to your streaming media presentations by including some text. RealText supports hyperlinks, so text in the RealPlayer can link to Web pages or to other streaming media presentations. These links can also go to different parts of the current presentation, allowing RealText to be used as a navigational tool.

RealText supports many of the same functions that you use in your word processor, such as different fonts, font sizes, colors, bold, italics, and underline. You can even create special effects, such as drop shadows, with a little extra effort.

RealText is an XML-compliant language that uses a simple set of tags, much like HTML. If you've ever done any HTML coding, you should have no trouble picking up the RealText syntax because the syntax of RealText is very similar to HTML code. If you've never used HTML code before, you still should be able to pick up RealText very quickly because you only have to learn a few simple tags — the rest is plain text.

How RealText Works

RealText files are plain text files that tell the RealPlayer how and when to display the desired text. These files use a simple markup language and take the file extension .rt. The RealText markup language includes a number of tags that describe the overall size and shape of the presentation, when to display certain elements in the file, and the display characteristics of each piece of text, such as font, size, color, and so on.

On the CD-ROM   The example RealText files in this chapter are included on the CD in the RealText directory.

RealText tags are enclosed in angle brackets, just like HTML. For instance, every RealText file must begin and end with <window> tags, as follows:

```
<window>
    This is an extremely simple RealText file.
</window>
```

This RealText file (simplest.rt in the RealText directory on the CD) contains just enough information to display a single line of text in the RealPlayer. Many variables such as window size, type, font, font size, and font color have been left out and, therefore, assume default values. Note how the file begins with a <window> tag and ends with a </window> tag. You should type this file into a text editor and save it with a .rt extension or double-click the simplest.rt file on the CD to see how this file displays.

Now that you've seen how simple a RealText file can be, I've added some new elements to showcase some of the features of RealText:

```
<window duration="30" bgcolor="yellow">
??????
<time begin="1"/>This file shows some basic RealText features.
<time begin="3"/><p>Note the yellow background...
<time begin="6"/><p>You can use <b>bold</b>, <i>italics</i>,
    and <u>underline</u>.</p>
```

```
<time begin="9"/><p><center>Text can be centered.</center></p>
<time begin="11"/><clear/>
<time begin="12"/>You can clear the screen and start over again.<br/>
<time begin="15"/><font size="+2">Text can be large...</font><br/>
<time begin="16"/><font size="-2">or small</font><br/><br/>
<time begin="19"/><font face="arial">and of course</font><br/>
<time begin="20"/><font face="courier">you can use</font><br/>
<time begin="21"/><font face="verdana">different fonts.</font><br/><br/>
<time begin="23"/><font face="helvetica" size="+1">Pretty nifty, don't you
think?</font>
?????
</window>
```

In this example (basic_features.rt in the RealText directory on the CD), a number of RealText tags are used. Each tag may in turn have one or more *attributes*, such as a font having a size and typeface. This file introduces a number of RealText concepts:

✦ **Duration:** The window tag may have a `duration` attribute that determines the length of the presentation.

✦ **Background color:** The window tag may have a `bgcolor` attribute that specifies the window background color.

✦ **Timing:** Text is made to display at different times by using the `<time/>` tag with the `begin` attribute.

✦ **Positioning:** Using paragraph `<p>` and line break `<br/>` tags, text can be laid out according to your wishes. Additionally you can position text at exact pixel locations using the `<pos>` tag.

✦ **Appearance:** Using `<font>` tags with `face` and `size` attributes, or simple bold `<b>`, italics `<i>`, and underline `<u>` tags, the appearance of the text can be manipulated.

The first line of code establishes that the presentation lasts 30 seconds and that the background color should be yellow. Each line following begins with a time reference, followed with some text. The text on each line may have some formatting or appearance tags, such as `<b>` for bold or `<i>` for italics. The sixth line of code is a special command to clear the display window. If you watch this RealText presentation, you see that each line of text is displayed at the time specified with the `begin` attribute, using whatever positioning or formatting information is included before the next time tag.

The code in this example creates a RealText presentation that runs for 30 seconds and displays 11 lines of text in various ways. The whole presentation is under a kilobyte — in fact, it is exactly 834 bytes, or 6,672 bits. Divide this number by the duration of the file, and you get an average bit rate of 222 bps! Compare that to the mind-boggling bit rates of raw audio and video (1,378 Kbps and 26MBs respectively), or even to the simplest audio codecs that require 5 Kbps, which is still over 20 times the bit rate of this RealText file. You can get a lot of mileage out of RealText without a significant impact on bandwidth.

The RealText markup language provides additional tags that add functionality, such as being able to launch another presentation, launching another RealPlayer, e-mail links, and linking to Web pages. You can also make the text move up or down, or from side to side. You can even place text at exact pixel locations in the display window. Before you delve into the more advanced functionality of RealText, you must first learn about the different window types RealText offers, how RealText is authored, and how RealText syntax works.

RealText Window Types

RealText presentations can have a number of different behaviors. For example, text can be made to crawl from left to right or scroll up the screen. For the sake of convenience, these RealText behaviors have been grouped into different *window types*. Each window type has certain default behaviors.

When you author RealText presentations, you start by choosing a suitable window type and specifying the values for the behaviors included with that window type. The full list of available window types is as follows:

> **Note**   The window types listed here use capitalization and no spaces for consistency with the RealText Authoring Guide. When specifying the type of attribute in your files, capitalization is unnecessary; however, you *must not use spaces,* otherwise the type goes unrecognized, and the generic type is assumed.

✦ **ScrollingNews:** This type of window scrolls the text up the screen.

✦ **TelePrompter:** Text in this type of window automatically moves up when the bottom of the window is reached.

✦ **TickerTape:** TickerTape windows contain only two lines of text, an upper and a lower, that scroll from right to left.

✦ **Marquee:** Marquee windows are similar to TickerTape windows, but only scroll a single line of text, from right to left, centered in the display window.

✦ **Generic:** The most flexible window type, generic windows can scroll, crawl, and accept any timing, positioning, or timing tags. If no window type is specified, the generic window type is assumed.

> **On the CD-ROM**   Examples of RealText files are included on the CD in the RealText directory. You should watch each example and take a quick look at the code in a text editor as you read through the following descriptions.

The following sections provide a brief overview of each of the available RealText window types. After these descriptions, RealText authoring is discussed. This includes an explanation of the RealText markup language and a step-by-step section that explains in detail how to author various types of RealText files.

ScrollingNews windows

Text in a ScrollingNews window scrolls up the screen. You can specify how quickly the text scrolls by setting the `scrollrate` attribute in the `<window>` tag. If you do not specify a `scrollrate` attribute, the default value is 10. ScrollingNews windows cannot loop.

Timing tags are optional in ScrollingNews windows. If no timing tags are specified, all the text is displayed, starting in the top-left corner. The formatting and spacing tags are applied, and the text is then scrolled up the window.

The first line of text in a ScrollingNews window is displayed by default at the top-left corner of the display. Unfortunately, this causes the text to immediately scroll off the display. If you want your text to begin scrolling from the bottom of the screen, you should precede your text with a number of line break tags (`<br/>`). You can see how this works by watching the scrollingnews.rt file on the CD and then examining the code in your text editor.

TelePrompter windows

TelePrompter text windows start writing text in the upper-left corner, moving down until the bottom of the display is reached. When the bottom is reached, the existing text is moved up just enough to display the new text. To see an example of a TelePrompter window, you should watch the teleprompter.rt file in the RealText directory on the CD and then examine the code in a text editor.

The TelePrompter window type is designed to use timing tags. For example, the following code snippet displays two lines of text, one at one second and another at five seconds:

```
<time begin="1"/>This line displays one second into the presentation.
<time begin="5"/>This line displays five seconds into the presentation.
```

Without the timing tags, all the text is displayed at once. Additionally, TelePrompter windows ignore any `scrollrate` or `crawlrate` attributes and cannot loop.

When using the TelePrompter window type, it is best to set your window height according to the font size of the text you plan to use. If your window height is not an even multiple of the font pixel height, partial lines are displayed at the top of the screen as the text is moved up, which makes the teleprompter window look unprofessional.

To determine an appropriate window height, determine the pixel height of the font size you plan on using, and multiply it by the number of lines you want displayed in your window. Table 23-1 located later in the chapter contains the pixel heights for all the font sizes available in RealText.

For example, in the `teleprompter.rt` file on the CD, I wanted up to be able to display up to five lines at a time using the default font size. Taking a quick look at Table 23-1 indicates that the default font size is 16 pixels, so multiplying that by five gives an optimal window height of 80 pixels. If you look at the source code for the `teleprompter.rt` file you'll see that's the case.

TickerTape windows

TickerTape windows move two lines of text from right to left, much as you'd expect. Text intended for the upper line must be surrounded by `<tu>` and `</tu>` tags; text for the lower line must be surrounded by `<tl>` and `</tl>` tags. Each text element can have separate appearance attributes, such as different colors, fonts, and so on. An example of the TickerTape window, `tickertape.rt` is included in the RealText directory on the CD.

The line break tag (`<br/>`) has special uses in the TickerTape window. The line break tag causes the text immediately following it to be displayed at the rightmost edge of the screen when the preceding text touches the left side of the screen. If the line break tag is used at the beginning of a file, the text begins crawling from the rightmost side of the window. Without an opening line break tag, the text begins crawling from the left side of the window and immediately disappears.

By definition, text in the upper and lower lines of TickerTape windows cannot overlap. If you have long lines of text, the text in the lower line will not appear until the upper line has been completely displayed. Don't think of TickerTape windows as having two separate lines; think of them as one continuous line of text that can be displayed either on the upper or lower line.

Tip   If you want two overlapping lines scrolling right to left, use two RealText Marquee windows instead of the TickerTape window type. Using this approach you can even specify different `crawlrate` attributes for each line.

TickerTape windows ignore any `scrollrate` attributes and loop by default. The loop is not immediate; a brief delay occurs between the end of the crawling text and the loop restarting. TickerTape windows also have a slightly different default color scheme, with a black background, white upper text, and green lower text.

Marquee windows

Marquee window types are very much like TickerTape windows, but only have a single line of text scrolling from left to right. The line break tag (`<br/>`) acts as it does in the TickerTape window, namely making the text immediately following the tag to begin crawling from the right side of the window.

Marquee text is always centered vertically in the window. You may want to use the information in Table 23-1 located later in this chapter to help you choose a window height. Marquee windows loop by default. For an example of a RealText marquee window, see the marquee.rt file in the RealText directory on the CD.

Generic windows

Generic windows are the most flexible of all RealText window types. You can make the text scroll, crawl from right to left, or even move diagonally by specifying both a `scrollrate` and a `crawlrate` attribute. Although you can use the scroll and crawl features of RealText, generic window types cannot loop.

You can position text at exact pixel locations using `<pos>` tag when using the generic window type, which allows precise control of your layout. You do this by specifying x and y coordinates as attributes of the tag, as follows:

```
<pos x="10" y="25" />This code puts text ten pixels from the top and 25
    pixels from the top left corner of the screen.
```

You cannot, however, use exact pixel locations if the text is moving.

The basic_features.rt file examined earlier was a generic window type. You can find this file in the RealText directory on the CD. A few more examples are included on the CD, each with a special feature:

✦ **Diagonal.rt.** Diagonally scrolling text

✦ **Positioning.rt.** Positions text using the `<pos>` tag

✦ **Drop_shadows.rt.** Creates the drop shadow effect by using the positioning feature

All of the example files listed above include clever ways of combining simple RealText tags to create interesting effects. You should open these files up in a text editor to see how these effects were accomplished. This will give you an idea of how RealText files are authored, which is covered in more detail in the following sections.

Authoring RealText Files

RealText files are authored in a text editor. No RealText authoring environments are available at this time, however RealText presentations are simple and straightforward enough that authoring in a text editor should not present any problems.

There's no set way to author RealText, but a basic approach is as follows:

1. **Select a window type.** RealText offers several default window types with slightly different behaviors. Select the type that suits your application and set the necessary `<window>` attributes.

2. **Enter your text.** Type in or cut and paste the desired text between the `<window>` and `</window>` tags.

3. **Format the text by selecting the fonts, sizes, and styles for your text.**

4. **If necessary, add timing tags to make parts of your file appear at different times.**

5. **Save your file with a** `.rt` **file extension; then test it locally by double-clicking on the file.** If it isn't displaying properly, modify the file until it does.

If you do not have a good simple text editor, trial versions of UltraEdit and BBEdit have been included on the CD. Both are extremely versatile text editors

If you choose to use UltraEdit, make sure to use the WORDLIST.TXT file included on the CD. This makes UltraEdit RealText-aware — if you type your tags correctly, they light up in different colors. If the tags don't light up, something is wrong. This feature can be extremely helpful when debugging files. Please note that UltraEdit is PC-only.

BBEdit can also be made to highlight correct RealText syntax, but unfortunately this is left as an exercise to the reader. Sorry!

Keep in mind the following rules when authoring RealText files.

✦ All RealText tags fall into one of two categories:

- **Unary tags.** These tags stand alone and *always* end with a forward slash. Examples are `<clear/>` and `<br/>`.

- **Binary tags.** These tags come in pairs and surround what they operate on. The opening tag contains no forward slash; the closing tag contains a forward slash before the tag name. Examples are `<window>` and `</window>` or `<center>` and `</center>`.

✦ Always use lowercase for tags and attributes.

✦ Always use quotation marks to enclose attribute values, for example `bgcolor="black"`.

✦ Always use the file extension `.rt` — do not use spaces in the file name.

✦ If you want to use certain characters in your presentation, such as angle brackets, ampersands, and a few others, you'll have to use special codes just like you do in HTML (see Bonus Chapter 2 "Special Characters in RealText" located on the CD-ROM).

✦ Last but not least, you can add comments to a RealText file by using standard HTML syntax, namely:

```
<!-- This is a comment -->
```

Throwing in a comment or two is a good idea, particularly if someone else is going to take a look at your code at some point. Don't go hog wild, though — comments are sent along with the rest of the file when it streams. If you include excessive commenting in your file, your file size and, therefore, the bit rate will be impacted.

That's about it. RealText is pretty simple. As soon as you learn about the different window types and the handful of RealText tags and attributes, you can author streaming text files to your heart's content.

RealText Syntax

Real Text files are delimited by the `<window>` and `</window>` tags. The first window tag may take a number of different attributes to describe what kind of RealText window it is, the window size, and other control attributes, such as whether or not to loop.

After the opening window tag and its attributes comes the body of the file that contains the text to be displayed along with any display and timing information. You can modify the appearance of the text by specifying fonts, colors, sizes, and whether the text should be bold, italic, or underlined. Text layout can also be specified by using a number of special positioning tags.

If you want your text to appear at specific times, you can do this by using the `<time/>` tag. The time tag can take both `begin` and `end` attributes. Last but not least, RealText provides for some advanced functionality with a set of command tags, for linking to other presentations, Web pages, and controlling playback of the RealPlayer.

Window attributes

Every RealText file must open with a `<window>` tag and end with a `</window>` tag. The opening `<window>` tag can take a number of attributes. Each attribute has a value, and the value should be enclosed in double quotation marks, such as:

```
<window duration="30" width="320" height="240" >
```

If you do not specify any window attributes, the default values are assumed. These default values are specified in Bonus Chapter 2 on the CD-ROM, and vary depending on the window type that you specify. Following is a full list of all the available window attributes.

Caution Some attributes are not available in certain window types. For example, you cannot set ScrollingNews windows to loop. For full documentation of attribute limitations, please refer to Bonus Chapter 2 on the CD-ROM.

✦ `type`. Specifies what kind of RealText window the presentation is. Acceptable values are `generic`, `scrollingnews`, `teleprompter`, `tickertape`, and `marquee`.

✦ `duration`. Determines the length of the presentation. The value should be specified in the `dd:hh:mm:ss.xyz` format where the values are the following:

   • **dd:** Days

   • **hh:** Hours

   • **mm:** Minutes

- ss: Seconds

- xyz: Milliseconds

If no decimal points or colons are used in the value, the value is assumed to be a number of seconds. Therefore, a minute and a half presentation could be written as either: `duration="90"` or `duration="1:30"`

✦ `width`. The width of the display window in pixels

✦ `height`. The height of the display window in pixels

✦ `bgcolor`. Specifies the background color of the display window. You can specify a predefined color name or an RGB hexadecimal value, preceded by a # sign. The predefined colors are: white, silver, gray, black, yellow, fuchsia, red, maroon , lime, olive, green, purple, aqua, teal, blue, and navy. A valid background color specificatin would be as follows:

`bgcolor="red"` or `bgcolor="#FF0000"`

✦ `scrollrate`. Determines how quickly text moves vertically up the screen. Negative values are not allowed.

✦ `crawlrate`. Determines how quickly the text moves horizontally from right to left. Negative values are not allowed.

Scroll and crawl rates can range from 0 to as high as you like, but values below 30 pixels per second work best. Because of the way RealText calculates time, some rates are better than others. In particular, 25, 20, 10, 8, 5, 4, 2, and 1 give the smoothest performance. If you want a rate faster than 30, use multiples of 20 or 25.

✦ `link`. Allows you to specify a color for text used as a link. You can specify a predetermined color or RGB value (as per `bgcolor`).

RealText links default to the color blue. If you're using a blue background color, be sure to set your link attribute in the window tag to a different color. In fact, you must always make sure that the background color and the link color are different if you want your links to be visible.

✦ `underline_hyperlinks`. Hyperlinks can be underlined or not depending on whether this attribute is set to `true` or `false`.

✦ `wordwrap`. Another true or false attribute, `wordwrap` determines whether text that reaches the edge of the window is wrapped to the next line or truncated. `wordwrap` has no effect in TickerTape or Marquee windows.

✦ `loop`. The TickerTape and Marquee windows can be set to loop with this attribute that you can set to `true` or `false`. This attribute has no effect in any other windows.

✦ `extraspaces`. Set this attribute to `use` or `ignore`. This attribute determines whether or not RealText pays attention to extra spaces in your file.

Tip

If you are having trouble with text alignment, try setting `extraspaces="ignore"`. This attribute defaults to `use`, which sometimes inserts spaces in unexpected places. For example, if you have a carriage return in your file and `extraspaces` is set to `use`, the carriage return shows up as a space in the displayed file.

✦ `version`. This specifies what version number of RealText must be used to display the file. This attribute is rarely used and is not necessary to display most English language files.

You don't have to specify all the attributes in your window tag. Any attribute you don't specify assumes a default value (see cross reference icon below). In general, it may suffice to specify a window type to suit your presentation and `height` and `width` attributes. After you've done that, it's time to add the text you want displayed, along with any appearance tags, which are covered in the next section.

Cross-Reference

For a full list of all the default attribute values, please refer to Bonus Chapter 2 located on the CD-ROM.

RealText appearance tags

The text in your RealText files can be styled by using a number of different tags. All appearance tags are binary tags, which means that they *must* have a closing tag. There are a number of tags that do not have any attributes, and one tag that can have a number of attributes. The tags that do not take any attributes are as follows:

✦ `<b></b>`: Specifies **bold** text

✦ `<i></i>`: Specifies *italics*

✦ `<u></u>`: Specifies <u>underlined</u> text

✦ `<s></s>`: Specifies ~~strikethrough~~ text (text with a line through the middle)

The <font> tag

The `<font>` tag is the most powerful appearance tag. The `<font>` tag can take a number of attributes that enable you to specify various characteristics for your text, such as size, color, and what typeface to use. You can specify multiple attributes in a single font tag. As an example, the following line of code would display the text in an Arial font, in white, on a black background, with the default character size:

```
<font color="white" face="arial" bgcolor="black">White Arial
    text on a black background.</font>
```

All font attributes can be changed throughout the presentation. Each time an attribute value is specified, it takes precedence over any previously specified attribute values. The available font attributes are as follows:

✦ color: Sets the color of the text. Acceptable values are the standard set of pre-determined colors (see bgcolor in the "Window attributes" section earlier in this chapter) or RGB values.

Caution

Make sure that your text is a different color than the background color — otherwise your text will not be visible.

✦ bgcolor: Sets the background color of the text. Acceptable values are the standard set of predetermined colors (see bgcolor in the "Window attributes" section earlier in this chapter) or RGB values.

✦ face: Sets the typeface of the text. Most common fonts are supported, though cross platform issues may arise. A list of all the fonts that use the US-ASCII or ISO-8859-1 character set along with the defaults used on the Mac and Unix platforms is included in Bonus Chapter 2 on the CD-ROM.

Caution

When specifying a font name, be sure to type the font name in exactly, *including spaces*. You don't have to use capitalization, but without the spaces RealText will not recognize the font name.

✦ size: Specifies the size of the text. You can specify an absolute or relative size. RealText supports seven different sizes. Please refer to Table 23-1 for details about absolute and relative sizes and how they correspond to actual pixel size.

✦ charset: Enables you to specify a non-standard character set. You can author RealText presentations in Chinese, Korean, Japanese, and many other character sets. Please refer to Bonus Chapter 2 on the CD-ROM for a full list of accepted character sets.

Table 23-1 RealText Font Size Information		
Relative Size	**Absolute Size**	**Pixel Size Reference**
-2	1	12 pixels
-1	2	14 pixels
(default)	3	16 pixels
+1	4	20 pixels
+2	5	24 pixels
+3	6	36 pixels
+4	7	48 pixels

Using the <font> tag

The <font> tag is a binary tag, which means that it always takes a closing </font> tag. The opening tag can have one or more attributes. The attribute values in the font tag apply to all text enclosed by the opening and closing font tags. You can also stack and nest the font tag. Type the following code snippet into your text editor, save it with a .rt file extension and watch the result:

```
<window extraspaces="ignore">
    <font face="arial">This text will be printed using the arial font.<br/>
    <font color="blue">This text will be arial and blue.<br/>
    <font size="+2" color="yellow">This text wil be large, arial, and
        yellow, temporarily overriding the previous color attribute.<font/>
    <br/><br/>
```

Because the previous font tag has been closed, this text will no longer be yellow - it will be blue. And the size reverts back to the default.

```
    <br/><br/>
    <time begin="5"/>
    <clear/>
```

Note the clear tag clears the screen, but not the remaining active font tag, specifying the Arial typeface.

```
<br/>
    </font>
```

This last closing font tag turns off the face information, leaving the default face, size, and color.

```
<br/>
</window>
```

A font tag precedes the first line of text, which specifies the Arial font. The next line also contains a font tag, which specifies the color blue. Any text after these two tags will be blue *and* use the Arial font. The third line of text specifies a larger font size and changes the text color to yellow. This color attribute takes precedence over the previous color attribute.

The closing font tag on the next line ends the scope of the closest font tag, which specified the increased size and yellow text. The color reverts to blue, the previously specified color attribute, and the size back to default since there is no other font tag specifying size. The clear tag clears the screen but does not shut off any existing active font tags. Font tags remain active until a closing font tag is reached. When there are no longer any active font tags, the default font information is used.

Positioning tags

RealText offers several tags to customize text layout, most of which should be immediately familiar to anyone who has looked at HTML code:

✦ `<br/>`: The line break tag adds a carriage return to the display, causing text to be displayed on the next line. The line break tag is a unary tag, which means it takes a closing slash and does not need a closing tag.

In TickerTape and Marquee windows, the line break tag causes the next line of text to start crawling from the right side of the window when the previous text touches the left edge of the window. If the previous text is longer than the width of the window, the line break tag inserts a few tabs before displaying the next line.

✦ `<p></p>`: The paragraph tag adds space between text, but not in the same way that you may be used to in HTML. The paragraph tag works by printing two blank lines before the next line of text.

In TickerTape and Marquee windows, the paragraph tag acts just like a line break tag, causing the next line of text to start crawling from the right side of the window when the previous text touches the left edge of the window. If the previous text is longer than the width of the window, the paragraph tag inserts a few tabs before displaying the next line.

Note   The `<p>` tag, in the strict legal sense, is a binary tag and therefore should require the `</p>` tag. In practice the closing tag isn't necessary — in fact, it changes the behavior of the tags. A `<p>` tag acts like two line breaks if prior text is visible, a single line break otherwise. The tricky part is that the `</p>` tag acts the same way. This can lead to undesirable spacing. To avoid the somewhat unpredictable behavior of `<p>` tags, you may want to use a double `<br/>` tag instead.

✦ `<ol></ol>`: The ordered list tags are provided for HTML compatibility so that HTML documents can be displayed as RealText. Like HTML, the tags indent text, but unlike HTML numbers are not added to each line.

✦ `<ul></ul>`: Similar to the ordered list tags, unordered list tags also indent text, but unlike HTML bullets are not added.

✦ `<li></li>`: List item tags are provided for HTML compatibility, but in RealText they function as line break (`<br/>`) tags.

✦ `<hr/>`: The horizontal rule tag is provided for HTML compatibility but does not draw a horizontal line. It acts like two line break (`<br/>`) tags.

✦ `<center></center>`: The center tags horizontally center the enclosed text and have no effect in the TickerTape or Marquee windows.

Text enclosed by center tags is assumed to be on a new line. If the text is not preceded by a line breaking tag, such as `<br/>`, `<p>`, or `<hr/>`, the center tag forces a line break. The closing center tag always causes a line break.

✦ `<pre></pre>`: The preformatted text tags work the same as they do in HTML. Text enclosed by preformatted tags is displayed in the courier font at the current font size. All white space, such as tabs and line breaks, is used.

> **Note**
>
> RealText does not center lines until it can determine the exact line length. Sometimes when RealText is streamed, a line may be spread across multiple packets. In this case, the line is displayed flush left until the complete line has been delivered, at which point it will be centered.

✦ `<pos/>`: The position tag allows you to specify absolute pixel positions for your text relative to the top left of your presentation window. It takes horizontal (x) and vertical (y) attributes, though only one attribute is required. It is a unary tag, so requires the closing slash:

```
<pos x="10" y="25"/>This text is displayed ten pixels from
    the left and 25 pixels from the top of the display
    window.
```

> **Note**
>
> The position tag is only available in non-moving windows, such as when the `scrollrate` and `crawlrate` are zero. This should give you enough information to use the positioning tags. For additional information, see Bonus Chapter 2 on the CD-ROM in this book or the RealText Authoring Guide, available from the RealNetworks Web site (`www.realnetworks.com`).

Using timing tags in RealText

Timing tags (`<time />`) are used to make text appear and disappear at specific times in the presentation. If you do not use timing tags, RealText tries to display all the text as quickly as it can. Timing tags are unary tags, which means that they require a closing slash and no closing tag is used. Timing tags have two attributes:

✦ `begin`: The time to begin displaying the text

✦ `end`: The time to finish displaying or erase text

`Begin` and `end` values should be specified in the `dd:hh:mm:ss.xyz` format where

✦ `dd`: Days

✦ `hh`: Hours

✦ `mm`: Minutes

✦ `ss`: Seconds

✦ `xyz`: Milliseconds

If no decimal points or colons are used, the value is assumed to be a number of seconds.

Timing tags can have one or both attributes. The timing tags operate on all text until the next timing tag is encountered. The following are examples of timing tags:

```
<time begin="5"/>This text is displayed 5 seconds into the
presentation
<time begin="6.0" end="10.5"/>This text appears at six
    seconds and disappears at 10.5 seconds
```

Both `begin` and `end` attributes remain active until a subsequent timing tag over-rides them. If you do not specify a `begin` attribute, the begin time is inherited from the previous timing tag, or is assumed to be the beginning of the presentation if the `begin` attribute has not yet been specified. Consider the following code:

```
This text is displayed immediately and stays on the
    screen until the end of the presentation or the next
    clear tag, because there is no begin or end time
    specified<br/><br/>
<time begin="3.0" end="15"/>This text appears at three
    seconds and disappears at 15 seconds<br/><br/>
<time end="10"/>This has no start time and therefore
    "inherits" the previous line's start time of three
    seconds. However, this text disappears at 10
    seconds.<br/><br/>
```

If no `end` attribute is specified, the `end` attribute value is assumed to be the end of the presentation or until the next `<clear/>` tag. If you specify an `end` attribute in a timing tag and want additional text to be displayed after the first piece ends, you must specify a new `end` attribute. Consider the following code snippet:

```
<time begin="1"/>This text will be displayed at one second,
    and stay on screen until the next clear tag or until the
    end of the presentation.<br/>
<time begin="6.0" end="10.5"/>This text appears at six
    seconds and disappears at 10.5 seconds.<br/>
<time begin="12"/>This text will not be displayed because the
    end attribute is still set at 10.5 seconds, which is
    before the start time.
<time begin="12" end="20"/>This text will be displayed as
    expected, beginning at 12 seconds and ending at 20.
```

 Note   The clear tag clears the screen even if text on-screen has an end time that has not yet elapsed.

Timing tags are fairly straightforward as long as you're careful with your end times. Timing tags are primarily for use in windows without movement, although there is no rule against using timing tags in windows that scroll or crawl. If you use timing tags in moving windows, the effect is to make the text visible at the appointed time. Type the following code into a text editor, save with a `.rt` extension, and observe the behavior:

```
<window type="marquee">
    <br/>
```

This is normal marquee behavior. The line break tag moves the text to the right side of the window, where it begins to crawl to the left.

```
</window>

<window type="marquee">
   <br/>
   <time begin="5"/>The line break tag again moves the text
   to the right side of the screen. It begins to crawl, but
   is not made visible until 5 seconds into the presentation,
   at which point it has already crawled into view.
</window>
```

Using timing tags in windows with movement can be tricky, but with a little effort just about anything can be accomplished. You can also manipulate RealText files globally by using SMIL (see Chapter 32) to achieve complex timing effects.

RealText command tags

RealText provides a number of command tags to perform advanced tasks. The command tags vary from the simple clear tag, which clears the current display screen, to a number of commands to link to other presentations and to control the RealPlayer.

The <clear/> tag

The clear tag clears the current display screen. Any subsequent text is displayed in the top-left corner of the screen, unless there are subsequent positioning tags.

The clear tag clears the screen even if text on-screen has an end time that has not yet elapsed. The clear tag does not, however, reset any font information. Any font attributes remain active for subsequent text.

Linking to other presentations or applications using anchor tags

RealText offers a few ways to link to other presentations and applications using the anchor syntax familiar to HTML users:

```
<a href="URL or command" target="application"> ... </a>
```

The anchor tag has two attributes:

✦ href: Takes the URL of the document or presentation you want to link to or takes the command you want to send to the RealPlayer.

✦ target: Tells RealText to send the command to the current RealPlayer, a secondary RealPlayer, or a browser.

Tip

Links by default are underlined in RealText presentations. You can override this by setting the underline_hyperlinks attribute in the window tag to "false".

You can create a number of different links with the RealText anchor tag, such as e-mail links, linking to other presentations, or using RealText as a navigational tool by linking to other parts of the presentation.

Creating a mail link

One of the simplest links you can create using the RealText anchor tag is an e-mail link. You can put an e-mail link in your RealText presentation with the following code:

```
<a href="mailto:address">Email me!</a>
```

Opening a URL in RealPlayer or a browser

To open another document from a RealText file, you have to specify the location of the document and whether you want a browser or the RealPlayer to open the document.

You can specify the location of a document by using a fully qualified URL for the `href` attribute or use relative paths like what you do in HTML. All the following are valid anchor tags:

```
<a href="newfile.rt">Links to a realtext presentation in the
    same directory as the current file</a>
<a href=<"../upone.rm">Links to a RealMedia file one
    directory above the current file
<a href="http://www.myserver.com/index.html">Links to a file
    called index.html on the www.myserver.com server</a>
```

If you do not specify a target, the RealPlayer assumes that the file is to be opened by the viewer's Web browser. The first two links above may not open properly if the user's browser is not configured correctly. You can specify that the link should be opened in the RealPlayer by using the target attribute:

```
<a href="newfile.rt" target="_player">
```

This text links to newfile.rt which is in the same directory as the current file, and plays it back in the RealPlayer.

```
</a>
<a href="rtsp://www.myserver.com/myfile.rm" target="_player">
```

This text links to the file myfile.rm on www.myserver.com, and plays it back in the RealPlayer.

```
</a>
```

You can also specify `target="_browser"` to target the viewer's Web browser, but this is not necessary because the browser is the default.

RealPlayer control commands

You can use links in your RealText to control playback of the RealPlayer. You must specify the target as "_player" and use one of the following href attributes:

✦ command:pause(): Pauses the RealPlayer.

✦ command:play(): Resumes play of the RealPlayer.

✦ command:seek(dd:hh:mm:ss.xyz): Seeks to the desired location in the current presentation.

Some sample RealPlayer commands:

```
<a href="command:pause()" target="_player">Pause the
    RealPlayer</a>
<a href="command:play()" target="_player">Resume playback</a>
<a href="command:seek(2:30)" target="_player">Seek two
    minutes and thirty seconds into the presentation</a>
```

You can see this code in action by watching the RealPlayer_control.rt file on the CD in the RealText directory.

Using the openwindow command to open new RealPlayer windows

The ability to open multiple RealPlayer windows began with the release of RealPlayer 7.0 in 2000. When a new window is opened, playback in the original window stops, and playback in the new window begins. You can open new windows via RealText by using the anchor tag with the following syntax:

```
<a href="command:openwindow(name, URL [, playmode=value,
playmode=value...])" target="_player">Open a new player</a>
```

Older versions of the RealPlayer do not support multiple windows. You can add version="1.4" to the <window> tag to cause older versions to ask the user to upgrade their players.

The openwindow command is slightly different in that it takes a few parameters. The name and URL parameters are required; additional playmode parameters are optional. Note that the openwindow parameters are not quoted.

If you have a URL that has commas, parentheses, or any other special characters, you *must* enclose it in single quotation marks.

In addition to the name and URL parameters, the optional playmode parameter can take several different name-value pairs. The full list of openwindow command parameters is as follows:

✦ name: The name parameter comes first and specifies which window to open. The name can be a predefined name or a user-defined name. The predefined names are as follows:

- self **or** _current: Opens the specified URL in the current RealPlayer window.

- _new **or** _blank. Opens a new RealPlayer window.

In addition to the predefined names, you can specify a name for the RealPlayer window. If a RealPlayer window is already open with that name, the presentation is opened in that window. If no current RealPlayer is using that name, a new RealPlayer window is opened and assigned the user-defined name.

✦ URL: The URL is the location of the presentation to be opened. The URL must be fully qualified, including the transport protocol such as rtsp:// or http://. Relative URLs do not work in the openwindow command.

✦ playmode: The RealPlayer has a number of playback attributes that can be accessed by the openwindow command. These attributes include zoom level, whether or not the player is autosized, and whether or not the player stays on top of other windows while playing.

- zoomlevel. Determines how large the playback window is. The options are normal, double, and full. Double doubles the original screen size of the presentation and full plays the presentation back in fullscreen mode.

- autosize. When autosize is set to true, the RealPlayer opens to the smallest size possible to play back the linked presentation The RealPlayer controls are not visible unless the user mouses over the presentation. If autosize is set to false, the RealPlayer opens in compact mode, which is just large enough to display both the linked presentation and the RealPlayer controls.

- ontopwhileplaying. Set to true or false, this parameter determines if the RealPlayer remains on top of other windows during playback or if the window can be hidden.

You can use any combination of these attributes in your openwindow command. For example, this first example opens up myfile.rm in a new window, playing at double the presentation's original size:

```
<a href="command:openwindow(_new,
    rtsp://www.myserver.com/myfile.rm, zoomlevel=double)"
    target="_player")Open myfile.rm in a new player</a>
```

The next example opens up the file myfile.rm in a new window called "video" and makes sure it always plays on top:

```
<a href="command:openwindow(video,
    rtsp://www.myserver.com/myfile.rm,
    ontopwhileplaying=true)" target="_player")Open myfile.rm
    in a new window called video</a>
```

This last example uses two `playmode` attributes. `Myfile.rm` is played back double-size and autosized so that the video only has a thin frame around it:

```
<a href="command:openwindow(video,
    rtsp://www.myserver.com/myfile.rm, zoomlevel=double,
    autosize=true)" target="_player")Open myfile.rm in a new
    window, auto-sized and double original size</a>
```

The <required> tag

In theory, streaming RealText files should perform exactly the same way as local files. Unfortunately, packets can be lost in transit on the Internet. If a complete block of text is lost, the RealPlayer displays an ellipsis (. . .) to indicate missing text.

To avoid this, RealText provides a `<required></required>` tag to indicate text that absolutely, positively has to be displayed. When this tag is used, the RealPlayer halts the presentation and waits until the data has been received before resuming playback. Under most circumstances, the `<required>` tag should not be necessary.

Creating a RealText Presentation

Creating a RealText presentation is simple. Decide on a window type, set your window attributes correctly, and then add a bunch of text in between your window tags. You'll probably want to add some font information, some positioning information, and maybe some timing tags.

The following example shows how you can create two RealText windows, one of which opens up the other. For my examples (included on the CD), I'll be creating a generic window that opens a small marquee window. If you want to create different types of windows or use different colors, feel free to experiment!

These files are available on the CD-ROM in the RealText directory, named mymarquee.rt and mygeneric.rt.

First, create a simple stand-alone RealText file.

1. **Open a text editor.**

2. **Set up your window attributes.** I set my attributes to the following:

```
<window type="marquee"
        bgcolor="yellow"
        extraspaces="ignore"
        >
```

You can type all of the above on a single line. I prefer the attributes on separate lines for readability. I also find it easier to debug files when the window attributes are on separate lines.

3. **Make it a legal file by closing the window tag a few lines below the open window tag.**

```
</window>
```

4. **Save the file.** I saved my file as mymarquee.rt. At this point you can test the file. Not a lot happens, but you should not get any errors. You should at least see the background color that you specified, and if you specified any height or width parameters the window should open to the appropriate size.

   If you get errors at this point, there is something wrong with your window tags. Make sure all your attributes are typed correctly, using no spaces, and with double quotation marks around all your values. Make sure the first window tag does *not* have a closing slash, and that there is a closing `</window>` tag.

   The RealText renderer might give you some indication of where it thinks the problem is, such as "Error near line 2." It isn't always accurate, but it should point you in the right direction. Most errors in RealText are generated by misspellings or by missing slashes.

5. **Add some text to the window.** I used a blue Arial font, sized up a bit. My code is listed below — feel free to try out other font, color, and font size variables in your own file (and of course you may not agree with my text message).

```
<font face="arial" color="blue" size="+2">I love the
    Streaming Media Bible</font>
```

   Again, this can be on a single line or divided up for readability.

6. **Save your file and test it.** Your text message should appear in the top-left corner of your display window. If you're using a window with movement, such as a marquee window, the text should immediately start scrolling or crawling. If you're using a window type with movement and want the text to start at the right or from the bottom, you're going to have to insert line breaks in the next step. If you're using a static window type, skip to Step 9.

   If your text isn't displaying, make sure that the color of the text and the background are different. Make sure that all your attributes are typed correctly, with double quotation marks around all the values. Make sure that any binary tags like the font tag have closing tags.

7. **If you're using a moving window and want the text to start from the right side or the bottom, insert line breaks.** I'm using a marquee window, so a single line break tag starts the text from the right hand side. If you're using a ScrollingNews window, you must add a number of line breaks, depending on your window height. You can place the line breaks before the font tag or before the text. In this case I prefer the line breaks before the font tag, so my code now looks like this:

```
<br/>
<font face="arial" color="blue" size="+2">I love the
    Streaming Media Bible</font>
```

8. **Save your file and test it.** That's much better, isn't it? If you're using a Scrolling News window and need to add more line breaks, go ahead and do it now. Test, test, test.

9. **Fine tune any parameters.** Personally, I always fine-tune my files as I go along, so I'm going to change the width of the window and speed up the crawl rate a bit. I changed the width by adding `width="150"` and sped up the crawl rate by adding `crawlrate="20"` to my window attributes. You can do the same with your window or try experimenting with other window attributes. My code now looks like this:

```
<window type="marquee"
        width="150"
        crawlrate="20"
        bgcolor="yellow"
        extraspaces="ignore"
      >
      <font face="arial" color="blue" size="+2"><br/>I love
          the Streaming Media Bible</font>
</window>
```

10. **Save your work and test it.** Perfect!

Now it's time to create a second RealText presentation that contains a link to the first presentation. For my second presentation, I decided on a generic window type using a blue background with yellow lettering.

1. **Open a new file in your editor (or modify the** `generic.rt` **file) and save it as a** `.rt` **file.** I saved my file as `mygeneric.rt`.

2. **Type in the appropriate window tags and attributes.** My code is below. Feel free to try different window types and background colors:

```
<window type="generic"
        bgcolor="blue"
        extraspaces="ignore"
      >

</window>
```

In my case, I didn't have to specify the "generic" type, because it is the default, but doing it this way leaves no confusion.

3. **Type in some text after your open window tag.**

   `Howdy!`

4. **Save and test.**

   You should see your text displayed in the top left corner of your window. In my case, the black type is hard to read on the blue background that I chose. I'm going to change the font to Arial, the text color to yellow, increase the size, and what the heck — center the text, as well. Feel free to join me, or try other formatting. Except for the variables you choose to change, the code should look like the following:

```
<window type="generic"
        bgcolor="blue"
        extraspaces="ignore"
      >
    <center>
    <font face="arial" color="yellow" size="+2">
    Howdy!
    </font>
    </center>
</window>
```

The center tags can surround the text, or they can also encapsulate the font tags. It doesn't really matter. If you only want certain text centered, you should put the center tags immediately around that text. If you want a whole section or presentation centered, place the center tags around the section.

Since I want my whole presentation centered, I put my tags outside the font tags.

Be sure to close all your binary tags, such as center tags and font tags. And if you're going to nest your tags, make sure that you keep track of which closing tag belongs to which opening tag to avoid trouble later. Indenting your code helps a lot.

5. **Save and test.** Perfect!

6. **Choose a color for your links.** You can do this by adding a link attribute to your window tag. If you don't mind blue links, you can skip this step and move on to step 7. In my case, since I chose a blue background, I *have to* change the color of my links or they won't be visible on the blue background. My code now looks like this – feel free to substitute a different link color:

```
<window type="generic"
        bgcolor="blue"
        link="yellow"
        extraspaces="ignore"
      >
    <center>
    <font face="arial" color="yellow" size="+2">
    Howdy!
    </font>
    </center>
</window>
```

7. **Add the code to link to the first window.** In my case, I want the link a couple of lines below the first line so I added a few line break tags. Here's what I added, after the first line of text:

```
<br/>
<br/>

<a href="mymarquee.rt" target="_player">Show the love</a>
```

Make sure you substitute the name of your first file for mymarquee.rt if you called your first file something else. Also, feel free to use different text for the link. The line break tags I added are only for aesthetic reasons — you don't need them.

8. **Save and test.** The file should now have a second line of text, underlined, that when clicked links to the first file you created. My code ended up looking like this:

```
<window type="generic"
        bgcolor="blue"
        link="yellow"
        extraspaces="ignore"
        >
    <center>
    <font face="arial" color="yellow" size="+2">
        Howdy!
        <br/>
        <br/>

        <a href="mymarquee.rt" target="_player">Show the

            love</a>
    </font>
    </center>
</window>
```

So there you are. If your file is not working, check to make sure that all the attributes are spelled correctly and that all the values have double quotation marks around them. If your link isn't working make sure your filename is correct and the path is correct if they're not in the same directory.

As an exercise, try changing the code to open a second RealPlayer window instead of opening the presentation in the same RealPlayer. To do this, you would use the openwindow command. You can do this with local files using the following syntax:

```
<a href="command:openwindow(new,c:\\mymarquee.rt)" target="_player">
```

This of course assumes that the file you want to link to is in the base directory of your C drive, and the back slashes assume a Windows machine. With a little tinkering you should be able to get this to work on your machine.

Streaming Live RealText

You can use the RealText broadcast application to stream RealText live. Live text streams are perfect for information that continually changes, such as stock tickers or radio play lists. The live broadcast application sends the new text information to the server, which then broadcasts this information to the live audience.

Caution   The RealText broadcast application is an unsupported feature of RealText. It works fine in most situations and is used often, but RealNetworks does not provide technical support for any problems that you may encounter.

The RealText broadcast application requires information about three different components before it can begin broadcasting:

✦ **Server.** You must supply a valid RealServer name, port, username, and password.

✦ **File names.** You must supply a name for the live text stream as well as a local file to be monitored for new text

✦ **Window attributes.** You must define all the window attributes for the live text window, such as type, height, width, and so on.

After the RealText broadcast application has all the necessary information, it establishes a connection to the server and begins monitoring the local file you specified as the location for new text. When you want to broadcast new text, you simply save the new text to the locally monitored file. The RealText broadcast application detects the new information and sends the complete contents of the file to the RealServer.

The RealText broadcast application ships with the RealSystem Authoring Guide, available from the RealNetworks site (`www.realnetworks.com`). The version provided runs on any 32-bit Windows operating system. The C++ code is available if you want to compile it and run it on a different operating system.

Running the RealText broadcast application

The live RealText application is named evlvtxt2.exe. It requires a few shared libraries to run, which you can find in the authoring kit or perhaps already installed on your computer if you have other RealSystem components installed. The necessary libraries are listed in Table 23-2. The live RealText application can run from any directory on the encoding machine, as long as these libraries are in the same directory.

Tip   To save time and more importantly avoid typing errors, create a directory called `c:\livetext` and copy the libraries and live RealText executable program there. The live RealText application asks for information that requires full paths to be entered. It's much easier to type `c:\livetext` than `"c:\Program Files\Real\Authoring Kit\RealTextBroadcastFiles\."`

Table 23-2	
Live RealText Shared Libraries	
Windows 32-Bit	*UNIX*
rtli3260.dll	rtlive.so.6.0
encn3260.dll	encnet.so.6.0
sdpp3260.dll	sdpplin.so.6.0
auth3260.dll	authmgr.so.6.0
rn5a3260.dll	rn5auth.so.6.0

After you locate all the libraries and the live RealText executable and copied them into the same directory, you're ready to run the RealText broadcast application. If you're running the application on a windows machine, double-click the executable file to start it up. If you're running under UNIX, type in the name of the file you compiled. The remainder of this section assumes the reader is running the application under Windows, though the behavior and appearance of the application under UNIX should be identical.

When you start up the RealText broadcast application, a DOS window opens, like the one in Figure 23-1.

Figure 23-1: The Live RealText encoder

The live RealText encoder then asks you for the parameters it needs for the broadcast. To begin with, it asks for server information. Your RealSystem administrator should provide the following information to you:

✦ **Host.** The host is the name of the RealServer that will be broadcasting your text. You can use a DNS name such as `my.realserver.com` or an IP address such as `192.168.0.127`.

✦ **Port.** The port that the RealServer uses for live broadcasts, typically 4040.

✦ **Username.** A valid username on the RealServer.

✦ **Password.** Without the proper password, the RealText broadcast application cannot connect to the server.

✦ **Stream filename.** This is the name of the live stream, such as `livetext.rt`.

✦ **Input filename.** This is the name of a local file you want the RealText broadcast application to monitor for new text.

Tip

The file to be monitored can be anywhere on the encoding machine, but the RealText broadcast application seems to work best if the file is in the same directory as the encoding application. Call it superstition, call it experience — it just works.

✦ **Frequency.** You can specify how often the RealText broadcasting application checks the local file for changes. The default is once every second.

The encoder then needs to set the window attributes for the live broadcast. You can set each attribute individually, or you can use the default settings. For a complete list of default settings, please see Bonus Chapter 2 on the CD-ROM. If you want to use custom attribute settings, you'll be asked about each attribute individually. For each attribute, enter the desired value or press Enter to use the default value.

Caution

Do not put attribute values in quotation marks when using the RealText broadcast application.

The last item the RealText broadcast application asks for is an expected average bit rate. For most applications, the default value of 1000 bps works just fine. After this value is entered, the application attempts to establish a connection to the server. You'll see some setup information on the screen, as shown in Figure 23-2.

If the application can connect to the server, it sends the contents of the local file and begins the monitoring process. The broadcast application checks to see if the contents have changed once every second (or whatever interval you specified during the setup) and sends the contents of the entire file every time a change is made. During this broadcast, your encoding window should resemble Figure 23-3.

This indicates that the Real Text broadcast application
has successfully established a connection with the RealServer

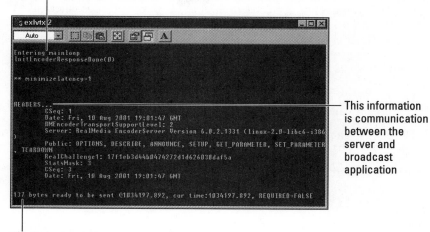

This information
is communication
between the
server and
broadcast
application

This is the local file information about to be sent

Figure 23-2: After you enter all necessary parameters, the RealText broadcast
application attempts to establish a connection to the RealServer.

Each time a change to the file is detected,
the contents of the file are sent to the server.

The encoder also indicates when no change has been detected.

Figure 23-3: The RealText broadcast application in operation

> **Tip**
>
> If the RealText broadcast application fails, chances are that you entered some of the server information incorrectly. Unfortunately, the RealText broadcast application provides virtually no feedback or error messaging. Make absolutely sure that you have all the server information correct, and the broadcast application should work just fine.

Alternatively, you can use a single long command line to start the RealText broadcast application instead of stepping through the questions one at a time. The format for the command line is as follows:

```
exlvtxt2.exe <host> <port> <username> <password>
    <streamfilename> <sourcefilename> <file-polling period>
    <RealText window type> <window width> <window height>
    <window bgcolor> <loopText (true or false)>
    <extra spaces (ignore or use)> <crawlrate> <scrollrate>
    <do wordwrap> <underline hyperlinks (true or false)>
    <link color> <expected avg bitrate>
```

> **Note**
>
> The command line format is the same for UNIX, as long as you substitute the name of the compiled file for exlvtxt2.exe.

You must specify a value for *every* parameter, separated by spaces, without quotation marks. You must specify a value even for those attributes you can ignore in the window tag. A command line call to the RealText broadcast application would look like this:

```
exlvtxt2.exe my.realserver.com 4040 MyUsername MyPassword
    mylivetext.rt livetext.txt 3 generic 300 200 blue false
    ignore 0 0 do true yellow 1000
```

If you are not in the same directory as the RealText broadcast application, you must specify full paths for the exlvtxt2.exe application (or whatever you named the executable under UNIX) and the local file that you want the application to monitor.

> **Tip**
>
> If you plan on using the RealText broadcast application often, saving a command line version in a file is a good idea. Doing so makes restarting the application easier if any problems occur. On a Windows machine, simply save the command line in a file with a .bat (batch file) extension. Unix machines can save to any file and run the file as a script.

If during a live broadcast you need to supply a RealText version number to take advantage of new features such as opening additional RealPlayer windows or using different character sets, you can specify it during the interactive setup by appending ?version=*number* to the stream file name as follows:

```
stream filename (the name RealPlayers will use to view the
    stream): livetext.rt?version=1.4
```

Similarly, on the command line, you specify the version number by typing the following:

```
exlvtxt2.exe my.realserver.com 4040 MyUsername MyPassword
    mylivetext.rt?verion=1.4 livetext.txt 3 generic 300 200
    blue false ignore 0 0 do true yellow 1000
```

Stopping the RealText broadcast application

To end your live text broadcast, simply type a dollar sign ( ) as the first character of your local text file, and the RealText broadcast application stops. You don't have to clear the file or do anything else — simply put a dollar sign in the very first character of the top line of your file.

Using tags in live RealText applications

All the positioning, layout, and font tagsthat can be used in a static (non-live) RealText file can be used in a live RealText file. All you have to do is put them in the local file that the RealText broadcast application is monitoring. For example, your local file could contain the following code:

```
<clear/>
<font face="arial" size="+2">
This will broadcast just fine!
</font>
```

Notice that no window tags (`<window></window>`) are in this file. The RealText broadcast application automatically creates these tags from the information you supply when you start up the application and should not be included in your file.

Tip   Always put a `<clear/>` tag at the top of your live RealText file. The `<clear/>` tag clears the screen each time new text is broadcast.

You can also use any command tags. To put a link to your site and an e-mail link into a live broadcast, you could use the following code:

```
<clear/>
<a href="http://www.mywebserver.com">Check out our site</a>
<br/>
<a href="mailto:me@myserver.com">Tell us what you think about
    our broadcast</a>
```

Timing tags should not be used during live broadcasts. The timeline during live broadcasts is based on when the broadcast application starts relative to the system clock, not relative to zero. A quick glance at Figure 23-3 shows that the broadcast in that particular instance started at 1034379.338 seconds, so if you put in a time tag to display something at ten seconds, you'd never see it!

You shouldn't need timing tags anyway, because during a live broadcast you simply save the new text when you want it to be broadcast, and it automatically happens. Any movement or looping information is calculated for you automatically.

Summary

RealText is a low bit rate, full-featured implementation of streaming text. It only works in RealPlayer G2 or more recent, but most of the installed RealPlayers are G2 or higher anyway. RealText is a lightweight technology that you can use to add interest and interactivity to your RealPlayer presentations.

✦ RealText is authored in a simple text editor.

✦ A number of different window types are available.

✦ A RealText file is enclosed in `<window></window>` tags. The opening tags take a number of global attributes, including height, width, type of presentation, and so on.

✦ RealText provides a number of tags that enable you to modify the layout, appearance, and timing of your RealText presentations.

✦ RealText provides anchor tags that can link to other presentations, Web pages, send e-mail, and even control playback of the RealPlayer.

✦ RealText can be broadcast live by using the RealText broadcast application.

✦   ✦   ✦

Streaming Images with RealPix

RealNetworks opened up their streaming system in 1998 to include text and pictures as well as third-party data types. This new system was known as RealSystem G2 and remains the basis of the RealSystem today. During this process RealNetworks created RealPix, a proprietary data type for handling the streaming and rendering of images.

RealPix appeared at the same time as RealText (see Chapter 23). RealPix comprises a simple markup language for authoring RealPix presentations, along with software to enable the RealSystem to stream and render RealPix presentations. RealPix is built in to all RealServer and RealPlayer releases after 1998.

Note RealPix is only supported by the RealSystem and requires the RealPlayer G2 (6.0) or above. It is a proprietary implementation, not currently supported by any other streaming platform. The RealPix Authoring Guide is available from the RealNetworks Web site (www.realnetworks.com).

Streaming images instead of video has a number of advantages:

◆ **Lower framerate:** Images are streamed at a drastically lower framerate than video. Because of this, each individual frame can be much higher quality.

◆ **Client-side render:** Rendering even the simplest transitions between scenes is very difficult in low bit rate video encoding. For example, crossfades between scenes usually suffer heavy quality losses when encoded at low bit rates. The quality loss is not a limitation of the user's computer — it's a limitation of video codecs.

However, even computers that are underpowered by today's standards can crossfade between two pictures without any trouble. RealPix takes advantage of this capability by streaming high quality images and performing the transitions in the RealPlayer. Rendering the transitions between images in this manner provides a much higher quality image than encoded video streams of the same content.

✦ **Image caching:** Images used in RealPix presentations are cached locally and therefore can be reused throughout the presentation without being down-loaded again.

RealPix is ideal for authoring slideshow presentations such as showing off vacation photos, or Microsoft PowerPoint presentations. RealPix presentations can be authored in any text editor using a simple XML-compliant markup language. You specify the images that you'll be working with, and when and how you want the images to be displayed. You can perform a number of effects in RealPix, such as fading between images and zooming into pictures.

RealNetworks provides a couple of authoring tools that utilize RealPix technology. RealSlideshow combines RealPix, RealAudio, RealText, and SMIL technology to create slideshow presentations that include audio and text captions. RealPresenter allows you to export your PowerPoint slides, audio, and video directly into a multimedia presentation. Both RealSlideshow and RealPresenter are available from the RealNetworks Web site (www.RealNetworks.com).

This chapter, however, teaches you how to author RealPix presentations from scratch so that you understand how the technology works. Once you have a grasp on what the technology involves, you'll be able to author more effective streaming media presentations.

How RealPix Works

RealPix files are plain text files that tell the RealPlayer how and when to display the desired images. These files use a simple markup language and take the file extension .rp. The RealPix markup language consists of a handful of tags that allow you to define which images you are using in your presentation, as well as how you want them displayed.

On the CD-ROM   The RealPix file examples in this chapter are included in the RealPix directory on the CD.

All RealPix tags are enclosed in angle brackets. For example, every RealPix file must begin and end with <imfl></imfl> tags. The following code is a simple RealPix file that displays a single image and then fades out.

RealPix files must be enclosed in `<imfl></imfl>` tags. A `<head/>` tag defines the global characteristics of the presentation such as window width and height, bit rate, and so on. After the `<head/>` tag, you list the images you'll be using in the presentation with `<image/>` tags. Finally you list when you want images to appear and what effects you want performed. The following code is a simple RealPix presentation, included on the CD as simple.rp:

```
<imfl>
    <head width="320"
          height="240"
          duration="10"
          bitrate="20000"
          timeformat="dd:hh:mm:ss.xyz"
          />

    <!-- define the image(s) -->
    <image handle="1" name="images/cabin_sun.jpg" />

    <!-- begin presentation -->
    <fadein start="0" target="1" duration="1" />
    <fadeout start="7" duration="3" />
</imfl>
```

Note The `<head/>` tag is written across multiple lines in this example for legibility. RealPix ignores whitespace and treats it as one line. Personally, I find it easier to read and debug RealPix files when they're formatted this way.

The entire file is enclosed within the `<imfl>` and `</imfl>` tags. The basic parameters are laid out in the `<head/>` tag, such as the height and width of the presentation, along with the duration, bit rate, and time format.

Next, a single image is defined using the `<image/>` tag. The image is given a *handle*, which is a number that is used to refer to the image throughout the rest of the RealPix file.

Finally, the presentation itself consists of two commands, one to fade in the image at the start of the file, and the second to fade out the image at the end of the presentation. The next example includes another image and a few more effects to show you some of the possibilities of RealPix:

```
<imfl>
    <head width="320"
          height="240"
          duration="30"
          bitrate="20000"
          timeformat="dd:hh:mm:ss.xyz"
          />
<!-- define the image(s) -->
    <image handle="1" name="images/cabin_sun.jpg" />
```

```
        <image handle="2" name="images/cabin_frost.jpg" />

    <!-- begin presentation -->
        <fadein start="0" target="1" duration="1" />
        <crossfade start="5" target="2" duration="1" />
        <wipe start="10" target="1" duration="1" type="normal"
            direction="left" />
        <viewchange start="15" duration="4"
            srcx="250" srcy="180" srch="120" srcw="160"/>
        <viewchange start="20" duration="4"
            srcx="250" srcy="180" srch="120" srcw="160"
            dstx="110" dsty="100" dsth="45" dstw="60"/>
        <crossfade start="24" target="2" duration="1" />
        <fadeout start="27" duration="3" />
    </imfl>
```

In this example (RealPix_effects.rp on the CD), two images are defined, and three new RealPix tags are used. These tags showcase some of the transition effects available in RealPix:

✦ `<crossfade/>`. Fades between the current image and the image specified by the "target" parameter.

✦ `<wipe/>`. Transitions between the current image and the image specified by the "target" parameter using a "wipe" effect. When wipe effects are used, one image appears to either push another image off the screen or slide over another image.

✦ `<viewchange/>`. Allows complex image effects such as zooms and pans.

Two other tags complete the RealPix markup language, `<fill/>` and `<animate/>`. `<fill/>` is used to fill areas with color; `<animate/>` is used to animate of GIF files. Though it may seem like a limited set, you can create incredibly rich presentations with RealPix commands.

Authoring RealPix Files — An Overview

There are a number of steps involved in authoring RealPix presentations, which break down into three basic categories: image preparation, writing RealPix code, and fine-tuning the presentation for bandwidth usage. The process may be iterative. Depending on the performance of your RealPix file you might fine tune by tweaking your code, or you may go back and change your image files. The actual steps are as follows:

1. **Prepare your images.** Edit, resize, compress, and optimize your images for streaming.

2. **Define the global parameters for the presentation.**

3. **Define the images to be used in the presentation.** Each image you want to use needs to be defined using an `<image/>` tag.

4. **Set up the presentation using the effects tags.** The effects tags determine when, where, and how the images are displayed.

5. **Calculate bandwidth usage and optimize if necessary.** You can calculate your bandwidth usage by using the RealPix bandwidth calculator. The RealPix bandwidth calculator is a tool provided by RealNetworks. Using the bandwidth calculator you can determine if your presentation will stream smoothly to your intended audience.

Image Preparation

RealPix supports JPEG, PNG, and GIF images. Because the frame rate of RealPix is so low, each image used may be of fairly high quality. However, because you still may be authoring for dial-up modem users, you need to ensure that the images are small enough to be delivered in time.

A 28.8K modem provides a theoretical maximum bandwidth of 28,800 bps. Likewise a 56K modem has a theoretical maximum of 56,000. In reality, the bandwidth available is generally much lower. For a 28.8K modem, 20,000 bps is a safe estimate. To calculate how long a 320 × 240 100K JPEG file may take to download, you can do a little math, first converting bytes to bits, then dividing by the throughput of the modem:

```
100 K * 8 bits/byte = 800 Kb
800 Kb / 20 Kbps= 40 seconds
```

This shows that a 100KB file (a reasonably high-quality 320 × 240 JPEG) takes about 40 seconds to download. This is unacceptable to most viewers. The audience is used to the presentation buffering for 5–10 seconds. Working backwards, this buffering time would give us:

```
5 seconds * 20 kbps = 100 Kb
100 kb / 8bits/byte = 12.5 KB
     => 10 seconds = 25 KB
```

Therefore, if you are authoring for 28.8K modem users, and want between five and ten second gaps between each image you should aim for images in the 10–30K range. You can do this by either making the images smaller or by sacrificing image quality and using heavier image compression. Table 24-1 shows some good target image file sizes for different bit rates, assuming a target buffering time of 5–7 seconds per slide.

Table 24-1
Target Image File Sizes for Different Bitrates *

Presentation	Target image stream bit rate	Target image file size
28.8 Slideshow (no audio)	20 Kbps	10–15K per slide
28.8 Slideshow with audio	12 Kbps (plus 8 Kbps audio)	7–10K per slide
56K Slideshow	32 Kbps	20–30K per slide
56K Slideshow with audio	24 Kbps (plus 8 Kbps audio)	15–22K per slide
256K DSL Slideshow	220 Kbps	140–210K per slide
256K DSL Slideshow with audio	200 Kbps (plus 20 Kbps audio)	125–180K per slide

* Assumes a target buffering time of 5–7 seconds per slide

Your images should be resized to the presentation window size and saved at an appropriate quality level to achieve the target image file size.

Tip

In general, you should maintain different sets of images during the authoring process. You should always keep the high-quality originals in a separate directory so that you can return to them in case you need to re-edit. The second set should be your "working" images, which you'll use to preview the presentation locally and to calculate bandwidth usage.

After you have a working set of images, you can begin writing the RealPix code to display the images when, where and how you want.

Writing RealPix Code

RealPix presentations can be authored in any text editor. It's a simple language, but you need to keep a few things in mind:

✦ With the exception of the `<imfl></imfl>` tags that enclose your presentation, all RealPix tags are *unary*, which means all tags must contain a closing slash:

```
<tag attribute="value" [attribute="value"] />
```

✦ Attributes should be separated by spaces (not commas).

✦ Always use lower case for tags and attributes.

✦ Always use double quotes to enclose attribute values:

```
bgcolor="black"
```

✦ Always use the file extension `.rp` — do not use spaces in the file name.

✦ Comments use the standard HTML syntax, namely

```
<!-- This is a comment -->
```

Note Throwing in a few comments into your code is always a good idea, particularly if someone else may have to work on it at some point. Comments can let people know what you were trying to accomplish with your RealPix code.

On the CD-ROM If you do not have a good simple text editor, trial versions of UltraEdit and BBEdit have been included on the CD. Both are extremely versatile text editors.

If you choose to use UltraEdit, make sure to use the WORDLIST.TXT file included on the CD. This makes UltraEdit RealPix-aware — if you type tags in correctly, they light up in different colors. If the tags don't light up, something is wrong. This feature can be extremely helpful when debugging files. Please note that UltraEdit is PC-only.

BBEdit can also be made to highlight correct RealPix syntax, but unfortunately this is left as an exercise to the reader. Sorry!

RealPix tags

This section presents all the RealPix tags and their accompanying attributes. Some attributes can be used in multiple tags. Attributes that are used in multiple tags are explained the first time they arise.

The <imfl></imfl> tag

This tag is the only binary tag, meaning it requires the closing tag. It is used to delimit RealPix presentations.

The <head/> tag

The `<head/>` tag specifies the global attributes of the RealPix file. Many different attributes can be specified, a few of which are required.

Required attributes

The following attributes must be specified in the `<head/>` tag of every RealPix presentation. In fact, a minimum RealPix `<head/>` tag should look something like this:

```
<head duration="1:00"
      width="240"
      height="180"
      bitrate="12000"
      />
```

Note The `<head/>` tag is written across multiple lines for legibility. RealPix ignores whitespace and treats it as one line. Personally, I find files formatted this way easier to read and debug, if necessary.

✦ **duration:** Determines the length of the presentation. The value should be specified in the "dd:hh:mm:ss.xyz" format where

- `dd`: Days
- `hh`: Hours
- `mm`: Minutes
- `ss`: Seconds
- `xyz`: Milliseconds

If no decimal points or colons are used, the value is assumed to be a number of seconds. Therefore, a presentation lasting a minute and a half could be written as either

```
duration="90" or duration="1:30"
```

✦ **width:** The width of the display window in pixels.

✦ **height:** The height of the display window in pixels.

Note If the RealPix presentation is used as part of a SMIL presentation, the SMIL region width and height attributes take precedence over the settings in the RealPix file.

✦ **bitrate:** Specifies the maximum bit rate the RealPix file should utilize.

Optional attributes

The rest of the attributes are optional. Some have default values such as `timeformat` and `background-color`; others do not.

✦ `timeformat`: Specifies whether time references in the body of the file are wrtten in milliseconds or in dd:hh:mm:ss:xyz format. The default is milliseconds.

✦ `preroll`: Sets the number of seconds the RealPix presentation buffers before playback.

Note The RealSystem always calculates how long it will take to adequately buffer the first image. If this is longer than the preroll setting, the preroll setting is ignored. It is therefore only necessary to specify preroll if you desire an artificially long preroll.

✦ `background-color`: Specifies the background color of the display window. The default is black. You can either specify a predefined color name, or an RGB hexadecimal value preceded by a # sign. See "Using color in RealPix" later in this chapter.

✦ `title`: Allows you to specify title information for the clip.

✦ author: Allows you to specify author information for the clip.

✦ copyright: Allows you to specify copyright information for the clip.

✦ url: Specifies a URL that the presentation links to when the viewer clicks on the display window. All URLs are sent to the viewer's Web browser, unless the command:openwindow() syntax is used (see "Opening new RealPlayer windows" later in this chapter). URLs can also be set in individual transitions, which override this setting. Only fully qualified URLs should be used, such as

```
url=http://smacktastic.tv
```

✦ aspect: Set to either true or false, this specifies whether the images used are stretched to fit if they are shaped differently than the display window. The default is "true."

With the aspect attribute set to false, all pictures are stretched to fill the display window, no matter how distorted they may become. This attribute can be overriden in each individual transition. See "Controlling Aspect Ratios in RealPix" later in this chapter.

✦ maxfps: Determines the maximum number of frames per second used in transition effects. The RealPlayer automatically renders transitions at the best possible quality, so this tag is not necessary unless you wish to use it as a special effect. For instance, setting maxfps="3" makes transitions look choppy instead of smooth. Maxfps can be temporarily overridden in individual transitions just like the aspect attribute.

<image/> tags

The <image/> tag is used to define the images used in your presentation. Each image tag must specify the location of the image and assign it a unique number, which is used throughout the rest of the presentation to refer to the image. The image tag attributes are as follows:

✦ name: Defines the location of the image file relative to the location of the RealPix file. File names and directory paths are case-sensitive. Do not use spaces in your file names. Relative directory references like the dot-dot construct (../) are legal.

✦ handle: Assigns a unique number to the image. This number is then used by transition tags to reference the image. The handle *must* be an integer — no letters or symbols can be used.

 Make sure each image has a unique number. If the same number is assigned to more than one image, only the last image defined with that number is utilized.

The following are legal image tags:

```
<image name="images/cabin_sun.jpg" handle="1" />
<image handle="2001" name="../graphics/syd.jpg" />
```

The following are not:

```
<image handle="A1" name="images/erin.jpg" />
<image name="new images/jake.jpg" handle="7" />
```

The first illegal image definition has a letter in the handle name; the second has a space in the file path.

Transition tags

After you've defined all of your images, you can begin displaying them using the transitions available in RealPix. Each transition has its own set of attributes, though all transitions use more or less the same attributes. For instance, each transition has a start attribute, which defines when the transition starts. Transition attributes are as follows:

✦ `start`: Specifies the start time of the effect.

✦ `target`: Specifies the image to transition to.

✦ `duration`: Specifies how long the transition takes.

✦ `color`: Specifies a color to use in the `<fadeout/>` and `<fill/>` tags. See "Using color in RealPix" later in this chapter.

✦ `srcx, srcy, srcw, srch`: Defines the area of the source image the transition works with. See "Defining source image and display window areas" later in this chapter.

✦ `dstx, dsty, dstw, dsth`: Defines the rectangular area of the display window where the transition occurs. See "Defining source image and display window areas" later in this chapter.

The following three tags can be used to temporarily override settings in the `<head/>` tag for the duration of the transition.

✦ `url`

✦ `aspect`

✦ `maxfps`

Most of the above attributes are fairly self-explanatory. The trickiest part of RealPix authoring, however, is understanding how to define specific areas of the display window and source image for advanced transition effects. This is the topic of the next section.

Defining source image and display window areas

When using transitions in RealPix, the default behavior is to use the complete source image and display using the whole display window. How it is displayed depends on the aspect setting (see "Controlling aspect ratios in RealPix"). There are times, however, when you may want to display only part of an image, or perhaps show two images at once in the display window. You can do both of these by utilizing the source image attributes (srcx, srcy, srcw, srch) and display window attributes (dstx, dsty, dstw, dsth).

Specifying a particular area of the source image or the display window involves specifying the x and y pixel values of the top left-hand corner of the rectangle you want, and then specifying a height and width. All values are measured from the top left corner of the display window and original source image, which is referred to as (0,0). From this corner x values are measured to the right and y values measured down.

RealPix is only capable of defining rectangular areas at this time. Figure 24-1 shows a RealPix presentation (fade-in.rp in the RealPix directory on the CD) that uses different display window areas and how they are referenced.

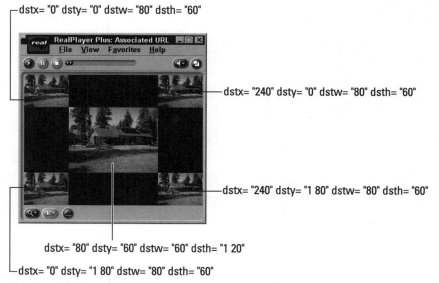

Figure 24-1: Specifying different areas of the display window.

Working with different areas of the source image works in the same way. You specify the section of the image you want to use in the transition.

Controlling aspect ratios in RealPix

When you're working with RealPix, be careful of the aspect ratio of your images. The *aspect ratio* is the ratio of the width to the height of your image.

By default, RealPix does not stretch any images to fit display windows. Instead, the image is made as large as possible until it fills either the vertical or horizontal dimension. If the aspect ratio of the image is slightly different from the aspect ratio of the display window, the extra room in the display is filled by black stripes.

Alternately, RealPix can be made to ignore the source image's native aspect ratio and stretch it to fill the entire display window. If the aspect ratios are similar, this effect might not be noticeable. If the aspect ratios are noticeably different, the image will appear distorted, stretched in either the vertical or horizontal direction. Figure 24-2 shows the results of different aspect attribute settings when the display window and source image have different aspect ratios.

a) scrx="60" scry="20" scrw="180" scrh="180"

b) scrx="60" scry="20" scrw="180" scrh="180" aspect="true"

c) scrx="60" scry="20" scrw="180" scrh="180" aspect="false"

d) scrx="60" scry="20" scrw="180" scrh="180"
dstx="70" dsty="20" dstw="180" dsth="180"

Figure 24-2: Specifying an area of the source image and different aspect settings: a) original 320 × 240 image and desired square section; b) source image displayed with aspect="true"; c) with aspect="false"; d) displayed using display window attributes.

You can set how a RealPix presentation treats aspect ratios in either the `<head/>` tag or on a case-by-case basis in the transition tags. Any settings in transition tags last only for the duration of the transition, after which it reverts to the setting in the `<head/>` tag. The default is always `true`.

For most applications, you'll want to leave the aspect attribute set to its default of true. If you decide to set it to false, be careful — the stretched images may look unprofessional.

The <fadein/> and <crossfade/> tag

The `<fadein/>` and `<crossfade/>` tags perform the exact same effect — fading from the existing color or image to the next. You must specify the `start`, `target`, and `duration` attributes — all others are optional. The `<fadein/>` and `<crossfade/>` tags do not take a color attribute.

Tip

If you want images to appear immediately instead of fading in, use the `<fadein/>` or `<crossfade/>` tag and set the duration attribute to zero.

You can do multiple fade-ins at the same time, or overlap cross-fade effects, though the result may be a bit unpredictable if images overlap. By specifying display window attributes you can fade-in to different areas of the display window. You can see different fade-in effects by watching the fade-in.rp file included on the CD, in the RealPix directory.

The <fadeout/> tag

The `<fadeout/>` tag simply fades the contents of the current display window to a specified color. The only required attributes are `start` and `duration`; if no `color` attribute is specified the display window is faded out to black, such as in the following example:

```
<fadeout start="25" duration="5" />
```

You can fade out rectangular portions of the display window by specifying destination window attributes.

The <wipe/> tag

The `<wipe/>` tag specifies a transition whereby the new image either "pushes" the previous image off screen, or the new image is revealed beneath the previous image. The wipe can happen from either the left or right sides, as well as up or down.

The `<wipe/>` tag requires the `start`, `duration`, and `target` attributes, as well as two additional attributes, `type` and `direction`. The `type` attribute must be either `"push"` or `"normal"`; The direction must be either `"left"`, `"right"`, `"up"`, or `"down"`. A typical `<wipe/>` tag would be as follows:

```
<wipe start="5" duration="3" target="2" type="push"
      direction="right" />
```

If you specify a specific portion of the display window using the display window attributes, the wipe effect is done only in the specified area. You can do multiple wipes simultaneously. You can see the different wipe effects as well as multiple simultaneous wipes by watching the wipes.rp file included on the CD, in the RealPix directory.

The <viewchange/> tag

The <viewchange/> enables you to do zooming and panning effects. It does not take a target attribute because it is assumed that the effect is done on the current image. Because <viewchange/> operates on the current image, you must first display an image using some other effect before you can perform any <viewchange/> effect.

Using the <viewchange/> tag can be a little tricky. It all depends on how you define the source and the display (destination) windows. Zoom and pan effects can be done by varying the source image attributes and/or the destination image attributes. The confusing part is that completely different effects occur depending on which attributes you change.

Pans and zooms can be combined to produce complex effects. A couple of simple rules of thumb to remember when using the <viewchange/> effect are as follows:

✦ If you're changing the width or height attributes (srcw, srch, dstw, or dsth), you're changing the size of the source image or display area, which results in a zoom effect.

✦ If you're changing the x or y attributes (srcx, srcy, dstx, or dsty), you're moving around an image, which results in a panning effect.

✦ If you're changing a combination of attributes, you're performing a complex effect.

After you get the hang of it, the <viewchange/> tag is a lot of fun.

Zooms

Zoom effects can be done in a number of ways. You can increase or decrease the size of the source image window or the display window, or change them both at the same time. Depending on what settings you specify, the effect can be dramatically different.

The simplest case is when the display window stays the same and the size of the source image window changes. If the display window stays the same, and the source image window is decreased, the effect is that of a zoom in, because the smaller area of the source image is *stretched* to fit the same display window. This is illustrated in Figure 24-3.

Conversely, you can zoom out of an image by selecting a larger source image window. Increasing the size of the source window produces a zoom out because more of the source picture has to fit into the same display window. This effect is illustrated in Figure 24-4.

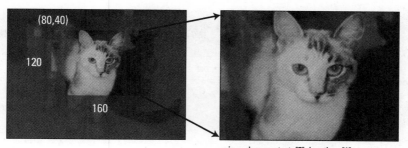

<view change start="5" duration="1"
srcx="80" srcy="40" srcw="160" srch="120"/>

Figure 24-3: Using `<viewchange/>` to zoom into an image by specifying a smaller source image window.

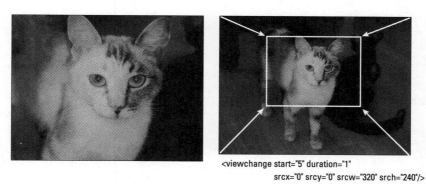

<viewchange start="5" duration="1"
srcx="0" srcy="0" srcw="320" srch="240"/>

Figure 24-4: Using `<viewchange/>` to zoom out of an image by specifying a larger source image window.

A slightly different way to produce zoom effects is to keep the source image attributes the same, and to change the display window attributes. You can accomplish very complicated zooms by changing both the source image and display window attributes at the same time. Table 24-2 is a matrix of the possible different zoom effects possible by changing the source window and display window attributes.

Table 24-2
Zoom Effects Using `<viewchange/>`

Display window Area	Source image area	Resultant zoom effect
Held constant	Reduced	Zoom in (the smaller source area is stretched to fit the same display window).
Held constant	Increased	Zoom out (the larger source image must be shrunk to fit the same display window).
Increased	Held constant	Zoom in (the same source image is stretched to fill a larger display window).
Reduced	Held constant	Zoom out (the same source image is shrunk to fit a smaller display window).
Reduced	Reduced	Depends on the percentage of each increase.
Reduced	Increased	Extreme zoom out (more of the source image has to be fit into an even smaller display window).
Increased	Reduced	Extreme zoom in (less of the source image has to be stretched to fit an even larger display window).
Increased	Increased	Depends on the percentage of each increase.

Pans

Panning across an image is not quite as tricky as zooming, because you don't really have to worry about the display window attributes. You simply choose the start and end points of your pan effect, and away you go.

Because you can only pan to the edges of an image, you have to either start with an image that is larger than your display window, or zoom in to give yourself some room to work with. Either way, the process is as follows:

1. **Specify the area you wish to pan from, using the source image attributes** (`srcx`, `srcy`, `srcw`,`srch`). Remember, the `<viewchange/>` tag operates on the current image, so you'll have to use another effect to get to the portion of the source image you want to begin your pan from, such as a fade in.

2. **To pan across the image, use the source image attributes to set the destination of the pan in the** `<viewchange/>` **tag.** Only the `srcx` and `srcy` attributes should change — otherwise you're combining a zoom and a pan.

Figure 24-5 illustrates how the pans in the cats_pan.rp file on the CD were constructed. Note that the second pan combines both a pan and a zoom, since the source image width and height attributes change. Because the tags enclose a larger area than the previous view, the effect is a slight zoom out.

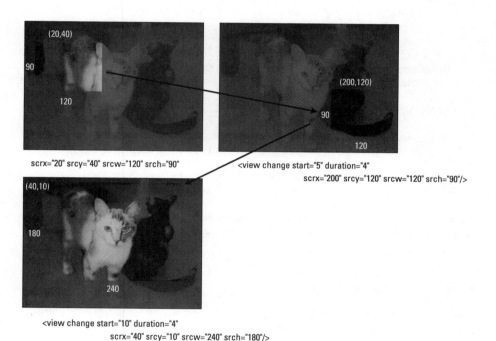

Figure 24-5: Setting `<viewchange/>` parameters for panning (and zooming) effects.

Special tags

The two tags described here are used in very specific situations and are not strictly transitions.

The `<fill/>` tag

The `<fill/>` tag is used to fill the screen with a color. It requires a `start` attribute, as well as a `color` attribute. Fill commands happen immediately — you cannot specify duration. If you want a color to slowly appear, use the `<fadeout/>` transition instead.

Optionally, you can fill only a portion of the display screen by using the display window attributes.

The <animate/> tag

The animate tag is used to trigger the animation of GIF files that contain multiple frames. It can also be used to display GIF images. If an image is displayed using the <animate/> tag, it appears immediately and begins animating according to the attributes set. If you wish to bring in the GIF file using a different transition, first use a different transition tag to bring in the GIF file and then begin the animation with the <animate/> tag.

The <animate/> tag requires a start, duration, and target attribute. All other attributes are optional. The maxfps attribute can be used to set the rate at which the GIF cycles through its frames. Here are a few examples of <animate/> tags:

```
<animate start="0" duration="30" target="1" />
```

This tag causes the GIF image with the handle "1" to appear at time zero, and animate for 30 seconds, provided it is not covered up by another image.

```
<fadein  start="5" duration="1"  target="12" />
<animate start="8" duration="30" target="12" maxfps="1" />
```

This combination of tags fades in the GIF image with the handle "12" and then begins animating it a few seconds later, cycling though one frame of the GIF animation every second.

Using color in RealPix

Colors used in RealPix attributes may be specified by either using a predefined color or specifying a hexadecimal value preceded by a # sign:

```
color="red" or background-color="#669933"
```

The predefined colors are

```
white, silver, gray, black, yellow, fuchsia, red, maroon,
lime, olive, green, purple, aqua, teal, blue, and navy.
```

Transparency in RealPix

The transparency features of GIF and PNG files are supported in RealPix. Any colors or images beneath an image with transparency show through. Transparency is not, however, supported in SMIL 1.0. If your RealPix presentation is part of a SMIL 1.0 presentation, media in other regions are not visible "through" the RealPix region.

Note Transparency *is* supported in SMIL 2.0.

Opening new RealPlayer windows

RealPix can open up new instances of the RealPlayer via the url attribute. The url attribute can be specified globally in the <head/> tag, or separately in transition tags. When the viewer clicks on the display screen, a RealPlayer is opened and the specified URL is played. The syntax is as follows:

```
url="command:openwindow(name, URL [,playmode=value][,playmode=value][...])"
```

Caution Older versions of the RealPlayer do not support multiple windows. You can use the <switch> statement in SMIL to author an alternative presentation for people with older players.

Cross-Reference SMIL is covered in chapters 26 through 32 of this book.

The name and URL parameters are required; additional playmode parameters are optional. Note that the openwindow parameters are usually not quoted; however if you have a URL that contains commas or parentheses or other special characters, you must enclose the URL in *single* quotes.

✦ name: The name parameter comes first, and specifies which window to open. It can either be a predefined or a user-defined name. The predefined names are as follows:

- _self or _current: Opens the specified URL in the current RealPlayer window.

- _new or _blank: Opens a new RealPlayer window.

In addition to the predefined names, you can specify a name for the RealPlayer window. If a RealPlayer window is already open with that name, the presentation is opened in that window. If no current RealPlayer is using that name, a new RealPlayer window is opened and assigned the user-defined name.

✦ URL: The location of the presentation to be opened. The URL must be fully qualified, including the transport protocal such as rtsp:// or http://, such as:

```
http://my.webserver.com/myfile.smil
rtsp://my.realserver.com/myfile.rp
```

Note Relative URLs do not work in the openwindow **command.**

✦ `playmode`: The RealPlayer has a number of playback attributes that can be accessed by the openwindow command. These include the zoom level, whether or not the player is "autosized," and whether or not the player stays on top of other windows while playing.

- `zoomlevel`: Determines how large the playback window is. The options are `"normal"`, `"double"`, and `"full"`. `"double"` doubles the screensize, while `"full"` plays the presentation back in fullscreen mode.

- `autosize`: When `autosize` is set to `true`, the RealPlayer opens to the smallest size possible to play back the linked presentation. The RealPlayer controls are not visible unless the user mouses over the presentation. If `autosize` is set to `false`, the RealPlayer opens in compact mode, which is just large enough to display both the linked presentation and the RealPlayer controls.

- `ontopwhileplaying`: Set to `"true"` or `"false"`, it determines whether the RealPlayer remains on top of other windows during playback, or whether it can be hidden.

You can use any combination of these parameters in your url attribute. For instance, this first example sets the url to open up myfile.rm in a new window, playing at double its original size:

```
url="command:openwindow(_new,
    rtsp://myserver.com/myfile.rm, zoomlevel=double)"
```

This next example sets the url to open myfile.rm in a new window called "video" and makes sure it always plays on top:

```
url="command:openwindow(video,
    rtsp://myserver.com/myfile.rm, ontopwhileplaying=true)"
```

This last example uses two playmode attributes. Myfile.rm will be played back double its original size, and autosized so that the video only has a thin frame around it:

```
url="command:openwindow(video,
    rtsp://myserver.com/myfile.rm, zoomlevel=double,
autosize=true)"
```

RealPix Bandwidth Considerations

Authoring the most compelling RealPix presentation in the world doesn't do you a bit of good if it does not stream well to your viewers. You have to ensure that the amount of data you're trying to send them doesn't exceed their maximum bandwidth.

The first step is actually preparing your images as discussed earlier (see "Image Preparation" earlier in this chapter). After you've written your RealPix code, you need to use the RealPix bandwidth calculator to ensure the presentation will stream smoothly. The RealPix bandwidth calculator is a Microsoft Excel spreadsheet application that takes your RealPix file as input, and analyzes its performance based on your image files and the settings in your `<head/>` tag.

If you've been diligent thus far, you probably won't have too many problems with the bandwidth calculator. If you've been using images straight off the scanner, chances are you are going to be surprised at what the bandwidth calculator is going to tell you.

One thing to remember is the actual throughputs your users receive may vary from the manufacturer's specifications. You'll have to think about who your audience is and what type of presentation you should be authoring. In addition, the audience you target determines the bandwidth limitations.

Many people, especially in work environments, have access to relatively fast Internet connections. However, dial-up users may have slow connections, so you may want to consider authoring different presentations for those users. You'll want to take special care estimating bandwidth requirements for presentations that have multiple streams playing in parallel. Bonus Chapter 1 on the CD-ROM has recommended settings for most kinds of presentations.

Using the RealPix bandwidth calculator

The RealPix bandwidth calculator reads in the `bitrate` and `preroll` attributes you specify in the `<head/>` tag of your presentation, then finds all the images you are using and calculates how long each one will take to download. After it has calculated the time necessary to download all the images in the presentation, it compares these calculated times to when you've scheduled each image to appear. By comparing the actual time required for each image to download to the scheduled time for each displayed image, the bandwidth calculator can indicate whether your file will stream smoothly or not.

For example, let's say you have authored the following RealPix file:

```
<imfl>
    <head width="320"
          height="240"
          duration="10"
          bitrate="20000"
          preroll="7"
          timeformat="dd:hh:mm:ss.xyz"
          />

<!-- define the image(s) -->
    <image handle="1" name="images/cabin_sun.jpg" />

<!-- begin presentation -->
    <fadein start="0" target="1" duration="1" />
    <fadeout start="7" duration="3" />
</imfl>
```

The bandwidth calculator can extract the bit rate and pre-roll information from the `<head/>` tag, find out the size of the image, and do a little math to establish whether the presentation will stream smoothly. First, to figure out how long it takes to download the image it can divide the file size by the bandwidth (assuming the image is 17K):

```
17 K * (8 bits/byte) / 20 Kbps = 6.8 seconds to download
```

Next, it can determine that there are 7 seconds of pre-roll, and that the image should be displayed at time 0. In this case, the presentation will stream smoothly because the image can be downloaded during the pre-roll period.

The bandwidth calculator repeats this calculation for every image in the file, and gives an indication when problems arise by turning values red in the display. The bandwidth calculator lets you change values interactively to see how they affect your presentation, for instance increasing your pre-roll or increasing the bit rate. Using this interactivity, you can figure out how to make your presentation stream smoothly. Figure 24-6 is an illustration of the bandwidth calculator.

Note   The RealPix bandwidth calculator is a Windows-only application. If you're on Mac or Unix, you'll have to either calculate the download times by hand or test it from the server. You can use the values in Table 24-1 to estimate your RealPix file performance.

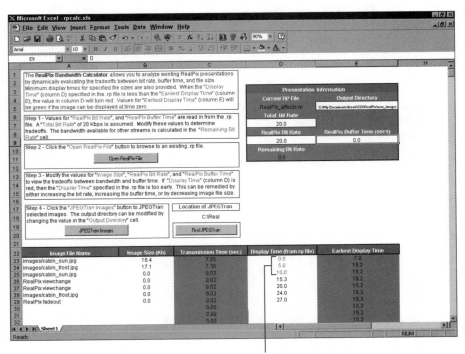

Display times shown in red indicate problems

Figure 24-6: The RealPix bandwidth calculator.

To use the RealPix bandwidth calculator, do the following:

1. **Open rpcalc.xls.**

2. **Enter the target bitrate in cell D7.** This defaults to 20 Kbps for modem users.

3. **Open your RealPix file by clicking the Open RealPix File button under Step 2.**

4. **Check display times.** Any images scheduled to be displayed before they are fully downloaded have their display times shown in red. If you want your presentation to stream properly, you must not have any red display times.

5. **Modify values.** You can modify any values in the bandwidth calculator to see how your file would be affected. By playing with the values in the bandwidth calculator, you can see how long folks will have to wait for each problem image, or how small you'd have to make your image to display in the given pre-roll time.

Setting a pre-roll time in your RealPix presentation does not guarantee the buffer time. If the pre-roll time is not sufficient to download the first image, RealPix ignores it and buffers as long as it needs to recieve the first image.

The bandwidth calculator looks for the pre-roll attribute in the `<head/>` tag and uses that as the RealPix Buffer Time in cell E-9. Because pre-roll is not a required attribute, it usually defaults to zero in the bandwidth calculator.

With the RealPix Buffer Time set to zero, you can see how long your presentation needs to buffer by looking at the Earliest Display Time for your first image in cell E-23. If this value is acceptable, enter it as the RealPix Buffer Time variable. If it is not, enter an acceptable value in the RealPix Buffer Time variable, and change the Image Size variable of your first image to see how small you have to make your first image. Once you have the first image's Display Time showing in black, you can move on to the rest of your images.

If other images still have Display Time shown in red, you must either delay the image or reduce its file size until the Display Time is shown in black. You can enter values in the Image Size or Display Time columns to see how you'll have to modify your presentation timing or image file size.

Using the RealPix bandwidth calculator may seem awkward at first, but it is extremely important to master if you want your RealPix presentations to stream properly. RealPix can be an incredibly powerful technology, but it is entirely possible to author presentations that look fine locally but do not stream well. Even after you've fine-tuned your presentation by using the bandwidth calculator, you should test your presentation streaming from a server, using a modem or whatever your intended audience is using.

Creating a RealPix File

Creating a RealPix file is easy, but making sure it streams smoothly can be a little tricky. This exercise walks you through the steps necessary to create a smoothly streaming RealPix file.

1. **First, choose your images.** You'll want to prepare them by resizing them and compressing them until they're within the recommended filesizes detailed in Table 24-1.

   Remember, the sizes recommended in Table 24-1 are based on 5–7 seconds of download time per image. You can use larger files if you think the audience is prepared to wait for them.

2. **Open a text editor.**

3. **Type the** `<imfl>` **and** `</imfl>` **tags.**

4. **Set up the global attributes in the** `<head/>` **tag.** At a minimum, you'll need to specify the `width`, `height`, `duration`, and `bitrate`. You may want to specify a `title`, `author`, and `copyright`; also if you prefer working in seconds as opposed to milliseconds you should specify the `timeformat`.

   ```
   <head  width="320"
          height="240"
          duration="30"
          bitrate="20000"
          timeformat="dd:hh:mm:ss.xyz"
          />
   ```

5. **Define all your images.** Each one should have an `<image/>` tag specifying the location of the file and a unique handle.

   ```
   <image handle="1" name="images/mypix-1.jpg" />
   <image handle="2" name="images/mypix-2.jpg" />
   etc.
   ```

Tip   All the examples in this chapter have the images in a directory separate from the RealPix code, as do the files on the CD. You should adhere to this practice as well. It makes working on files much easier by keeping separate file types *separate*.

6. **Save the file and test it.** Nothing much happens, except you should see a black screen for the duration of your file. If there are any errors in your file, RealPix will report them.

   This process is a good idea because it makes sure that all your image tags are legal. RealPix does a reasonable job with error reporting, but testing at regular intervals helps localize and trap any potential errors early on.

7. **Provided your file is error-free, you may begin adding transitions.** Most RealPix files begin with the first file fading in:

```
<fadein start="0" duration="1" target="1" />
```

This line of code assumes the first image you want displayed was given the handle "1". Of course you can use any handle numbers you want, but assigning numbers in the order you want to display them makes things easier.

8. **Add a few more transitions, leaving five second gaps between them.** This is a good starting point. You may have to move them later after checking with the bandwidth calculator, but if you kept the image file sizes down, you should be able to maintain five second gaps between them.

9. **Save your file after every five transitions or so and test it so that you can localize any errors that pop up.** Not only that, you'll lose less data if your computer crashes.

10. **After you've added all your transitions, save your file and test it.** If it looks and acts like you expect it to, run it through the bandwidth calculator to see if it will stream smoothly.

11. **Open** `rpcalc.xls` **in Microsoft Excel.**

12. **Open your file by clicking on the Open RealPix File button.** The bandwidth calculator automatically reads in the bitrate setting, and finds all the images used in the file.

13. **Unless you specified a pre-roll, the RealPix Buffer Time value defaults to zero.** You can find out how long the file needs to buffer by looking at the Earliest Display Time displayed next to your first image.

    If this is an acceptable buffer time, go ahead and enter this number for your RealPix Buffer Time. If it is not, you're going to have to reduce the file size of your first image, or use a different first image.

14. **After you have a suitable RealPix Buffer Time, look at the Display Time column of numbers.** If all your display times are displayed in black, go to the head of the class! Skip straight to step 16.

    Any numbers displayed in red indicate a problem. To fix any of these problems, you must either delay the display of the image until the Earliest Display Time listed for that image, or reduce its file size.

You can change values in the RealPix Bandwidth calculator to see how they affect the overall file, but this does not change the values inside the actual RealPix file. Use the bandwidth calculator as a guide; then amend your RealPix code and test again.

15. **If you have to make edits to your RealPix code, do so, save it, and test it locally.** If it still plays back well, re-load it into the RealPix bandwidth calculator and check it again. Go back to Step 12.

16. **Once all your display times are displayed in black, your file is ready to stream.** Load the file and the accompanying images up to the RealServer, being careful to maintain any directory structures.

Streaming Live RealPix

RealPix can be streamed live using the RealPix broadcast application. The application works by checking a directory every second for an updated image. If the image has been updated, it is sent to the server. You cannot specify transitions when using the broadcast application — the transitions automatically alternate between a cross-fade and push-wipe.

 Caution The RealPix broadcast application is an unsupported feature. RealNetworks does not provide technical support for any problems you may encounter.

The RealPix broadcast application requires information about three different items before it can begin broadcasting:

✦ **Server:** You must supply a valid RealServer name, port, username, and password.

✦ **File names:** You must supply a name for the live stream, as well as the image file name to be monitored.

✦ <head/> **attributes:** You must define all the required attributes for the live RealPix stream, such as width, height, and bitrate.

Once the RealPix broadcast application has the information it needs, it establishes a connection to the server and sends the image file you specified to be monitored. When you want to send a new image, you simply save a new image on top of the monitored file. The RealPix broadcast application detects the image change and sends the new image to the RealServer.

The RealPix broadcast application ships with the RealSystem Authoring Guide, available from the RealNetworks site (www.realnetworks.com). The version provided runs on any 32-bit Windows operating system. The C++ code is available if you want to compile it and run it on a different operating system.

Running the RealPix broadcast application

The live RealPix application is named exlivpix.exe. It requires a few shared libraries to run, which can be found either in the authoring kit or perhaps already installed on your computer if you have other RealSystem components installed. The necessary libraries are listed in Table 24-3. The RealPix broadcast application can run from any directory on the encoding machine, as long as these libraries are in the same directory.

Tip

It's a good idea to create a directory called `c:\livepix` and copy the libraries and live RealPix executable there. The live RealPix application asks for information that requires full paths to be entered. It's much easier to type `c:\livepix` than `c:\Program Files\Real\Authoring Kit\RealPixBroadcastFiles\`.

Table 24-3
Live RealPix Shared Libraries

Windows 32-Bit	UNIX
px1i3260.dll	pxlive.so.6.0
pxcg3260.dll	pxcgif2.so.6.0
pxcj3260.dll	pxcjpeg2.so.6.0
encn3260.dll	encnet.so.6.0
sdpp3260.dll	sdpplin.so.6.0
auth3260.dll	authmgr.so.6.0
rn5a3260.dll	rn5auth.so.6.0

After you locate all the libraries and the live RealPix executable and copy them into the same directory, you're ready to run the broadcast application. If you're running under UNIX, you'll have to compile the source code before you can run the program. The remainder of this section assumes the reader is running the application under Windows, though the behavior and appearance of the application under UNIX should be identical.

To start the RealPix broadcast application, you have to type a long command line with the following parameters:

```
exlivpix.exe server port filename imgname width height
    bitrate username password
```

✦ `server`: This is the name of the RealServer broadcasting your images. You can use a DNS name such as `my.realserver.com` or an IP address such as 192.168.0.127.

✦ `port`: The port that the RealServer uses for live broadcasts; the default is 4040.

✦ `filename`: The name of the live stream, such as livepix.rt.

✦ `imgname`: The name of the image you want the RealPix broadcast application to monitor.

Tip   The file to be monitored can be anywhere on the encoding machine, but works best if it is in the same directory as the encoding application. Call it superstition, call it experience — it's what works.

✦ width: The width of the live RealPix presentation in pixels.

✦ height: The height of the live RealPix presentation in pixels.

✦ bitrate: The bitrate at which you want the RealPix presentation to stream.

✦ username: A valid username on the RealServer.

✦ password: The correct password for the username. Without the proper password, the broadcast application will not be able to connect to the server.

Caution   The RealPix broadcast application is a simple application. It does not hide your password onscreen, so be careful.

You must specify a value for *every* parameter, separated by spaces, without quotes. A command line call to the RealPix broadcast application would therefore look like this:

```
exlivpix.exe my.realserver.com 4040 livepix.rp liveslide.jpg
    320 240 20000 MyUsername MyPassword
```

If you are not in the same directory as the RealPix broadcast application, you must specify full paths for the exlivpix.exe and the image you want the application to monitor.

Tip   It's always a good idea to save the command line in a file. This makes it easier to restart the application if there are any problems. On a Windows machine, simply save the command line in a file with a .bat (batch file) extension. Unix machines can save to any file and run the file as a script.

When you start up the RealPix broadcast application, it should look like Figure 24-7.

Tip   If for some reason the RealPix broadcast application fails, chances are that you entered some of the server information incorrectly. Unfortunately the RealPix broadcast application provides virtually no feedback or error messaging. Make absolutely sure you have all the server information correct and the broadcast application should work just fine.

The application connects to the server, sends the image and begins the monitoring process. The broadcast application checks the image every second and re-sends it every time a change is made.

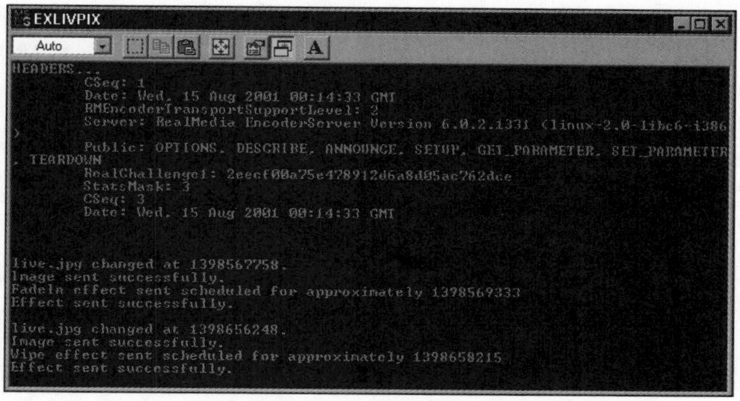

Figure 24-7: The RealPix broadcast application in operation.

Stopping the RealPix broadcast application

To end your live text broadcast, type q in the command console window. Alternately, you can simply delete the file that is being monitored or change its name. As soon as the broadcast application cannot find the file specified in the command line, it stops the broadcast.

Live RealPix considerations

Be sure your images are small enough to be broadcast at the specified bit rate. All images are eventually broadcast, but large files will take much longer to reach your audience. Be sure to prepare your images carefully to avoid unnecessary delays for your viewers. Table 24-1 should be helpful in this regard.

Summary

RealPix presentations can be more compelling than RealVideo because the low bitrate allows each image to be reasonably high quality. Since the transitions are rendered on the viewer's machine, they are very high quality. RealPix provides a rich set of transitions that enable you to create interesting effects.

✦ Images for RealPix presentations should be resized and compressed to an appropriate file size for the intended bitrate.

✦ RealPix presentations use a simple markup language to tell the RealPlayer how and when to display the desired images.

✦ With the exception of the `<imfl><imfl/>` tag, all RealPix tags are unary and require the closing slash — for example, `<image/>`.

✦ The global parameters of the RealPix presentation are set in the `<head/>` tag.

✦ All RealPix presentations require the `duration`, `width`, `height`, and `bitrate` attributes — all other attributes are optional.

✦ All images must be defined with an `<image/>` tag and assigned a unique handle.

✦ Transition tags are used to display images in different manners.

✦ All RealPix presentations should be checked using the RealPix bandwidth calculator to see if they'll stream properly.

✦ Images can be streamed live using the RealPix broadcast application.

✦   ✦   ✦

Other Data Types

In addition to audio, video, and the data types that have been discussed up to this point, there are others at your disposal such as 3-D text, streaming screen capture codecs, and specialized video codecs. These data types tend to be somewhat specialized in their application, but you should be aware that they exist.

Some data types require special equipment, while others are merely custom plug-ins for the players and encoders. Some require specialized authoring tools. Many are limited in their platform support.

In this chapter, you'll learn about a few special application audio data types.

Next, some special video data types are covered, including a 360-degree interactive data type, and a 3-D video data type. Remember 3-D glasses? You haven't seen the last of them.

Finally, presentation data types are discussed. Presentation data types include screen capture codecs (enable you to capture everything displayed a computer screen) and a whiteboard data type that allows you to capture everything written on a whiteboard — useful for training, meetings, and a number of other applications.

This chapter should by no means be considered a definitive list of everything available. Many custom data types are available, depending on the platform on which you're working. However, this should give you an idea of what is possible using the vendors' SDKs to create custom applications.

Audio Data Types

All three streaming media platforms offer excellent audio codecs. However, there are numerous instances when you might want to control the access rights to your content. The recent controversy surrounding downloadable music underscored the need to protect the rights of copyright holders. Using an audio data type with built-in rights management provides security for your content so that it cannot be traded or swapped illegally.

A couple of audio data types include digital rights management built into the solution. Another audio data type offers the ability to stream MIDI (Musical Instrument Digital Interface) information instead of encoded audio streams. The data rate is extremely low, and the quality usually fairly high.

Audible

Audible is essentially a plug-in that combines encryption and streaming audio codecs that enable people to download audio entertainment, such as books on tape, in a secured manner. Because the content is encrypted, it cannot be listened to unless it has been legitimately paid for. It also cannot be listened to on another computer. After you purchase the content, you can either listen to the content being streamed across the Internet, or download the content to your computer and transfer it to a portable device for listening away from your computer.

Audible provides plug-ins for both the RealPlayer and Windows Media Player. The plug-in for the RealPlayer automatically installs when you attempt to listen to audible content; the Windows Media Player filter can be downloaded from Audible's Web site (www.audible.com).

Audible technology is not available for use by third parties — it is a proprietary implementation. However, audible technology is a great example of how streaming media can be put to use in a reasonably cross-platform manner to provide a useful service.

Liquid Audio

Liquid Audio was developed to address the specific needs of the music industry, particularly rights management of digital music on the Internet. The Liquid Audio system includes a complete audio production environment, digital rights management system, a proprietary Liquid Audio player, and plug-ins for the RealPlayer and Windows Media Player. Figure 25-1 shows the Liquid Audio plug-in for the RealPlayer.

The Liquid Audio production environment is much more than a simple encoder. It includes sophisticated pre-processing and variety of codecs. The Liquid Audio system also allows you to associate a variety of metadata with a song or CD, including cover art, liner notes, lyrics, writing credits, production credits, and so on.

Figure 25-1: The Liquid Audio plug-in inside the RealPlayer

The Liquid Audio digital rights management system enables you to set rules for CDs and songs. You can set rules in a number of different ways, including providing short streaming samples or lower quality versions for free. After you set the rules for the content, you upload it to a Liquid Audio server, which manages the DRM functionality.

The Liquid Audio server can work in tandem with the RealServer or Windows Media Server — free versions may be offered in a streaming format, but secure downloads are handled by the Liquid Audio server.

Streaming MIDI with Crescendo

Music sequencing programs control keyboards, samplers, and other digital musical equipment by using MIDI (Musical Instrument Digital Interface) data. Instead of recording the actual sounds, sequencing programs store information about how the music was played, such as which notes were used and when they were played. This information is then stored in MIDI files (`.mid`).

Because MIDI data is relatively low bit rate, it is a perfect candidate for streaming across the Internet. Many computer sound cards come with built-in MIDI synthesizer capabilities; the listener's computer can play the streamed MIDI data without any additional external hardware. If the user does not have built-in MIDI capabilities, free software MIDI synthesizers can be downloaded online such as Yamaha's MIDplug (`www.yamaha-xg.com`) and Crescendo Forte (`www.liveupdate.com`).

MIDI playback capabilities are somewhat limited. Only digital musical instrument information can be sequenced. You cannot, for instance, record vocals into a MIDI file. Additionally, different MIDI implementations use different sounds, so you cannot guarantee exactly what a MIDI file sounds like played back on someone else's computer unless you know exactly what MIDI playback device they're using.

The RealSystem can stream MIDI files via the Crescendo plug-in. The RealServer uses the Crescendo Forte plug-in to stream MIDI files. This plug-in is available from the Live Update Web site (www.liveupdate.com). Once you have purchased and installed the Crescendo Forte plug-in for your RealServer, you can place MIDI files on your RealServer and stream them just as you would any other file. You can reference them directly, or use them as an element inside a SMIL file.

SMIL is covered in detail in Chapters 27–31.

Listeners must download a plug-in for the RealPlayer before they can play back streamed MIDI files. This is taken care of automatically by the RealSystem Auto Update functionality.

Although both the QuickTime and Windows Media players can play local MIDI files, neither can play streaming MIDI files.

Video Data Types

A couple of specialized video data types exist that could be of interest to a streaming media professional. BeHere TotalView has been used at sporting events and music concerts (see Chapter 39). iSee3D is a true 3-D video codec that utilizes cutting edge imaging technology.

BeHere TotalView

BeHere TotalView technology creates an interactive video experience. Users have the ability to zoom in, out, and move around in a 360-degree radius through the video. The video is shot using a special camera and software that turns a 360-degree panoramic view into a continuous strip of video (see Figure 25-2). This video can then be encoded and played back as streaming media.

As the audience watches the video, they can adjust their viewing angle by dragging their cursor back and forth over the video display. The display changes as if the camera were being moved. In fact, the camera never moves — only the portion of the video that is being displayed to the viewer changes.

Because the entire 360-degree view must be streamed, TotalView requires higher bit rates to achieve the same quality as standard video shot at the same screen size. In addition to the screen that the viewer is watching, there are approximately another four screens worth of image data that also must be sent.

Figure 25-2: The BeHere TotalView system
Image courtesy of BeHere Technolgies, Inc.

BeHere technology is incorporated into the RealPlayer and QuickTime player, and can be played back in the Windows Media Format via an ActiveX control embedded in Internet Explorer. BeHere can only be streamed live using the RealSystem Producer and Windows Media Technologies Encoder.

The equipment necessary to produce BeHere TotalView events can be purchased or rented from BeHere Technologies. For more information on the TotalView system, please refer to the BeHere Web site (www.behere.com).

iSee3D

iSee3D streaming technology grew out of iSee3D's medical imaging technology, which was developed to give surgeons better views during minimally invasive surgery procedures. The technology, which involves special camera lenses and encoding equipment, was re-purposed into a streaming data type.

The technology works with both the RealPlayer and the Windows Media player. You can watch the content in either interlaced mode (requiring specially synchronized glasses), anaglyph mode (using the traditional red/blue glasses) or in standard two-dimensional mode. Please see the iSee3D Web site for further information (www.isee3d.com).

Presentation Data Types

There are a number of applications where the presentation data types discussed in this section can be used, such as distance learning or business communications. In each of these situations, information is often transferred a screen at a time. The screen size required to make presentations useful is far too large for a video codec to handle gracefully.

These presentation data types take advantage of the fact that though the screen is large, there is very little motion. The color palette can be reduced dramatically compared to standard video as well. Even though they display at a large screen size, the data rates can be kept low.

Screen capture codecs

Screen capture codecs are designed to encode the information that is displayed to a computer screen into a video-like presentation. The frame rates they can achieve depend on the bit rate, the screen size, and the number of colors they try to display.

Screen capture codecs do a good job by taking some short cuts. Because of the short cuts, you should avoid doing several things when recording a presentation using a screen capture codec. For example, as with video codecs, avoid excessive motion. Other things that can drastically reduce the quality of your encodes are:

✦ Opening and closing windows often

✦ Dragging windows across the screen

✦ Scrolling up and down windows. If you must move down a page in a window, use the Page Down or Page Up buttons instead.

✦ Playing videos

The best quality encodes are obtained by slow, graceful movements on screen. This may not be the easiest thing to get used to, but it definitely improves the quality of your screen capture encodes. Other things you should consider doing are:

✦ Reducing the display size of your screen. The larger the display size, the more data there is for the codec to encode. Reducing the screen size to 800 × 600 or even 640 × 480 improves your encoding quality. Alternatively, try selecting a reduced area of the screen to encode if the software allows it.

✦ Reducing the number of colors displayed. Try to change the number of colors to 256.

One last thing to beware of is that screen capture encoding is a very CPU intensive operation. Make sure you have a fast computer to handle the encoding, and try not to run any unnecessary programs. Refer to each manufacturer's Web site for minimum recommended hardware specifications.

Windows Media Technologies' Screen Capture

Windows Media Technologies added a screen capture codec to Windows Media Encoder Version 7.0. This enabled the direct capture of screen actions by re-encoding of AVI files produced by other screen capture utilities.

Setting up a live encode from the screen involves a couple of simple steps:

✦ Setting up a source group that includes screen capture

✦ Selecting a profile that utilizes the screen capture codec

When you're set up to go, you simply start the encoder and record your session.

Setting up Windows Media screen capture

1. **Open the Windows Media Encoder and open up the Session Properties window by typing Alt+Enter.**

2. **This opens up the Session Properties window.** Make sure that the Sources tab is selected, and click on the New button to create a new source group. This brings up the New Source Group window (see Figure 25-3).

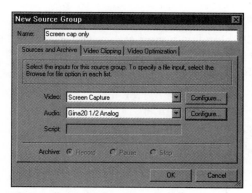

Figure 25-3: Setting up a new source group for screen capture in the Windows Media Encoder

3. **Choose Screen Capture from the drop-down menu and click the Configure button if you want to encode something less that full screen (see Figure 25-4).** Encoding smaller regions of the screen produces higher quality encodes.

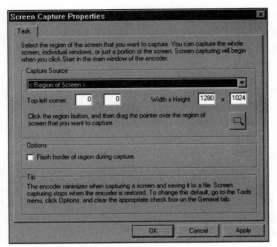

Figure 25-4: The Windows Media Screen
Capture Properties window

4. **If you specified a reduced region to capture, click Apply to return to the New Source Group window.**

5. **If you want to record audio along with your screen capture, make sure that your audio source is also properly configured.**

6. **Click OK to return to the Session Properties window of the encoder.**

   You now have your source group configured for screen capture. Now all you have to do is choose or create an appropriate profile.

7. **In the Session Properties window, click the Profiles tab to bring up the profile selection box (see Figure 25-5).** Choose an appropriate profile or create your own specialized profile.

   The Windows Media Encoder comes with three Screen Capture profile presets. You may want to start with one of these and modify as necessary. Save any modifications for later use.

8. **Click on the Output tab and set up your broadcast parameters or your archive file name.**

9. **Click OK to return to the main Windows Media Encoder window.**

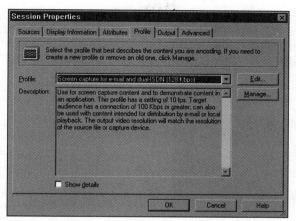

Figure 25-5: Selecting an appropriate profile for screen capture in the Windows Media Encoder

When you're ready, click Start on the encoder. It hides from view and encodes whatever happens on screen as per your instructions in Step 3. To end your encoding session, simply restore the Windows Media Encoder window by clicking on the icon in the start bar.

If you have AVI files that you created with other screen capture utilities, you can encode them using the screen capture codec by selecting the file as the input when you select your source group. You can take advantage of the streaming capabilities and codec efficiencies of the Windows Media Screen Capture without having to recreate your screen capture movies from scratch.

ScreenWatch 3.0

ScreenWatch is a product developed by OPTX International for encoding screen-based presentations. It works as a stand-alone program for creating screen capture files, or with the RealSystem and Windows Media Technologies.

When used with the RealSystem, the ScreenWatch system can be used to create on-demand screen capture files or broadcast live directly to a RealServer using the live webcasting module. Both the on-demand files and the live versions can be used in SMIL presentations along with other data types.

To use ScreenWatch files with the Windows Media system, the files must be converted using the ScreenWatch conversion utility. This utility combines the ScreenWatch files with audio WAV files to create Windows Media WMV files, using the Windows Media Screen Capture codec. Live broadcast is not supported in the Windows Media format.

The ScreenWatch system does not record audio. This must be done in a separate application such as the RealSystem Producer or any audio editing program. To find out more about the ScreenWatch system, please refer to the ScreenWatch Web site (www.screenwatch.com).

Mimio

Mimio technology combines ultrasonic technology and streaming technology to come up with a cool application. The Mimio system uses special hardware that attaches to your whiteboard and special sensors that attach to your whiteboard markers and erasers to capture everything written on or erased from a white board.

The information written on the whiteboard is captured in a proprietary file format called INK files. These INK files can be watched locally using the Mimio player, or exported as Windows Media files on the Windows platform, or saved as QuickTime movie files on the Mac.

For live broadcast situations, Mimio has a system called boardCast that works with the RealSystem. This involves a plug-in for the RealServer, a plug-in for the RealPlayer that is automatically installed if viewers don't have it already, and the Mimio boardCast Producer, which combines Mimio files with audio files and outputs to the RealMedia format.

To find out more about the Mimio system, visit the Mimio Web site (www.mimio.com).

Summary

Many special application data types exist — this chapter only covered a few. Because these data types are special applications, they often are not supported by all three streaming platforms, and sometimes do not offer Mac support.

✦ Windows Media offers its own built-in screen capture codec.

✦ To use the Windows Media screen capture codec, simply set the screen up as a source and choose an appropriate encoding profile.

✦ BeHere TotalView technology is supported on all three streaming platforms.

✦ Total View enables viewers to adjust their point of view across 360-degrees, as well as zooming in and out.

This chapter concludes Part VI of this book. The next part introduces you to SMIL, the Synchronized Multimedia Integration Language. SMIL can be used to combine multiple data types into a single presentation.

✦   ✦   ✦

SMIL (Synchronized Multimedia Integration Language)

SMIL – An Overview

SMIL (pronounced smile), the Synchronized Multimedia Integration Language, was developed in 1998 under the auspices of the World Wide Web Consortium (W3C) to address the needs of multimedia authors working on the Internet. It was developed with input from many different companies, including Apple, Philips, Lucent, Netscape, and RealNetworks, as well as prestigious research organizations, such as Columbia University and CWI (the Netherlands) and INRIA (France).

SMIL was developed because a need was recognized for a multimedia authoring language that addressed multiple concurrent data types, interactivity, presentation layout, and timing concerns. The W3C was chosen as the organization to lead the effort because of their success with previous Internet standardization efforts, such as HTML and XML. The W3C's resulting recommendation, SMIL 1.0, was released in 1998.

The first commercial implementation of SMIL was RealNetworks' RealSystem G2. In addition to using SMIL as the layout language, it also introduced RealText and RealPix, which were new streaming data types designed to take advantage of the power of SMIL.

The SMIL 2.0 recommendation, approved in August 2001, incorporates more features and functionality than SMIL 1.0. It also introduces the concept of profiles, which allows multimedia authors to author one presentation for a variety of different streaming-enabled devices. Broad cross industry support for SMIL 2.0 included participation from Adobe, Macromedia, Microsoft, Intel, IBM, Nokia, and Panasonic as well as from the original participants.

SMIL: An Overview

SMIL is a simple, XML-based markup language that enables multimedia authors to combine multiple data types into a single presentation. The language itself is simple and straightforward, consisting of tags in angle brackets, such as `<smil>`. This set of tags enables the author to define the layout of a presentation, as well as all the necessary timing information. Because SMIL is XML-compliant, it should look familiar to anyone who has ever examined HTML code.

SMIL presentations are divided into two sections. The first section is the header section, where the author defines the global characteristics of the presentation, such as width and height, as well as areas of the screen (regions) where different parts of the presentation should be displayed. Metadata can also be specified in the header section.

Tip   Metadata is information *about* a file, such as the title, author, and copyright of a file.

The second section is the body, where all the timing information is specified. Clips can be played in *sequence,* one after the other, or in *parallel*, at the same time. Alternatively the author can specify exact *begin* and *end* times for each clip. The body section can also contain tags that specify which streams to send depending on the viewer's bandwidth, language preference, or player version. Listing 26-1 is a simple SMIL file that plays an audio file, which is followed by a video file.

Listing 26-1: A simple SMIL file

```
<smil>

    <head>
        <root-layout width="320" height="240"/>
    </head>

    <body>
        <seq>
            <audio src="rtsp://my.server.com/audio.rm"/>
            <video src="rtsp://your.server.com/video.rm"/>
        </seq>
    </body>

</smil>
```

All SMIL files must begin and end with the `<smil></smil>` tags. After the opening `<smil>` tag, the layout of the presentation is defined in the header section. The header section is enclosed with `<head></head>` tags, and contains a single line of code which defines the size of the presentation. In this case, the size of the presentation is 320 × 240.

Following the header section is the body section, which is enclosed by the `<body></body>` tags. In this body section, two media streams are contained within `<seq></seq>` tags, which specifies that they are to be played in sequence. In this presentation, the `audio.rm` file on `my.server.com` is played, followed by the `video.rm` file on `your.server.com`.

The preceding example is not so revolutionary. In fact, you might be tempted to ask why eleven lines of code were necessary to play two simple files back to back when you could accomplish the same thing with two lines of code in a metafile. To answer this, take a look at a typical television program and break it down into its component parts.

Figure 26-1 is an artist's rendition of a typical sports program. It may look like any other television program, but a closer inspection reveals that it is a particularly information-rich presentation. The announcer talks about the day's sporting events. As he speaks, photos of the various stories are displayed over his shoulder. During the whole presentation, scores from various leagues are displayed along the bottom of the screen. Last but not least, the sports network's logo is displayed in the lower right hand corner — a persistent reminder of who owns the broadcast.

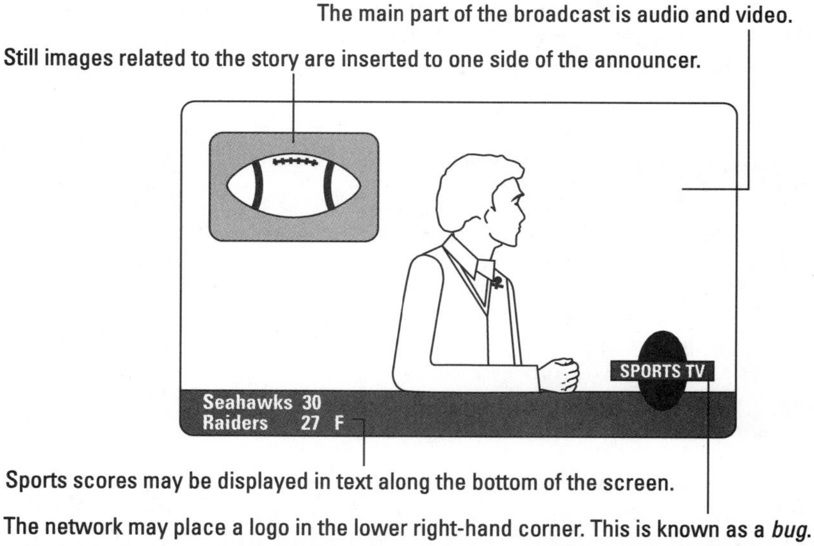

The main part of the broadcast is audio and video.

Still images related to the story are inserted to one side of the announcer.

Seahawks 30
Raiders 27 F

SPORTS TV

Sports scores may be displayed in text along the bottom of the screen.

The network may place a logo in the lower right-hand corner. This is known as a *bug*.

Figure 26-1: A typical sports television broadcast consists of different types of media.

We see the program as a single presentation, but it actually consists of four separate elements:

✦ **Video:** The announcer is a continuous video stream.

✦ **Changing images:** Different photos are used to illustrate each story.

✦ **Text:** The sports scores along the bottom provide additional text information.

✦ **Persistent image:** The logo in the lower right hand corner that never changes.

Before the television program can be broadcast, it must be assembled in the television studio from the individual parts. The four separate elements are produced individually and combined using powerful video broadcasting tools. The resulting video is sent to the television station's antenna or satellite and broadcast to the audience.

This modularity gives the program a large degree of flexibility. By separating the program into its component parts, different people can be assigned to different parts of the broadcast. A few simple keystrokes can change whether the images are displayed on the right or left. The scores along the bottom can be made to disappear if desired. The component parts can also be re-used. The sports scores could be used in the evening news, or the broadcast could be licensed to a third party with the logo in the lower right-hand corner removed.

SMIL mirrors this modularity in software. By allowing the author to specify multiple data types and different regions, a large degree of flexibility is provided. Streams can be combined and re-used, moved around in both time and space. This flexibility provides not only a large degree of freedom for the author, but more importantly, significant bandwidth savings, which enables the creation of rich multimedia presentations at low bandwidths.

The Advantages of SMIL

If the sports program in Figure 26-1 is encoded as a unified video stream, the quality suffers at low bit rates. In particular, the text along the bottom of the screen will be illegible. The still images are compromised because they are treated as part of the full motion video, even though the frame rate of the still images is much, much lower. The video quality suffers because the changing text at the bottom and the changing images add considerable motion to the frame.

If the program is separated into its component parts, significant gains in quality can be realized:

✦ The text along the bottom, for instance, could be sent as a text stream at less than 1 Kbps. The text would be displayed perfectly clearly, and the removal of this motion from the video frame would improve the quality of the video encode.

✦ The still images illustrating the stories could be sent as individual images. Since the image only changes every 15 seconds or so, the quality of each image could be very high.

✦ The logo in the lower right-hand corner could be sent as a single high-quality image at the beginning of the broadcast.

✦ With all the extraneous components removed, the remaining video frame has much less motion, so the result should be a higher quality video encode.

In addition to the potential quality gains, SMIL offers additional flexibility. Since the Internet is an international medium, people may be tuning in from different countries. Using SMIL you can specify different streams to be sent to different audience members based on a language setting in their player. Or, you could send them a different presentation based on their connection speed to the Internet.

The next few chapters introduce the functionality and power of SMIL. Don't let its simplicity fool you — you can author very sophisticated presentations within the framework it defines.

How SMIL Works

SMIL files are simple text files just like HTML files. They can either reside on Web servers or streaming media servers. Depending on the level of support and the data types used inside the presentations, SMIL files can be played back by a variety of different players.

Caution

Even though SMIL is an open framework, the implementations of it have been somewhat proprietary. For instance, the RealPlayer renders SMIL files but not if they contain data types that the RealPlayer does not support. The QuickTime player supports *most* of SMIL 1.0, and Internet Explorer has limited support for SMIL 2.0 (for more on SMIL 2.0 please turn to Chapter 32). While it is hoped that there is more interoperability in the future, this topic is still a bit of a minefield for the time being. Proceed with caution.

As soon as the player or browser has the complete SMIL file, it looks at the header section to find out what the layout of the presentation is. After the header section has been analyzed, the player looks at the body section and begins buffering the streams that are to be played back first. The player then attempts to play back all the streams using the timing constraints specified in the file.

Going back to the example in Listing 26-1, the player would size its display window to 320 × 240, as specified in the `<root-layout>` tag. The player would then begin buffering the first stream, `audio.rm` from `my.server.com`. As the end of `audio.rm` approached, the player would then begin buffering `video.rm` from `your.server.com`. When `audio.rm` finished playing, `video.rm` would immediately begin playing without any intervening buffering time.

SMIL does not have any built-in bandwidth management. Listing 26-1 assumes the viewer has sufficient bandwidth to accommodate both the streams included in the presentation. This can be a problem particularly when streams are played in parallel — in which case, the viewer must have sufficient bandwidth to accommodate both streams *at the same time*.

You must author your SMIL presentations carefully and test them under real-world conditions to make sure they stream properly. Judicious use of the various timing tags in SMIL should avert any potential bandwidth problems.

Summary

SMIL is a simple markup language designed as an open framework to author multimedia presentations for the Internet. It provides a method for authors to define layout and timing parameters, as well as advanced commands that enable the presentation to be modified according to the viewer's language preference, Internet connection speed, and player version.

The next chapter looks at the syntax of SMIL, and how SMIL presentations are put together. Remember the following basic points from this chapter.

✦ SMIL was developed by a number of companies working together with the W3C.

✦ SMIL is an XML-compliant markup language.

✦ SMIL files have two parts: the header and body sections.

✦ The header section specifies layout information and metadata.

✦ The body section specifies the timing of the presentation.

✦ SMIL is an open framework, but implementations have been proprietary.

✦　　✦　　✦

SMIL Syntax

SMIL is a deceptively simple yet extremely powerful markup language. There are only a handful of tags to learn, and a few basic rules to follow. Once you have a firm grasp of these, you should be able to author a wide variety of multimedia presentations.

SMIL is an XML-compliant language and therefore uses commands in angle brackets, which are called tags. Tags may take one or more attributes, which are separated by spaces. Each attribute, in turn, takes a value enclosed in double quotation marks. The following is a typical SMIL tag:

```
<root-layout width="250" height="230"/>
```

This `<root-layout/>` tag, which defines the displayed size of a SMIL presentation, has two attributes, `width` and `height`, each of which has a value enclosed in double quotation marks. Now that you know what a SMIL tag looks like, read on to learn more about some basic XML rules.

Basic Rules

Because SMIL is an XML-compliant language, some simple rules must always be followed:

- ✦ Tags are case-sensitive. All SMIL 1.0 tags are lower case — SMIL 2.0 introduces some tags that contain uppercase characters
- ✦ All tag attributes must be separated by spaces, and their values enclosed in double quotation marks
- ✦ The order the attributes are listed in is irrelevant
- ✦ Extra white space in SMIL files is ignored
- ✦ Unary tags take the closing slash, such as:

```
<img src="images/myimage.jpg" />
```

✦ Binary tags come in pairs, the second tag taking the preceding slash, such as:

```
<smil>
... other SMIL tags
</smil>
```

✦ Comments use standard HTML format, such as:

```
<!-- comments are a good idea -->
```

> **Note** Even though SMIL files can be extremely simple, it's always a good idea to insert a few comments into the code, particularly if different people may be working on the code. In particular, nested timing tags can be particularly complex — a word or two about the original author's intent never go amiss.

✦ All SMIL files should take the `.smil` or `.smi` file extension.

Unary tags versus binary tags

There are two types of tags in SMIL, unary and binary. *Unary tags* are self-contained, consisting of the tag name, one or more attributes with values, and a closing slash, all enclosed in angle brackets. All the necessary operational information is contained within the tag itself. For instance, use the `<video/>` tag as follows to specify what video clip to play:

```
<video src="video/myvideo.rm" region="videoscreen"
       begin="10s" repeat="3" fill="remove" />
```

This tag references a video named `myvideo.rm` in the video directory that is to be played back in the videoscreen region of this presentation. It is to be played back ten seconds from the beginning of the SMIL presentation, repeated three times, and then removed from the videoscreen region.

Binary tags, on the other hand, operate in pairs. The first tag does not take a slash, and the second tag, known as a closing tag, takes a slash preceding the tag name. Binary tags enclose one or more SMIL tags and act on all of them. Binary tags can be thought of as "grouping" tags because they operate on the tags they enclose as a group.

Binary tags may also take attributes just as unary tags do. As an example, consider the following code:

```
<par endsync="first">
  <audio src="audio/myvoiceover.rm" />
  <video src="video/myvideo.rm" />
</par>
```

Note that the first `<par>` tag has an attribute, and the closing `</par>` tag has the preceding slash. This code excerpt specifies that two clips, `myvoiceover.rm` and `myvideo.rm` are to be played in parallel, and to stop playback of the two clips whenever the shortest clip ends.

To complicate things slightly, some tags can be both unary and binary. For example, if we wanted to link the video clip in the sample above to a Web page, we could use the linking capabilities of SMIL as follows:

```
<video src="video/myvideo.rm" region="videoscreen"
    begin="10s" repeat="3" fill="remove" >
    <anchor href="http://www.myserver.com" />
</video>
```

The `<anchor/>` tag specifies that if a user clicks on the video screen, it links to a Web page. The `<video>` tag, in this case, does not take a closing slash; instead it takes the binary form and uses the `</video>` tag, since it must enclose the anchor information. In fact, multiple `<anchor/>` tags can be specified, each linking a different screen area or time during the video that is to be linked to a particular presentation. The `<video></video>` tags must enclose all the tags that pertain to the video clip being referenced.

This is a fairly specialized case. Most tags are either unary or binary. For tags that can go either way, you should have no trouble deciding whether to use tags in their unary or binary form. As a rule, simply remember that unary tags are self-contained, whereas binary tags enclose the other tags that they operate on.

Using special characters

Because angle brackets, quotation marks, and ampersands are part of the SMIL syntax, you must use special character codes if you want to include these characters in your presentation. Table 27-1 lists the codes required to use these characters.

Table 27-1
Predefined Special Characters in SMIL

Character	Code required	Appearance
Left angle bracket ("less-than" sign)	&lt	<
Right angle bracket ("greater-than" sign)	&gt	>
Double quote (quotation marks)	&quote	"
Single quote (apostrophe)	&apos	'
Ampersand	&amp	&

As an example of using special characters, assume you wanted to specify the following title for your SMIL presentation:

```
The <cow> says "moo!"
```

You can specify metadata using the `<meta/>` tag. However, since the above title has special characters in it, you would use the following code:

```
<meta name="title"
      content="The &lt;cow&gt; says &quote;moo!&quote;" />
```

A Simple SMIL File

Now that you've learned the basic rules of SMIL, you are ready to take a look at a simple SMIL file to learn how SMIL presentations are organized. To start off, have a look at the SMIL code in Listing 27-1.

On the CD-ROM The following SMIL code is included on the CD in the SMIL directory, `simple.smil`.

Listing 27-1: A Simple SMIL File

```
<smil>

    <head>
        <meta name="title" content="My SMIL Presentation" />

        <layout>
            <root-layout width="340" height="260" />
            <region id="background" top="0" left="0"
                    width="340" height="260" z-index="0" />
            <region id="video" top="10" left="10"
                    width="320" height="240" z-index="1" />
        </layout>
    </head>

    <body>

<!-- display the background image first,  -->
<!-- then the audio and video in parallel -->

        <par>
            <seq>
                <img src="images/my_bkgnd.gif"
                        region="background" dur="7s" fill="freeze"/>

                <par>
```

```
                <audio src="audio/my_music.rm" />
                <video src="video/my_video.rm"
                       region="video" />
            </par>
          </seq>
        </par>

      </body>

    </smil>
```

Note This code listing has been formatted for clarity purposes. White space is ignored in SMIL files. Though it is not strictly necessary, I highly recommend using good formatting and indenting practice when authoring SMIL files. Because there are no decent SMIL authoring tools or debuggers (yet), making your code clean and easy to read will save you (or some other poor soul) hours of agonizing later.

All SMIL files must begin and end with the `<smil></smil>` tags. The file is divided into two sections: the header section and the body section. The header section, enclosed by `<head></head>` tags, contains a title for the presentation, as well as layout information. The body section, enclosed by `<body></body>` tags, contains the timing information for the presentation.

In Listing 27-1, a background image is displayed for seven seconds, followed by an audio and a video file, which are played in parallel. This example presents a number of tags and attributes that are discussed in detail in the following sections and chapters.

Cross-Reference Chapter 28 deals with SMIL layout concerns. Chapter 29 deals with timing in SMIL. Chapter 30 explores strategies for effective SMIL file authoring.

The Header Section

The header section contains all the metadata and layout information of a SMIL presentation. It is enclosed by the `<head></head>` tags and must contain one or more of the following tags:

✦ `<meta/>` — Allows the author to specify metadata, such as title, author, copyright, and so on, for the presentation.

✦ `<layout></layout>` — If the presentation has layout data specified, it must be enclosed in these tags. One or more of the following tags must be enclosed by the `<layout></layout>` tags:

    • `<root-layout/>` — Specifies the size of the display window for the presentation.

    • `<region/>` — Allows the author to specify a region in which to display streams. A SMIL presentation can have many regions.

The header section is not required in a SMIL presentation. If no layout information is specified, the player resizes automatically to accommodate each clip. If clips are played back in parallel, the display window is made large enough to accommodate all the streams without overlapping, and the streams are displayed side by side.

If a SMIL presentation contains any visual streams, such as images or video, you should always specify layout information. Even though it isn't required, without it, you have no guarantee of what your presentation will look like.

Note The exception to the rule is when you embed SMIL presentations into Web pages using HTML to do your layout. In this case, the layout section *must* be omitted. The player uses the region information specified in the embedded players. See Chapter 31 for more information.

The <meta /> tag

The `<meta />` tag is used to specify metadata. A separate tag must be used for each piece of information specified. Each `<meta />` tag takes two attributes, `name` and `content`, as follows:

```
<meta name="title" content="My Summer Vacation" />
<meta name="author" content="Steve Mack" />
```

Virtually any information can be placed inside a `<meta />` tag. Depending on the player implementation, different things are done with the metadata. Table 27-2 lists the metadata values recognized and used by the RealPlayer.

Note As of December 2001 the QuickTime player ignores the `<meta/>` tag. For more information about SMIL support in the QuicktTime player please check the Apple website (`www.apple.com`).

Table 27-2
<meta /> Attributes and Values Recognized by the RealPlayer

Attribute	Value	Function
name	title	Presentation title when clip info is displayed
	author	Presentation author when clip info is displayed
	copyright	Presentation copyright when clip info is displayed
	abstract	A description of the presentation — displayed when Help ⇨ About this Presentation is chosen from the RealPlayer menu
	base	Specifies a URL to prepend to all relative URLs used in the presentation
content	any string of text	The value assigned to the particular name attribute

You are free to define your own metadata name values. For instance, you could define search terms by defining a new name value called `search` and then listing relevant terms in the content attribute:

```
<meta name="search" content="smil, music, free, mp3" />
```

This file could then be parsed by any XML-aware search engine and indexed according to the values of the content attribute.

Note   The RealPlayer displays all metadata when you choose About this Presentation from the Help menu.

The layout section

If a SMIL presentation contains layout information, it must be enclosed by the `<layout></layout>` tags. A `<root-layout />` and one or more `<region />` tags must also be specified.

The <root-layout /> tag

The `<root-layout />` tag is used to specify the width and height of the display window. Optionally, a background color can also be specified. The syntax is as follows:

```
<root-layout width="320" height="240"
              [background-color="green"] />
```

All other regions defined in the layout section define their positions relative to the upper left-hand corner of the root-layout. When specifying colors in SMIL, you can use a predefined color or use a hexadecimal RGB value preceded by a pound sign (see "Using colors in SMIL" later in this chapter).

The <region /> tag

The `<region/>` tag defines rectangular regions in which streams may be displayed. Regions are defined by specifying the x and y coordinates of the top left corner and the width and height of the region.

The top left corner of the region is defined in relation to the top left corner of the root-layout. The top left corner of the root-layout is defined as (0,0) with x values increasing to the right and y values increasing as you move down. Each region may also take a number of additional attributes, such as `id`, `z-index`, and `background-color`.

Cross-Reference   For a full discussion on all the possibilities of the `<region />` tag, see Chapter 28.

Using colors in SMIL

When using colors in SMIL, you can either specify a predefined color name or use any RGB hexadecimal value, preceded by a # sign:

```
"red" or "#669933"
```

The predefined colors are white, silver, gray, black, yellow, fuchsia, red, maroon, lime, olive, green, purple, aqua, teal, blue, and navy.

The Body Section

The body section is where all the clip sources and timing information are specified in your SMIL file. Each clip must have its own source tag, along with a number of attributes. A typical source tag is as follows:

```
<video src="video/my_video.rm" region="video" begin="5s"
       duration="3:00" fill="freeze" />
```

This tag defines a video clip called my_video.rm that is played back in the video region. It begins playback five seconds into the presentation and plays for three minutes. The fill attribute specifies that, after the completion of playback, the video is left "frozen" on the last frame in the video region.

Only the src attribute is required, though each clip's source tag should also specify a region in which to play back the clip. While it is not strictly necessary, without a region assignment, the author has no guarantees about what the presentation will look like.

Note   Audio sources do not require a region attribute.

Clips can be grouped together and played in parallel or in sequence. They can have begin and end times relative to the master timeline, as shown previously, or relative to the clip's internal timeline. Additional attributes can specify how the clip is to be displayed, metadata for the clip, as well as advanced options such as whether or not the clip should be displayed based on the viewer's language preference. The following sections provide more detail about referencing clips in SMIL presentations.

Specifying clips

To reference clips, you can use a number of tags. All these tags can take additional attributes, any number of which may be included to specify additional information about how to display the clip. Table 27-3 lists the tags available to refer to clips in the body section of SMIL files.

Table 27-3
Clip Source Tags

Tag	Used for
`<animation />`	Animation clips
`<audio />`	Audio clips
`<img />`	Single still images
`<ref />`	Generic reference tag used to refer to any other media not covered by other tags
`<text />`	Static text files
`<textstream />`	Streaming text files (RealText)
`<video />`	Video files

In fact, all the tags in Table 27-3 are equivalent. They only have different names to illustrate the type of data being referenced. Other than for clarity's sake, there is no real reason why you couldn't use the `<ref />` tag for all your data.

Each clip source tag must specify the clip location using the `src` attribute. The value of the `src` attribute can be either a fully qualified or a relative URL. In addition to the required `src` attribute, a handful of other attributes are available. Table 27-4 lists the attributes available for clip source tags.

Note You cannot use relative URLs when authoring SMIL presentations for the QuickTime player unless the documents they refer to are in the same directory as the SMIL file.

Table 27-4
Clip Source Tag Attributes

Attribute	Value	Used for
`src`	Any valid fully qualified or relative URL (QuickTime exception — see Note Icon above)	Specifies the location of the clip.
`region`	Any region name defined in the presentation	Assigns a playback area for the clip.
`begin`	Any valid SMIL timing reference (see "Timing References in SMIL")	Specifies the begin time of the clip relative to the master timeline.

Continued

Table 27-4 *(continued)*

Attribute	Value	Used for
end	Any valid SMIL timing reference (see "Timing References in SMIL")	Specifies the end time of the clip relative to the master timeline.
dur	Any valid SMIL timing reference (see "Timing References in SMIL") or "indefinite." Indefinite durations make the clip appear as a live clip, and disable the RealPlayer timeline slider. (See Chapter 31.)	Specifies the duration of a clip. Do not use with the end attribute.
clip-begin	Any valid SMIL timing reference (see "Timing References in SMIL")	Specifies the starting point of the clip on the clip's internal timeline.
clip-end	Any valid SMIL timing reference (see "Timing References in SMIL")	Specifies the ending point of the clip on the clip's internal timeline.
fill	Freeze or remove (Default is remove.)	Specifies whether the stream is to be left displayed or removed from the region upon completion of playback.
id	Any text string	Specifies a name for a clip that can be used by other tags for reference.
repeat	Any integer value or "indefinite"	Specifies number of times to repeat a stream, or to repeat indefinitely.
title	Any text string	Specifies title metadata for the clip.
author	Any text string	Specifies author metadata for the clip.
copyright	Any text string	Specifies copyright metadata for the clip.
abstract	Any text string	Specifies abstract metadata for the clip.
system-bitrate	Any integer representing bps, such as 20000 for 28.8 modems	Specifies a bit rate threshold for presentations using the advanced <switch/> tag.

Attribute	Value	Used for
system-captions	On **or** off	Specifies whether or not the stream is to be displayed if captions are present.
system-language	Any valid SMIL language code (See Chapter 31.)	Specifies a language that must match the player's language preference for the stream to be played back.

Some sample clip references are as follows:

```
<audio src="audio/my_audio.rm" dur="60" />
```

This audio clip plays back for 60 seconds and then stops.

```
<video src="video/my_video.rm" region="video"
    fill="freeze" />
```

This video clip will be played back in the region named video. When the video reaches the end, the last frame remains displayed in the region.

```
<animation src="anim/cartoon.swf" region="topleft"
    repeat="5" />
```

This animation is played back in the region named topleft five times, after which the animation disappears from the display.

Clip references can have as many attributes as necessary, provided they do not conflict. For instance, you should not specify duration using the dur attribute if you've specified an end or clip-end attribute. Here's a clip definition that uses a lot of attributes:

```
<video src="video/looper.rm" region="tvscreen"
        clip-begin="10" clip-end="40" repeat="5"
        fill="freeze" id="theloop"
        title="The ever-looping clip" />
```

The section of this video between 10 and 40 seconds plays five times in a region called tvscreen. After the clip finishes looping, the final frame remains displayed in the region. The title specified overrides any title specified in the header. Last but not least, an id attribute is provided so that a <par></par> group can reference this clip as a group ending sync point (see Chapter 29).

RealPlayer src attribute extensions

The RealPlayer has `src` attribute extensions that can be used with the `<img />` tag. When using these extensions, follow the `src` attribute with a question mark (?), and separate multiple extensions by ampersands (&). The following image tags illustrate the use of the RealPlayer extensions:

```
<img src="images/my_image.jpg?reliable=true" />
<img src="link.jpg?url=http://myserver.com&target=_browser" />
<img src="play.jpg?url=command:play()&target=_player" />
```

Table 27-5 lists all the available image extensions.

	Table 27-5	
	RealPlayer src Attribute Extensions	
Attribute	**Values**	**Used For**
bgcolor	Any valid pre-defined color or RGB value preceded by a pound sign (#).	Setting a background color behind a transparent GIF file.
bitrate	Any integer representing bps, such as 20000 for 28.8 modems.	Sets the bit rate at which the image should be streamed. Can be simpler than assembling a complete RealPix presentation when sending a single image.
reliable	True	Ensures delivery of the image. Playback of presentation halts if transmission problems occur.
target	_browser	Sets the viewer's Web browser as the target for the url attribute.
	_player	Sets the RealPlayer as the target for the url attribute.
url	Any valid fully qualified URL, such as http://www.myserver.com or rtsp://www.myrealserver.com	Sends the destination URL to the specified target when image is clicked.
	command:play( )	Begins RealPlayer playback when image is clicked.
	command:pause( )	Pauses the RealPlayer when image is clicked.
	command:stop( )	Stops the RealPlayer when image is clicked.
	command:seek(dd:hh:mm:ss.xyz)	Starts the RealPlayer playing when image is clicked.

Timing in SMIL

Timing can be specified in SMIL in a number of ways:

✦ **Playing clips in parallel.** Clips can be grouped inside `<par></par>` tags to be played back concurrently.

✦ **Playing clips in sequence.** Clips can be played one after another by placing them inside `<seq></seq>` tags.

✦ **Specifying timing in the clip source.** Each clip can have timing information specified in reference to itself, or to the group it is included in.

✦ **Synchronizing groups of clips.** Clips can be delayed as a group, or made to end when other clips end.

All of these methods can be combined in simple or very complex timing arrangements. If neither `<par></par>` tags nor `<seq></seq>` tags are specified, the default behavior is to display the clips in sequence.

Playing clips in parallel

If you wish to play a number of clips simultaneously (for instance, a voiceover along with a slideshow presentation), you can do so by grouping a number of clips within `<par></par>` tags, as follows:

```
<par>
  ... one or more stream references
  ... to be played simultaneously
</par>
```

Playing clips in sequence

If you want clips to be played in sequence (for instance, a series of music videos on a music channel), you would use `<seq></seq>` tags to group your clips as follows:

```
<seq>
  ... one or more stream references
  ... to be played sequentially
</seq>
```

Timing references in SMIL

When specifying timing references in SMIL, you can use either the standard dd:hh:mm:ss.xyz format or a value followed by a shorthand abbreviation indicating what units the value represents. The acceptable abbreviations are as follows:

✦ h for hours

✦ min for minutes

✦ s for seconds

✦ ms for milliseconds

If no abbreviation is used, standard time format is assumed. The value does not have to be an integer — decimal points can be used. Table 27-6 lists some timing references and what they translate to.

Table 27-6 SMIL Timing References	
Time	*Translation*
"5s"	5 seconds
"5.0"	5 seconds
"5000ms"	5 seconds
"90"	90 seconds
"1:30"	90 seconds
"1.5m"	90 seconds
".025h"	90 seconds

Using timing tags in clips

A number of attributes can be used to specify timing, such as `begin`, `end`, `dur`, `clip-begin`, and `clip-end`. Each takes a SMIL timing reference and has a slightly different behavior (depending on where the clip is located in the presentation).

Cross-Reference

A full discussion of timing in SMIL can be found in Chapter 29.

In particular, the `begin` and `end` attributes have different behaviors depending on whether the clip is contained within a `<par></par>` group or a `<seq></seq>` group. Here are a few clip definitions using timing attributes, followed by explanations of each:

```
<audio src="my_audio.rm" clip-begin="5" dur="30" />
```

In this case, the playback of `my_audio.rm` begins five seconds into the clip — the first five seconds of `my_audio.rm` are not played back in this case. Playback continues for 30 seconds.

```
<video src="my_video.rm" begin="10s" />
```

The `begin` attribute acts differently depending on where the clip is located. Essentially, it means "begin playing back this clip ten seconds after the start." The tricky part is determining when the "start" is:

✦ If the clip is contained within a `<par></par>` group, playback begins 10 seconds after group playback begins.

✦ If the clip is contaned within a `<seq></seq>` group, playback begins 10 seconds after the previous clip in the group ends.

```
<audio src="my_audio.rm" begin="5" clip-begin="30"
       clip-end="60" />
```

This clip combines internal timing references with a master timeline reference. The `clip-begin` and `clip-end` tags specify that the section of the clip beginning at 30 seconds and ending at the 60 second mark of the clip is played. The play back begins five seconds after the previous clip, or five seconds after the `<par></par>` group begins playback.

Summary

SMIL syntax is fairly simple but can be used to create complex multimedia presentations. As long as you remember where to put your closing slashes, you should have no problems. The next chapter covers SMIL layout in greater detail.

✦ Unary tags take the closing slash; binary tags take a preceding slash in the closing tag.

✦ All attribute values should be enclosed in double quotation marks.

✦ The header section contains metadata and layout information.

✦ The header section is optional.

✦ The body section contains all the clip references and timing information.

✦ Clips can be grouped and played back in parallel or in sequence.

✦ Timing attributes can be specified relative to the clip's internal timeline or the presentation's master timeline.

✦ Timing in SMIL can be specified either in standard time format or using shorthand abbreviations indicating the units.

✦　　✦　　✦

Laying Out Your Presentation Using SMIL

The header section provides an opportunity for you to lay out your SMIL presentation by allowing you to specify different regions in which you can play back your streams. You can specify a root-layout, which defines the overall size of the presentation. You can also specify as many other regions of different sizes and background colors as you like.

You don't have to specify additional regions, but if you don't, there is no guarantee your presentation will play back the way you expect it to. Without defined regions, you have no control over the placement of your streams.

Laying out your presentation makes sense not only from an aesthetic sense but also from a programming standpoint. If you author your presentation well, you can easily modify it with a few simple edits. Once you begin to realize the power of SMIL layout and timing, you'll understand the value of using layouts.

When you deal with SMIL layouts, you have to think in three dimensions. Regions can be placed in the two dimensions defined by the root-layout, and have a "z-index" that determines where they fall along the third dimensional axis.

SMIL layouts can be thought of as a three dimensional axis. The width and left attributes of layout tags are along the x-axis, the height and top attributes along the y-axis, and the z-index falls on the z-axis. This is illustrated in Figure 28-1.

Any layout attributes that are not specified default to a value of zero. Therefore, if a z-index is not defined, it defaults to zero. Similarly, if top and left attributes are not specified their values default to zero, making the region's upper left-hand corner correspond to the top left-hand corner of the root-layout.

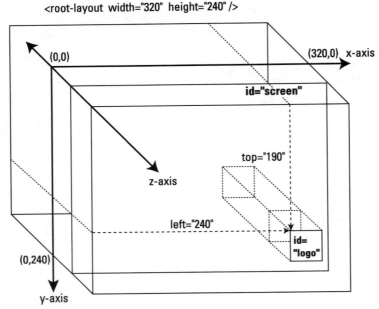

`<region id="screen" width="320" height="240" z-index="1" />`
`<region id="logo" width="40" height="40" top="190" left="240" z-index="2" />`

Figure 28-1: The three axes of a SMIL presentation. Figures with a higher z-index sit "on top" of regions with a lower z-index.

The Root-Layout Region

The root-layout region is where you set the global parameters of your layout. You must specify a width and height, and can (optionally) specify a background color. The syntax, as described in Chapter 27, is as follows:

```
<root-layout width="320" height="240"
    [background-color="green"] />
```

Both the `width` and `height` attributes are required. When specifying a background color, you may specify any pre-defined color or use a hexadecimal RGB value preceded by a # sign.

Caution Streams cannot be played back in the root-layout. If you neglect to define additional playback regions, your player will open up large enough to accommodate the root-layout region plus space to accommodate all additional streams without overlapping.

When defining your root-layout, you may want to consider using an aspect ratio that looks good in full-screen mode. Most computers are now powerful enough to play full-screen presentations, and most media players do a pretty good job of rendering files full screen. If you want to avoid black space at the top and bottom or on the sides, you should use an aspect ratio of 4:3 such as 640 × 480, 320 × 240, or 240 × 180.

Defining Playback Regions

The power of SMIL layouts lies in the region definitions. Any number of rectangular regions can be defined, each with its own set of playback attributes. Since the root-layout region can not be used for playback, at least one region must be specified in the layout section. A region definition looks like this:

```
<region id="background" width="320" height="240" z-index="0"
    background-color="blue" fit="fill" />
```

The full set of `<region/>` tag attributes is as follows:

- ✦ `id`. Assigns a name to the region
- ✦ `width`. Defines the width or the region
- ✦ `height`. Defines the height of the region
- ✦ `top`. Defines the y coordinate of the upper left-hand corner of the region relative to the top left-hand corner of the root-layout
- ✦ `left`. Defines the x coordinate of the upper left-hand corner of the region relative to the top left-hand corner of the root-layout
- ✦ `z-index`. Defines the layer number of the region. Higher numbers are displayed on "top" of lower numbers
- ✦ `background-color`. Defines a background color for the region
- ✦ `fit`. Defines how streams are displayed in regions with aspect ratios that are different from the stream's native aspect ratio

These attributes are discussed in depth in the following sections.

Naming regions with the id attribute

Each region must have a unique name specified by the `id` attribute. This name is used in the body section to target streams to particular regions. Any text string can be used.

Tip   Although any name can be used for a region id, use descriptive names. Regions with `id` names such as "background," "logo," and "video" are much more intuitive than "1," "a," or "first" — particularly if someone else may be taking a look at your code.

If for some reason more than one region ends up with the same id, the presentation will fail. When creating SMIL files, it is tempting to "copy & paste" region definitions to save typing — which is fine as long as you ensure each region has a unique id attribute.

Sizing and placing regions with the width, height, top, and left attributes

The width, height, top, and left attributes define where the region is placed in the root-layout. These attributes can be defined as pixel values or as percentages. If percentages are used, they are calculated as percentages of the root-layout dimensions.

If the top and left attributes are undefined, they default to a value of zero, which places the upper left-hand corner of the region in the top left-hand corner of the root-layout. The width and height also default to zero if they are not defined, but that would be a mighty small region. A few sample region definitions are illustrated in Figure 28-2.

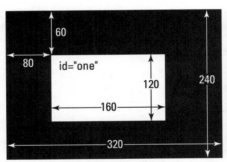

(a) <region id="one" width="160" height="120" left="80" top="60"/>

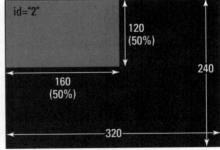

(b) <region id="2" width="50%" height="50%" background-color="red"/>

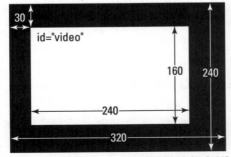

(c) <region id="video" width="240" height="160" left="30" top="30" z-Index="10" fit="fill"/>

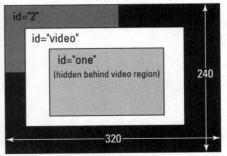

(d) all three regions displayed concurrently

Figure 28-2: Three region definitions (a, b, c) assuming a root-layout of 320 × 240 and how they would be layered if displayed concurrently (d).

In the first region definition, `width`, `height`, `top`, and `left` are all defined. The second region has its dimensions specified in percentages. Also, since no `top` or `left` attribute is specified, these two attributes both assume a default value of zero. This second region also has a red background.

The third region introduces the z-index tag. Since this third region has a z-index of ten, it would be displayed on top of the other two layers, which have no z-index specified.

Caution

Sometimes SMIL can be overly flexible. For instance, you may use negative values for the `top` and `left` attributes. Also, you can define regions with dimensions that exceed the size of your root-layout. While it's nice to have no restrictions, be warned that SMIL will not warn you if you decide to become adventurous with your dimensional attributes.

A region's size attributes override any dimensions defined in individual streams. For instance, if you have a RealPix stream with dimensions of 320 × 240 and assign it to a region that is 100 × 400, the RealPix stream will be resized according to the fit attribute. For more on this, see "How clips fit into regions" later in this chapter.

Defining layers using the z-index attribute

The `z-index` attribute defines where the region sits on the z-axis. This determines which "layer" the region is in, and therefore which region is rendered "on top" of another layer if they overlap and are playing concurrent streams. Regions with higher `z-index` numbers are rendered on top of regions with lower `z-index` numbers.

The `z-index` values may be positive or negative, and use decimal points. Regions that do not overlap may share a `z-index` number.

Tip

If your presentation has many layers, group them numerically. For instance, place background elements on layers numbered 1–10. Place middle elements in the tens or twenties, and layers that absolutely must be on top, in the nineties or hundreds. This may seem like overkill, but when you're working with 20 or more layers, every bit of organization helps.

Setting background colors

If you want to set a background color, you can do so by using the `background-color` attribute. You can either specify a predefined color name or an RGB hexadecimal value preceded by a # sign as follows:

```
background-color="red" or background-color="#669933"
```

The default background color for all regions is black. SMIL 1.0 has no provision for transparency, though SMIL 2.0 does (see Chapter 32 for more information).

A strange side effect of specifying a background color for a region is that it causes the region to become visible as soon as the presentation begins. In fact, if you define a region with a background color, it will become visible at the beginning of the presentation even if no streams are targeted to it! Consider the original `simple.smil` code from Chapter 27:

On the CD-ROM

The following SMIL behaviors are illustrated with files on the CD in the SMIL directory, named simple.smil, simple_background_color.smil, and simple_ weirdness.smil.

```
<smil>

    <head>

        <meta name="title" content="My SMIL presentation" />

        <layout>
            <root-layout width="340" height="260" />
            <region id="background" top="0" left="0"
                    width="340" height="260" z-index="0" />
            <region id="video" top="10" left="10"
                    width="320" height="240" z-index="1" />
        </layout>
    </head>

    <body>

<!-- display the background image first,  -->
<!-- then the audio and video in parallel -->

        <par>
            <seq>
                <img src="images/my_bkgnd.gif"
                     region="background" dur="7s" fill="freeze"/>

                <par>
                    <audio src="audio/my_music.rm" />
                    <video src="video/my_video.rm"
                            region="video" />
                </par>
            </seq>
        </par>

    </body>
</smil>
```

When simple.smil is played back, it begins by displaying the background for seven seconds. After that, the video is played back in the video region, which is rendered on top of the background layer because of its higher z-index. It will display the video differently if you change the video region definition to include a background color as follows:

```
<region id="video" top="10" left="10" width="320"
        height="240" z-index="1" background-color="green" />
```

Playing back this file (simple_background_color.smil on the CD), you see that the region is now visible from the beginning of the file, obscuring the background slide. This last example adds a region to the simple.smil file that has no streams targeted to it. The new region is defined as follows:

```
<region id="weird" top="100" left="100" width="100"
        height="100" z-index="10" background-color="green" />
```

Playing back this file (simple_weirdness.smil on the CD) shows that the region is rendered from the beginning of the file, even though no streams are ever targeted to this region! This is strange behavior at best, but part of the SMIL 1.0 definition. You can use this behavior in some creative ways, but the real answer is that this behavior is entirely controllable in SMIL 2.0.

If you want to use background colors but not have the regions visible until the stream begins playback, consider using the background color attribute of the stream if it is available.

How clips fit into regions

The `fit` attribute of the region tag defines how to display streams in regions with aspect ratios different from the stream's native aspect ratio. There are five acceptable values:

✦ `fill`. The stream is played back filling the entire region. The stream will be stretched if the aspect ratios of the stream and region do not match.

✦ `hidden`. The stream is kept at its original size, and played back with its upper left-hand corner placed in the top left-hand corner of the region. If the stream's original size exceeds the region dimensions in any way, portions of the stream will not be visible.

✦ `meet`. The stream is scaled, preserving its original aspect ratio, until one of the region's dimensions is met and the second dimension remains within the region boundaries. If any extra space is on the sides or bottom, the region's background color is displayed.

✦ `slice`. The stream is scaled until one dimension meets the region boundary with the other exceeding the boundary. The portion that exceeds the boundary is not shown.

✦ `scroll`. The stream is displayed at its original encoded size with the upper left-hand corner placed in the top left-hand corner of the root-layout. If the stream exceeds either of the dimensions, scroll bars are displayed as necessary.

The default value is hidden. How these values affect image display is best explained with illustrations. Figures 28-3 through 28-7 illustrate the various fit attributes.

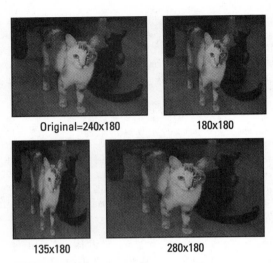

Original=240x180   180x180

135x180   280x180

Figure 28-3: How fit="fill" affects image display.

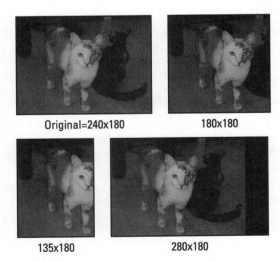

Original=240x180   180x180

135x180   280x180

Figure 28-4: How fit="hidden" affects image display.

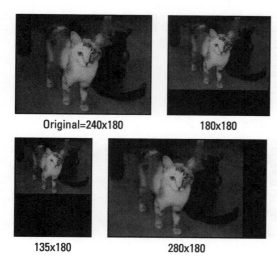

Original=240x180   180x180

135x180   280x180

Figure 28-5: How `fit="meet"` affects image display.

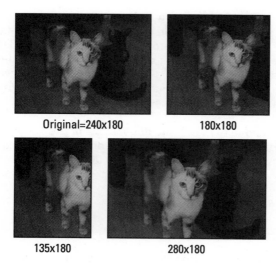

Original=240x180   180x180

135x180   280x180

Figure 28-6: How `fit="slice"` affects image display.

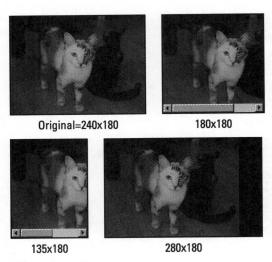

Original=240x180   180x180

135x180   280x180

Figure 28-7: How `fit="scroll"` affects image display.

Each `fit` value affects images in a slightly different way. If you don't ever want to see any blank space around your streams, you should use either the `fill`, `hidden`, or `slice` values. Then again, the `fill` value can distort streams significantly if the aspect ratio of the stream and the region differ significantly. Also, with the `hidden` and `slice` values, your images stand a good chance of being cropped in some way. The `meet` value always shows the entire image without distortion, but might leave blank space at the side or bottom.

Ideally you want your region dimensions to match the dimensions of the stream. This way the stream will not be scaled or cropped. Scaling not only produces ugly results but is also computationally complex, which can lead to degraded playback performance.

Summary

SMIL layout is accomplished in the header section through the definition of a root-layout and one or more regions in which to play back streams. In the next chapter, you'll find out all about timing in SMIL.

✦ Streams cannot be played back in the root-layout region.

✦ Each defined region must have a unique name specified via the `id` attribute.

✦ The region's name is used in the body section to place streams in specific regions.

✦ The `z-index` attribute can be used to define how different regions overlap.

✦ The `fit` attribute specifies how streams will be displayed in regions — different values can provide significantly different results.

✦ You can define as many regions as you want, and regions can be re-used by different clips.

✦　　✦　　✦

Synchronizing Your Streams in SMIL

◆ ◆ ◆ ◆

In This Chapter

Grouping clips for timing purposes

Specifying timing in SMIL tags

Repeating clips or groups in SMIL

◆ ◆ ◆ ◆

SMIL offers a number of different ways to add timing to your presentations. Clips can be grouped so that they play back in parallel or in sequence. These groups can be nested to enable complex timing combinations.

SMIL tags may also take timing attributes that can be applied to individual clips or to groups. These attributes can operate relative to the master timeline of the presentation or relative to the clip's internal timeline. SMIL also provides for looping in presentations using the `repeat` attribute. This attribute can be applied to individual clips or entire groups.

This chapter explains tags used to group clips together and then discusses timing attributes, many of which can be used in both clip reference tags and grouping tags.

In addition, this chapter explains the `fill` attribute, which determines what happens to visual clips when they are finished playing back — they can either be removed from view, or the last frame of the stream can be kept visible in the region. Using `fill="freeze"` to keep static images visible is an excellent way to conserve bandwidth.

Finally, this chapter discusses looping clips or groups of clips.

Grouping Clips for Timing Purposes

Two tags are used in SMIL to group clips together — the `<par></par>` tags and the `<seq></seq>` tags. The first set is used when a group of clips are to be played back in parallel, and the second for groups that are to be played back sequentially.

These tags can be nested, which means you can have "groups within groups." Groups of clips playing in parallel can play back in sequence, and vice-versa. Combining these two simple grouping tags with timing attributes enables very complex timing models.

Playing clips sequentially

To play clips back in sequence, surround the clip references with `<seq></seq>` tags, as follows:

```
<seq>
... one or more stream references
... to be played sequentially
</seq>
```

Clips within the `<seq></seq>` group play back one after the other. By definition, the playback of clips (or groups) within a `<seq></seq>` group can never overlap. If you want more than one clip to play at a time, you should use a `<par></par>` group and timing attributes instead of the `<seq></seq>` group. Timing attributes can also be used in `<seq>` tags (see "Using the begin and end attributes" later in this chapter).

Tip   Judicious use of the `<seq></seq>` tags can be very useful when trying to conserve bandwidth. Playing clips in parallel can tax your bandwidth requirements.

Playing clips back in parallel

To play back a number of clips at the same time, simply surround the clip references with `<par></par>` tags, as follows:

```
<par>
... one or more stream references
... to be played simultaneously
</par>
```

The clips inside the `<par></par>` group do not have to be played back strictly in parallel. They can have further timing constraints placed on them via timing attributes in the clip reference tags or in the opening `<par>` tag. Essentially, the clips do not have to start or end at the same times, but if at any point you want clips to stream simultaneously you should put them inside `<par></par>` tags.

Tip   Always put a set of `<par></par>` tags around your entire presentation. This establishes a "master timeline," which means the presentation is treated as one continuous program. Without the master timeline, the presentation is treated as a sequence of individual files, and the player rebuffers between each clip.

Ending parallel groups

By default, parallel groups end when the longest clip contained within the group finishes playback. Alternatively, you might want to have the group end when the shortest clip finishes, or when a particular clip is finished. SMIL provides an attribute called `endsync` specifically for the purpose of ending parallel groups when a specific clip ends.

The `endsync` attribute may take one of three values:

✦ `endsync="first"`: Ends the group when the shortest clip finishes playback

✦ `endsync="last"`: Ends the group when the longest clip finishes playback

✦ `endsync="id(clip id)"`: Ends the group when the clip referenced by `clip-id` finishes playback

The default behavior of `<par></par>` groups is `endsync="last"`. If you use `endsync="id(clip id)"`, all clips stop playback when the designated clip finishes playing back, regardless of the other clips' timing attributes. As an example, take a look at the following code:

```
<par endsync="id(exit)" >
    <video src="video/news.rm" region="screen" id="exit" />
    <animation src="anim/logo.swf" region="logo"
            repeat="indefinite" fill="freeze" />
</par>
```

In this example, the animation loops indefinitely until the video is finished playing back. If the group did not have the `endsync` attribute specified, the group would never finish, because the animation would loop forever.

Tip   The `endsync` attribute can be handy when one of the clips in your parallel group is a live stream.

Nesting groups of clips

Groups can be nested within each other. The order of the groups greatly affects the playback order of the clips. To illustrate this, consider the following groupings:

```
<par>
    <seq>
        <video region="top" src="one.rm" dur="30" />
        <video region="top" src="two.rm" dur="30" />
    </seq>
    <seq>
        <audio src="a.rm" dur="1:00" />
        <audio src="b.rm" dur="1:00" />
    </seq>
</par>
```

In this example, two sequential groups are contained within a parallel group. Therefore the two sequential groups play at the same time. This means `one.rm` and `a.rm` begin playback at the same time. Since the duration of `one.rm` was set to 30 seconds, 30 seconds into the group `two.rm` begins playback. One minute into the presentation, both `two.rm` and `a.rm` end, and `b.rm` begins playback. The parallel group remains active until `b.rm` finishes playback.

In the following example, two parallel groups are contained within a sequential group.

```
<seq>
   <par>
      <video region="top" src="one.rm" dur="30" />
      <video region="bottom" src="two.rm" dur="30" />
   </par>
   <par>
      <audio src="a.rm" dur="1:00" />
      <audio src="b.rm" dur="1:00" />
   </par>
</seq>
```

In this case the first parallel group plays, followed by the second parallel group. The two video clips play in parallel, which is why they are now targeted to different regions. After 30 seconds, they both finish, and the next parallel group becomes active. In the second group, two audio sources play simultaneously.

```
<par>
   <video region="top" src="one.rm" dur="30" />

   <seq>
         <video region="top" src="two.rm" dur="30" />
         <audio src="a.rm" dur="1:00" />
   </seq>

   <audio src="b.rm" dur="1:00" />
</par>
```

When playback begins, `one.rm`, `two.rm`, and `b.rm` all begin playback. Thirty seconds in, both `one.rm` and `two.rm` are done; `a.rm` begins playback because it follows `two.rm` in a sequential group. For the next 30 seconds, both audio tracks play, until a minute into the presentation, when `b.rm` ends and leaves `a.rm` playing on its own.

Groups may be nested but not overlapped. Consider the following:

```
<seq>
   <video region="top" src="one.rm" dur="30" />
<par>
   <video region="top" src="two.rm" dur="30" />
</seq>
   <audio src="a.rm" dur="1:00" />
</par>
```

This is a mess. It is unclear what is supposed to happen; in this case, the player actually reports a missing tag error. Code like this generally results from sloppy editing of code, particularly when the formatting is unclear.

Tip Always use indenting to set groups apart. This makes your code easier to read and debug, and reduces the chances of error.

Grouping and nesting provide powerful timing capabilities. Combine them with timing attributes and you should be able to create any timing schemes you require.

Specifying Timing in SMIL Tags

When you use timing attributes in SMIL tags, you can specify timing relative to the presentation timeline (the master timeline) or the clip's internal timeline. The difference is subtle but very important:

✦ If you're specifying timing in relation to other clips in the presentation, you're working with the master timeline, and should use the `begin` and `end` attributes.

✦ If you're specifying timing in relation to a single clip — that is, specifying a point in the clip at which you'd like to begin or end playback — you're working on the clip's internal timeline and should use the `clip-begin` and `clip-end` attributes.

Timing values in SMIL can be specified in either normal timing format (dd:hh:mm:ss.xyz) or by using a number followed by a shorthand abbreviation indicating what units the value represents. The acceptable abbreviations are as follows:

✦ h for hours

✦ min for minutes

✦ s for seconds

✦ ms for milliseconds

If no abbreviation is used, standard time format is assumed. The value does not have to be an integer — decimal points can be used.

Using the begin and end attributes

The `begin` and `end` attributes set timing constraints relative to the master timeline. They are used as follows:

```
<audio src="music/my_music.rm" begin="30" end="5:00" />
```

If this line of code stands alone in a SMIL presentation, playback of `mymusic.rm` begins 30 seconds after the start of the presentation, and ends 5 minutes after the start of the presentation. This means that only 4 minutes and 30 seconds of the clip is played, starting at the beginning of the clip.

Clips in sequential groups are treated individually. Since the clips are played back in sequence, and not overlapped, each clip occupies its own section of the master timeline. Therefore, `begin` and `end` attributes are calculated in reference to the previous clip, not the sequential group as a whole.

So if the previous clip is in a `<seq></seq>` group, the `begin` attribute inserts a 30 second gap between the previous clip and the current clip, and the `end` attribute ends playback 5 minutes from the end of the previous clip. Again, only 4 minutes and 30 seconds of the clip are played.

Clips in parallel groups share a section of the master timeline; therefore, `begin` and `end` attributes are calculated from the start of the group. If the above clip is included in a `<par></par>` group, the clip begins playback 30 seconds after the parallel group begins playback, not from the absolute beginning of the presentation.

This is not necessarily intuitive and the source of many a timing woe. It's always best to think of `<par></par>` groups as units. All `begin` and `end` attributes should be thought of as relative only to the clips in the same group. With sequential groups, it's just the opposite — they should be thought of as individual clips with timing attributes referenced only to the previous clip.

Tip   The `begin` and `end` attributes don't really make sense used with clips that are grouped together in sequential groups. Use the `clip-begin` and `clip-end` attributes to select the section of the clip you wish played back instead.

The `begin` and `end` attributes may also be used in group tags, as follows:

```
<par begin="5" end="20">
  ...clips
</par>
or
<seq begin="5" end="20">
  ... clips
</seq>
```

When timing attributes are used in group tags, the attributes operate on the group as a whole. Playback of clips in the group is delayed 5 seconds from the previous clip or group, and ends after 15 seconds of playback.

The group actually "starts" when the previous clip or group ends, but playback of the clips contained within the group is delayed 5 seconds by the `begin` attribute. The group ends 20 seconds after it starts, as determined by the `end` attribute. Therefore, any clips in the group play for only 15 seconds.

Using the clip-begin and clip-end attributes

The `clip-begin` and `clip-end` attributes are much more straightforward than the `begin` and `end` attributes, because they only operate on the clip that is being referenced. Think of them as specifying a start and end point inside the clip, which enables you to choose the section of the clip you want displayed:

```
<video src="my_video.rm" region="video" clip-begin="20"
    clip-end="45" />
```

This reference chooses the 25 seconds beginning at the 20-second mark and ending at the 45-second mark of the clip for playback, and displays it in the video region.

You are free to mix and match the `clip-begin` and `clip-end` attributes with the `begin` and `end` attributes:

```
<video src="my_video.rm" region="video" begin="10" end="1:00"
    clip-begin="20" clip-end="45" />
```

This reference selects the same 25 seconds of video to display, but delays playback 10 seconds from the end of the previous clip or the start of the <par></par> group. Note that the clip isn't supposed to end until one minute, which is longer than our video clip selection. In this case, the clip finishes playback before the end attribute comes into play. This could be modified using the `fill` attribute, discussed later in the chapter.

Setting clip duration

Another way of specifying playback times is by using the `dur` attribute to set a clip duration. Instead of using a `clip-end` attribute in the preceding clip, you could just as easily set a 25-second duration:

```
<video src="my_video.rm" region="video" clip-begin="20"
    dur="25" />
```

This is exactly equivalent to the clip reference in the previous section. Which method you choose to employ is completely up to you. The `dur` attribute may also be used in grouping tags to set group durations:

```
<par begin="5" dur="2:00">
    ...clips
</par>
```

You may also specify an indefinite duration. In the RealPlayer, this causes the stream to appear to be a live stream. This disables the user's ability to seek through the presentation, which may or may not be desirable. Be careful — clips with indefinite durations can cause problems in `<par></par>` groups without some sort of additional timing constraint. For instance:

```
<par>
   <video src="my_video.rm" region="video" clip-begin="20"
         />
   <textstream src="text/my_captions.rm" region="subtititles"
         />
   <audio src="audio/bkgnd_music.rm" dur="indefinite" />
</par>
```

The previous `<par></par>` group never ends, because the audio clip has an indefinite duration. A better approach is

```
<par endsync="id(vid)">
   <video src="my_video.rm" region="video" clip-begin="20"
         id="vid" />
   <textstream src="text/my_captions.rm" region="subtititles"
         />
   <audio src="audio/bkgnd_music.rm" dur="indefinite" />
</par>
```

Now the group terminates when the video clip finishes playback.

Note   The indefinite duration only works in RealPlayer 8 and higher.

There may be times when you want something to remain on the screen for an indefinite amount of time without the added headache of having to worry about the potential downside of the indefinite duration attribute. An excellent alternative is to use the `fill` attribute to "freeze" a clip in a region.

Using the fill attribute

The `fill` attribute determines what happens to a clip and the region it occupies when the clip reaches its end. There are two options:

   ✦ `fill="remove"`: This is the default behavior, with the clip and its region being removed completely from the display.

   ✦ `fill="freeze"`: Alternatively the clip can be frozen in the region. The clip remains on display until the end of the presentation, unless something is rendered on top of it.

Using `fill="freeze"` is an excellent way to conserve bandwidth. If your presentation has a persistent background or logo image, it can be streamed and then "frozen" in position. After the image has loaded, the stream is finished. One less stream means more bandwidth for other elements. You would do this as follows:

```
<par>
   <seq>
      <img src="images/bkgnd.jpg" region="background"
          fill="freeze" />
      <img src=""images/logo.jpg" region="logo"
          fill="freeze" />
         <par>
            ... streaming clips here
         </par>
   </seq>
</par>
```

First set up a `<par></par>` group to establish a master timeline, and within that, set up a sequential group because you want to do the following:

1. Load the background.

2. Load the logo.

3. Start the rest of the presentation.

Because you want to follow these steps in order, a `<seq></seq>` group makes sense. After both the static elements have been loaded and frozen into position, you are free to use all available bandwidth for streaming content.

Cross-Reference Chapter 30 discusses other effective methods of authoring SMIL files.

Repeating Clips or Groups in SMIL

Clips or entire groups of clips can be repeated using the `repeat` attribute. You can either specify a specific number of repeats, or have it loop indefinitely, as follows:

```
<video src="video/loop.rm" region="screen" repeat="10" />
```

or

```
<par repeat="indefinite">
   <video src="video/advertisement.rm" region="screen" />
</par>
```

In the first example, the video plays ten times. In the second example, the video loops indefinitely until the presentation is stopped. Alternatively, a duration or end attribute can be specified:

```
<par repeat="indefinite" dur="1:00:00" >
    <video src="video/advertisement.rm" region="screen" />
</par>
```

In this last case, the video loops for one hour.

Note   The indefinite repeat only works in RealPlayer 8 and higher.

Summary

SMIL provides a number of attributes and grouping tags that allow you to create presentations with complex timing.

✦ Clips in `<par></par>` groups play back in parallel.

✦ Clips in `<seq></seq>` groups play back sequentially.

✦ Groups may be nested but not overlapped.

✦ The begin and end attributes specify timing relative to the master timeline.

✦ The clip-begin and clip-end attributes specify timing relative to the clip's internal timeline.

✦ "Freezing" clips on screen by using the fill attribute is an excellent approach for bandwidth conservation.

Now that you've learned about layout and timing, it's time to begin the authoring process. The next chapter walks you through some strategies for successful SMIL file authoring.

✦   ✦   ✦

Authoring Effective SMIL Files

Although SMIL is a simple language, authoring SMIL files effectively can be a daunting task. It is entirely possible to author files that look fantastic on your desktop machine but grind to a frustrating halt when streamed across a network.

The largest task facing the SMIL author is bandwidth management. Combining multiple data types into a compelling presentation is only part the process — the trickier part is ensuring that they stream smoothly to the intended audience.

The goal of the presentation and who the intended audience is determines the outcome of the three steps a SMIL author must take: media preparation, layout, and timing.

Currently, there are a few tools available with graphical user interfaces for authoring SMIL files, such as the GriNS editor from Oratrix, Fluition from Confluent Technologies, and GoLive 6 from Adobe Systems. However, these tools have not been around for very long, and as such can be somewhat limited or slightly unintuitive.

As convenient as these tools can be, it is still important to understand how SMIL files are authored and, more importantly, how they can be optimized. This chapter teaches you how to author SMIL files by hand for that reason.

Some of the tips and tricks revealed in this chapter may seem like standard programming practice — often that is what they are. For example, good indenting makes your code much easier to read and therefore to debug.

The effective SMIL author combines good programming practices, economical presentation design, and careful stream preparation to provide the best multimedia experience within the given bandwidth limitations.

Bandwidth Management

Bandwidth is everything. You've heard it before, but the problem becomes more acute when you're working with multiple streaming files in a single presentation. Instead of an encoder taking care of everything and handing you a file that is ready to stream, you must sharpen your pencil and figure out the implications of your presentation design.

Since you may have multiple streams playing simultaneously, you have to consider whether the streams can stream simultaneously to your entire audience. As an example, consider a SMIL presentation of a keynote presentation from a conference. At a minimum, the presentation would most likely consist of a number of different elements:

✦ **Video of the speaker giving the presentation.** The video and audio would most likely be encoded into a single stream.

✦ **The speaker's slideshow presentation.**

✦ **A user interface.** The video and slideshow streams may be placed inside some sort of branded interface, possibly with links to more information.

Only two of the three streams have to be streamed in parallel, because the user interface can be downloaded and displayed before the video and slideshow streams begin. The difficulty arises when you have to deliver streams in parallel.

Let's say the video and audio were encoded as a single stream for a 28.8K audience using a target bit rate of 20 Kbps. The slideshow presentation could be authored in RealPix at a bit rate of say 12 Kbps. If we add those together, we get a total bit rate of 32 Kbps, which eliminates any possibility whatsoever of this presentation streaming to a 28.8K modem user.

To make this presentation work over a 28.8K modem, you must get the total bit rate under 20 Kbps, or 22 Kbps if you're feeling adventurous. You can compromise one or both streams, in any way that reduces the overall bit rate while maintaining an acceptable level of quality. If you reduce the bit rate of the video, for instance, you may want to reduce the screen size. The same goes for the slide show.

On the other hand, you might decide that this presentation is not suited for 28.8K modem users. Or you might decide to author separate presentations for low and high bit rate users, so that each user gets the highest possible quality. This, however, is time consuming, and time is one thing no one has enough of these days.

The trick is to plan ahead so that you don't waste time at any point in the process. To do this, you have to know about some of the hidden overheads that accompany streaming media steams.

Hidden Overheads

A number of things occur behind the scenes of streaming media systems that can add latency to your presentation. These fall into two main categories:

✦ **Player-server overheads** — Time-consuming interaction between the media player and server that are hidden from the viewer

✦ **Bit rate fluctuations in streams** — Data types such as Flash and RealPix can wreak havoc with the best designed presentations because their bit rates are variable and subject to large fluctuations.

Player-server overheads

When a media player receives a SMIL file, it requests header information for each and every file that is going to be played in the near future. How the player defines "near future" depends on the particular player, but it can potentially ask for information about every stream in your presentation.

The header information is small, but if you have a number of streams, the incremental delays can add up. If the streams are coming from different servers, the problem can be exacerbated because each time the media player encounters a different server, it must do a DNS lookup to locate the server, which takes time.

The amount of overhead is also highly dependent on the protocol used to deliver the stream. RTSP (Real Time Streaming Protocol) is a well-behaved streaming protocol, because it was designed to operate within allotted bit rate restrictions, meaning it never uses more bandwidth than it is supposed to. HTTP, on the other hand, was not designed for streaming and, therefore, does not have any bit rate controls. HTTP sends as many packets as possible until all bandwidth is consumed. This is not the behavior you want if a number of streams share bandwidth. Also, with HTTP there is also a significant amount of TCP/IP overhead, which are low-level networking messages.

Many media players can use HTTP as a transport protocol. HTTP can be a double-edged sword, however, because it is designed to continually re-request packets that are lost in transit. The problem is this can take up additional bandwidth and delay the playback of the presentation. As a general rule, avoid using HTTP in your presentations for stream delivery. Stick with RTSP, which was designed to deliver streaming media efficiently.

Note   Many firewalls block RTSP traffic. Most players fall back to the HTTP protocol when this occurs. So even if you design your presentation to use the RTSP protocol, the player may automatically switch to HTTP to circumvent firewall issues.

Bit rate fluctuations in streams

Another hidden overhead lurks inside the streams themselves. Most streaming codecs are designed to encode streams using a constant bit rate (CBR), though variable bit rate (VBR) codecs usually produce higher quality streams. VBR codecs use fewer bits during portions of the stream and more bits during others. This makes them "spiky," which means if you graph the bit rate requirements over time, spikes would appear where the bit rate was higher. If you don't have enough overhead to accommodate these bandwidth spikes, the presentation must rebuffer.

Some data types are spiky in nature no matter what you do. Flash animation can be a notorious offender if you're not careful. These streams begin by streaming the graphical elements in the presentation followed by the instructions with which to animate them. Averaged over time, the overall bit rate looks manageable because streaming the instructions takes up negligible bandwidth. The initial buffering, however, can far exceed the bit rate.

 Cross-Reference To learn how to author Flash animations that stream well, please refer to Chapter 22.

RealText is also a spiky data type, although the spikes are nowhere near as large as with animation. This is because RealText presentations are delivered all at once, even if there are text events in the file that don't happen until much later. A RealText file can be very small, but if you use HTTP to "stream" it, the impact on your bandwidth can be noticeable. When you have little or no overhead, every single bit counts.

Of course no one expects you to avoid animation or text in your presentations. They are both excellent multimedia data types. The key is to make sure you design enough time and space to allow for effective delivery of all your data types.

Strategies for Success

The first and most important thing to think about when designing a presentation is your target audience. This puts a ceiling on the bandwidth you'll have available to you as an author. You may want to consider authoring more than one version if you are catering to a wide variety of bit rates. You don't necessarily have to author a separate presentation for each and every possibility, but it probably is worth your while to author both a low and a high bit rate version.

After you've decided on your target audience(s) and bit rate(s), you need to decide what data types you want to use. At this point, you must ask yourself, "What is most important in this presentation?" For instance, if you are authoring a presentation of a keynote speech with a slideshow, you can go one of three ways:

✦ Use a high quality combined audio/video stream and stream the slides via text.

✦ Use a medium quality combined audio/video stream and stream the slides as pictures.

✦ Use only the speaker's voiceover to encode an audio stream and stream high-quality slides.

Though it may seem that video of the speaker is most important and most desirable, at low bit rates the quality may not be compelling enough to warrant surrendering the majority of the bit rate to the combined audio/video stream. Don't be afraid to break with convention — just because most presentations on the Internet may be offered in a particular format does not necessarily mean it is the best format. It's up to you to decide what the best format for your content is.

After you've decided on the data types to use, allot bandwidth to the various streams. Static items should not be streamed during the body of the presentation. They should be loaded at the beginning of the presentation and "frozen" into their regions using the `fill="freeze"` attribute, so you don't need to include them in your rough bit rate calculations. However, any time you plan on streaming anything in parallel, you must decide how much of the available bandwidth to assign to each stream. After you settle on target bit rates for each individual stream, it's time to prepare your media. The target bit rates determine appropriate screen sizes, image sizes, and so on. If you exceed your bit budget on any one stream, you have to make up for it by economizing elsewhere.

You'll need to set up your regions, the sizes of which are determined by the prepared media streams. Then you have to set up the timing of your streams in the body of the SMIL file. This is where you can make or break a SMIL presentation. Bringing in too many streams at once can be a recipe for disaster. Allowing a little breathing room for each stream gives you a much greater chance of success.

Lastly, and most importantly, you must test your SMIL presentation from a streaming server to ensure that it streams smoothly across a network. The best-laid plans can fall to pieces when confronted with an overtaxed network.

Media Preparation

Preparing your media involves a delicate tradeoff between quality and reliability. The slimmer your stream, the better chance it has of being streamed successfully over troublesome networks. However, as the bit rate of a stream decreases, the number of bits available is reduced, thereby compromising the quality.

An important adage to remember is "a bird in the hand is worth two in the bush." A beautiful presentation is useless if it re-buffers every five seconds. Err on the side of caution, because the few extra bits that add that extra polish may be the bits that bottleneck the presentation.

Audio

With audio files, you don't have much of a choice with your bit rates because audio codecs come in predetermined bit rates. One thing to be careful of is that these pre-determined bit rates are designed to take up all available bandwidth at a given target bit rate. You must customize the settings to ensure you get the bit rate you require.

For example, if you choose a 28.8K target audience, the RealProducer defaults to a 20 Kbps codec for music content and a 16 Kbps codec for voice content. If you're going to be playing the audio in parallel with any other stream, you may want the audio to be only 8 Kbps or perhaps 6.5 Kbps. You have to change the default setting or create a template in whatever audio editing system you're working in to choose the appropriate codec.

 For more information about choosing bit rates when encoding files, please refer to Chapter 13 and Chapter 14.

Video

Video files are similar to audio in that the default templates for target bit rates assume you want to give the video stream as much bandwidth as possible. If you're playing the video in parallel with another stream, this is not the case. Again, you're going to have to modify the preset or create a new template to achieve the bit rate you require.

Because the bit rate you're using may be smaller than normal, you may want to consider a smaller screen size to maintain an acceptable quality level. For example, you would normally encode an audio/visual stream for a 56K modem audience at 240×180 or 176×132, assuming an available bit rate of 32 Kbps. If you wanted to stream this in parallel with a slideshow encoded at 12 Kbps, your total available bit rate for the audio/visual stream is effectively only 20 Kbps, so you may want to consider reducing your screen size to 160×120.

Another thing to consider would be encoding the video using a reduced frame rate, possibly even reducing the video to a slideshow presentation. This may sound drastic, but for certain presentations, a large slide show might be more effective than a small blurry video.

 For more information on recommended bit rates and audio codecs, please refer to Appendix B. For more information on recommended screen sizes and frame rates, please refer to Chapter 12.

Images

Plenty of good image compression programs are available, such as Macromedia Fireworks and Adobe Photoshop. If you plan on working with a lot of images, you should invest in one. They can achieve drastically better results at much-reduced file sizes. Many also offer a preview facility whereby you can see the degradation as you shrink the file size.

For a table of target image file sizes, please turn to Chapter 24.

Animation

Streaming animation (Flash, not animated `.gif` files) is tricky. Watch out for the image elements that are being animated and the number of key frames. Flash offers a way to set image quality during export — the settings here have a large effect on the buffering time and average bit rate of the presentation. Also, reducing the number of key frames greatly affects the bandwidth consumption of Flash files.

All Flash animation files must be tuned before they are streamed. Flash files can be tuned when they are exported from the Flash authoring tool. Tuning helps ensure that Flash files stream at the bit rate you specify. However, if the animation cannot truly stream at the specified rate, it compensates by prebuffering for a very long time. You have to make sure that your presentation streams at the required bit rate without an unusually high preroll.

For more information about tuning Flash animation files and ways to author effective streaming Flash files, please turn to Chapter 22.

Good Programming Practice

An often overlooked but very important aspect of SMIL authoring is something that is inculcated into aspiring programmers from the first day they start writing code: good programming practice. SMIL isn't exactly a programming language, but the same rules should still apply. Following a few simple consistent rules and developing a style make the authoring process smoother in the long run.

Format your code

Any code that has different sections and, particularly, code that includes binary tags that require a closing tag can benefit from good formatting. Separate different sections of your code with blank lines. SMIL ignores extra white space in the file, and a few extra carriage returns in the file won't impact your bit rate — however it does make your code much easier to read and debug.

While you're adding a few blank lines for legibility, you should indent your code. Any time you have a group of tags enclosed by a pair of tags, it's a good idea to indent the code enclosed by the tags. That way it's immediately obvious where the group begins and ends, and easier to detect if a closing tag is missing or misplaced. Take a look at the two code snippets in code Listing 30-1 for an example.

Listing 30-1: Good versus Bad Code Formatting

code snippet (a)

```
<body>
<par>
<seq>
<img src="your.jpg" region="bgimage_region" fill="freeze" />
<img src="your_logo.gif" region="Logo" fill="freeze" />
<par>
<video id="clip 2" src="your.rm" region="Video"
fill="freeze" />
<textstream id="clip 4" src="your.rt" region="RealText"
fill="freeze" />
</par>
</seq>
</par>
</body>
```

code snippet (b)

```
<body>
<par>
    <seq>
        <img src="your.jpg" region="bgimage_region"
            fill="freeze" />
        <img src="your_logo.gif" region="Logo"
            fill="freeze" />
        <par>
            <video id="clip 2" src="your.rm" region="Video"
                fill="freeze" />
            <textstream id="clip 4" src="your.rt"
                region="RealText" fill="freeze" />
        </par>
    </seq>
</par>
</body>
```

If you stare long enough at code snippet (a), you can decipher what is supposed to happen, but it isn't immediately obvious. What's more, the three group closing tags at the end of the snippet are hard to match to their opening tags. Code snippet (b), on the other hand, is much clearer and it is a cinch to see where each group begins and ends.

Use comments

While it may seem petty to ask you to supply a few comments in your files, let me be clear: There is nothing more frustrating than sloppy code — especially when you can't decipher what the original author's intent was. How would you feel if people were constantly sending you SMIL files that "didn't work" without the slightest indication of what the file would do if it did work?

Comments are necessary in two situations. First, as a guide to what the code is supposed to accomplish. Second, to point out any tricks or shortcuts the original author may have used that are not immediately obvious to the casual observer.

You don't have to go overboard, because comments are streamed along with the rest of the SMIL code — a few simple pointers will do. You'll appreciate it yourself when you revisit the code six months later. Here's a helpful comment:

```
<!-- load background, then play video and slides in parallel -->
```

Use intuitive names

Choosing names should be a simple and straightforward task. Don't try to save a few keystrokes by naming your regions with a letter or number. Give them meaningful names that someone else can easily decipher. What you're trying to do is create code that is easy to understand so that you can debug or modify it quickly and simply.

If your presentation uses a logo graphic, use the following names:

+ logoRegion for the region the logo is targeted to

+ logoStream for the clip id if it needs to be referenced by other streams

+ logo_40 × 40.jpg for the actual image, which appears to be 40 × 40 pixels in size

Use an intuitive directory structure

When you begin building your presentation, it is tempting to put all the elements in a single directory. You might start off with a handful of images and a video stream. As your presentation becomes more and more complex, additional elements are added to the directory until, before you know it, you've got a mess on your hands.

The best way to organize things is to have only the SMIL file in the top-level directory, and all other elements in separate directoriesnamed video, images, audio, and so on. Again, this may seem like nitpicking, but you'll love yourself in six months when you return to the project for some reason or other and don't have to spend time figuring out where files are.

Effective Clip Sequencing

After you've prepared your media and set up the header section of your presentation, it's time to begin sequencing your clips. At this point, you should take a serious look at your presentation and figure out exactly what has to be seen and when. While you're doing this, you should bear the following in mind:

✦ Clips running in parallel share bandwidth — running clips in sequence lets each stream have maximum bandwidth.

✦ Clips in parallel groups are treated as a unit.

✦ Static elements don't have to run in parallel — they can be brought in and "frozen" in place using `fill="freeze"`.

Sequential versus parallel groups

When you watch a presentation, it is often easy to think of the whole thing as a unit. This lends itself to organizing the clips in the presentation in one large parallel group, perhaps with some clips delayed slightly to begin a bit later. But it turns out that this is not the best approach. The best way to illustrate is with an example.

Imagine you're assembling a presentation that has a background image, a logo, a video stream, and an image stream. Your first attempt at a body for this file might look something like this:

```
<par>
    <img src="images/bkgnd.jpg" region="bkgndRegion" />
    <img src="images/logo.jpg" region="logoRegion" />
    <video src="video/keynote.rm" region="videoRegion" />
    <img src="images/slides.rp" region="slidesRegion" />
</par>
```

Assuming you're working with limited bandwidth, you might run into problems at the very beginning of the file because everything is going to try to stream at once. You might try to delay the video and slides a bit by using begin attributes:

```
<par>
    <img src="images/bkgnd.jpg" region="bkgndRegion" />
    <img src="images/logo.jpg" region="logoRegion" />
    <video src="video/keynote.rm" region="videoRegion"
        begin="5" />
    <img src="images/slides.rp" region="slidesRegion"
        begin="5" />
</par>
```

Now the video and slide show clips won't begin until five seconds into the presentation. The problem is, since the video and slide show clips are in a parallel group , the media player treats them as a unit. The media player requests header information for all the streams in the parallel group, and possibly even buffers the video from the beginning of the presentation.

If you take a step back from the presentation, you should realize that the background and logo don't need to run in parallel with the video and slides. In fact, because they're over and done with quickly, you may as well get them out of the way. So, pull them out of the parallel group. You also want them to load before the video and slides begin, so enclose the two groups inside a <seq></seq> group:

```
<seq>
    <img src="images/bkgnd.jpg" region="bkgndRegion" />
    <img src="images/logo.jpg" region="logoRegion" />
    <par>
        <video src="video/keynote.rm" region="videoRegion" />
        <img src="images/slides.rp" region="slidesRegion" />
    </par>
</seq>
```

When a SMIL player executes this code, it loads the background, then the logo, after which the video and slideshow presentations run in parallel. Note that the five second delay using the begin attribute is no longer necessary. Also, since the <par></par> group comes after a few sequential clips, the player should not bother to buffer the video and slides until a few seconds later. During this time the two images have the complete bandwidth available to them and download quickly.

The only problem with this code is that the background and logo are removed from the screen before the video and slides are displayed. In fact the background disappears before the logo displays. What we really want them to do is stay in their respective regions until the presentation is over. This is where the fill="freeze" attribute comes in.

Freezing static elements

In the previous example, two graphic elements needed to remain visible until the end of the presentation. This is precisely what fill="freeze" is for. Any static elements should be brought in and frozen using this attribute as follows:

```
<seq>
    <img src="images/bkgnd.jpg" region="bkgndRegion
        fill="freeze" />
    <img src="images/logo.jpg" region="logoRegion"
        fill="freeze" />
    <par>
        <video src="video/keynote.rm" region="videoRegion" />
        <img src="images/slides.rp" region="slidesRegion" />
    </par>
</seq>
```

Now the background graphic and logo images remain visible. You might even want to add the same attribute to the video and slides streams so that when the streams finish they won't disappear from the presentation.

Testing your SMIL file

Once you've arrived at what you think is an effective sequencing of your clips, and the presentation runs locally without any problems, it's time for the real test — streaming from a server. No matter how well your presentation appears to work locally, it may grind to a halt when streamed across a network. There are no bandwidth constraints running off your local drive. To truly test your presentation you must load it onto a server and try streaming it across a network.

If your presentation is being authored for a dial-up modem audience, it is crucial that you test with a modem. Streaming your presentation across your internal network only tells you whether whether or not anyone else on your network can watch it. It tells you nothing about the real-world woes faced by a dial-up user.

Tip

The RealProducer Plus ships with a Bandwidth Simulator that allows you to simulate modem performance and even packet loss. It can be a handy shortcut in your testing process, but still no substitute for real-world testing.

If your presentation buffers too long or if it rebuffers mid-presentation, you're going to have to do a little debugging to figure out which stream is giving you all the trouble. After you've narrowed the problem down to a particular clip or group, you must either modify the SMIL file or the actual stream until your presentation streams well to your intended audience.

SMIL file debugging

The best approach when authoring SMIL files is to test at numerous points in the process. If there are any syntax problems, the file will not play back. The player generally returns an error message that indicates where in the file the problem was encountered. In most cases, the problem is a simple typographical error or a missing or mismatched closing tag.

After you've eliminated all syntax errors, you must test the file's performance across a network. If your presentation runs fine locally but has performance problems across a network, you need to isolate the problem clip or group. You can do this as you author, by testing the presentation each time you add a new clip or group (although this can be time consuming).

Another way to locate problem areas in your SMIL code is to comment out sections of your code until the performance problem disappears, and then to add the clips or groups back in one at a time until the problem re-appears. For example, imagine you had with the code example from earlier in the chapter:

```
<par>
   <seq>
      <img src="images/bkgnd.jpg" region="bkgndRegion" />
      <img src="images/logo.jpg" region="logoRegion" />
      <par>
```

```
            <video src="video/keynote.rm" region="videoRegion"/>
            <img src="images/slides.rp" region="slidesRegion" />
        </par>
    </seq>
</par>
```

The first thing to try would be removing the `<par></par>` group that contains the video and image streams as follows:

```
<par>
    <seq>
        <img src="images/bkgnd.jpg" region="bkgndRegion" />
        <img src="images/logo.jpg" region="logoRegion" />
<!-- removed for debugging purposes
        <par>
            <video src="video/keynote.rm" region="videoRegion"/>
            <img src="images/slides.rp" region="slidesRegion" />
        </par>
*** end of debugging -->
    </seq>
</par>
```

Note that the comment begins with `<!--` and continues across multiple lines until the closing `-->`. Also note how the comment is obvious so that removing it or moving it around is easy — and you're not likely to leave it in by mistake. If you're using a text editor with syntax highlighting, the section you remove should be grayed out or a different color.

When this code is played back, you'll be able to see if the first two clips perform satisfactorily. If they do, move the debugging comments to surround only clip 4, so that you've added clip 3 back to the equation, like so:

```
<par>
    <seq>
        <img src="images/bkgnd.jpg" region="bkgndRegion" />
        <img src="images/logo.jpg" region="logoRegion" />
        <par>
            <video src="video/keynote.rm" region="videoRegion"/>
<!-- removed for debugging purposes
            <img src="images/slides.rp" region="slidesRegion" />
*** end of debugging -->
        </par>
    </seq>
</par>
```

You have now added clip 3 for testing purposes, without adding clip 4. In the same manner, you can isolate any clip or group of clips. Continue doing this until you've identified the problem. Once you've isolated the problem, you can modify the clips or the SMIL code to obtain the performance you're after. Debugging performance problems can be tedious, which is why it is preferable to carefully plan in advance and to err on the side of caution when allotting bandwidth.

Fixing SMIL File Bandwidth Problems

If your presentation looks fine locally but won't stream across a network, you have bandwidth problems. This problem falls into one of two categories:

✦ Too many streams at once

✦ Streams too close together

If streams playing in a parallel group is causing the problem, chances are too many streams are competing for bandwidth. Even if your calculations say that there is enough room for all the streams, there may be hidden overheads you aren't aware of that are causing the problem. In this situation, you must either remove one or more streams from the parallel group or reduce the bit rate of one or more streams until the parallel group ceases to be a problem.

If streams playing in sequence is causing the problem, you're trying to play them too close together. Again, it might all look fine on paper and playback locally from your hard drive, but network delivery is completely different. Your choices in this case are to either remove a stream from the presentation or to increase the amount of time between streams loading by using timing attributes such as dur, begin, end, and so on. Consider the following example:

```
<par>
    <seq>
        <img src="images/bkgnd.jpg" region="bkgndRegion"
            fill="freeze" dur="1" />
        <img src="images/logo.jpg" region="logoRegion"
            fill="freeze" dur="1" />
        <par>
            <video src="video/keynote.rm" region="videoRegion"/>
            <img src="images/slides.rp" region="slidesRegion" />
        </par>
    </seq>
</par>
```

This example has been used throughout the presentation, but now duration attributes of one second have been added to the two images. The desired behavior of this presentation is for the background to load; one second later, the logo to load; and then one second later, for the video and slides to start playing back in parallel. Chances are that this presentation will either rebuffer before the video playback, or have an unusually long preroll. Why?

The performance of this presentation is player-dependent, but this is what probably would happen:

1. **Player receives SMIL file, parses it, and decides one of two things:**

   a. It must buffer all the streams.

   b. It only needs to buffer the streams before the parallel group.

2. **If it chooses option a, the amount of preroll is dependent on the sizes of the background and logo images.** If each image takes 3–4 seconds to download, and video playback requires 5–7 seconds of preroll, the player could buffer for as long as 15 seconds, which may be unacceptable.

If the player chooses option b, it buffers the first two images for 6–8 seconds and then begins playback. Once playback begins, the player then realizes it must buffer the video and slides. The problem is that there are only two seconds in which to do so. The player would have to rebuffer after the second image. Of course, this might not be immediately noticeable because the images are static, but the desired behavior of having the video play back starting at 3 seconds would not occur.

Figure 30-1 illustrates these two scenarios.

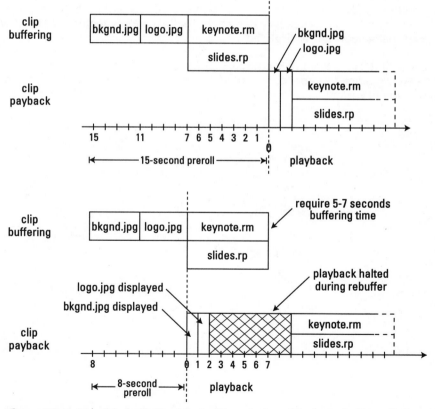

Figure 30-1: Possible buffering/playback scenarios: (a) player buffers all clips before playback; (b) player buffers images and rebuffers during playback.

The solution to this problem lies in spreading out the clips. Doing this gains you a number of advantages. First of all, by delaying the playback of the video until 10 seconds or so into the presentation, the player will most likely decide *not* to pre-buffer the video alongside the images — it will wait until after the presentation has begun. Second, since the player decides not to buffer the video along with the images, all the available bandwidth is used to download the images, so they will download faster. Third, the player will most likely pre-buffer both images before playback begins, therefore when the presentation does begin, the first 10 seconds of the presentation can be used to pre-buffer the video and image streams in the parallel group.

You might consider "camouflaging" the 10-second gap by adding some text, or using an animated GIF for the background or logo image. Text is an excellent data type for this purpose because it is extremely low bit rate.

 Tip

People are generally prepared to wait for streams provided they see something happening. It's much better to show them something quickly and then add elements one by one, even if it takes time, rather than making them wait 15–20 seconds before anything is displayed.

Figure 30-2 illustrates two alternative scenarios for this presentation that stand a much better chance of smooth streaming. Code for example b would look something like the following.

```
<par>
   <seq>
      <img src="images/bkgnd.jpg" region="bkgndRegion"
         fill="freeze" dur="3" />
      <img src="images/logo.jpg" region="logoRegion"
         fill="freeze" dur="3" />
      <textstream src="text/topics.rt" region="textRegion"
         fill="freeze" dur="5" />
      <par>
         <video src="video/keynote.rm" region="videoRegion"/>
         <img src="images/slides.rp" region="slidesRegion" />
      </par>
   </seq>
</par>
```

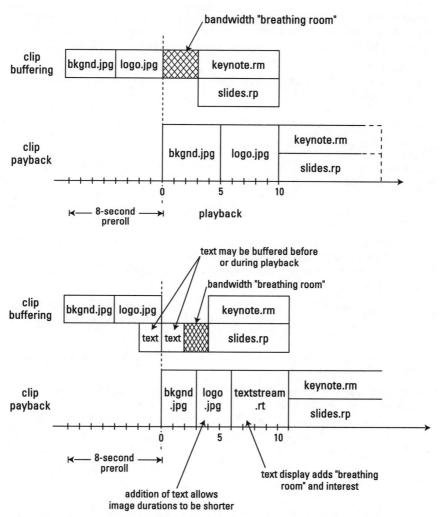

Figure 30-2: Improved playback scenarios: (a) images with longer durations; (b) Text stream added for interest and pacing.

Authoring a SMIL File

Authoring a SMIL file depends largely on the type of presentation you are designing, but there are a number of good habits you should get yourself into. This simple example assumes you're working on the example used throughout this chapter, whereby you are authoring a presentation of a keynote speech, which includes slides from the speaker's presentation. The presentation uses a background image, your company logo, and some text for pacing and interest as suggested in the previous section.

1. **First you have to decide on the target audience.** In this case, assume the audience has at least a 56K modem. Taking a quick glance at the suggested target bit rates in Appendix B, you see that you have approximately 32 Kbps to work with.

   Because the only streams that absolutely must run in parallel are the video stream (which of course includes the audio as well) and the slides, the sum of their bit rates must not exceed 32 Kbps. Encoding video stream at anything less than 20 Kbps would compromise the quality and size too much, so assign 20 Kbps to the video, which leaves 12 Kbps for the slides.

2. **Now it's time to prepare your media:**

   Assuming that there isn't too much motion in the video frame, the video should be encoded at either 176×132 or 160×120. The code below assumes a screen size of 176×132. The image quality should be acceptable at this screen size. Also, assuming there is no music in the presentation, you should, use a voice codec.

   The slides should be prepared at either 320×240 or 240×180, depending on how often they change. If they change often, choose the smaller screen size for higher quality images. The code below assumes the smaller screen size of 240×180.

   The images should be compressed as much as possible and resized to the sizes you want. The code below assumes a background image size of 480×300 and a logo size of 60×60.

   The streaming text file should be prepared. The code in Step 3 assumes a presentation size of 160×135.

3. **After your media is ready to go, you can begin the SMIL authoring process.** Start off with the tags you know you'll need: `<smil></smil>` tags, `<head></head>` tags, `<body></body>` tags, and `<par></par>` tags to establish a master timeline. While you're at it, throw in a few comments. Your code should look like this:

```
<smil>
<!-- keynote speech 9/30/01. -->

    <head>

    </head>

    <body>
<!-- bring in the background, then logo, then text,
and finally play the video and slides in parallel -->

        <par>

        </par>

    </body>
</smil>
```

4. **Believe it or not, you could test your code at this point.** Nothing would happen, but if you mistyped any tags, the player would complain.

Add your region definitions. Use a root layout that accomodates a 240 × 180 slide show, a 160 × 120 video, the logo, and a text area that you can use as a table of contents. If you choose a root-layout size of 480 × 300 and put the video and text on the left and slides on the right, the layout definitions should look like the following:

```
<layout>
    <root-layout width="480" height="300" />
    <region id="bkgndRegion" width="480" height="300" />
    <region id="videoRegion" left="15" top="25"
            width="176" height="132" z-index="10" />
    <region id="textRegion" left="15" top="160"
            width="160" height="135" z-index="1" />
    <region id="logoRegion" left="395" top="220"
            width="60" height="60" z-index="1" />
    <region id="slidesRegion" left="215" top="25"
            width="240" height="180" z-index="10" />
</layout>
```

Note that background colors are not defined with the regions so they all assume the default black background. Also, no fit attributes have been specified, so they assume the default value of `hidden`. You can do this since you're preparing all your media specifically to fit in these regions. To make the code more modular, you might want to add `fit="fill"` to all the region definitions.

Also note that since no regions overlap, they could all share a `z-index` attribute. In this case, the video and slides have been bumped up to `z-index` 10 to ensure that they are on top of everything else. The background region assumes the default value of zero. The text and logo share `z-index` 1.

5. **You can test again at this point.** If you do, the player should open up to the size of your root-layout region. If anything is wrong, the player returns an error message.

6. **Provided the player is happy with all your layout definitions, it's time to start adding clips.** Start by adding the first three elements, without the video. Bring them in sequentially, letting each clip play three seconds. Your body section should look like this:

```
    <body>
<!-- bring in the background, then logo, then text,
and finally play the video and slides in parallel -->

        <par>
          <seq>
            <img src="images/bkgnd.jpg"
              region="bkgndRegion" dur="3" fill="freeze"/>
            <img src="images/logo.jpg"
              region="logoRegion" dur="3" fill="freeze"/>
```

```
            <textstream src="text/seekpoints.rt"
                region="textRegion" dur="5" fill="freeze"/>
        </seq>

    </par>

</body>
```

7. **Test your code.** You want to make sure that there are no syntax errors, which the player flags with error messages, and also that the presentation flows as you expected. Testing now saves heartaches later. If you're syntax error free, and the presentation looks and flows like it is supposed to, you can move on to Step 8.

   If you encounter any problems, such as region size mismatches or clip orders, fix them now before you move on.

8. **Add the video and slides streams.** You want them to play in parallel, so they must be added in a parallel group. The entire file should now look like Listing 30-2.

Listing 30-2: **Step-by-Step Example Code**

```
<smil>
<!-- keynote speech 9/30/01. -->

    <head>
        <layout>
            <root-layout width="480" height="300" />

            <region id="bkgndRegion" width="480" height="300" />
            <region id="videoRegion" left="15" top="25"
                    width="160" height="120" z-index="10" />
             <region id="textRegion" left="15" top="160"
                    width="160" height="135" z-index="1" />
            <region id="logoRegion" left="395" top="220"
                    width="60" height="60" z-index="1" />
            <region id="slidesRegion" left="215" top="25"
                    width="240" height="180" z-index="10" />
        </layout>
    </head>

    <body>
<!-- bring in the background, then logo, then text,
and finally play the video and slides in parallel -->

        <par>
            <seq>
                <img src="images/bkgnd.jpg" region="bkgndRegion"
                    dur="3" fill="freeze" />
                <img src="images/logo.jpg" region="logoRegion"
                    dur="3" fill="freeze" />
```

```
        <textstream src="text/seekpoints.rt"
             region="textRegion" dur="5" fill="freeze" />

        <par>
           <video src="video/keynote.rm"
                region="videoRegion" fill="freeze" />
           <img src="images/slides.rp"
                region="slidesRegion" fill="freeze" />
        </par>

     </seq>
   </par>

  </body>
</smil>
```

9. **Test your file locally to make sure there are no syntax errors and that it looks and flows like you expected.** If so, move on to Step 10, the biggest hurdle.

10. **Move all your files onto a server and test.** Be sure you maintain the directory structure you set up on your local computer and that all the files you need are transferred to the server. If files are missing or not where they're supposed to be, the player returns an error message.

If you're targeting dial-up modem users, as in this presentation, it is crucial that you dial up and try streaming the presentation across a modem. If it does stream, congratulations, the combination of media preparation and careful design has paid off and you're ready to put a link to the presentation on a public server.

If it doesn't stream, then it's time to do some debugging. Comment out parts of the code until you find the culprit, and fix as necessary.

Authoring SMIL for QuickTime

 Expert The following section was contributed by Steven Dryall, President and CTO of Confluent Technologies Inc., creators of the SMIL authoring tool Fluition. For contact information, please turn to Bonus Chapter 6 on the CD-ROM.

QuickTime officially supports SMIL 1.0 as of Version 4.1. However, even though SMIL 1.0 is a "standard," there are differences in implementation between the major streaming platforms. To author SMIL files for the QuickTime player, to understanding these differences is necessary.

This section examines the presentation created in the preceding step-by-step example in this chapter and explains the steps required to make it QuickTime compliant.

Use QuickTime compatible media files

It may be obvious, but in the example, there are two files that will not work with QuickTime. Both the keynote speech and the slide show are RealMedia files. These must either be converted to a QuickTime format (in the case of the video) or displayed using a different approach (in the case of the slides).

The example uses streaming text as a navigation scheme. This could easily be implemented using a QuickTime chapter list. Because that is a QuickTime-specific feature and not directly related to SMIL, it is left as an exercise to the reader.

The slide show can be recreated by using the built-in capabilities of SMIL. You cannot perform the same transitions that you can with RealPix, but the most important part of the slideshow is the timing of the slides. Doing so is easily accomplished by using SMIL. (See Step 3 of "SMIL timing in QuickTime.")

SMIL layout in QuickTime

The layout information of the presentation remains the same. QuickTime supports all root layout and region tags and attributes.

SMIL timing in QuickTime

To begin with, have a look at code in Listing 30-2 used to sequence the presentation. The code used to bring in the two images at the start works fine in a QuickTime player, and this example won't be covering how to implement the RealText navigation scheme as a QuickTime chapter list. It's the content in the `<par>` group that must be changed.

First of all, you must use a `.mov` file for the video. If you're going to progressively download the file, you can use a regular movie. If you're going to stream the video, you must use a reference movie that refers to the streaming movie.

Next, the slideshow must be changed to a QuickTime compatible format. Instead of using RealPix, you can use SMIL timing to load the slides. The following code shows how this could be done, using the same region that the RealPix stream was targeted to:

```
<seq>
    <img src="slide1.jpg" region="slidesRegion" dur="00:00:10" />
    <img src="slide2.jpg" region="slidesRegion" dur="00:00:05" />
    <img src="slide3.jpg" region="slidesRegion" dur="00:00:10" />
</seq>
```

This code plays three slides — the first slide for 10 seconds, the second slide for 5 seconds, and finally the third slide plays for 10 seconds. You can see how the entire slideshow can easily be re-created in this manner.

This simple example should give you an idea of how just about any SMIL presentation you can think of can be authored in such a way that the QuickTime player can play it back. The only thing you have to be careful of is to use QuickTime supported data types.

Making your presentation accessible to viewers

QuickTime SMIL presentations can be streamed or progressively downloaded. Using a streaming server for the video files can improve the quality of the final experience for the viewer, because streaming servers are better equipped to handle the task. However, it is possible that you may not have access to a streaming server, in which case progressive downloading is your only option.

The key difference between a streaming version and a progressively downloaded version is how the streaming elements are referenced inside the SMIL code. In the streaming version, the video files being streamed are referenced using a fully qualified URL to the streaming server, such as:

```
<video src="rtsp://quicktime.yourdomain.com/keynote.mov"
       region="videoRegion" fill="freeze"/>
```

For progressively downloaded presentations, you would place all the files on your Web server, and reference them locally:

```
<video src="keynote.mov" region="videoRegion" fill="freeze"/>
```

Regardless of which delivery method you use, you want to save your SMIL presentation as a self-contained movie. When you save SMIL presentations, the QuickTime player acts slightly differently than when you save other QuickTime presentations. Self-contained SMIL presentations do not contain the individual pieces of media — they contain only the references necessary to assemble the presentation.

Make sure to save your presentation using the `.mov` extension, not `.smil`. Doing so ensures that the QuickTime player is used to play back the presentation, not the RealPlayer (or Internet Explorer in some cases). After the SMIL presentation has been saved the self-contained movie file can then be treated as any other QuickTime file and linked to from a Web page or embedded into a Web page.

Summary

Authoring effective SMIL files is as much planning as it is implementation, particularly if you're authoring for lower bit rates. The key is to design within the given bandwidth constraints, as opposed to trying to fit a beautiful design down a constricted Internet connection.

✦ Bandwidth management is key to successful SMIL presentations.

✦ Sometimes hidden overheads can interfere with your available bandwidth.

✦ Player-server interactions and bit rate fluctuations in streams are two common hidden overheads.

✦ Allot the available bandwidth according to the importance of the streams and the design goals of the presentation.

✦ Prepare your streams carefully and err on the side of caution with bit rates.

✦ Good programming practice, such as effective comments and indenting your code makes your code more modular as well as making debugging easier.

✦ Use sequential grouping for your clips whenever possible.

✦ Using `fill="freeze"` is an excellent way to keep static clips visible.

✦ Test your SMIL file by the network connection the intended audience will be using.

✦ Debug your SMIL code by commenting out sections until you find the problem areas or clips.

✦ Bandwidth problems are usually caused by either too many clips playing in parallel, or attempting to play clips in sequence too quickly.

In the next chapter, you'll learn about some advanced SMIL techniques that not only allow you to add interactivity to your presentation, but also to author for multiple bit rates inside the same file.

✦　　✦　　✦

Advanced SMIL Techniques

T he last few chapters introduced you to the basic rules for authoring SMIL files, including syntax, layout, and timing rules. Now it is time to learn about the advanced features of SMIL.

First, this chapter covers linking in SMIL. You can link to other presentations or to Web pages. This is done with a simple tag that turns the entire clip into a link, or with a more powerful tag that allows specified regions of a presentation, known as "hotspots," to be the active link area. Temporal attributes can also be specified in these tags so that links may be active for specific time periods.

The chapter also covers the <switch> tag, which allows the player to make choices based on user settings. This enables you to author multiple presentations inside a single SMIL file. For instance, the same presentation could display different video clips based on the viewer's bandwidth or preferred language setting.

The system-captions attribute provides another method of authoring files based on user settings. Sections of the SMIL code can be executed or ignored depending on whether or not the user has indicated a preference for captions.

Because SMIL is an extensible language, both RealNetworks and Apple have added special functionality to SMIL that only their players recognize — these extensions are also discussed in this chapter.

The RealPlayer extensions allow player control, control of the player cache, ad insertion, and some extra tag functionality. The QuickTime extensions allow access to various features of the QuickTime player from within the SMIL file.

Last but not least, embedding SMIL presentations in Web pages is discussed.

Linking to Other Presentations

SMIL offers two different tags for linking purposes. One should be very familiar to anyone who has authored a Web page; the other is a similar but far more powerful version.

Linking using the `<a>` tag

The `<a>` tag is a binary tag, which means it takes a closing `</a>` tag, and links whatever it encloses to the value specified in the `href` attribute. The syntax is as follows:

```
<a href="url" show="value" >
    <img src="images/smacktastic.jpg" region="logoRegion"
        fill="freeze" />
</a>
```

Caution   The `<a>` tag can only surround a single clip.

The `href` attribute can take any valid relative or fully qualified URL. Optionally, the `<a>` tag may also take a `show` attribute. The `show` attribute may take one of the following values:

✦ `replace` — The default, assumes the URL is to be played by the player, replacing the currently playing presentation

✦ `new` — Sends the URL to the viewer's browser while keeping the player running

✦ `pause` — Sends the URL to the viewer's browser and pauses playback

A code example using the `<a>` tag is as follows:

```
<a href="http://smacktastic.tv" show="new" >
    <img src="images/smacktastic.jpg" region="logoRegion"
        fill="freeze" />
</a>
```

This code links the `smacktastic.jpg` image to the Smacktastic Web site for the entire time that the image is visible. In this case, `fill="freeze"` has been specified, so the link remains active until the end of the file or until a region with a higher `z-index` covers the image.

In this code example the `show` attribute has the value `"new."` This means when the image is clicked the Smacktastic Web site address is sent to the viewer's browser, and playback of the SMIL presentation continues uninterrupted. If instead the `show` attribute had the value `"pause,"` the media player pauses when the image is clicked, and again the Smacktastic Web site address is sent to the viewer's browser.

Linking using the <anchor/> tag

The <anchor> tag is similar to the <a> tag, but has the added ability to define "hotspots." This means that a certain area or timed section of a clip — instead of the whole clip — can link to another clip or Web page.

Specifying hotspot areas

Hotspots in SMIL 1.0 must be rectangular (not so in SMIL 2.0 — see Chapter 32). The hotspots are defined by specifying coordinates that position the top left-hand and bottom right-hand corners of the rectangular hotspot. Each coordinate value represents the number of pixels measured from the top left-hand corner of the region. Alternatively coordinates can be specified as percentages of the clip's width and height. Figure 31-1 illustrates how these coordinates are specified.

```
<img src="images/cabin.jpg" region="imageRegion" fill="freeze" >
  <anchor href="http://smacktastic.tv/cabin.html"
          coords="140,130,600,290" show="new" />
</img>
```

Figure 31-1: Specifying the coordinates of a hotspot. Coordinates are listed in the following order: top, left, right, bottom.

Specifying temporal attributes

Hotspots may also have timing attributes associated with them. You can specify a begin or end time or both. Hotspots defined without a start time are assumed to begin at the start of the file; those without an end time are assumed to end at the end of the file. Hotspots with particular begin and end times are known as temporal hotspots. Figure 31-2 illustrates some example temporal hotspots.

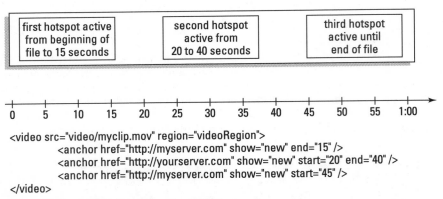

```
<video src="video/myclip.mov" region="videoRegion">
        <anchor href="http://myserver.com" show="new" end="15" />
        <anchor href="http://yourserver.com" show="new" start="20" end="40" />
        <anchor href="http://myserver.com" show="new" start="45" />
</video>
```

Figure 31-2: Specifying active times for hotspots

Example hotspot definitions

Hotspot attributes can be mixed and matched in any way you like. You can specify both temporal and spatial attributes in the same tag, and clip references can have multiple hotspots defined within them.

Since multiple hotspots can be defined for each clip, <anchor/> tags use a slightly different syntax than <a></a> tags. In this case, the clip reference tags must enclose the defined hotspot(s). This was discussed briefly in Chapter 27 — this is the special case where clip reference tags take the binary form.

For example, in most cases, the <video/> tag is unary, meaning it takes a closing slash and no closing tag. When defining hotspots in a video, however, it takes the binary form. Take a look at the following code:

```
<video src="video/myVideo.rm" region="videoRegion" >
    <anchor href="http://smacktastic.tv" show="new"
            begin="5" end="20" />
</video>

<video src="video/myVideo.rm" region="videoRegion" >
    <anchor href="http://smacktastic.tv" show="new"
            begin="5" end="20" />
    <anchor href="http://smacktastic.tv" show="new" begin="30"
            coords="0,0,160,120" />
</video>
```

First, notice how the `<video>` tag no longer takes the closing slash. Instead, after the `<anchor/>` tag, there is a closing `</video>` tag. In the first example, the hotspot has temporal attributes, which link the entire clip region to the specified URL from five seconds into the clip until 20 seconds into the clip. In the second example, two hotspots are defined — the first duplicates the behavior of the first example, the second becomes active after 30 seconds and links the area defined by the coordinates to the specified URL. If the resolution of this video is 320 × 240, the coordinates specify the top left-hand quadrant of the video.

Caution Be careful when defining your hotspot coordinates and timing attributes. SMIL will let you define hotspots that overlap, but how the player decides to treat them is fairly unpredictable.

The complete set of attributes for the `<anchor/>` tag is as follows:

✦ `href` — Specifies the URL the clip links to

✦ `show` — Defines how and where the URL should be displayed. As with the `<a>` tag, it can take one of three values:

 • `replace` — The default, assumes the URL is to be played by the player, replacing the currently playing presentation

 • `new` — Sends the URL to the viewer's browser while keeping the player running

 • `pause` — Sends the URL to the viewer's browser and pauses playback

✦ `id` — Allows a name to be specified so that the `<anchor/>` may be referred to by other links

✦ `begin` — Specifies when the anchor becomes active, relative to when the clip begins playback

✦ `end` — Specifies when the anchor stops being active, relative to when the clip begins playback

✦ `coords="top, left, right, bottom"` — Allows the specification of a rectangular sub-section of the clip region to become active. Four numbers are required; the first two define the top left-hand corner, while the second two define the bottom right-hand corner of the rectangle (refer to Figure 31-1). The coordinates may be specified as exact pixel values or as percentages of the region's dimensions.

Switching Between Choices

SMIL provides a mechanism for decision making within files using the `<switch>` tag. The decisions are made based on internal player settings, such as preferred language, system bitrate, or player version.

The `<switch>` tag is binary, meaning it takes a closing `</switch>` tag. Within these tags, a number of options are listed, each with a test attribute. The player analyzes each option, in order, and executes the first option it finds with an appropriate value. After it executes the option, the rest of the entries in the `<switch>` statement are ignored.

The `<switch>` tag can be used to choose between individual clips or whole groups. `<switch>` statements may be used in the body or header of a SMIL file to choose between alternate layouts (as demonstrated in the next section).

In case none of the other groups or clips can be executed, you should always include a final default option without a test attribute when using the `<switch>` statement. The default option should always be listed last, because `<switch>` statements are parsed in the order they're listed — the first statement that passes the test is executed, and the rest of the switch group is ignored.

The three attributes you can test for are as follows:

✦ `system-bitrate`: An integer value representing bits per second which is tested against the media player's internal setting. If the attribute value is less than the player setting, the clip or group is played.

✦ `system-language`: A two-letter language code which is tested against the player language setting.

✦ `system-required`: Tests the attribute against the player version.

These attributes can be combined to test for multiple requirements for certain streams, groups, or layouts.

Switching based on user bandwidth

When you install a media player, you are generally asked to supply the speed at which you connect to the Internet. The player then saves this setting to use when it communicates with servers so that the highest quality stream can be sent. This setting can also be used to choose between different clips in a SMIL presentation.

Imagine, for example that you had two versions of a clip — one encoded at a broadband 300 Kbps bit rate, and the other, a low bandwidth 56 Kbps version. If you wanted to make sure folks with a fast connection got the higher quality clip and the dial-up folks got the lower quality clip, you could use the following code:

```
<switch>
    <video src="video/myclip_256.rm" region="videoRegion"
        system-bitrate="200000" />
    <video src="video/myclip_32.rm" region="videoRegion" />
</switch>
```

The player would check its own system-bit rate and as long as it was greater than 200,000 bps (DSL or above), the broadband clip would be played back. Note how the second clip does not have a `system-bitrate` attribute — this way at least one clip is always played back.

Chances are, though, that if you had two versions of a video, one at 300 Kbps and one at 32 Kbps, they would have different screen sizes. You would probably want to target them to different sized regions. You could do that by specifying two regions in the layout, and targeting the appropriate region. However, you might want the entire root-layout to change based on people's connection speed. You could accomplish that by using a `<switch>` tag in the header section:

```
<head>
   <switch>
      <layout system-bitrate="200000">
         <root-layout width="480" height="360" />
         <region id="hiVideoRegion" top="10" left="10"
                 width="320" height="240" />
      </layout>
      <layout>
         <root-layout width="320" height="240" />
         <region id="loVideoRegion" top="10" left="10"
                 width="176" height="132" />
      </layout>
   </switch>
<head>
```

Now the player sets up the root layout and region depending on the player's `system-bitrate` attribute. Note how the second `<layout>` group does not have a test attribute — it is the default layout for players that do not have system bit rates of 200 Kbps or above. This code can be combined with the `<switch>` tag shown earlier, provided the regions targeted are changed to reflect the regions defined in this layout section.

Caution Even though only one of the layout sections above is used, all regions still require unique names. You should name them differently, anyway, for clarity's sake.

Switching based on user language setting

Switching based on language setting works exactly the same as switching based on system bit rate, but in this case the system language setting must match exactly the setting in the player. The language setting is based on a short international code for the language.

Cross-Reference The full listing of SMIL language codes is listed in Bonus Chapter 2 located on the CD-ROM.

If you wanted to switch your presentation's narration based on the viewer's language setting, you could do it as follows (the following example assumes the audio has been encoded separately from the video):

```
<par>
    <video src="video/travel.rm" region="videoRegion" />
    <switch>
        <audio src="audio/narr_fr.rm" system-language="fr" />
        <audio src="audio/narr_de.rm" system-language="de" />
        <audio src="audio/narr_es.rm" system-language="es" />
        <audio src="audio/narr_ja.rm" system-language="ja" />
        <audio src="audio/narr_en.rm" />
    </switch>
</par>
```

The video plays regardless of language setting, but the audio narration is chosen depending on the viewer's chosen language. This presentation offers French (fr), German (de), Spanish (es), Japanese (ja), and English versions of the narration. Note that the English version is the default, with no system-language requirement.

If you had multiple clips that were language dependent, you could use the <switch> statement with groups:

```
<par>
    <switch>
        <par system-language="fr">
            <audio src="audio/narr_fr.rm" />
            <video src="video/travel_fr.rm" region="videoRegion"
                />
        </par>
        <par system-language="es">
            <audio src="audio/narr_es.rm" />
            <video src="video/travel_es.rm" region="videoRegion"
                />
        </par>
        <par>
            <audio src="audio/narr_en.rm" />
            <video src="video/travel_en.rm" region="videoRegion"
                />
        </par>
    </switch>
</par>
```

Switching based on player version

Different versions of players have different capabilities that you may want to take advantage of without compromising the presentation for those who don't have the most recent player. If you want to author a presentation that takes advantage of the latest player features but retains backwards compatibility, you would author your presentation with a `<switch>` statement that has one section using the latest features, and another section that uses the standard SMIL features.

Caution This feature has not been implemented in all SMIL players. Please consult your player documentation for details.

If you want to author your presentation so that it plays different streams based on the player version, you must specify an XML namespace in your presentation, and then test using the `system-required` attribute. Declaring the XML namespace is done in the very beginning of your file, in the `<smil>` tag as follows:

```
<smil xmlns:cv="http://features.real.com/systemComponent">
```

Note The previous namespace declaration assumes you are authoring for the RealPlayer. You would use a different declaration for other players. See "QuickTime SMIL extensions" later in this chapter for the code required for the QuickTime namespace.

The letters between the `xmlns:` and the equals sign are used by the player to reference the XML namespace. In the previous code example, this statement notifies the RealPlayer that the presentation uses an extension called `systemComponent`. The player doesn't actually visit the specified URL — this is used merely as a unique identifier.

After you have specified the XML namespace, the RealPlayer uses the letters `cv` to reference the namespace and test for a player version as follows (line breaks inserted for clarity):

```
<switch>
    <par system-required="cv" cv:systemComponent=
        "http://features.real.com/?feature;player=6.0.9.584">
        <video src="video/myclip_NewFeatures.rm"
            region="videoRegion" />
    </par>
    <par>
        <video src="video/myclip_generic.rm"
            region="videoRegion" />
    </par>
</switch>
```

Many of the advanced RealPlayer SMIL extensions require a recent RealPlayer. You may want to consider authoring your presentations so that people with older players can see an alternate presentation.

Working with Captions

SMIL includes a parameter `system-captions` that allows you to choose whether or not to play back caption streams if they are available, based on the viewer's player setting. When the player has the captions preference set to "on," any clip or group with the `system-captions` attribute set to "on" is played. You can also set the `system-captions` attribute to "off" for clips or groups that only should be played when the player's captions preference is set to "off."

If you wanted to have closed-caption text under your news video, you would author a text stream and only turn the text stream on when captions were requested, as follows:

```
<par>
    <video src="video/news.rm" region="videoRegion" />
    <textstream src="text/captions.rm" region="captionsRegion"
            system-captions="on" />
</par>
```

The `system-captions` attribute can also be used in group tags. For example, if you wanted to get fancy, you could encode a different video stream that omits the audio to accompany the captions. After all, the audio uses up valuable bandwidth — you may as well dedicate those extra bits to the video encoding. The SMIL code would look like this:

```
<par system-captions="on" >
    <video src="video/news_noAudio.rm" region="videoRegion" />
    <textstream src="text/captions.rm" region="captionsRegion"
            />
</par>
<par>
    <video src="video/news.rm" region="videoRegion" />
</par>
```

The RealPlayer also has an extension to SMIL allowing the `system-captions` attribute to be used in the layout tag as well (see "Using system-captions in the <layout> tag," later in this chapter).

RealPlayer SMIL Extensions

RealNetworks has without a doubt been the most aggressive proponent of SMIL technology. To this end, they have implemented a number of extensions to basic SMIL 1.0 technology that offer additional functionality:

✦ **RealPlayer Control:** Issues RealPlayer commands from within SMIL presentations.

✦ **Additional image** src **attributes:** Enables extra control of image delivery and control of the RealPlayer.

✦ **RealPlayer Cache Control:** Requires a special protocol, CHTTP, which old players do not support.

✦ **Using infinite duration to fake live broadcasts:** The RealPlayer treats presentations with dur="infinite" as live streams, which can be useful.

✦ **Ad Insertion:** Ads can be automatically inserted into SMIL presentations.

✦ **Use of** system-captions **attribute in the** <layout> **tag:** Allows custom layouts based on whether or not the captions feature is being used.

RealPlayer control

You can issue commands to the RealPlayer in two ways. You can open up new RealPlayer windows via the <a> and <anchor> tags, and control RealPlayer playback via the src attribute of the <img/> tag. Opening up new RealPlayer windows utilizes special syntax in the href attribute of the anchor tags, while RealPlayer control occurs via extensions to the src attribute of the <img/> tag. These capabilities are discussed in more detail in the following sections.

Popping up new RealPlayer windows

New RealPlayer windows can be launched using the hyperlink tags, <a> and <anchor>. The syntax is as follows:

```
<a href="command:openwindow(name, URL,
        [,playmode=value][,playmode=value...])">
   {clip being linked}
</a>

<clip reference without closing slash>
   <anchor href="command:openwindow(name, URL,
           [,playmode=value][,playmode=value...])"
           {additional anchor attributes} />
<closing clip tag />
```

The href attribute simply takes the value command:openwindow() with a number of parameters. This functionality works exactly as popping up windows in RealPix does. The parameters and possible values are listed in Table 31-1.

Table 31-1
RealPlayer command: openwindow() parameters

Parameter	Required?	Value	Notes
Name	Yes	_self or _current	Opens URL in current RealPlayer.
		_new or _blank	Opens URL in a new RealPlayer.
		A user-defined name, such as name=video	If a RealPlayer is currently open with the user-defined name, the URL is opened in that window.
			If no RealPlayer is currently open with that name, a new player is opened and assigned the user-defined name, and the URL is played in that player.
URL	Yes	Any valid, fully qualified URL such as http://www. myserver.com or rtsp://www. yourserver.com	Relative URLs are not valid.
Autosize	No	True or false	Set to true or false, specifies whether the RealPlayer should be played back in autosize mode.
Zoomlevel	No	True or false	Set to normal, double, or full, specifies whether the RealPlayer should play back the specified URL normal size, double sized, or full screen.
Ontopwhileplaying	No	True or false	Set to true or false, specifies whether the RealPlayer should always be on top while playing.

Some examples of syntax are as follows:

```
<a href="command:openwindow(_new,
        rtsp://my.realserver.com/myvideo.rm)">
  <img src="myvideo.gif" region="myVideoButton"/>
</a>

<video src="rtsp://my.realserver.com/keynote.rm"
      region="video">
  <anchor href="command:openwindow(_current,
          rtsp://my.realserver.com/keynote.rm,
          zoomlevel=double)" show="replace" />
</video>
```

The first example links the image `myvideo.gif` to a video clip called `myvideo.rm`. If the image is clicked, the video begins playback in a new RealPlayer window. The second example links a video clip to a double-sized version of itself, which plays back in the same player.

Additional attributes for the `<anchor>` tag can be specified, such as spatial coordinates or timing constraints. For example, if a logo appeared in the bottom right-hand corner of a video for a specified amount of time, you could pop-up a new player using that logo as a key with the following code:

```
<video src="rtsp://my.realserver.com/videoWithLogo.rm"
      region="video">
  <anchor href="command:openwindow(logoCompanyWindow,
      rtsp://logocompany.realserver.com/logovideo.rm)"
      coords="75%,75%,100%,100%" begin="1:00" end="2:30" />
```

</video>RealPlayer playback control

RealPlayer playback control occurs via extensions to the `src` attribute of the `<img>` tag. You can stop, pause, play, or seek to a specific location in the presentation. They are discussed in the following section.

src attribute extensions of the <img> tag

The RealPlayer has `src` attribute extensions that can be used with the `<img />` tag. When using these extensions, you must append a question mark (?) to the clip url, followed by an attribute and its value. If you use multiple extensions you must separate them with ampersands (&). The syntax is as follows:

```
<img src="{clip url}?attribute=value[&attribute=value]"/>
```

The following image tags illustrate the use of the RealPlayer extensions:

```
<img src="images/my_image.jpg?reliable=true" />
<img src="link.jpg?url=http://www.myserver.com&target=_browser" />
<img src="play.jpg?url=command:play()&target=_player" />
```

Caution   These extensions to the SMIL language are proprietary to the RealPlayer's implementation of SMIL. They only work in RealPlayer 7 and higher. Additionally, they only work with still images. You cannot use these extensions when using a RealPix file as your source.

The first example tells the RealPlayer that the image must be delivered in full before the presentation can proceed. This can be useful for important images such as presentation backgrounds or company logos. Note, however that ensuring reliable delivery may result in the presentation being delayed if transmission problems occur.

The second example links an image to a Web page, and displays the linked page in a browser. This duplicates functionality available with the `<a>` and `<anchor>` tags. The last example links an image to a RealPlayer command. In this case when the image is clicked, the RealPlayer begins playback. You can also stop, pause, and seek to a specified location.

Table 31-2 lists all the available image `src` attribute extensions. Remember to separate multiple extensions by an ampersand (&).

Table 31-2
src Attribute Extensions for the `<img>` Tag

Attribute	Values	Used for
Bgcolor	Any valid pre-defined color or RGB value preceded by a pound sign (#).	Setting a background color behind a transparent GIF file.
Bitrate	Any integer representing bits per second — that is, 20000 for 28.8K modems	Sets the bit rate at which the image should be streamed.
Reliable	True	Ensures delivery of the image. Playback of presentation halts if transmission problems occur. Can be set to false, but that is the default behavior.
Target	_browser	Sets the viewer's Web browser as the target for the url attribute.
	_player	Sets the RealPlayer as the target for the url attribute.

Attribute	Values	Used for

url	Any valid fully qualified URL, such as
	
	`http://www.myserver.com`
	
	or
	
	`rtsp://www.myrealserver.com`
		Sends the destination URL to the specified target when image is clicked.

	`command:play()`	Begins RealPlayer playback when image is clicked.
	`command:pause()`	Pauses the RealPlayer when image is clicked.
	`command:stop()`	Stops the RealPlayer when image is clicked.
	`command:seek` `(dd:hh:mm:ss.xyz)`	Starts the RealPlayer playing when an image is clicked.

Using the RealPlayer cache

The RealPlayer has the ability to cache any clip delivered via the HTTP protocol. The author can specify which clips should be cached. Caching can be beneficial if viewers return to your site often to watch multimedia presentations that share common elements.

For instance, if you provide a daily news update that always has the same background and logo images, you could specify that these two images be cached on the viewer's computer. When the viewer returns, they no longer need to download the images. This might lead to an improvement in their viewing experience if it allows the video to begin playback sooner.

To utilize the RealPlayer cache, all you have to do is specify the clip reference using the CHTTP protocol, as follows:

```
<img src="chttp://myserver.com/bkgnd.gif" region="image"/>
```

Caution The RealPlayer cache only works in RealPlayer 7 and higher. If you wish to utilize the RealPlayer cache while supporting older players, you must author an alternative presentation that does not use the CHTTP protocol, and use the `<switch>` tag to determine player version. See "Switching based on player version."

When the RealPlayer encounters a clip that uses the CHTTP protocol, it checks the RealPlayer cache to see if it has a copy of the clip. If it does, it uses the clip in its cache. If not, it requests the clip via HTTP, and stores a copy in its cache for later use.

The RealPlayer supports the same HTTP header fields that Web browsers use to control expiration of files. These fields allow the author to decide how long clips are cached for. Since the RealPlayer uses the same fields, you can use images served off Web servers while maintaining the caching directives that have already been set up.

For a full discussion of all available caching parameters, refer to the RealSystem Production Guide, available from the RealNetworks Web site (www. realnetworks.com).

Using indefinite durations

You may have read in Chapter 29 about setting a duration for a clip or group. It was also briefly mentioned that you could set dur="infinite." This attribute setting has a particular side effect in the RealPlayer — it disables the RealPlayer timeline slider, and makes the stream appear to be a live stream.

Caution   The side effect described only occurs in RealPlayer 8 and above. Earlier versions of the RealPlayer ignore the duration attribute if it is set to "infinite".

Any clip with an infinite duration continues playing until the end of the clip is reached, at which point the last frame is frozen in the display region and the timeline continues advancing until the viewer clicks the stop button or some other event stops playback.

This behavior can be useful to make static presentations appear live, or to disable the viewer from searching through a stream. For instance, some of the controversy surrounding music on the Internet concerns listeners being able to hear what ever they want when they want it (imagine that). Live broadcasts are deemed acceptable because the listener cannot "skip over" the advertising or fast-forward to the song he or she wishes to hear. Many Internet radio stations, however, are automated and not at all live. To soothe the various regulatory agencies' ire, these stations can set dur="infinite" in their presentations and thereby not allow seeking to particular songs. It remains to be seen if this is acceptable to the aforementioned agencies, of course, but it does address one of their largest concerns.

Inserting ads

RealNetworks has added a tag to insert banner ads into your SMIL presentation. The <RealAdInsert> tag works in conjunction with the RealServer to insert URLs for the advertisements into the SMIL code. The RealServer, in turn, typically gets the URL information for ads from a third party advertising solution.

SMIL files that utilize the `<RealAd Insert>` tag must reside in a special RealServer directory named `adtag`. SMIL files in this directory are assumed to have one or more `<RealAdInsert>`tags. The RealServer parses the SMIL code and replaces each instance of the `<RealAdInsert>` tag with an `<img>` tag containing the URL for the banner and any additional display information you specified.

To use the `<RealAdInsert>` tag you must work closely with your RealServer system administrator. The administrator is in charge of setting up the `adtag` directory on the server. Each subdirectory may have a slightly different behavior. In addition, the RealServer has automatic ad insertion capabilities that you may be able to take advantage of.

To use the `<RealAdInsert>` tag, you must define a region for the banner, and then specify any additional image tag information you require. In the body of your SMIL file, instead of specifying a particular image to use, you would use the `<RealAdInsert>` tag so that the RealServer would insert the appropriate image. The code in your SMIL file might look like this:

```
<body>
   <par>
      <RealAdInsert region="adBanner" fill="freeze"/>
      <video src="rtsp://myrealserver.com/keynote.rm"
             region="videoRegion"/>
   </par>
</body>
```

However, when the RealPlayer received the SMIL from the RealServer, it would now look like this (line breaks added for clarity):

```
<body>
   <par>
      <img
       src="chttp://some.adserver.com/foo/annoyingbanner.gif?
       url=http://www.annoying.com&target=_new&reliable=true"
       region="adBanner" fill="freeze"/>
      <video src="rtsp://myrealserver.com/keynote.rm"
             region="videoRegion"/>
   </par>
</body>
```

The RealServer replaces the `<RealAdInsert>` tag with an `img` tag that contains the URL of the banner ad file, the URL the banner links to, and ensures the banner ad is delivered reliably. Note that attributes specified in the `<RealAdInsert>` tag are included in the image tag that replaces the `<RealAdInsert>` tag.

The RealServer can also serve rotating banner ads, sending new ad images and URLs at a preset interval. This rotation interval is set in the RealServer advertising extension. To use rotating ad banners, set a `dur` attribute in the `<RealAdInsert>` tag. This tells the RealServer that the ad banner should be rotated throughout its duration. For live presentations, you can specify `dur="infinite."` For all other presentations, you should specify a duration equal to the length of your presentation.

Cross-Reference   For more on the RealServer advertising extension, see Chapter 21 and the RealServer Administration Guide, available from the RealNetworks Web site (`www.realnetworks.com`).

Using system-captions in the `<layout>` tag

Using the `system-captions` attribute to decide whether or not a clip was played back was discussed earlier in this chapter. This takes care of the clip, but the problem is that the root-layout is generally designed to accommodate all the streams — if some streams are not played back, the layout might not be optimal. You might wish to define two separate layouts based on whether or not captions are requested. You can do this by specifying two separate layouts and placing a `system-captions` attribute in the first layout tag:

```
<layout system-captions="on">
    <root-layout width="320" height="280" />
    <region id="videoRegionCaptions" width="320" height="240"
        />
    <region id="captionsRegion" width="320" height="40"
            top="320" />
</layout>
<layout>
    <root-layout width="320" height="240" />
    <region id="videoRegion" width="320" height="240" />
</layout>
```

If the user has the captions preference set to on, the root-layout is defined large enough to accommodate both the video and the captions clips. If not, the root-layout is defined slightly smaller to compensate.

Caution   You can have multiple layout regions, but you must still use unique region names even though some of the regions are not used.

Since you must use unique names when defining multiple regions, you have to be careful about targeting the correct region in the body section. This example supplies two video clip reference tags: one to use if the captions are turned on targeting the region defined in the captions layout, and the other to target the region defined in the non-captions layout:

```
<par>

<!-- play the video in the regular region
```

```
                          if system captions are off -->
     <video src="video/news.rm" region="videoRegion"
            system-captions="off"/>

   <!-- otherwise play the video and captions
           streams in their respective regions -->
     <video src="video/news.rm" region="videoRegionCaptions"
            system-captions="on"/>
     <textstream src="text/captions.rm" region="captionsRegion"
            system-captions="on" />
   </par>
```

Note how two video streams are contained within the parallel group, but only one ever plays at a time, because of the `system-captions` attribute.

QuickTime SMIL Extensions

 Note   This section assumes the reader has a certain level of familiarity with theQuickTime player and authoring QuickTime files. For more on the QuickTime authoring process, please see Chapter 30 or refer to the Apple Web site (`www.apple.com`).

Apple's QuickTime player has some support for SMIL 1.0, which began with Version 4.1 of the QuickTime player. The QuickTime player also has its own set of extensions. Using these extensions requires a namespace definition, which must be included in the `<smil>` tag at the beginning of your presentation, as follows:

```
<smil xmlns:qt=
    "http://www.apple.com/quicktime/resources/smilextensions">
```

As stated earlier in the chapter, the letters between the `xmlns:` and the equals sign are used by the player to reference the XML namespace. The QuickTime player does not access the URL — it is merely used as a unique identifier. Once the namespace has been declared, the player can use `qt=` in tags to use the QuickTime Extensions. The QuickTime extensions are as follows:

✦ `autoplay` — Determines whether the presentation should play back or wait for the user to press the Play button. This extension is used in the `<smil>` tag as follows:

```
<smil xmlns:qt=
"http://www.apple.com/quicktime/resources/smilextensions"
    qt:autoplay="true">
```

✦ `bitrate` — Used to specify the birate of a particular clip. This enables the QuickTime player to determine how much of the clip to buffer. It is used in the clip reference tag and specified in bits per second, as follows:

```
<video src="myVideo.mov" qt:bitrate="56000" />
```

✦ chapter — Enables the author to specify a name for a particular media element. This name is read by the QuickTime player and is accesible in the controller pop-up list. The viewer can then jump to any "chapter." Chapters are specified as follows:

```
<video src="Intro.mov" region="videoRegion"
       qt:chapter="Introduction"/>
<video src="Chap1.mov" region="videoRegion "
       qt:chapter="Chapter 1" />
<video src="Chap2.mov" region="videoRegion "
       qt:chapter="Chapter 2" />
```

✦ chapter-mode — This specifies whether the QuickTime slider time represents the duration of the whole presentation or the duration of the current chapter. The value must be either all for the whole presentation or clip for the current chapter. This extension is also used in the <smil> tag:

```
<smil xmlns:qt="http://www.apple.com/quicktime/
      resources/smilextensions" qt:chapter-mode="all">
```

✦ composite-mode — Used to specify the graphics mode of an element, which is used to determine transparency. It has a number of possible values. The general syntax is as follows:

```
<img src="myImage.gif" region="imageRegion"
     qt:composite-mode="mode[;value]" />
```

Some modes require values, while others do not. The different modes are as follows:

- copy, none, or direct — specifies no transparency

- blend — used along with a percentage to specify how opaque the element is, with 100 percent specifying complete opacity. The syntax is as follows:

```
<img src="myImage.gif" region="imageRegion"
     qt:composite-mode="blend;75%" />
```

- transparent-color — Specifies a color to use as a chroma key. The specified color is rendered transparent. The color specification may be any of the predetermined colors or an RGB value preceded by a pound (#) sign. The syntax is as follows:

```
<img src="myImage.gif" region="imageRegion"
     qt:composite-mode="transparent-color;green" />
```

- alpha, straight-alpha, premultiplied-white-alpha, premultiplied-black-alpha — Indicates the image's internal alpha channel that should be used. These modes must have a percentage specified, as follows:

```
<img src="myImage.gif" region="imageRegion"
     qt:composite-mode="alpha,60%" />
```

- `straight-alpha-blend` — Specifies an image with an internal alpha channel as a separate component, and that an additional level of transparency should be applied to the whole image. Requires a percentage:

```
<img src="myImage.gif" region="imageRegion"
    qt:composite-mode="straight-alpha-blend,80%" />
```

✦ `fullscreen` — Used to specify the size the QuickTime player should play the presentation at. It has a number of possible values. The general syntax is as follows:

```
<smil xmlns:qt=
"http://www.apple.com/quicktime/resources/smilextensions"
    qt:fullscreen="value" />
```

The different values are as follows:

- **false** — Disables full screen mode

- **normal** — Plays the presentation at the original authored size

- **double** — Plays the presentation at double the authored size

- **half** — Plays the presentation at half the authored size

- **full** — Plays the presentation full screen.

- **current** — Plays the presentation at the current player size

✦ `immediate-instantiation` — This specifies whether the clips in the presentation should all be downloaded (or streamed) in advance or whether they should be downloaded (or streamed) as they are needed. This extension can be used in the `<smil>` tag or in individual clip reference tags. Selective use of this extension can ensure that clips are ready to play when they are needed. The syntax is as follows:

```
<smil xmlns:qt=
"http://www.apple.com/quicktime/resources/smilextensions"
    qt:immediate-instantiation="true">
<img src="bkgnd.png" region="bkgndRegion"
    qt:immediate-instantiation="true"/>
```

✦ `next` — Specifies the URL of the next clip to play when the current SMIL presentation finishes. It can be a relative or fully qualified URL. It is used in the SMIL tag, as follows:

```
<smil xmlns:qt=
"http://www.apple.com/quicktime/resources/smilextensions"
    qt:next="nextChapter.smil">
```

✦ `preroll` — Used to specify the number of seconds to pre-roll a clip.

```
<video src="myVideo.mov" qt:preroll="10" />
```

✦ `system-mime-type-supported` — Used to specify the MIME type needed to be able to play back the clip. This can be used in a `<switch>` statement to choose between different media types, for instance:

```
<switch>
    <video src="qtmovie.mov"
        qt:system-mime-type-supported="video/quicktime"/>
    <video src="mpegmovie.mpg"
        qt:system-mime-type-supported="video/mpeg" />
    <img src="cantplay.jpg" />
</switch>
```

✦ `target` — Specifies whether the target of an href paramenter in an `<a>` or `<anchor>` tag is a new browser, a browser frame, or a QuickTime player. This extension is used along with the `show="new"` attribute.

```
<a href="http://myserver.com/thenextone.smi" show="new"
    qt:target="quicktimeplayer">
    <img src="OpenNewSMIL.gif" region="r2" dur="5:00" />
</a>
```

✦ `time-slider` — Specifies whether or not the QuickTime time slider should be included. It is specified in the `<smil>` tag, and defaults to `"false"`.

```
<smil xmlns:qt=
"http://www.apple.com/quicktime/resources/smilextensions"
        qt:time-slider="true">
```

Embedding SMIL Presentations in Web Pages

The simplest way to embed a SMIL presentation in a Web page is to embed the particular player you're authoring for, and then play back the SMIL presentation in the embedded player. The presentation looks and acts the same as it does in the player.

The other way this can be accomplished if you're authoring for the RealPlayer is by using HTML for the layout and then playing back the presentation using the regions defined in the HTML. Some find this preferable because of the ready availability of HTML authoring tools. Either way, the process is reasonably straightforward. The only thing you must remember is that if you're using HTML for the layout, you must remove the layout section from your SMIL code.

The following sections go into more detail about how to accomplish both methods of embedding presentations into Web pages, including the HTML code. Please bear in mind that HTML is slightly different from SMIL in that the unary tags to not take the closing slash, for example:

```
<param name="src" value="cabin.smil">
```

Embedding files with SMIL layout

If you decide to use the layout capabilities in SMIL and to merely embed a player in a Web page, the process is exactly like the one described in Chapter 16. All you have to do is use either the Netscape plug-in or the Active X control, and specify the SMIL file as your source file.

On the CD-ROM The following examples are included on the CD, in the SMIL directory. The SMIL version is called cabin.smil; the HTML version is called cabin.html.

As an example, consider a simple SMIL file that includes a slideshow, a RealText stream, and an audio stream. The code for this file, cabin.smil, is listed in Listing 31-1.

Listing 31-1: **Original SMIL File (cabin.smil)**

```
<smil>

   <head>
      <meta name="title" content="Our Cabin in Montana" />

      <layout>
         <root-layout width="340" height="280" />
         <region id="slidesRegion" top="10" left="10"
                 width="320" height="240" />
         <region id="textRegion" top="255" left="10"
                 width="320" height="20" />
      </layout>
   </head>

   <body>

<!-- everything in parallel, text & pix offset 3 seconds  -->

   <par>
      <audio src="audio/my_music.rm" />
      <a href="http://smacktastic.tv/cabin/index.html"
            show="new">
       <img src="images/cabin.rp" region="slidesRegion"
            begin="3" fill="freeze"/>
      </a>
      <textstream src="text/cabin.rt" region="textRegion"
            begin="3" fill="freeze" />
   </par>

   </body>
</smil>
```

The code listing for a simple embedded player that plays the original SMIL file in a Web page is shown in Listing 31-2.

Listing 31-2: **Code for Embedding RealPlayer to Play cabin.smil**

```
<html>
   <head>
      <title>Embedded Player using SMIL layout </title>
      <meta http-equiv="Content-Type" content="text/html;
            charset=iso-8859-1">
   </head>

   <body>

   <center>
   <h1>This page contains an embedded RealPlayer
           that simply plays back the entire SMIL file.</h1>

<!-- the first object definition defines
     the playback window -->

       <object ID=RVOCX
classid="clsid:CFCDAA03-8BE4-11cf-B84B-0020AFBBCCFA"
        width=340 height=280>
         <param name="src" value="cabin_w_layout.rpm">
         <param name="controls" value="ImageWindow">
         <param name="autostart" value="true">
         <param name="console" value="_master">
         <embed width="340" height="280"
               src="cabin_w_layout.rpm"
               controls="ImageWindow" console="_master" >
         </embed>
       </object>

       <br>

<!-- the second object defines the player controls -->

       <object ID=RVOCX
classid="clsid:CFCDAA03-8BE4-11cf-B84B-0020AFBBCCFA"
        width=340 height=40>
         <param name="controls" value="ControlPanel">
         <param name="console" value="_master">
          <embed width="340" height="40"
               src="cabin_w_layout.rpm"
               controls="ControlPanel" console="_master" >
```

```
        </embed>
      </object>
    </center>
    </body>
</html>
```

In the HTML code Listing 31-2, two are objects defined — the first object tag defines the playback window, and the second object tag defines the player controls. Note how each object tag also includes an embed tag for Netscape plug-in compatibility. All the objects link to a `.rpm` file, which is a metafile that points to the actual SMIL presentation.

For more information about embedding players in web pages, please refer to Chapter 16.

The second object definition in Listing 31-2 is not entirely necessary unless you want to give your viewers control of the presentation. The width and height of the first object match the settings in the SMIL file. If the dimensions of the embedded object do not match the dimensions of the SMIL presentation, the presentation is squeezed or stretched to fit the settings in the HTML object.

The HTML code in Listing 31-2 (included on the CD as cabin.smil) could be brought into an HTML editor where other elements could be added, such as images and text. To embed a SMIL presentation that plays back in the QuickTime player, you would do much the same thing, but use the proper `classid` value to load the embedded QuickTime player.

For more on authoring SMIL files for the QuickTime player, see "Authoring SMIL files for the QuickTime player," in Chapter 30.

Embedding SMIL files using HTML layout

There may be times when you want to use the layout capabilities of HTML. When using HTML for your layout, you embed an object for each region used in the SMIL presentation. Each of these embedded players must have a `region` parameter whose value is the name of the region targeted in the SMIL file.

The following examples are included on the CD in the SMIL directory. The embedded version using a table layout is called cabin_table.html, the version using frames is called cabin_frames.html. Both use cabin_nolayout.smil, which has had the layout section surgically removed.

Using the same SMIL example as before, you could embed the objects in a table, each object in its own table cell or in the same cell. Alternatively, you can even embed objects in different frames.

The most important thing to remember when using HTML to do your layout is that you *must* remove the layout section from the SMIL file. If you leave it in by mistake, the presentation does not behave as expected. Audio streams are played back, since they do not require regions, but any clips targeted to regions are not displayed. Listing 31-3 lists the HTML code used to embed the SMIL presentation in an HTML table.

Listing 31-3: HTML Code for Embedded RealPlayer Using HTML Layout for a SMIL Presentation

```
<html>
   <head>
   <title>SMIL playback using HTML table layout</title>
<meta http-equiv="Content-Type" content="text/html;
      charset=iso-8859-1">
   </head>

   <body>
   <center>
   <h1>This page embeds different regions into different
      table cells </h1>
   <br>
   <table>
      <tr>
         <td>
            <object ID=RVOCX width=320 height=240
      classid="clsid:CFCDAA03-8BE4-11cf-B84B-0020AFBBCCFA">
            <param name="controls" value="ImageWindow">
            <param name="console" value="master">
            <param name="region" value="slidesRegion">
            <embed width="320" height="240"
               src="cabin_w_layout.rpm"
               region="slidesRegion"
               controls="ImageWindow" console="_master" >
            </embed>
            </object>
         </td>
         <td>
            <object ID=RVOCX width=320 height=20
      classid="clsid:CFCDAA03-8BE4-11cf-B84B-0020AFBBCCFA">
            <param name="controls" value="ImageWindow">
            <param name="console"  value="master">
            <param name="region" value="textRegion">
            <embed width="320" height="20"
               src="cabin_w_layout.rpm"
```

```
                    region="textRegion"
                    controls="ImageWindow" console="_master" >
             </embed>
         </object>
         <p>
         <object ID=RVOCX width=320 height=40
     classid="clsid:CFCDAA03-8BE4-11cf-B84B-0020AFBBCCFA">
             <param name="src" value="cabin_nolayout.smil">
             <param name="controls" value="ControlPanel">
             <param name="autostart" value="true">
             <param name="console" value="master">
             <embed width="320" height="40"
                 src="cabin_w_layout.rpm"
                 controls="ControlPanel" console="_master">
             </embed>
         </object>
     </td>
   </tr>
 </table>
 </center>
 </body>

</html>
```

In Listing 31-3, three separate embedded objects exist — two define playback regions, and one defines the player controls. You do not have to define a playback object for the audio stream since it does not require a region. Only one of the embedded ActiveX objects lists the SMIL file in the `src` attribute — in this case, the object that defines the playback controls, which also sets the `autostart` attribute to true. The `src` attribute must be defined in every instance of the Netscape plug-in.

Listing 31-4 lists the SMIL file, now without the layout section and the anchor tag removed.

 Caution In the RealPlayer, both the `<a>` and `<anchor>` tags cease to function when the layout section of a SMIL file has been removed. Because you *must* remove the layout section when you use HTML for your layout, any anchor tags in your code will no longer work. Linking still images using the `src` attribute extensions, however, does work.

Listing 31-4: **SMIL File for Embedded Play Using HTML Layout**

```
<smil>

   <head>
```

Continued

Listing 31-4 *(continued)*

```
        <meta name="title" content="Our Cabin in Montana" />
<!-- layout done via HTML -->
    </head>

    <body>

<!-- everything parallel, text & pix offset 3 seconds -->

    <par>
        <audio src="audio/my_music.rm" />
        <img src="images/cabin.rp" region="slidesRegion"
                begin="3" fill="freeze"/>
        <textstream src="text/cabin.rt" region="textRegion"
                begin="3" fill="freeze"/>
    </par>

    </body>
</smil>
```

Summary

SMIL offers a number of advanced features, and in addition, the Real and QuickTime players offer extensions to that functionality. This advanced functionality adds a significant amount of flexibility and modularity to SMIL as a language — and there's even more on the way. The next chapter delves into SMIL 2.0, which offers another order of magnitude's worth of authoring power.

✦ Linking in SMIL can be done via the <a> tag and the <anchor/> tag.

✦ The <a> tag links a whole clip, the <anchor/> tag defines a hotspot in the clip which can have temporal and spatial constraints.

✦ The <switch> tag allows choices to be made in the SMIL presentation based on the viewer's player settings, such as language preference.

✦ You can also make choices in your SMIL presentations based on required bit rate, and player version required using the <switch> tag.

✦ SMIL also offers support for captions via the system-captions attribute. This allows choice between clips (and layout in the RealPlayer).

✦ The RealPlayer has extended SMIL functionality that allows RealPlayer control, caching, ad insertion, and files of infinite duration masquerading as live presentations.

✦ The QuickTime player also has extended SMIL functionality that allows acces to QuickTime authoring features, such as chapters, next clip, control of instantiation, alpha channels, and more.

✦ SMIL files can be embedded into Web pages as full SMIL files utilizing SMIL layout, or utilizing HTML layout.

✦ When using HTML layout, be sure to remove the layout section from your SMIL files.

✦ Neither `<a>` or `<anchor>` tags work in SMIL files that do not contain layout information. Be sure to do your linking in HTML when you use HTML to do your layout.

✦   ✦   ✦

What's New in SMIL 2.0

 Expert David Warner, the technical editor for *SMIL: Adding Multimedia to the Web*, contributed the information in this chapter. This chapter is intended to give you a broad overview of what is possible with SMIL 2.0. For further information, please consult one of the references listed in Bonus Chapter 5 on the CD or the W3C Web site (`www.w3.org/TR/smil20`).

SMIL 1.0 provided you with a very clever way to create simple multimedia presentations, but lacked several features found in most other multimedia authoring environments. The recent release of the SMIL 2.0 specification attempts to address some of the shortcomings of the first version.

In this chapter, I explain some of the major changes in SMIL 2.0, which are divided into three major categories:

✦ Grammar

✦ Layout

✦ Timing

After discussing the three main divisions of SMIL 2.0, I provide the inside scoop on what players currently recognize SMIL 2.0 and what tools are available to build SMIL 2.0 presentations.

SMIL 2.0 Grammar

Before you see any new functional features in SMIL 2.0, the first change that will probably strike you is the grammar: the way a SMIL 2.0 file reads.

Few changes have been made in the SMIL grammar between SMIL 1.0 and SMIL 2.0. The biggest change is the switch to the use of *camel case* for tags that have two or more words. Where SMIL 1.0 tags separated words with a dash, SMIL 2.0 removes the dash and capitalizes the letter of the second word. For example, the SMIL 1.0 tag `background-color` becomes `backgroundColor` in SMIL 2.0.

For the sake of backwards compatibility, SMIL 1.0 tags are recognized with either dashes or camel case, though you should probably use camel case. SMIL 2.0 tags must be written using camel case.

The new camel case syntax has two notable exceptions: the `z-index` and `root-layout` properties, for some reason, retain their dashes in SMIL 2.0. Now that the change in grammar is out of the way, let's look at the features that make SMIL 2.0 interesting. First on the list are new layout specifications that enable greater interactivity and more flexibility.

SMIL 2.0 Layout

In addition to all the changes that have been made to the SMIL timing model, SMIL 2.0 has a number of new features for the visual presentation.

Animation

The biggest addition to SMIL 2.0 layout is the ability to animate regions containing any media. Using SMIL 2.0, you can animate a number of different things:

✦ **Position of the media.** A media clip or region can move during a presentation, even as it is playing a clip.

✦ **Size of the media.** The size of media clips or regions can change dynamically.

✦ **Audio volume of the media.** The volume of a clip can change throughout a presentation.

✦ **Background color of the media.** The background color of a region can change throughout a presentation.

These animations are done through the `<animate/>`, `<animateMotion/>`, `<animateColor/>`, or `<set/>` tags. I focus on the `<animate/>` tag, because the latter three tags all use similar syntax to the `<animate/>` tag.

The `<animate/>` tag can appear in one of two places, but the location is always somewhere within the body of a SMIL document. First, the `<animate/>` tag can appear within the source tag of the media tag it affects:

```
<video src="video1.mpeg" id="vid1" region="vidregion">
  <animate .../>
</video>
```

Alternatively, the `<animate/>` tag can appear alone, behaving similarly to a media tag. The following example plays a video, then an animation, and then another video:

```
<seq>
  <video src="video1.mpeg" region="vidregion"/>
  <animate .../>
  <video src="video2.mpeg" region="vidregion"/>
</seq>
```

Just like a media tag, you can use common timing attributes, such as `begin`, `end`, and `dur` to control the timing of your animation. To choose what you want to animate, you set the `targetElement` attribute of the `<animate/>` tag to the `id` of the clip or region you want to animate, then set the `attributeName` attribute of the `<animate/>` tag to the attribute you want to animate. For example, to animate the width of a video clip with an `id` of "vid1", you use the following code:

```
<animate targetElement="vid1" attributeName="width" .../>
```

You then choose animation values:

✦ **Using the** `to` **and** `from` **attributes.** To change the width from 100 to 200, set `from` to 100 and `to` to 200. Both attributes specify a starting and ending value for whatever is being animated. You can also use negative values. For example, if you want to slide something off-screen you can change its `left` value to –200.

✦ **Using the** `by` **attribute.** To make the width of the clip or region you're animating 50 pixels larger, set the `by` attribute to 50. The value of the `by` attribute is added to the value of whatever attribute is being animated. You can use negative numbers to shrink the value you are animating.

✦ **Using a list of values in the** `values` **attribute.** Finally, you can make a list of values and enter them into the `values` attribute. By using the `calcMode` attribute, you can specify how those values are used.

For each of these animation methods, you should use the `dur` attribute to specify how long the animation should take. Without a `dur` value, the change takes place instantaneously.

Using the to and from attributes

Use the `to` and `from` attributes if your animation should always begin in the same place. For example, if you have an image that you want to start at the left edge of the screen and move 20 pixels to the right, you would use the following `<animate/>` tag:

```
<animate targetElement="img1" attributeName="left" from="0"
to="20" dur="5s" .../>
```

When this animation is activated, if the image is not already at the left edge of the screen, it immediately appears there to begin the animation. It then moves 20 pixels to the right during the next 5 seconds.

Using the by attribute

If you want your animation to begin wherever the object currently is, rather than jumping to a beginning spot, use the by attribute. The by attribute does not specify a starting value, only an amount to change the value by. So, if you want your image to move 20 pixels further right each time the animation is activated, use the following code:

```
<animate targetElement="img1" attributeName="right" by="20"
dur="5s" .../>
```

When this animation is activated, the image moves 20 pixels to the right, regardless of where it starts. If the animation is activated a second time, the image will be 40 pixels right of its starting point.

Using the values and calcMode attributes

Finally, you can use the values and calcMode attributes to create a multistep animation. For example, imagine you want an image to start at the top of the screen, move 50 pixels down, and then bounce 10 pixels back up. To do this, you are going to set up 3 values in your values attribute: the top of the screen, 50 pixels down, and 10 pixels up. So, your <animate/> tag will look like this:

```
<animate targetElement="img1" attributeName="top"
values="0,50,40" dur="6s" .../>
```

After you have your values set, you need to decide how the image should move through them. To do this, add the calcMode attribute. The following list shows how different calcMode values affect your animation:

✦ discrete. Attribute used when there is no animation between the different values. If no calcMode is defined, the animation defaults to discrete.

```
<animate targetElement="img1" attributeName="top"
    values="0,50,40" dur="6s" calcMode="discrete" ... />
```

In this example, the image will start at 0, jumps 50 pixels down at 3 seconds, and at 6 seconds appears 40 pixels from the top of the region.

✦ linear. Attribute used to make the image spend an even amount of time between each value.

```
<animate targetElement="img1" attributeName="top"
    values="0,50,40" dur="6s" calcMode="linear" ... />
```

In this example the image spends the first 3 seconds of the animation moving from 0 to 50 pixels, and the second 3 seconds moving from 50 to 40 pixels. Because the image must travel 50 pixels in the first 3 seconds it moves faster than in the second 3 seconds, where it only has to move 10 pixels.

✦ `paced`. Attribute used to ensure that the image moves through each of the points while maintaining a constant speed.

```
<animate targetElement="img1" attributeName="top"
        values="0,50,40" dur="6s" calcMode="paced" ... />
```

In this example, the image needs to move a total of 60 pixels over the course of 6 seconds, or 10 pixels per second. Therefore, the image spends 5 seconds moving from 0 to 50 and then 1 second moving from 50 up to 40.

```
<animate targetElement="img1" attributeName="top"
values="0,50,40" calcMode="paced" dur="6s" .../>
```

SMIL 2.0 also supports animating along curves and accelerating or decelerating animations by setting the `calcMode` to `spline`. The `spline` value uses a system of defining a curve called a spline curve. Creating spline curves is a tad more complex than the other values, and requires the addition of other attributes to the `<animate/>` tag.

For more information about spline curve animation, please refer to one of the references listed in Bonus Chapter 5 on the CD-ROM. *SMIL: Adding Multimedia to the Web* has a section dedicated to working with spline curves.

The other three animation tags are variations on the `<animate/>` tag with specific focuses:

✦ `animateColor`: This tag changes the background color of regions or media.

✦ `animateMotion`: This tag animates both the horizontal and vertical position of the tag's target.

✦ `set`: This tag changes the target value immediately, with no animation from the current value.

These new animation tags open up possibilities for much more dynamic SMIL presentations.

Other layout changes

A few other changes have been made to layout within SMIL 2.0. These features are fairly straightforward, but still add substantial functionality to your SMIL presentations. For more information about these changes please refer to one of the references listed in Bonus Chapter 5 on the CD-ROM or the W3C Web site (`www.w3.org/TR/smil20`).

Multiple windows

In SMIL 2.0, multiple player windows can be controlled by a single SMIL file. You can make a new window with the `<topLayout>` element, which functions similarly to the `<root-layout/>` element within your `<layout>`. You can tell the window when to open or close using the open and close attributes. Any regions that should appear within the new window are created as child elements of the `<topLayout>` element.

For example, the following `<layout>` defines a separate 160 × 120 window, with a `<region/>` of the same size inside the new window:

```
<layout>
   <root-layout width="400" height="300"/>
   <topLayout width="160" height="120" open="onStart"
              close="onRequest">
      <region id="mywindow" width="160" height="120" left="0"
              top="0" />
   </topLayout>
</layout>
```

In the previous example, the new window appears as soon as the presentation begins, even if nothing is playing in the new window. It then persists until the user closes it. If you would rather have the window appear only if media is playing within it and disappear once the media is done, you would change the open and close values:

```
<topLayout width="160" height="120" open="whenActive"
        close="whenNotActive">
   ...
</topLayout>
```

Refer to one of the SMIL 2.0 resources mentioned in Bonus Chapter 5 on the CD-ROM for more information on using the `<topLayout>` tag.

Hierarchical layout

SMIL 2.0 allows any region to have one or more child regions. Child regions appear within the frame of the parent region. Hierarchical regions can be very useful for animation. For example, if you have a video file that you want to play in a graphical frame, you could animate both the video and the frame together by animating a parent region that contains both media, rather than animating the two pieces separately. Here is how the layout for that example would look:

```
<layout>
   <region id="main" width="400" height="300">
      <region id="frame" width="400" height="300" left="0"
         top="0"/>
      <region id="video" width="320" height="240" left="40"
         top="30"/>
   </region>
</layout>
```

Notice how the region tag with the id="main" takes the binary form, which means it does not take a closing slash in the opening tag, and therefore requires a closing `</region>` tag. This region definition encloses the following two region definitions by using the binary form. Being able to group clips and regions in this way saves time and cuts down on potential errors.

Area tags

The `<anchor/>` tag of SMIL 1.0 has been deprecated in favor of the new area tag for creating hyperlinks in a portion of a media file. Though very similar to the anchor tag in most respects, one new feature the `<area/>` tag adds is the ability to define non-rectangular hot spots, such as circles or polygons. This can be handy if you only want to link a very specific region of the media clip, and that region happens to be oddly shaped.

The following example shows how you could link to a circular area of a video to a web page. Circles are defined by the x and y coordinates of their center and a radius:

```
<video src="myVideo.rm" region="video">
   <area shape="circle" coords="240,180,40"
      href="http://my.network.com"/>
</video>
```

The `coords` attribute specifies that the center of this circle is at (240, 180). In a 320×240 region this is in the lower-right corner, where a network logo generally is. For more information on using the `<area/>` tag, refer to one of the SMIL 2.0 resources mentioned in Bonus Chapter 5 on the CD-ROM.

SMIL 2.0 Timing

Even though SMIL 1.0 has reasonably powerful timing abilities, it is nowhere near as flexible and powerful as multimedia authors demand. SMIL 2.0 adds new functionality to the timing capabilities of SMIL in the following areas:

- ✦ **Interactivity:** Enables a presentation to react in new ways to mouse clicks and key presses.
- ✦ **Transitions:** Enables transitions between any two media clips playing in the same region.
- ✦ **Synchronization:** Allows for much greater flexibility with regards to synchronization.

Interactivity

The most exciting new feature of SMIL 2.0 is the ability to create more interactive presentations. In SMIL 1.0, interactivity within a single presentation was limited to the ability to seek within the presentation. All clips in SMIL 1.0 presentations were fixed with respect to the master timeline of the presentation. If you stopped the presentation or fast-forwarded to a particular point in the presentation, all the clips were affected.

In SMIL 2.0, clips do not have to be fixed to the master timeline. Media clips can begin or end with a mouse click without affecting the rest of the clips included in the presentation. For example, a user could flip through a slideshow of images at her leisure while background music plays. This additional layer of interactivity is accomplished through additional timing options, called event timing and access key timing, and a new tag called the exclusive (`<excl>`) tag.

Event timing

The new timing options in SMIL 2.0 extend the existing timing tags, such as `begin` and `end`, to allow the use of references to events as well as times. This means that a video could start playing when the user clicks a graphic or presses a key. The following example shows a line from a SMIL 2.0 file in which a video file plays when a clip or region with an `id` of `skippy` is clicked:

```
<video src="myvideo.mpg" region="videoregion"
       begin="skippy.activateEvent"/>
```

In this example, the `begin` attribute contains the `id skippy` followed by `activateEvent`. The `activateEvent` value is the mouse click. SMIL 2.0 recognizes additional events, such as another element beginning or ending playback or a mouse hovering over an element, among others.

 Note   SMIL 2.0 does not distinguish between a mouse click and the release of a mouse button, nor does it specify which to recognize for the `activateEvent` value.

Access key timing

Another timing option specifies that playback should begin or end on the press of a particular key. The following example shows a line from a SMIL 2.0 file in which an audio file plays when the p key is pressed:

```
<audio src="myaudio.au" begin="accesskey(p)"/>
```

The `accesskey` event is case-sensitive, so the previous example recognizes the key p, but not the P key. Happily, if you want an item to recognize more than one event, you can simply make a list of events separated by semi-colons. In the following code, a video file begins playing if the user presses either the p or P keys, or clicks on the actual video:

```
<video src="myvideo.mpg" region="videoregion" id="me"
begin="me.activateEvent; accesskey(p); accesskey(P)"/>
```

This new event-based timing opens up a huge range of possibilities beyond the linear presentation model of SMIL 1.0. However, the structure of SMIL files needs to be updated as well to allow for nonlinear presentations. This is where the new exclusive tag comes in handy.

Utilizing the exclusive timing tag

The exclusive tag, `<excl>`, is a new timing tag that is similar to the `<par>`, `<seq>`, or `<switch>` tags. For any list of elements within an exclusive tag, only one element may play at a given time. If an element is playing, and another element is begun by an event, the first element stops. Elements within an exclusive tag do not begin playback until triggered by an event. In the following example, one of three videos plays back, depending on whether the user presses the 1, 2, or 3 key:

```
<excl>
  <video src="video1" region="videoregion"
      begin="accesskey(1)"/>
  <video src="video2" region="videoregion"
      begin="accesskey(2)"/>
  <video src="video3" region="videoregion"
      begin="accesskey(3)"/>
</excl>
```

In this example, the author doesn't need to worry about setting up end attributes for each of the video clips. If the first video is playing, and the user pushes the 2 key, the first video automatically stops, and the second video begins playing.

The new interactivity features of SMIL 2.0 can have significant impact on a presentation's bandwidth consumption. Interactivity can make it more difficult for authors to predict how bandwidth will be used over the course of a presentation. Consider all possible combinations of a presentation and the subsequent drain on bandwidth. There's no point in adding interactivity if it ends up grinding the presentation to a halt due to bandwidth limitations.

Transitions

SMIL 2.0 adds the ability to do transitions between any two media in a given region. Previously this was only possible in the RealPlayer implementation of SMIL, and even then only between images in a RealPix file. Now, not only can you transition from image to image, but you can also transition from video to video, from an image to a video or animation, or any other combination you can come up with.

You can specify transitions in SMIL 2.0 in two ways: in-line and in the head section of the SMIL document. An in-line transition enables you to transition between two clips by adding a `fill="transition"` to the first clip and a `transitionFilter` tag to the second clip. Thus, to crossfade from one video clip into a second video clip, you would use the following code:

```
<seq>
<video src="vid1.mpeg" region="videoregion"
       fill="transition"/>
<video src="vid2.mpeg" region="videoregion">
   <transitionFilter type="fade" subtype="crossfade"
       dur="2s"/>
</video>
</seq>
```

This code causes the first video to freeze when it ends and crossfade to the second video. Notice that there are two properties of the transitionFilter tag to set the kind of transition you want: type and subtype. SMIL 2.0 supports all of the hundreds of SMPTE (Society of Motion Picture and Television Engineers) transitions, which are organized into types and subtypes to make them easier to find.

If you plan to use the same transition more than once in a presentation, setting up a transition in the head of your document is a good idea. For example, if you want to fade to black at the end of the first video and then fade back in at the beginning of the second, you would add the following code to the document heading:

```
<transition id="fadetoblack" type="fade"
     subtype="fadeToColor" fadeColor="black" dur="1s"/>
<transition id="fadefromblack" type="fade"
     subtype="fadeFromColor" fadeColor="black" dur="1s"/>
```

You can now refer to these transitions by their id attributes using the transIn and transOut attributes of any media tag:

```
<seq>
    <video src="vid1.mpeg" region="videoregion"
          transOut="fadetoblack"/>
    <video src="vid2.mpeg" region="videoregion"
          transIn="fadefromblack"/>
</seq>
```

Although transitions do not offer sweeping changes like interactivity or animation, they do make a presentation look much more polished.

Synchronization behavior

SMIL 1.0 expected all media to be perfectly synchronized at all times. In a streaming environment, packet loss meant that presentations would often have to stop to wait for information that had not arrived in time. SMIL 2.0 recognizes that there are often times when synchronization is not as important, and offers the author greater flexibility in this regard.

Some of the new synchronization behaviors that can be set to any media or timing block are:

✦ Allowing media to fall out of sync within a specified amount of time

✦ Allowing media to fall out of sync completely with each other

✦ Setting media on a separate time line from the main presentation

These settings allow greater flexibility for items that only need a moderate level of synchronization, such as a slide show with a voice commentary, and open up new possibilities, such as a background music track on a separate timeline that keeps playing while the user interacts with the presentation.

Other SMIL 2.0 changes

You find a number of other changes in SMIL 2.0. These features are handy because they can make presentations faster and easier to use. For more information about these features please refer to one of the references listed in Bonus Chapter 5 on the CD-ROM or the W3C Web site (www.w3.org/TR/smil20).

Preloading media

Authors can now preload portions of media or entire media files during a presentation. This feature is very useful when used with the new interactivity in SMIL 2.0. For example, if a user is presented with an option to play three video clips, the presentation can be preloading the first 10 seconds of all three videos to ensure that playback of any video begins as soon as the user selects one.

Improved accessibility features

A number of new features in SMIL 2.0 enable presentations to be more handicapped-accessible. Some of these features are:

* The ability to tab between links with the author able to set the tab order

* The ability to set a key to launch a given link

* Switch settings for both text captions and audio descriptions

These features are important to make sure that presenting information within a SMIL file does not prohibit people with disabilities from viewing the presentation.

SMIL 2.0 Implementations

SMIL 2.0 is already available in a few major players, such as the RealPlayer and Internet Explorer. SMIL 2.0 is designed to be configurable for different players and devices through a system of *modules* and *profiles*.

Modules are pieces of the SMIL language, such as the animation module, which includes all of the tags that make animation possible. Profiles are collections of modules used by a player. For instance, a player that plays the SMIL 2.0 Language profile can use all of the major modules of SMIL 2.0. Another profile, called the SMIL 2.0 Basic profile, is intended for smaller devices, such as PDAs or cell phones. A player can choose to support a given profile or decide to use just certain modules from SMIL 2.0.

RealPlayer

RealNetworks' RealOne Player is the first major media player to support the SMIL 2.0 Language profile. RealNetworks has been a strong advocate of SMIL, has been a part of the W3C group that created the SMIL specification, and has supported SMIL 1.0 for many years, so it should come as no surprise that RealNetworks has a thorough implementation of SMIL 2.0 in the RealPlayer. In addition, RealNetworks finally supports transparency between data types in a SMIL presentation and has even used SMIL 2.0's extensible architecture to add some tags of its own. These tags add some interesting features to SMIL, such as the ability to animate the transparency level of a datatype.

Internet Explorer

Microsoft has also been involved in the W3C group in charge of SMIL for several years, though only recently did they support SMIL in their products. Their approach to SMIL is somewhat different from RealNetworks' approach. Rather than playing SMIL within the Windows Media Player, Microsoft has been working with the W3C to create a new profile called XHTML+SMIL, which embeds several of the SMIL 2.0 timing and animation modules into HTML pages.

Microsoft first supported the draft versions of several SMIL 2.0 modules in Internet Explorer 5.5 through HTML+TIME, an antecedent to XHTML+SMIL. In Internet Explorer 6, Microsoft has implemented the working draft version of the XHTML+SMIL profile.

For more information about the XHTML+SMIL profile please see the specification on the W3C site (www.w3.org/TR/XHTMLplusSMIL). For information about Microsoft's implementation, please refer to the Microsoft Web site (http://msdn.microsoft.com/library/default.asp?url=/workshop/author/behaviors/reference/time2/htime_node_entry.asp).

QuickTime

At the time of writing, QuickTime still supports SMIL 1.0, though we hope to see Apple introduce SMIL 2.0 support within QuickTime soon.

SMIL 2.0 Tools

One of the problems with SMIL 1.0 was the relative scarcity of tool choices to help authors build presentations. With all the added complexity of SMIL 2.0, the need for a high-quality authoring environment is even greater. However, the choices are still quite limited.

However, I'm not saying that you can't find any good tools. Oratrix (`www.oratrix.com/`), a company with ties to the W3C group that created SMIL, sells a very powerful tool called GRiNS. The learning curve for GRiNS is a bit steep, because it assumes a deep familiarity with SMIL to build anything more complex than presentations based on a few pre-built templates. However, with a good understanding of the SMIL language, GRiNS can be a very useful environment to develop in because it offers a graphical authoring environment. Authoring SMIL presentations in a graphical environment can be much more intuitive than typing code into a text editor.

GoLive 6, the most recent version of Adobe's HTML-authoring tool (`www.adobe.com`), can also build SMIL presentations. The current tools for building HTML are extended to SMIL, allowing visual editing, code editing, or a tree-structured view of the code. In addition, a graphical timeline allows authors to build the body of their presentations. Unfortunately, GoLive 6 only authors SMIL 1.0 presentations.

RealNetworks has also created a small editor called SMILGen that is available for Windows or Linux. SMILGen is a rather basic tool that constructs SMIL code through the use of dialog boxes.

Summary

SMIL 2.0 is a major update to the language that adds a number of powerful features. SMIL now offers many of the features found in other multimedia environments, but still approaches the problem of multimedia development from a very unique angle.

✦ SMIL 2.0 has an updated grammar that makes use of camel case for attribute names with more than one word.

✦ SMIL 2.0 layout is much more dynamic with the addition of animation, multiple windows, and hierarchical regions.

✦ With interactivity, SMIL 2.0 documents are no longer tied to a linear timeline.

✦ SMIL 2.0 can create smooth transitions between any two media files.

✦ SMIL 2.0 allows the author to improve the user experience with improved synchronization, file preloading, and accessibility support.

✦ SMIL 2.0 is supported in the RealOne Player and Internet Explorer 6.

✦   ✦   ✦

Broadcasting on the Internet

Planning for Live Broadcasts

Live broadcasts are different from on-demand files in a number of ways — the most obvious being that with live broadcasts, you don't get a second chance. Everything must work perfectly.

The fact of the matter is, nothing ever does. As a veteran of hundreds of live Internet broadcasts, and hundreds more live events before that, I can safely speak with authority when I say flawless live events do not exist. Something always goes wrong. The key is being prepared to deal with this eventuality.

Redundancy is the first step in preparing for a live broadcast. For every link in the broadcast chain, you should have a backup plan. The backup plan extends from the microphones and cameras all the way to spare servers. Each link is a potential point of failure — and, therefore, you must have a plan of action if and when it fails.

Live broadcasts present other areas of concern. For example, you may want to revise your encoding parameters to decrease the chance of rebuffering. In the authoring stage, you may want to simplify your Web site to steer people directly to the live streams. Serving is a particularly important area, because poor server architecture can limit the success of your event.

To help prevent problems, you should test everything often and as early as possible. Test the connectivity between the site and your server weeks in advance. Test the equipment before it leaves your business and again as soon as you set it up on site. You should test user interfaces, the Web pages, Web servers, and media servers. You can't test too much.

Before any of this happens, you'll need to find out a few things to see if a live broadcast is even possible.

Before You Say Yes

When someone suggests a live broadcast, you need to find out the details before you agree to participate. First, you need to find out whether there is connectivity available on site, because lack of it makes a broadcast impossible, and having it installed can be a time-consuming process. Second, and nearly as important, you need permission to broadcast. This permission may need to come from multiple sources — make sure that you cover your bases unless you feel the need for a lawsuit. Last but not least consider your budget. Live broadcasts can get expensive for a number of reasons (discussed later). At the end of the day, someone needs to cover the costs. Figure 33-1 shows a flow chart for the preliminary planning process for a live event.

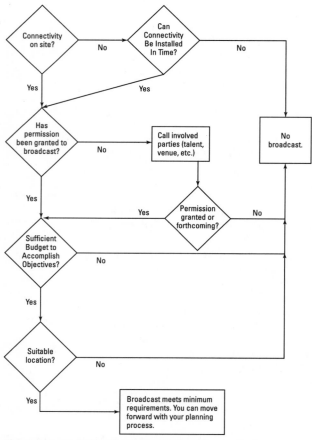

Figure 33-1: A flowchart illustrating the preliminary decision-making process necessary for a successful live broadcast

Connectivity

If you are broadcasting from a remote location, the first hurdle you must clear is connectivity. Somehow you have to get the encoded streams or raw audio and video from the location to your broadcast center. You can use two basic approaches:

✦ Encode on site and send encoded stream(s) back to your servers.

✦ Send raw audio back to your broadcast operations center (BOC) to be encoded.

Each scenario has benefits and drawbacks. Encoding on site is cheaper but involves lugging a bunch of computer gear to the remote site and requires sufficient Internet connectivity. Sending raw feeds puts the encoding back into the safe surrounds of the BOC, but doing so can be expensive.

If your broadcast is audio-only, a couple of solutions can be used to send good quality audio over telephone or ISDN lines. Phone lines can suffice for voice content; ISDN lines can transmit a very high-quality stereo audio signal that is sufficient for music broadcasts.

When video is involved, most people choose to encode on site and send encoded feeds back to the BOC because of the expense of sending raw video. Satellite up-link time costs approximately $1,000 an hour. Fiber links can also be used to send raw video, but their availability is limited and they are expensive, too.

Encoding video on site is relatively cost effective. Depending on the amount of outbound connectivity you require, an ISDN line may suffice. If you require more bandwidth, DSL and Frame Relay lines can be provisioned. The biggest problem is the amount of time it takes to install connectivity if the location does not have an existing Internet connection.

Getting connected

If you have to install connectivity at your site, beware. Doing so involves the local phone company, and we all know how frustrating that can be. Having time on your side is important. Any connectivity install needs *at least* a six-week lead-time, and that's if you like biting your nails. Planning on 8–12 weeks for an install is more realistic.

Call the local phone company as soon as you have any inkling at all that you may need to install connectivity. They may tell you that they're backed up six months on DSL installs, which may kill your live broadcast right then and there. On the other hand, the phone company may say six weeks, in which case you should plan on eight.

Be nice, but be persistent. If they say they'll arrive at 9 a.m., you should be there at 8 a.m. and plan to be there all day. If you miss your appointment, you may not be rescheduled for another six weeks. Test the line as soon as it is active, preferably while the technician is still there. ISDN in particular can be very tricky, giving the phone technician every indication that it works when, in fact, it doesn't.

Tip Make sure that you have the long distance service turned on for ISDN installs if you're going to be calling long distance. It is not activated unless you specifically ask for it, and without it you're stranded.

Swimming upstream

Installing connectivity is not always enough — whether or not the connectivity will suffice depends on the type of connectivity you install. With dial-up modems, ISDN, and Frame Relay lines, you have dedicated bandwidth from the remote location all the way back to your servers. The data is sent via phone company switches (or the Frame Relay Cloud) and does not hit the public Internet at any point.

The same does not hold true for DSL or T1 lines because they are usually terminated at a local ISP. Getting from the local ISP to your servers may or may not be a simple task. It depends entirely on the ISP's connectivity to the Internet backbone and how many "hops" occur between your servers and the ISP. Every time your data hits a new router as it travels across the Internet is considered a hop. Too many hops and your data can be delayed or lost in transit.

The success of your broadcast depends entirely on the quality of your connectivity; therefore, testing is important. If you're attempting to send broadband streams of 300 Kbps or more across the public Internet, you are asking for trouble. If, however, you're trying to send 100 Kbps streams, you have a good chance of getting your broadcast to work — but you're going to want to test in advance.

When doing remote broadcasts that involve the public Internet, being on good terms with your senior network administrator is paramount. He or she can give you an idea of the chances of success for your event, given the connectivity parameters. If you aren't given a 100% guarantee of success, you figure out a different way to do the broadcast or cancel the event.

Permission

One area that is often overlooked but very important is getting legal clearances for broadcasts. In the early days, someone showing up with a laptop and encoding an event without a soul knowing or caring wasn't uncommon. When people started noticing, scrawled notes on the back of napkins were accepted as "legal contracts." These days, you're likely to end up with a summons on your desk if you attempt a broadcast without the proper paperwork.

The amount of clearance necessary varies for different types of broadcasts, but areas you should be aware of that may need legal attention are:

✦ **Talent.** The speaker(s) or musical groups must give permission to broadcast.

✦ **Business Rights.** The talent may have an existing contract with another party, such as a record company, that restricts their performing rights.

✦ **Venue.** You may have to pay a location fee or obtain permission for your broadcast.

✦ **Organizations.** Many organizations are tasked with charging fees for broadcasts, such as ASCAP, BMI, SESAC, and so on.

✦ **Unions.** Unions may charge additional fees if a broadcast is taking place.

You need to ensure that you are covered in all these areas. Negotiations for fees and permissions can be as time consuming as installing connectivity, so the sooner you or your legal department gets started, the better.

Budget

You should ensure that there is sufficient budget to cover all your expenses before you agree to produce a live broadcast. Live broadcasts can get expensive for a couple of reasons:

✦ **Production costs.** Shipping, travel, accomodation, fees, and connectivity can add up quickly.

✦ **Bandwidth costs.** Live events attract larger audiences, so you may need to increase your peak capacity. Also, total throughput is large and adds to the eventual bandwidth bill.

The costs behind broadcast can be looked at differently depending on whether the broadcast is for commercial purposes or for a company's internal use. Commercial broadcasts in theory have to pay for themselves, while corporate broadcasts can be seen in the context of a larger budget, and even be seen as a cost-saving device.

Commercial broadcasts

Commercial broadcast costs can be recuperated a number of ways. Advertising is the first obvious choice, but the math usually doesn't pencil out. For example, assume you're broadcasting a music concert live, re-broadcasting it the following day, and then placing the concert on demand for a month following the two live broadcasts.

For a medium-sized event, a budget of $10,000 would be average. Assuming that you had 10,000 viewers for each of the live broadcasts, and 100,000 viewers during the month of on-demand viewing, and further assuming a $20 CPM rate (which is optimistic), the revenue generated from advertising would be

```
120,000 * $20 per 1,000 views = $2,400
```

For a more in-depth discussion about advertising and streaming media, please turn to Chapter 21.

You can see that there's a significant shortfall between expenditure and revenue. Looked at in a different manner, you'd have a half million viewers to pay for the production expenses, and that's assuming a $20 CPM.

Sponsorship is a better option, because exclusive sponsorships usually command a higher premium than ads. Pay-per-view is of course the Holy Grail of Internet broadcasting, but most people are simply not yet willing to pay for broadcasts on the Internet, even when major acts are involved.

Depending on who ends up with the rights to the broadcast, commercial broadcasts can also be seen as a way to amass a library of content that can be leveraged. For example, radio and television stations often retain the rights to events they broadcast. These broadcasts can later be licensed to other entities, or released on CD or DVD.

The bottom line is that someone has to foot the bill for the live broadcast because there are certain hard costs that must be paid. Because the business model for Internet broadcasts hasn't yet been fully worked out, the only way to justify an Internet broadcast at this point is to assume a certain amount of the expense will not be recuperated in hard cash. This shortfall must be seen as marketing expenditure or as an acquisition expense if you can retain rights to the broadcast. Someone must decide whether or not the broadcast makes sense seen in this light.

Corporate broadcasts

Many businesses use Internet broadcasting as a cost savings device. For example, a company may decide to stream a company meeting live and then provide access to the archived version instead of sending videotapes to branch offices. Companies can often take advantage of existing internal bandwidth, unlike companies that broadcast entertainment on the public Internet.

Location scouting

If you're about to spend a considerable amount of money on a live broadcast from a remote location, you must scout the location and make sure that it is suitable. You should do this with the production manager and the manager of the venue, so you can discuss where your equipment will be located, where power can be found, where connectivity can be brought in, and so on. Even if the location is ideal and provides no particular challenges, you'll be better off on the day of show (preferably the day before) when you can stroll in and know where everything is located.

A more likely scenario is that one or more issues arise during the location walk-through. Dealing with these issues in advance instead of discovering them on the day of the show helps you to know what sort of situation you're walking into. Time is at a premium in live broadcast situations, so anything that saves time is valuable.

How Live Broadcasts Differ from On Demand

Live broadcasts place strain on each step of the streaming media process, from creation all the way through serving. Table 33-1 summarizes the main concerns a live broadcast introduces to the streaming media process.

Table 33-1
How Each Stage of the Streaming Media Process is Affected During a Live Broadcast

Creation	Encoding	Authoring	Serving
• All streams created simultaneously.	• Longer listening times mean longer sustained througput required, which suggests being conservative with bit rates.	• Web sites may need to be simplified to improve access to streams.	• Increased bandwidth demands.
• More equipment required.		• Web sites may need to be simplified to reduce impact on Web servers.	• Increased server license demands (RealSystem only).
• Additional crew required.	• Faster machines required to encode in real-time.		• More servers needed.
• Backup equipment required.	• Back-up machines required in case of failure.	• Player presentation should be authored conservatively, not using cutting edge technology or excessive bit rates.	• Load balancing system crucial.
• Remote broadcasts place a strain upon equipment.			
• Remote broadcast environments may not offer the facilities or control of a studio.		• Stand-alone players tend to be more stable, which limits the authoring possibilities.	
• You may want to create additional content to precede and follow the actual show.			
• You may need a special communications system for crew members.			

Most of these concerns can be taken care of if you take the time to prepare for a live broadcast. The following few sections provide a brief overview of how each stage of the streaming media process is affected. Chapters 34 through 37 address each stage in more detail.

Creation

Live broadcasts require a considerable amount of extra effort in the creation stage, because the broadcast happens once. Instead of being able to record your presentation one piece at a time and edit it together later, you have to combine all the parts of the broadcast in real-time. The amount of equipment you need increases dramatically, and you'll need additional crew to operate the equipment.

Remote broadcasts present an additional challenge because you are not working within the cozy confines of your studio. You have to ensure that there is adequate space to work in, as well as adequate power. You may need a special communications system if crewmembers are working in different locations.

You also may need to produce additional content, such as a pre-show for early birds, or have a host or emcee to give the broadcast a professional feel. The extra production does not have to be excessive, but it should be thought about during your planning process.

Chapter 34 addresses live broadcast concerns during the creation stage in more depth.

Encoding

In theory, there should be no real difference between the encoding parameters you set for an on-demand file and a live broadcast. In practice, however, you may want to be that extra bit more conservative with your settings for a couple of reasons:

✦ The longer a modem is connected, the higher the probability it will re-negotiate to a lower transmission speed.

✦ Sustaining high bit rates for long periods of time across the public Internet without rebuffering is difficult.

You do not need to scale back dramatically; however, live events are not good places to push the envelope. You must also have backup encoding equipment available in case of equipment failure.

Chapter 35 addresses live broadcast concerns during the encoding stage in more depth.

Authoring

Authoring for live broadcasts actually breaks down into two different areas — the Web site and the presentation. The line between the two gets blurry when the media player is embedded in a Web page. Essentially what you want to do is make it as easy as possible for folks to get to the live stream, and once they tune in that they get the best possible experience.

In both areas, you should err on the side of caution. This means keeping your Web pages lean so that they load quickly for your viewers and don't put an excessive strain on your Web servers. You should also keep your streaming interfaces simple for the same reason.

You also should consider whether you want to embed your presentation in a Web page, because in general streaming media presentations are more stable when played back in stand-alone streaming media players.

 Chapter 36 addresses live broadcast concerns during the authoring stage in more depth.

Serving

Serving is subject to the most strain and is the hardest to test. Although other areas are tricky, you can generally avoid the worst problems by careful planning and having a few pieces of backup equipment. Server problems don't appear until the heat of the moment, when the whole world is trying to access your broadcast at the same time. Simulating the crushing loads that your servers are under during a live broadcast is very difficult.

You also have to ensure that you have the capacity, both on the licensing and on the bandwidth front, to handle the event. Increased bandwidth capacity and additional server licenses must be arranged well in advance, and unfortunately, both increased capacity and additional licenses often must be paid for whether the increased capacity is used or not.

 Chapter 37 addresses live broadcast concerns during the serving stage in more depth.

The Importance of Testing

I cannot stress enough how important it is to test at every step of your production. The key to solving problems is having enough time to come up with a creative solution. The earlier you detect potential problems, the more time you'll have to fix them (and test again).

Test the connectivity as soon as it is installed. First, test to see if it works at all and then test to see if it can handle a sustained load. You should plan on encoding a file with the same specs you plan on using during the broadcast for at least a half-hour. If you plan on sending multiple streams, you should send as many streams as you plan on encoding during the show.

Have the folks at your BOC (broadcast operations center) check the quality and packet statistics. Make sure that the connection is clean and the server does not disconnect. You should work closely with your network administrator at this point. He or she'll be able to take a close look at the connection and point out any potential problems.

All the production equipment should be tested before it leaves the office and tested again as soon as it is set up on site. The user interface, both Web page and/or player should be tested throughout the design process, especially via dial-up modem if the broadcast will be targeting dial-up users.

On the day of show you should stage a full run though, testing all cameras, all microphones, and all the encoders. All the backup equipment should be set up, tested, and ready to swap out with a faulty component at a moment's notice.

The best-case scenario is that the backup systems won't be necessary. Worst case — well, let's assume you're prepared for the worst. If you're careful and take the advice of the next few chapters, you will be.

Summary

Live broadcasts are a bit more challenging than on-demand files because you only get one shot at it. For precisely that reason, you have to be prepared to deal with any problems that arise. If you take a little time to prepare and test as much as possible, you'll probably be fine.

✦ Connectivity is the first thing to worry about — you've gotta have it.

✦ Legal clearances are a close second.

✦ Make sure that someone is prepared to foot the bill.

✦ Make sure that you've got all the equipment you need, including backups.

✦ Don't go crazy with your encoding settings — play it safe.

✦ Ditto for authoring — be conservative.

✦ Make sure that you've got the server capacity — both licensing and bandwidth.

✦ Test. Test again. Again. I mean it.

✦   ✦   ✦

Content Creation for Live Broadcasts

The creation stage is where live broadcasts differ most from on-demand production. The location can be unfamiliar and unfriendly. More equipment is necessary because everything happens at once. Tensions run high because everyone, especially the talent, knows that you can't stop and start over again.

Remote broadcasts put a strain on equipment, because the location may not be as hospitable as your studio. The equipment may be spread out across an entire location, and inaccessible at certain times. If you're working in a music venue, it may be filled with cigarette smoke and condensation.

Your equipment probably will take a beating, either at the event or in transit. Cards can wiggle loose from motherboards. Monitors can crack. Hard drives can crash. Luggage can disappear. It's all part of the rich tapestry of a live broadcast, and why you need to have backup plans.

Before you set up your equipment, you need to secure a location for your on-site base of operations. This base is going to serve as your studio for the duration of your broadcast, so it must have everything necessary for your broadcast. You should also establish where your cameras can be placed and where your cable runs can go.

Live broadcasts can introduce new elements, such as a communications system, for the on-site crew and back to your Broadcast Operations Center (BOC). You may want a host to keep the broadcast moving along, or music to play before and after the show. Anyone can encode a live stream — a truly successful broadcast is the one that goes the extra mile to be entertaining.

After your equipment is set up, tested, and ready to go, the countdown begins.

Location

If you're doing a live broadcast from the comfort of your own studio, you won't have too much more to worry about other than being able to accommodate the extra equipment the broadcast requires. In addition, you'll have to make sure that your studio facility has connectivity to your local area network, so you can get the encoded streams to your server.

If, however, you're doing a broadcast from somewhere off-site, there are a number of issues you have to be concerned with:

✦ **Protection.** Your equipment should be protected from the elements, both natural and criminal.

✦ **Power.** You'll need plenty of power to run all your equipment.

✦ **Connectivity.** You have to be within reach of the Internet connectivity.

✦ **Proximity to Media Feeds.** The output of all the cameras and audio gear has to be wired to the encoding equipment.

✦ **Camera Locations.** You want the best camera positions you can get.

First, secure a safe place for your equipment. Indoor locations don't usually present much of a problem; outdoor broadcasts can be tricky. Make sure that your location is adequately covered. Bright sunny days can wreak as much havoc on equipment as rain. If you're out in the open on a sunny day, the temperature can affect computer performance, and monitors are all but impossible to see.

Often, you won't have much of a choice as to where you set up your gear. Many large events are strictly controlled by the production staff who guard every square inch of the backstage area. These people must be courted and cajoled, starting as early as possible. With a bit of persistence, you should be able to get what you need.

Luckily, most of what you need can be brought to you. Long extensions cords can provide power, and Ethernet cables can be run 150 meters with little or no signal degradation. The only thing to worry about is protecting these cable runs.

The raw media feeds are the biggest problems. You should always use high-quality cables in live situations, and every cable *must* be shielded, because so much electricity is running around. Every cable carrying a voltage is a potential source of interference for your audio and video signals. Additionally, the longer your cables, the more antenna-like they become. Shielded cables provide a good deal of protection from external interference, but aren't perfect. For this reason it's a good idea to stay as close as possible to the audiovisual sources, so these cable runs can be kept short.

Camera Placement

The placement of your cameras depends on how many you have and what sort of access you are given by the production manager. Although live broadcasts can be done with a single camera, having more than one camera helps to keep a broadcast interesting. A three-camera shoot is fairly standard in the industry and strikes a balance between coverage and manageability.

You don't need to follow any hard-set rules on camera placement, but here are some helpful guidelines:

✦ Always have an *establishment* shot — a wide shot that shows the entire stage. This shot gives your audience a sense of scale and location.

✦ The next camera should be able to provide a close-up. Close-ups add visual interest and get the audience involved in the broadcast.

✦ A third camera can provide a medium shot or a close-up from a different angle.

✦ Try not to shoot people from below — it's an unflattering angle.

✦ Similarly, make sure you're high enough above the audience so that an unexpected hat or "girlfriend-on-shoulders" doesn't destroy your camera angle.

✦ Try not to block audience sight lines. You want to be unobtrusive, and you don't want your cameramen being pelted with abuse (or worse).

✦ Make sure that your camera placements are secure and not liable to be bumped by the audience. Have protective barriers put around your camera placements.

✦ Vibration can be a problem. Try to get on separate risers from other equipment and crewmembers and avoid placements on top of any part of the PA.

Camera placement is often determined by the show format. For example, if you were filming a talk show, you'd want to get close-ups of both the host and guest, along with your establishment shot. Other times the production manager may decide where the cameras go based on where they are the safest and least obtrusive. You need to discuss camera placement early on in the production, preferably during the location scout.

Tip The sooner you can do a location scout, the sooner you can begin to address potential issues. Try to do a location walkthrough during the early planning stages of the broadcast.

Equipment

The equipment list for a live broadcast isn't that different from what you use in your everyday on-demand productions. The biggest difference is that you must have backup systems available in case of equipment failure. If you're producing a remote broadcast, you have to be prepared because you don't have the luxury of being able to run to your supply closet to grab another extension cord.

You may need some additional pieces of equipment that you don't normally use. If you're going to do a multicamera shoot, you'll need a switcher to be able to switch between different camera feeds. You may want to record a copy of the master output other than the encoded version, in which case you'll need a video recording deck. If you don't do many live broadcasts, renting the extra equipment you need may be more cost effective than purchasing it. Whatever you decide to use, make sure that you are prepared for equipment failure.

Be prepared

To truly be prepared for the worst that can happen, have a backup for everything. Having a backup doesn't necessarily mean that you have to double your equipment list. For example, on a three-camera shoot you should bring four cameras. If you need two lavaliere microphones for the talent, bring a third.

In theory, you should bring a spare for everything but doing so is not always practical. Also, some equipment is much less likely to break, and therefore, less likely to need replacing. Rack-mounted, solid-state equipment, such as compressors, are very unlikely to break when compared to fragile computer monitors, XLR cables, or microphones. Use common sense to determine what is absolutely necessary. At the very minimum bring a case full of extra cables, adapters, and tools so that you can fix components that break (see "The Dookie Kit" sidebar).

The Dookie Kit

Once upon a time at the company where I previously worked, I traveled regularly to remote locations to broadcast various events. My coworkers and I built a padded, shock-mounted flight case for all the equipment we needed to do the broadcast. Upon arrival to a new location, we often faced varying conditions — computers that refused to boot up, cables that stopped working, missing power cables, you name it.

We slowly built up a case that contained just about everything you might ever need to fix whatever might go wrong. Somewhere along the way it was dubbed "the dookie kit." It saved our bacon on more than one occasion. Want to know what was inside it?

✦ Spare microphone

✦ Spare XLR cables — usually four 25-footers

✦ Male-to-female and female-to-male XLR adapters — 2 of each

✦ Male XLR to ¼ inch TRS cables, Female XLR to ¼ inch TRS cables — 2 of each

✦ ¼ inch TRS cables — four 10-footers

✦ A selection of audio adapters, such as RCA to mini, XLR to ¼ inch, ¼ inch to mini, and so on

✦ Isolation transformer

✦ Two video humbuckers

✦ BNC video cables — four 25-footers

✦ BNC to RCA adapters

✦ Spare Ethernet cables and a couple of crossover cables

✦ Spare ISDN modem, later a spare DSL LAN modem

✦ Spare PS2 and VGA cables

✦ Spare mouse

✦ Spare NIC card, sound card, video capture card (all ended up being used at some point)

✦ An array of CD-ROMS, including operating system(s), soundcard drivers, video capture card drivers, encoding and editing software, TELNET and FTP software, and so on

✦ Blank floppy discs

✦ 50-foot grounded extension cord and a spare power strip, plus a handful of ground lifters

✦ Soldering kit, small tool kit, cable ties

✦ Flashlight, batteries

✦ Sharpie permanent markers and masking tape

✦ Cheap plastic phone

✦ 100-foot phone extension cord (RJ11)

✦ Earplugs, band-aids, and a bottle of ibuprofen

✦ Black gaffer's tape, white cloth tape, and tons of duct tape — of course

Shipping

Unless you're only driving across town and can throw what you need into the back of your car, you're going to have to pack your equipment up in cases that are suitable for travel. These cases have to be sturdy, well padded, and preferably have wheels, because this stuff gets heavy quickly.

Fortunately, you have plenty options available, manufactured specifically to transport computer or audio equipment. Cases come in all shapes, sizes, and colors with all sorts of different features. The most important feature to look for is padding. You can count on the case being dropped once or twice. Cases have even been known to be pierced by forklifts and survive. For your peace of mind, nothing is better than a good flight case.

Connecting your equipment to the in-house systems

Unless you're providing all the production on site, at some point you're going to have to get connected to the audio and video systems. In some cases, you may bring all the cameras and take an audio feed from the PA system. Other times, you may be taking both audio and video feeds from the in-house production team. Regardless, at some point your equipment has to be connected to theirs.

All professional equipment, be it audio or video, is designed to be interconnected reasonably painlessly. For video feeds, all you need to do is to be very nice to the technical director and ask for a video feed. He or she generally has extra feeds available — if not, you may need to rent a distribution amplifier to split the video feed. Try to determine if you need to do so as early as possible, for instance during the location scout.

Audio can be slightly tricky because of a phenomenon known as *ground hum*. A full technical explanation of what ground hum is and why it occurs would take up too much room and bore most of you to death. Suffice it to say that the problem exists because wall current alternates at 60 Hz, which is well within our hearing range. If equipment is incorrectly grounded or if there is a difference in ground potential between two pieces of equipment, some current may "leak" into the system, causing a nasty hum.

Taking two steps can eliminate most grounding problems. First, make sure that you are getting your power from the same circuit that the in-house PA system is. Second, make sure that you use balanced cables. These two simple steps should keep you hum-free 99 percent of the time. If for some reason a hum problem does occur, you can use an isolating transformer.

An *isolating transformer* transmits the audio signal without physically connecting the two pieces of equipment plugged into it. Isolating transformers do this by exploiting a phenomenon known as *inductive coupling*. Because the two pieces of equipment are not actually connected, there is no ground differential, no current leakage, and no nasty hum. You can pick up isolating transformers from your local home recording equipment vendor. Isolating transformers can be invaluable in live situations (see "The Dookie Kit" sidebar).

Video signals are also susceptible to grounding problems, though nowhere near as often as audio. With video, grounding problems are visible as *hum bars* in the picture, which may hold still or slowly move up or down the picture. To solve video grounding problems you can use a *video humbucker* or an *isolating video distribution amplifier*. It's a good idea to have a couple of video humbuckers on hand for live broadcasts.

 Cross-Reference   See Bonus Chapter 5 on the CD-ROM for a list of equipment vendors.

Ambient microphones

If you're broadcasting a music event, and you truly want to capture the "live" sound, you should use ambient microphones. Ambient mics are used to capture the ambience of a music venue and are absolutely necessary for two reasons:

✦ To capture the audience response and sense of space

✦ To capture the full musical program, some of which may not be coming through the PA system

The reason people attend live events is to witness the spectacle of it all, and to participate in the crowd euphoria. The crowd makes noise, and without that noise, a live broadcast falls flat. At the actual event this ambience doesn't need to be captured, so no microphones need to face the crowd. For the purposes of your broadcast, however, you absolutely need a microphone either facing or in the crowd.

The second reason ambient mics are necessary has to do with the size of the venue and the type of music being performed. If you're in a small venue, and the music is fairly loud, some of the loudness you hear may not be coming from the PA — it may be coming directly from the instrument or the amplifier. For example, when a rock group plays in a small venue, the guitars are rarely amplified by the PA. The guitar amplifiers generate a sufficient volume level on their own.

If you're getting your audio feed directly from the PA, what you'll get is vocals, snare drum, and bass drum. This is obviously not what you want. You want to hear what everyone at the venue can hear. An ambient mic (or two) can compensate for what's missing in the PA mix and makes the broadcast sound more natural and alive.

At large venues, such as theaters or arenas, every instrument is run through the PA. In this case, you won't need the ambient mics for musical balance, but you'll want them to add a sense of space to your audio.

Ambient microphone placement

The placement of your ambient microphones depends on whether you are using a single microphone or a pair. For true stereo, you should always use a matched pair of microphones. If you are archiving the recording for later use, you should use a pair. However, if your budget is limited, a single mic can suffice.

Microphone placement is an art; however, you should follow a few simple guidelines:

✦ Hang them somewhere they can pick up the sound coming from the stage as well as the crowd noise in between songs.

✦ Be careful not to hang them too close to the audience — you may end up listening to a conversation instead of the band.

✦ If you decide to use two microphones, the safest way to avoid phase cancellation is to hang them next to each other with the diaphragms at a 90-degree angle to each other (see Figure 34-1).

✦ Try to keep the ambient microphones reasonably close to the stage. Sound travels 110 feet per second, so if your microphones are 30 feet from the stage, the ambient microphone sound will be one-quarter of a second behind the PA feed.

Figure 34-1 illustrates sample ambient microphone placement.

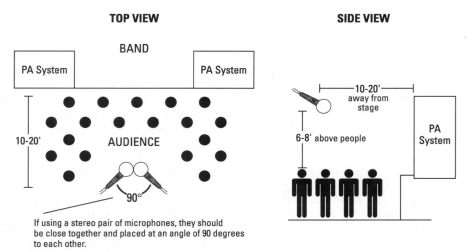

Figure 34-1: Sample ambient microphone placement

Setting ambient microphone level

The ambient microphones should be plugged into your mixing desk along with the feed from the PA system. You must then balance the levels between the two. The relative balance between the PA feed and the ambient mics is determined by how good the ambient mics sound. Your can take one of two approaches:

✦ Base the master mix on the PA feed and use the ambient mics to add a live feel

✦ Base the master mix on the ambient mics and use the PA feed to add clarity to the vocals and drums

Some venues sound great, and others are huge echo boxes designed to torture attendees. If you're in a good sounding room, you should start off with the ambient mics and add the PA feed little by little until the vocals sit slightly on top of the mix. If you're in a nasty concrete box, you should start with the PA feed and add just enough ambience to take the clinical edge off the mix. Both the PA feed and the ambient mics can of course be processed using EQ and compression. Compression, in particular, can make a mix feel a bit more "together."

 Cross-Reference For a full discussion about audio processing, including EQ and compression, please turn to Chapter 8.

If your ambient mics are too far from the stage, you may notice a slight time difference between the PA system feed and the ambient mics. If this is very slight, it will not be too noticeable, and can in fact add a sense of space to the mix. If your ambient mics are too far from the stage, for instance 50 feet or more, you'll have to keep them very low in the mix. Fifty feet is nearly a half-second delay, which is far too noticeable for most people.

The Crew

The scale of your production determines the number of crew you use at a live event. Generally you'll want a camera operator for each camera you have at the event. You should also break down the responsibilities for different portions of the event.

Again, it depends on the size of the event, but at a minimum you should have the following crew:

✦ **Line producer.** Responsible for the overall coordination of the event. May also double as technical director

✦ **Encoding technician.** Responsible for all the encoders and the on-site connectivity

- ✦ **A/V technician.** Responsible for all the audiovisual equipment and the cables
- ✦ **Camera operator(s).** One for each camera, though not absolutely necessary, is what you should aim for

If the size of the broadcast merits it, you may also want the following:

- ✦ **Soundman.** Responsible for the online audio mix
- ✦ **Technical director.** The person who switches between the different cameras and communicates with the camera crew via intercom
- ✦ **Gophers.** People who can be sent on errands, to "go for" whatever it is that has to be done
- ✦ **Camera assistant(s).** Used to feed cable to roving cameramen, change tapes, fix things that go wrong
- ✦ **Tape op.** On a large broadcast where you may be taping multiple camera angles, it is best to assign this responsibility to one person

As tempting as it may be, you should try not to scrimp on crew. Crews are expensive, but can really help make your event a success. As mentioned before, the one luxury you don't have at a live event is time, and having a crew that is sufficiently large enough to accomplish the task at hand is paramount.

Tip   The crew should dress in black — this makes them less visible on camera.

Communicating at Live Events

Though it may be stating the obvious, having good lines of communication at live events is very important. For broadcasts to run smoothly, everybody involved has to know what is going on. This is especially the case when things break down, but even when things are running smoothly, knowing that is the case can keep them running that way.

Communicating inside the venue

Generally, most of the crew should have headphones on, connected to a central intercom system. These systems allow two-way communication by everyone in the broadcast, no matter where they are located. These systems either require separate cabling or can be run through the camera cables of certain systems. They can be rented from any good a/v rental house.

Communicating with the broadcast operations center (BOC)

Having a line of communication open to the BOC in case any server or encoder problems occur is necessary. Cell phones have become ubiquitous in the last five years, but sometimes reception problems can render them useless. Broadcasting from loud locations can also hinder cell phones usefulness. Land lines are marginally more useful, because they do not have reception problems. However, they still have problems in loud locations, and of course long distance fees factor in to the cost.

Instant messaging systems can be extremely useful. Theses systems are very low bit rate, so they do not interfere with the encoding bandwidth. They can be perfectly silent and don't require any reception. What's more, phone numbers or settings are easier to remember when they're written down in front of you.

Producing The Show

After you've got everything set up and ready to go, the countdown begins. A common mistake many people make is waiting until the last minute to crank up the production. This assumes that no one arrives early to the Webcasts, and that no problems will occur when the broadcast starts up.

Pre-show

You're there, the equipment is ready to go, and your crew is itching to get started. You should begin your broadcast no less than one hour before the scheduled kick-off time. This allows any bugs to be shaken out of the system, allows your cameramen to get comfortable in their positions, and puts something on the screen for the early arrivals to the Webcast.

What should you show? Well, people go to live events to see the main attraction *and* to interact with folks. So a little crowd surfing by the cameramen isn't a bad thing. What should the audience be hearing? Most venues provide incidental music before shows or conference presentations. However, you should be prepared: Bring your own CD player along with some appropriate music to play.

If you really want to make your Webcast special, you should have a host. The host doesn't even need to appear on camera. Because people are listening in from all different time zones, sometimes having a simple announcement leading up to the video is nice:

"Hi and thanks for tuning in to our Webcast from the Showbox in Seattle. The show should be starting in about fifteen minutes."

You have a somewhat captive audience, so you may as well use the time wisely. Tell them about any upcoming shows you've got. Tell them about your wonderful sponsor. Tell them about your Web site. Talk to them! Make them feel welcome.

During the show

After the show begins, you need to communicate with all your crew on a continual basis, choosing camera angles, giving suggestions for coverage, and warning them about potential problems. This is where the communication system comes into play. Cameramen can also use the communication system to ask for help or ask to be relieved during daylong shoots.

The director should warn the cameramen against using extreme close-ups, and excessive camera movement. The temptation for most cameramen is to zoom in as tight as possible, because it's an intimate shot. The problem is that with live broadcasts there the performers tend to move around a lot. To keep the performer centered in the frame, the cameraman is forced to continually move the camera. This kind of shot is used all the time in music videos and on television, but it is extremely hard to encode.

A better approach is to use medium close ups or even medium shots, and to hold the camera as steady as possible. This type of shot is not as engaging as an extreme close up, but it encodes much better. There is no sense in getting shots that do not encode well. You can keep interest levels up by cutting to other camera angles instead of using movement in the shot.

For a discussion which camera shots work best and why, please turn to Chapter 5.

The director should also try to curb the temptation to cut from camera angle to camera angle as quickly as possible. For low bit rate encoding this can be as bad as movement in the frame — in fact, it's just as bad because each time the director switches to a new shot, the encoder has to drop a new key frame. If too many key frames are used the overall encoding quality will suffer.

For a discussion of video codecs please turn to Chapter 3.

Live broadcasts have to strike a balance between what is visually interesting and what encodes well. It can be very difficult trying to convince cameramen that they should pull back from the subject, and just as difficult convincing directors that they should only cut once every ten seconds. Luckily encoding quality is improving on a daily basis, and soon the quality will match what we're used to with traditional media such as television and DVDs.

Post-show

If it has been a good show, people may not want to "leave" immediately. They may hang around a bit, just to see if anything else is going to happen. This time is ideal time to thank them for coming — and for sticking around to the end. This is another area where having a host can make your broadcast come alive. Additionally, you can promote other shows you have coming up, promote your Web site, and thank your sponsors over and over again.

Summary

Producing a live broadcast requires a lot of planning, equipment, and cooperation. They can be absolutely terrifying if poorly executed, and very gratifying when done well.

✦ Make sure that the location has access to power, connectivity, and the media feeds. Select a well-protected location to keep your equipment safe from the elements.

✦ Choose camera placements that provide the best coverage and the most secure locations.

✦ Make sure that you have a backup plan for any major pieces of equipment.

✦ Assemble a case full of spare cables, tools, and odds and ends.

✦ Always use balanced cables in broadcast situations.

✦ Always use ambient mics when broadcasting musical events.

✦ Always start your Webcasts an hour or more before the published start time.

✦   ✦   ✦

Encoding for Live Broadcasts

Encoding live broadcasts can be a carefree affair as long as you have the right equipment and the connectivity has been carefully tested beforehand. After the encoder establishes a connection to the server, it should maintain the connection for the duration of the broadcast.

If the encoder should become disconnected for any reason, simply restart the encoder. However, when the encoder disconnects, the server assumes that the broadcast is over and kicks the audience members off the broadcast.

Both the RealSystem and Windows Media have redundancy schemes to combat this unfortunate side effect. Multiple encoders can be used to prevent encoder mishaps. This requires additional encoders, which means more equipment (and connectivity) onsite. If the broadcast is an absolutely, positively, got-to-happen event, you should think about using multiple encoders to implement stream redundancy.

Before you start worrying about redundancy, you first have to think about what sort of equipment you're going to use to encode and how you're going to transport that equipment to the live broadcast site.

Live Encoding Equipment

The equipment you use to encode your live broadcast can be the same equipment you use to encode on your desktop. If you're broadcasting from your studio, you may be using your desktop equipment. However, if your broadcast is taking place at a remote location, desktop systems simply do not travel well.

You should build a rack-mounted encoding solution that you can roll into the back of a truck or hand off to a cargo company. To protect your equipment, your encoding equipment should be shipped in a liberally padded flight case.

Rack-mounted solutions

The most compact and protected way to move your equipment around is to use a flight-case with a standard 19-inch equipment rack mounted inside. Because the equipment you're transporting is delicate, you should make sure that the rack is suspended by padded foam for extra protection.

How tall to make the rack depends on how much equipment you're going to include and the size of the encoding machines. (See the following sidebar for more information on building a rack-mounted encoder.). A typical flight-cased system should include the following:

✦ Power distribution/protection unit

✦ Audio compressor(s)

✦ Audio distribution amplifier

✦ Video distribution amplifier

✦ Keyboard/video/mouse switching unit

✦ Encoding machines

You may also want to include:

✦ A panel with dedicated audio and video inputs

✦ Rack-mounted keyboard drawer and mouse

✦ Drawer to store a flat panel monitor

The most important element of the flight case is the amount of protection it offers your equipment. You can count on the case being dropped, knocked over, and generally mishandled by every cargo handler that comes into contact with it, fragile stickers notwithstanding. Spend the extra money to ensure that the rack is *floated* on a bed of foam. Floated equipment racks have a layer of foam between the equipment rack and the flightcase.

Avoid building equipment racks more than five feet tall, because taller the rack, the higher the center of gravity. If your rack is too tall, a pebble in the road can cause the case to topple onto its side. Not only is this extremely bad for the equipment, but these racks tend to be so heavy that they are very difficult to set upright again without a little help. If you keep your racks short, you can maneuver them more easily, and they are less likely spill.

Building a Rack-Mounted Encoder

Computers have been available in rack-mounted formats for years now. Essentially, a rack-mounted format is a desktop computer turned on its side with a couple of rack ears on the side so that they can be screwed into a standard 19-inch equipment rack.

Rack-mounted solutions are used at ISPs because they're the most efficient way to house a lot of computers in the same room. ISPs charge customers for the amount of rack space their computers occupy. The more rack space the computers occupy, the higher the *rack space charge*. Motherboard manufacturers realized this and decided to work with rack-mount case manufacturers to create smaller and smaller rack-based servers. Smaller computers take up less rack space, thereby incurring a smaller rack space charge. However, for live encoding solutions you don't necessarily want to use the smallest rack-mounted computers available.

How small is too small?

Rack space is measured in U (units). Each U is 1.75 inches, so a 2U case is 3.5 inches tall, and a 3U case is 5.25 inches tall. Most cards that are installed in computers are about 4 inches tall, so you must mount cards sideways to fit them into anything smaller than a 3U case. To accommodate the need to mount cards sideways, motherboard manufacturers came up with all kinds of designs. Manufacturers also tried to include more and more functionality built in to the motherboard, such as a built-in NIC or built-in soundcard capabilities.

The problem with functionality built in to the motherboard is that it is very difficult, if not downright impossible to fix. If your network interface goes down on a machine that uses a separate NIC, you simply swap the NIC out for a replacement, and you're back on the air. If a built-in NIC goes awry, you have to send the motherboard back to the manufacturer.

Note: You can always drop a NIC card into a computer that has a defective on-board NIC interface, provided you have an extra slot, and provided you can disable the built-in interface. This can be problematic on some operating systems.

Of course, smaller cases (in theory) mean that you can take more encoders along. In fact, this can be a preferable solution because swapping out a card takes at least five to ten minutes, while a back-up encoder can be up and running in seconds. However, not everyone's budget allows for extra encoding boxes.

Personally, I prefer to build slightly bigger boxes with cards, instead of small boxes with extensive on-board functionality. To get enough cards in (NIC, sound card, video capture card, VGA card) this pretty much limits you to a 4U case. If you're willing to live with some on-board functionality, a good 2U case comes with a PCI riser that accepts 3 PCI cards. Choose a motherboard with a built in VGA adapter, because they are least likely to fail, in my experience.

If you're building your own boxes, use parts from reputable manufacturers, not the cheapest ones you can find. Quality does have a price tag, and saving a few bucks up front won't justify a blown soundcard in the middle of a broadcast.

Multiple stream solutions

Recently, a number of manufacturers have come out with encoding solutions that can produce multiple streams from a single box. This drastically reduces the amount of equipment required on site. Not only that, but these multiple-stream encoding solutions also generally offer various degrees of pre-processing for the audio and video signals.

These features are not cheap. The price tags range from $10 – $40,000 depending on the configuration. You should ask yourself several questions before you hand over your credit card:

✦ How big is the install base?

✦ How long has the company been around?

✦ Is the cost competitive when compared to building your own?

✦ Can individual parts be replaced, or is the entire product a custom solution?

You can take a look for yourself here:

✦ **NetStreamer by DPS.** www.dps.com

✦ **Niagra Streaming Systems by Viewcast.** www.viewcast.com

✦ **StreamFactory by Pinnacle Systems.** www.pinnaclesys.com

The savings in shipping costs or rack space can be considerable when compared to what these boxes replace. As with any other major investment, you must decide if the advantages to a multiple stream solution outweigh the disadvantages.

Live Stream Redundancy

The weakest link in a streaming media broadcast traditionally has been the encoder-server connection. The major streaming platforms failed to include provisions for redundancy until recently. Now you can run multiple encoders and have the server switch to a backup stream if the first stream fails.

Using multiple sources does not necessarily guarantee success. For example, if one encoder fails because of connectivity problems at a remote site, backup encoders may share the same fate unless they are using different connectivity.

As a last resort, you should also have a static file that the server can broadcast in case your live sources fail. Television stations have please stand by or we're experiencing technical difficulties clips for precisely the same reasons.

RealSystem iQ

The RealSystem enables you to have as many redundant sources as you like. All you have to do is to append a unique number to each version of the live stream you provide to the server, and use the redundant mount point in your link. The redundant mount point is used to indicate to the RealServer that more than one version of the stream is being encoded to the server.

For example, if you wanted to provide two feeds of a keynote address broadcast, you would use two encoders, naming the first file keynote.rm.1 and the second keynote.rm.2. The numbers appended to the redundant files do not determine the order in which they are used — the numbers are merely identifiers. The encoders send the live streams to the same server, just like any other encoded stream.

When linking to the file, you must specify the redundant mount point, like this:

```
http://my.realserver.com:8080/ramgen/redundant/keynote.rm
```

Using the redundant mount point tells the RealServer that there are multiple versions of the live stream to choose from. The RealServer automatically switches to another stream if one of the streams fails.

The above example assumes the default RealServer HTTP port, redundant mount point, and that no path was specified in the encoders. All these settings are configurable, so your link may be slightly different. The generic syntax for linking to a redundant broadcast is as follows:

```
http://server:HTTP port/ramgen/redundant mount point/path/filename
```

or if you're linking directly to the stream in a SMIL presentation or in a .ram file:

```
rtsp://server/redundant mount point/path/filename
```

All of the RealServer redundancy settings are configurable. For full documentation on using redundant files in live broadcasts, please refer to the RealServer Administration Guide, available from the RealNetworks Web site (www.realnetworks.com).

 Cross-Reference The RealSystem supports the use of a static fallback file. For more information about this feature, see Chapter 38.

QuickTime

The QuickTime streaming server has no built-in support for live stream redundancy. However, QuickTime broadcasts can take advantage of the redundancy capabilities of the RealServer, albeit with some limitations. Even though the RealServer accepts live streams from Sorenson Broadcaster, the software application used to encode live QuickTime files, these files cannot be served using the redundancy feature. Neither can live broadcasts generated by the QuickTime PlaylistBroadcaster.

The only live QuickTime broadcasts that can be served using the redundancy feature are simulated live broadcasts of QuickTime using the G2SLTA application that is included with the RealServer. Redundancy can be achieved by using multiple instances of the G2SLTA application.

If a simulated live broadcast of a QuickTime file fails and a redundant stream is available, the RealServer switches to the redundant stream. If a viewer is using a RealPlayer to view the presentation, it re-buffers and continues playback. However, if a viewer is using the QuickTime player to view the presentation, he must press stop and then play to continue watching the broadcast. For full documentation on the limitations of using redundancy with QuickTime live broadcasts, please refer to the RealServer Administration Guide, available from the RealNetworks Web site (www.realnetworks.com).

 Note The RealPlayer can only play back QuickTime files that have been encoded with an open standards codec, such as H.263.

Windows Media Technology

The Windows Media Services server can support redundant live sources by taking advantage of the way that Windows Media creates different types of programming. You can create redundancy for your broadcast by setting up a *program* that consists of two or versions of the same live stream and specifying that the program should loop. If the first live stream listed in the program becomes unavailable, the program moves to the next stream, which happens to be another version live stream.

The slightly confusing aspect to this is that Windows Media programs are accessed via Windows Media *stations*, which are multicast streams. However, if the Windows Media player cannot connect to a station via multicast, it automatically switches to unicast. So even though you're setting up a multicast station, your unicast audience will be able to see your broadcast.

For full documentation about how to set up Windows Media stations and programs, please refer to the documentation that installs with Windows Media Services, which is available from the Windows Media Web site (www.microsoft.com/windows/windowsmedia).

Choosing Your Bit Rates

When setting up an encoder for a live broadcast, you should be conservative with the bit rate settings. It's tempting to try and send the highest possible quality stream, but you have to consider what actually constitutes the best experience. People are willing to settle for slightly inferior quality provided that the delivery is constant. If the stream has to re-buffer often, the audience may become frustrated and leave.

Live broadcasts last longer than the average on-demand file. Because people watch longer, they are more tempted to surf, answer e-mail, chat, and all sorts of other bandwidth consuming activities. The higher the bit rate of your live stream, the greater the chance that it may suffer from competition for bandwidth.

Competition for bandwidth is particularly fierce for modem users. As discussed in Chapter 33, the longer a user has been connected to the Internet, the more likely the modem is to renegotiate. The available bandwidth may be quite different from when the initial connection was originally made a few hours ago.

Broadband users do not have this problem, because their connectivity is relatively constant. However, sustaining high bit rates for extended periods of time is still difficult. But just because doing so is difficult doesn't mean that you should not cater to a broadband audience — it just means that instead of attempting to deliver megabit streams, you should consider limiting the bit rates to 100-300 Kbps. As the infrastructure of the Internet continues to improve, this situation will change. The best approach is to use the SureStream or multi-bit rate technologies of the RealSystem or Windows Media Technology to ensure that viewers can fall back to a lower bit rate if the full bit rate becomes impossible to sustain.

 Cross-Reference For a full discussion about RealNetworks SureStream technology and Windows Media Multiple Bitrate (MBR) files, please turn to Chapter 13.

Summary

Live encoding is not that much different from ordinary encoding. In the next chapter, you'll find out about authoring issues.

✦ Encoding solutions for remote broadcasts should be rack-mounted in padded flight cases.

✦ Don't build your racks too tall.

✦ Some encoding solutions can provide multiple streams (and formats) from a single box.

✦ The RealServer allows multiple live sources to be used for redundancy.

✦ RealServer can also serve redundant QuickTime broadcasts, but this functionality is somewhat limited.

✦ Both the RealSystem and Windows Media Technologies allow static fallback files to be used in case of live stream failure.

✦ Be conservative with your bit rate.

✦ Use SureStream or multi-bit rate encoding profiles for your live streams.

✦　　✦　　✦

Authoring for Live Broadcasts

The authoring stage for live broadcasts does not differ that much from authoring for any on-demand file. However, you must keep in mind that the concentration of traffic is much higher during a live broadcast and that economy in design can be a very good thing.

First, consider whether you're going to use an embedded player or a stand-alone player. Embedded players are very tempting, but cross-platform and OS issues may lead you to consider a pop-up player instead.

If you decide to author a presentation in your player with SMIL, refer to the process that is described in the SMIL section of this book in Chapters 27 through 31. All you have to do is link to live sources instead of linking to on-demand files. You should err on the side of caution when designing your SMIL presentations — if you're conservative with your bit rates your presentation has a far greater chance of success.

Most folks try to offset some of the costs associated with a live broadcast by selling advertising or securing a sponsorship. This generally involves adding some sort of banner ad or logo into your presentation. Integrating advertising or sponsorship messaging into your presentation can be done in a number of ways.

Cross-Reference Inserting advertising into your streams is discussed in Chapter 21.

The best approach is to get people into the broadcast as quickly as possible. You can provide links to the Web site in the player for users to explore when there is a lull in the broadcast.

Embedded Versus Stand-Alone Players

When authoring for a live broadcast, you first need to decide whether to use an embedded or a stand-alone player. Each method has its own set of benefits and idiosyncrasies — you have to figure out whether the benefits of an embedded player outweigh the potential problems.

Embedded players have the benefit of allowing the design of the broadcast to be done in HTML. Most companies already have a Web design team with all the tools they need to throw together a well designed page, thus saving time, money, and resources. When media players are embedded, the branding of the particular player can be hidden. The audience doesn't really have to know what sort of player they're using, as long as they have the correct plug-in installed.

When you install a media player, it generally asks you which browser you are using. The install program for the media player usually finds your browser and registers the media player as a plug-in. The operative word in that last sentence is *usually*. If the player doesn't register with the browser for some reason or other, the viewer could get an error message when trying to watch the broadcast.

The other place a media player has to register is with the operating system. Registering your media player with the operating system is what allows your player to pop-up automatically when you click on a media file. The operating system checks a list of file types and finds out what program is associated with the particular file you click on. Media players generally have less problem registering with the operating system than they do registering with Web browsers.

The other problem with embedded players is that with all the different browsers out there, authoring code that works on every possible OS/browser combination can be tricky. Not that it's impossible — far from it. You can do a lot of sleuthing with JavaScript and construct your Web pages accordingly. Using a stand-alone player, however, is very simple and straightforward.

In my experience, pop-up players are more reliable. I've been involved with many live broadcasts that use embedded players. I always maintain a list of direct links to the streams that bypass the embedded player. The first thing I do when problems arise is to check the live stream in a stand-alone player. More often than not the stream works just fine in the stand-alone player. Whether the cause of the problem is poor authoring, browser-player incompatibilities, or just bad ju-ju is hard to determine.

To be honest, things have improved in the last few years. Media players seem to be doing a better job registering themselves with the browsers. Perhaps its superstition, but I still prefer using stand-alone players during live broadcasts. Anything I can do to reduce the possibility of error is something worth doing.

I've lost this battle many a time. Embedded players are just too desirable from a branding standpoint. I understand this and merely register my concerns, which too often are proven true on the day of broadcast.

Tip

As a compromise to the embed versus stand-alone issue, I would heartily recommend that if you absolutely, positively must embed the player for a live broadcast, consider placing a link on the page to trigger a stand-alone player — just in case.

Linking to Live Broadcasts

Linking to live broadcasts is trivial. You use the same syntax as linking to on-demand presentations, with a few minor differences depending on the platform you are using.

QuickTime

When you link to live QuickTime presentations, you simply link to the Session Description Protocol (SDP) file created by the broadcast application you are using. This small text file contains all the information the QuickTime player needs to play the live stream. After the SDP files are created, they must be uploaded to the QuickTime server. You then can link to the file in a number of ways:

✦ Link directly to the SDP file via RTSP using the `qtsrc` parameter

✦ Link directly to the SDP file via RTSP using the `href` parameter

✦ Link to a Fast Start reference movie that references the SDP file using the `src` parameter

✦ Link to a Fast Start reference movie that references the SDP file using the `qtsrc` parameter

✦ Link to a Fast Start reference movie that references the SDP file using the `href` parameter

Caution

When linking directly to an SDP file, you must leave off the `.sdp` file extension.

If you are broadcasting a conference keynote speech, you should set up the broadcast parameters in your broadcasting application and create an SDP file with an appropriate name, such as spring_keynote_2002.sdp. Then place this SDP file on the QuickTime server in the Movies directory. Provided you were using the default settings of the QuickTime server, you could link directly to this movie by using RTSP as follows:

```
<object classid="clsid:02BF25D5-8C17-4B23-BC80-D3488ABDDC6B"
    width="240" height="196"
    codebase="http://www.apple.com/qtactivex/qtplugin.cab">
    <param name="src"
          value="rtsp://my.quicktimeserver.com/spring_keynote_2002">
    <embed src="placeholder.mov" type="image/x-macpaint"
          width="240" height="196"
          qtsrc="rtsp://my.quicktimeserver.com/spring_keynote_2002" >
    </embed>
</object>
```

 Caution

When using the Netscape plug-in, never link directly to a stream using the RTSP protocol with the `src` parameter. If you do, the browser attempts to download the movie, and because most browsers do not support RTSP the results are unpredictable at best. Using the `qtsrc` parameter guarantees that the URL is handed off to the QuickTime player. This is not an issue with the ActiveX control, because the `classid` parameter guarantees the QuickTime plug-in receives the value of the `src` parameter.

If you want to launch a pop-up player, you can do so by using the `target` parameter:

```
<object classid="clsid:02BF25D5-8C17-4B23-BC80-D3488ABDDC6B"
    width="240" height="196"
    codebase="http://www.apple.com/qtactivex/qtplugin.cab">
    <param name="src"
          value="rtsp://my.quicktimeserver.com/spring_keynote_2002">
    <param name="target" value="quicktimeplayer">
    <embed src="placeholder.mov" type="image/x-macpaint"
        width="240" height="196" target="quicktimeplayer"
        qtsrc="rtsp://my.quicktimeserver.com/spring_keynote_2002" >
    </embed>
</object>
```

 Note

The `qtsrc` parameter only works with QuickTime Version 4 or later. Older players use the file in the `src` parameter. Using a graphic that says "You need QuickTime 4 or later to view this content" is a good idea. You must use a QuickTime image format to ensure that the QuickTime plug-in is loaded.

If you want to link the presentation from an image, you can do so by using the `href` parameter. In this case, the file specified in the `src` parameter is loaded and displayed. When the image is clicked, the QuickTime player begins playback of the file specified by the `href` parameter according to the `target` parameter:

```
<object classid="clsid:02BF25D5-8C17-4B23-BC80-D3488ABDDC6B"
    width="240" height="196"
    codebase="http://www.apple.com/qtactivex/qtplugin.cab">
    <param name="src" value="displayed.mov">
    <param name="href"
          value="rtsp://my.quicktimeserver.com/spring_keynote_2002">
    <param name="target" value="quicktimeplayer">
mov   <embed src="displayed.mov" type="image/x-macpaint"
```

```
    width="240" height="196" target="quicktimeplayer"
    href="rtsp://my.quicktimeserver.com/spring_keynote_2002" >
  </embed>
</object>
```

This example launches the presentation in a pop-up player.

If you're using a Fast Start reference movie to reference the live stream, you can specify it as a `qtsrc` parameter or directly in the `src` parameter (Fast Start reference movies are small text files that live on your Web server and, therefore, use the HTTP protocol). You can also specify it in the `href` parameter if you want to launch the presentation by clicking on an image (ActiveX code left out for simplicity):

```
<embed src="spring_keynote_2002_ref.mov" height="336"
    width="240" >

<embed src="placeholder. mov" type="image/x-macpaint"
    height="336" width="240"
    qtsrc="spring_keynote_2002_ref.mov" >

<embed src="placeholder. mov" type="image/x-macpaint"
    height="336" width="240" target="myself"
    href="spring_keynote_2002_ref.mov" >
```

The first example links directly to the Fast Start reference movie, the second example displays the place holder image if the user does not have QuickTime 4 or better, and the last example begins playback only after the viewer clicks the image.

With so many different options, you may be slightly confused as to how to employ the best method. The method you should use depends on what your biggest concerns are:

✦ If you're worried about older players, use the `qtsrc` parameter with an image that contains an upgrade message in the `src` parameter.

✦ If you want to use a QuickTime poster to trigger the broadcast, use an image in the `src` parameter and place the link to the stream in the `href` parameter.

✦ If the broadcast is linked from more than one location, create a master Fast Start reference movie, and host it at a single location. This allows you to make changes to it without having to notify everyone who is linking to the presentation.

It's also a great idea to use the `pluginspage` parameter so that viewers are notified if they do not have the QuickTime player installed, like so:

```
<embed src="upgrademessage.mov" type="image/x-macpaint"
    height="336" width="240"
    qtsrc="http://my.MasterWebServer.com/master_ref.mov"
    pluginspage="http://www.apple.com/quicktime/download/" >
```

Tip   Similarly, it's a good idea to use the `codebase` parameter in the ActiveX control.

As a last note, QuickTime broadcasts may also be hosted on a RealServer. The only difference is the SDP file lives on the RealServer. Because QuickTime broadcasts are published separately from RealMedia broadcasts, you'd need to specify the correct mount point if you used a direct RTSP reference. If the default QuickTime mount point were used, a direct RTSP reference would look like this:

```
rtsp://your.realserver.com/qtencoder/spring_keynote_2002
```

RealSystem

When you link to a live stream coming from a RealServer, you can use any of the linking options discussed in Chapter 15 of this book:

✦ Link to a `.ram` file to open a stand-alone player.

✦ Link to a `.rpm` file to use an embedded player.

✦ Link directly to a RealMedia file (`.ra`, `.rm`, et.al) using the `ramgen` function on the RealServer to open a pop-up player.

✦ Link directly to a RealMedia file (`.ra`, `.rm`, et.al) using the `ramgen` function on the RealServer to use an embedded player by using the `embed` attribute.

Note   The RealServer can also host QuickTime broadcasts. To link to QuickTime broadcasts, use the syntax described in the previous section.

The only difference is that when you reference live streams, you have to use the proper mount point specified in the RealServer Administrator. Also, if you're using `ramgen`, you must use the RealServer HTTP port. Both the live stream mount point and the HTTP port can be custom configured by your system administrator. Assuming the default values for both the mount point and HTTP port, the following example is a sample link to live Real content:

```
http://your.server.com:8080/ramgen/encoder/yourlivefile.rm
```

Used directly in a Web page, this link opens a stand-alone player. You can use the following link in a Web page to play back a live stream in an embedded player, using the `embed` attribute:

```
http://my.server.com:8080/ramgen/encoder/embedded.rm?embed
```

If you wanted to manually link to a file using a .ram, .rpm, or a SMIL file, you could link directly to the stream as follows:

```
rtsp://your.server.com/encoder/yourlivefile.rm
```

Used in a .ram file, the link opens a pop-up player. If it were placed in a .rpm file, it would use an embedded player, as long as plug-in code was included in the page. If you used this link in a SMIL file, it would play back in whatever region it was targeted to. The SMIL file would have to be linked via ramgen, a .ram file or .rpm file to determine whether the player was embedded or not.

Windows Media Technologies

Linking to live Windows Media streams is very straightforward. When you broadcast using Windows Media Technologies, you define a unique publishing point for each live stream. These publishing points are defined by using the Windows Media Administrator.

When you define the broadcast publishing points, you specify a unique alias and a path the server uses to establish a connection to the Windows Media Encoder (or station in the case of multicast). To link to the broadcast, all you have to do is use the correct alias in the file reference of your .asx file.

If you wanted to broadcast a Madonna concert, you would set up a publishing point on your server and specify "madonna" as the alias. To access the stream, your .asx file would look like this:

```
<ASX version = "3.0">
   <entry>
      <ref href="mms://my.wmtserver.com/madonna" />
   </entry>
</ASX>
```

If you wanted to embed your presentation, you would reference the .asx file from within an <object> tag. If you wanted to open a stand-alone player, you'd reference the .asx file from an <a> tag.

Live Broadcasts Utilizing SMIL

Using SMIL in live broadcasts is no different than using SMIL in on-demand situations. All you have to do is reference the live streams from within the presentation as you would any other stream. There are a few obvious limitations:

✦ You cannot use the repeat attribute with live sources

✦ You cannot use the clip-begin or clip-end attributes with live sources

Other than that, you are free to do what you want. You can place the live source(s) within a <seq> group to play things before and after the broadcast. You can place the source(s) within a <par> group to play or display elements concurrently with a broadcast. You can mix and match on-demand clips with live sources.

You must be very careful when running streams in parallel. If the combined bit rate of the streams running in parallel exceeds the viewer's maximum bit rate, you condemn him or her to an infinite cycle of rebuffering.

Synchronizing Multiple Live Sources in SMIL

Note   `wallclock` functionality only works in the RealPlayer.

If you have more than one live source in a SMIL file, and you want them to be synchronized, you can use the `wallclock` attribute. This ensures that if the live sources are started at slightly different times, the player receiving the broadcast synchronizes them as if they were started concurrently. All you have to do is append the `wallclock` attribute to the stream reference and use the same name value for each stream that needs to be synchronized. For example:

```
<par>
  <video src="rtsp://my.realserver.com/live/voiceover.rm?wallclock=sync"/>
  <img src="rtsp://my.realserver.com/live/slides.rp?wallclock=sync"/>
</par>
```

Because `wallclock="sync"` is specified in each of these references, the player ensures that these two streams are played back in perfect sync. You should keep in mind the following items when synchronizing live streams:

✦ The RealSystem uses the audio stream to sync to, so the audio encoder should be the last live source you start up. All other streams are forced to wait for the audio.

✦ The RealSystem uses internal timestamps from for synchronization purposes, so all streams to be synchronized must be broadcast from the same computer, or from computers that have been previously synchronized.

✦ `wallclock` synchronization works with all RealNetworks proprietary data types, such as RealAudio, RealVideo, RealText, and RealPix, but not necessarily with other datatypes. .See the RealNetworks Web site for more information (`www.realnetworks.com`).

Web Site Concerns

An often-overlooked part of any broadcast is the Web site the viewers must traverse before they can get to the broadcast. Two main issues arise in live broadcast situations:

✦ How many pages must the user click through to find the broadcast?

✦ How heavy are these pages? Do they contain a lot of images or animation?

As tempting as leading the audience through your freshly redesigned site may be, you should really get the audience connected to the broadcast as soon as possible. Making the audience jump through too many hoops leaves a bad taste in their mouth.

Getting folks to the broadcast as quickly as possible is also practical. If you've got a truly popular broadcast on your hands, your Web servers may see more traffic than they've ever seen before. The number of hits per second could increase by a couple of orders of magnitude.

When Web servers are under this kind of strain, every piece of content served adds to the problem. If your Web site is particularly image heavy, you could be faced with a bottleneck at the front entrance to your broadcast. What's worse, if your Web site goes down, no more audience members can get to your broadcast until you get the Web page with the links to the broadcast back up.

According to the *Wall Street Journal,* during the tragic events that transpired at the World Trade Center, both the MSNBC and CNN Web sites pulled almost all the images off their home pages to cope with the crushing loads their servers were under. RealNetworks did the same for President Clinton's testimony broadcast. It ain't pretty, but these are practical steps taken by people who are used to dealing with vast amounts of traffic.

Of course, removing all the images from your Web site is a drastic step, and one not lightly taken. The steps you should take depend on the scale of your broadcast and the scalability of your Web server architecture. A site that is front-heavy with graphics and animation is like putting a turnstile in front of a stampede — both foolish and dangerous.

Summary

Authoring for live broadcasts isn't significantly different from authoring for on-demand presentations. However, you may want to think about how the large spike in traffic will affect your Web servers and streaming servers. The leaner the code, the safer you'll be. In the next chapter, I discuss server strategies for live broadcasts.

✦ Embedded player or pop-up player? Design considerations lean towards the former, experience towards the latter. Offer both if possible.

✦ Linking to live broadcasts isn't much different than linking to on-demand presentations.

✦ Linking to QuickTime broadcasts involves linking to the SDP (Session Description Protocol) file.

✦ Linking to RealSystem broadcasts involves linking directly to the files, linking to metafiles, or using `ramgen` to have the RealServer generate metafiles.

✦ Linking to Window Media broadcasts involves linking to the publishing point alias in an ASX file.

✦ Live broadcasts may be referenced from within SMIL files

✦ Don't make your audience search for the link to the live broadcast.

✦ Try to keep your Web site lean and mean during broadcasts.

✦   ✦   ✦

Serving Live Broadcasts

Serving live broadcasts is probably the most crucial stage of the live broadcasting process. Although serving live broadcasts does not differ significantly from serving on-demand files, serving live events is what really tests your server architecture.

On-demand serving is spread out over days, weeks, and months. Live broadcasts are tightly focused events that deal with a much higher number of requests per second as the event starts up as well as an extremely high rate of through-put for an extended period of time.

This chapter takes a look at some of the quantities involved with live broadcasts — from attendance through bandwidth requirements. After you recover sufficiently, you can read on to find out about ways to plan for the coming onslaught.

All the serving models discussed in the book thus far assume that streams are being unicast. In unicast situations, each audience member is sent a unique copy of the stream. This makes sense with on-demand files, because people watch different streams at different times.

However, if you're broadcasting in a closed environment, such as a corporate LAN, you should definitely consider multicasting the event. *Multicasting* is an Internet broadcasting technique that enables a single broadcast stream to be shared among all users instead of each user receiving an individual copy. Multicast on the public Internet is not really a viable option currently, but that may change in the years to come. In controlled environments, multicast broadcasts are the way to go.

Big Numbers, Small Numbers

Live broadcasts tax your system in a number of ways, the foremost being bandwidth. Imagine three different broadcasts — a distance learning course, a corporate meeting, and a rock concert. Each live broadcast attracts a different audience size, with different connectivity characteristics. Table 37-1 breaks out the approximate numbers associated with each.

Table 37-1 Bandwidth Numbers for Three Different Broadcasts				
Type of broadcast	*Attendance*	*Audience connection speeds*	*Total concurrent bandwidth (in bits per second)*	*Total throughput for 1 hour broadcast (in bytes)*
Distance Learning	50	32 Kbps	1.56 Mbps	702MB
Small Corporate Broadcast	250	75% @ 32 Kbps, 25% @ 80 Kbps	11 Mbps	4.85GB
Large Entertainment Broadcast	5,000	10% @ 20 Kbps, 75% @ 32 Kbps, 10% @ 80 Kbps, 5% @ 300 Kbps	240 Mbps	105GB

Even the smallest educational broadcast can generate numbers that merit some thought. The distance learning broadcast requires more than one T1 line's worth of connectivity to support a paltry 50 attendees. A corporate broadcast attended by 250 employees, even with most viewers on dial-up connections and without a true broadband stream (300 Kbps+) soaks the company LAN and requires over a 10Mbit Internet connection.

Large broadcasts are where the numbers get very scary. For an hour-long show with 5,000 attendees, assuming only 5 percent watch the broadband stream, you're now staring at 240 Mbps concurrent bandwidth. You need approximately 8 T3s to support that kind of throughput.

Look at it another way — if you haggle a lot you may get a rate of a penny per Megabyte data transfer fee. At that rate, you're looking at $1,000 an hour for your broadcast, which is equivalent to a satellite uplink fee.

Now, what sort of revenue can you expect? Banner ads are sold by the thousand, which is referred to as a CPM (clicks per thousand) rate. If you rotate the ads every minute, each person sees 60 ads, for a total of 300,000 ad impressions. If you can get a $20 CPM, which is unheard of in this post-dot-bomb world, you make:

```
$20 * 300 (thousands) = $6,000
```

While not an insignificant amount of money, this revenue is not going to cover your costs. Your costs may include production costs ($5,000–$50,000), development costs (~$2,500), licensing costs ($500–$1,500), setup fees (~$500), and many other hidden fees that arise during a live broadcast.

Of course, there are other ways to sell a broadcast. Sponsorships pay more than ads, pay-per-view is a possibility, and some vendors may be willing to cut their rates as long as they can share the PR spotlight.

Live broadcasts are not a hopeless scenario, but they merit serious thought before blindly moving forward. For example, cutting out the broadband streams in the preceding example would cut your bandwidth requirements (and therefore costs) by 20 percent, assuming those viewers watched the 80 Kbps stream instead. The tradeoff between cost and customer satisfaction is one only you (and your accountants) can make.

An alternative method of Internet broadcasting known as *Peer-to-Peer streaming* has recently been developed. Peer-to-peer streaming involves forwarding live broadcasts from player to player, instead of every stream coming from a centralized server. For more information about peer-to-peer streaming, see the "Peer-to-Peer Streaming" sidebar.

Live Server Redundancy

You need redundancy more than ever in a live broadcast scenario. You need it to handle the spike in traffic, and you need it in case a server goes down. If your event is as popular as you hoped, there's a good chance one of your servers *may* go down. Servers die during live events because of the surge in traffic, just like light bulbs blow when you turn them on because of the surge of electricity.

Using multiple servers

If you're expecting any kind of serious traffic, you need to use multiple servers. The question is how to distribute the live stream to all the servers you use to broadcast your event. With on-demand content, you merely copy files from one computer to the next. During live broadcasts the copying must happen as the file is being encoded.

Peer-to-Peer Streaming by Brett Bekritsky

Peer to-peer streaming is a new approach to Webcasting, which gives content owners the ability to reach larger audiences using less bandwidth and fewer resources. The underlying concept behind peer-to-peer streaming is that, during a live broadcast, the streams need not originate from one central server. Instead, it they can cascade.

How it works

During a peer-to-peer Webcast, the first few users to connect get the stream from the originating server. They then forward the stream to the next set of audience members who request it, and these audience members in turn forward it to other new audience members. From the broadcaster's perspective, the bandwidth requirements are drastically reduced, which reduces the cost of delivering the Webcast.

Each participant in a peer-to-peer Webcast acts as both a viewer and a sender. Software at a central site maintains and manages the broadcast in real time, and connects new audience members to the viewer who is in the best position to pass along the stream. Both geography and available bandwidth are taken into consideration when pairing audience members to current listeners. The entire process is transparent to the audience. They enjoy the broadcast without interruption even as they distribute it to other audience members. The quality of the stream is never compromised.

Benefits of peer-to-peer streaming

Broadcasters who use peer-to-peer streaming benefit in a number of ways. Not only is it less expensive, but also it's software-only, meaning that no new hardware or personnel is needed to manage the Webcasts. Best of all, peer-to-peer realizes the original promise of the Internet, that all of us would be exchanging information and entertaining one another online without worrying about cost. With peer-to-peer software, a good-quality laptop, and some sort of input device (a microphone, camera, or CD player, for example) you can be broadcasting in 15 minutes. All that's missing in the audience.

Brett Bekritsky manages Advertising and Corporate Communications for AllCast, the company that invented peer-to-peer streaming and holds the patent (US patent No. US5884031).

Generally speaking, a stream that is being encoded live to a master server must be distributed to a number of distribution servers. These distribution servers are then used to serve the streams to viewers. A general distributed network is illustrated in Figure 37-1.

You can accomplish a number of goals by using a distributed server architecture.

✦ The server load is distributed among a number of servers so that no single machine is under duress.

✦ The bandwidth requirements for a broadcast can be geographically distributed, thereby alleviating potential bottlenecks.

✦ If one server does go down, the users can be redirected to a different server.

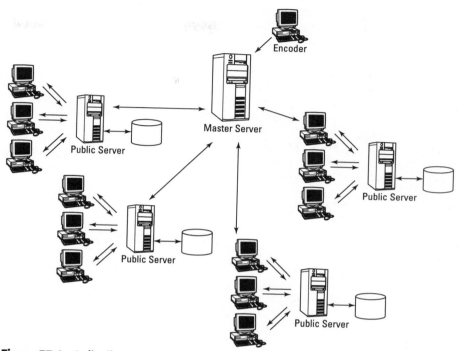

Figure 37-1: A distributed server architecture

Distributed server architectures are a necessary part of any large-scale live broadcast. All three major platforms can do this, but use slightly different methodologies and terminology to describe how they do it. The following sections discuss how to set up distributed serving architectures on each of the three major streaming platforms.

Cross-Reference For more general information about serving (including a discussion of unicasting and multicasting), please turn to Chapter 18.

QuickTime

The QuickTime server uses the concept of *relays* to forward live streams from one server to the next. Any server can stream and relay live streams to other servers. Servers use relay configuration files to determine what and where streams should be relayed and use SDP (Session Description Protocol) files to determine what files can be streamed. In relay situations, the SDP file must be slightly modified to reflect the source of the stream.

Relay configuration files

When the QuickTime server is started, it checks for relay configuration files in the /etc/streaming directory. The server accepts and forwards streams as specified in these files. Each relay configuration file is a simple text file that lists the source of the file to be relayed and also lists one or more destinations to which the file must be forwarded.

Modified SDP files

QuickTime servers use SDP files to locate the source of a stream. When Sorenson Broadcaster, the software application that encodes live QuickTime streams, creates the original SDP file, it uses the IP address of the machine that it is broadcasting from to set the source variable. Streaming servers receiving the live stream from relay servers need a copy of the SDP file, but the source variable must be changed to reflect the IP address of the relay machine instead of the original broadcasting machine. You can do so in any text editor.

Assume your computers had the IP addresses as outlined in Figure 37-2.

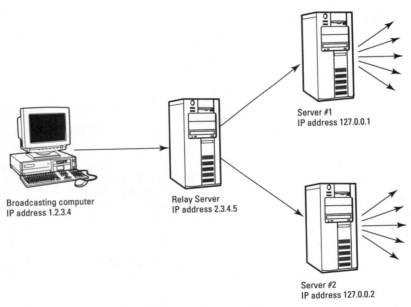

Server #1
IP address 127.0.0.1

Broadcasting computer
IP address 1.2.3.4

Relay Server
IP address 2.3.4.5

Server #2
IP address 127.0.0.2

Figure 37-2: A simple QuickTime relay scenario

You need to create a relay configuration file for the relay server. The relay configuration needs three lines, one to specify the source, and two to specify the two destinations. It would look something like this:

```
relay_source "in_addr=1.2.3.1 src_addr=2.3.4.5
    in_ports=7298 7300 ttl=15"
```

```
relay_destination "dest_addr=127.0.0.2 out_addr=2.3.4.5
    dest_ports=7298 7300 ttl=15"
relay_destination "dest_addr=127.0.0.3 out_addr=2.3.4.5
    dest_ports=7298 7300 ttl=15"
```

The first line specifies that the source of the broadcast is the machine with IP address 1.2.3.4, and the streams use ports 7298 and 7300. You must specify a port for each track that is being relayed (in this case the movie stream has two tracks; the audio and the video). The second and third lines specify two destination machine IP addresses as well as the ports to use and a *time-to-live* variable, which determines how far data packets can travel across a network. This information is all that the server needs to relay the live stream.

Note   Line breaks are for clarity — you should have only three lines in the actual configuration file. Don't use carriage returns.

The streaming servers need a SDP file to be able to serve the stream. The original SDP file references the broadcast machine. The SDP files for the streaming servers must be changed to reference the relay machine instead of the broadcasting machine. If you opened the SDP file up in a text editor, you should see the following code:

```
c=IN IP4 1.2.3.1
```

Change this code to the relay server IP address, because the relay server is the live stream source for the two streaming servers:

```
c=IN IP4 2.3.4.5
```

When viewers request the live stream from the servers #1 and #2 (don't forget to omit the .sdp file extension), the streaming servers know that the stream requested is coming from IP address 2.3.4.5. The relay server knows from the relay configuration file that the stream is coming from IP address 1.2.3.4, though it doesn't know whether the stream is coming from a broadcaster or another relay machine.

The relay server can also serve the stream to audience members. Generally you don't want to serve the public from the relay server, because you don't want to put the relay server under any strain. If the relay server crashes, all the relayed streams crash along with it.

Relay configurations can get as complicated as you like, and can use both unicast and multicast protocols. Multicast is discussed later on in this chapter. For more information on the configuration of QuickTime server relays, please refer to the Apple Web site (www.apple.com).

RealSystem iQ

The RealSystem uses the concept of *splitting* to describe how multiple servers can be used to host live streams. Splitting architectures consist of two kinds of machines — *transmitters* and *receivers*. Much like the QuickTime relay architecture, servers can be both transmitters and receivers.

The RealServer is configured via a browser-based user interface. All you have to do is specify the host name or IP address of the other servers that you want to transmit to or receive from, and you are ready to go. As soon as the transmitters and receivers are configured, you can request live streams from the receivers by using any of the linking methods that I describe in Chapter 36.

Configuring transmitters

To turn your server into a transmitter, add one or more receivers via your RealSystem Administrator. To do this, all you have to do is click on the Splitting option, choose Transmitter, and enter a few values, such as the IP address of the intended receivers. Figure 37-3 shows how transmitters can be configured using the RealSystem Administrator.

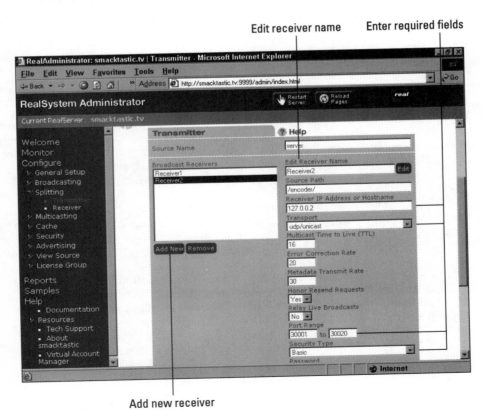

Figure 37-3: Configuring a transmitter using the RealSystem Administrator

You must specify a port range, a password, and IP address of the receiving computers. If you want the transmission to be secured, you can specify a security type. Transmitters and receivers must use the same values in these parameters. You can also specify a number of optional parameters, depending on your exact configuration. For a full description of all the transmitter parameters, please refer to the RealSystem Server Administration Guide, available from the RealNetworks Web site (www.realnetworks.com).

After you're done with the settings, click Apply. Your RealServer is ready to transmit live streams to receiving computers (as shown in the following figure).

Configuring receivers

Setting up a receiver is very similar to setting up a transmitter. You do so by using the RealSystem administrator, this time choosing Receiver from under the Splitting option. Again, you must enter a few values including the IP address of the transmitter. You can also specify a different mount point for received streams. Figure 37-4 shows how you configure a receiver using the RealSystem Administrator.

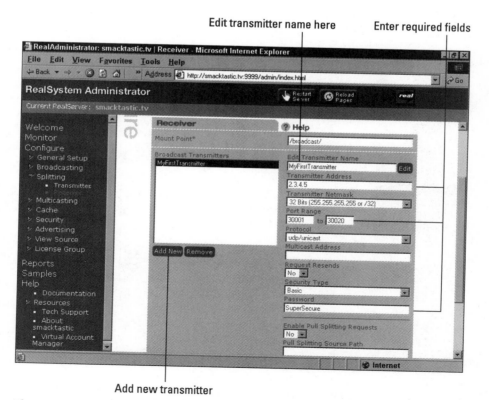

Figure 37-4: Configuring a receiver by using the RealSystem Administrator.

You must use the same port range, password, and security type as the transmitter or the splitting process will fail. You can configure a number of optional parameters, such as error correction rate and time to live, depending on your exact configuration. For a full description of all the transmitter parameters, please refer to the RealSystem Server Administration Guide, available from the RealNetworks Web site (www.realnetworks.com).

After you're done with the receiver settings, click Apply and your RealServer is ready to receive streams from a transmitter. These streams are then broadcast to the audience. The transmitter can also serve streams to audience members, but in general you don't want to serve the public from the transmitter, because if the transmitter crashes, all the receivers lose their live feeds.

Assume that the same situation as the QuickTime example, but with the terminology changed to reflect the RealSystem metaphor.

Figure 37-5 illustrates a simple splitting scenario where an encoding computer sends a stream to a transmitter, which then forwards the stream to two receivers. The two receivers then serve the live stream to audience members.

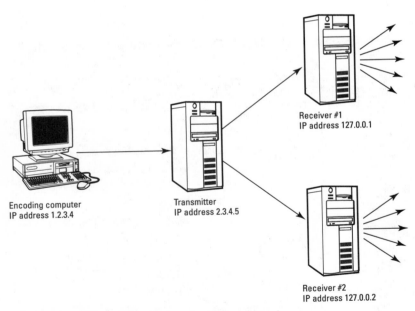

Receiver #1
IP address 127.0.0.1

Receiver #2
IP address 127.0.0.2

Encoding computer
IP address 1.2.3.4

Transmitter
IP address 2.3.4.5

Figure 37-5: A simple RealSystem splitting scenario

To enable the scenario illustrated in Figure 37-5, you must set up the transmitter to forward the live stream to the two receivers. You must also set up the two receivers to receive the stream from the transmitter. Configuring a RealServer to be a receiver or transmitter is done via the RealSystem Administrator, which is a browser-based user interface. You can connect to any RealServer remotely using the following syntax:

```
http://your.realserver.com:{admin port}/admin/index.html
```

The admin port is configured during the setup process. After you connect to your RealServer using this URL in your browser, you are asked for a username and password. Assuming you provide a valid username and password, you are presented with the RealSystem Administrator interface where you can configure the server to be a transmitter, receiver, or both.

First, you need to set up the transmitter to send streams to the receivers. The following steps are illustrated in Figure 37-3:

1. **Open your browser and log in to the RealSystem Administrator on the server you wish configure as a transmitter server and click on the Splitting option.**

2. **Select Transmitters.**

3. **Add a new receiver by clicking the Add New button.** A new receiver is created with a default name Receiver1. You can change this name by typing in a new one in the Edit Receiver Name box and clicking the Edit button.

4. **Enter the IP address of the receiver, along with a transport setting, a port range, a security type, and a password.** You can use the default settings for the transport, port range, and security type as long as they agree with the settings on the receiver.

5. **Click Apply.**

6. **Repeat Steps 3 through 5 to configure the second receiver.**

7. **Your server is now configured to transmit live streams to the two receivers.**

Next you have to set up the two receivers to receive streams from the transmitter. The following steps are illustrated in Figure 37-3:

1. **Log into the RealSystem Administrator on the server you want to configure as the first receiver and click on the Splitting option.**

2. **Select Receiver.**

3. **Add a new transmitter by clicking the Add New button.** A new transmitter is created with a default name Transmitter1. You can change this by typing in a new one in the Edit Receiver Name box and clicking the Edit button.

4. **Enter the IP address of the transmitter, along with a port range, a protocol, a security type, and a password.** You can use the default settings for the port range, protocol, and security type as long as they agree with the settings on the receiver. The password must agree with the password set on the transmitter.

5. **Click Apply.**

6. **Repeat Steps 1 through 5 on the second receiver to configure it to receive streams from the transmitter.**

7. **Your servers are now configured to receive live streams from the transmitter.**

To link to broadcasts on the receivers, you can use any of the linking methods described in Chapter 36. In this case, because the mount point on the receivers was left as the default, a `ramgen` link to a live file called `keynote.rm` looks like this (assuming the receiver was using the default HTTP port 8080):

```
<a href="http://127.0.0.1:8080/ramgen
    /broadcast/keynote.rm">Click here to tune in.</a>
```

RealSystem iQ splitting defaults to a push system, whereby live streams are automatically propagated out to all receivers, regardless of whether the receivers have clients requesting the streams or not. Alternatively, splitter architectures can be configured to use a pull mode, where streams are not propagated until a request is received.

RealSystem iQ splitting can be configured in a number of different ways. You can use multiple transmitters, multicast, and other options. For a full description of all the capabilities of RealSystem iQ splitting, check out the RealSystem Server Administration Guide, available from the RealNetworks Web site at `www.realnetworks.com`.

Windows Media Services

Windows Media Services defines access to live streams by means of broadcast publishing points. Broadcast publishing points are virtual directories on the Windows Media server that are used to provide access to live streams. The key to implementing a distributed Windows Media architecture is in the way sources for publishing points are defined. The source for a publishing point can be an encoder, a publishing point on a different server, or a remote *station*, which is Windows Media terminology for a multicast.

Defining publishing points

When you define a publishing point on a Windows Media server, you supply an alias, a path type, and a URL to the stream source. The alias must always be unique; the path type and URL vary slightly depending on what the source is:

✦ **Remote encoder.** Choose Windows Media Encoder for the path type and specify the URL as follows:

```
mms://{name or IP address of encoder}:{encoder port}
```

✦ **Remote broadcast publishing point.** Choose Remote publishing point for the path type and specify the URL as follows:

```
mms://{name or IP address of remote server}/{remote
publishing point alias}
```

✦ **Remote station.** Choose Remote station for the path type and specify the URL as follows:

```
mms://{name or IP address of remote server}/{remote station
name}
```

Broadcast publishing points are defined via the Windows Media Administrator, by using the Quick Start wizard or manually. The next section walks you through an example of how to set up a distributed server architecture using broadcast publishing points.

Setting up Windows Media Publishing Points

Figure 37-6 illustrates a distributed Windows Media Services architecture where the first server uses the Windows Media Encoder as its source, and the second two servers use the first server as their source. The second two servers are used to serve the audience.

Configuring Widows Media Services is done via the Windows Media Administrator, which is a browser-based interface you use to administer servers remotely.

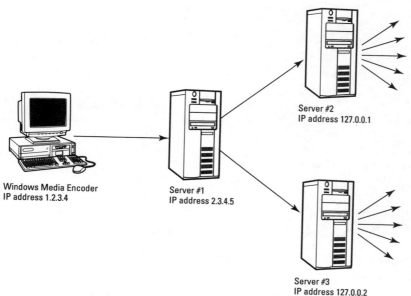

Windows Media Encoder
IP address 1.2.3.4

Server #1
IP address 2.3.4.5

Server #2
IP address 127.0.0.1

Server #3
IP address 127.0.0.2

Figure 37-6: A distributed Windows Media Services architecture

For this example, assume your Windows Media Encoder is set up to broadcast on the standard port. First you must configure a publishing point for the live stream on Server #1, then configure publishing points on Servers #2 and #3 that reference Server#1 as their source. The following steps are illustrated in Figure 37-7:

1. **Open your Windows Media Administrator and connect to Server #1.** You do this by selecting the server from the drop-down menu on the left-hand side of the interface. If the server has not yet been configured for your Windows Media Administrator, click the "Add new server" button and specify the necessary information.

2. **Click Unicast Publishing Points.** Make sure that the Use wizard... checkbox is *not* checked, click Broadcast and then select new from the drop-down menu. This action brings up the New Broadcast Publishing Point screen.

3. **Specify an alias, the path type, and the URL of the encoder.** Figure 37-7 uses the alias LiveStream. The path type is set to Windows Media Encoder and the server URL is typed in, using the HTTP protocol. Click OK. Server #1 is now ready to serve the live broadcast.

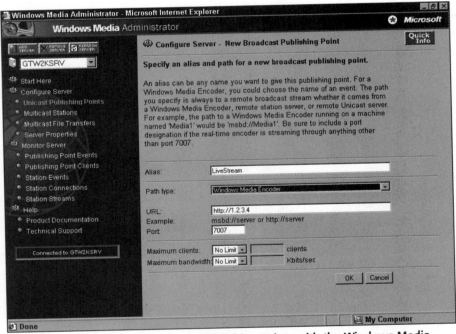

Figure 37-7: Configuring Broadcast Publishing Points with the Windows Media Administrator

Caution   Windows Media Encoder 7.0 and 7.1 no longer support the `msbd` protocol, only HTTP.

Next you have to configure the two other servers to use Server #1 as the source for their broadcast publishing points. Continue using the Windows Media Administrator, but now you must connect to the other two servers.

1. **Connect to Server #2 by choosing Server #2 from the drop-down menu or by adding a new server.**

2. **Click Unicast Publishing Points.** Make sure that the Use wizard... checkbox is **not** checked, click Broadcast and select new from the drop-down menu.

3. **Specify an alias, the path type, and the URL of the encoder.** This time set the Path type to Remote Windows Media Publishing Point and use the IP address for Server #1.

Caution

Make sure that you use the mms protocol when specifying the URL of a remote publishing point or station.

4. **Click OK.** Server #2 is now ready to serve live streams that originate from the encoder at 1.2.3.4 and are published by the server at 2.3.4.5.

5. **Repeat Steps 1 through 4 for Server #3 to complete your setup.** Voilà!

To link to the broadcasts on any of the servers, you can use any of the linking methods discussed in Chapter 36. In general, whether you link directly to the file or via an ASX file, the link to the file would look like this:

```
mms://{server IP or name}/{broadcast publishing alias}
```

Live server load balancing

The only other piece of the puzzle missing is some way to steer audience members to different servers. You can do so in a number of different ways, which break down into roughly three methods:

✦ **Hardware/appliance load balancing**: Commonly referred to as layer 4 switches, though some dispute the accuracy of the term.

✦ **Software load balancing:** Requests are routed via a single computer that forwards the requests to servers.

✦ **Dynamic URL generation:** In which the clients are sent URLs that are constructed on the fly by software.

✦ **DNS Round robin:** A balancing system that feature of DNS tables that allow you to map a single host name to a number of IP addresses.

The first two methods are excellent and can be used in combination for extra caution; the third method is now outdated and should be avoided. A full discussion of each of these methods is beyond the scope of this book. It's really more of a networking issue, which is what your network administrators are so well paid to know. In the interest of comprehensiveness, a brief description of each follows.

Hardware load balancing

Hardware load balancing makes use of the low-level information contained in the data packets streaming across the Internet to make intelligent decisions about where the data should be sent.

Standard routers send the data to the correct destination computer. That's all they do. Layer 4 switches look deeper into the individual data packets and determine what sort of traffic it is. They figure out not only which computer the data is destined for, but also what application running on the computer the data is intended for.

These switches provide load-balancing programmability by allowing you to group a number of servers into one virtual server. Traffic sent to the IP address of the virtual server is distributed among the group of servers. The switch maintains a running tally of how much traffic is sent to each server and, therefore, can make intelligent decisions about which computer should receive the next request.

In addition to load balancing, hardware load balancing adds a level of security, because the virtual server does not exist, and the IP addresses of the actual servers need not be published.

Software load balancing

You can use software to load balance your server requests. Software load balancing is similar to hardware load balancing in that all incoming traffic is addressed to the load-balancing computer, and then distributed across the servers. The load balancer keeps a list of all available servers and how many streams have been sent to each server.

Software load balancing also adds a level of security much the same way a hardware load balancer does, since the IP addresses of the actual servers are never revealed.

Cross-Reference   For a tutorial about how to load balance the RealServer using the Linux Virtual Server (LVS), please turn to Chapter 38.

Dynamic URL generation

Dynamic URL generation can be done in a number of different ways, by using different software approaches such as cgi or php. The way it works is that instead of a viewer requesting a static metafile from a Web server, they issue a request to a small software routine that assembles a metafile (or SMIL file) on-the-fly based upon known information about the servers.

For example, if you had a server farm consisting of three servers, you could write a program that assembled URLs by simply substituting the server names in a round-robin fashion. The problem with this method is that the program doesn't know when a server goes down — it carries on with its round-robin substitution regardless.

You can build a bit of intelligence into the system by having the URL generator do a table look-up instead of hard-coding the server names into the program. You can then write other programs to monitor the status of the servers and remove non-functioning servers from the table. This way, the URL generator always sends requests to operating servers.

Any decent network engineer can throw one of these programs together with a bit of help from you to teach them what streaming URLs should look like. They're already used to monitoring servers — that's what those pagers are for.

DNS round robin

DNS round robin exploits a loophole in the DNS system whereby a hostname can be assigned to multiple IP addresses. As requests come into the DNS table, the IP address returned is varied in a round-robin fashion.

This system has a number of flaws. First of all, updating a DNS table entry is a time consuming process, because the change has to propagate across the entire Internet. Second, most operating systems cache DNS table lookups. If a server goes down, rebooting is the only way to get your computer to query DNS for a different IP address.

DNS round robin is now completely superseded by the other options available. Avoid it like the plague, especially in live broadcast scenarios.

Live stream latency

One item that should be mentioned is live stream latency. When you watch a baseball game live on television, it only takes a fraction of a second for the signal to bounce off each satellite, and perhaps a fraction of a second to traverse the miles of cable to your house. The total delay between the crack of the bat and being displayed on your screen may be as long as a second or two.

Internet broadcast latency is a lot worse. First of all, the media players themselves buffer for five to seven seconds. Second, when multiple servers are used (particularly if they are geographically disbursed), there may be additional buffering to compensate for erratic bandwidth availability. Last but not least, the Internet can introduce a significant amount of latency, particularly when rebuffering occurs.

Therefore, at a live broadcast, no one is hearing the *exact* same thing at the *exact* same time. Does it matter? Yes and no. If you're hoping for a high degree of interactivity, then latency can be troublesome. If it's more of a standard broadcast, then, for the most part, people are unaware of the fact that they are behind their fellow audience members.

Multicasting

In live broadcast situations, you have a large number of people all watching the same stream. Using traditional unicast broadcasting, each audience member is sent a unique copy of the stream. A better approach would be to send out the broadcast on a single channel that all the viewers can tune in to. This is precisely the approach that multicast uses.

How multicasting works

Unicast streams are sent to a single user, whose IP address is stamped on each packet. Routers on the Internet or LAN use this information to deliver the packets to a particular computer. Multicast streams are different. They are sent to a multicast IP address. Packets with multicast addresses are forwarded to all routers instead of to a particular computer.

To receive a multicast, a media player simply tunes in to a particular multicast IP address. The local router sends each media player listening to the multicast a copy of the stream. The difference is that only a single stream has to traverse the distance from the server to the local router. Figure 37-8 illustrates the difference between unicast and multicast.

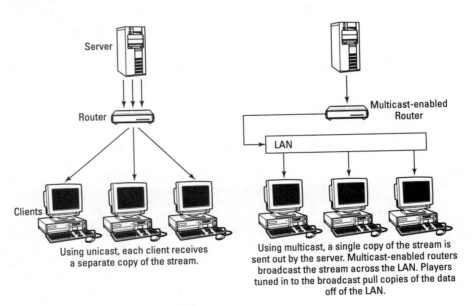

Using unicast, each client receives a separate copy of the stream.

Using multicast, a single copy of the stream is sent out by the server. Multicast-enabled routers broadcast the stream across the LAN. Players tuned in to the broadcast pull copies of the data off of the LAN.

Figure 37-8: Unicast versus multicast

The obvious benefit to multicasting is that the traffic requirements are much lower when using multicast. Only a single copy of the stream has to be sent out rather than hundreds or thousands. The only problem with multicasting across the Internet is that every single router involved must be multicast-enabled, which is not yet the case.

Multicasts make an enormous amount of sense on LANs where a single network administrator has control of all the routers. In situations like these, broadband streams can be multicast across a LAN with minimal impact on traffic congestion.

Configurations that combine multicast and unicast can be used to minimize bandwidth and maximize coverage. For example, you can multicast inside your LAN, unicast to the public Internet, and send a single stream via unicast to a second server that multicast to another LAN.

Multicasting support

All three major platforms provide support for multicasting. As usual, they all approach the problem in a slightly different way, using slightly different terminology.

QuickTime simply uses multicast addresses to determine whether or not a stream is to be multicast. The servers can relay streams via multicast or unicast. Linking to multicasts are just links to multicast IP addresses. The source of the multicast is a Sorenson Broadcaster or a relay server.

The RealSystem supports two types of multicasting — back-channel multicasting and scalable multicasting. *Back-channel* multicasting maintains a connection to every multicast client so that interaction is possible. *Scalable* multicasting does not maintain a connection with each client. Both types offer SureStream support, but without the stream switching capability.

Windows Media refers to multicasts as *stations*. Stations are multicast streams that contain one or more *programs*. Programs, in turn, contain one or more streams. In addition, they use the concept of *distribution stations* that move streams via unicast from one multicast server to another. Programs can contain live streams or archived streams to be played back in a live fashion.

Both the RealSystem and Windows media offer protocol rollover, whereby viewers who cannot receive broadcasts via multicast can attempt to receive the broadcast via unicast.

A full discussion of how each platform implements multicasting is beyond the scope of this book. Rest assured that none of the implementations are particularly complicated. With a bit of patience you can be multicasting on your LAN in no time at all.

Does the Broadcast Really Have to be Live?

One way to avoid a lot of the headache involved with live broadcasts is to cheat. In many instances, the live broadcast does not need to coincide with the actual event. Obviously there are instances when live must mean *live* — but not always.

If the event can be taped for later broadcast, the nightmare of on-site connectivity is completely avoided, as is the cost. So, too, is the worry about encoding machines. You can encode the file later at your leisure. If something goes wrong with the encoding, you can simply start over. You still are faced with the same bandwidth issues to stream the broadcast, but eliminating two out of three problem issues definitely merits consideration.

All three platforms offer methods of faking live broadcasts — and of course, they all use slightly different terminology. For complete descriptions of all the options available and how to implement these methods, please refer to the appropriate server manual. A brief overview of each platform follows.

QuickTime PlaylistBroadcaster

The QuickTime server offers the ability to broadcast playlists. Playlists are created using the Server Administrator. You choose the files that you want to broadcast and then choose a play mode. Three play modes are available:

✦ **Sequential.** The files are played in order one time.

✦ **Sequential looped.** Same as sequential, but the presentation loops indefinitely.

✦ **Weighted random.** Each file is assigned a weight between 1 and 10 that determines how often it is played. Playback is continuous.

After you set up your playlist, you can start or stop playback via the Server Administrator. All media contained in a playlist must be of the same type, contain the same number of tracks, and use the *exact* same encoding specs, such as bit rate, screen size, and so on.

RealSystem G2SLTA

The RealSystem calls their method the G2SLTA, which is an acronym for the G2 Simulated Live Transfer Agent. This method is a command line-only program that sends on-demand files to the server as if they were live files. It can rebroadcast a single file or a playlist, which is a simple text file that contains a list of files to be rebroadcast. This playlist can be created in any text editor or created dynamically, and it can be edited while the G2SLTA is broadcasting.

The G2SLTA can play the files sequentially or in random order, and it can specify title, author and copyright information. All the files contained in the playlist must be of the same type and have the *exact* same encoding parameters, such as bit rate, screen size, SureStream specs, and so on.

Windows Media stations

Windows media uses the concept of stations that contain one or more programs to broadcast on-demand content in a simulated live fashion. Stations must contain at least one program; programs must contain at least one file. Programs can be set to play the files sequentially a number of times or looped indefinitely.

Stations are by definition multicast streams, but can be configured to rollover to unicast if multicast is unavailable. Stations and programs are created, edited, and controlled via the Windows Media Administrator.

Summary

Solid server architecture is crucial to the success of your live broadcast, because live broadcasts put your servers under abnormal stress. Building redundancy into your architecture and having some form of load balancing is crucial.

✦ Live broadcasts can place an enormous strain on your servers.

✦ The economics of live broadcasts on the Internet generally come up a bit short.

✦ Server redundancy using a distributed architecture spreads out the load and reduces bandwidth bottlenecks.

✦ All three platforms can implement distributed architectures.

✦ Load balancing should be employed, preferably by using a combination of hardware appliances (layer 4 switches) and dynamic URL generation.

✦ Avoid DNS round robin.

✦ Multicasting can lead to enormous bandwidth savings by sending out only a single copy of a live broadcast that viewers can tune in to.

✦ Multicasting on the public Internet is a virtual impossibility at this point, because all routers must be multicast-enabled.

✦ Broadcasts on an internal LAN should always take advantage of multicasting.

✦ Live broadcasts don't necessarily have to be *live* — they can be a rebroadcast of an on-demand file.

✦ Rebroadcasting on-demand files eliminates two of the headaches of live broadcasting — the encoding and the on-site connectivity.

✦ All three platforms support rebroadcasts.

✦   ✦   ✦

Case Studies

A Radio Station — KING FM

Classic KING FM (www.king.org) made Internet history on December 12, 1995, when it became the first classical music radio station to stream its signal live over the Internet, 24 hours a day, 7 days a week. In fact, KING FM began streaming high-quality classical programming before most radio shows of any genre got online.

Of course, unbeknownst to KING FM, its signal had been streaming long before that. Earlier that summer a small company then known as Progressive Networks had been running extended tests on its software system by streaming classical music, day and night.

Back in those days, a portable stereo system hung out a window, connected to a computer across the room. The radio feed was encoded and broadcast across the Internet, without KING-FM's knowledge. (Full disclosure: the author was responsible for this inexcusable act of piracy.) The only major problems occurred when electrical storms moved in, and the resultant FM signal shifts in the middle of the night compromised the audio quality.

As soon as the system was working well enough to demonstrate, the folks from KING FM were called up and given a demonstration of the technology. Even though you could see them wince when they heard the audio quality, they realized that the technology could only improve and decided to go public with the signal.

Many years and many codec improvements later, KING FM continues to stream and is consistently one of the highest rated radio stations on the Internet. Its infrastructure is simple and efficient and is now basically self-sustaining.

Production

Radio stations have a distinct advantage over other companies that are trying to put media on the Internet — radio stations already produce a signal that is ready to encode. Producing an Internet stream merely involves taking a split from the broadcast signal and feeding it to their encoder of choice.

The equipment necessary to produce the KING FM stream is modest to say the least. The room it is done in measures approximately 6 × 8 feet; most people would consider it a closet. Nevertheless, it has everything you need to get a radio station on the Internet. Figure 38-1 is a snapshot of KING-FM's Internet facilities.

Figure 38-1: The KING FM Internet production room. Note the modest equipment setup, which includes good speakers and a good amplifier, a good microphone, and a small mixing board.

Then again, nothing is ever as simple as it first seems. Classic KING FM did not simply want to repurpose their terrestrial broadcast. From the very beginning, KING FM wanted to derive revenue from their Internet venture. Having been in the radio business for years, they realized that advertising would provide the necessary revenue stream.

Ad removal/insertion

Classic KING FM did not want to stream the advertisements that it sold to its local clients. The people at KING FM saw the available ad space as an additional revenue stream, and therefore, wanted to remove the ads from the terrestrial signal and replace them with Internet-only ads. The Internet offered them a potentially global audience, and they wanted to exploit that fact. Even if their audience turned out to be mostly local, they still did not want to give their local terrestrial advertisers something that they did not pay for.

The problem was, the station hadn't sold the ads yet, and at that point (1995) selling Internet ads was unheard of. The station had no ads to insert into the Internet stream, but did not want to give the valuable space away for free. As an interim solution, KING-FM cleverly constructed a switching system that sensed when ads were being played on the terrestrial signal and swapped the audio signal over to a multi-CD player that was loaded with a number of classical CDs playing nonstop in random mode.

This interim solution worked fairly well, except for the odd time when the CD player would jam or skip and someone at KING FM had to give it a swift kick. The solution was not optimal, though, because the transition to the CD player was abrupt — as was switching back to the live feed. Nevertheless, the rough transition did not stop people from listening. Today, the switching system is still in use, although the circuit has been improved a number of times. Instead of switching to a CD player, the switching system now switches to their automated advertising software.

KING FM runs a mixture of traditional advertisements, Internet-only ads, sponsorship messages, and promotional clips. These promotional messages are inserted automatically by a software system that senses what is known as a *tertiary tone* embedded in the broadcast signal. When the software system senses a tone, the software automatically inserts predetermined spots into the stream. KING FM runs two separate instances of the software, one for the terrestrial stream and one for the Internet feed.

Signal preprocessing

Not much signal processing is required because the signal is already produced to a very high standard. Before the signal is encoded it is lightly compressed using a Behringer Composer stereo compressor. Although compressing the dynamic range of classical music is never truly desirable, the dynamic range of the lower bit rate streams is much smaller than the recorded dynamic range. To make sure that the quietest sections are audible, the signal must be lightly compressed.

Encoding

The partnership between KING FM and RealNetworks continues to this day. Because Classic KING FM is a not-for-profit enterprise, they work with the RealImpact group. RealImpact is a division of RealNetworks dedicated to helping progressive organizations utilize the Internet. In this case, RealImpact provides encoding services and bandwidth.

The audio signal arrives via a dedicated high-quality audio line provided by the local phone company. After some light preprocessing, the signal is fed into a Linux-based encoder equipped with a Sound Blaster Live! soundcard. KING FM has always been run on Linux encoders because of the rock-solid reliability that they provide.

The encoded stream is sent to the server cluster that resides in the same room. Many different codecs and bit rates have been experimented with over the years. During one particular early experiment, an encoded stream was played over the air in place of CDs to see if listeners would notice the difference. Listeners did not notice, and this experiment was a turning point in KING FM's commitment to encoded audio.

As codec technology improved sufficiently, the staff at KING-FM decided that a single, high-quality 20 Kbps mono signal would enable KING FM to reach the most listeners, given the bandwidth restrictions their budget placed upon them. Because the majority of listeners are listening through small plastic speakers and at low volume, higher bit rate codecs do not add much to the equation.

Authoring

Classic KING FM has never been one to get too fancy with its user interface. They believe that people listening to their Internet stream are listening to it just as they would a traditional radio — using it as a background for their daily work routine. This is amply reflected in their traffic and usage patterns (see the "How Successful is KING FM?" section later in this chapter).

Because the Classic KING FM online operation is essentially a one-man show, the majority of the effort is placed on the Web site, which is a major promotional outlet for them. The audio-only streams are left to speak for themselves. Advertising and promotional work are done in the audio stream, where they are most effective (see the "Internet Audio — Dead or Alive" sidebar in Chapter 21).

Expert Tutorial: Load Balancing Streaming Servers Using the Linux Virtual Server by Mark Winter

With KING FM, we started out years ago with a single server, but as demand grew, we added more servers to cope with the increased loads. Initially, DNS round robin was used to load balance, but DNS round robin is never an optimal solution. However, it was quick and easy to implement and served us well in the short term.

Eventually, it became apparent that we needed a more robust solution. The demand for KING FM grew from around 200 simultaneous connections to over 2,500 connections in a one-month period, so we decided to try out load balancing by using LVS (the Linux Virtual Server). With LVS, throwing additional servers into the rotation to keep up with demand is easy.

This Tutorial assumes that you know a bit about the Linux operating system. It's not difficult, but I'm going to skip over some of the nitty-gritty, such as installing a patch on your kernel. If you want more information, check out any of the excellent documentation available online (`www.linuxvirtualserver.org/Documents.html`).

LVS benefits

The Linux Virtual Server allows you to load balance a number of servers by clustering them behind a single *virtual* server. The load balancing takes place at the operating system level. Load balancing at the operating system level is great for a number of reasons:

✦ LVS is easy to administer and configure.

✦ LVS is well documented.

✦ LVS is incredibly scalable.

✦ The actual IP addresses of the servers are not public and are, therefore, protected.

✦ LVS is very reliable.

✦ Best of all, it's free!

Taking all these things into account, we decided to give it a shot.

LVS IP forwarding options

LVS can use a number of different IP forwarding modes. Three kinds of IP forwarding are built into Linux:

✦ **Virtual Server via Network Address Translation (NAT):** Where requests and responses go through the LVS director box. By using this method, your LVS machine can become a bottleneck because all inbound and outbound packets go through the LVS machine. However, this method is easy to set up on all types of operating systems, and only the director box needs to be configured.

✦ **Virtual Server via Direct Routing:** Is very robust and has high throughput because only acknowledgment traffic goes through the director box.

Continued

Continued

✦ **Virtual Server via IP Tunneling:** Works only on Linux, similar to Direct Routing but used for machines on different segments (different locations).

In our case, we decided to use Direct Routing because with this method your servers aren't bottlenecked by a Firewall/NAT box but are still secure because of the private addressing.

LVS load balancing options

Using LVS, you can decide how the virtual server chooses which server to send the latest request to. You can use a number of options:

✦ **Round robin:** Where requests are assigned in a predetermined order.

✦ **Weighted round robin:** Where requests are assigned in a predetermined order, with the added ability to assign a *weight* to each server, corresponding to the processing power of each server.

✦ **Least connections:** Where the server with the least amount of connections is assigned the next request.

✦ **Weighted least connections:** Same as least connections but with the ability to specify a weight for each server according to processing power.

✦ **Locality based least connections:** Designed for caching servers.

✦ **Destination hashing:** An algorithm used for Web caches. This option is useful if you want clients to connect to the same Web server for each subsequent request.

✦ **Source hashing:** For load balancing across multiple firewalls.

We use weighted round robin with a weight of 10 for all the servers and adjust the weight setting if a machine starts acting up. Alternatively, if you want to pull a server out of rotation, all you have to do is set the weight to 0.

We have experimented with weighted least connections, but in a couple of instances it caused some strange weighting problems. For instance, if a new machine was thrown into rotation, all connections were sent to it. For our purposes, weighted round robin has proved very reliable.

Installing LVS

Setting up your servers using LVS is a little tricky at first, but after you get the hang of it, you'll find that it's really very simple. First, you must have a server that is dedicated to balancing the load amongst the streaming servers, in this case RealServers, but you can use the same approach on Web/download servers.

Check out Joseph Mack's HOWTO (no relation to the author) here:

```
www.linuxvirtualserver.org/Joseph.Mack/HOWTO/LVS-HOWTO.html
```

To Implement LVS, you have to apply a patch to your Linux kernel. Doing so means adding some software to the original configuration to give the kernel LVS functionality. Patching a

Linux kernel is simple. I won't go into detail here. If you don't know how to patch your kernel, you're probably not reading this! Patch your kernel, rebuild it, and you're ready to go.

You can get the patch here:

```
http://linux-vs.org/software/ipvs-1.0.8-2.2.19.tar.gz
```

Configuring LVS

LVS utilizes the built-in IP forwarding capabilities of the Linux operating system. So to use LVS, you have to turn on this functionality, specify the type of scheduling you want to use, and specify the servers to which you want packets forwarded to.

Using LVS you'll become intimately familiar with `ipvsadm`, which is the configuration program for LVS (**ip** **v**irtual **s**erver **adm**inistrator). With `ipvsadm` you can add and remove servers to/from your cluster, apply different weights to servers, and so on.

One of the things you need to do if you're running a RealServer LVS cluster is use the Persistence feature. The RealPlayer must keep a TCP connection to the RealServer for control purposes, so you want to make sure that players continue talking to the server they started off with. You can do this by specifying the `-p` switch in the `ipvsadm` command.

Another thing to bear in mind is that the RealServer accepts packet requests on a number of different ports. Because Linux IP forwarding is done on a port basis, you have to make sure that you forward all the appropriate ports.

The easiest way to keep track of all this is to use a built-in feature of Linux called firewall marking. This feature enables you to specify a group of ports, all of which are marked as okay to forward. Define the group using the `ipchains` command and then specify the number of the group you defined in the `ipvsadm` command.

Running LVS

The following example is for a 2.2 Linux kernel.

1. **Set the type of IP forwarding, in this case direct routing, by typing the following command:**

```
echo 1 > /proc/sys/net/ipv4/ip_forward
```

2. **Load the scheduling module, in this case weighted round robin (wrr):**

```
/sbin/modprobe ip_vs_wrr
```

3. **Specify the ports you want forwarded by defining a firewall marker group.** You need an `ipchains` command for each port.

```
/sbin/ipchains -F
/sbin/ipchains -A input -d <LVS server IP address>/32 554 -p
    tcp -m 1
```

Continued

Continued

```
/sbin/ipchains -A input -d <LVS server IP address>/32 3030 -p
     tcp -m 1
... {make sure you have an ipchains statement for each port you
want forwarded}
```

4. Using `ipvsadm`, specify persistence and the scheduling algorithm:

   /sbin/ipvsadm -A -f 1 -p -s wrr

5. Specify the IP addresses of the streaming servers. You need a separate
   `ipvsadm` command for each server:

```
/sbin/ipvsadm -a -f 1 -r <Server IP address>
```

At this point, your LVS server begins to forward incoming packets on the marked ports to the servers, using the load balancing method you specified.

Obviously, you don't want to have to do each of these steps every time you boot your machine. Ideally you should create a `rc.lvs` file that is called at boot time. Code Listing 38-1 lists the contents of this file. Please note that I've hidden the actual IP address of our LVS director machine, which is specified in the VIP parameter. Also, the three RealServers in this example have IP addresses specified in the three RIP variables, You would substitute your server IP addresses for these variables.

Code Listing 38-1: A Sample rc.lvs Startup file

```sh
#!/bin/sh
# Setup IP Addresses
VIP="207.xxx.xxx.xxx"
RIP_1="192.168.22.70"
RIP_2="192.168.22.71"
RIP_3="192.168.22.72"

# Load needed modules
BALANCE="wrr"
/sbin/modprobe ip_masq_mfw
/sbin/modprobe ip_vs_$BALANCE

# Define the ports you want forwarded, using firewall marking
/sbin/ipchains -F
/sbin/ipchains -A input -d ${VIP}/32 554 -p tcp -m 1
/sbin/ipchains -A input -d ${VIP}/32 3030 -p tcp -m 1
/sbin/ipchains -A input -d ${VIP}/32 7070 -p tcp -m 1
/sbin/ipchains -A input -d ${VIP}/32 8080 -p tcp -m 1
/sbin/ipchains -A input -s 0.0.0.0/0 6970:7170 -d ${VIP}/32 -p
udp -m 1
```

```
# Setup the LVS to listen to the marked ports, specify
# persistence, and the type of balancing desired
/sbin/ipvsadm -C
/sbin/ipvsadm -A -f 1 -p -s $BALANCE

# Setup the real server
/sbin/ipvsadm -a -f 1 -r ${RIP_1}
/sbin/ipvsadm -a -f 1 -r ${RIP_2}
/sbin/ipvsadm -a -f 1 -r ${RIP_3}
```

Bear in mind that when you use LVS with RealServer clusters, you need to makes sure to have IPBINDINGS set correctly in your `rmserver.cfg` file. If your IPBINDINGS are not setup in the correct order, the source address of the packets will be from the nonroutable IP address.

```
<List Name="IPBindings">
    <Var Address_1="<your server IP address>"/>
    <Var Address_2="127.0.0.1"/>
    <Var Address_3="192.168.22.71"/>
</List>
```

Finally, you want to make sure to set up nonarping on your streaming servers. Explaining why is a little hairy — the basic idea is that you don't want the RealServers responding directly to client requests. You want all requests to be routed via the LVS director box. To set up nonarping on a 2.2 Linux box here's what we used in `rc.local`:

```
# The following is used with LVS
echo "1" > /proc/sys/net/ipv4/conf/all/hidden
echo "1" > /proc/sys/net/ipv4/conf/lo/hidden
/sbin/ifconfig lo:0 207.xxx.xxx.xxx netmask 255.255.255.255
```

That's it! If all goes well, you should be up and running with a super-cool virtual server that load balances your streaming servers. LVS can be used to load balance Web servers, too, so don't be afraid to use LVS for all sorts of applications.

Mark Winter has been working at RealNetworks for far too long now. His current title is "Superhero in Training," and he can actually be reached at `justice@real.com`.

Serving

Linux-based servers have served KING FM for years. Linux-based servers were chosen, like the encoder, for their reliability. As word got out, the audience grew from a handful to a considerable size. One thing KING FM has always had is an audience larger than there are streams to serve them. Eventually, the KING FM servers had to have limits put on them as bandwidth requirements got out of hand.

These days, the KING FM streams are served out of a single box with four separate servers inside it. The servers are part of a Linux Virtual Server (LVS) group. One server is used as the load balancer, and the other three are used as RealServers. (See the Expert Tutorial, "Load Balancing Streaming Servers Using the Linus Virtual Server.")

The servers are more than enough to handle the load — in fact they're coasting most of the time. This is one key to KING FM's streaming architecture — because the servers are never under duress, they rarely fail. There's plenty of redundancy built into the system so that even if a server fails, the other servers are more than adequate to sustain the user load.

How Successful is KING-FM?

In short, KING-FM's streaming media infrastructure works wonderfully. The simplest way to illustrate their success is to look at some of the numbers:

✦ Over 10,000 unique listeners a day during the week; over 5,000 unique listeners a day on the weekends

✦ Average listening times of 75 minutes per listener during the week

✦ Over 2500 concurrent viewers at any given point during the week

These numbers would probably be significantly higher if it were not for the bandwidth restrictions. Because Classic KING FM is a not-for-profit enterprise and operates with a very small staff (one person dedicated to their online presence), its ability to grow its market and expand online activity is limited.

The station's experiments with advertising have also proven successful, particularly for customers who are trying to drive people to their Web sites. Some of their advertisers have had more success with their Internet ads than they did with the ads on the terrestrial broadcast signal. This makes sense, because folks listening online are far more likely to click over to a Web site than someone listening on the drive home. In fact, some feel that Internet radio is the much sought-after killer-app. For one Internet radio veteran's opinion, please see the "Internet Radio: Dead or Alive?" sidebar at the end of this chapter.

Classic KING FM is busy building for the future. A single channel, nonprofit terrestrial radio station has a tough road ahead of it. In spite of having tremendous listener numbers, the station needs to grow and provide more. By building new systems and working on new business models, hopefully KING FM can expand its brand and reach more listeners.

A particularly rich resource is available through the local Seattle classical music performing groups. As the traditional recording industry continues its contraction of classical music offerings, they find themselves with fewer traditional outlets and a need to develop other avenues. KING FM hopes to be at the forefront of these efforts. In these days of direct satellite and DMX radio, Classic KING FM realizes it must stretch limited resources to ensure the station's survival.

If you'd like to find out more about Classic KING FM, feel free to visit their Web site (www.king.org) or contact them directly via e-mail at web@king.org.

Internet Radio — Dead or Alive? By Todd Herman

A well-dressed woman at a swank LA club asked me: "Does the Internet actually improve radio?" "It does and it doesn't," I said, attempting to sound equally swanky. The real answer is it can — but right now, it isn't. Let me buy you a drink and I'll explain.

What's wrong with traditional radio?

Why does traditional radio bother you? One reason might be that they play songs that you think don't fit in. Another might be because you hear the same songs over and over again. Here is the ugly truth — they do both things on purpose because they have to.

In order to sell advertising, radio stations attempt to reach demographic cells: male or female, 12–17, 18–34, 25–54, etc. That means that stations need 18 year olds *and* 34 year olds to listen to the same station — which is against nature. 18 and 34 year olds don't go to the same clubs and they don't hang out together. Stations attempt to walk the line and program for both groups because they need to sell advertising.

This severely limits what music a station can play. It's why all music on classic rock radio stations is the same, and why all urban and oldies stations sound alike They all use the same research (and radio is likely one of the most researched of all industries). It is also the reason you are so practiced at quickly punching the buttons on your radio when a song comes on that bothers you.

It gets even ruder. Stations may want you to go away — honestly. If a station seeking men, 25–54, suddenly starts seeing a number of younger men tuning in they will modify their programming to more strongly appeal to men 25–54. A program director will accomplish this by removing the music that would likely appeal to the unwanted demographic.

Why make people go away? Aren't more people better for advertisers? Don't they want all those people to hear their ads? Not necessarily. Someone advertising skateboards won't waste money talking to men over the age of (I'll be kind here, all you Peter Pans), let's say, 30. If the Skateboard Company buys an ad seeking men under 30, it's a waste of money if a bunch of 50-year-old men hear the message. Why not just focus on men, 22–25 and play a whole bunch of their music? Advertisers won't purchase ads to reach such a small demographic cell. Why don't broadcasters just build more stations? Simple: The broadcast spectrum is finite and hence there are a limited number of frequencies available. These days when a broadcast group wants to expand there is only one way to do so: Buy another station. As more stations are owned by fewer and fewer companies the similarity in programming becomes even more pronounced. This, in turn results in the listener doing more station surfing.

Continued

Continued

Can Internet Radio still change the World?

The Internet allows a focus unheard of in traditional radio, making it possible to "narrowcast." Technology today enables Internet radio stations to let the listener choose the music — right down to whether they want the album version or radio edit of their favorite Rolling Stones' song. The ability to let the listener choose the music theoretically eliminates all of the limits listed above; listeners hear only what they want, advertisers can significantly focus their message and radio stations can fire their program directors. It's a powerful possibility and the technology isn't brain surgery, but it won't be used for a while.

Record Companies, performer unions, and some artists are extremely worried about the Internet because digital technology allows people to do awful things like make copies of songs and post them online for anyone to download (record company translation: to steal). This limits the amount of personalization Internet radio stations currently allow. Until the legal problems are worked out, personalization of music will be a risky business.

When those issues are worked out and enough people are actually using Internet radio, it will be interesting to see how many people want to program their own stations and how many will want it done for them. I'm betting on the latter. VCR's have been around for 20 years and the majority of the VCR users I know still can't program the things — and don't want to learn how to. I think, for the next ten years or so, the same will prove true with Internet radio and consumers will want it programmed for them.

To me, the most exciting aspect of Internet Radio is the ability to finally have radio that is completely unique and no longer the red-headed stepchild of television. Instead of the same old DJs telling us the time and temperature, we can have real personalities communicating with wit and passion — and allow the listeners to choose who they like. For each news story that we hear, our browser will automatically take us to a corresponding Web site where we can interact and learn more. Internet radio will change the world — if its creators aren't lazy.

Is Internet radio a gamble?

As cool as all the technology sounds, should you place a bet on Internet-enabled radio at your local NASDAQ casino? I'll let your broker advise you on investments — I will only tell you what I think. When the big companies like ABC, Clear Channel, and Entercomm get the right tools at their disposal and learn to use them, they will have the opportunity to move into a whole new realm of creativity and revenue streams. I think these companies, who have made billions in radio, are in the best position to capitalize on the future — if they are able to see that it is not enough to simply simulcast a radio signal. The technology to focus ads, to let listeners choose what they hear, to add interactivity to a broadcast, to mix visual images with the audio broadcast can mean a quantum leap in what we think of today as radio. I hope it does. It will be up to the large groups to lead the way.

I know this. Digital technology changes everything eventually and it will change radio. Radio will eventually make more money using tools that we currently associate with the Internet — one day soon it will be the way things are done. My bet is on digitally enabled radio, not just Internet radio. The least it will do is enable broadcasters to make more money and the most it will do is morph radio into something entirely new.

If you are considering building an Internet radio station I have this advice. Only do it out of love. I think the chances of independent Internet radio stations winning in business get slimmer every day as Yahoo! buys Launch.com, Loudeye buys theDial and the big boys like Clear Channel really get into the game — with more than just simulcasts of their traditional broadcasts. However, consumer taste is king and if you have something different, something that is not just good, but great, then dive in. But please be creative — and brilliant.

Summing it all up

✦ **Can the Internet improve radio?** Quite possibly, but it hasn't even scratched the surface yet. The technology exists to change radio completely. It will be up to the big boys to decide whether they use that technology or stick with the status quo.

✦ **Should you bet on Internet radio?** Ask you broker. I am betting on digital technology plus consumer love of and loyalty to radio as a medium. If it were up to me, I'd be changing radio today.

✦ **Should you launch an Internet Radio Station?** Only if you recognize the odds are stacked against you and you have something the world must experience.

Todd Herman has been in radio since 1991 and was most recently the CEO of theDial, a groundbreaking Internet Radio company that pioneered a new level of entertainment interactivity and was among the first to welcome top brands like Proctor & Gamble, Sears, Muzak, and Hewlett Packard into the World of Internet radio. TheDial, which was acquired by Loudeye Technologies, continues to provide private labeled Internet radio to the Web's largest sites. In the early 90s, before changing Internet Radio, Herman helped modify the world of talk radio as a leading edge purveyor of the Hot Talk format. As a host, he is proud to have been banned from the Utah State House for life. He may be reached at Todd@mediagasm.com.

Summary

Creating an online radio presence does not present a gargantuan task. In fact, judging by how well KING FM's system works, if you plan well your system can pretty much run without assistance.

✦ Radio signals do not need much preprocessing because the signal is already broadcast quality.

✦ You do not need a roomful of equipment — unless the room is very small.

✦ Because the dynamic range of low bitrate audio streams is smaller than recorded classical music, light compression of the audio signal is a good idea so that the quiet parts of the recordings can be heard.

✦ If you have got programming that people want, they'll listen for extended periods of time.

✦ You do not have to kill yourself over a dazzling visual presentation.

✦ If you are using the RealSystem, Linux encoders and servers are a great choice for reliability.

✦ LVS is powerful, flexible, and free but requires a degree of Linux familiarity to implement.

✦   ✦   ✦

A Large-Scale Event – U2 Live from Notre Dame

As I have said throughout this book, live events are very tricky because you don't get a second chance. Any mistakes can jeopardize the entire broadcast. The pressure is bad enough during run-of-the-mill live events — it is even worse when you work with one of the biggest bands in the world.

The U2 broadcast was a joint effort between U2.com (the band's official Web site), Tiscali, (a large European ISP) and RealNetworks. Tiscali agreed to host the special Webcast Web site as well as the streams for European viewers. RealNetworks agreed to provide the streaming technology, host the streams for U.S. audience members, and cover on-site production costs.

The U2 Elevation tour was a stripped-down affair compared to the band's previous few outings. Instead of massive stadiums and huge production values, the band decided to opt for a simplified stage design and more intimate settings. The shows were done in the round, with audience members on all sides of a large heart-shaped stage that allowed the band to circulate through the audience.

Each band member had a camera trained on him for the entire show. These camera feeds were fed to the projection screens in black and white to match the look and feel of the band's latest CD release. The stage had four projection screens at the front and two screens each on the other three sides. Figure 39-1 shows an aerial view of the stage layout and the location of various elements of the Webcast production.

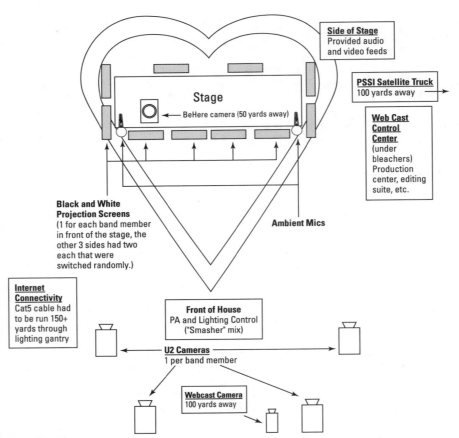

Figure 39-1: An aerial view of the U2 Webcast stage and equipment layout

The idea was to encode the four cameras trained on the band members and stream these to the Internet, along with a Smasher Mix, which contained all four camera feeds, one in each corner of the video. In addition, the band wanted to have a wide shot of the whole stage available for the Internet audience. The Webcast team had to provide a camera and operator for this stream. Last but not least the band wanted a BeHere camera feed that viewers could interact with. For people connecting at low bit rates, they also wanted to provide a higher quality audio-only stream.

In addition to the live event, U2.com also wanted to produce a series of interviews, possibly including band members, to give viewers a sense of what it was like to prepare for an event of this magnitude.

The entire event was to be broadcast live on October 10, 2001, at 9 p.m. Eastern time, with a rebroadcast the next day at 9 p.m. central European time.

The Plan

My company was contracted to produce the event. My responsibilities, many of which were evolving up until the last minute, included:

✦ Managing and acquiring on-site connectivity for the event.

✦ Managing a satellite crew, if necessary.

✦ Liasing with the band's production crew and acquiring the necessary audio and video signals for the broadcast, on-site power, locations, and so on.

✦ Augmenting existing video feeds with a wide shot; augmenting audio with the addition of ambient mics and appropriate preprocessing.

✦ Delivering these feeds, via satellite or encoded via IP connectivity, to the Real Broadcast Network (RBN) for distribution.

✦ Authoring and implementation of a SMIL user interface for the Webcast.

✦ Management and implementation of the BeHere camera feed.

✦ On-site crew and equipment for preshow interview taping.

✦ On-site editing facilities for interview editing and encoding.

All in all, this undertaking initially appeared to be a relatively straightforward live event. However, the project was given the initial go ahead (via a long distance call from a pub in the U.K.) on September 5, 2001 and was supposed to be broadcast live from the University of Notre Dame's Joyce Center on October 10, 2001. This meant five weeks in which to organize a major broadcast — a fairly narrow window with little margin for error.

Connectivity

Because the broadcast was being done from a remote location and with a constricted time window, first I had to establish whether connectivity was available and how reliable it was. Because a number of different streams were being offered at different bitrates to viewers, a lot of connectivity was required:

✦ 4 individual camera feeds at 80/56/28.8K SureStream

✦ "Smasher Mix" at 80/56/28.8K SureStream

✦ "Smasher Mix" at 200K broadband

✦ Wide angle shot at 80/56/28.8K SureStream

✦ Wide angle shot at 200K broadband

✦ BeHere Camera at 80/56/28.8K SureStream

✦ BeHere Camera at 200K broadband

✦ Audio-only mix at 32K SureStream

Altogether, approximately two megabits of dependable throughput was needed between the Joyce Center and the RBN Broadcast Operations Center (BOC). If you have tried to watch broadband streams across the Internet, you can imagine that the prospect of back hauling ten times that amount of data across the Internet for three hours left all involved more than a bit nervous.

Setting up the IP connection

The University of Notre Dame was immediately contacted. The director of Web administration informed us that WNDU, the local television affiliate owned by the university had fiber connectivity between the Joyce Center and the station. The station also had DS3 connectivity to the Internet. The problem was the fiber pairs were traditionally used to send video feeds to the television station; they were not used to send IP data.

In theory, IP data could be sent over fiber, but this theory would have to be tested. Unfortunately, the equipment necessary to do the test had to be purchased via mail order. The equipment at Joyce Center was state-of-the-art circa 1990, and the adapters needed were no longer readily available.

The folks at Notre Dame and WNDU did not want to order equipment or invest significant amounts of time researching the situation unless they were going to be paid for it. After some discussion, all parties involved agreed that a certain minimum expense would be covered, regardless of whether the connectivity checked out or not.

The backup — A satellite connection

Satellite connectivity was not considered at the outset because of the number of feeds. Each raw video feed would have to be bounced off a satellite transponder, at an estimated cost of $1,000 an hour, which gets expensive very quickly when you've got six video feeds. However, with the uncertain connectivity picture at Notre Dame, the satellite option had to be pursued as an alternative.

In addition to traditional satellite connectivity, we explored the possibility of sending IP data over satellite and transmitting compressed feeds. Sending compressed MPEG2 video via satellite enables the transmission of multiple video feeds via a single transponder. Although using any type of compression in your signal chain is not desirable, in this case, the slight reduction in quality was offset by the reduction in cost.

The vendor we were working with, Production & Satellite Services (PSSI), said that it could send six video feeds along with a limited amount of IP connectivity all through a single satellite transponder, bringing the cost within reasonable bounds. Though this option is more expensive than IP connectivity, it is much more reliable — a necessary element in this equation.

The solution — A combination

The IP connectivity at Notre Dame checked out just fine, with 10 Mbps connectivity between the Joyce Center and WNDU. In addition, the connectivity between WDNU and RBN looked excellent, with very low latency and virtually no packet loss. However, the idea of sending 2 Mbps across the public Internet left me feeling distinctly uneasy. The satellite truck was expensive but reliable. I decided to use the satellite truck for all the video feeds, and IP connectivity for backup.

The exception was the BeHere camera, which required a local encoding setup. The encoded feed of this camera had to be sent back to RBN via IP. We decided to send this encoded feed two ways, one via satellite IP connectivity and the other via traditional Internet connectivity. This gave us some redundancy; satellite IP connectivity had not been extensively tested by the PSSI or RBN. If the satellite IP connectivity failed, we had the local connectivity to fall back on.

Production

Excessive on-site production wasn't necessary; most of the video feeds were coming directly from the existing production. The wide shot had to be provided by my crew, as well as a camera and lighting setup for the potential interviews. A small editing system also needed to be provided. We brought two cameras, a lightweight portable camera for the interviews, and a higher quality camera for the wide shot.

For the audio feed, enough equipment to supply a good live mix had to be supplied. This equipment included a pair of ambient mics, a good quality mixer, and an audio signal multiprocessor to treat the mix. We also brought a trunk full of audio and video cables and adapters to deal with the eventualities that always crop up at a live broadcast. In addition, because there would be a small local LAN on site, some networking equipment and lots of cable were also brought. In fact, we brought a 1,000-foot box of Cat5 cable — we used it all.

For a full list of all the equipment used, see the "U2 Broadcast Equipment List."

U2 Broadcast Equipment List

The U2 broadcast from Notre Dame University involved a fairly typical amount of equipment on-site. Thanks to understanding airline personnel and light packing by the crew, much of the equipment came along on the plane. You can imagine the look on the luggage examiners when we tried to explain what a raid array was. Thankfully, the rest was shipped on the ground.

The equipment rack that was shipped included the following:

✦ 2 Fuhrman power conditioners

✦ Rane 26-B splitter-mixer

Continued

Continued

- ✦ Presonus ACP-22 compressor
- ✦ Mackie 1202 mixer
- ✦ Orban Optimod 6200 Audio Processor
- ✦ Kramer Electronics video switcher
- ✦ Dual-processor video capture machine with a Miro DC-50 card, with breakout box and 36GB raid array, running Vegas Video
- ✦ Dual-processor BeHere encoding machine with BeHere card and Sound Blaster Live! audio card
- ✦ Flat-panel display
- ✦ Keyboard/mouse/monitor switcher
- ✦ Two small network hubs

Other equipment included the following:

- ✦ Sony DSR-300 camera and tripod
- ✦ Sony DVX-1000 camera and tripod
- ✦ Arri three-point lighting kit with various filters, gels, and so on.
- ✦ Video d/a
- ✦ Four wired lavaliere mikes
- ✦ Sennheiser shotgun microphone & boom, windsock and power supply
- ✦ Small pair of computer speakers for reference
- ✦ Two pairs of high-quality headphones, one Sehhneiser, one Sony
- ✦ Various cables and adapters, including:
  - Over 200 feet of audio cable
  - Over 500 feet of video cable
  - Various adapters and turnarounds
- ✦ Box of 1,000 foot of Cat5 cable for network wiring, crimping tool, Cat5 plugs
- ✦ Plenty of gaffer's tape & duct tape
- ✦ Large bottle of pain killers

In addition to all this, a satellite truck was contracted from PSSI, which included all the necessary gear to do high-quality MPEG2 encoding. The truck also included hundreds of feet of audio and video cabling that was absolutely crucial to the success of the broadcast. The other ingredient that PSSI added to the broadcast was highly-qualified and motivated engineers.

Encoding

Because most of the video feeds were going to be sent via satellite to RBN, the encoding would not be taking place on-site. Instead, the video feeds would be encoded at the RBN BOC. Doing so was preferable for a number of reasons:

✦ Encoding racks did not have to be shipped to Notre Dame, avoiding unnecessary expense and equipment wear and tear.

✦ The RBN BOC is a controlled environment with plenty of redundancy built in.

✦ Sending raw video back to RBN meant that the raw video feeds could be taped there for backup instead of having to ship expensive beta decks to the site.

The BeHere camera, however, had to be encoded on site. Because the BeHere camera is a proprietary system, the raw video feed cannot be sent via satellite. The feed must be encoded locally and sent via IP to a server. To this end, a relatively inexpensive computer was configured as a BeHere encoder, tested in Seattle, and then shipped to Notre Dame along with the rest of the production equipment. The feed was encoded and archived locally.

On site, we discovered that the camera and the encoding machines needed to be quite far apart, requiring a much longer cable. BeHere Technologies had a special 200-foot cable available — for an added premium. Needless to say, the cable had to be shipped overnight to arrive in time for the broadcast.

Any interview footage that was filmed in the days preceding the live broadcast had to be edited and encoded on-site and then FTPed to RBN. My crew edited the raw footage and exported encoded versions directly from the video-editing platform using the required encoding specifications.

Authoring

Originally, my company was slated to author a SMIL presentation to be used for showcasing the various streams. Because of the difficulty involved organizing an event of this caliber when the involved parties are separated by a nine-hour time difference, the decision was made that all authoring would be done by Tiscali, who chose to use embedded players and simple metafiles instead of SMIL.

Unfortunately, this decision would later come back to haunt Tiscali, because due to their inexperience with streaming media and live events, they made a number of basic mistakes that were ridiculously hard to correct.

Their inexperience led them to create an interface that was unintuitive and difficult to navigate. For example, when a viewer chose a stream to watch, he or she was taken to a page that contained only that stream. To view any of the other camera angles, he or she had to hit a very small back button. The reason that all the camera angles were not available on the same page remains somewhat of a mystery.

The issues were doubly complicated because some streams were to be made available to all viewers, and others were to be available to U2.com members or RealNetworks GoldPass members (now known as RealOne). Depending on the user's IP address, Tiscali was supposed to generate different pages and send viewers to different servers. What actually happened during the live event was another thing altogether.

Viewers were repeatedly asked to supply a password or join U2.com each time they went back to the page that contained all the camera angles. Even though some of the camera feeds were available free of charge, it appeared otherwise. Savvy users who simply closed the pop-up U2.com membership window could sometimes watch streams that were reserved for members. The user interface was confusing and poorly implemented, and as we were to eventually find out, it was combined with a Web hosting architecture that works fine for Web pages but terribly for live events.

Serving

All the streams originated at the RBN BOC and then split out to various distribution servers. In addition to the RBN U.S. network, streams were also split to the Tiscali master servers, which would, in turn, distribute those streams to public servers to serve European customers.

The encoded BeHere stream was sent back via IP to the same servers at RBN that were splitting out to the public servers and Tiscali servers. To enable redundancy for this stream, a small server was set up on-site, which then transmitted two streams back to RBN — one stream was sent via satellite IP multicast, the other stream was sent via unicast across the WNDU DS3.

Did It Work?

All the video and audio was delivered to RBN without a hitch. Not a single encoder failed, nor did any connectivity problems occur. RBN successfully sent all streams to the Tiscali network without a problem.

The on-site crew filmed a number of exclusive interviews with various crewmembers and fans, edited and encoded them, and sent them back up to RBN for on-demand distribution. The satellite IP connectivity worked flawlessly, and there were no problems sending the BeHere camera stream via the Internet.

The Tiscali redirection scheme left a lot to be desired. To begin with, every viewer could see all the streams, regardless of whether they were U2.com or GoldPass members or not. Initially, all viewers were sent to the European Tiscali servers, including audience members from the United States. Solving these problems proved to be unnecessarily complex.

The problem was two-fold. First, the Tiscali site used cookies to plant information on viewers' browsers, and these cookies were being set wrong from the start of the broadcast. The problem was that we couldn't simply reset the cookies.

Second, the Tiscali Web architecture is designed as a multilevel cache. Therefore, correcting errors was not instantaneous; doing so was a time-consuming process that involved waiting for the corrected pages to propagate throughout the Tiscali network. Not only that, unless viewers cleared their browser cache, they never received the pages with the corrected links — essentially locking some viewers out of the broadcast for the duration of the event.

Even with all the problems that were encountered, the Webcast was, by all indications, a success, with over a quarter of a million accesses and over 10,000 concurrent streams from the U.S. servers alone on the first night. The full show was rebroadcast the following day and then placed on-demand for U2.com and GoldPass members for three weeks.

Still — it must be asked — how many people would have seen the show had there not been the redirection problems?

What Went Wrong — What Went Right

I have mentioned numerous times that things always go wrong during live broadcasts, and this Webcast was no exception. In fact, at some points, it seemed that this event was plagued and perhaps was not meant to happen. Then again, most producers always feel this way leading up to a broadcast. In fact, if everything runs too smoothly, that is when you really get nervous.

This broadcast started out with an extremely tight window in which to get everything arranged. The fact that everything worked on the night of the show is a testament to all the people involved, especially when you consider what went wrong:

✦ The fiber connectors to the WNDU fiber lines had to be custom ordered from a mail-order catalog, delaying connectivity testing by a week.

✦ Business terms could not be definitively decided upon until eight days before the broadcast. Without business terms, we had no budget. Without a budget, vendors could not be booked, flights and accommodations could not be reserved, crew could not be booked, and so on.

✦ Even after the business terms were agreed upon, contractual haggling continued until four days before the broadcast. The constant haggling changed the equipment requirements on an almost daily basis. In fact, the haggling continued up to 45 minutes before the broadcast, giving me a king-sized headache.

✦ The band's representatives threatened to cancel the broadcast numerous times. I was forced to have two cell phones going at all times — one for the RealNetworks London office, one for communication with the RBN BOC.

✦ The World Trade Center attack occurred during the preparation stage for the concert, making flying and shipping arrangements nearly impossible and taking the best part of a week out of everyone's schedules.

✦ U2 production crew only provided PAL SDI video feeds — complicating equipment issues.

✦ The satellite company (PSSI) could not get IP connectivity working reliably as late as four days before the broadcast.

✦ The equipment rack missed its shipping connection, delaying its arrival to the following day. Then, if that was not bad enough, the equipment rack was delayed a second time, making everyone on-site extremely nervous.

✦ Connectivity was on opposite side of arena, requiring a 150 yard Cat5 cable run across the lighting catwalk.

✦ U2.com representatives were completely unsatisfied with the broadcast plan and insisted that more satellite time be booked for testing and that more crew be flown out.

✦ WNDU decided that they had to be paid in advance for the connectivity, in cash, or they would disconnect us. This, of course, had not been discussed previously.

✦ Connectivity (WNDU DS3) went down completely for eight hours the day before the show — this was *after* they had been paid.

✦ Tiscali could not replicate the streams from RBN as late as one day before the event.

✦ The preroll advertisement that Tiscali had sold to offset their investment was not shown. They were given the code to create a multiclip .ram file, but did not have time to implement it for the live broadcast (it was later attached to the front of the on-demand streams).

✦ Someone on the opposite phase of the same satellite transponder was sending such a strong signal that the IP connectivity did not work up until three hours before going live.

✦ One hour before showtime, one of the video feeds from the U2 crew failed. The failure was in U2's equipment. The crew scrambled and got the video feed working again in 20 minutes.

✦ The U2 production crew changed the video feeds to color instead of black and white because the projection screens were not used during some songs. The band insisted that the video footage had to be black and white. 45 minutes before kickoff, the band threatened (again) to cancel the event. Eventually band management intervened and decided color was just fine. (Removing color from NTSC feeds would have been simple — but not from PAL SDI feeds due to the scarcity of PAL equipment in the U.S.).

This short list does not even begin to cover the minutiae of the event. There was a lot of inexperience involved in this event that led to many misunderstandings and much frustration on the part of the people who knew what had to be done. Tempers flared often, and harsh words were exchanged.

At the end of the day, however, everyone feels better after a successful broadcast. After the broadcast was up and running, the Webcast ran smoothly. Band management watched the streamed event instead of the live show. The audio quality was unparalleled. Best of all, the band put on a superb show that left the entire audience, both in attendance and online, entirely rapt.

Summary

As stressful as this event was, nothing beats combing through the newsgroups the next day and reading that your broadcast had "awesome audio quality" or that someone's player "never even rebuffered!" Certainly some viewers were frustrated by the bad links that were distributed, and the labyrinthine Web site design, but for the most part, a lot of people got to see and/or hear one of their favorite bands playing a great show.

✦ Multiplexing MPEG2 feeds over a single satellite transponder is a relatively cost-efficient way of sending video long distances.

✦ IP via satellite is tricky but doable; As soon as the feed is up it stays that way, provided someone on the same transponder isn't sending too strong of a signal.

✦ Never, ever, ever let anyone else control the access to your streams, particularly an ISP who has never done a large-scale live event.

✦ Don't let intermediaries come between the production crews. Let the audio folks talk to the audio folks and the video folks talk to the video folks. The business people should stay out of the conversation.

✦ Make sure that a technical person is present at all the business meetings and design meetings to make sure that unrealistic promises are not made and that the production crew knows exactly what is expected.

✦ Think twice before agreeing to do an event with less than six weeks before the event — I know I will from now on.

✦ If you don't get a large enough budget, politely refuse the broadcast. You'll end up spending the money anyway and then having to extract the money from the client.

✦   ✦   ✦

Appendixes

Streaming Media File Sizes

Streaming media is an amazing achievement because of the drastic file size reduction that must occur to be able to stream the files in real time. However, as the number or length of the files increases, the amount of storage and bandwidth required also rises.

Table A-1 lists a number of different common bit rates used in streaming media and some of the different numbers associated with each bit rate. Taking the simplest example, a small 22 Kbps file intended for a 28.8 modem viewer may seem innocuous on its own, but if over 50 people try to listen or watch the same stream concurrently, the resulting bandwidth is enough to plug a T-1 line.

Obviously, as the target bit rate increases, the numbers also increase. SureStream files and Multiple Bit Rate files are particularly nasty, in that the overall bit rate is actually the sum the bit rates of all the streams contained within the file.

Table A-1 gives you an idea of the storage and bandwidth requirements you may encounter with your streaming media.

Table A-1
Streaming Media File Sizes

Bit Rate (Connectivity)	File Size per one minute file	Amount of storage per hour's worth of content	Amount of storage per GB	Maximum concurrent streams per T-1 line (1.5 Mbps)	Approximate maximum concurrent streams 10 Mbps leg (LAN)	Connectivity required for 100 concurrent streams (in Mbps)	Connectivity required for 1000 concurrent streams (in Mbps)
22 (28.8 modem)	165 KB	9.67MB	106 hrs	52	340	2.2	21.5
34 (56K modem)	255 KB	15MB	68.5 hrs	34	220	3.3	33
45 (single ISDN)	338 KB	19.8MB	51.8 hrs	24	166	4.4	44
80 (dual ISDN)	600 KB	35.2MB	29 hrs	14	93	7.8	78
150 (corporate LAN)	1.1MB	66MB	15.5 hrs	7	50	14.7	146
225 (256K DSL line)	1.65MB	99MB	10.4 hrs	5	33	22	220
350 (384K cable/ DSL line)	2.56MB	153.8MB	6.7 hrs	3	21	34.2	342

Bit Rate (Connectivity)	File Size per one minute file	Amount of storage per hour's worth of content	Amount of storage per GB	Maximum concurrent streams per T-1 line (1.5 Mbps)	Approximate maximum concurrent streams 10 Mbps leg (LAN)	Connectivity required for 100 concurrent streams (in Mbps)	Connectivity required for 1000 concurrent streams (in Mbps)
RealSystem 28/56K Sure Stream (34 + 20 + 15 + 12 = 81 kbps)	608 KB	35.6MB	28.8 hrs	34 – 52, depending on users	220 – 340, depending on users	3.3 (max)	33 (max)
RealSystem 28/56/80K SureStream (140 Kbps) or Windows Media Video for 28/ 56/ISDN (139 Kbps)	1MB	62MB	16.6 hrs	14 – 50, depending on users	93 – 340, depending on users	7.8 (max)	78 (max)

Recommended Target Bit Rates and Audio Settings

Choosing your encoder settings involves striking a delicate balance between the highest possible quality and the maximum bit rate that your audience can safely receive.

If you're streaming a live broadcast, long files, or to people who are geographically far away, be conservative with your bit rate. The higher the bit rate, the more difficult it is to sustain for an extended period. Exactly what this maximum bit rate should be is a point of some contention between the platforms.

After you've chosen your target bit rate, you have to decide how much of that to allot to the audio. Whatever you don't use for audio is used by the video codec. Although using the lowest possible audio bit rate is tempting, you should be aware that audiences are far more tolerant of low quality video when the audio quality is acceptable.

Maximum Bit Rates

In general, you should always leave 20 to 30 percent of the total available bit rate for error correction, transport overheads, and other Internet activity. Leaving this amount provides a sufficiently large safety margin for smooth streaming.

Table B-1 lists the maximum recommended bit rates for various connection speeds. For the most part, the recommended maximum target bit rates are very similar for both the RealSystem and Windows Media platforms, with Windows

Media Technologies tending to slightly more aggressive at the lower bit rates. Windows Media Technology does offer presets with slightly lower total bit rates if you decide you want to play it safe.

Note   Apple does not publish recommended maximum bit rates for streaming QuickTime files.

Table B-1
Recommended Maximum Target Bit Rates

Connection Speed	RealSystem*	Windows Media Technology**
28.8 modem	20 Kbps	24 Kbps
56K modem	34 Kbps	37 Kbps
Single ISDN	45 Kbps	50 Kbps
Dual ISDN	80 Kbps	100 Kbps
Corporate LAN	150 Kbps	150 Kbps
256K DSL	225 Kbps	225 Kbps
384K DSL	350 Kbps	350 Kbps

* Quoted from the RealSystem Production Guide

** Taken from the default Windows Media Encoder settings

Audio Codecs

The audio codec you choose also impacts video quality, because the video codec is allotted the leftover bandwidth. The higher the bit rate of your audio codec, the smaller the number of bits left over for the video stream. When choosing your audio codec, keep in mind that audio quality affects how people perceive video. Low-quality video is far more tolerable with a decent soundtrack.

You also choose a codec that is appropriate for your content. Voice codecs should be used only on files that have no music whatsoever or music that is used only in the background. If you're unsure, stick with a music codec.

Tables B-2 and B-3 list codec suggestions for different connection speeds and different types of content.

Note   The following choices are entirely subjective. In particular, I prefer higher fidelity to frequency response. I find that the codecs with higher frequency responses have a "lisping" quality that I find distracting. Therefore, I opt for lower sampling rates on the Windows Media codecs. For low bit rates, I recommend mono codecs. Your mileage may vary.

Table B-2
Recommended Audio Codecs — Voice Content

Connection Speed	QuickTime	RealSystem	Windows Media Technology
28.8 modem voice	Qualcomm PureVoice SmartRate, mono, 16bit, 11,025	16 Kbps voice	16 Kbps ACELP.net
28.8 modem, video with voiceover	Qualcomm PureVoice Half Rate, mono, 16bit, 11,025,	6.5 Kbps voice	6.5 Kbps ACELP.net
56K modem voice	Qualcomm PureVoice SmartRate, mono, 16bit, 11,025	16 Kbps voice	16 Kbps ACELP.net
56K modem, video with voiceover	Qualcomm PureVoice Half Rate, mono, 16bit, 11,025,	8.5 Kbps voice	8.5 Kbps ACELP.net
Single ISDN voice mono	Qualcomm PureVoice SmartRate, mono, 16bit, 22.050	32 Kbps voice	WMA 32 Kbps, 44 KHz,
Single ISDN, video with voiceover	Qualcomm PureVoice SmartRate, mono, 16bit, 11,025	8.5 Kbps voice	8.5 Kbps ACELP.net
Dual ISDN voice mono	Qualcomm PureVoice SmartRate, mono, 16bit, 44,100	64 Kbps voice	WMA 48 Kbps, 44 KHz,
Dual ISDN, video with voiceover	Qualcomm PureVoice SmartRate, mono, 16bit, 11,025	16 Kbps voice	16 Kbps ACELP.net
Corporate LAN voice	Qualcomm PureVoice SmartRate, mono, 16bit, 44,100	64 Kbps voice	WMA 48 Kbps, 44 KHz, mono

Continued

Table B-2 *(continued)*

Connection Speed	QuickTime	RealSystem	Windows Media Technology
Corporate LAN, video with voiceover	Qualcomm PureVoice SmartRate, mono, 16bit, 22.050	32 Kbps voice	WMA 32 Kbps, 44 KHz, mono
256K DSL and above voice	Qualcomm PureVoice SmartRate, mono, 16bit, 44,100	64 Kbps voice	WMA 48 Kbps, 44 KHz, mono
256K DSL and above, video with voiceover	Qualcomm PureVoice SmartRate, mono, 16bit, 22.050	32 Kbps voice	WMA 32 Kbps s, 44 KHz, mono

Table B-3
Recommended Audio Codecs — Music Content

Connection Speed	QuickTime	RealSystem	Windows Media Technology
28.8K modem music	Qdesign Music 2, 20 Kbps, 16bit mono or stereo	20 Kbps music (mono or RA8 stereo)	WMA V8, 20 Kbps, 22 KHz, mono or stereo
28.8K modem, video with music content	Qdesign Music 2, 8 Kbps, 16bit mono	8 Kbps music	WMA V8, 8 Kbps, 8 KHz
56K modem music	Qdesign Music 2, 32 Kbps, 16bit stereo	32 Kbps music RA8 stereo	WMA V8, 32 Kbps, 32 KHz, stereo
56K modem, video with music content	Qdesign Music 2, 10 or 12 Kbps, 16bit mono	8 Kbps or 11 Kbps music	WMA V8, 10 Kbps, 11 KHz or 12 Kbps, 16 KHz mono
Single ISDN music	Qdesign Music 2, 40 Kbps, 16bit stereo	44 Kbps music (mono or RA8 stereo)	WMA V8, 40 Kbps, 32 KHz, stereo
Single ISDN, video with music content	Qdesign Music 2, 10 or 12 Kbps	11 Kbps music	WMA V8, 10 Kbps, 11 KHz or 12 Kbps, 16 KHz mono
Dual ISDN music	Qdesign Music 2, 48 Kbps, 16bit stereo	64 Kbps RA8 stereo	WMA V8, 64 Kbps, 44 KHz or 80 Kbps, 44 KHz, stereo

Connection Speed	QuickTime	RealSystem	Windows Media Technology
Dual ISDN, video with music content	Qdesign Music 2, 20 Kbps	20 Kbps RA8 stereo	WMA V8, 20 Kbps, 22 KHz, mono or stereo
Corporate LAN music	Qdesign Music 2, 48 Kbps, 16bit stereo	96 Kbps RA8 stereo	WMA V8, 80 Kbps, 44 KHz or 96 Kbps, 44 KHz, stereo
Corporate LAN, video with music content	Qdesign Music 2, 32 Kbps, 16bit stereo	32 Kbps RA8 stereo	WMA V8, 32 Kbps, 32 KHz, stereo
256K DSL and above music	Qdesign Music 2, 48 Kbps, 16bit stereo	96 Kbps RA8 stereo	WMA V8, 80 Kbps, 44 KHz or 96 Kbps, 44 KHz, stereo
256K DSL and above, video with music content	Qdesign Music 2, 32 Kbps, 16bit stereo	32 Kbps RA8 stereo	WMA V8, 32 Kbps, 32 KHz, stereo

Note   Mono codecs are always higher fidelity and generally have a higher frequency range, but obviously they're not stereo.

✦   ✦   ✦

A Simple Audio/Video Production Suite

If you're serious about trying to produce high-quality streaming media files, the fact is that you're going to have to invest in some equipment. The bad news is you're going to have to spend some money; the good news is you don't have to break the bank to look and sound like the pros.

But before you start shopping, you have to figure out where you're going to put all your new toys. Although stacking them up on your desk is tempting, you really should find a dedicated location for your production suite. If you plan on shooting video, you should also have a dedicated video shoot room.

As soon as you've earmarked locations for the equipment, your next step is to break out the credit card. If you know exactly what you want (or if you decide to buy anything listed here), you can put those Internet search engines to work and find the lowest price. However, you may want to buy from your local music store or camera shop — if the equipment doesn't work, it will be easier to bring it back.

Everything listed in this appendix has been chosen because of my own experience and the price-to-performance ratio. Plenty of other makes and models are available, and I'm sure that they can do the job as well or better. Also, I've tried to pick manufacturers that have a proven track record. However, situations change, as do prices, model numbers, and features. This guide is meant to help you get started.

Location

If at all possible, you should reserve a separate, closed space for your production suite. Having such a space is important not only for noise considerations during recording, but also for noise that your co-workers must suffer while you play your recordings over and over again.

Of course, make sure that the space you choose has plenty of electricity and ventilation, because all this gear heats up a room quickly. If you can't spare a separate room, you can do wonders with portable *acoustic baffles*. Acoustic baffles are sound-absorbent panels, often made of some sort of foam, which improve the acoustics of a room by absorbing sound that would otherwise be reflected.

Audio considerations

One problem with traditional office spaces is that the rooms are small and square, both of which are ill suited to recording. Small, square rooms have bad frequency and echo characteristics. You can make the best of a bad situation by using:

✦ **Acoustic foam.** You can significantly attenuate the echo by attaching acoustic foam tiles to the wall. Even tiny spaces can be made acceptable with enough foam tiles.

✦ **Bass traps.** Small rooms are succeptible to bass build-up, particularly in the corners. Custom bass traps help solve this. You can purchase bass traps in numerous configurations.

✦ **Fabric.** Hanging draperies on bare walls improves the sound characteristics of small rooms. Placing a tablecloth on the table also helps.

Another problematic issue is ventilation noise. Our brains tune out white noise sources, such as air conditioners and computer fans. If you have noise reduction capabilities in your audio editing software, you can use the software to remove the unwanted noise, but a better approach is to remove the noise sources. Installing low-noise ventilation diffusers and ducting is the best solution, though expensive. Otherwise, turn off the ventilation during recording sessions if you can.

Another problem to consider is co-worker noise. Consider buying a recording sign for use during recording sessions. Not only does the sign add an air of authenticity to the proceedings, but it also discourages excessive noisemaking.

Video considerations

If you're going to be shooting indoors, reserve a room for your video shoots. Video shoots require a lot of elbowroom, ceiling height, ventilation, and electricity. As with the audio studio, noise is always a problem, so try to choose a location as far away from foot traffic as possible.

Being able to hang your lights from the ceiling is a luxury few of us can afford; however, getting wiring and equipment off the floor helps a lot. Even if you're not going to hang your lights, you need to have a lot of headroom for ventilation purposes — lights heat up a room *very* quickly.

Audio Equipment

Audio equipment is very reasonably priced these days, and the results obtained from better equipment are immediately noticeable. Much of the processing that has been discussed in this book can be done in your audio editing software, but you may want to consider some external hardware regardless. At the minimum, you will need a good set of monitors and a microphone. You should also consider treating yourself to a mixing desk and a compressor.

Note   Prices listed here are manufacturer's list prices — in general they are quite a bit cheaper in stores (as much as half off list price), and many of these items can be found on auction sites such as eBay (www.ebay.com) or digibid (www.digibid.com).

Monitors

If you cannot accurately hear what you are producing, you cannot effectively apply the processing that is necessary. You should invest in a good set of monitors as well as a good set of headphones to spare people in the area from having to listen to the same thing over and over again.

I've only listed powered monitors, because powered monitors do not require a separate amplifier — they're self-*powered*.

Powered monitors

✦ **Genelec 1030a.** Definitely overkill for most applications, but the author won't leave home without them. $2200/pr, www.genelec.com.

✦ **Mackie HR824.** Another great Mackie product. Again, probably overkill but a lot of fun. $1600/pr, www.mackie.com.

✦ JBL LS25P. Good sounding, medium-priced monitors. $800/pr, www.jbl.com.

✦ **Yamaha MS10.** Good sounding, aggressivley priced monitors from Yamaha. $340/pr, www.yamaha.com/proaudio/index.htm.

✦ **Cambridge SoundWorks "SoundWorks."** Excellent value for the money in a multimedia speaker setup. $99, www.hifi.com.

Headphones

✦ **Sony 7500 series.** The 7506 are studio reference headphones and excellent; the 7505 and 7502 are cheaper but still very good. $160, $125, and $99 respectively. `bpgprod.sel.sony.com`.

✦ **AKG K240.** Standard studio reference headphones, excellent sound. $220, `www.akg.com`.

Note Studio reference headphones are designed to reproduce the sound *accurately*, as opposed to flattering the sound with exaggerated bass or high frequency response.

Microphones

Don't expect to create great sounding streaming media if all you have is a cheap plastic microphone. Microphones come in all shapes and sizes. At the very least, buy yourself a good dynamic mic for all-around use. You may also want a lavaliere mic or two for video shoots, a shotgun mic for boom use during video shoots, or some high-quality condenser mics for studio work.

Dynamic microphones

✦ **Shure SM-58.** Without a doubt, the most famous microphone ever. Not only are they fabulous all-around microphones, these microphones are so durable you can practically hammer nails with them. No microphone collection is complete without one. $188, `www.shure.com`.

✦ **Shure SM-7B.** One of the standards in studio broadcasting. These mics are particularly prized because they do not exhibit the proximity effect and are practically immune to popping. $600, `www.shure.com`.

Note Microphone popping is discussed in Chapter 8.

✦ **Electrovoice RE-20.** Another industry standard, also very good with proximity and plosive consonants. $800, `www.electrovoice.com`.

Condenser microphones

✦ **Audio Technical 4033.** A great sounding condenser microphone that is surprisingly good for the price. $549, `www.audiotechnica.com`.

✦ **AKG 414.** A wonderful microphone with legendary clarity in the top end. $1000, `www.akg.com`.

Lavaliere microphones

✦ **Audio Technica 803b.** A great all-around lavaliere microphone at a reasonable price. $190, `www.audiotechnica.com`.

✦ **Shure MX 183.** A great sounding sounding lavaliere mic with classic shure performance. $275, www.shure.com.

Shotgun microphones

✦ **Sennheiser ME66.** This microphone delivers great performance for the price, but it can be very sensitive to handling noise. $250, www.sennheiser.com.

✦ **Audio Technica AT835B.** Audio Technica delivers the goods once again. $329, www.audiotechnica.com.

Mixing desks

You may think that you don't need a mixing desk. Then one day your boss comes in and tells you that you have to record a meeting, in which you need four microphones, audio from a computer, and a CD player for incidental music. You need a mixing desk.

✦ **Mackie 1202 VLZ Pro.** Some may say that I'm biased, because Mackie is a local company where I'm from. But the fact is Mackie makes excellent sounding equipment that can take an unusual amount of punishment. Another indispensable piece of equipment. $489, www.mackie.com.

✦ **Behringer MX802A.** Purists may scoff, but Behringer definitely excels in the bang-for-the-buck category. $125, www.behringer.com.

✦ **Spirit Folio RW5353.** Extremely small footprint, very portable, good sounding mixer. $199, www.soundcraft.com.

Hardware

For the most part, your recording and processing can be done in software. One piece of equipment that you should invest in, however, is a compressor. Compressors are invaluable during live broadcasts and minimize your day-to-day level adjustments. If you plan on doing any recording in the field, you should also invest in a DAT or MiniDisc recorder.

Compressors

✦ **Presonus Blue Max.** It's tiny, it's cheap, it's blue, and it has presets. What more could you ask for? $199, www.presonus.com.

✦ **FMR RNC 1773.** The RNC stands for "Really Nice Compressor." Has a "SuperNice" mode that is unbelievable, considering the price of this unit. $199, www.fmraudio.com.

✦ **dbx 266.** A nice sounding budget version of the classic dbx compressor. $189, www.dbxpro.com.

DAT Recorders

✦ **Tascam DA-P1.** A great portable DAT machine; another workhorse in the industry. You can find other portables, but none that offer the same level of functionality for the price. $2200, `www.tascam.com`.

✦ **Sony PCM M1.** A tiny portable DAT machine with some cool built in dynamics control. $1060, `bpgprod.sel.sony.com`.

Extras

You can buy plenty of extras, but you need to resist the temptation to buy gadgets until you've lived with your basic system awhile and have identified specific needs. You are going to have to buy some of the following:

✦ **Cables.** If you're not comfortable with a soldering iron, buy manufactured cables. Don't bother buying cheap versions from a hobby store. Buy them from a cable manufacturer or an audiovisual catalog. `www.sweetwater.com`, `www.avcable.com`.

✦ **Microphone stands.** Don't leave your microphones lying on the floor or stuffed in a drawer. Put them on a stand where they belong. Using a microphone stand drastically cuts down on handling noise.

✦ **Pop screen.** If you buy a high-quality condenser microphone, you should invest in a pop screen to reduce plosive consonants and to keep spittle off your expensive microphones. I'm not kidding.

✦ **Equipment rack.** Don't stack your equipment up on a desk. That's how it gets knocked off a desk and irreparably damaged.

✦ **Adapters.** Think like a boy scout — be prepared.

Video Equipment

Purchasing video equipment is costly. The truth is that you really do get what you pay for with most video equipment. Prices have been coming down considerably lately as a result of the explosive consumer demand, and many of the higher-end consumer cameras are entirely suitable for streaming media applications (though not broadcast).

Cameras

With the number of cameras available, the camera that's best for you depends largely on your budget. Make sure that you make a list of features you require (FireWire, manual adjustments, and so on.) Don't be sold on useless features that you don't need (100x digital zoom, in-camera effects, and so on).

Here's a list of good, solid, cameras that can give you years of dependable service.

✦ **Canon GL-1.** Excellent entry-level prosumer camera. $2699, www.canondv.com.

✦ **Canon XL-1.** The GL-1's big brother. Good all-around camera. $4699, www.canondv.com.

✦ **Sony DCR VX-2000.** The successor to the ubiquitous VX-1000. $2899, bpgprod.sel.sony.com.

✦ **Panasonic AG-DVC200.** Very, very nice camera with 1/2 CCDs. $8799, www.panasonic.com.

Extras

In addition to a camera, you're going to need a few extras to round out your video kit.

✦ **Tripod.** Bogen makes a whole line of excellent tripods. Buy the best one you can afford that supports your camera's weight. From about $150.

✦ **Studio1 Productions XLR-PRO.** Consumer-grade DV camcorders do not have professional-quality audio inputs on them. This gadget adds one or two XLR inputs, depending on the model. You need one of these. $249, www.studio1productions.com.

✦ **Lighting kit.** If you plan on shooting indoors, buy a simple lighting kit. Lowel makes a number of different kits ideal for basic lighting setups From about $500 on up, www.lowel.com.

✦ **Reflector (bounce board).** Reflectors are extremely valuable when shooting outdoors when you want to throw a bit of fill light on your subject. You can buy portable, folding, dual-sided versions that reflect different amounts of light from each side.

✦ **Good quality TV monitor.** Not absolutely necessary, but sometimes seeing your video on an interlaced TV monitor instead of the small screen your video editing software uses is nice. A monitor is also very useful if you're going to process your video using a video proc amp.

✦ **Proc amp.** Very useful for adjusting your video quality. Most video editing software and capture cards have software versions, but you can't beat a good proc amp. Studio 1 Productions makes excellent single and dual channel versions.

✦ **Cables.** As with the audio cables, don't buy cheap ones. You will end up replacing them and wishing that you had done so sooner.

Computer Hardware & Software

Deciding what platform you're going to base your production suite on is the first step. Both Mac and PC have valid reasons for being your platform of choice. Once upon a time the PC was a poor substitute when it came to multimedia creation, but these days it competes on just about every level. Appropriate multimedia software is also available on both platforms.

Hardware

In computer hardware, you can't have too much storage or a processor that's too fast. In general, you may want to stay away from the bleeding edge of technology, because hardware and software manufacturers may not have tested their wares on the latest releases. Try to stay a couple of notches back on the hardware front, for price and performance considerations.

Hard drives

As far as drives are concerned, you're fine with ATA drives if you're capturing DV content, because your maximum data rate is only about 4MB/s. If you're building a full-screen uncompressed quality capture system, you may want to consider SCSI drives to sustain the much higher data rates.

Hard drive technology has improved so much in the last few years it hardly bears mentioning, but make sure that you go for drives with a minimum 7200 rpm rotation speed, or even the 10K rpm drives. Not only does this help ensure that your video captures do not drop frames but also speeds up your rendering.

Sound cards

If you're setting up a full video-editing solution, you may have high-quality audio inputs built into your video capture system. If not, or if you're setting up an audio-only system, consider the following sound cards:

✦ **Echo Audio GINA.** Excellent system offering two inputs, eight outputs, all balanced, in a breakout box with a headphone jack. $495, www.echoaudio.com.

✦ **Echo Audio MIA.** Superb audio quality plus balanced inputs and outputs using ¼ inch connectors. Hallelujah! No more crappy ⅛ inch connectors! 24bit/96 kHz compatible, multiple virtual outputs, and all for under $250. Need I go on? $249, www.echoaudio.com.

✦ **SoundBlaster Live!.** Audio purists have been known to scoff at the mighty SoundBlaster, but it no longer deserves the reputation it once had. For the price, they're pretty darned good, but I really despise those ⅛ inch connectors. $59, www.soundblaster.com.

Video capture cards

If you're setting up a DV capture system, FireWire is definitely the way to go. Not only does it transfer the video digitally, but deck control is also built into the FireWire protocol. As long as your camera has a FireWire output (and you should make sure that it does), you can automate your captures, which is a real time saver.

If you're capturing from analog sources, you'll need a card that does analog inputs, and if you're planning on streaming live, you're going to need a card that captures uncompressed video at the screen size you need.

Unfortunately, most high-quality capture boards tend to use MJPEG compression, making them unsuitable for live applications. However, budget priced capture cards have improved quite a bit in recent times.

Caution

You should do extensive research into whatever card you plan to buy. Video capture cards are notorious for being incredibly finicky about what motherboards and chipsets they are compatible with. Some require specific PCI slots, disc controllers, and so on. The best resources for questions such as these are the user forums for each manufacturer.

FireWire cards

Because FireWire is a standard and FireWire cards are simple data transfer cards, quality doesn't really come into the equation. Make sure the card is OHCI-compliant.

✦ **ADS Pyro.** $49, `www.adstech.com`.

✦ **Adaptec FireConnect 4300.** $69, `www.adaptec.com`.

Budget/live capture cards

✦ **Winnov Videum series.** Winnov has a number of cards at various price points, all of which provide good quality. From $129, `www.winnov.com`.

✦ **Viewcast Osprey series.** Ubiquitous in the industry, Osprey has a number of cards, all of which are suitable for live streaming applications. From $99, `www.viewcast.com`.

Mid-price/high-quality capture cards

✦ **DPS Reality.** Unbelievable quality and a great breakout box. $2800, `www.dps.com`.

✦ **Pinnacle Systems DV 500 Plus.** Very good image quality, native DV codec support. $999, `www.pinnaclesys.com`.

✦ **Matrox RT2500.** Very good image quality, real-time hardware effects rendering, native DV support. $899, `www.matrox.com`.

✦ **Aurora Fuse.** Very good quality Mac capture card. $99, `www.auroravideosys.com`.

Software

At a minimum, you're going to need good audio and video editing software. Many video editing packages come with rudimentary audio editing capabilities that can handle quick fixes but are insufficient to really give you optimal quality.

Your software choices are determined to some extent by the platform you're working on.

Audio editing

✦ **Sound Forge.** Windows-only, author's favorite. See the trial version on CD. $499, www.sonicfoundry.com.

✦ **BIAS Peak.** Excellent Mac audio editing software. Check out the trial version on CD. From $99 for Peak Lite. www.bias-inc.com.

✦ **CoolEdit.** Very cool shareware audio editor. Slightly funky interface but does just about everything you need. $69, www.syntrillium.com.

Video Editing

✦ **Vegas Video.** Another solid product from Sonic Foundry (makers of Sound Forge). This software features real-time rendering, rendering directly to streaming versions of files, AVI 2.0 support, and so on. $599, www.sonicfoundry.com.

✦ **Video Factory.** Unbelievable functionality for the price. You even get a FireWire card for under $100. However, this product won't let you customize your streaming media presets. Try out the trial version on the CD. $99, www.sonicfoundry.com.

✦ **Premiere 6.0.** The latest version of Premiere includes excellent batch rendering functionality and AVI 2.0 support. Premiere 6.0 comes bundled with many decent capture cards. $599, www.adobe.com.

✦ **Final Cut Pro.** Excellent Mac video editing platform. $999, www.apple.com.

✦   ✦   ✦

What's on the CD-ROM

The CD-ROM included with this book is packed full of great software and some examples that you should find useful. The software included is as follows:

◆ Demo versions of Sonic Foundry's Video Factory, Batch Converter, and Sound Forge XP for Windows

◆ Trial version of Bias, Inc.'s Peak audio editing software for the Mac

◆ BBEdit and BBEdit Lite, text editors for the Mac

◆ UltraEdit text editor for the PC

In addition to the software, you also get:

◆ Files to use along with the Quick Start section

◆ Sample video files for encoding

◆ Sample HTML pages with embedded players, with and without JavaScript controls

◆ Examples of encoded streaming media files

◆ Sample RealText and RealPix files showcasing things you can do in each technology

◆ Sample SMIL files

By now you've probably already torn open the plastic envelope and installed every single piece of software offered on the CD-ROM. In fact, you're probably not even going to read this appendix. However, in the interest of completeness, here's what you'll find on the next few pages:

◆ System Requirements

◆ Using the CD with Windows and Macintosh

◆ What's on the CD

◆ Troubleshooting

System Requirements

If you've purchased your computer in the past two or three years, there should be no reason why you shouldn't be able to run any of the software packages included on the CD-ROM. If you're unsure about whether or not your machine is up to the task, here are a few guidelines:

Non-platform-specific guidelines:

✦ You can never have too much RAM. Though most applications will run with a minimum of 32MB, you really need at least 64MB to do live encoding, and if you're running Windows 2000 you should have at least 128MB.

✦ You can never have too much hard drive space. Some of the programs on this CD-ROM require up to 25MB of free space to install, and if you plan on doing any video capture you're going to need a lot of free hard drive space. At a minimum, you should have a 9GB hard drive with plenty of free space; if you have 20–40GB free, so much the better.

✦ The faster your processor, the better. Most of the included applications will run on a lowly 120 MHz processor, but if you plan on doing any live encoding you need a Pentium III or better on the PC platform or a 400 MHz processor or better on the Mac platform.

✦ You'll also need some sort of soundcard and speakers to be able to work with audio. Any soundcard and speakers will do, but better quality equipment produces better quality streaming media files.

To learn more about soundcards, please refer to Chapter 6 or Appendix C.

✦ If you plan on capturing video, you'll need a video capture card. Any capture card will do, but as with a soundcard, better quality capture cards produce higher quality streaming media files. You do not need a video capture card if you only plan on working with audio or with pre-existing digital video content.

To learn more about video capture cards, please refer to Chapter 6 or Appendix C.

✦ Of course, you'll need a CD-ROM and a modem or Ethernet card to access the Internet.

Using the CD with Windows

I'm hoping that you've installed software from a CD-ROM before, so that the following steps are second nature, but if not, here's how to access the CD-ROM:

1. Insert the CD into your computer's CD-ROM drive.

2. A window appears with the following options: Install, Explore, eBook, Links and Exit.

   Install: Gives you the option to install the supplied software and/or the author-created samples on the CD-ROM.

   Explore: Allows you to view the contents of the CD-ROM in its directory structure.

   Links: Opens a hyperlinked page of Web sites.

   Exit: Closes the autorun window.

If you do not have autorun enabled or if the autorun window does not appear, follow the steps below to access the CD.

1. **Click Start ⇨ Run.**

2. **In the dialog box that appears, type** d:\setup.exe, **where** d **is the letter of your CD-ROM drive.** This will bring up the autorun window described above.

3. **Choose the Install, Explore, Links, or Exit option from the menu.** (See Step 2 in the preceding list for a description of these options.)

Using the CD with the Mac OS

As per the section above, I'm hoping that you've installed software off a CD-ROM before. In case you haven't, follow these steps:

1. **Insert the CD into your CD-ROM drive.**

2. **Double-click the icon for the CD after it appears on the desktop.**

3. **Most programs come with installers; for those, simply open the program's folder on the CD and double-click the Install or Installer icon.** Note: To install some programs, just drag the program's folder from the CD window and drop it on your hard drive icon.

What's on the CD-ROM

The following sections provide a summary of the software and other materials you'll find on the CD-ROM.

Author-created materials

All author-created material from the book, including code listings and samples, are on the CD in the folder named "Author."

✦ **Audio:** Contains some sample audio files for use along with Chapter 8 of this book.

- **example.wav.** A short musical piece used for various examples

- **fourscore.wav.** A short speech sample used to demonstrate audio editing

- **pop_goes_the_weasel.wav.** A short speech sample used to demonstrate pop removal

- **well_recorded.wav.** A short speech sample used to demonstrate what well recorded file looks and sounds like

✦ **Authoring:** Contains source code for files discussed in Part IV of this book.

- **quicktime_dual.html.** Embedded QuickTime player using the Netscape plug-in and the ActiveX control

- **RealPlayer_activeX_with_controls.html.** Embedded RealPlayer using the ActiveX control (IE only)

- **RealPlayer_dual_with_controls.html.** Embedded RealPlayer using the Netscape plug-in and the ActiveX control

- **RealPlayer_netscape_plugin_basic.html.** Embedded RealPlayer using the Netscape plug-in

- **RealPlayer_netscape_plugin_with_controls.html.** Embedded RealPlayer using the Netscape plug-in

- **RealPlayer_parts.html.** HTML page showing what all the available components of the RealPlayer look like, using the ActiveX and Netscape plug-in

- **WMT_activeX_no_ui.html.** Windows Media Player without controls embedded using the ActiveX control

- **WMT_activeX_with_controls.html.** Windows Media Player with controls embedded using the ActiveX control

- **WMT_dual_with_controls.html.** Windows Media Player with controls embedded using the Netscape plug-in and the ActiveX control

✦ **Batch Processing:** Contains a number of batch processing script files, as discussed in Chapter 11 and Chapter 14.

- **audio_optimizer.bcs.** A script for use with Sonic Foundry Batch Converter 2.0

- **rm_batch_template.txt.** A template to use for encoding RealSystem files

- **wmt_batch_template.txt.** A template to use for encoding Windows Media files

✦ **Quick Start:** Contains an audio and video file to be used in the Quick Start section of the book.

- **audio_example.wav.** A short musical piece with a voiceover

- **ferrycrossing_160.avi.** A short video piece

✦ **RealPix:** Contains RealPix source files that are discussed in Chapter 24.

- **aspect_ratios.rp.** RealPix file showing the effect of different aspect ratios
- **fade-in.rp.** Simple RealPix file that fades in a single image
- **pan_zoom.rp.** RealPix file that demonstrates a pan and a zoom
- **Realpix_effects.rp.** RealPix file showcasing multiple RealPix effects
- **simple.rp.** Very basic RealPix file
- **wipes.rp.** RealPix file showcasing different wipe effects

✦ **RealText:** Contains RealText source files that are discussed in Chapter 23.

- **basic_features.rt.** Showcases basic RealText features
- **diagonal.rt.** Showcases text moving diagonally
- **drop shadow.rt.** Showcases a drop-shadow effect
- **Marquee.rt.** Showcases a Marquee-type RealText window
- **mymarquee.rt.** Another RealText marquee window
- **parent.rt.** Showcases how RealText can spawn child windows
- **positioning.rt.** Showcases positioning capabilities of RealText
- **RealPlayer_control.rt.** Showcases RealPlayer control via RealText
- **scrollingnews.rt.** A simple scrolling news RealText presentation
- **simplest.rt.** A very simple RealText file
- **teleprompter.rt.** A simple teleprompter window
- **tickertape.rt.** A simple tickertape RealText display

✦ **SMIL:** Contains SMIL source files that are discussed in Part VII of this book.

- **cabin.html.** A simple HTML page with an embedded SMIL presentation
- **cabin_HTML_layout.html.** A simple page that uses HTML to layout a SMIL presentation
- **cabin.smil.** A simple SMIL presentation
- **fit_demos.smil.** A SMIL presentation that showcases the different fit parameter values
- **hotspots.smil.** A presentation that showcases SMIL hotspots
- **simple.smil.** A very basic SMIL presentation

✦ **Video:** Contains sample video files for you to play around with.

- **sunsetferry_320_2997_u.avi.** A short video clip of Seattle ferries
- **seattle_320_2997_u.avi.** A short video clip of Seattle seen from the West

Applications

The following applications are included on the CD-ROM:

Windows applications

* **Batch Converter** from Sonic Foundry

Demo Version. Batch Converter is a great tool to automate your audio processing and encoding needs. It includes a full set of audio processing tools and enables you to export to any streaming media format.

✦ **Premiere** from Adobe

Trial Version. Premiere is a full-featured video editing platform with excellent batch processing capabilities.

✦ **Sound Forge XP Studio** from Sonic Foundry

Demo version. Sound Forge XP Studio is a full-function audio editing platform that enables you to enhance the quality of your audio clips and even export directly to any streaming media format you like.

✦ **Video Factory** from Sonic Foundry

Demo version. Video Factory is a simple, full-featured video editor. It also enables you to export directly to any streaming media format you like.

✦ **UltraEdit-32** from IDM

Shareware. UltraEdit is a super-cool text editor that you'll find invaluable for SMIL, HTML, RealPix, RealText, ASX, and any other text file you can think of.

Mac applications

✦ **BBEdit**

Demo version. BBEdit is the hands-down favorite for text editing on the Mac. Use it to edit SMIL, HTML, RealPix, RealText, ASX, and any other text file you can think of.

✦ **BBEdit Lite**

Freeware. BBEdit Lite is the free, scaled down version of BBEdit.

✦ **Peak VST** from Bias, Inc.

Trial version. Peak VST is a great audio editing platform that enables you to enhance the quality of your audio clips. It also allows you to export directly to QuickTime and RealAudio formats.

✦ **Premiere** from Adobe

Trial Version. Premiere is a full-featured video editing platform with excellent batch processing capabilities.

Shareware programs are fully functional, trial versions of copyrighted programs. If you like particular programs, register with their authors for a nominal fee and receive licenses, enhanced versions, and technical support. *Freeware programs* are copyrighted games, applications, and utilities that are free for personal use. Unlike shareware, these programs do not require a fee or provide technical support. *GNU software* is governed by its own license, which is included inside the folder of the GNU product. See the GNU license for more details.

Trial, demo, or *evaluation versions* are usually limited either by time or functionality (such as being unable to save projects). Some trial versions are very sensitive to system date changes. If you alter your computer's date, the programs will "time out" and will no longer be functional.

Troubleshooting

If you have difficulty installing or using any of the materials on the companion CD, try the following solutions. If they don't help, please refer to the software manufacturer's web site for further troubleshooting advice.

✦ **Turn off any anti-virus software that you may have running.** Installers sometimes mimic virus activity and can make your computer incorrectly believe that it is being infected by a virus. (Be sure to turn the anti-virus software back on later.)

✦ **Close all running programs.** The more programs you're running, the less memory is available to other programs. Installers also typically update files and programs; if you keep other programs running, installation may not work properly.

✦ **Reference the ReadMe:** Please refer to the ReadMe file located at the root of the CD-ROM for the latest product information at the time of publication.

If you still have trouble with the CD, please call the Hungry Minds Customer Care phone number: (800) 762-2974. Outside the United States, call 1 (317) 572-3994. You can also contact Hungry Minds Customer Care by e-mail at techsupdum@ hungryminds.com. Hungry Minds will provide technical support only for installation and other general quality control items; for technical support on the applications themselves, consult the program's vendor or author.

✦   ✦   ✦

Glossary

Artifact Artifacts are distortions such as jagged edges along diagonals or metallic sounds that are introduced into an audio or video file (or image) by the compression codec. Many artifacts can be reduced or masked by clever production techniques.

AVI 2.0 See OpenDML.

Backbone The main sections of the Internet that carry the bulk of the traffic are referred to as the backbone. How far your ISP is from the backbone can determine the type of streaming media quality you can send and receive.

BOC (Broadcast Operations Center) A generic term applied to the location where you serving operations take place. Also known as a NOC (Network Operations Center).

Boolean A variable that is either true or false. Boolean variables often use zero and one to represent true and false, with zero equal to false.

Broadband A loose term that refers to high-speed Internet connections. Broadband is generally anything above approximately 300kbps.

Cache RAM memory is much faster than retrieving data from hard drives, so computers store data that is used often in a software cache. Similarly, Internet caching technology stores the most accessed files in RAM memory of a dedicated cache machine instead of pulling the files off a hard drive. Also, these caching machines can be placed at the edges of a network so that the whole network does not have to be traversed.

Chrominance The color component of a video signal.

Codec A contraction of **co**mpressor-**de**compressor, or **co**der-**dec**oder, a codec is an algorithm used to reduce file sizes. Codecs use all sorts of perceptual models to help them maintain the integrity of the file.

Compression (audio) An audio signal processing technique whereby portions of audio programming that exceed a certain threshold are attenuated. Compression is often used to protect input levels from distortion caused by sudden peaks in the audio programming. It is also used to even out the overall levels throughout a program.

Compression (file size) A technique used to reduce the size of digitized files. Many common Internet file types such as JPEG, GIF, and PNG utilize compression to achieve their reduced file sizes. They use what is known as "lossy" compression, where the resulting file is only an approximation of the original. In loss-less compression, such as .zip files, the original file(s) can be recreated exactly.

Constant Bit Rate (CBR) An approach to encoding data that keeps the bit rate constant throughout. This approach is more suited to streaming media.

Cookie A small text file stored on the user's machine containing data that can be accessed by the browser via JavaScript. Some data, such as passwords or credit card numbers, is encrypted before being stored. Cookies allow browsers to remember things about you, such as your address. Contrary to popular belief, Web pages can only access cookies that were set by pages in the same domain. People cannot write surreptitious JavaScript code to steal information out of cookies set by other Web sites.

Decibel (dB) A unit of measure used in audio that measures the power of an audio signal. It is a logarithmic measure so each increase of 3 dB means a doubling of power. To complicate matters, there are various types of decibels: dBU, dBV, and so on. In this book, we are using the term in its most generic form.

De-interlacing A process that attempts to remove the artifacts from an interlaced signal. (See Interlacing.)

Difference frame In a compressed video sequence, a frame that contains only the information about the current frame that is different from the previous frame. Difference frames require key frames as a reference.

DNS (Dynamic Name Service or System) The system by which Internet server names, such as www.streamingmediabible.com are translated into IP addresses, such as 192.68.1.100.

DRM (Digital Rights Management) Digital rights management schemes are used to protect content from unlawful use. For example, some DRM schemes prevent you from swapping music with other people online, or from burning CDs.

Equalization (EQ) An audio signal processing technique that changes harmonic or tonal character by boosting or attenuating certain frequency ranges in an audio signal. Desired frequencies can be turned up, or boosted, while undesired frequencies or noise can be turned down, or attenuated. An everyday example would be the bass and treble adjustments on your home stereo.

Field One-half of an interlaced video frame, consisting of either the odd or the even numbered scan lines.

Firewall A security system designed to allow only certain kinds of traffic in and out of networks. They can be implemented in hardware or software, and can block data packets based on a number of different security criteria, such as port number or protocol type. Firewalls often block streaming media traffic because it uses non-standard port numbers.

FireWire See IEEE 1394.

Gain In audio terms, gain refers to the amount of amplification being applied. Similarly, the *gain structure* of an audio setup refers to the amount of amplification being applied at each stage.

Gating (noise gate) A form of audio signal processing where everything below a set threshold is muted. It can be useful as a noise reduction technique.

Headroom (audio) The difference between the maximum signal a system can reproduce without distortion and the standard operating level.

Hertz (Hz) A unit of measure, generally used for audio frequency. One cycle per second is equal to one Hertz (Hz). The human hearing range extends from 20-20,000Hz, or 20-20kHz. In this case, the "k" stands for 1000 instead of 1024 as is generally assumed in computer applications.

Hotspot A particular area or segment of a clip that links to another clip or presentation. Hotspots can be defined spatially and temporally.

IEEE Pronounced "I-triple-E", the Institute of Electrical and Electronics Engineers, Inc. An organization dedicated to promoting standards in computing and electrical engineering.

IEEE 1394 (also known as FireWire or iLink) A IEEE standard for exchanging digital information at rates of 100, 200, or 400 megabits per second. Originally developed by Apple and trademarked as FireWire, it was standardized by the IEEE 1394 working group. iLink is Sony's implementation of the IEEE 1394 standard.

iLink See IEEE 1394.

Interlacing The system used by television displays and cameras whereby each frame is divided up into odd lines and even lines. Each group of odd and even lines is referred to as a field. The combination of the two fields, displayed in rapid succession, makes up one frame of video. (See Field; De-interlacing.)

Inverse Telecine The process of removing the extra fields in a video signal that result from the Telecine process. Removing these redundant fields leads to greater encoding efficiency.

ISP (Internet Service Provider) A company that provides access to the Internet, often also offering server hosting, stream hosting, and so on.

Key frame In a compressed video sequence, a frame that contains information about the whole frame, as opposed to a difference frame. (See Difference frame.)

Luminance The black and white portion of a video signal.

Metadata A neologism from the Greek *meta* (among, with) and data, metadata is information about data. For example, the title, author, and copyright of a presentation are metadata associated with a presentation.

Metafile Similar to metadata, a metafile is a file that contains information about another file. Typically the metafile contains a "pointer" to the location of the file, such as a URL or a relative path.

MIDI (Musical Instrument Digital Interface) A standard used to exchange musical information between devices. Using MIDI, music sequencing software can control the playback of keyboards, samplers, or any other MIDI-compliant devices. MIDI data includes what notes to play, when to play them, how long to play them, how loud, what instrument to use, and so on. MIDI data can be streamed by the RealSystem utilizing the Crescendo Forte plug-in.

MIME type MIME (Multipurpose Internet Mail Extensions) types are used as a standard way of exchanging data over the Internet. An application can determine if it has appropriate rendering software to decode a file by looking at the MIME type. If it does not, it can hand off the file to a separate program (or plug-in). When you install new software, it generally "registers" itself for a number of different MIME types — sometimes conflicting with other applications.

Multicasting A method of broadcasting data across the Internet where packets use an address in the Multicast Address Space (224.0.0.0 through 239.255.255.255). These packets are forwarded indiscriminately across the Internet instead of forwarded to a particular user. All multicast audience members receive copies of the data packets from their local routers. All routers involved in a multicast must be "multicast-enabled."

NIC (Network Interface Card) A computer card that enables communication across a local area network.

NOC (Network Operations Center) See BOC.

Noise gate See Gating.

Normalization An audio signal processing technique that analyzes a file to discover exactly how much the volume can be turned up before distortion, and then applies that volume change. Some normalization routines allow the user to specify the level to 'normalize' to as a percentage of maximum allowable volume.

NTSC (National Television Standards Committee) The broadcast standard for television signals in the United States and most of Central and South America, which specifies 30 interlaced frames per second. Each frame consists of 525 horizontal lines of resolution.

NTSC 3/2 Pulldown Because of the differing frame rates (24 for film, 30 for NTSC) extra frames must be created. By scanning every other frame three times instead of twice, five fields are created from every two frames, yielding 60 fields total from 24 frames. The reverse process is known as Inverse Telecine (see Inverse Telecine). See Chapter 2 for a more detailed discussion.

OpenDML Also known as AVI 2.0, a standard that extends the AVI specification and effectively removes the 2 Gigabyte file size limit by allowing data to be written across multiple files.

Overscan The area of a broadcast video image that is normally hidden by the plastic surrounds of a television monitor. Sometimes this area can contain video noise and should be removed before encoding.

PAL (Phase Alternation by Line) The broadcast standard for television signals in most European countries, which specifies 25 interlaced frames per second. Each frame consists of 625 horizontal lines of resolution. PAL color is considered to be superior to NTSC.

Port (port numbers) Networking applications use ports to determine which application receives the data being sent. For example, Web browsers request data on port 80, which is assigned to HTTP traffic. When the request arrives at the destination server, it is handed to the Web server. In this manner many different servers can run on the same machine, each on a different port.

Proc amp Short for video processing amplifier. A proc amp is used to adjust the quality of a video signal by manipulating the brightness, contrast, and color content.

Protocol A set of rules that determine how programs exchange data over a network. Different protocols use different amounts and types of error correction, compression, encryption, and so on.

Q (in relation to audio equalization) The width of the frequency band to be affected by a parametric EQ operation. Q relates to the number of octaves — a Q of 1 means one octave, centered on the chosen frequency will be affected.

Render In video editing systems, the act of committing desired special effects or transitions to the hard drive. Some effects may not be visible until the section is rendered.

SDP (Session Description Protocol) file The file used to connect QuickTime players to live QuickTime streams. These files are created by the broadcast application and must be placed on the QuickTime streaming server in the configured media directory.

SECAM ("Systeme Electronique Couleur Avec Memoire" — Sequential Color and Memory) The broadcast standard for television signals in France, Australia, and a few other European countries, which specifies 25 interlaced frames per second, each frame containing 625 horizontal lines of resolution.

SMIL (Synchronized Multimedia Integration Language) An open, standardized language for combining multiple data types into a single multimedia presentation. SMIL is covered in detail in Part VII of this book.

SMPTE The Society of Motion Picture and Television Engineers.

SMPTE Timecode A standard used to synchronize different pieces of audiovisual equipment.

Telecine The process of transferring film content to video (see NTSC 3/2 Pulldown).

Time-to-live (TTL) The time-to-live variable is used during multicasts to determine how long a data packet is kept alive and forwarded to multicast enabled routers. The time-to-live variable therefore determines how far the packet travels. Short TTL times are used for local LAN multicasts, longer TTL variables are used for multiple-LAN and WAN multicasts.

URL (Uniform Resource Locator) The URL of a document specifies where a document is located and what protocol is to be used to retrieve it. The protocol precedes the :// and may be HTTP, FTP, RTSP, or any other valid protocol. Following the protocol is the IP address or name of the server, followed by the directory structure to follow to find the document.

Variable Bit Rate A system of encoding that allots variable amounts of bits to different sections of the file. Less bits are used to encode the low-motion sections, so that more bits can be used to encode the difficult, high-motion sections. Variable bit rate files in general are not suitable for streaming due to the large variation in data rate in the file.

Virtual Private Networks (VPNs) Disparate networks connected via the Internet in such a fashion that security is maintained.

Z-index Used in SMIL files, the z-index determines which layers are rendered on top of others. Layers with higher z-index numbers are "on top" of those with lower numbers. Negative numbers are allowed.

✦   ✦   ✦

Index